congratulations!

As a student purchasing the *Concepts of Programming Languages*, Sixth Edition, you are entitled to six months of prepaid access to the book's Companion Website. This prepaid subscription gives you full access to all student support areas of this Web site, including:

- An online language reference library, complete with reference material, links to compilers and the best Web sites for each supported language.
- Programming projects, that expand upon several of the projects in the textbook.
- Self-assessment quizzes to test your knowledge of the concepts in the textbook.

To access the *Concepts of Programming Languages* Companion Website for the first time:
You will need to register online using a computer with an Internet connection and a Web browser. The process takes just a couple of minutes and only needs to be completed once.

1. Go to **http://www.aw.com/sebesta**.
2. Click **Student Resources**.
3. Click the **Register** button.
4. Use a coin to scratch off the gray coating below and reveal your student access code.* Do not use a knife or other sharp object, which can damage the code.

*

5. On the registration page, enter your student access code. Do not type the dashes. You can use lowercase or uppercase.
6. Follow the on-screen instructions. If you need help at any time during the online registration process, simply click the **Need Help?** icon.
7. Once your personal Login Name and Password are confirmed, you can begin using the *Concepts of Programming Languages* Companion Website!

To log into the *Concepts of Programming Languages* Companion Website after you register:
You only need to register for this Companion Website once. After that, you can access the site by going to http://www.aw.com/sebesta, clicking "Student Resources," and providing your Login Name and Password when prompted.

***IMPORTANT:** The Access Code on this page can only be used once to establish a subscription to the *Concepts of Programming Languages*, Companion Website. This subscription is valid for six months upon activation, and is not transferable. If this access code has already been scratched off, it may no longer be valid. If this is the case, you can purchase a subscription by going to http://www.aw.com/sebesta and clicking "Student Resources."

Concepts of Programming Languages

SIXTH EDITION

Concepts of Programming Languages

SIXTH EDITION

Robert W. Sebesta

University of Colorado, Colorado Springs

PEARSON

Addison
Wesley

Boston San Francisco New York
London Toronto Sydney Tokyo Singapore Madrid
Mexico City Munich Paris Cape Town Hong Kong Montreal

Sponsoring Editor	Maite Suarez-Rivas
Project Editor	Katherine Harutunian
Senior Production Supervisor	Juliet Silveri
Production Services	Argosy Publishing
Cover Designer	Joyce Cosentino Wells
Text Design	Delgado Design, Inc.
Marketing Manager	Nathan Schultz
Senior Marketing Coordinator	Lesly Hershman
Print Buyer	Caroline Fell

Cover image © 2003 Norman Koren and James Gritz, PhotoDisc

Access the latest information about Addison-Wesley titles from our World Wide Web site:
http://www.aw.com/cs

Many of the designations used by manufacturers and sellers to distinguish their products are claimed as trademarks. Where those designations appear in this book, and the publisher was aware of a trademark claim, the designations have been printed in initial caps or all caps.

The programs and applications presented in this book have been included for their instructional value. They have been tested with care but are not guaranteed for any particular purpose. Neither the publisher nor the author offers any warranties or representations, nor do they accept any liabilities with respect to the programs or applications.

Library of Congress Cataloging-in-Publication Data

Sebesta, Robert W.
    Concepts of programming languages / Robert W. Sebesta.—6th ed.
      p. cm.
    Includes bibliographical references and index.
    ISBN 0-321-19362-8
    1. Programming languages (Electronic computers) I. Title.

QA76.7.S43 2003
005.13 21

For information on obtaining permission for the use of material from this work, please submit a written request to Pearson Education, Inc., Rights and Contracts Department, 75 Arlington Street, Suite 300, Boston, MA 02116 or fax your request to (617) 848-7047.

345678910-HT-060504

Preface

CHANGES TO THE SIXTH EDITION

The goals, overall structure, and approach of this sixth edition of *Concepts of Programming Languages* remain the same as those of the five earlier editions. The principal goal is to provide the reader with the tools necessary for the critical evaluation of existing and future programming languages. An additional goal is to prepare the reader for the study of compiler design. There were several sources of our motivations for the changes in the sixth edition. First, to maintain the currency of the material, much of the discussion of older programming languages has been removed. In its place is material on newer languages. Especially interesting historical information on older programming languages has been retained but placed in *historical side boxes*. Second, the material has been updated to reflect the fact that most students now come to this course with a basic understanding of object-oriented programming. We shortened the discussion of basics and expanded the discussion of advanced topics.

Third, reviewer comments have prompted several changes. For example, the material on functional programming languages has been reorganized and strengthened. Also, we have added a *programming exercises section at the end of most chapters* to give students experience with the concepts described in the book and to make the concepts more realistic and appealing. The book now has a new supplement: *a companion Web site* with a few small language manuals, interactive quizzes for students, and additional programming projects. Finally, *interviews with the designers of recent languages* that have achieved widespread use appear in several places in the book. These show the human side of language development.

Four specific changes distinguish the sixth edition text from its predecessor. First, the material on implementing subprograms has been condensed, largely because the virtual disappearance of Pascal and Modula-2, as well as the shrinking usage of Ada, has made the implementation of nested subprograms with static scoping less important. All of the relevant Pascal examples were rewritten in Ada. Second, Chapter 14 has been expanded to cover both exception handling and event handling. This change was motivated by the great increase in interest and importance of event handling that has come with the wide use of interactive Web documents. Third, the introduction to Smalltalk has been eliminated because we believe the syntactic details of Smalltalk are no longer relevant to the material of the book. Fourth, there are numerous significant changes motivated by the aging of existing programming languages and the emergence of new programming languages. There is now little mention of Modula-2, Pascal, and the ALGOLs. Also, the coverage of Ada and Fortran has been whittled down to the more interesting of their features that do not appear in other popular languages. New material on JavaScript, PHP, and C# has been added where appropriate. Finally, most chapters now include a new section, Programming Exercises.

THE VISION

This book describes the fundamental concepts of programming languages by discussing the design issues of the various language constructs, examining the design choices for these constructs in some of the most common languages, and critically comparing design alternatives.

Any serious study of programming languages requires an examination of some related topics, among which are formal methods of describing the syntax and semantics of programming languages, which are covered in Chapter 3. Also, implementation techniques for various language constructs must be considered: Lexical and syntax analysis are discussed in Chapter 4, and implementation of subprogram linkage is covered in Chapter 10. Implementation of some other language constructs is discussed in various other parts of the book.

The following paragraphs outline the contents of the sixth edition.

CHAPTER OUTLINES

Chapter 1 begins with a rationale for studying programming languages. It then discusses the criteria used for evaluating programming languages and language constructs. The primary influences on language design, common design tradeoffs, and the basic approaches to implementation are also examined.

Chapter 2 outlines the evolution of most of the important languages discussed in this book. Although no language is described completely, the origins, purposes, and contributions of each are discussed. This historical overview is valuable because it provides the background necessary to understanding the practical and theoretical basis for contemporary language design. It also motivates further study of language design and evaluation. In addition, because none of the remainder of the book depends on Chapter 2, it can be read on its own, independent of the other chapters.

Chapter 3 describes the primary formal method for describing the syntax of programming language, BNF. This is followed by a description of attribute grammars, which describe both the syntax and static semantics of languages. The difficult task of semantic description is then explored, including brief introductions to the three most common methods: operational, axiomatic, and denotational semantics.

Chapter 4 introduces lexical and syntax analysis. This chapter is targeted to those colleges that no longer require a compiler design course in their curricula. Like Chapter 2, this chapter stands alone and can be read independently of the rest of the book.

Chapters 5 through 14 describe in detail the design issues for the primary constructs of the imperative languages. In each case, the design choices for several example languages are presented and evaluated. Specifically, Chapter 5 covers the many characteristics of variables, Chapter 6 covers data types, and Chapter 7 explains expressions and assignment statements. Chapter 8 describes control statements, Chapters 9 and 10 discuss subprograms and their implementation. Chapter 11 examines data abstraction facilities. Chapter 12 provides an in-depth discussion of language features that support object-oriented programming (inheritance and dynamic method binding), Chapter 13 discusses concurrent program units, and Chapter 14 is about exception handling and event handling.

The last two chapters (15 and 16) describe two of the most important alternative programming paradigms: functional programming and logic programming. Chapter 15 presents an introduction to Scheme, including descriptions of some of its primitive functions, special forms, and functional forms, as well as some examples of simple functions written in Scheme. Brief introductions to COMMON LISP, ML, and Haskell are given to illustrate some different kinds of functional language. Chapter 16 introduces logic programming and the logic programming language, Prolog.

TO THE INSTRUCTOR

In the junior-level programming language course at the University of Colorado at Colorado Springs, the book is used as follows: We typically cover Chapters 1 and 3 in detail, and though students find it interesting and beneficial reading, Chapter 2 receives little lecture time due to its lack of hard technical content. Because no material in subsequent chapters depends on Chapter 2, as noted earlier, it can be skipped entirely, and because we require a course in compiler design, Chapter 4 is not covered.

Chapters 5 through 9 should be relatively easy for students with extensive programming experience in C++, Java, or C#. Chapters 10 through 14 are more challenging and require more detailed lectures.

Chapters 15 and 16 are entirely new to most students at the junior level. Ideally, language processors for Scheme and Prolog should be available for students required to learn the material in these chapters. Sufficient material is included to allow students to dabble with some simple programs.

Undergraduate courses will probably not be able to cover all of the last two chapters in detail. Graduate courses, however, by skipping over parts of the early chapters on imperative languages, will be able to completely discuss the nonimperative languages.

SUPPLEMENTAL MATERIALS

The following supplements are available to all readers of this book at www.aw.com/cssupport.

- A set of lecture notes slides. These slides are in the form of Microsoft PowerPoint source files, one for each of the chapters of the book.
- PowerPoint slides of all the figures in the book, should you wish to create your own lecture notes.
- A companion web site. With the sixth edition we are introducing a brand-new supplements package for students. To reinforce learning in the classroom, to assist with the hands-on lab component of this course, and/or to facilitate students in a distance learning situation, the edition will be accompanied by a comprehensive web site with the following content:

    1. Mini manuals (approximately 100-page tutorials) on a handful of languages. These will assume that the student knows how to program in some other language, giving the student enough information to complete the chapter materials in each language. Currently manuals are planned in C++, C, Java, and C#.
    2. Lab projects. A series of lab projects will be defined for each concept taught in the book. The solutions will be available exclusively to those teaching a course.
    3. Self-grading review exercises. Using the Addison-Wesley software engine, students can complete a series of multiple-choice and fill-in-the-blank exercises to check their understanding of the chapter just read.

Solutions to many of the problem sets are available only to qualified instructors. Please contact your local Addison-Wesley sales representative, or send e-mail to aw.cse@aw.com, for information about how to access them.

Language Processor Availability

Processors for and information about some of the programming languages discussed in this book can be found at the following web sites:

C#	http://microsoft.com
Java	http://java.sun.com
Haskell	http://haskell.org
Scheme	http://www.cs.rice.edu/CS/PLT/packages/drscheme/
Perl	http://www.perl.com

JavaScript is included in virtually all browsers; PHP is included in virtually all Web servers.

All this information is also included on the companion web site.

ACKNOWLEDGEMENTS

The suggestions from outstanding reviewers contributed greatly to this book's present form. In alphabetical order, they are:

Charles Dana, *California Polytechnic State University, San Luis Obispo*
Eric Joanis, *University of Toronto*
Donald H. Kraft, *Louisiana State University*
Dennis L. Mumaugh, *DePaul University*
Sibylle Schupp, *Rensselaer, Polytechnic Institute*
Neelam Soundarajan, *Ohio State University*
Ryan Stansifer, *Florida Institute of Technology*
Steve Stevenson, *Clemson University*
Virginia Teller, *Hunter College CUNY*
Salih Yurttas, *Texas A&M University*
Yang Wang, *Southwest Missouri State University*

Numerous other people provided input for the previous editions of *Concepts of Programming Languages* at various stages of its development. All of their comments were useful and greatly appreciated. In alphabetical order, they are: Vicki Allan, Henry Bauer, Carter Bays, Manuel E. Bermudez, Peter Brouwer, Margaret Burnett, Paosheng Chang, John Crenshaw, Barbara Ann Griem, Mary Lou Haag, Eileen Head, Ralph C. Hilzer, Hikyoo Koh, Jiang B. Liu, Meiliu Lu, Jon Mauney, Bruce R. Maxim, Robert McCoard, Michael G. Murphy, Andrew Oldroyd, Rebecca Parsons, Jeffery Popyack, Steven Rapkin, Hamilton Richard, Tom Sager, Joseph Schell, Mary Louise Soffa and John M. Weiss.

Maite Suarez-Rivas, Editor, Katherine Harutunian, Project Editor, and Juliet Silveri, Production Supervisor at Addison-Wesley, and Daniel Rausch at Argosy, all deserve my gratitude for their efforts to produce the sixth edition quickly, as well as help make it significantly more complete than the fifth.

Finally, I thank my children, Jake and Darcie, for their patience in enduring my absence from them throughout the endless hours of effort I invested in writing the six editions of this book.

ABOUT THE AUTHOR

Robert Sebesta is an Associate Professor in the Computer Science Department at the University of Colorado, Colorado Springs. Professor Sebesta received a B.S. in applied mathematics from the University of Colorado in Boulder and his M.S. and Ph.D. degrees in Compuer Science from the Pennsylvania State University. He has taught computer science for over 30 years. His professional interests are the design and evaluation of programming languages, compiler design, and software testing methods and tools. He is a member of the ACM and the IEEE Computer Society.

Contents

1

Preliminaries

CHAPTER OUTLINE

Before we begin discussing the concepts of programming languages, we must consider a few preliminaries. First we explain some reasons why computer science students and professional software developers should study general concepts of language design and evaluation. This discussion is valuable for those who believe that a working knowledge of one or two programming languages is sufficient for computer scientists. The major programming domains are then briefly described. Next, because the book evaluates language constructs and features, we present a list of criteria by which such judgments can be made. The two major influences on language design, machine architecture and program design methodologies, are then discussed. Next we describe a few of the major trade-offs that must be considered during language design.

Because this book is also about the implementation of programming languages, this chapter includes an overview of the most common approaches to implementation. Finally, we briefly describe a few examples of programming environments and discuss their impact on software production.

1.1 Reasons for Studying Concepts of Programming Languages

It is natural for students to wonder how they will benefit from the study of programming language concepts. After all, many other topics in computer science are worthy of serious study. The following is what we believe to be a compelling list of potential benefits of studying language concepts.

- *Increased capacity to express ideas.* It is widely believed that the depth at which we can think is influenced by the expressive power of the language in which we communicate our thoughts. Those with a limited grasp of natural language are limited in the complexity of their thoughts, particularly in depth of abstraction. In other words, it is difficult for people to conceptualize structures they cannot describe, verbally or in writing. Programmers in the process of developing software are similarly constrained. The language in which they develop software places limits on the kinds of control structures, data structures, and abstractions they can use; thus the forms of algorithms they can construct are also limited.

  Awareness of a wider variety of programming language features can reduce such limitations in software development. Programmers can increase the range of their software-development thought processes by learning new language constructs.

  It might be argued that learning the capabilities of other languages does not help a programmer who is forced to use a language that lacks those capabilities. That argument does not hold up, however, because often language constructs can be simulated in other languages that do not support those constructs directly.

For example, having learned the structure and uses of associative arrays in Perl (Wall et al., 2000), a C programmer might design structures that simulate associative arrays in that language.

The study of programming language concepts builds an appreciation for valuable language features and encourages programmers to use them.

The fact that many features of languages can be simulated in other languages does not lessen significantly the importance of designing languages with the best collection of features. It is always better to use a feature whose design has been integrated into a language than to use a simulation of that feature, which is often less elegant, more cumbersome, and less safe in a language that does not support it.

- *Improved background for choosing appropriate languages.* Many professional programmers have had little formal education in computer science; rather, they have learned programming on their own or through in-house training programs. Such training programs often teach one or two languages that are directly relevant to the current projects of the organization. Many other programmers received their formal training in the distant past. The languages they learned then are no longer used, and many features now available in programming languages were not widely known. The result of this background is that many programmers, when given a choice of languages for a new project, continue to use the language with which they are most familiar, even if it is poorly suited to new projects. If these programmers were familiar with the other languages available, and especially the particular features in those languages, they would be in a better position to make informed language choices.

- *Increased ability to learn new languages.* Computer programming is still a relatively young discipline, and design methodologies, software development tools, and programming languages are still in a state of continuous evolution. This makes software development an exciting profession, but it also means that continuous learning is essential. The process of learning a new programming language can be lengthy and difficult, especially for someone who is comfortable with only one or two languages and has never examined programming language concepts in general. Once a thorough understanding of the fundamental concepts of languages is acquired, it becomes far easier to see how these concepts are incorporated into the design of the language being learned.

For example, programmers who understand the concepts of object-oriented programming will have a much easier time learning Java (Gosling et al., 1996) than those who have never used those concepts. The same phenomenon occurs in natural languages. The better you know the grammar of your native language, the easier you will find it to learn a second natural language. Furthermore, learning a second language also has the beneficial side effect of teaching you more about your first language.

Finally, it is essential that practicing programmers know the vocabulary and fundamental concepts of programming languages so they can read and understand programming language manuals and promotional literature for languages and compilers.

- *Better understanding of the significance of implementation.* In learning the concepts of programming languages, it is both interesting and necessary to touch on the implementation issues that affect those concepts. In some cases, an understanding of implementation issues leads to an understanding of why languages are designed the way they are. This in turn leads to the ability to use a language more intelligently, as it was designed to be used. We can become better programmers by understanding the choices among programming language constructs and the consequences of those choices.

  Certain kinds of program bugs can only be found and fixed by a programmer who knows some related implementation details. Another benefit of understanding implementation issues is that it allows us to visualize how a computer executes various language constructs. This in turn fosters an understanding of the relative efficiency of alternative constructs that may be chosen for a program. For example, programmers who know little about how recursion is implemented often do not know that a recursive algorithm can be far slower than an equivalent iterative algorithm.

- *Overall advancement of computing.* Finally, there is a global view of computing that can justify the study of programming language concepts. Although it is usually possible to determine why a particular programming language became popular, it is not always clear, at least in retrospect, that the most popular languages are the best available. In some cases, it might be concluded that a language became widely used, at least in part, because those in positions to choose languages were not sufficiently familiar with programming language concepts.

  For example, many people believe it would have been better if ALGOL 60 (Backus et al., 1962) had displaced Fortran (ANSI, 1992) in the early 1960s, because it was more elegant and had much better control statements than Fortran, among other reasons. That it did not is due partly to the programmers and software development managers of that time, many of whom did not clearly understand the conceptual design of ALGOL 60. They found its description difficult to read (which it was) and even more difficult to understand. They did not appreciate the benefits of block structure, recursion, and well-structured control statements, so they failed to see the benefits of ALGOL 60 over Fortran.

  Of course, many other factors contributed to the lack of acceptance of ALGOL 60, as we will see in Chapter 2. However, the fact that computer users were generally unaware of the benefits of the language played a significant role.

In general, if those who choose languages were better informed, perhaps better languages would eventually squeeze out poorer ones.

1.2 Programming Domains

Computers have been applied to a myriad of different areas, from controlling nuclear power plants to storing the records of personal checkbooks. Because of this great diversity in computer use, programming languages with very different goals have been developed. In this section, we briefly discuss a few of the areas of computer applications and their associated languages.

1.2.1 Scientific Applications

The first digital computers, which appeared in the 1940s, were used and in fact invented for scientific applications. Typically, scientific applications have simple data structures but require large numbers of floating-point arithmetic computations. The most common data structures are arrays and matrices; the most common control structures are counting loops and selections. The high-level programming languages invented for scientific applications were designed to provide for those needs. Their competition was assembly language, so efficiency was a primary concern. The first language for scientific applications was Fortran. ALGOL 60 and most of its descendants were also intended for use in this area, though they were designed to be used in other related areas also. For some scientific applications where efficiency is the primary concern, like those that were common in the 1950s and 1960s, no subsequent language is significantly better than Fortran.

1.2.2 Business Applications

The use of computers for business applications began in the 1950s. Special computers were developed for this purpose, along with special languages. The first successful high-level language for business was COBOL (ANSI, 1985), the initial version of which appeared in 1960. It is still the most commonly used language for these applications. Business languages are characterized by facilities for producing elaborate reports, precise ways of describing and storing decimal numbers and character data, and the ability to specify decimal arithmetic operations.

With the advent of microcomputers came new ways for businesses, especially small businesses, to use computers. Two specific tools that can be used on small computers, spreadsheet systems and database systems, were developed for business and now are widely used.

There have been only limited developments in business application languages other than COBOL. Therefore, this book does not discuss business application languages other than to provide a history of the development of COBOL in Chapter 2.

1.2.3   Artificial Intelligence

Artificial intelligence (AI) is a broad area of computer applications characterized by the use of symbolic rather than numeric computations. Symbolic computation means that symbols, consisting of names rather than numbers, are manipulated. Also, symbolic computation is more conveniently done with linked lists of data rather than arrays. This kind of programming sometimes requires more flexibility than other programming domains. For example, in some AI applications the ability to create and execute code segments during execution is convenient.

The first widely used programming language developed for AI applications was the functional language LISP (McCarthy et al., 1965), which appeared in 1959. Most AI applications have been written in LISP or one of its close relatives. During the early 1970s, however, an alternative approach to these applications appeared—logic programming using the Prolog (Clocksin and Mellish, 1997) language. Scheme (Dybbig, 1996), a dialect of LISP, and Prolog are introduced in Chapters 15 and 16, respectively.

1.2.4   Systems Programming

The operating system and all of the programming support tools of a computer system are collectively known as its **systems software.** Systems software is used almost continuously and therefore must be efficient. Therefore, a language for this domain must provide fast execution. Furthermore, it must have low-level features that allow the software interfaces to external devices to be written.

In the 1960s and 1970s, some computer manufacturers, such as IBM, Digital, and Burroughs (now UNISYS), developed special machine-oriented high-level languages for systems software on their machines. For IBM mainframe computers, the language was PL/S, a dialect of PL/I; for Digital, it was BLISS, a language at a level just above assembly language; for Burroughs, it was Extended ALGOL.

The UNIX operating system is written almost entirely in C (ANSI, 1989), which has made it relatively easy to port, or move, to different machines. Some of the characteristics of C make it a good choice for systems programming. It is low level, it is execution efficient, and it does not burden the user with many safety restrictions. Systems programmers are often excellent programmers and do not believe they need such restrictions. Some nonsystems programmers, however, find C to be too dangerous to use on large, important software systems.

1.2.5   Scripting Languages

Scripting languages have evolved over the past 25 years. Early scripting languages were used by putting a list of commands, called a script, in a file to be executed. The first of these languages, named `sh` (for shell), began as a small collection of commands that were interpreted as calls to system subprograms that performed utility functions, such as file management and simple file filtering. To this basis were added variables, control flow statements, functions, and various other capabilities, and the result is a complete programming language. One of the most powerful and widely known of these is `ksh` (Bolsky and Korn, 1995), which was developed by David Korn at Bell Laboratories.

`awk` is another scripting language, developed by Al Aho, Brian Kernighan, and Peter Wienberger at Bell Laboratories (Aho et al., 1988). `awk` began as a report-generation language but later became a more general-purpose language. `tcl` is an extensible scripting language developed by John Ousterhout at the University of California at Berkeley (Ousterhout, 1994). `tcl` is now combined with `tk`, a language that provides a method of building X Window applications. The Perl language, developed by Larry Wall, was originally a combination of `sh` and `awk`. Perl has grown significantly since its beginnings, and is now a powerful though somewhat primitive programming language. Although it is still often called a scripting language, we prefer to think of it as an odd but full-fledged programming language. When the World Wide Web first became widely used, the use of Perl rose dramatically, primarily because it is a nearly ideal language for Common Gateway Interface (CGI) programming.

JavaScript (Flanagan, 1998) is a scripting language developed by Netscape for use in both Web servers and browsers. It has grown, both as a language and in popularity, in recent years. It is used mostly as a client-side scripting language. In that role, JavaScript code is embedded in HTML documents and is interpreted by a browser that finds the code in a document that is being displayed.

PHP (Converse and Park, 2000) is a scripting language designed by Rasmus Lerdorf for use on Web server systems. Like JavaScript, PHP code is embedded in HTML documents. This code is interpreted on the server before the document is sent to a requesting browser.

Perl, JavaScript, and PHP were not designed to be general-purpose programming languages. However, because they include some interesting features that may influence mainstream languages, we discuss these features in this book.

1.2.6   Special-Purpose Languages

A host of special-purpose languages have appeared over the past 40 years. They range from RPG, which is used to produce business reports, to APT, which is used for instructing programmable machine tools, to GPSS, which is used for systems simulation. This book does not discuss special-purpose languages, primarily because of their narrow applicability and the difficulty of comparing them with other languages.

1.3 Language Evaluation Criteria

As noted previously, the purpose of this book is to examine carefully the underlying concepts of the various constructs and capabilities of programming languages. We will also evaluate these features, focusing on their impact on the software development process, including maintenance. To do this, we need a set of evaluation criteria. Such a list of criteria is necessarily controversial, because it is virtually impossible to get even two computer scientists to agree on the value of some given language characteristic relative to others. In spite of these differences, most would agree that the criteria discussed in the following subsections are important.

Some of the characteristics that influence the most important of these criteria are shown in Table 1.1, and the criteria themselves are discussed in the following sections.

Note that some of these criteria are broad and somewhat vague, such as writability, whereas others are specific language constructs, for example, exception handling. Although the discussion may seem to imply that the criteria have equal importance, that implication is not intended, and it is clearly not the case.

1.3.1   Readability

Perhaps one of the most important criteria for judging a programming language is the ease with which programs can be read and understood. Before 1970, software development was largely thought of in terms of writing code. The primary positive characteristics of programming languages were efficiency and machine readability. Language constructs were designed more from the point of view of the computer than of computer users. In the 1970s,

Table 1.1

Language evaluation criteria and the characteristics that affect them.

	Criteria		
Characteristic	READABILITY	WRITABILITY	RELIABILITY
Simplicity/orthogonality	•	•	•
Control structures	•	•	•
Data types & structures	•	•	•
Syntax design	•	•	•
Support for abstraction		•	•
Expressivity		•	•
Type checking			•
Exception handling			•
Restricted aliasing			•

however, the software life cycle concept (Booch, 1987) was developed; coding was relegated to a much smaller role, and maintenance was recognized as a major part of the cycle, particularly in terms of cost. Because ease of maintenance is determined in large part by the readability of programs, readability became an important measure of the quality of programs and programming languages. This was an important juncture in the evolution of programming languages. There was a distinct crossover from focus on machine orientation to focus on human orientation.

Readability must be considered in the context of the problem domain. For example, if a program that describes a computation was written in a language not designed for such use, the program may be unnatural and convoluted, making it unusually difficult to read.

The following subsections describe characteristics that contribute to the readability of a programming language.

1.3.1.1 Overall Simplicity

The overall simplicity of a programming language strongly affects its readability. First of all, a language that has a large number of basic components is more difficult to learn than one with a small number of basic components. Programmers who must use a large language tend to learn a subset of the language and ignore its other features. This learning pattern is sometimes used to excuse the large number of language components, but that argument is not valid. Readability problems occur whenever the program's author has learned a different subset from that subset with which the reader is familiar.

A second complicating characteristic of a programming language is feature multiplicity—that is, having more than one way to accomplish a particular operation. For example, in Java a user can increment a simple integer variable in four different ways:

```
count = count + 1
count += 1
count++
++count
```

Although the last two statements have slightly different meaning from each other and from the others in some contexts, all four have the same meaning when used as stand-alone expressions. These variations are discussed in Chapter 7.

A third potential problem is operator overloading, in which a single operator symbol has more than one meaning. Although this is a useful feature, it can lead to reduced readability if users are allowed to create their own overloading and do not do it sensibly. For example, it is clearly acceptable to overload + to use it for both integer and floating-point addition. In fact, this overloading simplifies a language by reducing the number of operators. However, suppose the programmer defined + used between single-dimensioned array operands to mean the sum of all elements of both arrays. Because the usual meaning of vector addition is quite different from this, it would make the program more confusing for both the author and the program's readers. An even more extreme example of program confusion would be a user defining + between two vector operands to mean the difference between their respective first elements. Operator overloading is further discussed in Chapter 7.

Simplicity in languages can, of course, be carried too far. For example, the form and meaning of most assembly language statements are models of simplicity, as you can see when you consider the statements that appear in the next section. This very simplicity, however, makes assembly language programs less readable. Because they lack more complex control statements, their structure is less obvious; because their statements are simple, far more of them are required than equivalent programs in a high-level language. These same arguments apply to the less extreme case of high-level languages with inadequate control and data structuring constructs.

1.3.1.2 Orthogonality

Orthogonality in a programming language means that a relatively small set of primitive constructs can be combined in a relatively small number of ways to build the control and data structures of the language. Furthermore, every possible combination of primitives is legal and meaningful. For example, consider data types. Suppose a language has four primitive data types, integer, float, double, and character, and two type operators, array and pointer. If the two type operators can be applied to themselves and the four primitive data types, a large number of data structures can be defined. However, if pointers were not allowed to point to arrays, many of those possibilities would be eliminated.

The meaning of an orthogonal language feature is independent of the context of its appearance in a program. (The name *orthogonal* comes from the mathematical concept of orthogonal vectors, which are independent of each other.) Orthogonality follows from a symmetry of relationships among primitives. Pointers should be able to point to any type of variable or data structure. The lack of orthogonality leads to exceptions to the rules of the language.

We can illustrate the use of orthogonality as a design concept by comparing one aspect of the assembly languages of the IBM mainframe computers and the VAX series of superminicomputers. We consider a single simple situation: adding two 32-bit integer values that reside in either memory or registers and replacing one of the two values with the sum. The IBM mainframes have two instructions for this purpose, which have the forms

```
A    Reg1, memory_cell
AR   Reg1, Reg2
```

where Reg1 and Reg2 represent registers. The semantics of these are

```
Reg1 ← contents(Reg1) + contents(memory_cell)
Reg1 ← contents(Reg1) + contents(Reg2)
```

The VAX addition instruction for 32-bit integer values is

```
ADDL   operand_1, operand_2
```

whose semantics is

```
operand_2 ← contents(operand_1) + contents(operand_2)
```

In this case, either operand can be a register or a memory cell.

The VAX instruction design is orthogonal in that a single instruction can use either registers or memory cells as the operands. There are two ways to specify operands, which can be combined in all possible ways. The IBM design is not orthogonal. Only two operand combinations are legal out of four possibilities, and the two require different instructions, A and AR. The IBM design is more restricted and therefore less writable. For example, you cannot add two values and store the sum in a memory location. Furthermore, the IBM design is more difficult to learn because of the restrictions and the additional instruction.

Orthogonality is closely related to simplicity: The more orthogonal the design of a language, the fewer exceptions the language rules require. Fewer exceptions mean a higher degree of regularity in the design, which makes the language easier to learn, read, and understand. Anyone who has learned a significant part of the English language can testify to the difficulty of learning its many rule exceptions (for example, *i* before *e* except after *c*).

As examples of the lack of orthogonality in a high-level language, manifested as rule exceptions, consider the following rules in C. Although C has two kinds of structured data types, arrays and records (**struct**s), records can be returned from functions but arrays cannot. A member of a structure can be any data type except **void** or a structure of the same type. An array element can be any data type except **void** or a function. Parameters are passed by value, unless they are arrays, in which case they are, in effect, passed by reference (because the appearance of an array name without a subscript in a C program is interpreted to be the address of the array's first element). A simple addition expression, such as

```
a + b
```

usually means the values of a and b are fetched from memory and added. However, if a happens to be a pointer, the fetched value of b may be changed before the addition takes place. For example, if a points at a value that is two bytes long, b's value is multiplied by 2 before the addition takes place. The type of a, which is the left context of

```
+ b
```

forces the value of b to be modified before it is added to a.

Too much orthogonality can also cause problems. Perhaps the most orthogonal programming language is ALGOL 68 (van Wijngaarden et al., 1969). Every language construct in ALGOL 68 has a type, and there are no restrictions on those types. In addition, most constructs produce values. This combinational freedom allows extremely complex constructs. For example, a conditional can appear as the left side of an assignment, along with declarations and other assorted statements, as long as the result is an address. This extreme form of orthogonality leads to unnecessary complexity. Furthermore, because languages require a large number of primitives, a high degree of orthogonality results in an explosion of combinations. So, even if the combinations are simple, their sheer numbers lead to complexity.

Simplicity in a language, therefore, is at least in part the result of a combination of a relatively small number of primitive constructs and a limited use of the concept of orthogonality.

Some believe that functional languages offer a good combination of simplicity and orthogonality. A functional language, such as LISP, is one in which computations are made primarily by applying functions to given parameters. In contrast, in imperative languages such as C, C++, and Java, computations are usually specified with variables and assignment statements. Functional languages offer potentially the greatest overall simplicity because they can accomplish everything with a single construct, the function call, which can be combined with other function calls in simple ways. This simple elegance is the reason why some language researchers are attracted to functional languages as the primary alternative to complex nonfunctional languages such as C++. Other factors, such as efficiency, however, have prevented functional languages from becoming more widely used.

1.3.1.3 Control Statements

The structured programming revolution of the 1970s was in part a reaction to the poor readability caused by the inadequate control statements of some of the languages of the 1950s and 1960s. In particular, it became widely recognized that indiscriminate use of goto statements severely reduces program readability. A program that can be read from top to bottom is much easier to understand than a program that requires the reader to jump from one statement to some nonadjacent statement in order to follow the execution order. In certain languages, however, gotos that branch upward are sometimes necessary; for example, they are required to construct **while** loops in Fortran 77 (which are not part of the language). For example, consider the following nested loops, written in C:

```
while (incr < 20) {
   while (sum <= 100) {
      sum += incr;
   }
   incr++;
```

```
}
```

If C did not have a loop construct, this would be written as follows:

```
loop1:
  if (incr >= 20) go to out;
loop2:
 if (sum > 100) go to next;
  sum += incr;
  go to loop2;
next:
  incr++;
  go to loop1:
out:
```

The versions of BASIC and Fortran that were available in the early 1970s lacked the control statements that allow strong restrictions on the use of gotos, so writing highly readable programs in those languages was difficult. Most programming languages designed since the late 1960s, however, have included sufficient control statements, so the need for the goto statement has been greatly reduced, if not eliminated. Therefore, the control statement design of a language is now a less important factor in readability than it was in the past.

1.3.1.4 Data Types and Structures

The presence of adequate facilities for defining data types and data structures in a language is another significant aid to readability. For example, suppose a numeric type is used for an indicator flag because there is no Boolean type in the language. In such a language, we might have an assignment such as

```
timeOut = 1
```

whose meaning is unclear, whereas in a language that includes Boolean types, we would have

```
timeOut = true
```

whose meaning is perfectly clear. Similarly, record data types provide a method for representing employee records that is more readable than using a collection of similar arrays, one for each data item in an employee record, which is the required method in a language without records. For example, in Fortran 90, an array of employee records might be stored in the following arrays:

```
Character (Len = 30) Name (100)
Integer Age (100), Employee_Number (100)
Real Salary (100)
```

Then a particular employee is represented by the elements of these four arrays with the same subscript value.

1.3.1.5 Syntax Considerations

The syntax, or form, of the elements of a language has a significant effect on the readability of programs. The following are two examples of syntactic design choices that affect readability:

- *Identifier forms*. Restricting identifiers to very short lengths detracts from readability. If identifiers can have six characters at most, as in Fortran 77, it is often not possible to use connotative names for variables. A more extreme example is the original American National Standards Institute (ANSI) BASIC (ANSI, 1978b), in which an identifier could consist only of a single letter or a single letter followed by a single digit.

    Other design issues concerning identifier forms are discussed in Chapter 5.

- *Special words*. Program appearance and thus program readability are strongly influenced by the forms of a language's special words (for example, **while**, **class**, and **for**). Especially important is the method of forming compound statements, or statement groups, primarily in control constructs. Some languages have used matching pairs of special words or symbols to form groups. Pascal requires **begin-end** pairs to form groups for nearly all of its control constructs. C and its descendants use braces for the same purpose. All of these languages suffer because statement groups are always terminated in the same way, which makes it difficult to determine which group is being ended when an **end** or } appears. Fortran 95 and Ada make this clearer by using a distinct closing syntax for each type of statement group. For example, Ada uses **end if** to terminate a selection construct, and **end loop** to terminate a loop construct. This is an example of the conflict between simplicity that results in fewer reserved words, as in C++, and the greater readability that can result from using more reserved words, as in Ada.

    Another important issue is whether the special words of a language can be used as names for program variables. If so, the resulting programs can be very confusing. For example, in Fortran 95, special words such as Do and End are legal variable names, so the appearance of these words in a program may or may not connote something special.

- *Form and meaning*. Designing statements so that their appearance at least partially indicates their purpose is an obvious aid to readability. Semantics, or meaning, should follow directly from syntax, or form. In some cases, this principle is violated by two language constructs that are identical or similar in appearance but have different meanings, depending perhaps on context. In C, for example, the meaning of the reserved word **static** depends on the context of its appearance. If used on the definition of a variable inside a function, it means the variable is created at compile time. If used on the definition of a variable that is outside all functions, it means the variable is visible only in the file in which its definition appears; that is, it is not exported from that file.

One of the primary complaints about the shell commands of UNIX (Kernighan and Pike, 1984) is that their appearance does not always suggest their function. For example, the UNIX command grep can be deciphered only through prior knowledge, or perhaps cleverness and familiarity with the UNIX editor, ed. Its appearance connotes nothing to UNIX beginners. (In ed, the command /regular_expression/ searches for a substring that matches the regular expression. Preceding this with g makes it a global command, specifying that the scope of the search is the whole file being edited. Following the command with p specifies that lines with the matching substring are to be printed. So g/regular_expression/p, which can obviously be abbreviated as grep, prints all lines in a file that contain substrings that match the regular expression.)

1.3.2 Writability

Writability is a measure of how easily a language can be used to create programs for a chosen problem domain. Most of the language characteristics that affect readability also affect writability. This follows directly from the fact that the process of writing a program requires the programmer frequently to reread the part of the program that is already written.

As is the case with readability, writability must be considered in the context of the target problem domain of a language. It is simply not reasonable to compare the writability of two languages in the realm of a particular application when one was designed for that application and the other was not. For example, the writabilities of COBOL (ANSI, 1985) and Fortran are dramatically different for creating a program to deal with two-dimensional data structures, for which Fortran is ideal. Their writabilities are also quite different for producing financial reports with complex formats, for which COBOL was designed.

The following subsections describe the most important factors influencing the writability of a language.

1.3.2.1 Simplicity and Orthogonality

If a language has a large number of different constructs, some programmers may not be familiar with all of them. This can lead to a misuse of some features and a disuse of others that may be either more elegant or more efficient, or both, than those that are used. It may even be possible, as noted by Hoare (1973), to use unknown features accidentally, with bizarre results. Therefore, a smaller number of primitive constructs and a consistent set of rules for combining them (that is, orthogonality) is much better than simply having a large number of primitives. A programmer can design a solution to a complex problem after learning only a simple set of primitive constructs.

On the other hand, too much orthogonality can be a detriment to writability. Errors in writing programs can go undetected when nearly any combination of primitives is legal. This can lead to absurdities in code that cannot be discovered by the compiler.

1.3.2.2 Support for Abstraction

Briefly, **abstraction** means the ability to define and then use complicated structures or operations in ways that allow many of the details to be ignored. Abstraction is a key concept in contemporary programming language design. This is a reflection of the central role that abstraction plays in modern program design methodologies. The degree of abstraction allowed by a programming language and the naturalness of its expression are therefore very important to its writability. Programming languages can support two distinct categories of abstraction, process and data.

A simple example of process abstraction is the use of a subprogram to implement a sort algorithm that is required several times in a program. Without the subprogram, the sort code would have to be replicated in all places where it was needed, which would make the program much longer and more tedious to write. More importantly, if the subprogram were not used, the code that used the sort subprogram would be cluttered with the sort algorithm details, greatly obscuring the flow and overall intent of that code.

As an example of data abstraction, consider a binary tree that stores integer data in its nodes. Such a binary tree would usually be implemented in a language that does not support pointers and dynamic storage management with a heap, such as Fortran 77, as three parallel integer arrays, where two of the integers are used as subscripts to specify offspring nodes. In C++ and Java, these trees can be implemented by using an abstraction of a tree node in the form of a simple class with two pointers (or references) and an integer. The naturalness of the latter representation makes it much easier to write a program that uses binary trees in these languages than to write one in Fortran 77. It is a simple matter of the problem solution domain of the language being closer to the problem domain.

The overall support for abstraction is clearly an important factor in the writability of a language.

1.3.2.3 Expressivity

Expressivity in a language can refer to several different characteristics. In a language like APL, it means that there are very powerful operators that allow a great deal of computation to be accomplished with a very small program. It more commonly means that a language has relatively convenient, rather than cumbersome, ways of specifying computations. For example, in C, the notation `count++` is more convenient and shorter than `count = count + 1`. Also, the **and then** Boolean operator in Ada is a convenient way of specifying short-circuit evaluation of a Boolean expression. The inclusion of the **for** statement in Java makes writing counting loops easier than with the use of **while**, which is also possible. All of these increase the writability of a language.

1.3.3   Reliability

A program is said to be **reliable** if it performs to its specifications under all conditions. The following subsections describe several language features that have a significant effect on the reliability of programs in a given language.

1.3.3.1 Type Checking

Type checking is simply testing for type errors in a given program, either by the compiler or during program execution. Type checking is an important factor in language reliability. Because run-time type checking is expensive, compile-time checking is more desirable. Furthermore, the earlier errors in programs are detected, the less expensive it is to make the required repairs. The design of Java requires checks of the types of nearly all variables and expressions at compile time. This virtually eliminates type errors at run time in Java programs. Types and type checking are discussed in depth in Chapters 5 and 6.

One example of how failure to type check, at either compile time or run time, has led to countless program errors is the use of subprogram parameters in the original C language (Kernighan and Ritchie, 1978). In this language, the type of an actual parameter in a function call was not checked to determine whether its type matched that of the corresponding formal parameter in the function. An **int** type variable could be used as an actual parameter in a call to a function that expected a **float** type as its formal parameter, and neither the compiler nor the run-time system would have detected the inconsistency. This naturally led to problems, the source of which were often difficult to determine.[1] The current version of C (ISO, 1999) has eliminated this problem by requiring all parameters to be type checked. Subprograms and parameter-passing techniques are discussed in Chapter 9.

1.3.3.2 Exception Handling

The ability of a program to intercept run-time errors (as well as other unusual conditions detected by the program), take corrective measures, and then continue is a great aid to reliability. This language facility is called **exception handling.** Ada, C++, and Java include extensive capabilities for exception

---

[1] In response to this and other similar problems, UNIX systems include a utility program named `lint` that checks C programs for such problems.

handling, but such facilities are practically nonexistent in many widely used languages, such as C and Fortran. Exception handling is discussed in Chapter 14.

1.3.3.3 Aliasing

Loosely defined, **aliasing** is having two or more distinct referencing methods, or names, for the same memory cell. It is now widely accepted that aliasing is a dangerous feature in a programming language. Most programming languages allow some kind of aliasing—for example, union members and pointers set to point to the same variable in C. In both cases, two different program variables can refer to the same memory cell. Some kinds of aliasing, as described in Chapters 5 and 9, can be prohibited by the design of a language.

In some languages, aliasing is used to overcome deficiencies in the language's data abstraction facilities. Other languages greatly restrict aliasing to increase their reliability.

1.3.3.4 Readability and Writability

Both readability and writability influence reliability. A program written in a language that does not support natural ways to express the required algorithms will necessarily use unnatural approaches. Unnatural approaches will be less likely to be correct for all possible situations. The easier a program is to write, the more likely it is to be correct.

Readability affects reliability in both the writing and maintenance phases of the life cycle. Programs that are difficult to read are difficult both to write and to modify.

1.3.4   Cost

The ultimate total cost of a programming language is a function of many of its characteristics.

First, there is the cost of training programmers to use the language. This is a function of the simplicity and orthogonality of the language and the experience of the programmers. Though more powerful languages need not be harder to learn, they often are.

Second is the cost of writing programs in the language. This is a function of the writability of the language, which depends in part on its closeness in purpose to the particular application. The original efforts to design and implement high-level languages were driven by the desire to lower the costs of creating software.

Both the cost of training programmers and the cost of writing programs in a language can be significantly reduced in a good programming environment. Programming environments are discussed in Section 1.8.

Third is the cost of compiling programs in the language. A major impediment to the early use of Ada was the prohibitively high cost of running the first-generation Ada compilers. This problem was diminished by the appearance of better Ada compilers.

Fourth, the cost of executing programs written in a language is greatly influenced by that language's design. A language that requires many run-time type checks will prohibit fast code execution, regardless of the quality of the compiler. Although execution efficiency was the foremost concern in the design of early languages, it is now considered to be less important.

A simple trade-off can be made between compilation cost and execution speed of the compiled code. *Optimization* is the name given to the collection of techniques that compilers may use to decrease the size and/or increase the execution speed of the code they produce. If little or no optimization is done, compilation can be done much faster than if a significant effort is made to produce optimized code. The extra compilation effort results in faster code execution. The choice between the two alternatives is determined by the environment in which the compiler will be used. In a laboratory for beginning programming students, who use a great deal of compiling time but little code execution time (their programs are small and they must execute correctly only once), little or no optimization should be done. In a production environment, where completed programs are executed many times, it is better to pay the extra cost to optimize the code.

The fifth factor in the cost of a language is the cost of the language implementation system. One of the factors that explains the rapid acceptance of Java is that free compiler/interpreter systems have been available for it since soon after its design was first released. A language whose implementation system is either expensive or runs only on expensive hardware will have a much smaller chance of ever becoming widely used. For example, the high cost of first-generation Ada compilers helped prevent Ada from becoming popular in the early days.

Sixth is the cost of poor reliability. If the software fails in a critical system, such as a nuclear power plant or an X-ray machine, the cost could be very high. The failures of noncritical systems can also be very expensive in terms of lost future business or lawsuits over defective software systems.

The final consideration is the cost of maintaining programs, which includes both corrections and modifications to add new capabilities. The cost of software maintenance depends on a number of language characteristics but primarily readability. Because maintenance is often done by individuals other than the original author of the software, poor readability can make the task extremely challenging.

The importance of maintainability of software cannot be overstated. It has been estimated that, for large software systems with relatively long lifetimes, maintenance costs can be as high as two to four times as much as development costs (Sommerville, 2000).

Of all the contributors to language costs, three are most important: program development, maintenance, and reliability. Because these are functions of writability and readability, these two evaluation criteria are, in turn, the most important.

Of course, a number of other criteria could be used for evaluating programming languages. One example is portability, or the ease with which programs can be moved from one implementation to another. Portability is most strongly influenced by the degree of standardization of the language. Some languages, such as BASIC, are not standardized at all, making BASIC programs very difficult to move from one implementation to another. Standardization is a time-consuming and difficult process. A committee began work on producing a standard version of C++ in 1989. It was approved in 1998.

Generality (the applicability to a wide range of applications) and well-definedness (the completeness and precision of the language's official defining document) are two other criteria.

Most criteria, particularly readability, writability, and reliability, are neither precisely defined nor exactly measurable. They are useful concepts, however, and they provide valuable insight into the design and evaluation of programming languages.

A final note on evaluation criteria: Language design criteria are weighed differently from different perspectives. Language implementors are concerned primarily with the difficulty of implementing the constructs and features of the language. Language users are worried about writability first and readability later. Language designers are likely to emphasize elegance and the ability to attract widespread use. These characteristics sometimes conflict with one another.

1.4   Influences on Language Design

In addition to those factors described in Section 1.3, several other factors influence the basic design of programming languages. The most important of these are computer architecture and program design methodologies.

1.4.1   Computer Architecture

The basic architecture of computers has had a profound effect on language design. Most of the popular languages of the past 45 years have been designed around the prevalent computer architecture, called the von Neumann architecture, after one of its originators, John von Neumann (pronounced "von Noyman"). These languages are called **imperative** languages. In a von Neumann computer, both data and programs are stored in the same memory. The central processing unit (CPU), which actually executes instructions, is separate from the memory. Therefore, instructions and data must be piped, or transmitted, from memory to the CPU. Results of operations in the CPU must be moved back to memory. Nearly all digital computers built since the 1940s have been based on the von Neumann architecture. The overall structure of a von Neumann computer is shown in Figure 1.1.

Figure 1.1

The von Neumann
computer architecture

Central processing unit

Because of the von Neumann architecture, the central features of imperative languages are variables, which model the memory cells; assignment statements, which are based on the piping operation; and the iterative form of repetition, which is the most efficient way to implement repetition on this architecture. Operands in expressions are piped from memory to the CPU, and the result of evaluating the expression is piped back to the memory cell represented by the left side of the assignment. Iteration is fast on von Neumann computers because instructions are stored in adjacent cells of memory. This efficiency discourages the use of recursion for repetition, although recursion is often more natural.

As stated earlier, a functional, or applicative, language is one in which the primary means of computation is applying functions to given parameters. Programming can be done in a functional language without the kind of variables that are used in imperative languages, without assignment statements, and without iteration. Although many computer scientists have expounded on the myriad benefits of functional languages, such as LISP, it is unlikely that they will displace the imperative languages until a non–von Neumann computer is designed that will allow efficient execution of programs in functional languages. Among those who have bemoaned this fact, the most eloquent has been John Backus, the principal designer of the original version of Fortran (Backus, 1978).

The parallel architecture machines that have appeared over the past 20 years hold some promise for speeding the execution of functional programs, but so far it has not been enough to make them competitive with imperative programs. In fact, although there are elegant ways of using parallel architectures to execute functional programs, most parallel machines are used for imperative programs particularly those written in dialects of Fortran.

In spite of the fact that the structure of imperative programming languages is modeled on a machine architecture, rather than on the abilities and inclinations of the users of programming languages, some believe that using imperative languages is somehow more natural than using a functional language.

1.4.2 Programming Methodologies

The late 1960s and early 1970s brought an intense analysis, begun in large part by the structured programming movement, of both the software development process and programming language design.

An important reason for this research was the shift in the major cost of computing from hardware to software, as hardware costs decreased and programmer costs increased. Increases in programmer productivity were relatively small. In addition, progressively larger and more complex problems were being solved by computers. Rather than simply solving sets of equations to simulate satellite tracks, as in the early 1960s, programs were being written for large and complex tasks, such as controlling large petroleum refining facilities and providing worldwide airline reservation systems.

The new software development methodologies that emerged as a result of the research of the 1970s were called top-down design and stepwise refinement. The primary programming language deficiencies that were discovered were incompleteness of type checking and inadequacy of control statements (requiring the extensive use of gotos).

In the late 1970s, a shift from procedure-oriented to data-oriented program design methodologies began. Simply put, data-oriented methods emphasize data design, focusing on the use of abstract data types to solve problems.

For data abstraction to be used effectively in software system design, it must be supported by the languages used for implementation. The first language to provide even limited support for data abstraction was SIMULA 67 (Birtwistle et al., 1973), although that language certainly was not propelled to popularity because of it. The benefits of data abstraction were not widely recognized until the early 1970s. However, most languages designed since the late 1970s support data abstraction. Data abstraction is discussed in detail in Chapter 11.

The latest step in the evolution of data-oriented software development, which began in the early 1980s, is object-oriented design. Object-oriented methodology begins with data abstraction, which encapsulates processing with data objects and hides access to data, and adds inheritance and dynamic method binding. Inheritance is a powerful concept that greatly enhances the potential reuse of existing software, thereby providing the possibility of significant increases in software development productivity. This is an important factor in the increase in popularity of object-oriented languages. Dynamic (run-time) method binding allows more flexible use of inheritance.

Object-oriented programming developed along with a language that supported its concepts: Smalltalk (Goldberg and Robson, 1989). Although Smalltalk never became as widely used as some other languages, support for object-oriented programming is now part of most popular imperative languages, including Ada 95 (ARM, 1995), Java, and C++. Object-oriented concepts have also found their way into functional programming in CLOS (Bobrow et al., 1988) and logic programming in Prolog++ (Moss, 1994). Language support for object-oriented programming is discussed in detail in Chapter 12.

Procedure-oriented programming is, in a sense, the opposite of data-oriented programming. Although data-oriented methods now dominate software development, procedure-oriented methods have not been abandoned. On the contrary, a good deal of research has occurred in procedure-oriented programming in recent years, especially in the area of concurrency. These research efforts brought with them the need for language facilities for creating and controlling concurrent program units. Ada and Java include such capabilities. Concurrency is discussed in detail in Chapter 13.

1.5   Language Categories

Programming languages are often categorized into four bins: imperative, functional, logic, and object oriented. We have already discussed the characteristics of imperative and functional languages. We have also described how the most popular object-oriented languages grew out of imperative languages. Although the object-oriented software development paradigm differs greatly from the procedure-oriented paradigm usually used with imperative languages, the extensions to an imperative language required to support object-oriented programming are not overwhelming. For example, the expressions, assignment statements, and control statements of C and Java are nearly identical. (On the other hand, the arrays, subprograms, and semantics of Java are very different from those of C.)

Another kind of language, the visual language, forms another subcategory of the imperative languages. The most popular visual language is Visual BASIC (Schneider, 1999), which is now being replaced by Visual BASIC .NET (Balena, 2002). These languages (or their implementations) include capabilites for drag-and-drop generation of code segments. Such languages were once called fourth-generation languages, though that name has now fallen out of use. The characterizing feature of a visual language provides a simple way to generate graphical user interfaces to programs. For example, in Visual BASIC the code to produce a display of a form control, such as a button or text box, can be created with a single keystroke.

A logic programming language is an example of a rule-based language. In an imperative language, an algorithm is specified in great detail, and the specific order of execution of the instructions or statements must be included. In a rule-based language, rules are specified in no particular order, and the language implementation system must choose an execution order that produces the desired result. This approach to software development is radically different from those used with the other three kinds of languages and clearly requires a completely different kind of language. Prolog, the most commonly used logic programming language, and logic programming are discussed in Chapter 16.

Markup languages, such as HTML, are sometimes confused with programming languages. However, markup languages do not specify computations; rather, they describe the general appearance of documents. However, many of the design and evaluation criteria described in this chapter also apply to markup languages. After all, it is obviously important that markup code is easy to write and read. In spite of this, however, we do not discuss markup languages in this book.

1.6   Language Design Trade-offs

The programming language evaluation criteria described in Section 1.3 provide a framework for language design. Unfortunately, that framework is self-contradictory. In his insightful paper on language design, Hoare (1973) states that "there are so many important but conflicting criteria, that their reconciliation and satisfaction is a major engineering task."

Two criteria that conflict are reliability and cost of execution. For example, the Java language definition demands that all references to array elements be checked to ensure that the index or indices are in their legal ranges. This adds a great deal to the cost of execution of Java programs that contain large numbers of references to array elements. C does not require index range checking, so C programs execute faster than semantically equivalent Java programs, although Java programs are more reliable. The designers of Java traded execution efficiency for reliability.

As another example of conflicting criteria that leads directly to design trade-offs, consider the case of APL. APL includes a powerful set of operators for array operands. Because of the large number of operators, a significant number of new symbols had to be included in APL to represent the operators. Also, many APL operators can be used in a single long, complex expression. One result of this high degree of expressivity is that, for applications involving many array operations, APL is very writable. Indeed, a huge amount of computation can be specified in a very compact program. Another result is that APL programs have very poor readability. A compact and concise expression has a certain mathematical beauty but is difficult for anyone other than the person who wrote it to understand. The well-known author Daniel McCracken once noted that it took him four hours to read and understand a four-line APL program (McCracken, 1970). The designers of APL traded readability for writability.

The conflict between flexibility and safety is a common one in language design. Pascal variant records allow a memory cell to contain different type values at different times. For example, a cell may contain either a pointer or an integer. So a pointer value put in such a cell can be operated on as if it were an integer, using any operation defined for integer values. This provides a loophole in Pascal's type checking that allows a program to do arithmetic on pointers, which is sometimes convenient. However, this unchecked use of memory cells is, in general, a dangerous practice.

Examples of conflicts among language design (and evaluation) criteria abound; some are subtle, others are obvious. It is therefore clear that the task of choosing constructs and features when designing a programming language involves a collection of compromises and trade-offs.

1.7   Implementation Methods

As described in Section 1.4.1, two of the primary components of a computer are its internal memory and its processor. The internal memory is used to store programs and data. The processor is a collection of circuits that provides a realization of a set of primitive operations, or machine instructions, such as those for arithmetic and logic operations. In most computers, some of these instructions, which are sometimes called macroinstructions, are actually implemented with an even lower-level set of instructions called microinstructions. Because microinstructions are never seen by software, they will not be discussed further here.

The machine language of the computer is its set of macroinstructions. In the absence of other supporting software, its own machine language is the only language that most hardware computers "understand." Theoretically, a computer could be designed and built with a particular high-level language as its machine language, but it would be very complex and expensive. Furthermore, it would be highly inflexible, because it would be difficult (though not impossible) to use it with other high-level languages. The more practical machine design choice implements in hardware a very low-level language that provides the most commonly needed primitive operations and requires system software to create an interface to programs in higher-level languages.

A language implementation system cannot be the only software on a computer. Also required is a large collection of programs, called the operating system, which supplies higher-level primitives than those of the machine language. These primitives provide system resource management, input and output operations, a file management system, text and/or program editors, and a variety of other commonly needed functions. Because language implementation systems need many of the operating system facilities, they interface to the operating system rather than directly to the processor (in machine language).

The operating system and language implementations are layered over the machine language interface of a computer. These layers can be thought of as virtual computers, providing interfaces to the user at higher levels. For example, an operating system and a C compiler provide a virtual C computer. With other compilers, a machine can become other kinds of virtual computers. Most computer systems provide several different virtual computers. User programs form another layer over the top of the layer of virtual computers.

The layered view of a computer is shown in Figure 1.2.

The implementation systems of the first high-level programming languages, constructed in the late 1950s, were among the most complex software systems of that time. In the 1960s, intensive research efforts were made to understand and formalize the process of constructing these high-level language implementations. The greatest success of those efforts was in the area of syntax analysis, primarily because that part of the implementation process is an application of parts of automata theory and formal language theory that were then well understood.

Figure 1.2

Layered interface of virtual computers, provided by a typical computer system

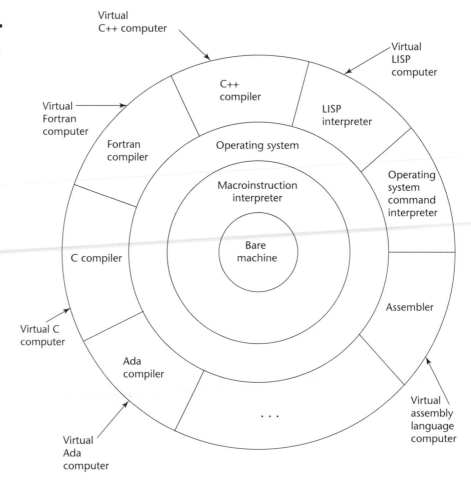

1.7.1 Compilation

Programming languages can be implemented by any of three general methods. At one extreme, programs can be translated into machine language, which can be executed directly on the computer. This is called a **compiler** implementation. This method has the advantage of very fast program execution, once the translation process is complete. Most production implementations of languages such as C, COBOL, and Ada are by compilers.

The language that a compiler translates is called the **source language**. The process of compilation takes place in several phases, the most important of which are shown in Figure 1.3.

Figure 1.3

The compilation process

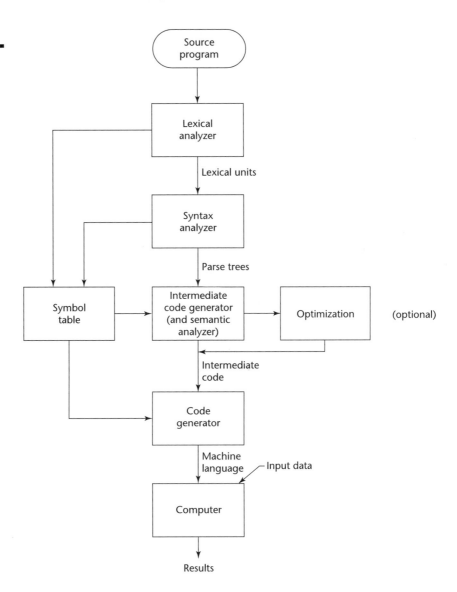

The lexical analyzer gathers the characters of the source program into lexical units. The lexical units of a program are identifiers, special words, operators, and punctuation symbols. The lexical analyzer ignores comments in the source program, because the compiler has no use for them.

The syntax analyzer takes the lexical units from the lexical analyzer and uses them to construct hierarchical structures called **parse trees**. These parse trees represent the syntactic structure of the program. In many cases, no actual parse tree structure is constructed; rather, the information that would be required to build a tree is generated and used. Both lexical units and parse trees are further discussed in Chapter 3. Both lexical analysis and syntax analysis, or parsing, are discussed in Chapter 4.

The intermediate code generator produces a program in a different language, at an intermediate level between the source program and the final output of the compiler, the machine language program. (Note that the words *program* and *code* are often used interchangeably.) Intermediate languages sometimes look very much like assembly languages and in fact sometimes are actual assembly languages. In other cases, the intermediate code is at a level somewhat higher than an assembly language. The semantic analyzer is an integral part of the intermediate code generator. The semantic analyzer checks for errors that are difficult if not impossible to detect during syntax analysis, such as type errors.

Optimization, which improves programs by making them smaller or faster or both, is often an optional part of compilation. In fact, some compilers are incapable of doing any significant optimization. This type of compiler would be used in situations where execution speed of the translated program is far less important than compilation speed. An example of such a situation is a computing laboratory for beginning programmers. In most commercial and industrial situations, execution speed is more important than compilation speed, so optimization is routinely desirable. Because many kinds of optimization are difficult to do on machine language, most optimization is done on the intermediate code.

The code generator translates the optimized intermediate code version of the program into an equivalent machine language program.

The symbol table serves as a database for the compilation process. The primary contents of the symbol table are the type and attribute information of each user-defined name in the program. This information is placed in the symbol table by the lexical and syntax analyzers and is used by the semantic analyzer and the code generator.

As stated above, although the machine language generated by a compiler can be executed directly on the hardware, it must nearly always be run along with some other code. Most user programs also require programs from the operating system. Among the most common of these are programs for input and output. The compiler builds calls to required system programs when they are needed by the user program. Before the machine language programs produced by a compiler can be executed, the required programs from the operating system must be found and linked to the user program. The linking operation connects the user program to the system programs by placing the addresses of the entry points of the system programs in the calls to them in the user program. The user and system code together are sometimes called a **load module,** or **executable image.** The process of collecting system programs and linking them to user programs is called **linking and loading,** or sometimes just **linking.** It is accomplished by a systems program called a **linker.**

In addition to systems programs, user programs must often be linked to previously compiled user programs that reside in libraries. So the linker not only links a given program to system programs, it may also link it to other user programs.

The execution of a machine code program on a von Neumann architecture computer occurs in a process called the **fetch-execute cycle.** As stated in Section 1.4.1, programs reside in memory but are executed in the CPU. Each instruction to be executed must be moved from memory to the processor. The address of the next instruction to be executed is maintained in a register called the **program counter.** The fetch-execute cycle can be simply described by the following algorithm:

```
initialize the program counter
repeat forever
        fetch the instruction pointed to by the program counter
        increment the program counter to point at the next instruction
        decode the instruction
        execute the instruction
end repeat
```

The "decode the instruction" step in the process above means the instruction is examined to determine what action it specifies. Program execution terminates when a stop instruction is encountered, although on an actual computer a stop instruction is rarely executed. Rather, control transfers from the operating system to a user program for its execution and then back to the operating system when the user program execution is complete. In a computer system in which more than one user program may be in memory at a given time, this process is far more complex.

The speed of the connection between a computer's memory and its processor usually determines the speed of the computer, because instructions often can be executed faster than they can be moved to the processor for execution. This connection is called the **von Neumann bottleneck;** it is the primary limiting factor in the speed of von Neumann architecture computers. The von Neumann bottleneck has been one of the primary motivations for the research and development of parallel computers.

1.7.2   Pure Interpretation

Pure interpretation lies at the opposite end (from compilation) of implementation methods. With this approach, programs are interpreted by another program called an interpreter, with no translation whatever. The interpreter program acts as a software simulation of a machine whose fetch-execute cycle deals with high-level language program statements rather than machine instructions. This software simulation obviously provides a virtual machine for the language.

Pure interpretation has the advantage of allowing easy implementation of many source-level debugging operations, because all run-time error messages can refer to source-level units. For example, if an array index is found to be out of range, the error message can easily indicate the source line and the name of the array. On the other hand, this method has the serious disadvantage that execution is 10 to 100 times slower than in compiled systems. The primary source of this slowness is the decoding of the high-level language statements, which are far more complex than machine language instructions (although there may be fewer statements than instructions in equivalent machine code). Furthermore, regardless of how many times a statement is executed, it must be decoded every time. Therefore, statement decoding, rather than the connection between the processor and memory, is the bottleneck of a pure interpreter.

Another disadvantage of pure interpretation is that it often requires more space. In addition to the source program, the symbol table must be present during interpretation. Furthermore, the source program may be stored in a form designed for easy access and modification rather than one that provides for minimal size.

Although some simple early languages of the 1960s (APL, SNOBOL, and LISP) were purely interpreted, by the 1980s, the approach was rarely used on high-level languages. However, in recent years pure interpretation has made a significant comeback with some Web scripting languages, such as JavaScript and PHP, which are now widely used.

The process of pure interpretation is shown in Figure 1.4.

Figure 1.4

Pure interpretation

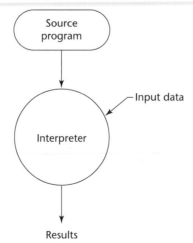

1.7.3   Hybrid Implementation Systems

Some language implementation systems are a compromise between compilers and pure interpreters; they translate high-level language programs to an intermediate language designed to allow easy interpretation. This method is faster than pure interpretation because the source language statements are decoded only once. Such implementations are called **hybrid implementation systems.**

The process used in a hybrid implementation system is shown in Figure 1.5. Instead of translating intermediate language code to machine code, it simply interprets the intermediate code.

Perl is implemented with a hybrid system. It evolved from the pure interpretive languages sh and awk, but is partially compiled to detect errors before interpretation and to simplify the interpreter.

Figure 1.5

Hybrid implementation system

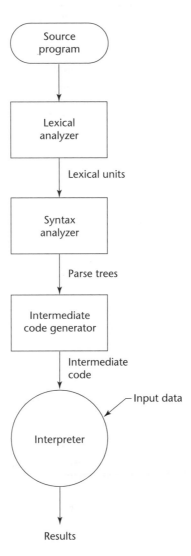

Initial implementations of Java were all hybrid. Its intermediate form, called **byte code**, provides portability to any machine that has a byte code interpreter and an associated run-time system. Together, these are called the Java Virtual Machine. There are now systems that translate Java byte code into machine code for faster execution. However, Java applets are always downloaded from the Web server in the form of byte code.

Sometimes an implementor may provide both compiled and interpreted implementations for a language. In these cases, the interpreter is used to develop and debug programs. Then, after a (relatively) bug-free state is reached, the programs are compiled to increase their execution speed.

1.8 Programming Environments

A programming environment is the collection of tools used in the development of software. This collection may consist of only a file system, a text editor, a linker, and a compiler. Or it may include a large collection of integrated tools, each accessed through a uniform user interface. In the latter case, the development and maintenance of software is greatly enhanced. Therefore, the characteristics of a programming language are not the only measure of the software development capability of a system. We now briefly describe several programming environments.

UNIX is an older programming environment, first distributed in the middle 1970s, built around a portable multiprogramming operating system. It provides a wide array of powerful support tools for software production and maintenance in a variety of languages. In the past, the most important feature absent from UNIX was a uniform interface among its tools. This made it more difficult to learn and to use. However, UNIX is now often used through a graphical interface that runs on top of UNIX. One example of such a graphical interface is the Common Desktop Environment (CDE).

Borland JBuilder is a programming environment that provides an integrated compiler, editor, debugger, and file system for Java development, where all four are accessed through a graphical interface. This is a complex and powerful system for creating Java software.

The latest step in the evolution of software development environments is represented by Microsoft Visual Studio .NET. This is a large and elaborate collection of software development tools, all used through a windowed interface. This system can be used to develop software in any one of the five .NET languages, C#, Visual BASIC .NET, JScript, J#, or managed C++.

SUMMARY

The study of programming languages is valuable for a number of important reasons: It increases our capacity to use different constructs in writing programs, enables us to choose languages for projects more intelligently, and makes learning new languages easier.

Computers are used in a wide variety of problem-solving domains. The design and evaluation of a particular programming language is highly dependent on the domain in which it is to be used.

Among the most important criteria for evaluating languages are readability, writability, reliability, and overall cost. These will be the basis on which we examine and judge the various language features discussed in the remainder of the book.

The major influences on language design have been machine architecture and software design methodologies.

Designing a programming language is primarily an engineering feat, in which a long list of trade-offs must be made among features, constructs, and capabilities.

The major methods of implementing programming languages are compilation, pure interpretation, and hybrid implementation.

Programming environments have become important parts of software development systems, in which the language is just one of the components.

REVIEW QUESTIONS

1. Why is it useful for a programmer to have some background in language design, even though he or she may never actually design a programming language?

2. How can knowledge of programming language characteristics benefit the whole computing community?

3. What programming language has dominated scientific computing over the past 40 years?

4. What programming language has dominated business applications over the past 40 years?

5. What programming language has dominated artificial intelligence over the past 40 years?

6. In what language is UNIX written?

7. What is the disadvantage of having too many features in a language?

8. How can user-defined operator overloading harm the readability of a program?

9. What is one example of a lack of orthogonality in the design of C?

10. What language used orthogonality as a primary design criterion?

11. What primitive control statement is used to build more complicated control statements in languages that lack them?

12. What readability problem is caused by using the same closing reserved word for more than one kind of control statement?

13. What construct of a programming language provides process abstraction?

14. What does it mean for a program to be reliable?

15. Why is type checking the parameters of a subprogram important?

16. What is aliasing?

17. What is exception handling?

18. Why is readability important to writability?

19. How is the cost of compilers for a given language related to the design of that language?

20. What has been the strongest influence on programming language design over the past 45 years?

21. What is the name of the category of programming languages whose structure is dictated by the von Neumann computer architecture?

22. What two programming language deficiencies were discovered as a result of the research in software development in the 1970s?

23. What are the three fundamental features of an object-oriented programming language?

24. What language was the first to support the three fundamental features of object-oriented programming?

25. What is an example of two language design criteria that are in direct conflict with each other?

26. What are the three general methods of implementing a programming language?

27. Which produces faster program execution, a compiler or a pure interpreter?

28. What role does the symbol table play in a compiler?

29. What does a linker do?

30. Why is the von Neumann bottleneck important?

31. What are the advantages in implementing a language with a pure interpreter?

PROBLEM SET

1. Do you believe our thinking capabilities are influenced by our language? Support your opinion.

2. What are some features of specific programming languages you know whose rationales are a mystery to you?

3. What arguments can you make for the idea of a single language for all programming domains?

4. What arguments can you make against the idea of a single language for all programming domains?

5. Name and explain another criterion by which languages can be judged (in addition to those discussed in this chapter).

6. What common programming language statement, in your opinion, is most detrimental to readability?

7. Java uses a right brace to mark the end of all compound statements. What are the arguments for and against this design?

8. Many languages distinguish between uppercase and lowercase in user-defined names. What are the pros and cons of this design decision?

9. Explain the different aspects of the cost of a programming language.

10. What are the arguments for writing efficient programs even though hardware is relatively inexpensive?

11. Describe some design trade-offs between efficiency and safety in some language you know.

12. What major features would a perfect programming language include, in your opinion?

13. Was the first high-level programming language you learned implemented with a pure interpreter, a hybrid implementation system, or a compiler? (You would not necessarily know this without research.)

14. Describe the advantages and disadvantages of some programming environment you have used.

15. How do type declaration statements for simple variables affect the readability of a language, considering that some languages do not require them?

16. Write an evaluation of some programming language you know, using the criteria described in this chapter.

17. Ada uses the semicolon to separate statements, while Java uses it to terminate statements. Which of these, in your opinion, is most natural and least likely to result in syntax errors? Support your answer.

18. Many contemporary languages allow two kinds of comments, one in which delimiters are used on both ends (for multiple-line comments), and one in which a delimiter marks only the beginning of the comment (for one-line comments). Discuss the advantages and disadvantages of each of these with respect to our criteria.

2

Evolution of the Major Programming Languages

T his chapter follows chronologically the development of a collection of programming languages, exploring the environment in which each was designed and focusing on the contributions of the language and the motivation for its development. Overall language descriptions are not included; rather, we discuss only the new features introduced by each language. Of particular interest are the features that most influenced subsequent languages or the field of computer science.

This chapter does not include an in-depth discussion of any language feature or concept; that is left for later chapters. Brief, informal explanations of features will suffice for our trek through the development of these languages.

The choice as to which languages to discuss here was subjective, and many readers will unhappily note the absence of one or more of their favorites. However, to keep this historical coverage to a reasonable size, it was necessary to leave out several languages that some regard highly. The choices were based on our estimate of each language's importance to language development and the computing world as a whole. We also include brief discussions of some other languages that are referenced later in the book.

This chapter includes listings of 12 complete example programs, each in a different language. None of these programs are described in this chapter; they are meant simply to illustrate the appearance of programs in these languages. Readers familiar with any of the common imperative languages should be able to read and understand most of the code in these programs, except those in LISP, COBOL, and Smalltalk. (The LISP example is discussed in Chapter 15.) The same problem is solved by the Fortran, ALGOL 60, PL/I, BASIC, Pascal, C, Ada, Java, and JavaScript programs. Note that most of the contemporary languages in this list support dynamic arrays, but because of the simplicity of the example problem, we did not use them in the example programs. Also, in the Fortran 95 program, we avoided using the features that could have avoided the use of loops altogether, in part to keep the program simple and readable and in part just to illustrate the basic loop structure of the language.

Figure 2.1 is a chart of the genealogy of the high-level languages discussed in this chapter.

2.1   Zuse's Plankalkül

The first programming language discussed in this chapter is highly unusual in several respects. For one thing, it was never implemented. Furthermore, although developed in 1945, its description was not published until 1972. Because so few people were familiar with the language, some of its capabilities did not appear in other languages until 15 years after Plankalkül's development.

2.1.1   Historical Background

Between 1936 and 1945, the German scientist Konrad Zuse (pronounced "Tsoo-zuh") built a series of complex and sophisticated computers from

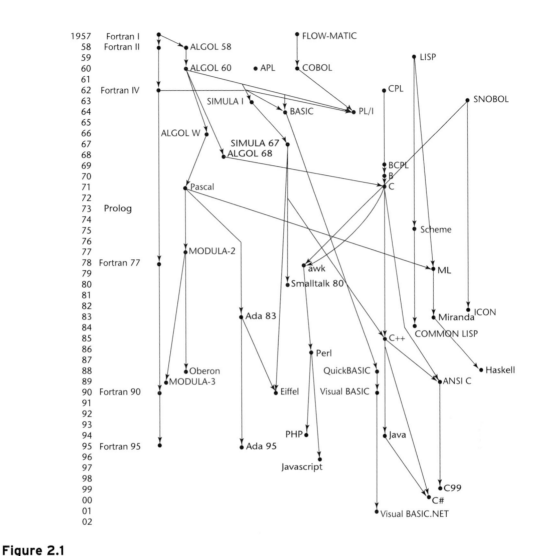

Figure 2.1

Genealogy of common high-level programming languages

electromechanical relays. By early 1945, the war had destroyed all but one of his latest models, the Z4, so he moved to a remote Bavarian village, Hinterstein, and his research group members went their separate ways.

Working alone, Zuse embarked on an effort to develop a language for expressing computations, a project he had begun in 1943 as a proposal for his Ph.D. dissertation. He named this language Plankalkül, which means program calculus. In a lengthy manuscript dated 1945 but not published until 1972 (Zuse, 1972), Zuse defined Plankalkül and wrote algorithms in the language for a wide variety of problems.

2.1.2 Language Overview

Plankalkül was remarkably complete, with some of its most advanced features in the area of data structures. The simplest data type in Plankalkül was the single bit. From the bit type were built types for integer and floating-point numeric types. The floating-point type used twos-complement notation and the "hidden bit" scheme currently used to avoid storing the most significant bit of the normalized fraction part of a value.

In addition to these usual scalar types, Plankalkül included arrays and records. The records could use recursion to include other records as elements.

Although the language had no explicit goto, it did include an iterative statement similar to the Ada **for**. It also had the command **Fin** with a superscript that specified a jump out of a given number of iteration loop nestings or to the beginning of a new iteration cycle. Plankalkül included a selection statement, but it did not allow an else clause.

One of the most interesting features of Zuse's programs was the inclusion of mathematical expressions showing the relationships between program variables. These expressions stated what would be true during execution at the points in the code where they appeared. These are very similar to the assertions used in the Eiffel programming language (Meyer, 1992) and in axiomatic semantics, which is discussed in Chapter 3.

Zuse's manuscript contained programs of far greater complexity than any written prior to 1945. Included were programs to sort arrays of numbers; test the connectivity of a given graph; carry out integer and floating-point operations, including square root; and perform syntax analysis on logic formulas that had parentheses and operators in six different levels of precedence. Perhaps most remarkable were his 49 pages of algorithms for playing chess, a game in which he was not an expert.

If a computer scientist had found Zuse's description of Plankalkül in the early 1950s, the single aspect of the language that would have hindered its implementation as defined would have been the notation. Each statement consisted of either two or three lines of code. The first line was most like the statements of current languages. The second line, which was optional, contained the subscripts of the array references in the first line. It is interesting to note that the same method of indicating subscripts was used by Charles Babbage in programs for his Analytical Engine in the mid-nineteenth century. The last line of each Plankalkül statement contained the type names for the variables mentioned in the first line. This notation is quite intimidating when first seen.

The following example assignment statement, which assigns the value of the expression A[4]+1 to A[5], illustrates this notation. The row labeled V is for subscripts, and the row labeled S is for the data types. In this example, 1.n means an integer of *n* bits:

```
    | A + 1 => A
V   | 4         5
S   | 1.n       1.n
```

We can only speculate on the direction that programming language design might have taken if Zuse's work had been widely known in 1945 or even 1950. It is also interesting to consider how his work might have been different had he done it in a peaceful environment surrounded by other scientists, rather than in Germany in 1945 in virtual isolation.

2.2   Minimal Hardware Programming: Pseudocodes

The computers that became available in the late 1940s and early 1950s were far less usable than those of today. In addition to being slow, unreliable, expensive, and having extremely small memories, the machines of that time were difficult to program because of the lack of supporting software.

There were no high-level programming languages or even assembly languages, so programming was done in machine code, which is both tedious and error-prone. Among its problems is the use of numeric codes for specifying instructions. For example, an ADD instruction might be specified by the code 14 rather than a connotative textual name, even if only a single letter. This makes programs very difficult to read. A more serious problem is absolute addressing, which makes programs very difficult to modify. For example, suppose we have a machine language program that is stored in memory. Many of the instructions in such a program refer to other locations within the program, usually to reference data or to indicate the targets of branch instructions. Inserting an instruction at any position in the program other than at the end invalidates the correctness of all instructions that refer to addresses beyond the insertion point, because those addresses must be increased to make room for the new instruction. To make the addition correctly, all those instructions that refer to addresses that follow the addition must be found and modified. A similar problem occurs with deletion of an instruction. In this case, however, machine languages often include a "no operation" instruction that can replace deleted instructions, thereby avoiding the problem.

These are standard problems with all machine languages and were the primary motivations for inventing assemblers and assembly languages. In addition, most programming problems of that time were numerical and required floating-point arithmetic operations and indexing of some sort to allow the convenient use of arrays. Neither of these capabilities, however, was included in the architecture of the computers of the late 1940s and early 1950s. These deficiencies naturally led to the development of somewhat higher-level languages.

2.2.1 Short Code

The first of these new languages, named Short Code, was developed by John Mauchly in 1949 for the BINAC computer. Short Code was later transferred to a UNIVAC I computer and, for several years, was one of the primary means of programming those machines. Although little is known of the original Short Code because its complete description was never published, a programming manual for the UNIVAC I version did survive (Remington-Rand, 1952). It is safe to assume that the two versions were very similar.

The UNIVAC I had words that had 72 bits, grouped as 12 six-bit bytes. Short Code consisted of coded versions of mathematical expressions that were to be evaluated. The codes were byte-pair values, and most equations fit into a word. Some of the codes were

```
01  -        06  abs value    1n  (n+2)nd power
02  )        07  +            2n  (n+2)nd root
03  =        08  pause        4n  if <= n
04  /        09  (            58  print and tab
```

Variables, or memory locations, were named with byte-pair codes, as were locations to be used as constants. For example, X0 and Y0 could be variables. The statement

```
X0 = SQRT(ABS(Y0))
```

would be coded in a word as 00 X0 03 20 06 Y0. The initial 00 was used as padding to fill the word. Interestingly, there was no multiplication code; multiplication was indicated by simply placing the two operands next to each other, as in algebra.

Short Code was not translated to machine code; rather, it was implemented with a pure interpreter. At the time, this process was called automatic programming. It clearly simplified the programming process but at the expense of execution time. Short Code interpretation was approximately fifty times slower than machine code.

2.2.2 Speedcoding

In other places, interpretive systems were being developed that extended machine languages to include floating-point operations. The Speedcoding system developed by John Backus for the IBM 701 is an example of such a system (Backus, 1954). The Speedcoding interpreter effectively converted the 701 to a virtual three-address floating-point calculator. The system included pseudoinstructions for the four arithmetic operations on floating-point data, as well as operations such as square root, sine, arc tangent, exponent, and logarithm. Conditional and unconditional branches and input/output conversions were also part of the virtual architecture. To get an idea of the limitations of such systems, consider that the remaining usable memory after loading the interpreter was only 700 words and that the add instruction took 4.2 milliseconds to execute. On the other hand, Speedcoding included the novel facility of automatically incrementing address registers. This facility did not appear in hardware until the UNIVAC 1107 computers of 1962. Because of such features, matrix multiplication could be done in 12 Speedcoding instructions. Backus claimed that problems that could take two weeks to program in machine code could be programmed in a few hours using Speedcoding.

2.2.3 The UNIVAC "Compiling" System

Between 1951 and 1953, a team led by Grace Hopper at UNIVAC developed a series of "compiling" systems named A-0, A-1, and A-2 that expanded a pseudocode into machine code subprograms in the same way as macros are expanded into assembly language. The pseudocode source for these "compilers" was still quite primitive, although even this was a great improvement over machine code because it made source programs much shorter. Wilkes (1952) independently suggested a similar process.

2.2.4 Related Work

Other means of easing the task of programming were being developed at about the same time. At Cambridge University, David J. Wheeler developed a method of using blocks of relocatable addresses to partially solve the problem of absolute addressing (Wheeler, 1950), and later, Maurice V. Wilkes (also at Cambridge) extended the idea to design an assembly program that could combine chosen subroutines and allocate storage (Wilkes et al., 1951, 1957). This was indeed an important and fundamental advance.

We should also mention that assembly languages, which are quite different from the pseudocodes mentioned, evolved during the early 1950s. However, they had little impact on the design of high-level languages.

2.3   The IBM 704 and Fortran

Certainly one of the greatest single advances in computing came with the introduction of the IBM 704 in 1954, in large measure because its capabilities prompted the development of Fortran. One could argue that if it had not been IBM with the 704 and Fortran, it would soon thereafter have been some other organization with a similar computer and related high-level language. However, IBM was the first with both the foresight and the resources to undertake these developments.

2.3.1   Historical Background

One of the primary reasons why interpretive systems were tolerated from the late 1940s to the mid-1950s was the lack of floating-point hardware in the available computers. All floating-point operations had to be simulated in software, a very time-consuming process. Because so much processor time was spent in software floating-point processing, the overhead of interpretation and the simulation of indexing were relatively insignificant. As long as floating-point had to be done by software, interpretation was an acceptable expense. However, many programmers of that time never used interpretive systems, preferring the efficiency of hand-coded machine (or assembly) language. The announcement of the IBM 704 system, with both indexing and floating-point instructions in hardware, heralded the end of the interpretive era, at least for scientific computation. The inclusion of floating-point hardware removed the hiding place for the cost of interpretation.

Although Fortran is often credited with being the first compiled high-level language, the question of who deserves credit for implementing the first such language is somewhat open. Knuth and Pardo (1977) give the credit to Alick E. Glennie for his Autocode compiler for the Manchester Mark I computer. Glennie developed the compiler at Fort Halstead, Royal Armaments Research Establishment, in England. The compiler was operational by September 1952. However, according to John Backus (Wexelblat, 1981, p. 26), Glennie's Autocode was so low level and machine oriented that it should not be considered a compiled system. Backus gives the credit to Laning and Zierler at Massachusetts Institute of Technology.

The Laning and Zierler system (Laning and Zierler, 1954) was the first algebraic translation system to be implemented. By algebraic we mean that it translated arithmetic expressions, used function calls for mathematical functions, and included subscripted variable references. The system was implemented on the MIT Whirlwind computer, in experimental prototype form, in the summer of 1952, and in a more usable form by May 1953. The translator generated a subroutine call to code each formula, or expression, in the program. The source language was easy to read, and the only actual machine instructions included were for branching. Although this work preceded the work on Fortran, it never escaped MIT.

In spite of these earlier works, the first widely accepted compiled high-level language was Fortran. The following subsections chronicle this important development.

2.3.2   Design Process

Even before the 704 system was announced in May 1954, plans were begun for Fortran. By November 1954, John Backus and his group at IBM had produced the report entitled "The IBM Mathematical FORmula TRANslating System: Fortran" (IBM, 1954). This document described the first version of Fortran, which we refer to as Fortran 0, prior to its implementation. It also boldly stated that Fortran would provide the efficiency of hand-coded programs and the ease of programming of the interpretive pseudocode systems. In another burst of optimism, the document stated that Fortran would eliminate coding errors and the debugging process. Based on this premise, the first Fortran compiler included little syntax error checking.

The environment in which Fortran was developed was as follows: (1) Computers were still small, slow, and relatively unreliable. (2) The primary use of computers was for scientific computations. (3) There were no existing efficient ways to program computers. (4) Because of the high cost of computers compared to the cost of programmers, speed of the generated object code was the primary goal of the first Fortran compilers. The characteristics of the early versions of Fortran follow directly from this environment.

2.3.3 Fortran I Overview

Fortran 0 was modified during the implementation period, which began in January 1955 and continued until the release of the compiler in April 1957. The implemented language, which we call Fortran I, is described in the first Fortran *Programmer's Reference Manual*, published in October 1956 (IBM, 1956). Fortran I included input/output formatting, variable names of up to six characters (it had been just two in Fortran 0), user-defined subroutines, although they could not be separately compiled, the If selection statement, and the Do loop statement.

Fortran 0 included a logical If statement whose Boolean expression used relational operators in their algebraic form—for example, > for "greater than." The 704 character set did not include characters such as >, so these relational operators had to be replaced. Because the machine had a three-way branch instruction based on the comparison of the value in a storage location with the value in a register, the original logical If was replaced with the arithmetic selection, which has the form

```
If (arithmetic expression) N1, N2, N3
```

where N1, N2, and N3 are statement labels. If the value of the expression is negative, the branch is to N1; if zero, it is to N2; if greater than zero, to N3. This statement is still part of Fortran.

The form of the Fortran I iterative (loop) statement was

```
Do N1 variable = first_value, last_value
```

where N1 was the label of the last statement of the body of the loop, and the statement on the line following the Do was the first.

As with the If statement, the 704 had a single instruction to implement the Do. Because the instruction was designed for posttest loops, Fortran I's Do was designed in that way. A pretest loop could have been implemented on the 704, but that would have required one additional machine instruction, and because efficiency was the overriding concern in the design of Fortran, it was not done.

All of Fortran I's control statements were based on 704 instructions. It is not clear whether the 704 designers dictated the control statement design of Fortran I or whether the designers of Fortran I suggested these instructions to the 704 designers.

There were no data-typing statements in the Fortran I language. Variables whose names began with I, J, K, L, M, and N were implicitly integer type, and all others were implicitly floating-point. The choice of the letters for this convention was based on the fact that at that time integers were used primarily as subscripts, and scientists usually used i, j, and k for subscripts. To be generous, Fortran's designers threw in the three additional letters.

The most audacious claim made by the Fortran development group during the design of the language was that the machine code produced by the compiler would be about as efficient as what could be produced by hand.[1] This, more than anything else, made skeptics of potential users and prevented a great deal of interest in Fortran before its actual release. To almost everyone's surprise, however, the Fortran development group nearly achieved its goal in efficiency. The largest part of the 18 worker-years of effort used to construct the first compiler had been spent on optimization, and the results were remarkably effective.

The early success of Fortran is shown by the results of a survey made in April 1958. At that time, roughly half of the code being written for 704s was being done in Fortran, in spite of the extreme skepticism of most of the programming world only a year earlier.

2.3.4   Fortran II

The Fortran II compiler was distributed in the spring of 1958. It fixed many of the bugs in the Fortran I compilation system and added some significant features to the language, the most important being the independent compilation of subroutines. Without independent compilation, any change in a program requires that the entire program be recompiled. Fortran I's lack of independent compilation capability, coupled with the poor reliability of the 704, placed a practical restriction on the length of programs to about 300 to 400 lines (Wexelblat, 1981, p. 68). Longer programs had a poor chance of being compiled completely before a machine failure occurred. The capability of including precompiled machine language versions of subprograms shortened the compilation process considerably.

2.3.5   Fortrans IV, 77, 90, and 95

A Fortran III was developed, but it was never widely distributed. Fortran IV, however, became one of the most widely used programming languages of its

---

[1]In fact, the Fortran team believed that the code generated by their compiler could be no less than half as fast as handwritten machine code, or the language would not be adopted by users.

time. It evolved over the period 1960 to 1962 and was standardized as Fortran 66 (ANSI, 1966), although that name is rarely used. Fortran IV was an improvement over Fortran II in many ways. Among its most important additions were explicit type declarations for variables, a logical `If` construct, and the capability of passing subprograms as parameters to other subprograms.

Fortran IV was replaced by Fortran 77, which became the new standard in 1978 (ANSI, 1978a). Fortran 77 retained most of the features of Fortran IV and added character string handling, logical loop control statements, and an `If` with an optional `Else` clause.

Fortran 90 (ANSI, 1992) is dramatically different from Fortran 77. The most significant changes are briefly described in the following paragraphs.

A collection of functions is built in for array operations. These include `Dotproduct`, `Matmul`, `Transpose`, `Maxval`, `Minval`, `Product`, and `Sum`, whose meanings are obvious from their names. These are just a few of the most useful functions available.

Arrays can be dynamically allocated and deallocated on command if they have been declared to be `Allocatable`. This is a radical departure from earlier Fortrans, which had only static data. A form of records, called derived types, is included. Pointers are also part of Fortran 90.

New control statements have been added: `Case` is a multiple selection statement, `Exit` is used to depart prematurely from a loop, and `Cycle` is used to transfer control to the bottom of a loop but not out.

Subprograms can be recursive and also have optional and keyword parameters.

A module facility has been added that is similar to the packages of Ada. Modules can contain data declarations and subprograms, each of which can be either `Private` or `Public` to regulate external access.

One new concept that is included in the Fortran 90 definition is that of removing language features from earlier versions. While Fortran 90 includes all of the features of Fortran 77, it has two lists of features that may be eliminated in future versions of Fortran. The obsolescent features list has features that may be eliminated in the next version of Fortran after 90. Included in this list are such things as the arithmetic `If` and the assigned `Goto` statements. The deprecated features list has features that may be eliminated in the second subsequent version after 90. Included in this list are the `Common`, `Equivalence`, and computed `Goto` statements as well as statement functions.

Fortran 90 included two simple syntactic changes that altered the appearance of both programs and the literature describing the language. First, the required fixed format of code, which required the use of specific character positions for specific parts of statements was dropped. For example, statement labels could appear only in the first five positions and statements could not begin before the seventh position. This rigid formatting of code was designed around the use of punch cards. The second change was that the official spelling of FORTRAN became Fortran. This change was accompanied by the change in convention of using all uppercase letters for keywords and identifiers in Fortran programs. Now, the convention is that uppercase letters begin keywords and identifiers, but lowercase is used otherwise.

The latest version of Fortran, Fortran 95 (ANSI, 1997), continues the evolution of the language. A new iteration construct, `Forall`, which is included to ease the task of parallelizing Fortran programs. Several features of Fortran 90 are absent from Fortran 95—among these are the `Pause`, `Assign`, and assigned `Goto` statements. In addition, several other features have been placed on the "obsolescent" list, among them the arithmetic `If` and computed `Goto` statements. These will be considered for removal at the next revision of the language.

2.3.6   Evaluation

The original Fortran design team thought of language design only as a necessary prelude to the critical task of designing the translator. Further, it never occurred to them that Fortran would be used on computers not manufactured by IBM. Indeed, they were forced to consider building Fortran compilers for other IBM machines only because the successor to the 704, the 709, was announced before the 704 Fortran compiler was released. The effect that Fortran has had on the use of computers, along with the fact that all subsequent programming languages owe a debt to Fortran, are indeed impressive in light of the modest goals of its designers.

One of the features of Fortran I, and all of its successors before 90, that allows highly optimizing compilers is that the types and storage for all variables are fixed before run time. No new variables or space can be allocated during run time. This is a sacrifice of flexibility to simplicity and efficiency. It eliminates the possibility of recursive subprograms and makes it difficult to implement data structures that grow or change shape dynamically. Of course, the kinds of programs that were being built at the time of the development of the early versions of Fortran were primarily numerical in nature and were simple in comparison with recent software projects. Therefore, the sacrifice was not a great one.

The overall success of Fortran is difficult to overstate: It dramatically changed forever the way computers are used. This is, of course, in large part due to its being the first widely used high-level language. In comparison with concepts and languages developed later, early versions of Fortran suffer in a variety of ways, as should be expected. After all, it would not be fair to compare the performance and comfort of a 1910 Model T Ford with the performance and comfort of a 2003 Ford Thunderbird. Nevertheless, in spite of the inadequacies of Fortran, the momentum of the huge investment in Fortran software, among other factors, has kept it among the most widely used of all high-level languages.

Alan Perlis, one of the designers of ALGOL 60, said of Fortran in 1978, "Fortran is the *lingua franca* of the computing world. It is the language of the streets in the best sense of the word, not in the prostitutional sense of the word. And it has survived and will survive because it has turned out to be a remarkably useful part of a very vital commerce" (Wexelblat, 1981, p. 161).

The following is an example of a Fortran 95 program:

```
Program Example

! Fortran 95 Example program
!  Input:  An integer, List_Len, where List_Len is less
!          than 100, followed by List_Len-Integer values
!  Output: The number of input values that are greater
!          than the average of all input values
Implicit none
Integer :: Int_List(99)
Integer :: List_Len, Counter, Sum, Average, Result
Result= 0
Sum = 0
Read *, List_Len
If ((List_Len > 0) .AND. (List_Len < 100)) Then
! Read input data into an array and compute its sum
   Do Counter = 1, List_Len
      Read *, Int_List(Counter)
      Sum = Sum + Int_List(Counter)
   End Do
! Compute the average
   Average = Sum / List_Len
! Count the values that are greater than the average
   Do Counter = 1, List_Len
      If (Int_List(Counter) > Average) Then
         Result = Result + 1
      End If
   End Do
! Print the result
   Print *, 'Number of values > Average is:', Result
Else
   Print *, 'Error - list length value is not legal'
End If
End Program Example
```

2.4 Functional Programming: LISP

The first functional programming language was invented to provide language features for list processing, the need for which grew out of the first applications in the area of artificial intelligence (AI).

2.4.1 The Beginnings of Artificial Intelligence and List Processing

Interest in AI appeared in the mid-1950s in a number of places. Some of this interest grew out of linguistics, some from psychology, and some from mathematics. Linguists were concerned with natural language processing. Psychologists were interested in modeling human information storage and retrieval, along with other fundamental processes of the brain. Mathematicians were interested in mechanizing certain intelligent processes, such as theorem proving. All of these investigations arrived at the same conclusion: Some method must be developed to allow computers to process symbolic data in linked lists. At the time, most computation was on numeric data in arrays.

The concept of list processing was developed by Allen Newell, J. C. Shaw, and Herbert Simon. It was first published in a classic paper that describes one of the first AI programs, the Logical Theorist,[2] and a language in which it could be implemented (Newell and Simon, 1956). The language, named IPL-I (Information Processing Language I), was never implemented. The next version, IPL-II, was implemented on a Rand Corporation Johnniac computer. Development of IPL continued until 1960, when the description of IPL-V was published (Newell and Tonge, 1960). The low level of the IPL languages prevented their widespread use. They were actually assembly languages for a hypothetical computer, implemented with an interpreter, in which list-processing instructions were included. The first implementation was on the obscure Johnniac machine, another factor that kept the IPL languages from becoming popular.

The contributions of the IPL languages were in their list design, and their demonstration that list processing was feasible and useful.

IBM became interested in AI in the mid-1950s and chose theorem proving as a demonstration area. At the time, the Fortran project was still under way. The high cost of the Fortran I compiler convinced IBM that their list processing should be attached to Fortran, rather than in the form of a new language. Thus, the Fortran List Processing Language (FLPL) was designed and implemented as an extension to Fortran. FLPL was used to construct a theorem prover for plane geometry, which was then considered the easiest area for mechanical theorem proving.

2.4.2   LISP Design Process

John McCarthy of MIT took a summer position at the IBM Information Research Department in 1958. His goal for the summer was to investigate symbolic computations and develop a set of requirements for doing such computations. As a pilot example problem area, he chose differentiation of algebraic expressions. From this study came a list of language requirements. Among them were the control flow methods of mathematical functions: recursion and conditional expressions. The only available high-level language of the time, Fortran I, had neither of these.

Another requirement that grew from the symbolic differentiation investigation was the need for dynamically allocated linked lists and some kind of implicit deallocation of abandoned lists. McCarthy simply would not allow

---

[2]Logical Theorist discovered proofs for theorems in propositional calculus.

his elegant algorithm for differentiation to be cluttered with explicit deallocation statements.

Because FLPL did not support recursion, conditional expressions, dynamic storage allocation, or implicit deallocation, it was clear to McCarthy that a new language was required.

When McCarthy returned to MIT in the fall of 1958, he and Marvin Minsky formed the MIT AI Project, with funding from the Research Laboratory for Electronics. The first important effort of the project was to produce a system for list processing. It was to be used initially to implement a program proposed by McCarthy called the Advice Taker.[3] This application became the impetus for the development of the list-processing language LISP. The first version of LISP is sometimes called pure LISP because it is a purely functional language. In the following section, we describe the development of pure LISP.

2.4.3 Language Overview

2.4.3.1 Data Structures

Pure LISP has only two kinds of data structures: atoms and lists. Atoms are either symbols, which have the form of identifiers, or numeric literals. The concept of storing symbolic information in linked lists is natural and was used in IPL-II. Such structures allow insertions and deletions at any point, operations that were then thought to be a necessary part of list processing. As it eventually developed, however, LISP rarely requires these operations.

Lists are specified by delimiting their elements with parentheses. Simple lists, in which elements are restricted to atoms, have the form

(A B C D)

Nested list structures are also specified by parentheses. For example, the list

(A (B C) D (E (F G)))

is composed of four elements. The first is the atom A; the second is the sublist (B C); the third is the atom D; the fourth is the sublist (E (F G)), which has as its second element the sublist (F G).

Internally, lists are usually stored as single-linked list structures, in which each node has two pointers and represents a list element. A node for an atom has its first pointer pointing to some representation of the atom, such as its symbol or numeric value, or the pointer to a sublist. A node for a sublist element has its first pointer pointing to the first node of the sublist. In both cas-

---

[3]Advice Taker represented information with sentences written in a formal language and used a logical inferencing process to decide what to do.

es, the second pointer of a node points to the next element of the list. A list is referenced by a pointer to its first element.

The internal representations of the two lists shown earlier are depicted in Figure 2.2. Note that the elements of a list are shown horizontally. The last element of a list has no successor, so its link is NIL, which is represented in Figure 2.2 as a diagonal line in the element. Sublists are shown with the same structure.

2.4.3.2 Processes in Functional Programming

LISP was designed as a functional programming language. All computation in a purely functional program is accomplished by applying functions to arguments. Neither the assignment statements nor the variables that abound in imperative language programs are necessary in functional language programs. Furthermore, iterative processes can be specified with recursive function calls, making loops unnecessary. These basic concepts of functional programming make it significantly different from programming in an imperative language.

2.4.3.3 The Syntax of LISP

LISP is very different from the imperative languages, both because it is a functional programming language and because LISP programs look so different from those in languages like Java or C++. For example, the syntax of Java

Figure 2.2

Internal representation
of two LISP lists

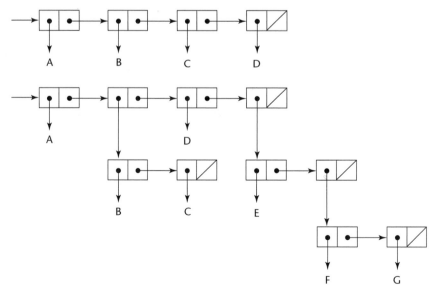

is a complicated mixture of English and algebra, while LISP's syntax is a model of simplicity. Program code and data have exactly the same form: parenthesized lists. Consider again the list

(A B C D)

When interpreted as data, it is a list of four elements. When viewed as code, it is the application of the function named A to the three parameters B, C, and D.

2.4.4 Evaluation

LISP completely dominated AI applications for a quarter of a century. It is still the most widely used language for AI. Much of the cause of LISP's reputation for being highly inefficient has been eliminated. Many contemporary implementations are compiled, and the resulting code is much faster than running the source code on an interpreter. In addition to its success in AI, LISP pioneered functional programming, which has proven to be a lively area of research in programming languages. As stated in Chapter 1, many programming language researchers believe functional programming is a much better approach to software development than the use of imperative languages.

During the 1970s and early 1980s, a large number of different dialects of LISP were developed and used. This led to the familiar problem of portability. To rectify this situation, a standard version named COMMON LISP was developed (Steele, 1984).

Scheme, a dialect of LISP, and functional programming are discussed below and at length in Chapter 15. The following is an example of a LISP program.

```
; LISP Example function
; The following code defines a LISP predicate function,
; that  takes two lists as arguments and returns True
; if the two lists are equal, and NIL (false)otherwise
(DEFUN equal_lists (lis1 lis2)
  (COND
    ((ATOM lis1) (EQ lis1 lis2))
    ((ATOM lis2) NIL)
    ((equal_lists (CAR lis1) (CAR lis2))
        (equal_lists (CDR lis1) (CDR lis2)))
    (T NIL)
  )
)
```

2.4.5 Two Descendants of LISP

Two dialects of LISP are now commonly used, Scheme and COMMON LISP. These are briefly discussed in the following subsections.

2.4.5.1 Scheme

The Scheme language emerged from MIT in the mid-1970s (Sussman and Steele, 1975). It is characterized by its small size, its exclusive use of static scoping (discussed in Chapter 5), and its treatment of functions as first-class entities. As first-class entities, Scheme functions can be the values of expressions and elements of lists; they can be assigned to variables, passed as parameters, and returned as the values of function applications. Early versions of LISP did not provide all of these capabilities, nor did they use static scoping.

As a small language with simple syntax and semantics, Scheme is well suited to educational applications, such as courses in functional programming and general introductions to programming. As mentioned before, Scheme is described in some detail in Chapter 15.

2.4.5.2 COMMON LISP

COMMON LISP (Steele, 1984) was created in an effort to combine the features of several dialects of LISP developed in the early 1980s, including Scheme, into a single language. Being such an amalgam, COMMON LISP is a large and complex language. Its basis, however, is pure LISP, so its syntax, primitive functions, and fundamental nature come from that language.

Recognizing the flexibility provided by dynamic scoping as well as the simplicity of static scoping, COMMON LISP allows both. The default scoping for variables is static, but by declaring a variable to be **special**, that variable becomes dynamically scoped.

COMMON LISP has a large number of data types and structures, including records, arrays, complex numbers, and character strings. It also has a form of packages for modularizing collections of functions and data providing access control.

COMMON LISP is further described in Chapter 15.

2.4.6 Related Languages

ML (*Meta*Language) (Ullman, 1998) was originally designed in the 1980s by Robin Milner at the University of Edinburgh as a metalanguage for a program verification system named Logic for Computable Functions (LCF) (Milner et al., 1990). ML is primarily a functional language, but it also supports imperative programming. Unlike LISP and Scheme, the type of every variable and expression in ML can be determined at compile time. Types are associated with objects rather than names. Types of expressions are inferred from the context of the expression, as discussed in Chapter 7.

Unlike LISP and Scheme, ML does not use the parenthesized functional syntax that originated with lambda expressions. Rather, the syntax of ML resembles that of the imperative languages such as Java and C++.

Miranda was developed by David Turner at the University of Kent in Canterbury, England, in the early 1980s (Turner, 1986). Miranda is based partly on the languages ML, SASL, and KRC. Haskell (Hudak and Fasel, 1992) is based in large part on Miranda. Like Miranda, it is a purely functional language, having no variables and no assignment statement. Another distinguishing characteristic of Haskell is its use of lazy evaluation. No expression is evaluated until its value is required. This leads to some surprising capabilities in the language.

Both ML and Haskell are briefly discussed in Chapter 15.

2.5   The First Step Toward Sophistication: ALGOL 60

ALGOL 60 has had a great influence on subsequent programming languages and is therefore of central importance in any historical review of languages.

2.5.1   Historical Background

ALGOL 60 came into being as a result of efforts to design a universal language. By late 1954, the Laning and Zierler algebraic system had been in operation for over a year, and the first report on Fortran had been published. Fortran became a reality in 1957, and several other high-level languages were being developed. Most notable among them were IT, which was designed by Alan Perlis at Carnegie Tech, and two languages for the UNIVAC computers, MATH-MATIC and UNICODE. The proliferation of languages made communication among users difficult. Furthermore, the new languages were all growing up around single architectures, some for UNIVAC computers and some for IBM 700-series machines. In response to this language proliferation, several major computer-user groups in the United States, including SHARE (the IBM scientific user group) and USE (UNIVAC Scientific Exchange, the large-scale UNIVAC scientific user group), submitted a petition to the Association for Computing Machinery (ACM) on May 10, 1957, to form a committee to study and recommend action to create a universal programming language. Although Fortran might have been a candidate, it could not become a universal language, because at the time it was solely owned by IBM.

Previously, in 1955, GAMM (a German acronym for Society for Applied Mathematics and Mechanics) had also formed a committee to design one universal, machine-independent, algorithmic language for use on all kinds of computers. The desire for this new language was in part due to the Europeans' fear of being dominated by IBM. By late 1957, however, the appearance of several high-level languages in the United States convinced the GAMM subcommittee that their effort had to be widened to include the Americans, and a letter of invitation was sent to ACM. In April 1958, after Fritz Bauer of GAMM presented the formal proposal to ACM, the two groups officially agreed to a joint language design project.

2.5.2 Early Design Process

GAMM and ACM decided that the joint design effort should be made at a meeting to which each group would send four members. The meeting, which was held in Zurich from May 27 to June 1, 1958, began with the following goals for the new language:

- The syntax of the language should be as close as possible to standard mathematical notation, and programs written in it should be readable with little further explanation.
- It should be possible to use the language for the description of computing processes in publications.
- Programs in the new language must be mechanically translatable into machine language.

The first goal indicates that the new language was to be used for scientific programming, which was the primary computer application area at that time. The second was something entirely new to the computing business. The last goal is an obvious necessity for any programming language.

Depending on how it is viewed, the Zurich meeting either produced momentous results or endless arguments. Actually, it did both. The meeting itself involved innumerable compromises, both among individuals and between the two sides of the Atlantic. In some cases, the compromises were not so much over great issues as they were over spheres of influence. The question of whether to use a comma (the European method) or a period (the American method) for a decimal point is one example.

2.5.3 ALGOL 58 Overview

The language designed at the Zurich meeting was named the International Algorithmic Language (IAL). It was suggested during the design that the language be named ALGOL, for ALGOrithmic Language, but the name was rejected because it did not reflect the international scope of the committee. During the following year, however, the name was changed to ALGOL, and the language subsequently became known as ALGOL 58.

In many ways, ALGOL 58 was a descendant of Fortran, which is quite natural. It generalized many of Fortran's features and added several new constructs and concepts. Some of the generalizations had to do with the goal of not tying the language to any particular machine, and others were attempts to make the language more flexible and powerful. A rare combination of simplicity and elegance emerged from the effort.

ALGOL 58 formalized the concept of data type, although only variables that were not floating-point required explicit declaration. It added the idea of compound statements, which most subsequent languages incorporated. Some features of Fortran that were generalized were the following: Identifiers were allowed to have any length, as opposed to Fortran I's restriction to six or fewer characters; any number of array dimensions was allowed, unlike Fortran I's limitation to no more than three; the lower bound of arrays could be specified by the programmer, whereas in Fortran it was implicitly 1; nested selection statements were allowed, which was not the case in Fortran I.

ALGOL 58 acquired the assignment operator in a rather unusual way. Zuse used the form

```
expression ⇒ variable
```

for the assignment statement in Plankalkül. Although Plankalkül had not yet been published, some of the European members of the ALGOL 58 committee were familiar with the language. The committee dabbled with the Plankalkül assignment form but, because of arguments about character limitations, the greater-than symbol was changed to a colon. Then, largely at the insistence of the Americans, the whole statement was turned around to the form

```
variable := expression
```

The Europeans preferred the opposite form.

2.5.4   Reception of the ALGOL 58 Report

Publication of the ALGOL 58 report (Perlis and Samelson, 1958) in December 1958 was greeted with a good deal of enthusiasm. In the United States, the new language was viewed more as a collection of ideas for programming language design than as a universal standard language. Actually, the ALGOL 58 report was not meant to be a finished product but rather a preliminary document for international discussion. Nevertheless, three major design and implementation efforts used the report as their basis. At the University of Michigan, the MAD language was born (Arden et al., 1961). The U.S. Naval Electronics Group produced the NELIAC language (Huskey et al., 1963). At System Development Corporation, JOVIAL was designed and implemented (Shaw, 1963). JOVIAL, an acronym for Jules' Own Version of the International Algebraic Language, represents the only language based on ALGOL 58 to achieve widespread use (Jules was Jules I. Schwartz, one of JOVIAL's designers). JOVIAL became widely used because it was the official scientific language for the U.S. Air Force for a quarter of a century.

The rest of the U.S. computing community was not so kind to the new language. At first, both IBM and its major scientific user group, SHARE, seemed to embrace ALGOL 58. IBM began an implementation shortly after the report was published, and SHARE formed a subcommittee, SHARE IAL, to study the language. The subcommittee subsequently recommended that

ACM standardize ALGOL 58 and that IBM implement it for all of the 700 series computers. The enthusiasm was short-lived, however. By spring 1959, both IBM and SHARE, through their Fortran experience, had had enough of the pain and expense of getting a new language started, both in terms of developing and using the first-generation compilers and in terms of training users in the new language and persuading them to use it. By the middle of 1959, both IBM and SHARE had developed such a vested interest in Fortran that they decided to retain it as *the* scientific language for the IBM 700 series machines, thereby abandoning ALGOL 58.

2.5.5   ALGOL 60 Design Process

During 1959, ALGOL 58 was furiously debated in both Europe and the United States. Large numbers of suggested modifications and additions were published in the European *ALGOL Bulletin* and in *Communications of the ACM*. One of the most important events of 1959 was the presentation of the work of the Zurich committee to the International Conference on Information Processing, for there Backus introduced his new notation for describing the syntax of programming languages, which later became known as BNF (for Backus-Naur form). BNF is described in detail in Chapter 3.

In January 1960, the second ALGOL meeting was held, this time in Paris. The work of this meeting was to debate the 80 suggestions that had been formally submitted for consideration. Peter Naur of Denmark had become heavily involved in the development of ALGOL, even though he had not been a member of the Zurich group. It was Naur who created and published the *ALGOL Bulletin*. He spent a good deal of time studying Backus's paper that introduced BNF and decided that BNF should be used to describe formally the results of the 1960 meeting. After making a few relatively minor changes to BNF, he wrote a description of the new proposed language in BNF and handed it out to the members of the 1960 group at the beginning of the meeting.

2.5.6   ALGOL 60 Overview

Although the 1960 meeting lasted only six days, the modifications made to ALGOL 58 were dramatic. Among the most important new developments were the following:

- The concept of block structure was introduced. This allowed the programmer to localize parts of programs by introducing new data environments, or scopes.
- Two different means of passing parameters to subprograms were allowed: pass by value and pass by name.
- Procedures were allowed to be recursive. The ALGOL 58 description was unclear on this issue. Note that although this recursion was

new for the imperative languages, LISP had already provided recursive functions in 1959.

- Stack-dynamic arrays were allowed. A stack-dynamic array is one for which the subscript range or ranges are specified by variables, so that the size of the array is set at the time storage is allocated to the array, which happens when the declaration is reached during execution. Stack-dynamic arrays are described in detail in Chapter 6.

Several features that might have had a dramatic impact on the success or failure of the language were proposed but rejected. Most important among these were input and output statements with formatting, which were omitted because they were thought to be too machine dependent.

The ALGOL 60 report was published in May 1960 (Naur, 1960). A number of ambiguities still remained in the language description, and a third meeting was scheduled for April 1962 in Rome to address the problems. At this meeting the group dealt only with problems; no additions to the language were allowed. The results of this meeting were published under the title "Revised Report on the Algorithmic Language ALGOL 60" (Backus et al., 1962).

2.5.7 ALGOL 60 Evaluation

In some ways, ALGOL 60 was a great success; in other ways, it was a dismal failure. It succeeded in becoming, almost immediately, the only acceptable formal means of communicating algorithms in computing literature, and it remained for over twenty years the sole language for publishing algorithms. Every imperative programming language designed since 1960 owes something to ALGOL 60. In fact, most are direct or indirect descendants; examples are PL/I, SIMULA 67, ALGOL 68, C, Pascal, Ada, C++, and Java.

The ALGOL 58/ALGOL 60 design effort included a long list of firsts. It was the first time that an international group attempted to design a programming language. It was the first language that was designed to be machine independent. It was also the first language whose syntax was formally described. This successful use of the BNF formalism initiated several important fields of computer science: formal languages, parsing theory, and compiler design. Finally, the structure of ALGOL 60 affected machine architecture. In the most striking example of this, an extension of the language was used as the systems language of a series of large-scale computers, the Burroughs B5000, B6000, and B7000 machines, which were designed with a hardware stack to implement efficiently the block structure and recursive procedures of the language.

On the other side of the coin, ALGOL 60 never achieved widespread use in the United States. Even in Europe, where it was more popular than in the United States, it never became the dominant language. There are a number of reasons for its lack of acceptance. For one thing, some of the features of ALGOL 60 turned out to be too flexible; they made understanding difficult and implementation inefficient. The best example of this is the pass-by-name method of passing parameters to subprograms, which is explained in Chapter 9. The difficulties of implementing ALGOL 60 are evidenced by Rutishauser's statement in 1967 that few if any implementations included the full ALGOL 60 language (Rutishauser, 1967, p. 8).

The lack of input and output statements in the language was another major reason for its lack of acceptance. Implementation-dependent input/output made programs difficult to port to other computers.

One of the most important contributions to computer science that is associated with ALGOL 60, BNF, was also a factor in its lack of acceptance. Although BNF is now considered a simple and elegant means of syntax description, to the world of 1960 it seemed strange and complicated.

Finally, although there were many other problems, the entrenchment of Fortran among users and the lack of support by IBM were probably the most important factors in ALGOL 60's failure to gain widespread use.

The ALGOL 60 effort was never really complete, in the sense that ambiguities and obscurities were always a part of the language description (Knuth, 1967).

The following is an example of an ALGOL 60 program:

```
comment ALGOL 60 Example Program
 Input:   An integer, listlen, where listlen is less than
          100, followed by listlen-integer values
 Output: The number of input values that are greater than
          the average of all the input values   ;
begin
  integer array intlist [1:99];
  integer listlen, counter, sum, average, result;
  sum := 0;
  result := 0;
  readint (listlen);
  if (listlen > 0) ∧ (listlen < 100) then
    begin
comment Read input into an array and compute the average;
    for counter := 1 step 1 until listlen do
      begin
      readint (intlist[counter]);
      sum := sum + intlist[counter]
      end;
comment Compute the average;
    average := sum / listlen;
comment Count the input values that are > average;
    for counter := 1 step 1 until listlen do
      if intlist[counter] > average
        then result := result + 1;
comment Print result;
    printstring("The number of values > average is:");
    printint (result)
```

Figure 2.3

Genealogy of
ALGOL 60

Fortran I (1957)

ALGOL 58 (1958)

ALGOL 60 (1960)

```
      end
   else
      printstring ("Error—input list length is not legal");
end
```

The ancestry of ALGOL 60 is shown in Figure 2.3.

2.6   Computerizing Business Records: COBOL

The story of COBOL is strange indeed. Although it has been used more than any other programming language, COBOL has had little effect on the design of subsequent languages, except for PL/I. It may still be the most widely used language,[4] although it is difficult to be sure one way or the other. Perhaps the most important reason why COBOL has had little influence is that few have attempted to design a new language for business applications since it appeared. That may be a tribute to how well COBOL's capabilities meet the needs of its application area. Another reason is that a great deal of growth in business computing over the past 15 years has occurred in small businesses. In these businesses, very little software development has taken place. Instead, most of the software used is purchased as off-the-shelf packages for various general business applications.

2.6.1   Historical Background

The beginning of COBOL is somewhat similar to that of ALGOL 60, in the sense that the language was designed by a committee of people meeting for relatively short periods of time. The state of business computing at the time, which was 1959, was similar to the state of scientific computing several years earlier, when Fortran was being designed. One compiled language for business applications, FLOW-MATIC, had been implemented in 1957, but it belonged to one manufacturer, UNIVAC, and was designed for that company's computers. Another language, AIMACO, was being used by the U.S. Air Force, but it was only a minor variation of FLOW-MATIC. IBM had designed a programming language for business applications, COMTRAN (COMmercial TRANslator), but it had not yet been implemented. Several other language design projects were being planned.

---

[4] In the late 1990s, in a study associated with the Y2K problem, it was estimated that there were approximately 800 million lines of COBOL in use in the 22 square miles of Manhattan.

2.6.2   FLOW-MATIC

The origins of FLOW-MATIC are worth at least a brief discussion, because it was the primary progenitor of COBOL. In December 1953, Grace Hopper at Remington-Rand UNIVAC produced a proposal that was indeed prophetic. It suggested that "mathematical programs should be written in mathematical notation, data processing programs should be written in English statements" (Wexelblat, 1981, p. 16). Unfortunately, it was impossible in 1953 to convince nonprogrammers that a computer could be made to understand English words. It was not until 1955 that a similar proposal had some hope of being funded by UNIVAC management, and even then it took a prototype system to do the final convincing. Part of this selling process involved compiling and running a small program, first using English keywords, then using French keywords, and then using German keywords. This demonstration was considered remarkable by UNIVAC management and was a prime factor in their acceptance of Hopper's proposal.

2.6.3   COBOL Design Process

The first formal meeting on the subject of a common language for business applications, which was sponsored by the Department of Defense, was held at the Pentagon on May 28 and 29, 1959 (exactly one year after the Zurich ALGOL meeting). The consensus of the group was that the language, then named CBL (for Common Business Language), should have the following general characteristics. Most agreed that it should use English as much as possible, although a few argued for a more mathematical notation. The language must be easy to use, even at the expense of being less powerful, in order to broaden the base of those who could program computers. In addition to making the language easy to use, it was believed that the use of English would allow managers to read programs. Finally, the design should not be overly restricted by the problems of its implementation.

One of the overriding concerns at the meeting was that steps to create this universal language should be taken quickly, as a lot of work was already being done to create new business languages. In addition to the existing languages, RCA and Sylvania were working on their own business applications languages. It was clear that the longer it took to produce a universal language, the more difficult it would be for the language to become widely used. On this basis, it was decided that there should be a quick study of existing languages. For this task, the Short Range Committee was formed.

There were early decisions to separate the statements of the language into two categories—data description and executable operations—and to have statements in these two categories reside in different parts of programs. One of the debates of the Short Range Committee was over the inclusion of subscripts. Many committee members argued that subscripts were too complex for the people in data processing, who were thought to be mathematically naive. Similar arguments revolved around whether arithmetic expressions should be included. The final report of the Short Range Committee, which was completed in December 1959, described a language that was later named COBOL 60.

The language specifications for COBOL 60, published by the Government Printing Office in April 1960 (Department of Defense, 1960), were described as "initial." Revised versions were published in 1961 and 1962 (Department of Defense, 1961, 1962). The language was standardized by the American National Standards Institute (ANSI) group in 1968. The next two revisions were standardized by ANSI in 1974 and 1985. The language continues to evolve today.

2.6.4 Evaluation

The COBOL language originated a number of novel concepts, some of which eventually appeared in other languages. For example, the DEFINE verb of COBOL 60 was the first high-level language construct for macros. More important, hierarchical data structures, which first appeared in Plankalkül, were first implemented in COBOL. They have been included in virtually every imperative language designed since then. COBOL was also the first language that allowed names to be truly connotative, because it allowed both long names (up to 30 characters) and word-connector characters (hyphens).

Overall, the data division is the strong part of COBOL's design, whereas the procedure division is relatively weak. Every variable is defined in detail in the data division, including the number of decimal digits and the location of the implied decimal point. File records are also described with this level of detail, as are lines to be output to a printer, which makes COBOL ideal for printing accounting reports. Perhaps the most important weakness of the procedure division lies in its lack of functions. Versions of COBOL prior to the 1974 standard also did not allow subprograms with parameters.

Our final comment on COBOL: It was the first programming language whose use was mandated by the Department of Defense (DoD). This mandate came after its initial development, because COBOL was not designed specifically for the DoD. In spite of its merits, COBOL probably would not have survived without that mandate. The poor performance of the early compilers simply made it too expensive to use. Eventually, of course, people learned more about designing compilers, and computers became much faster, cheaper, and had much larger memories. Together, these factors have made COBOL a great success, inside and outside DoD. Its appearance led to the electronic mechanization of accounting, an important revolution by any measure.

The following is an example of a COBOL program. This program reads a file named BAL-FWD-FILE that contains inventory information about a certain collection of items. Among other things, each item record includes the number currently on hand (BAL-ON-HAND) and the item's reorder point (BAL-REORDER-POINT). The reorder point is the threshold number of items on hand at which more must be ordered. The program produces a list of items that must be reordered as a file named REORDER-LISTING.

```
IDENTIFICATION DIVISION.
PROGRAM-ID. PRODUCE-REORDER-LISTING.

ENVIRONMENT DIVISION.
CONFIGURATION SECTION.
SOURCE-COMPUTER. DEC-VAX.
OBJECT-COMPUTER. DEC-VAX.
INPUT-OUTPUT SECTION.
FILE-CONTROL.
    SELECT BAL-FWD-FILE   ASSIGN TO READER.
    SELECT REORDER-LISTING  ASSIGN TO LOCAL-PRINTER.

DATA DIVISION.
FILE SECTION.
FD  BAL-FWD-FILE
    LABEL RECORDS ARE STANDARD
    RECORD CONTAINS 80 CHARACTERS.

01  BAL-FWD-CARD.
    02 BAL-ITEM-NO        PICTURE IS 9(5).
    02 BAL-ITEM-DESC      PICTURE IS X(20).
    02 FILLER             PICTURE IS X(5).
    02 BAL-UNIT-PRICE     PICTURE IS 999V99.
    02 BAL-REORDER-POINT  PICTURE IS 9(5).
    02 BAL-ON-HAND        PICTURE IS 9(5).
    02 BAL-ON-ORDER       PICTURE IS 9(5).
    02 FILLER             PICTURE IS X(30).

FD  REORDER-LISTING
    LABEL RECORDS ARE STANDARD
    RECORD CONTAINS 132 CHARACTERS.

01  REORDER-LINE.
    02 RL-ITEM-NO         PICTURE IS Z(5).
    02 FILLER             PICTURE IS X(5).
    02 RL-ITEM-DESC       PICTURE IS X(20).
    02 FILLER             PICTURE IS X(5).
    02 RL-UNIT-PRICE      PICTURE IS ZZZ.99.
    02 FILLER             PICTURE IS X(5).
    02 RL-AVAILABLE-STOCK PICTURE IS Z(5).
    02 FILLER             PICTURE IS X(5).
    02 RL-REORDER-POINT   PICTURE IS Z(5).
    02 FILLER             PICTURE IS X(71).
```

```
WORKING-STORAGE SECTION.
01  SWITCHES.
    02 CARD-EOF-SWITCH     PICTURE IS X.
01  WORK-FIELDS.
    02 AVAILABLE-STOCK     PICTURE IS 9(5).

PROCEDURE DIVISION.
000-PRODUCE-REORDER-LISTING.
    OPEN INPUT BAL-FWD-FILE.
    OPEN OUTPUT REORDER-LISTING.
    MOVE "N" TO CARD-EOF-SWITCH.
    PERFORM 100-PRODUCE-REORDER-LINE
        UNTIL CARD-EOF-SWITCH IS EQUAL TO "Y".
    CLOSE BAL-FWD-FILE.
    CLOSE REORDER-LISTING.
    STOP RUN.


100-PRODUCE-REORDER-LINE.
    PERFORM 110-READ-INVENTORY-RECORD.
    IF CARD-EOF-SWITCH IS NOT EQUAL TO "Y"
        PERFORM 120-CALCULATE-AVAILABLE-STOCK
        IF AVAILABLE-STOCK IS LESS THAN BAL-REORDER-POINT
            PERFORM 130-PRINT-REORDER-LINE.


110-READ-INVENTORY-RECORD.
    READ BAL-FWD-FILE RECORD
        AT END
            MOVE "Y" TO CARD-EOF-SWITCH.


120-CALCULATE-AVAILABLE-STOCK.
    ADD BAL-ON-HAND BAL-ON-ORDER
        GIVING AVAILABLE-STOCK.


130-PRINT-REORDER-LINE.
    MOVE SPACE             TO REORDER-LINE.
    MOVE BAL-ITEM-NO       TO RL-ITEM-NO.
    MOVE BAL-ITEM-DESC     TO RL-ITEM-DESC.
    MOVE BAL-UNIT-PRICE    TO RL-UNIT-PRICE.
    MOVE AVAILABLE-STOCK   TO RL-AVAILABLE-STOCK.
    MOVE BAL-REORDER-POINT TO RL-REORDER-POINT.
    WRITE REORDER-LINE.
```

The ancestry of COBOL is shown in Figure 2.4.

Figure 2.4
_____

Genealogy of COBOL

● FLOW-MATIC (1957)

● COBOL (1960)

2.7   The Beginnings of Timesharing: BASIC

BASIC (Mather and Waite, 1971) is another programming language that has enjoyed widespread use but has gotten little respect. Like COBOL, it has largely been ignored by computer scientists. Also, like COBOL, in its earliest versions it was inelegant and included only a meager set of control statements.

BASIC was very popular on microcomputers in the late 1970s and early 1980s. This followed directly from two of the main characteristics of BASIC: It is easy for beginners to learn, especially those who are not science oriented, and its smaller dialects can be implemented on computers with very small memories. A strong resurgence in the use of BASIC began with the appearance of Visual BASIC (Microsoft, 1991) in the early 1990s.

2.7.1   Design Process

BASIC (Beginner's All-purpose Symbolic Instruction Code) was designed at Dartmouth College (now Dartmouth University) in New Hampshire by two mathematicians, John Kemeny and Thomas Kurtz, who were involved in the early 1960s in producing compilers for a variety of dialects of Fortran and ALGOL 60. Their science students had little trouble learning or using those languages in their work.

However, Dartmouth was primarily a liberal arts institution, where science and engineering students made up only about 25 percent of the student body. It was decided in the spring of 1963 to design a new language especially for liberal arts students. This new language would use terminals as the method of computer access. The goals of the system were

1. It must be easy for nonscience students to learn and use.
2. It must be pleasant and friendly.
3. It must provide fast turnaround for homework.
4. It must allow free and private access.
5. It must consider user time more important than computer time.

The last goal was indeed a revolutionary concept. It was based at least partly on the belief that computers would become significantly cheaper as time went on, which, of course, they did.

The combination of the second, third, and fourth goals led to the time-shared aspect of BASIC. Only with individual access through terminals by numerous simultaneous users could these goals be met in the early 1960s.

How did you get from writing a shell program to collaborating with Microsoft? Tripod and Ruby are the same thing. After I signed a deal with Bill Gates, I changed the name of the prototype from Tripod to Ruby. I then used the Ruby prototype as prototypes should be used: as a disposable model for constructing release-quality code. Which is what I did. MS took the release version of Ruby and added QuickBASIC to it, creating VB. All of those original innovations were in Tripod/Ruby.

RUBY AS THE INCUBATOR FOR VISUAL BASIC

Let's revisit your interest in early Windows and that DLL feature. The DLL wasn't a thing, it was a facility in the OS. It allowed a programmer to build code objects that could be linked to at run time as opposed to only at compile time. This is what allowed me to invent the dynamically extensible parts of VB, where controls can be added by third-party vendors.

The Ruby product embodied many significant advances in software design, but two of them stand out as exceptionally successful. As I mentioned, the dynamic linking capability of Windows had always intrigued me, but having the tools and knowing what to do with them were two different things. With Ruby, I finally found two practical uses for dynamic linking, and the original program contained both. First, the language was both installable and could be extended dynamically. Second, the palette of gizmos could be added to dynamically.

Was your language in Ruby the first to have a dynamic linked library and to be linked to a visual front end? As far as I know, yes.

Using a simple example, what would this enable a programmer to do with his or her program? Purchase a control, such as a grid control,

from a third-party vendor, install it on his or her computer, and have the grid control appear as an integral part of the language, including the visual programming front end.

Why do they call you "the father of Visual Basic"? Ruby came with a small language, one suited only for executing the dozen or so simple commands that a shell program needs. However, this language was implemented as a chain of DLLs, any number of which could be installed at run time. The internal parser would identify a verb and then pass it along the chain of DLLs until one of them acknowledged that it knew how to process the verb. If all of the DLLs passed, there was a syntax error. From our earliest discussions, both Microsoft and I had entertained the idea of growing the language, possibly even replacing it altogether with a "real" language. C was the candidate most frequently mentioned, but eventually, Microsoft took advantage of this dynamic interface to unplug our little shell language and replace it entirely with QuickBasic. This new marriage of language to visual front end was static and permanent, and although the original dynamic interface made the coupling possible, it was lost in the process.

> **"**MSDOS.exe was the shell program for the first few releases of Windows. It was a terrible program, and I believed that it could be improved dramatically, and I was the guy to do it. In my spare time I immediately began to write a better shell program than the one Windows came with.**"**

SOME FINAL COMMENTS ON NEW IDEAS

In the world of programming and programming tools, including languages and environments, what projects most interest you? I'm interested in creating programming tools that are designed to help users instead of programmers.

What's the most critical rule, famous quote, or design idea to keep in mind? Bridges are not built by engineers. They are built by ironworkers.

Similarly, software programs are not built by engineers. They are built by programmers.

probably displace the older language over the next few years. It is also possible that the significant difference between Visual BASIC and VB .NET will cause some users to move to a different language, such as C# (see Section 2.19).

The following is an example of a BASIC program:

```
REM   BASIC Example Program
REM   Input:  An integer, listlen, where listlen is less
REM           than 100, followed by listlen-integer values
REM   Output: The number of input values that are greater
REM           than the average of all input values
  DIM intlist(99)
  result = 0
  sum = 0
  INPUT listlen
  IF listlen > 0 AND listlen < 100 THEN
REM  Read input into an array and compute the sum
    FOR counter = 1 TO listlen
      INPUT intlist(counter)
      sum = sum + intlist(counter)
    NEXT counter
REM  Compute the average
    average = sum / listlen
REM  Count the number of input values that are > average
    FOR counter = 1 TO listlen
      IF intlist(counter) > average
        THEN result = result + 1
    NEXT counter
REM  Print the result
    PRINT "The number of values that are > average is:";
          result
  ELSE
    PRINT "Error—input list length is not legal"
  END IF
END
```

The ancestry of BASIC is shown in Figure 2.5.

2.8   Everything for Everybody: PL/I

PL/I represents the first large-scale attempt to design a language that could be used for a broad spectrum of application areas. All previous and most subsequent languages have focused on one particular application area, such as science, artificial intelligence, or business.

2.8.1   Historical Background

Like Fortran, PL/I was developed as an IBM product. By the early 1960s, the users of computers in industry had settled into two separate and quite differ-

Figure 2.5

Genealogy of BASIC

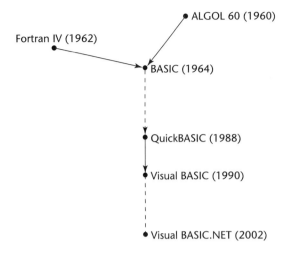

ent camps. From the IBM point of view, scientific programmers could use either the large-scale 7090 or the small-scale 1620 IBM computers. This group used floating-point and arrays extensively. Fortran was the primary language, although some assembly language was also used. They had their own user group, SHARE, and had little contact with anyone who worked on business applications.

For business applications, people used the large 7080 or the small 1401 IBM computers. They needed the decimal and character string data types as well as elaborate and efficient input and output facilities. They used COBOL, although in early 1963 when the PL/I story begins, the conversion from assembly language to COBOL was far from complete. This category of users also had its own user group, GUIDE, and seldom had contact with scientific users.

In early 1963, IBM planners perceived the beginnings of a change in this situation. The two widely separated groups were moving toward each other in ways that were thought certain to create problems. Scientists began to gather large files of data to be processed. This data required more sophisticated and more efficient input and output facilities. Business applications people began to use regression analysis to build management information systems, which required floating-point data and arrays. It began to appear that computing installations would soon require two separate computers, supporting two very different programming languages.

These perceptions quite naturally led to the concept of designing a single universal computer that would be capable of doing both floating-point and decimal arithmetic, and therefore both scientific and business applications. Thus was born the concept of the IBM System/360 line of computers. Along with this came the idea of a programming language that could be used for both business and scientific applications. For good measure, systems programming and list processing were thrown in as capabilities. Therefore, the new language was to replace Fortran, COBOL, LISP, and the systems applications of assembly language.

2.8.2 Design Process

The design effort began when IBM and SHARE formed the Advanced Language Development Committee of the SHARE Fortran Project in October 1963. This new committee quickly met and formed a subcommittee called the 3 × 3 Committee, so named because it had three members from IBM and three from SHARE. The 3 × 3 Committee met for three or four days every other week to design the language.

As with the Short Range Committee for COBOL, the initial design was scheduled for completion in a remarkably short time. Apparently, regardless of the scope of a language design effort, in the early 1960s the prevailing belief was that it could be done in three months. The first version of PL/I, which was then named Fortran VI, was supposed to be completed by December, less than three months after the committee was formed. The committee pleaded successfully on two different occasions for extensions, moving the due date back to January and then to late February 1964.

The initial design concept was that the new language would be an extension of Fortran IV, maintaining compatibility, but that goal was dropped quickly along with the name Fortran VI. Until 1965, the language was known as NPL, an acronym for New Programming Language. The first published report on NPL was given at the SHARE meeting of March 1964. A more complete description followed in April, and the version that would actually be implemented was published in December 1964 (IBM, 1964) by the compiler group at the IBM Hursley Laboratory in England, which was chosen to do the implementation. In 1965, the name was changed to PL/I to avoid the confusion of the name NPL with the National Physical Laboratory in England. If the compiler had been developed outside the United Kingdom, the name might have remained NPL.

2.8.3 Language Overview

Perhaps the best single-sentence description of PL/I is that it included what were then considered the best parts of ALGOL 60 (recursion and block structure), Fortran IV (separate compilation with communication through global data), and COBOL 60 (data structures, input/output, and report-generating facilities), along with a few new constructs, all somehow blended together. We will not attempt, even in an abbreviated way, to discuss all the features of the language, or even its most controversial constructs. Instead, we will mention briefly some of the language's contributions to the pool of knowledge of programming languages.

PL/I was the first programming language to have the following facilities:

- Programs were allowed to create concurrently executing subprograms. Although this was a good idea, it was poorly developed in PL/I.
- It was possible to detect and handle 23 different types of exceptions, or run-time errors.
- Procedures were allowed to be used recursively, but the capability could be disabled, allowing more efficient linkage for nonrecursive procedures.
- Pointers were included as a data type.
- Cross sections of arrays could be referenced. For example, the third row of a matrix could be referenced as if it were a vector.

2.8.4 Evaluation

Any evaluation of PL/I must begin by recognizing the ambitiousness of the design effort. In retrospect, it appears naive to think that so many constructs could have been combined successfully. However, that judgment must be tempered by acknowledging that there was little language design experience at the time. Overall, the design of PL/I was based on the premise that any construct that was useful and could be implemented should be included, with insufficient concern about how the many features would behave when thrown together. Edsger Dijkstra, in his Turing Award Lecture (Dijkstra, 1972), made one of the strongest criticisms of the complexity of PL/I: "I absolutely fail to see how we can keep our growing programs firmly within our intellectual grip when by its sheer baroqueness the programming language—our basic tool, mind you!—already escapes our intellectual control."

In addition to the problem with the complexity due to its large size, PL/I suffered from a number of what are now considered to be poorly designed constructs. Among these were pointers, exception handling, and concurrency, although we must point out that in each of these cases the construct was something new.

In terms of usage, PL/I must be considered at least a partial success. In the 1970s, it enjoyed significant use in both business and scientific applications. It was also widely used during that time as an instructional vehicle in colleges, primarily in several subset forms, such as PL/C (Cornell, 1977) and PL/CS (Conway and Constable, 1976).

The following is an example of a PL/I program:

```
/* PL/I PROGRAM EXAMPLE
 INPUT:  AN INTEGER, LISTLEN, WHERE LISTLEN IS LESS THAN
         100, FOLLOWED BY LISTLEN-INTEGER VALUES
 OUTPUT: THE NUMBER OF INPUT VALUES THAT ARE GREATER THAN
```

```
                        THE AVERAGE OF ALL INPUT VALUES    */
      PLIEX: PROCEDURE OPTIONS (MAIN);
        DECLARE INTLIST (1:99) FIXED.
        DECLARE (LISTLEN, COUNTER, SUM, AVERAGE, RESULT) FIXED;
        SUM = 0;
        RESULT = 0;
        GET LIST (LISTLEN);
        IF (LISTLEN > 0) & (LISTLEN < 100) THEN
          DO;
   /* READ INPUT DATA INTO AN ARRAY AND COMPUTE THE SUM */
          DO COUNTER = 1 TO LISTLEN;
            GET LIST (INTLIST (COUNTER));
            SUM = SUM + INTLIST (COUNTER);
          END;
   /* COMPUTE THE AVERAGE */
          AVERAGE = SUM / LISTLEN;
   /* COUNT THE NUMBER OF VALUES THAT ARE > AVERAGE */
          DO COUNTER = 1 TO LISTLEN;
            IF INTLIST (COUNTER) > AVERAGE THEN
              RESULT = RESULT + 1;
          END;
   /* PRINT RESULT */
          PUT SKIP LIST ('THE NUMBER OF VALUES > AVERAGE IS:');
          PUT LIST (RESULT);
          END;
        ELSE
          PUT SKIP LIST ('ERROR—INPUT LIST LENGTH IS ILLEGAL');
        END PLIEX;
```

The ancestry of PL/I is shown in Figure 2.6.

2.9   Two Early Dynamic Languages: APL and SNOBOL

The structure of this section is different from that shared by the other sections of the chapter because the languages discussed here are so different. Neither APL nor SNOBOL were based on any previous language, and neither had much influence on later mainstream languages (although the J language is based on APL, and ICON (Griswold and Griswold, 1983) is based on SNOBOL). Both APL and SNOBOL are used later in the book to illustrate and contrast some of their features with those of more conventional languages. This is why they are briefly discussed here.

In appearance and in purpose, APL and SNOBOL are very different. They share two common characteristics, however: dynamic typing and

Figure 2.6

Genealogy of PL/I

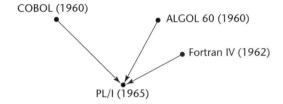

dynamic storage allocation. Variables in both languages are essentially untyped. A variable acquires a type when it is assigned a value, at which time it assumes the type of the value assigned. Storage is allocated to a variable only when it is assigned a value, because before that there is no way to know the amount of storage that will be needed.

2.9.1 Origins and Characteristics of APL

APL (Brown et al., 1988) was designed around 1960 by Kenneth E. Iverson at IBM. It was not originally designed to be an implemented programming language, but rather was intended to be a vehicle for describing computer architecture. APL was first described in the book from which it gets its name, *A Programming Language* (Iverson, 1962). In the mid-1960s, the first implementation of APL was developed at IBM.

APL has a large number of powerful operators, which created a problem for implementors. The first means of using APL was through IBM printing terminals. These terminals had special print balls that provided the odd character set required by the language. One reason APL has so many operators is that it allows arrays to be manipulated as if they were scalar variables. For example, the transpose of any matrix is done with a single operator. The large collection of operators provides very high expressivity but also makes APL programs difficult to read. This led people to think of APL as a language that is best used for "throw-away" programming. Although programs can be written quickly, they should be discarded after being used because they will be difficult to maintain.

APL has been around for forty years and is still used today, though not widely. Furthermore, it has not changed a great deal over its lifetime.

2.9.2 Origins and Characteristics of SNOBOL

SNOBOL (pronounced "snowball") (Griswold et al., 1971) was designed in the early 1960s by three people at Bell Laboratories: D. J. Farber, R. E. Griswold, and F. P. Polensky (Farber et al., 1964). It was designed specifically for text processing. The heart of SNOBOL is a collection of powerful operations for string pattern matching. One of the early applications of SNOBOL was for writing text editors. Because the dynamic nature of

SNOBOL makes it slower than some other languages, it is no longer used for such programs. However, SNOBOL is still a live and supported language that is used for a variety of text processing tasks in a number of different application areas.

2.10   The Beginnings of Data Abstraction: SIMULA 67

Although SIMULA 67 never achieved widespread use and had little impact on the programmers and computing of its time, some of the concepts it introduced make it historically important.

2.10.1   Design Process

Two Norwegians, Kristen Nygaard and Ole-Johan Dahl, developed the language SIMULA I between 1962 and 1964 at the Norwegian Computing Center (NCC). They were primarily interested in using computers for simulation, but also worked in operations research. SIMULA I was designed exclusively for system simulation and was first implemented in late 1964 on a UNIVAC 1107 computer.

As soon as the SIMULA I implementation was completed, Nygaard and Dahl began efforts to extend the language by adding new features and modifying some existing constructs in order to make the language useful for general-purpose applications. The result of this work was SIMULA 67, whose design was first presented publicly in March 1967 (Dahl and Nygaard, 1967). We will discuss only SIMULA 67, although some of the features of interest in SIMULA 67 are also in SIMULA I.

2.10.2   Language Overview

SIMULA 67 is an extension of ALGOL 60, taking both block structure and the control statements from that language. The primary deficiency of ALGOL 60 (and other languages at that time) for simulation applications is the design of its subprograms. Simulation requires subprograms that are allowed to restart at the position where they previously stopped. Subprograms with this kind of control are known as coroutines because the caller and called subprograms have a somewhat equal relationship with each other, rather than the rigid hierarchical relationship they usually have in imperative languages.

To provide support for coroutines in SIMULA 67, the class construct was developed. This was an important development because the concept of data abstraction began with it. The basic idea of a class is that a data structure and the routines that manipulate that data structure are packaged together. Furthermore, a class definition is only a template for a data structure and as such is distinct from a class instance, so a program can create and use any number of instances of a particular class. Class instances can contain local data. They can also include code that is executed at creation time, which can initialize some data structure of the class instance.

A more thorough discussion of classes and class instances is presented in Chapter 11. It is interesting to note that the important concept of data abstraction was not developed and attributed to the class construct until 1972, when Hoare (1972) recognized the connection.

The ancestry of SIMULA 67 is shown in Figure 2.7.

2.11   Orthogonal Design: ALGOL 68

ALGOL 68 was the source of several new ideas in language design, some of which were subsequently adopted by other languages. We include it here for that reason, even though it never achieved widespread use in either Europe or the United States.

2.11.1   Design Process

The development of the ALGOL family did not end when the revised report appeared in 1962, although it was six years until the next design iteration was published. The resulting language, ALGOL 68 (van Wijngaarden et al., 1969), was dramatically different from its predecessor.

One of the most interesting innovations of ALGOL 68 was one of its primary design criteria: orthogonality. Recall our discussion of orthogonality in Chapter 1. The use of orthogonality resulted in several innovative features of ALGOL 68, two of which are described in the following section.

2.11.2   Language Overview

One important result of orthogonality in ALGOL 68 was its inclusion of user-defined data types. Earlier languages, such as Fortran, included only a few basic data structures. PL/I included a large number of data structures,

Figure 2.7

Genealogy of SIMULA 67

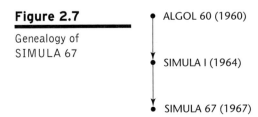

- ALGOL 60 (1960)
- SIMULA I (1964)
- SIMULA 67 (1967)

which made it harder to learn and difficult to implement, but it obviously could not provide an appropriate data structure for every application.

The approach of ALGOL 68 to data structures was to provide a few primitive types and structures and allow the user to combine those primitives into a large number of different structures. This provision for user-defined data types was carried over to some extent into all of the major imperative languages designed since then. User-defined data types are valuable because they allow the user to design data abstractions that fit particular problems very closely. All aspects of data typing are discussed in Chapter 6.

As another first in the area of data types, ALGOL 68 introduced the kind of dynamic arrays that will be termed implicit heap-dynamic in Chapter 5. A dynamic array is one in which the declaration does not specify subscript bounds. Assignments to a dynamic array cause allocation of required storage. In ALGOL 68, dynamic arrays are called **flex** arrays. For example, the declaration

```
flex [1:0] int list
```

states that list is a dynamic array of integers with a single subscript whose lower bound is 1, but it allocates no storage. The aggregate assignment

```
list := (3, 5, 6, 2)
```

causes list to be allocated sufficient storage for four integers, effectively changing its bounds to [1:4].

2.11.3   Evaluation

ALGOL 68 includes a significant number of features that had not been previously used. Its use of orthogonality, which some may argue was overdone, was nevertheless revolutionary. Many of the features that were introduced in ALGOL 68 became part of subsequent languages.

ALGOL 68 repeated one of the sins of ALGOL 60, however, and that was an important factor in its lack of widespread acceptance. The language was described using an elegant and concise but also unknown metalanguage. Before one could read the language-describing document (van Wijngaarden et al., 1969), he or she had to learn the new metalanguage, called van Wijngaarden grammars. To make matters worse, the designers invented a collection of words to explain the grammar and the language. For example, keywords are called *indicants*, substring extraction is called *trimming*, and the process of procedure execution is called a *coercion of deproceduring*, which might be meek, firm, or something else.

It is natural to contrast the design of PL/I with that of ALGOL 68. ALGOL 68 achieved writability by the principle of orthogonality: a few primitive concepts and the unrestricted use of a few combining mechanisms. PL/I achieved writability by including a large number of fixed constructs. ALGOL 68 extended the elegant simplicity of ALGOL 60, whereas PL/I simply threw together the features of several languages to attain its goals. Of course, it must be kept in mind that the goal of PL/I was to provide a unified tool for a broad class of problems; on the other hand, ALGOL 68 was targeted to a single class: scientific applications.

PL/I achieved far greater acceptance than ALGOL 68, due largely to IBM's promotional efforts and the problems of understanding and implementing ALGOL 68. Implementation was a difficult problem for both, but PL/I had the resources of IBM to apply to constructing a compiler. ALGOL 68 enjoyed no such benefactor.

The ancestry of ALGOL 68 is shown in Figure 2.8.

2.12 Some Early Descendants of the ALGOLs

All imperative languages, including the imperative/object-oriented languages such as C++ and Java, owe some of their design to ALGOL 60 and/or ALGOL 68. This section discusses some of early descendants of these languages.

2.12.1 Simplicity by Design: Pascal

2.12.1.1 Historical Background

Niklaus Wirth (Wirth is pronounced "Virt") was a member of the International Federation of Information Processing (IFIP) Working Group 2.1, which was created to continue the development of ALGOL in the mid-1960s. In August 1965, Wirth and C. A. R. ("Tony") Hoare contributed to that effort by presenting to the group a somewhat modest proposal for additions and modifications to ALGOL 60 (Wirth and Hoare, 1966). The majority of the group rejected the proposal as being too small an advance over ALGOL 60. Instead, a much more complex proposed revision was developed, which eventually became ALGOL 68. Wirth, along with a few other group members, did not believe that the ALGOL 68 report should have been released, based on the complexity of both the language and the metalanguage used to describe it. This position later proved to have some validity because the ALGOL 68 documents, and therefore the language, were indeed found by the computing community to be very difficult to understand.

The Wirth and Hoare version of ALGOL 60 was named ALGOL-W. It was implemented at Stanford University and was used primarily as an instructional vehicle, but only at a few universities. The primary contributions of

Figure 2.8

Genealogy of
ALGOL 68

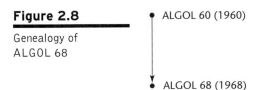

ALGOL 60 (1960)

ALGOL 68 (1968)

ALGOL-W were the value-result method of passing parameters and the **case** statement for multiple selection. The value-result method is an alternative to ALGOL 60's pass-by-name method. Both are discussed in Chapter 9. The **case** statement is discussed in Chapter 8.

Wirth's next major design effort, again based on ALGOL 60, was his most successful: Pascal. The original published definition of Pascal appeared in 1971 (Wirth, 1971). This version was modified somewhat in the implementation process and is described in Wirth (1973). The features that are often ascribed to Pascal in fact came from earlier languages. For example, user-defined data types were introduced in ALGOL 68, the **case** statement in ALGOL-W, and Pascal's records are similar to those of COBOL and PL/I.

2.12.1.2 Evaluation

The largest impact of Pascal was on the teaching of programming. In 1970, most students of computer science, engineering, and science were introduced to programming with Fortran, although some universities used PL/I, languages based on PL/I, and ALGOL-W. By the mid-1970s, Pascal had become the most widely used language for this purpose. This was quite natural, although perhaps not predictable, because Pascal had, in fact, been designed specifically for teaching programming. It was not until the late 1990s that Pascal was no longer the most commonly used language for teaching programming in colleges and universities.

Because Pascal was designed as a teaching language, it lacks several features that are essential for many kinds of applications. The best example of this is the impossibility of writing a subprogram that takes as a parameter an array of variable length. Another example is the lack of any separate compilation capability. These deficiencies naturally led to many nonstandard dialects, such as Turbo Pascal.

Pascal's popularity, for both teaching programming and other applications, was based primarily on its remarkable combination of simplicity and expressivity. Although there are some insecurities in Pascal, as we discuss in later chapters, it is still a relatively safe language, particularly when compared with Fortran or C. By the mid-1990s, the popularity of Pascal was on the decline, both in industry and in universities.

The following is an example of a Pascal program:

```
{Pascal Example Program
  Input:  An integer, listlen, where listlen is less than
          100, followed by listlen-integer values
  Output: The number of input values that are greater than
          the average of all input values }
program pasex (input, output);
  type intlisttype = array [1..99] of integer;
  var
```

```
      intlist : intlisttype;
      listlen, counter, sum, average, result : integer;
  begin
  result := 0;
  sum := 0;
  readln (listlen);
  if ((listlen > 0) and (listlen < 100)) then
      begin
{ Read input into an array and compute the sum }
      for counter := 1 to listlen do
        begin
        readln (intlist[counter]);
        sum := sum + intlist[counter]
        end;
{ Compute the average }
      average := sum / listlen;
{ Count the number of input values that are > average }
      for counter := 1 to listlen do
        if (intlist[counter] > average) then
          result := result + 1;
{ Print the result }
      writeln ('The number of values > average is:',
                result)
      end { of the then clause of if (( listlen > 0 ... }
    else
      writeln ('Error—input list length is not legal')
  end.
```

The ancestry of Pascal is shown in Figure 2.9.

2.12.2 A Portable Systems Language: C

Like Pascal, C contributed little to the previously known collection of language features, but it has been very widely used over a long period of time.

Figure 2.9

Genealogy of Pascal

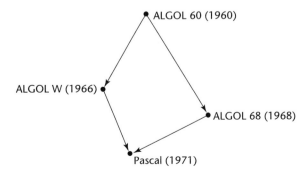

ALGOL 60 (1960)

ALGOL W (1966)

ALGOL 68 (1968)

Pascal (1971)

Although originally designed for systems programming, C is well suited for a wide variety of applications.

2.12.2.1 Historical Background

C's ancestors include CPL, BCPL, B, and ALGOL 68. CPL was developed at Cambridge University in the early 1960s. BCPL is a simple systems language developed by Martin Richards in 1967 (Richards, 1969).

The first work on the UNIX operating system was done in the late 1960s by Ken Thompson at Bell Laboratories. The first version was written in assembly language. The first high-level language implemented under UNIX was B, which was based on BCPL. B was designed and implemented by Thompson in 1970.

Neither BCPL nor B is a typed language, which is an oddity among high-level languages, although both are much lower level than a language such as Java. Being untyped means that all data are considered machine words, which, although extremely simple, leads to many complications and insecurities. For example, there is the problem of specifying floating-point rather than integer arithmetic in an expression. In one implementation of BCPL, the operands of a floating-point operation were preceded by periods. Operands not preceded by periods were considered to be integers. An alternative to this would have been to use different symbols for the floating-point operations.

This problem, along with several others, led to the development of a new typed language based on B. Originally called NB but later named C, it was designed and implemented by Dennis Ritchie at Bell Laboratories in 1972 (Kernighan and Ritchie, 1978). In some cases through BCPL, and in other cases directly, C was influenced by ALGOL 68. This is seen in its **for** and **switch** statements, in its assigning operators, and in its treatment of pointers.

The only "standard" for C in its first decade and a half was the book by Kernighan and Ritchie (1978).[5] Over that time span the language slowly evolved, with different implementors adding different features. In 1989, ANSI produced an official description of C (ANSI, 1989), which included many of the features that implementors had already incorporated into the language. This standard was updated in 1999 (ISO, 1999). This new version includes a few significant changes to the language. The 1989 version, which has long been called ANSI C, should now be called C89; we will refer to the 1999 version as C99.

2.12.2.2 Evaluation

C has adequate control statements and data-structuring facilities to allow its use in many application areas. It also has a rich set of operators that provide a high degree of expressiveness.

One of the most important reasons why C is both liked and disliked is its lack of complete type checking. For example, functions can be written for

---

[5]This language is often referred to as "K & R C."

which parameters are not type checked. Those who like C appreciate the flexibility; those who do not like it find it too insecure. A major reason for its great increase in popularity in the 1980s is that a compiler for it is part of the widely used UNIX operating system. This inclusion in UNIX provides an inexpensive (often free with UNIX) and quite good compiler that is available to programmers on many different kinds of computers.

The following is an example of a C program:

```c
/* C Example Program
   Input:  An integer, listlen, where listlen is less than
           100, followed by listlen-integer values
   Output: The number of input values that are greater than
           the average of all input values */
void main (){
  int intlist[98], listlen, counter, sum, average, result;
  sum = 0;
  result = 0;
  scanf("%d", &listlen);
  if ((listlen > 0) && (listlen < 100)) {
/* Read input into an array and compute the sum */
    for (counter = 0; counter < listlen; counter++) {
      scanf("%d", &intlist[counter]);
      sum = sum + intlist[counter];
    }
/* Compute the average */
    average = sum / listlen;
/* Count the input values that are > average */
    for (counter = 0; counter < listlen; counter++)
      if (intlist[counter] > average) result++;
/* Print result */
    printf("Number of values > average is:%d\n", result);
  }
  else
    printf("Error—input list length is not legal\n");
}
```

The ancestry of C is shown in Figure 2.10.

2.12.3 Other Early ALGOL Descendants

This section briefly discusses the origins and characteristics of a few other early ALGOL descendants.

2.12.3.1 Modula-2

After Pascal, Niklaus Wirth designed Modula, which resulted from his experimentations with concurrency (Wirth, 1976). No compiler for Modula was ever released, and its development was discontinued soon after its

Figure 2.10

Genealogy of C

publication. Wirth, however, did not abandon language design. His focus changed to building a language that was meant to be the single language for a new computer system that later was called Lilith. While the computer itself was never a commercial success, the language, Modula-2, was (Wirth, 1985).

The primary distinguishing features of Modula-2, whose design was based on Pascal and Modula, were modules, which provide support for abstract data types, procedures as types, low-level facilities for systems programming, and coroutines, as well as some syntactic features that were improvements over those of Pascal.

Modula-2 achieved widespread use in the late 1980s and early 1990s as a teaching language in universities. It also was used, at least for a few years, in various industrial application areas.

2.12.3.2 Oberon

Oberon, which is loosely based on Modula-2, is the most recent language designed by Niklaus Wirth. The latest version of Oberon is named Oberon-2 (Mössenbock, 1993).

Wirth's passion for simplicity in programming languages is stunningly evident in the design of Oberon. Although some features were added to Modula-2 to get Oberon, a larger number of features were subtracted, putting Oberon in stark contrast to C++ and Ada 95. Oberon is, in terms of complexity and size, the opposite of those two languages.

The main feature added to Modula-2 to get Oberon is type extension, which supports object-oriented programming. Among the removed features are variant records, opaque types, enumeration types, subrange types, the `CARDINAL` type, noninteger array indexes, the **with** statement, and the **for** statement. It is remarkable to find a language that is significantly smaller and less complex than its predecessor, but Oberon is exactly that.

2.13   Programming Based on Logic: Prolog

Simply put, logic programming is the use of a formal logic notation to communicate computational processes to a computer. Predicate calculus is the notation used in current logic programming languages.

Programming in logic programming languages is nonprocedural. Programs in such languages do not state exactly *how* a result is to be computed but rather describe the form of the result. What is needed to provide this capability for logic programming languages is a concise means of supplying the computer with both the relevant information and an inferencing process for computing desirable results. Predicate calculus supplies the basic form of communication to the computer, and the proof method named resolution, developed first by Robinson (1965), supplies the inferencing technique.

2.13.1   Design Process

During the very early 1970s, Alain Colmerauer and Phillippe Roussel in the Artificial Intelligence Group at the University of Aix-Marseille, together with Robert Kowalski of the Department of Artificial Intelligence at the University of Edinburgh, developed the fundamental design of Prolog. The primary components of Prolog are a method for specifying predicate calculus propositions and an implementation of a restricted form of resolution. Both predicate calculus and resolution are described in Chapter 16. The first Prolog interpreter was developed at Marseille in 1972. The version of the language that was implemented is described in Roussel (1975). The name Prolog is from *programming logic*.

2.13.2   Language Overview

Prolog programs consist of collections of statements. Prolog has only a few kinds of statements, but they can be complex.

One common use of Prolog is as a kind of intelligent database. This application provides a simple framework for discussing the Prolog language.

The database of a Prolog program consists of two kinds of statements, facts and rules. Examples of fact statements are

```
mother(joanne, jake).
father(vern, joanne).
```

which state that `joanne` is the `mother` of `jake`, and `vern` is the `father` of `joanne`.

An example of a rule statement is

```
grandparent(X, Z) :- parent(X, Y), parent(Y, Z).
```

which states that it can be deduced that `X` is the `grandparent` of `Z` if it is true that `X` is the `parent` of `Y` and `Y` is the parent of `Z`, for some specific values for the variables `X`, `Y`, and `Z`.

The Prolog database can be interactively queried with goal statements, an example of which is

```
father(bob, darcie).
```

which asks if `bob` is the `father` of `darcie`. When such a query, or goal, is presented to the Prolog system, it uses its resolution process to attempt to determine the truth of the statement. If it can conclude that the goal is true, it displays "true." If it cannot prove it, it displays "false."

2.13.3   Evaluation

In the 1980s, there was a relatively small group of computer scientists who believed that logic programming provided the best hope for escaping from the imperative languages, and also from the enormous problem of producing the large amount of reliable software that is needed. So far, however, there are two major reasons why logic programming has not become more widely used. First, as with some other nonimperative approaches, logic programming thus far has proven to be highly inefficient. Second, it has been shown to be an effective method for only a few relatively small areas of application: certain kinds of database management systems and some areas of AI.

There is a dialect of Prolog that supports object-oriented programming, Prolog++ (Moss, 1994). Logic programming and Prolog are described in greater detail in Chapter 16.

2.14 History's Largest Design Effort: Ada

The Ada language is the result of the most extensive and most expensive language design effort ever undertaken. The Ada language was developed for the Department of Defense (DoD), so the state of their computing environment was instrumental in determining its form.

2.14.1 Historical Background

By 1974, over half of the applications of computers in DoD were embedded systems. An embedded system is one in which the computer hardware is embedded in the device it controls or for which it provides services. Software costs were rising rapidly, primarily because of the increasing complexity of systems. More than 450 different programming languages were in use for DoD projects, and none of them were standardized by DoD. Every defense contractor could define a new and different language for every contract.[6] Because of this language proliferation, application software was rarely reused. Furthermore, no software development tools were created (because they are usually language dependent). A great many languages were in use, but none was actually suitable for embedded systems applications. For these reasons, the Army, Navy, and Air Force each independently proposed in 1974 the development of a single high-level language for embedded systems.

2.14.2 Design Process

Noting this widespread interest, Malcolm Currie, Director of Defense Research and Engineering, in January 1975, formed the High-Order Language Working Group (HOLWG), initially headed by Lt. Col. William Whitaker of the Air Force. The HOLWG had representatives from all of the military services and liaisons with Great Britain, France, and West Germany. Its initial charter was to

- Identify the requirements for a new DoD high-level language.
- Evaluate existing languages to determine whether there was a viable candidate.
- Recommend adoption or implementation of a minimal set of programming languages.

In April 1975, the HOLWG produced the Strawman requirements document for the new language (Department of Defense, 1975a). This was distributed to military branches, federal agencies, selected industrial and university representatives, and interested parties in Europe.

The Strawman document was followed by Woodenman (Department of Defense, 1975b) in August 1975 and Tinman (Department of Defense, 1976)

---

[6]This was largely a result of the widespread use of assembly language for embedded systems, along with the fact that most embedded systems used specialized processors.

in January 1976. The Tinman document was considered a complete set of requirements for a language with the desired characteristics. The principal author of these documents was David Fisher of the Institute for Defense Analysis. The group of participants in the effort was large, numbering over 200, with representatives from over forty organizations outside DoD. In January 1977, the Tinman document was replaced by the Ironman requirements document (Department of Defense, 1977), which was nearly equivalent in content but had a somewhat different format.

In April 1977, the Ironman document was used as the basis for an unrestricted request for proposals, which was then made public, thereby making Ada the first language to be designed by competitive contract. In July 1977, four of the proposing contractors—Softech, SRI International, Cii Honeywell/Bull, and Intermetrics—were chosen to produce, independently and in parallel, Phase 1 of the language design. All four of the resulting design proposals were based on Pascal.

When the six-month Phase 1 was completed in February 1978, there was a two-month evaluation by 400 volunteers in 80 review teams scattered around the world. The result of this evaluation was that two finalists— Intermetrics and Cii Honeywell/Bull—were chosen to go on to Phase 2 of the development.

In June 1978, the next iteration of the requirements document, Steelman, was released (Department of Defense, 1978).

At the end of Phase 2, another two-month evaluation was done, and in May 1979 the Cii Honeywell/Bull language design was chosen as the winner. Interestingly, the winner was the only foreign competitor among the final four. The Cii Honeywell/Bull design team in France was led by Jean Ichbiah.

In the spring of 1979, Jack Cooper of the Navy Materiel Command recommended the name for the new language, Ada, which was then adopted. Augusta Ada Byron (1815–1851), Countess of Lovelace, mathematician, and daughter of poet Lord Byron, is generally recognized as being the world's first programmer. She worked with Charles Babbage on his mechanical computers, the Difference and Analytical Engines, writing programs for several numerical processes.

Phase 3 of the Ada design project began with the selection of the winning design. The design and the rationale for it were published by ACM in its *SIGPLAN Notices* (ACM, 1979) and distributed to a readership of over 10,000 people. A public test and evaluation conference was held in October 1979 in Boston, with representatives from over 100 organizations from the United States and Europe. By November, more than 500 language reports had been received from 15 different countries. Most of the reports suggested small modifications rather than drastic changes and outright rejections. Based on the language reports, the next version of the requirements specification, the Stoneman document (Department of Defense, 1980a) was released in February 1980.

A revised version of the language design was completed in July 1980 and was accepted as MIL-STD 1815, the standard *Ada Language Reference*

Manual. The number 1815 was chosen because it was the year of the birth of Augusta Ada Lovelace. Another revised version of the *Ada Language Reference Manual* was released in July 1982. In 1983, the American National Standards Institute standardized Ada. This "final" official version is described in Goos and Hartmanis (1983). The Ada language design was then frozen for at least five years.

2.14.3 Language Overview

This section briefly describes four of the major features of the Ada language. Because we use the language in many examples throughout the remainder of the book, other features will be described along the way.

Packages in the Ada language provide the means for encapsulating data objects, specifications for data types, and procedures. This, in turn, provides the support for the use of data abstraction in program design, as described in Chapter 11.

The Ada language includes extensive facilities for exception handling, which allow the programmer to gain control after any one of a wide variety of exceptions, or run-time errors, has been detected. Exception handling is discussed in Chapter 14.

Program units can be generic in Ada. For example, it is possible to write a sort procedure that uses an unspecified type for the data to be sorted. Such a generic procedure must be instantiated for a specified type before it can be used. This is done with a statement that causes the compiler to generate a version of the procedure with the given type. The availability of such generic units increases the range of program units that might be reused, rather than duplicated, by programmers. Generics are discussed in Chapters 9 and 11.

The Ada language also provides for concurrent execution of special program units, named tasks, using the rendezvous mechanism. Rendezvous is the name of a method of intertask communication and synchronization. Concurrency is discussed in Chapter 13.

2.14.4 Evaluation

Perhaps the most important aspects of the design of the Ada language to consider are the following:

- Because the design was competitive, there was no limit on participation.
- The Ada language embodies most of the concepts of software engineering and language design of the late 1970s. Although one can question the actual methods used to incorporate these features, as well as the wisdom of including such a large number of features in a language, most agree that the features are valuable.
- Although many people did not initially realize it, the development of a compiler for the Ada language was a difficult task. Only in 1985,

almost four years after the language design was completed, did truly usable Ada compilers begin to appear.

The most serious criticism of Ada in its first few years was that it was too large and too complex. In particular, Hoare has stated that it should not be used for any application where reliability is critical (Hoare, 1981), which is precisely the type of applications for which it was designed. On the other hand, others have praised it as the epitome of language design for its time. In fact, even Hoare eventually softened his view of the language.

The following is an example of an Ada program:

```
-- Ada Example Program
-- Input:  An integer, List_Len, where List_Len is less
--           than 100, followed by List_Len-integer values
-- Output: The number of input values that are greater
--           than the average of all input values
with Ada.Text_IO, Ada.Integer.Text_IO;
use Ada.Text_IO, Ada.Integer.Text_IO;
procedure Ada_Ex is
  type Int_List_Type is array (1..99) of Integer;
  Int_List : Int_List_Type;
  List_Len, Sum, Average, Result : Integer;
begin
  Result:= 0;
  Sum := 0;
  Get (List_Len);
  if (List_Len > 0) and (List_Len < 100) then
-- Read input data into an array and compute the sum
    for Counter := 1 .. List_Len loop
      Get (Int_List(Counter));
      Sum := Sum + Int_List(Counter);
    end loop;
-- Compute the average
    Average := Sum / List_Len;
-- Count the number of values that are > average
    for Counter := 1 .. List_Len loop
      if Int_List(Counter) > Average then
        Result:= Result+ 1;
      end if;
    end loop;
-- Print result
    Put ("The number of values > average is:");
    Put (Result);
    New_Line;
  else
```

```
        Put_Line ("Error—input list length is not legal");
      end if;
  end Ada_Ex;
```

2.14.5 Ada 95

A revision effort for Ada began in 1988 with the establishment of the Ada 9X project by the Ada Joint Program Office. The Ada 9X project had three phases: the determination of the requirements for the revised language, the actual development of the definition of the revised language, and the transition into use of the revised language. The requirements were published by the Department of Defense (1990).

The requirements focused on four areas of the language: interfacing (especially into graphical user interfaces), support for object-oriented programming, more flexible libraries, and better control mechanisms for shared data.

Two of the most important new features of the new version of Ada, named Ada 95, are described briefly in the following paragraphs. In the remainder of the book, we will use the name Ada 83 for the original version and Ada 95 (its actual name) for the later version when it is important to distinguish between the two versions. In discussions of language features common to both versions, we will use the name Ada. The Ada 95 standard language is defined in ARM (1995).

The type derivation mechanism of Ada 83 is extended to allow the adding of new components to those derived from a tagged parent type. This provides for inheritance, a key ingredient in object-oriented programming languages. Dynamic binding of subprogram calls to subprogram definitions is accomplished through subprogram dispatching, which is based on the tag value of derived types through classwide types. This feature provides for polymorphism, another principal feature of object-oriented programming. These features of Ada 95 are discussed in Chapter 12.

The rendezvous mechanism of Ada 83 provided only cumbersome means of sharing data among concurrent processes. It was necessary to introduce a new task to control access to the shared data. The protected objects of Ada 95 offer an attractive alternative to this. The shared data is encapsulated in a syntactic structure that controls all access to the data, either by rendezvous or by subprogram call. The new features of Ada 95 for concurrency and shared data are discussed in Chapter 13.

It is widely believed that the popularity of Ada 95 suffered because the Department of Defense no longer requires its use in military software systems. There are, of course, other factors that have hindered its growth in popularity. Most important among these is the widespread acceptance of C++ for object-oriented programming, which occurred before Ada 95 was released.

The ancestry of Ada is shown in Figure 2.11.

Figure 2.11

Genealogy of Ada

- Pascal (1971)
- Ada 83 (1983)
- Ada 95 (1995)

2.15   Object-Oriented Programming: Smalltalk

As discussed in Chapter 1, object-oriented programming includes data abstraction as one of its three fundamental characteristics, the other two being inheritance and dynamic binding.

Inheritance appeared in a limited form in SIMULA 67, whose classes can be defined in hierarchies. Inheritance provides an effective method of code reuse.

The unit control concept of object-oriented programming is loosely modeled on the idea that programs simulate the real world, a legacy of its origins in SIMULA 67. Because much of the real world is populated by objects, a simulation of such a world must include simulated objects. In fact, a language based on the concepts of real-world simulation need only include a model of objects that can send and receive messages and react to the messages they receive.

The essence of object-oriented programming is solving problems by identifying the real-world objects of the problem and the processing required of those objects, and then creating simulations of those objects, their processes, and the required communications between the objects. Abstract data types, dynamic binding, and inheritance are the concepts that make object-oriented problem solving not only possible but also convenient and effective.

2.15.1   Design Process

The concepts that led to the development of Smalltalk originated in the Ph.D. dissertation work of Alan Kay in the late 1960s at the University of Utah (Kay, 1969). Kay had remarkable foresight in predicting the future availability of powerful desktop computers. Recall that the first microcomputer systems were not marketed until the mid-1970s, and they were only remotely related to the machines envisioned by Kay, which were seen to execute a million or more instructions per second and contain several megabytes of memory. Such machines, in the form of workstations, became widely available only in the early 1980s.

Kay believed that desktop computers would be used by nonprogrammers and thus would need very powerful human interfacing capabilities. The computers of the late 1960s were largely batch-oriented and were used exclusively by professional programmers and scientists. For use by nonprogrammers, Kay determined, a computer would have to be highly interactive and use sophisticated graphics in its interface to users. Some of the graphics concepts came from the LOGO experience of Seymour Papert, in which graphics were used to aid children in the use of computers (Papert, 1980).

Kay originally envisioned a system he called Dynabook, which was meant to be a general information processor. It was based in part on the Flex language, which he had helped design. Flex was based primarily on SIMULA 67. Dynabook was based on the paradigm of the typical desk, on which there are a number of papers, some partially covered. The top sheet is often the focus of attention, with the others temporarily out of focus. The display of Dynabook would model this scene, using screen windows. The user would interact with such a display both through a keyboard and by touching the screen with his or her fingers. After the preliminary design of Dynabook earned him a Ph.D., Kay's goal became to see such a machine constructed.

Kay found his way to the Xerox Palo Alto Research Center (Xerox PARC) and presented his ideas on Dynabook. This led to his employment there and the subsequent birth of the Learning Research Group at Xerox. The first charge of the group was to design a language to support Kay's programming paradigm and implement it on the best personal computer then available. These efforts resulted in an "Interim" Dynabook, consisting of the Xerox Alto hardware and the Smalltalk-72 software. Together, they formed a research tool for further development. A number of research projects were conducted with this system, including several experiments to teach programming to children. Along with the experiments came further developments, leading to a sequence of languages that ended with Smalltalk-80, which is the version discussed in this book. As the language grew, so did the power of the hardware on which it resided. By 1980, both the language and the Xerox hardware nearly matched the early vision of Alan Kay.

2.15.2 Language Overview

The program units of Smalltalk are objects. Objects are structures that encapsulate local data and a collection of operations called methods that is available to other objects. A method specifies the reaction of the object when it receives a particular message that corresponds to that method. The Smalltalk world is populated by nothing but objects, from integer constants to large complex software systems.

All computing in Smalltalk is done by the same uniform technique: sending a message to an object to invoke one of its methods. A reply to a message is an object, which returns the requested information or simply notifies the sender that the requested processing has been completed. The fundamental difference between a message and a subprogram call is this: A message is sent to a data object, which then is processed by code associated with the object; a subprogram call usually sends the data to be processed to a subprogram code unit.

From the simulation point of view, which is never far away, Smalltalk is a simulation of a collection of computers (objects) that communicate with each other (through messages). Each object is an abstraction of a computer in the sense that it stores data and provides processing capability for manipulating that data. In addition, objects can send and receive messages. In essence, those are the fundamental capabilities of computers: to store and manipulate data and to communicate.

In Smalltalk, object abstractions are classes, which are very similar to the classes of SIMULA 67. Instances of the class can be created and are then the objects of the program. Each object has its own local data and represents a different instance of its class. The only difference between two objects of the same class is the state of their local variables.

As in SIMULA 67, class hierarchies can be designed in Smalltalk. Subclasses of a given class are refinements of it, inheriting the functionality and local variables of the parent class, or superclass. Subclasses can add new local memory and functionality and modify or hide inherited functionality.

As briefly discussed in Chapter 1, Smalltalk is not just a language, it is also a complete software development environment. The interface to the environment is highly graphical, making heavy use of multiple overlaid windows, pop-up menus, and a mouse input device.

2.15.3 Evaluation

Smalltalk has done a great deal to promote two separate aspects of computing. The windowing systems that are now the dominant method of user interfaces to software systems grew out of Smalltalk. Today, the most significant software design methodologies and programming languages are object oriented. Although the origin of some of the ideas of object-oriented languages came from SIMULA 67, they reached maturation only in Smalltalk. It is clear that Smalltalk's impact on the computing world is extensive and will be long-lived.

The following is an example of a Smalltalk class definition:

```
"Smalltalk Example Program"
"The following is a class definition, instantiations of
which can draw equilateral polygons of any number of sides"
class name                    Polygon
superclass                    Object
instance variable names       ourPen
```

```
                                        numSides
                                        sideLength
"Class methods"
  "Create an instance"
  new
      ^ super new getPen

  "Get a pen for drawing polygons"
  getPen
      ourPen <- Pen new defaultNib: 2

  "Instance methods"
  "Draw a polygon"
  draw
      numSides timesRepeat: [ourPen go: sideLength;
                                    turn: 360 // numSides]

  "Set length of sides"
  length: len
      sideLength <- len

  "Set number of sides"
  sides: num
      numSides <- num
```

The ancestry of Smalltalk is shown in Figure 2.12.

Figure 2.12

Genealogy of
Smalltalk

ALGOL 58 (1958)

ALGOL 60 (1960)

SIMULA I (1964)

SIMULA 67 (1967)

Smalltalk-80 (1980)

2.16   Combining Imperative and Object-Oriented Features: C++

The origins of C were discussed in Section 2.12; the origins of Smalltalk were discussed in Section 2.15. C++ builds language facilities on top of C to support much of what Smalltalk pioneered. C++ has evolved from C through a sequence of modifications to improve its imperative features and additions to support object-oriented programming.

2.16.1   Design Process

The first step from C toward C++ was made by Bjarne Stroustrup at Bell Laboratories in 1980. Modifications included the addition of function parameter type checking and conversion and, more significantly, classes, which are related to those of SIMULA 67 and Smalltalk. Also included were derived classes, public/private access control of inherited components, constructor and destructor methods, and friend classes. During 1981, inline functions, default parameters, and overloading of the assignment operator were added. The resulting language was called C with Classes and is described in Stroustrup (1983).

It is useful to consider some goals of C with Classes. The primary goal was to provide a language in which programs could be organized as they could be organized in SIMULA 67, that is, with classes and inheritance. Another important goal was that there should be no performance penalty, relative to C. So that C with Classes could be used for every application for which C could be used, but virtually none of the insecure features of C would be removed. For example, array index range checking was not even considered because a significant performance disadvantage, relative to C, would result.

By 1984, this language was extended by the inclusion of virtual methods, which provide dynamic binding of method calls to specific method definitions; method name and operator overloading; and reference types. This version of the language was called C++. It is described in Stroustrup (1984).

In 1985, the first available implementation appeared, a system named Cfront, which translates C++ programs into C programs. This version of Cfront and the version of C++ it implemented were named Release 1.0. It is described in Stroustrup (1986).

Between 1985 and 1989, C++ continued to evolve, based largely on user reactions to the first distributed implementation. This next version was named Release 2.0. Its Cfront implementation was released in June 1989. The most important features added to C++ Release 2.0 were support for multiple inheritance (classes with more than one parent class) and abstract classes, along with some other enhancements. Abstract classes are described in Chapter 12.

Release 3.0 of C++ evolved between 1989 and 1990. It added templates, which provide parameterized types, and exception handling. The current version of C++, which was standardized in 1998, is described in ISO (1998).

In 2002, Microsoft released its .NET computing platform, which includes a new version of C++, named managed C++, or MC++. MC++ extends C++ to provide access to the functionality of the .NET Framework. This provides garbage collection of objects, among other things. Because .NET does not support multiple inheritance, neither does MC++.

2.16.2 Language Overview

C++ provides two constructs that define types, classes, and structs, with little difference between the two. In practice, structs that include method definitions are rarely used. Multiple inheritance is supported. In C++, methods are often called member functions.

Because C++ allows both functions and methods, it supports both procedural and object-oriented programming.

Operators in C++ can be overloaded, meaning the user can create operators for existing operators on user-defined types. C++ methods can also be overloaded, meaning the user can define more than one method with the same name, provided either the numbers or types of their parameters are different.

Dynamic binding in C++ is provided by virtual methods. These methods define type-dependent operations, using overloaded methods, within a collection of classes that are related through inheritance. A pointer to an object of class A can also point to objects of classes that have class A as an ancestor. When this pointer points to an overloaded virtual method, the method of the current type is chosen dynamically.

Both methods and classes can be templated, which means that they can be parameterized. For example, a method can be written as a templated method to allow it to have versions for a variety of parameter types. Classes enjoy the same flexibility.

C++ includes exception handling that is significantly different from that of Ada. One difference is that hardware-detectable exceptions cannot be handled. The exception handling of C++ is discussed in Chapter 14.

2.16.3 Evaluation

C++ rapidly became and remains a very popular language. One factor in its popularity is the availability of good and inexpensive compilers. Another factor in favor of the popularity of C++ is that it is almost completely backward compatible with C (meaning that C programs can be, with few changes, compiled as C++ programs), and in most implementations it is possible to link C++ code with C code. This meant that it was relatively easy for the many C programmers to learn C++. Finally, at the time object-oriented programming began to receive widespread interest, C++ was the only language that was available that was suitable for large commercial software projects.

On the negative side, because C++ is a very large and complex language, it clearly suffers drawbacks similar to those of PL/I. It inherited most of the insecurities of C, which make it less safe than languages such as Ada and Java. Finally, in part because of its basis in C, C++ is more like PL/I than ALGOL 68 in that it is more of a collection of ideas thrown together than the result of an overall language design plan.

The object-oriented features of C++ are described in far more detail in Chapter 12.

The ancestry of C++ is shown in Figure 2.13.

2.16.4 A Related Language: Eiffel

Eiffel is another hybrid language with both imperative and object-oriented features (Meyer, 1992). Eiffel was designed by a single person, Bertrand Meyer, who is French but lives in California. The language includes features to support abstract data types, inheritance, and dynamic binding, so it fully supports object-oriented programming. Perhaps the most distinguishing feature of Eiffel is the integrated use of assertions to enforce the "contract" between subprograms and their callers. It is an idea that was born in Plankalkül but ignored by most other languages designed since then. It is natural to compare Eiffel to C++. Eiffel is smaller and simpler than C++ but has nearly equal expressivity and writability. The reasons for the soaring popularity of C++, while Eiffel saw only limited use, are not difficult to determine. C++ is clearly the easiest way for software development organizations to move to object-oriented programming, because in many cases their developers already knew C. Eiffel enjoyed no such easy path to adoption. Also, for the first few years that use of C++ spread, the Cfront system was available and inexpensive. During its early years, Eiffel compilers were less available and more expensive. C++ had the backing of the prestigious Bell Laboratories, whereas Eiffel was backed by Bertrand Meyer and his relatively small software company, Interactive Software Engineering.

2.16.5 Another Related Language: Delphi

Delphi is a hybrid language, similar to C++ in that it was created by adding object-oriented support, among other things, to an existing imperative language. Delphi is derived from Pascal. Many of the differences between C++

Figure 2.13

The ancestry of C++

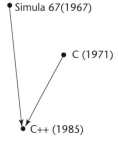

Simula 67(1967)

C (1971)

C++ (1985)

and Delphi are a result of the predecessor languages and the surrounding programming cultures from which they are derived. Because C is a powerful but potentially unsafe language, C++ also fits that description, at least in the areas of array subscript range checking, pointer arithmetic, and its numerous type coercions. Likewise, because Pascal is more elegant and safer than C, Delphi is more elegant and safer than C++. Delphi is also less complex than C++. For example, Delphi does not allow user-defined operator overloading, generic subprograms, and parameterized classes, all of which are part of C++.

Delphi, like Visual C++, provides a graphical user interface (GUI) to the developer and simple ways to create GUI interfaces to applications written in Delphi. Delphi was designed by Anders Hejlsberg, who had previously developed the Turbo Pascal system. Both of these were marketed and distributed by Borland. Hejlsberg was also the lead designer of C#.

2.17 An Imperative-Based Object-Oriented Language: Java

Java's designers started with C++, removed numerous constructs, changed some, and added a few others. The resulting language provides much of the power and flexibility of C++, but in a smaller, simpler, and safer language.

2.17.1 Design Process

Java, like many programming languages, was designed for an application for which there appeared to be no satisfactory existing language; in the case of Java, however, it was actually a sequence of applications, the first of which was the programming of embedded consumer electronic devices, such as toasters, microwave ovens, and interactive TV systems. It may not seem that reliability would be an important factor in the software for a microwave oven. If an oven had malfunctioning software, it probably would not pose a grave danger to anyone and probably would not lead to large legal settlements. However, if the software in a particular model was found to be erroneous after a million units had been manufactured and sold, their recall would entail significant cost. Therefore, reliability *is* an important characteristic of the software in consumer electronic products.

In 1990, Sun Microsystems decided that neither of the two programming languages they considered, C and C++, would be satisfactory for developing software for consumer electronic devices. Although C was relatively small, it did not provide support for object-oriented programming, which they deemed a necessity. C++ supported object-oriented programming, but it was judged to be too large and complex, in part because it also supported procedure-oriented programming. It was also believed that neither C nor C++ provided the necessary level of reliability. The design of Java was guided by the fundamental goal of providing greater simplicity and reliability than they believed were provided by C++.

Although the initial impetus for Java was consumer electronics, none of the products with which it was used in its early years were ever marketed. When the World Wide Web became widely used, starting in 1993, largely because of the new graphical browsers, Java was found to be a useful tool for Web programming. In its first few years in public use, the Web was Java's most common application.

The Java design team was headed by James Gosling, who had previously designed the UNIX emacs editor and the NeWS windowing system.

2.17.2 Language Overview

As we stated earlier, Java is based on C++ but was specifically designed to be smaller, simpler, and more reliable. Java has both classes and primitive types, which are not objects based on classes, as does C++. These include all of its scalar types, including those for integer, floating-point, Boolean, and character data. Objects are accessed through reference variables, but the primitive types are value types, exactly as the scalar values in purely imperative languages like C and Ada 83. Java arrays are instances of a predefined class, whereas in C++ they are not, although many C++ users build wrapper classes for arrays to add features like index range checking, which is implicit in Java.

Java does not have pointers, but its reference types provide some of the capabilities of pointers. These references are used to point to class instances—in fact, that is the only way class instances can be referenced. All objects are allocated on the heap. While pointers and references may seem a great deal alike, there are some important semantic differences. Pointers point to memory locations, but references point to objects. This makes any kind of arithmetic on references nonsense, eliminating that error-prone practice. The distinction between a pointer's value and the value to which it points is the responsibility of the programmer in many languages, in which pointers sometimes must be explicitly dereferenced. References are always implicitly dereferenced, when necessary. So they behave more like ordinary scalar variables.

Java has a primitive Boolean type, used mainly for the control expressions of its control statements (such as `if` and `while`). Unlike C and C++, arithmetic expressions cannot be used for control expressions. Java has no record, union, or enumeration types.

One significant difference between Java and many of its contemporaries that support object-oriented programming, including Ada 95 and C++, is that it is not possible to write stand-alone subprograms in Java. All Java subprograms are methods and are defined in classes. There is no construct in Java that is called a function or a subprogram. Furthermore, methods can only be called through a class or object, so, it does not support procedural programming.

Another important difference between C++ and Java is that C++ supports multiple inheritance directly in its class definitions. Some feel multiple inheritance leads to more complexity and confusion than it is worth. Java supports only single inheritance, although some of the benefits of multiple inheritance can be gained by using its interface construct.

Among the C++ constructs that were not copied into Java are structs, unions, and enumeration types.

Java includes a relatively simple form of concurrency control through its **synchronize** modifier, which can appear on methods and blocks. In either case, it causes a lock to be attached. The lock insures mutually exclusive access or execution. In Java it is relatively easy to create concurrent processes, which in Java are called *threads*.

Java uses implicit storage deallocation for its objects, often called *garbage collection*. This frees the programmer from being concerned with putting storage back in the heap when it is no longer needed. Programs written in languages that require explicit deallocation often suffer from what is sometimes called memory leakage, which means that storage is allocated but never deallocated. This can obviously lead to eventual depletion of all available storage.

Unlike C and C++, Java includes assignment type coercions (implicit type conversions) only if they are widening (from a "smaller" type to a "larger" type). So, **int** to **float** coercions are done, but **float** to **int** coercions are not.

2.17.3 Evaluation

The designers of Java did well at trimming out excess and/or unsafe features of C++. For example, the elimination of half of the assignment coercions that are done in C++ was clearly a step toward higher reliability. Index range checking of array accesses also makes the language safer. The addition of concurrency enhances the scope of applications that can be written in the language, as do the class libraries for applets, graphical user interfaces, database access, and networking.

Java's portability, at least in intermediate form, has often been attributed to the design of the language, but it is not. Any language could be translated to an intermediate form and "run" on any platform that had a virtual machine for that intermediate form. The price of this kind of portability is the cost of interpretation, which traditionally has been about an order of magnitude more than execution of machine code. The initial version of the Java interpreter, called the Java Virtual Machine (JVM), indeed was at least ten times slower than equivalent C programs. However, many Java programs are now translated to machine code before being executed, using Just In Time (JIT) compilers. This makes the efficiency of Java programs competitive with that of programs in compiled languages such as C++.

In its first few years, Java was widely used for programming World Wide Web pages. Before Java appeared, any significant computation required by a Web page was done through the Common Gateway Interface (CGI), using some application running on the Web server. Java applets are small programs that run on the Web client when it finds an applet call in the HTML of a page it is displaying. When called, the intermediate code form of the applet is downloaded from the server to the client, where it is interpreted. The output of an applet is placed in the browser display. This use of applets has declined in recent years, primarily because of the appearance of alternative technologies, such as the client-side scripting language, JavaScript.

The use of Java increased faster than that of any other programming language. Initially, this was due to its value in programming dynanmic Web documents. Another is that the compiler/interpreter system for Java has been free and easy to obtain on the Web. It is clear that one of the reasons for Java's rapid rise to prominence is simply that programmers like its design. There were always some developers who thought C++ was simply too large and complex to be practical and safe. Java offered them an alternative that has much of the power of C++, but in a simpler safer language. Java is now widely used in a wide variety of different applications areas.

The ancestry of Java is shown in Figure 2.14.

The following is an example of a Java program:

```
// Java Example Program
//  Input: An integer, listlen, where listlen is less
//         than 100, followed by length-integer values
// Output: The number of input data that are greater than
//         the average of all input values
import java.io.*;
class IntSort {
public static void main(String args[]) throws IOException {
  DataInputStream in = new DataInputStream(System.in);
  int listlen,
      counter,
      sum = 0,
      average,
      result = 0;
  int[] intlist = int[99];
  listlen = Integer.parseInt(in.readLine());
  if ((listlen > 0) && (listlen < 100)) {
/* Read input into an array and compute the sum  */
    for (counter = 0; counter < listlen; counter++) {
      intlist[counter] =
            Integer.valueOf(in.readLine()).intValue();
      sum += intlist[counter];
```

Figure 2.14

The ancestry of Java

C++ (1985)

Java (1994)

```
      }
/* Compute the average */
      average = sum / listlen;
/* Count the input values that are > average */
      for (counter = 0; counter < listlen; counter++)
        if (intlist[counter] > average) result++;
/* Print result */
        System.out.println(
            "\nNumber of values > average is:" + result);
      }  //** end of then clause of if ((listlen > 0) ...
      else System.out.println(
              "Error—input list length is not legal\n");
  }  //** end of method main
}  //** end of class IntSort
```

2.18   Scripting Languages for the Web: JavaScript and PHP

Use of the Web exploded in the mid-1990s after the first graphical browsers appeared. The need for computation associated with HTML documents, which by themselves are completely static, quickly became critical. Computation on the server end was made possible with the Common Gateway Interface, which allowed HTML documents to request the execution of programs on the server, with the results of such computations returned to the browser in the form of HTML documents. Computation on the browser end became available with the advent of Java applets. Both of these approaches are now slowly being replaced by newer technologies, in large part by scripting languages. This section briefly discusses two of the most popular of these, JavaScript, which is an HTML-resident client-side scripting language, and PHP, which is an HTML-resident server-side scripting language.

2.18.1   Origins and Characteristics of JavaScript

JavaScript, which was originally named LiveScript, was developed at Netscape. In late 1995, LiveScript became a joint venture of Netscape and Sun Microsystems and its name was changed to JavaScript. JavaScript has gone through extensive evolution, moving from version 1.0 to version 1.5 by adding many new features and capabilities. A language standard for JavaScript was developed in the late 1990s by the European Computer Manufacturers Association (ECMA) as ECMA-262. This standard has also been approved by the International Standards Organization (ISO) as ISO-16262. Microsoft's version of JavaScript is named JScript.

Although a JavaScript interpreter could be embedded in many different applications, its most common use is as an HTML-embedded client-side scripting language, whose primary use in Web programming is to create dynamic HTML documents. In spite of its name, JavaScript is related to Java only through the use of similar syntax. Java is strongly typed, which implies that the types of all variables can be determined at compile time, but JavaScript is dynamically typed. JavaScript's character strings and its arrays have dynamic length. Because of this, array indices are not checked for validity, although this is required in Java. Although Java fully supports object-oriented programming, JavaScript supports neither inheritance nor dynamic binding of method calls to methods.

Perhaps the most important use of JavaScript is in dynamically creating and modifying HTML documents. JavaScript defines an object hierarchy that matches a hierarchical model of an HTML document, which is defined by the Document Object Model. Elements of an HTML document are accessed through these objects, providing the basis for dynamic control of the elements of documents.

JavaScript is now a widely used tool for Web programming. In addition to its use for creating dynamic documents, it is also ideal for checking the validity of form inputs before the form data is sent to the server for processing.

Following is an example of a JavaScript script. Its appearance is odd, because it is embedded in an HTML document. This is by far the most common used of JavaScript. This program can be run with any Web browser that includes a recent version of a JavaScript interpreter.

```
<!DOCTYPE html PUBLIC "-//w3c//DTD XHTML 1.0 Strict//EN"
   "http://www.w3.org/TR/xhtml1/DTD/xhtml1-strict.dtd">
<!-- example.html
     Input: An integer, listLen, where listLen is less
            than 100, followed by listLen-numeric values
    Output: The number of input values that are greater
            than the average of all input values
    -->
<html>
<head><title> Example </title>
</head>
<body>
<script type = "text/javascript">
<!--
var intList = new Array(99);
var listLen, counter, sum = 0, result = 0;

listLen = prompt (
        "Please type the length of the input list", "");
if ((listLen > 0) && (listLen < 100)) {
// Get the input and compute its sum
   for (counter = 0; counter < listLen; counter++) {
      intList[counter] = prompt (
```

```
                              "Please type the next number", "");
            sum += parseInt(intList[counter]);
        }
// Compute the average
        average = sum / listLen;
// Count the input values that are > average
        for (counter = 0; counter < listLen; counter++)
            if (intList[counter] > average) result++;
// Display the results
        document.write("Number of values > average is: ",
                        result, "<br />");
    } else
        document.write(
            "Error - input list length is not legal <br />");
// -->
</script>
</body>
</html>
```

2.18.2 Origins and Characteristics of PHP

PHP was developed by Rasmus Lerdorf, a member of the Apache Group, in 1994. Its initial motivation was to provide a tool to help Lerdorf track visitors to his personal Web site. In 1995, he developed a package called Personal Home Page Tools, which became the first publicly distributed version of PHP. Originally, PHP was an acronym for Personal Home Page. Later, its user community began using the recursive name PHP: Hypertext Preprocessor, which subsequently forced the original name into obscurity. PHP is now developed, distributed, and supported as an open-source product. PHP processors are resident on most Web servers.

PHP is an HTML-embedded server side scripting language specifically designed for Web applications. PHP code is interpreted on the Web server when an HTML document in which it is embedded has been requested by a browser. PHP code often produces HTML code as output, which replaces the PHP code in the HTML document. Therefore, a Web browser never sees PHP code.

PHP is similar to JavaScript, in its syntactic appearance, in the dynamic nature of its strings and arrays, and in its use of dynamic typing. PHP's arrays are a combination of JavaScript's arrays and Perl's associative arrays.

PHP allows simple access to HTML form data, so form processing is easy with PHP. PHP provides support for many different database management systems. This makes it an excellent language for building programs that need Web access to databases.

2.19   A New Language for the New Millennium: C#

C#, along with the new development platform, .NET,[7] was announced by Microsoft in 2000. In January, 2002, production versions of both were released.

2.19.1   Design Process

C# is based on C++ and Java, but includes some ideas from Delphi and Visual BASIC. Its lead designer, Anders Hejlsberg, also designed Turbo Pascal and Delphi, which explains the Delphi parts of the heritage of C#.

The purpose of C# is to provide a language for component-based software development, specifically for such development in the .NET Framework. In this environment, components from a variety of languages can be easily combined to form systems. All of the .NET languages, which include C#, Visual BASIC .NET, Managed C++, J# .NET, and JScript .NET use the Common Type System (CTS). The CTS provides a common class library. All types in all five .NET languages inherit from a single class root, `System.Object`. Compilers that conform to the CTS specification create objects that can be combined into software systems. All five .NET languages are compiled into the same intermediate form, Intermediate Language (IL). Unlike Java, however, the IL is never interpreted. A Just-In-Time compiler is used to translate IL into machine code before it is executed.

2.19.2   Language Overview

Many believe that one of Java's most important advances over C++ lies in the fact that it excludes some of C++'s features. For example, C++ supports multiple inheritance, pointers, structs, **enum** types, operator overloading, and a goto statement, but Java includes none of these. The designers of C# obviously disagreed with this wholesale removal of features, for all of these except multiple inheritance have been brought back in the new language.

To the credit of C#'s designers, however, in several cases, the C# version of a C++ feature has been improved. For example, the **enum** types of C# are safer than those of C++, because they are never implicitly converted to integers. This allows them to be more type safe. The **struct** type was changed significantly, resulting in a truly useful construct, whereas in C++ it serves virtually no purpose. In C#, a struct is a lightweight class that does not support inheritance or subclassing. However, C# structs can implement interfaces and have constructors. They are value types, which means they are allocated on the run-time stack. All C# primitive types are implemented as structs.

C# takes a stab at improving the **switch** statement that is used in C, C++, and Java. In those languages, there is no implicit branch at the end of the selectable segments of code, which has caused innumerable program-

---

[7]The .NET development system is briefly discussed in Chapter 1.

ming errors. The problem stems from the fact that the programmer must remember to put a **break** statement in every selectable segment from which flow is to exit the structure, rather than going to the next selectable segment. Unfortunately, this makes the default action one that is rarely used in practice. The C# **switch** statement adds a single new requirement to the statement: Every nonempty case segment must end with an unconditional branch statement. So, if you want control to flow from one case segment to the next, it is necessary to use a goto statement to branch to the next case segment.

Although C++ includes function pointers, they share the lack of safety that is inherent in C++'s pointers to variables. C# includes a new type, delegates, which are both object-oriented and type-safe method references. Delegates are used for implementing event handlers and callbacks.[8] Callbacks are implemented in Java with interfaces; in C++, method pointers are used.

In C#, methods can take a variable number of parameters, as long as they are all the same type. This is specified by the use of a formal parameter of array type, preceded by the **params** reserved word.

Both C++ and Java use two distinct typing systems, one for primitives and one for objects. In addition to being confusing, this leads to frequent needs to convert values between the two systems, for example, to put a primitive value into a collection that stores objects. C# makes the conversion between values of the two typing systems partially implicit through the implicit boxing and unboxing operations, which are discussed in detail in Chapter 12.

Among the other features of C# are rectangular arrays, which are not supported in most programming languages, and a **foreach** statement, which is an iterator for arrays and collection objects. A similar **foreach** statement is found in Perl and PHP. Also, C# includes properties, which are an alternative to public data members. Properties are specified as data members with get and set methods, which are implicitly called when references and assignments are made to the associated data members.

2.19.3 Evaluation

C# was meant to be an advance over both C++ and Java as a general purpose programming language. Although it can be argued that some of its features are a step backwards, C# clearly includes some constructs that move it beyond its predecessors.

The primary intended application of C# is as the main language in the .NET environment. It is far too early to say with any certainty that C# will succeed in attracting a large number of users. However, given the huge effort being made by Microsoft to sell .NET, it appears that its chances at becoming widely used are excellent. Furthermore, some of its features will surely become adopted by programming languages of the near-term future.

The ancestry of C# is shown in Figure 2.15.

---

[8]When an object calls a method of another object and needs to be notified when that method has completed its task, it calls its caller back. This call is the *callback*.

Figure 2.15

The ancestry of C#

SUMMARY

We have investigated the development and the development environments of a number of the most important programming languages. This chapter should have given the reader a good perspective on current issues in language design. We hope to have set the stage for an in-depth discussion of the important features of contemporary languages.

BIBLIOGRAPHIC NOTES

Perhaps the most important source of historical information about the development of programming languages is *History of Programming Languages*, edited by Richard Wexelblat (Wexelblat, 1981). It contains the developmental background and environment of 13 important programming languages, as told by the designers themselves. A similar work resulted from a second "history" conference, this time published as a special issue of *ACM SIGPLAN Notices* (ACM, 1993a). In this work, the history and evolution of 13 more programming languages are discussed.

The paper "Early Development of Programming Languages" (Knuth and Pardo, 1977), which is part of the *Encyclopedia of Computer Science and Technology*, is an excellent 85-page work that details the development of languages up to and including Fortran. The paper includes example programs to demonstrate the features of many of those languages.

Another book of great interest is *Programming Languages: History and Fundamentals*, by Jean Sammet (Sammet, 1969). It is a 785-page work filled with details of 80 programming languages of the 1950s and 1960s. Sammet has also published several updates to her book, such as Sammet (1976).

REVIEW QUESTIONS

1. In what year was Plankalkül designed? In what year was that design published?

2. What two common data structures were included in Plankalkül?

3. How were the pseudocodes of the early 1950s implemented?

4. Speedcoding was invented to overcome two significant shortcomings of the computer hardware of the early 1950s. What were these two?

5. Why was the slowness of interpretation of programs acceptable in the early 1950s?

6. What hardware capability that first appeared in the IBM 704 computer strongly affected the evolution of programming languages? Explain why.

7. In what year was the Fortran design project begun?

8. What was the primary application area of computers at the time Fortran was designed?

9. What was the source of all of the control flow statements of Fortran I?

10. What was the most significant feature added to Fortran I to get Fortran II?

11. What control flow statements were added to Fortran IV to get Fortran 77?

12. Which version of Fortran was the first to have any sort of dynamic variables?

13. Which version of Fortran was the first to have character string handling?

14. Why were linguists interested in artificial intelligence in the late 1950s?

15. Where was LISP developed? By whom?

16. In what way are Scheme and COMMON LISP opposites of each other?

17. What dialect of LISP is used for introductory programming courses at some universities?

18. What two professional organizations together designed ALGOL 60?

19. In what version of ALGOL did block structure appear?

20. What missing language element of ALGOL 60 damaged its chances for widespread use?

21. What language was designed to describe the syntax of ALGOL 60?

22. On what language was COBOL based?

23. In what year did the COBOL design process begin?

24. What data structure appeared in COBOL that originated with Plankalkül?

25. What organization was most responsible for the early success of COBOL (in terms of extent of use)?

26. What user group was the target of the first version of BASIC?
27. Why was BASIC an important language in the early 1980s?
28. PL/I was designed to replace what two languages?
29. For what new line of computers was PL/I designed?
30. What features of SIMULA 67 are now important parts of some object-oriented languages?
31. What innovation of data structuring was introduced in ALGOL 68 but is often credited to Pascal?
32. What design criterion was used extensively in ALGOL 68?
33. What language introduced the **case** statement?
34. What operators in C were modeled on similar operators in ALGOL 68?
35. What are two characteristics of C that make it less safe than Pascal?
36. What is a nonprocedural language?
37. What are the two kinds of statements that populate a Prolog database?
38. What is the primary application area for which Ada was designed?
39. What are the concurrent program units of Ada called?
40. What Ada construct provides support for abstract data types?
41. What populates the Smalltalk world?
42. What three concepts are the basis for object-oriented programming?
43. Why does C++ include the features of C that are known to be unsafe?
44. What do the Ada and COBOL languages have in common?
45. What was the first application for Java?
46. What characteristic of Java is most evident in JavaScript?
47. How does the typing system of PHP and JavaScript differ from that of Java?
48. What array structure is included in C#, but not in C, C++, or Java?
49. What feature of Delphi's classes is included in C#?
50. What deficiency of the **switch** statement of C is addressed with the changes made by C# to that statement?

PROBLEM SET

1. What features of Plankalkül do you think would have had the greatest influence on Fortran 0 if the Fortran designers had been familiar with Plankalkül?
2. Determine the capabilities of Backus's 701 Speedcoding system, and compare them with those of a contemporary programmable hand calculator.

3. Write a short history of the A-0, A-1, and A-2 systems designed by Grace Hopper and her associates.

4. As a research project, compare the facilities of Fortran 0 with those of the Laning and Zierler system.

5. Which of the three original goals of the ALGOL design committee, in your opinion, was most difficult to achieve at that time?

6. Make an educated guess as to the most common syntax error in LISP programs.

7. LISP began as a pure functional language but gradually acquired more and more imperative features. Why?

8. Describe in detail the three most important reasons, in your opinion, why ALGOL 60 did not become a very widely used language.

9. Why, in your opinion, did COBOL allow long identifiers when Fortran and ALGOL did not?

10. Outline the major motivation of IBM in developing PL/I.

11. Was IBM's major motivation for developing PL/I correct, given the history of computers and language developments since 1964?

12. Describe, in your own words, the concept of orthogonality in programming language design.

13. What is the primary reason why PL/I became more widely used than ALGOL 68?

14. What are the arguments both for and against the idea of a typeless language?

15. Are there any logic programming languages, other than Prolog?

16. What is your opinion of the argument that languages that are too complex are too dangerous to use and we should therefore keep all languages small and simple?

17. Do you think language design by committee is a good idea? Support your opinion.

18. Languages continually evolve. What sort of restrictions do you think are appropriate for changes in programming languages? Compare your answers with the evolution of Fortran.

19. Build a table identifying all of the major language developments, together with when they occurred, in what language they first appeared, and the identities of the developers.

20. There have been some public interchanges between Microsoft and Sun concerning the design of Microsoft's J++ and C# and Sun's Java. Read some of these documents, which are available on their respective Web sites, and write an analysis of the disagreements concerning delegates.

3

Describing Syntax and Semantics

CHAPTER OUTLINE

This chapter covers the following topics. First, the terms *syntax* and *semantics* are defined. Then a detailed discussion of the most common method of describing syntax, context-free grammars (also known as Backus-Naur Form), is presented. Attribute grammars, which can be used to describe both the syntax and static semantics of programming languages, are discussed next. Finally, three formal methods of describing semantics—operational, axiomatic, and denotational semantics—are introduced. Because of the inherent complexity of the semantics description methods, our discussion of them will be brief. One could easily write an entire book on just one of the three (as several authors have).

3.1   Introduction

The task of providing a concise yet understandable description of a programming language is difficult but essential to the language's success. ALGOL 60 and ALGOL 68 were first presented using concise formal descriptions; in both cases, however, the descriptions were not easily understandable, partly because each used a new notation. The levels of acceptance of both languages suffered as a result. On the other hand, some languages have suffered the problem of having many slightly different dialects, a result of an understandable but informal and imprecise definition.

One of the problems in describing a language is the diversity of the people who must understand the description. Most new programming languages are subjected to a period of scrutiny by potential users before their designs are completed. The success of this feedback cycle depends heavily on the clarity of the description.

Programming language implementors obviously must be able to determine how the expressions, statements, and program units of a language are formed, and also their intended effect when executed. The difficulty of the job of implementors is in part determined by the clarity and precision of the language description.

Finally, language users must be able to determine how to encode software systems by referring to a language reference manual. Textbooks and courses enter into this process, but language manuals are usually the only authoritative printed information source about a language.

The study of programming languages, like the study of natural languages, can be divided into examinations of syntax and semantics. The **syntax** of a programming language is the form of its expressions, statements, and program units. Its **semantics** is the meaning of those expressions, statements, and program units. For example, the syntax of a Java **while** statement is

while (<boolean_expr>) <statement>

The semantics of this statement form is that when the current value of the Boolean expression is true, the embedded statement is executed. Then control implicitly returns to the Boolean expression to repeat the process.

Although they are often separated for discussion purposes, syntax and semantics are closely related. In a well-designed programming language, semantics should follow directly from syntax; that is, the form of a statement should strongly suggest what the statement is meant to accomplish.

Describing syntax is easier than describing semantics, partly because a concise and universally accepted notation is available for syntax description, but none has yet been developed for semantics.

3.2 The General Problem of Describing Syntax

A language, whether natural (such as English) or artificial (such as Java), is a set of strings of characters from some alphabet. The strings of a language are called **sentences** or statements. The syntax rules of a language specify which strings of characters from the language's alphabet are in the language. English, for example, has a large and complex collection of rules for specifying the syntax of its sentences. By comparison, even the largest and most complex programming languages are syntactically very simple.

Formal descriptions of the syntax of programming languages, for simplicity's sake, often do not include descriptions of the lowest-level syntactic units. These small units are called **lexemes**. The description of lexemes can be given by a lexical specification, which can be separate from the syntactic description of the language. The lexemes of a programming language include its identifiers, literals, operators, and special words. One can think of programs as strings of lexemes rather than of characters.

A **token** of a language is a category of its lexemes. For example, an identifier is a token that can have lexemes, or instances, such as sum and total. In some cases, a token has only a single possible lexeme. For example, the token for the arithmetic operator symbol +, which may have the name plus_op, has just one possible lexeme. Consider the following Java statement:

```
index = 2 * count + 17;
```

The lexemes and tokens of this statement are

Lexemes	Tokens
index	identifier
=	equal_sign
2	int_literal
*	mult_op
count	identifier
+	plus_op
17	int_ literal
;	semicolon

The example language descriptions in this chapter are very simple, and most include lexeme descriptions.

3.2.1   Language Recognizers

In general, languages can be formally defined in two distinct ways: by **recognition** and by **generation** (although neither provides a definition that is practical by itself for people trying to learn or even use a programming language). Suppose we have a language L that uses an alphabet Σ of characters. To formally define L using the recognition method, we would need to construct a mechanism R, called a recognition device, capable of reading strings of characters from the alphabet Σ. R would need to be designed so that it indicated that a given input string was or was not in L. In effect, R would either accept or reject the given string. Such devices are like filters, separating correct sentences from those that are incorrectly formed. If R, when fed any string of characters over Σ, accepts it only if it is in L, then R is a description of L. Because most useful languages are, for all practical purposes, infinite, this might seem like a lengthy and ineffective process. Recognition devices, however, are not used to enumerate all of the sentences of a language.

The syntax analysis part of a compiler is a recognizer for the language the compiler translates. In this role, the recognizer need not test all possible strings of characters from some set to determine whether each is in the language. Rather, it need only determine whether given programs are in the language. In effect then, the syntax analyzer determines whether the given programs are syntactically correct. Syntax analyzers, also known as parsers, are discussed in Chapter 4.

3.2.2   Language Generators

A language generator is a device that can be used to generate the sentences of a language. We can think of the generator as having a button that, when pushed, produces a sentence of the language. Because the particular sentence that is produced by a generator when its button is pushed is unpredictable, a generator seems to be a device of limited usefulness as a language descriptor. However, people prefer certain forms of generators over recognizers because they can more easily read and understand them. By contrast, the syntax-checking portion of a compiler (a language recognizer) is not as useful a language description for a programmer because it can only be used in trial-and-error mode. For example, to determine the correct syntax of a particular statement using a compiler, the programmer can only submit a guessed-at version and see whether the compiler accepts it. On the other hand, it is often possible to determine whether the syntax of a particular statement is correct by comparing it with the structure of the generator.

There is a close connection between formal generation and recognition devices for the same language. This was one of the seminal discoveries in computer science, and it led to much of what is now known about formal languages and compiler design theory. We return to the relationship of generators and recognizers in the next section.

3.3 Formal Methods of Describing Syntax

This section discusses the formal language generation mechanisms, usually called grammars, that are commonly used to describe the syntax of programming languages.

3.3.1 Backus-Naur Form and Context-Free Grammars

In the middle to late 1950s, two men, Noam Chomsky and John Backus, in unrelated research efforts, developed the same syntax description formalism, which subsequently became the most widely used method for programming language syntax.

3.3.1.1 Context-free Grammars

In the mid-1950s, Chomsky, a noted linguist, described four classes of generative devices or grammars that define four classes of languages (Chomsky, 1956, 1959). Two of these grammar classes, named context-free and regular, turned out to be useful for describing the syntax of programming languages. The tokens of programming languages can be described by regular grammars. Whole programming languages, with minor exceptions, can be described by context-free grammars. Because Chomsky was a linguist, his primary interest was the theoretical nature of natural languages. He had no interest at the time in the artificial languages used to communicate with computers. So it was not until later that his work was applied to programming languages.

3.3.1.2 Origins of Backus-Naur Form

Shortly after Chomsky's work on language classes, the ACM-GAMM group began designing ALGOL 58. A landmark paper describing ALGOL 58 was presented by John Backus, a prominent member of the ACM-GAMM group, at an international conference in 1959 (Backus, 1959). This paper introduced a new formal notation for specifying programming language syntax. The new notation was later modified slightly by Peter Naur for the description of ALGOL 60 (Naur, 1960). This revised method of syntax description became known as **Backus-Naur form,** or simply **BNF.**

BNF is a natural notation for describing syntax. In fact, something similar to BNF was used by Panini to describe the syntax of Sanskrit several hundred years before Christ (Ingerman, 1967).

Although the use of BNF in the ALGOL 60 report was not immediately accepted by computer users, it soon became and is still the most popular method of concisely describing programming language syntax.

It is remarkable that BNF is nearly identical to Chomsky's generative devices for context-free languages, called **context-free grammars.** In the remainder of the chapter, we refer to context-free grammars simply as grammars. Furthermore, the terms BNF and grammar are used interchangeably.

3.3.1.3 Fundamentals

A **metalanguage** is a language that is used to describe another language. BNF is a metalanguage for programming languages.

BNF uses abstractions for syntactic structures. A simple Java assignment statement, for example, might be represented by the abstraction <assign>. (Pointed brackets are often used to delimit names of abstractions.) The actual definition of <assign> may be given by

<assign> → <var> = <expression>

The symbol on the left side of the arrow, which is aptly called the left-hand side (LHS), is the abstraction being defined. The text to the right of the arrow is the definition of the LHS. It is called the right-hand side (RHS) and consists of some mixture of tokens, lexemes, and references to other abstractions. (Actually, tokens are also abstractions.) Altogether, the definition is called a **rule,** or **production.** In the example rule just given, the abstractions <var> and <expression> obviously must be defined before the <assign> definition becomes useful.

This particular rule specifies that the abstraction <assign> is defined as an instance of the abstraction <var>, followed by the lexeme =, followed by an instance of the abstraction <expression>. One example sentence whose syntactic structure is described by the rule is

```
total = sub1 + sub2
```

The abstractions in a BNF description, or grammar, are often called **nonterminal symbols,** or simply **nonterminals,** and the lexemes and tokens of the rules are called **terminal symbols,** or simply **terminals.** A BNF description, or **grammar,** is simply a collection of rules.

Nonterminal symbols can have two or more distinct definitions, representing two or more possible syntactic forms in the language. Multiple definitions can be written as a single rule, with the different definitions separated by the symbol |, meaning logical OR. For example, an Ada **if** statement can be described with the rules

<if_stmt> → **if** <logic_expr> **then** <stmt>

<if_stmt> → **if** <logic_expr> **then** <stmt> **else** <stmt>

or with the rule

<if_stmt> → **if** <logic_expr> **then** <stmt>

      | **if** <logic_expr> **then** <stmt> **else** <stmt>

Although BNF is simple, it is sufficiently powerful to describe the great majority of the syntax of programming languages. In particular, it can describe lists of similar constructs, the order in which different constructs must appear, nested structures to any depth, and even imply operator precedence, and operator associativity.

3.3.1.4 Describing Lists

Variable-length lists in mathematics are often written using an ellipsis (…); 1, 2, … is an example. BNF does not include the ellipsis, so an alternative method is required for describing lists of syntactic elements in programming languages (for example, a list of identifiers appearing on a data declaration statement). The most common alternative is recursion. A rule is **recursive** if its LHS appears in its RHS. The following rules illustrate how recursion is used to describe lists:

<ident_list> → identifier

| identifier , <ident_list>

This defines <ident_list> as either a single token (identifier) or an identifier followed by a comma followed by another instance of <ident_list>. Recursion is used to describe lists in many of the example grammars in the remainder of this chapter.

3.3.1.5 Grammars and Derivations

A grammar is a generative device for defining languages. The sentences of the language are generated through a sequence of applications of the rules, beginning with a special nonterminal of the grammar called the **start symbol.** A sentence generation is called a **derivation.** In a grammar for a complete programming language, the start symbol represents a complete program and is usually named <program>. The simple grammar shown in Example 3.1 is used to illustrate derivations:

EXAMPLE 3.1	A Grammar for a Small Language

<program> → **begin** <stmt_list> **end**
<stmt_list> → <stmt>
                   | <stmt> ; <stmt_list>
<stmt> → <var> = <expression>
<var> → A | B | C
<expression> → <var> + <var>
                   | <var> - <var>
                   | <var>

The language in Example 3.1 has only one statement form: assignment. A program consists of the special word **begin**, followed by a list of statements separated by semicolons, followed by the special word **end**. An expression is either a single variable, or two variables separated by either a + or – operator. The only variable names in this language are A, B, and C.

A derivation of a program in this language follows:

```
<program> => begin <stmt_list> end
          => begin <stmt> ; <stmt_list> end
          => begin <var> = <expression> ; <stmt_list> end
          => begin A = <expression> ; <stmt_list> end
          => begin A = <var> + <var> ; <stmt_list> end
          => begin A = B + <var> ; <stmt_list> end
          => begin A = B + C ; <stmt_list> end
          => begin A = B + C ; <stmt> end
          => begin A = B + C ; <var> = <expression> end
          => begin A = B + C ; B = <expression> end
          => begin A = B + C ; B = <var> end
          => begin A = B + C ; B = C end
```

This derivation, like all derivations, begins with the start symbol, in this case
<program>. The symbol => is read "derives." Each successive string in the
sequence is derived from the previous string by replacing one of the nonterminals with one of that nonterminal's definitions. Each of the strings in the
derivation, including <program>, is called a **sentential form.**

In this derivation, the replaced nonterminal is always the leftmost nonterminal in the previous sentential form. Derivations that use this order of
replacement are called **leftmost derivations.** The derivation continues until
the sentential form contains no nonterminals. That sentential form, consisting of only terminals, or lexemes, is the generated sentence.

In addition to leftmost, a derivation may be rightmost or in an order that
is neither leftmost nor rightmost. Derivation order has no effect on the language generated by a grammar.

By choosing alternative RHSs of rules with which to replace nonterminals in the derivation, different sentences in the language can be generated.
By exhaustively choosing all combinations of choices, we can generate the
entire language. This language, like most others, is infinite, so one cannot
generate *all* the sentences in the language in finite time.

Example 3.2 is another example of a grammar for part of a typical programming language:

EXAMPLE 3.2   A Grammar for Simple Assignment Statements

<assign> → <id> = <expr>
<id> → A | B | C
<expr> → <id> + <expr>
      | <id> * <expr>
        | (<expr>)
          | <id>

The grammar of Example 3.2 describes assignment statements whose right sides are arithmetic expressions with multiplication and addition operators and parentheses. For example, the statement

```
A = B * ( A + C )
```

is generated by the leftmost derivation:

```
<assign> => <id> = <expr>
         => A = <expr>
         => A = <id> * <expr>
         => A = B * <expr>
         => A = B * ( <expr> )
         => A = B * ( <id> + <expr> )
         => A = B * ( A + <expr> )
         => A = B * ( A + <id> )
         => A = B * ( A + C )
```

3.3.1.6 Parse Trees

One of the most attractive features of grammars is that they naturally describe the hierarchical syntactic structure of the sentences of the languages they define. These hierarchical structures are called **parse trees.** For example, the parse tree in Figure 3.1 shows the structure of the assignment statement derived above.

Every internal node of a parse tree is labeled with a nonterminal symbol; every leaf is labeled with a terminal symbol. Every subtree of a parse tree describes one instance of an abstraction in the sentence.

Figure 3.1

A parse tree for the simple statement
```
A = B * (A + C)
```

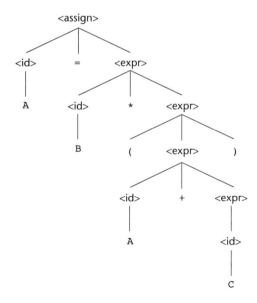

3.3.1.7 Ambiguity

A grammar that generates a sentential form for which there are two or more distinct parse trees is said to be **ambiguous.** Consider the grammar shown in Example 3.3, which is a minor variation of the grammar in Example 3.2.

EXAMPLE 3.3	An Ambiguous Grammar for Simple Assignment Statements

<assign> → <id> = <expr>
<id> → A | B | C
<expr> →<expr> + <expr>
     | <expr> * <expr>
     | (<expr>)
     | <id>

The grammar of Example 3.3 is ambiguous because the sentence

A = B + C * A

has two distinct parse trees, as shown in Figure 3.2. The ambiguity occurs because the grammar specifies slightly less syntactic structure than does the grammar of Example 3.2. Rather than allowing the parse tree of an expression to grow only on the right, this grammar allows growth on both the left and the right.

Syntactic ambiguity of language structures is a problem because compilers often base the semantics of those structures on their syntactic form. Specifically, the compiler decides what code to generate for a statement by examining its parse tree. If a language structure has more than one parse tree, then the meaning of the structure cannot be determined uniquely. This problem is discussed in two specific examples in the following three sections.

Figure 3.2

Two distinct parse trees for the same sentence,
A = B + (A * C)

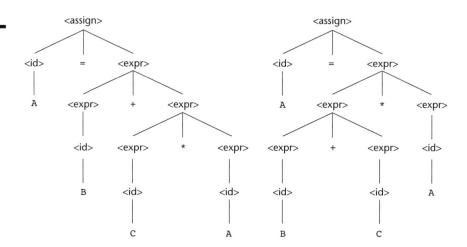

Some parsing algorithms can be based on ambiguous grammars. When such a parser encounters an ambiguous construct, its uses nongrammatical information provided by the designer to construct the correct parse tree. For example, some parser generation systems allow the compiler writer to provide all operator precedence and associativity information outside the grammar. In such systems, the grammar need not specify precedence or associativity rules and need not be unambiguous.

3.3.1.8 Operator Precedence

As stated earlier, a grammar can describe a certain syntactic structure so that part of the meaning of the structure can be determined from its parse tree. In particular, the fact that an operator in an arithmetic expression is generated lower in the parse tree (and therefore must be evaluated first) can be used to indicate that it has precedence over an operator produced higher up in the tree. In the first parse tree of Figure 3.2, for example, the multiplication operator is generated lower in the tree, which could indicate that it has precedence over the addition operator in the expression. The second parse tree, however, indicates just the opposite. It appears, therefore, that the two parse trees indicate conflicting precedence information.

Notice that although the grammar of Example 3.2 is not ambiguous, the precedence order of its operators is not the usual one. In this grammar, a parse tree of a sentence with multiple operators, regardless of the particular operators involved, has the rightmost operator in the expression at the lowest point in the parse tree, with the other operators in the tree moving progressively higher as one moves to the left in the expression. For example, in the parse tree in Figure 3.1, the plus operator is the rightmost operator in the expression and the lowest in the tree, giving it precedence over the multiplication operator to its left.

A grammar can be written to separate the addition and multiplication operators so they are consistently in a higher-to-lower ordering, respectively, in the parse tree. This ordering can be maintained regardless of the order in which the operators appear in an expression. The correct ordering is specified by using separate abstractions for the operands of the operators that have different precedence. This requires additional nonterminals and some new rules. The grammar of Example 3.4 is such a grammar.

EXAMPLE 3.4   An Unambiguous Grammar for Expressions

```
<assign> → <id> = <expr>
<id> → A | B | C
<expr> →  <expr> + <term>
       |  <term>
<term> → <term> * <factor>
       |  <factor>
<factor> → ( <expr> )
        |  <id>
```

The grammar in Example 3.4 generates the same language as the grammars of Examples 3.2 and 3.3, but it indicates the usual precedence order of multiplication and addition operators. The following derivation of the sentence A = B + C * A uses the grammar of Example 3.4:

```
<assign>  => <id> = <expr>
           => A = <expr>
           => A = <expr> + <term>
           => A = <term> + <term>
           => A = <factor> + <term>
           => A = <id> + <term>
           => A = B + <term>
           => A = B + <term> * <factor>
           => A = B + <factor> * <factor>
           => A = B + <id> * <factor>
           => A = B + C * <factor>
           => A = B + C * <id>
           => A = B + C * A
```

The unique parse tree for this sentence, using the grammar of Example 3.4, is shown in Figure 3.3.

The connection between parse trees and derivations is very close: Either can easily be constructed from the other. Every derivation with an unambiguous grammar has a unique parse tree, although that tree can be represented by different derivations. For example, the following derivation of the sentence A = B + C * A is different from the derivation of the same sentence given previously. This is a rightmost derivation, whereas the previous one is

Figure 3.3

The unique parse tree for A = B + (A * C) using an unambiguous grammar

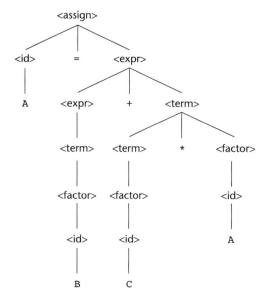

leftmost. Both of these derivations, however, are represented by the same parse tree.

```
<assign>  => <id> = <expr>
            => <id> = <expr> + <term>
            => <id> = <expr> + <term> * <factor>
            => <id> = <expr> + <term> * <id>
            => <id> = <expr> + <term> * A
            => <id> = <expr> + <factor> * A
            => <id> = <expr> + <id> * A
            => <id> = <expr> + C * A
            => <id> = <term> + C * A
            => <id> = <factor> + C * A
            => <id> = <id> + C * A
            => <id> = B + C * A
            => A = B + C * A
```

3.3.1.9 Associativity of Operators

Another interesting question concerning grammars for expressions is whether operator associativity is also correctly described; that is, do the parse trees for expressions with two or more adjacent occurrences of operators with equal precedence have those occurrences in proper hierarchical order? An example of an assignment statement with such an expression is

```
A = B + C + A
```

The parse tree for this sentence, as defined with the grammar of Example 3.4, is shown in Figure 3.4.

The parse tree of Figure 3.4 shows the left addition operator lower than the right addition operator. This is the correct order if addition is meant to be left associative, which is typical. In most cases, the associativity of addition in a computer is irrelevant. (In mathematics, addition is associative, which means that left and right associative orders of evaluation mean the same thing. That is, $(A + B) + C = A + (B + C)$.) Computer arithmetic is not always associative. Floating-point addition, for example, is not necessarily associative. In some situations, however, floating-point addition is not associative. Suppose floating-point values store seven digits of accuracy. Consider the problem of adding eleven numbers together, where one of the numbers is 10^7 and the other ten are 1. If the small numbers (the 1s) are each added to the large number, one at a time, there is no effect on that number, because the small numbers occur in the eighth digit of the large number. However, if the small numbers are first added together and the result is added to the large number, the result in seven-digit accuracy is $1.000001 * 10^7$. Subtraction and division are not associative, whether in mathematics or in a computer. Therefore, correct associativity may be essential for an expression that contains either of them.

Figure 3.4

A parse tree for A = B
+ (A + C) illustrating
the associativity of
addition

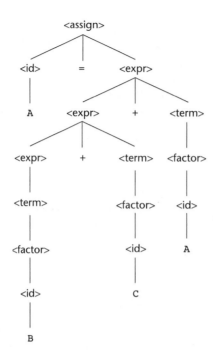

When a grammar rule has its LHS also appearing at the beginning of its RHS, the rule is said to be **left recursive.** This left recursion specifies left associativity. For example, the left recursion of the rules of the grammar of Example 3.4 causes it to make both addition and multiplication left associative.

In most languages that provide it, the exponentiation operator is right associative. To indicate right associativity, right recursion can be used. A grammar rule is **right recursive** if the LHS appears at the right end of the RHS. Rules such as

<factor> → <exp> ** <factor>
      | <exp>
<exp> → (<expr>)
     | id

could be used to describe exponentiation as a right-associative operator.

3.3.1.10 An Unambiguous Grammar for `if-then-else`

The BNF rules given in Section 3.3.1.3 for one particular form of **if-then-else** statement are repeated here:

<if_stmt> → **if** <logic_expr> **then** <stmt>
     | **if** <logic_expr> **then** <stmt> **else** <stmt>

If we also have <stmt> → <if_stmt>, this grammar is ambiguous. The simplest sentential form that illustrates this ambiguity is

if <logic_expr> **then if** <logic_expr> **then** <stmt> **else** <stmt>

The two parse trees in Figure 3.5 show the ambiguity of this sentential form. We will examine the practical problems associated with this else-association problem in Chapter 8.

We will now develop an unambiguous grammar that describes this **if** statement. The rule for **if** constructs in most languages is that an **else** clause, when present, is matched with the nearest previous unmatched **then**. Therefore, between a **then** and its matching **else**, there cannot be an **if** statement without an **else**. So, for this situation, statements must be distinguished between those that are matched and those that are unmatched, where unmatched statements are **else**-less **if**s and all other statements are matched. The problem with the grammar above is that it treats all statements as if they had equal syntactic significance; that is, as if they were all matched.

Figure 3.5

Two distinct parse trees for the same sentenial form

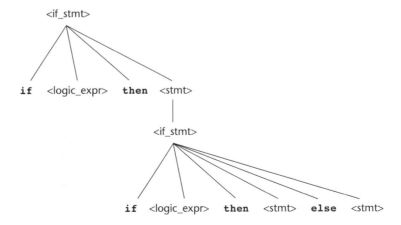

To reflect the different categories of statements, different abstractions, or nonterminals, must be used. The unambiguous grammar based on these ideas follows:

```
<stmt> → <matched> | <unmatched>
<matched> → if <logic_expr> then <matched> else <matched>
            | any non-if statement
<unmatched> → if <logic_expr> then <stmt>
              | if <logic_expr> then <matched> else <unmatched>
```

There is just one possible parse tree, using this grammar, for the sentence shown in Figure 3.5.

3.3.2   Extended BNF

Because of a few minor inconveniences in BNF, it has been extended in several ways. Most extended versions are called Extended BNF, or simply EBNF, even though they are not all exactly the same. The extensions do not enhance the descriptive power of BNF; they only increase its readability and writability.

Three extensions are commonly included in the various versions of EBNF. The first of these denotes an optional part of an RHS, which is delimited by brackets. For example, a C selection statement can be described as

```
<selection> → if ( <expression> ) <statement> [else <statement>]
```

Without the use of the brackets, the syntactic description of this statement would require two rules.

The second extension is the use of braces in an RHS to indicate that the enclosed part can be repeated indefinitely or left out altogether. This extension allows lists to be built with a single rule, instead of using recursion and two rules. For example, lists of identifiers separated by commas can be described by the following rule:

```
<ident_list> → <identifier> {, <identifier>}
```

This is a replacement of the recursion by a form of implied iteration; the part enclosed within braces can be iterated any number of times.

The third common extension deals with multiple-choice options. When a single element must be chosen from a group, the options are placed in parentheses and separated by the OR operator, |. For example,

```
<term> → <term> (* | / | %) <factor>
```

It would require three BNF rules to describe this structure. The brackets, braces, and parentheses in the EBNF extensions are metasymbols, which means they are notational tools and not terminal symbols in the syntactic entities they help describe. In cases where these metasymbols are also terminal symbols in the language being described, the instances that are terminal symbols can be underlined or quoted.

EXAMPLE 3.5   **BNF and EBNF Versions of an Expression Grammar**

BNF: <expr> → <expr> + <term>
                 | <expr> - <term>
                 | <term>
         <term> → <term> * <factor>
                 | <term> / <factor>
                 | <factor>
         <factor> → <exp> ** <factor>
                 | <exp>
         <exp> → <(<expr>)
                 | id
EBNF: <expr> → <term> {(+ | -) <term>}
         <term> → <factor> {(* | /) <factor>}
         <factor> → <exp> { ** <exp>}
         <exp> → (<expr>)
                 | id

The BNF rule

<expr> <expr> + <term>

clearly specifies—in fact forces—the + operator to be left associative. However, the EBNF version,

<expr> <term> { + <term> }

does not imply the direction of associativity. This problem is overcome in a syntax analyzer based on an EBNF grammar for expressions by designing the syntax analysis process to enforce the correct associativity. This is further discussed in Chapter 4.

Some versions of EBNF allow a numeric superscript to be attached to the right brace to indicate an upper limit to the number of times the enclosed part can be repeated. Also, some versions use a plus (+) superscript to indicate one or more repetitions. For example,

<compound> → **begin** <stmt> {<stmt>} **end**

and

<compound> → **begin** {<stmt>}$^+$ **end**

are equivalent.

In recent years, some variations on BNF and EBNF have appeared. Among these are the following.

- In place of the arrow, a colon is used and the RHS is placed on the next line.
- Instead of a vertical bar to separate alternative RHSs, they are simply placed on separate lines.

- In place of square brackets to indicate something being optional, the subscript $_{opt}$ is used. For example,

  ConstructorDeclarator $\rightarrow$ SimpleName (FormalParameterList$_{opt}$)

- Rather than using the | symbol in a parenthesized list of elements to indicate a choice, the words "one of" are used. For example,

  AssignmentOperator $\rightarrow$ one of

  $$= \quad *= \quad /= \quad \%= \quad += \quad -= \quad <<= \quad >>= \quad >>>= \quad \&= \quad \char`^= \quad |=$$

3.3.3 Grammars and Recognizers

Earlier in this chapter, we suggested that there was a close relationship between generation and recognition devices for a given language. In fact, given a context-free grammar, a recognizer for the language generated by the grammar can be algorithmically constructed. A number of software systems have been developed that perform this construction. Such systems allow the quick creation of the syntax analysis part of a compiler for a new language and are therefore quite valuable. One of the first of these syntax analyzer generators is named yacc (yet another compiler-compiler) (Johnson, 1975). There are now many such systems available.

3.4   Attribute Grammars

An **attribute grammar** is a device used to describe more of the structure of a programming language than can be described with a context-free grammar. An attribute grammar is an extension to a context-free grammar. The extension allows certain language rules to be conveniently described, such as type compatibility. Before we formally define the form of attribute grammars, we must clarify the concept of static semantics.

3.4.1 Static Semantics

There are some characteristics of the structure of programming languages that are difficult to describe with BNF, and some that are impossible. As an example of a language rule that is difficult to specify with BNF, consider type compatibility rules. In Java, for example, a floating-point value cannot be assigned to an integer type variable, although the opposite is legal. Although this restriction can be specified in BNF, it requires additional nonterminal symbols and rules. If all of the typing rules of Java were specified in BNF, the grammar would become too large to be useful because the size of the grammar determines the size of the parser.

As an example of a language rule that cannot be specified in BNF, consider the common rule that all variables must be declared before they are referenced. It can be proven that this rule cannot be specified in BNF. Another example is the rule that if the **end** of an Ada subprogram is followed by a name, that name must match the name of the subprogram.

These two problems exemplify the category of language rules called static semantics rules. The **static semantics** of a language is only indirectly related to the meaning of programs during execution; rather, it has to do with the legal forms of programs (syntax rather than semantics). In many cases, the static semantic rules of a language state its type constraints. Static semantics is so named because the analysis required to check these specifications can be done at compile time.

Because of the problems of describing static semantics with BNF, a variety of more powerful mechanisms has been devised for that task. One such mechanism, attribute grammars, was designed by Knuth (1968a) to describe both the syntax and the static semantics of programs.

Attribute grammars are a formal approach to both describing and checking the correctness of the static semantics of a program. Although they are not always used in a formal way in compiler design, the basic concepts of attribute grammars are at least informally used in every compiler (see Aho et al., (1986), Chapter 5).

Dynamic semantics is discussed in Section 3.5.

3.4.2 Basic Concepts

Attribute grammars are grammars to which have been added attributes, attribute computation functions, and predicate functions. **Attributes,** which are associated with grammar symbols, are similar to variables in the sense that they can have values assigned to them. **Attribute computation functions,** sometimes called semantic functions, are associated with grammar rules. They are used to specify how attribute values are computed. **Predicate functions,** which state some of the syntax and static semantic rules of the language, are associated with grammar rules.

These concepts will become clearer after we formally define attribute grammars and provide an example.

3.4.3 Attribute Grammars Defined

An attribute grammar is a grammar with the following additional features:

- Associated with each grammar symbol X is a set of attributes A(X). The set A(X) consists of two disjoint sets S(X) and I(X), called synthesized and inherited attributes, respectively. **Synthesized attributes** are used to pass semantic information up a parse tree, while **inherited attributes** pass semantic information down a tree.

- Associated with each grammar rule is a set of semantic functions and a possibly empty set of predicate functions over the attributes of the symbols in the grammar rule. For a rule $X_0 \rightarrow X_1 \ldots X_n$, the synthesized attributes of X_0 are computed with semantic functions of the form $S(X_0) = f(A(X_1), \ldots, A(X_n))$. So the value of a synthesized attribute on a parse tree node depends only on the values of the attributes on that node's children nodes. Inherited attributes of symbols X_j, $1 \leq j \leq n$ (in the rule above), are computed with a semantic function of the form $I(X_j) = f(A(X_0), \ldots, A(X_n))$. So the value of an inherited attribute on a parse tree node depends on the attribute values of that node's parent node and those of its sibling nodes. Note that, to avoid circularity, inherited attributes are often restricted to functions of the form $I(X_j) = f(A(X_0), \ldots, A(X_{(j-1)}))$. This form prevents an inherited attribute from depending on itself or on attributes to the right in the parse tree.

  A predicate function has the form of a Boolean expression on the attribute set $\{A(X_0), \ldots, A(X_n)\}$. The only derivations allowed with an attribute grammar are those in which every predicate associated with every nonterminal is true. A false predicate function value indicates a violation of the syntax or static semantics rules of the language.

A parse tree of an attribute grammar is the parse tree based on its underlying BNF grammar, with a possibly empty set of attribute values attached to each node. If all the attribute values in a parse tree have been computed, the tree is said to be **fully attributed.** Although in practice it is not always done this way, it is convenient to think of attribute values as being computed after the complete unattributed parse tree has been constructed by the compiler.

3.4.4   Intrinsic Attributes

Intrinsic attributes are synthesized attributes of leaf nodes whose values are determined outside the parse tree. For example, the type of an instance of a variable in a program could come from the symbol table, which is used to store variable names and their types. The contents of the symbol table are determined from earlier declaration statements. Initially, assuming that an unattributed parse tree has been constructed and that attribute values are desired, the only attributes with values are the intrinsic attributes of the leaf nodes. Given the intrinsic attribute values on a parse tree, the semantic functions can be used to compute the remaining attribute values.

3.4.5   Examples of Attribute Grammars

As a very simple example of how attribute grammars can be used to describe static semantics, consider the following fragment of an attribute grammar that describes the rule that the name on the **end** of an Ada procedure must match the procedure's name. The string attribute of <proc_name>, denoted by <proc_name>.string, is the actual string of characters that were found by the lexical analyzer. Notice that when there is more than one occurrence of a nonterminal in a syntax rule in an attribute grammar, the nonterminals are subscripted with brackets to distinguish them. Neither the subscripts nor the brackets are part of the described language.

Syntax rule: <proc_def> → **procedure** <proc_name>[1]
                                      <proc_body> **end**   <proc_name>[2];
Semantic rule: <proc_name>[1].string = <proc_name>[2].string

Next, consider a larger example of an attribute grammar. In this case, it is used to show how an attribute grammar can be used to check the type rules of a simple assignment statement. The syntax and semantics of this assignment statement are as follows: The only variable names are A, B, and C. The right side of the assignments can either be a variable or an expression in the form of a variable added to another variable. The variables can be one of two types: int or real. When there are two variables on the right side of an assignment, they need not be the same type. The type of the expression when the operand types are not the same is always real. When they are the same, the expression type is that of the operands. The type of the left side of the assignment must match the type of the right side. So the types of operands in the right side can be mixed, but the assignment is valid only if the LHS and the value resulting from evaluating the RHS have the same type. The attribute grammar specifies these semantic rules.

The syntax portion of our example attribute grammar is

<assign> → <var> = <expr>
<expr> → <var> + <var>
            | <var>
<var> → A | B | C

The attributes for the nonterminals in the example attribute grammar are described in the following paragraphs:

actual_type A synthesized attribute associated with the nonterminals <var> and <expr>. It is used to store the actual type, int or real in the example, of a variable or expression. In the case of a variable, the actual type is intrinsic. In the case of an expression, it is determined from the actual types of the child node or children nodes of the <expr> nonterminal.

expected_type An inherited attribute associated with the nonterminal <expr>. It is used to store the type, either int or real, that is expected for the expression, as determined by the type of the variable on the left side of the assignment statement.

The complete attribute grammar follows in Example 3.6.

EXAMPLE 3.6   An Attribute Grammar for Simple Assignment Statements

1. Syntax rule: <assign> → <var> = <expr>
   Semantic rule: <expr>.expected_type ← <var>.actual_type

2. Syntax rule: <expr> → <var>[2] + <var>[3]
   Semantic rule: <expr>.actual_type ←
   $\qquad$ if (<var>[2].actual_type = int) and
   $\qquad\quad$ (<var>[3].actual_type = int)
   $\qquad\qquad$ then int
   $\qquad\qquad$ else real
   $\qquad\quad$ end if
   Predicate: <expr>.actual_type = <expr>.expected_type

3. Syntax rule: <expr> → <var>
   Semantic rule: <expr>.actual_type ← <var>.actual_type
   Predicate: <expr>.actual_type = <expr>.expected_type

4. Syntax rule: <var> → A | B | C
   Semantic rule: <var>.actual_type ← look-up(<var>.string)

The look-up function looks up a given variable name in the symbol table and returns the variable's type.

An example of a parse tree of the sentence A = A + B generated by the grammar in Example 3.6 is shown in Figure 3.6. As in the grammar, bracketed numbers are added after the repeated node labels in the tree so they can be referenced unambiguously.

3.4.6   Computing Attribute Values

Now consider the process of decorating the parse tree with attributes. This could proceed in a completely top-down order, from the root to the leaves, if all attributes were inherited. Alternatively, it could proceed in a completely bottom-up order, from the leaves to the root, if all the attributes were synthesized. Because our grammar has both synthesized and inherited attributes, the evaluation process cannot be in any single direction. The following is an evaluation of the attributes, in an order in which it is possible to computer them.

1. <var>.actual_type ← look-up(A)   (Rule 4)
2. <expr>.expected_type ← <var>.actual_type   (Rule 1)
3. <var>[2].actual_type ← look-up(A)   (Rule 4)
   <var>[3].actual_type ← look-up(B)   (Rule 4)

Figure 3.6

A parse tree for
A = A + B

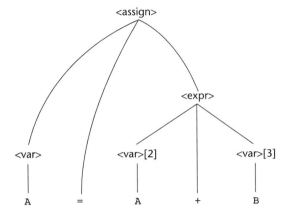

4. <expr>.actual_type ← either int or real (Rule 2)
5. <expr>.expected_type = <expr>.actual_type is either
                                    TRUE or FALSE (Rule 2)

The tree in Figure 3.7 shows the flow of attribute values in the example of Figure 3.6. Solid lines are used for the parse tree; dashed lines show attribute flow in the tree.

The tree in Figure 3.8 shows the final attribute values on the nodes. In this example, A is defined as a real and B is defined as an int.

Determining attribute evaluation order for the general case of an attribute grammar is a complex problem, requiring the construction of a dependency graph to show all attribute dependencies.

Figure 3.7

The flow of attributes in the tree

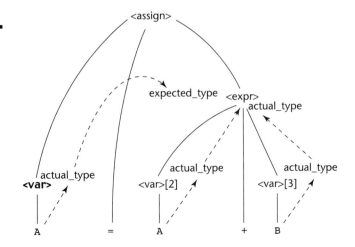

Figure 3.8

A fully attributed parse tree

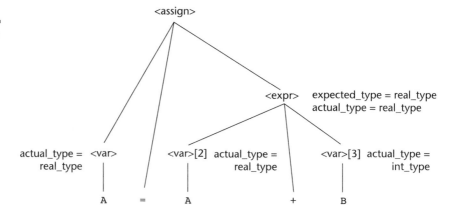

3.4.7 Evaluation

Checking the static semantic rules of a language is an essential part of all compilers. Even if a compiler writer has never heard of an attribute grammar, he or she would need to use the fundamental ideas of them to design the checks of static semantics rules for his or her compiler.

One of the main difficulties in using an attribute grammar to describe all of the syntax and static semantics of a real contemporary programming language is its size and complexity. The large number of attributes and semantic rules required for a complete programming language make such grammars difficult to write and read. Furthermore, the attribute values on a large parse tree are costly to evaluate. On the other hand, less formal attribute grammars are a powerful and commonly used tool for compiler writers, who are more interested in the process of producing a compiler than they are in formalism.

3.5 Describing the Meanings of Programs: Dynamic Semantics

We now turn to the difficult task of describing the **dynamic semantics,** or meaning, of expressions, statements, and program units. Because of the power and naturalness of the available notation, describing syntax is a relatively simple matter. On the other hand, no universally accepted notation has been devised for dynamic semantics. In this section, we briefly describe several of the methods that have been developed. For the remainder of this section, when we use the term *semantics*, we mean dynamic semantics; we will refer to static semantics as static semantics.

There are several different reasons why one may be concerned with describing semantics. First, programmers obviously need to know precisely what statements of a language do. But they usually find out by reading English explanations in language manuals. Such explanations are often imprecise and incomplete. Compiler writers also typically determine the semantics of the languages for which they are writing compilers from English descriptions. These informal descriptions are used because of the complexity of formal semantic descriptions. It is an obvious research goal to find a semantics formalism that could be used by programmers and compiler writers.

Scheme, a functional language described in Chapter 15, is one of only a few programming languages whose definition includes a formal semantics description. However, the method used is not one described in this chapter, as this chapter is focused on approaches that are suitable for imperative languages.

3.5.1 Operational Semantics

The idea behind **operational semantics** is to describe the meaning of a program by executing its statements on a machine, either real or simulated. The changes that occur in the machine's state when it executes a given statement define the meaning of that statement. Consider the simple case of a machine language instruction. Let the state of a computer be the values of all its registers and memory locations, including condition codes and status registers. If one simply records the state of the computer, executes the instruction for which the meaning is desired, and then examines the machine's new state, the semantics of that instruction is clear: It is represented by the change in the computer's state caused by the execution of the instruction.

3.5.1.1 The Basic Process

Describing the operational semantics of high-level language statements requires the construction of either a real or a virtual computer. Recall from Chapter 1 that the hardware of a computer is a pure interpreter for its machine language. A pure interpreter for any programming language can be constructed in software, which becomes a virtual computer for the language. The semantics of a high-level language can be described using a pure interpreter for the language. Unfortunately, there are two problems with this approach. First, the complexities and idiosyncrasies of the hardware computer and operating system that were used to run the pure interpreter would make the actions difficult to understand. Second, a semantic definition done this way would only be available to those with an identically configured computer.

These problems can be avoided by replacing the real computer with a low-level virtual computer, implemented as a software simulation. The registers, memory, status information, and execution process would all be simulated. The instruction set would be designed so that the semantics of each instruction was easy to describe and understand. In this way, the machine would be idealized and thus highly simplified, making its changes of state easy to understand.

Using the operational method to completely describe the semantics of a programming language L requires the construction of two components. First, a translator is needed to convert statements in L to the chosen low-level language. The other component is the virtual machine for that low-level language. The state changes in the virtual machine brought about by executing the code that results from translating a given statement in the high-level language defines the meaning of that statement. In effect, this approach describes the meaning of high-level language statements in terms of statements in a simpler, lower-level language.

This basic process of operational semantics is not unusual. In fact, the concept is frequently used in programming textbooks and programming language reference manuals. For example, the semantics of the C **for** construct can be described in terms of very simple statements, as in

C Statement	*Operational Semantics*
`for (expr1; expr2; expr3) {`	expr1;
`   ...`	loop: **if** expr2 $= 0$ **goto** out
`}`	...
	expr3;
	goto loop
	out: ...

The human reader of such a description is the virtual computer and is assumed to be able to correctly "execute" the instructions in the definition and recognize the effects of the "execution."

As an example of a low-level language that could be used for operational semantics, consider the following list of statements, which would be adequate for the simple control statements of a typical programming language.

ident = var
ident = ident **+** 1
ident = ident **-** 1
goto label
if var relop var **goto** label

In this list, relop is one of the relational operators from the set {=, <>, >, <, >=, <=}, ident is an identifier, and var is either an identifier or a constant. These statements are all simple and therefore easy to understand and implement.

A slight generalization of the three assignment statements above allows more general arithmetic expressions and assignment statements to be described. The new statements are

ident = var bin_op var
ident = un_op var

where bin_op is a binary arithmetic operator and un_op is a unary operator. Multiple arithmetic data types and automatic type conversions, of course, complicate this generalization somewhat. Adding just a few more relatively simple instructions would allow the semantics of arrays, records, pointers, and subprograms to be described.

In Chapter 8, the semantics of various control statements are described using operational semantics.

3.5.1.2 Evaluation

The first and most significant use of formal operational semantics was to describe the semantics of PL/I (Wegner, 1972). That particular abstract machine and the translation rules for PL/I were together named the Vienna Definition Language (VDL), after the city where IBM devised it.

Operational semantics provides an effective means of describing semantics for language users and language implementors, as long as the descriptions are kept simple and informal. The VDL description of PL/I, unfortunately, is so complex that it serves no practical purpose.

Operational semantics depends on programming languages of lower levels, not mathematics. The statements of one programming language are described in terms of the statements of a lower-level programming language. This approach can lead to circularities, in which concepts are indirectly defined in terms of themselves. The methods described in the following two sections are much more formal, in the sense that they are based on logic and mathematics, not programming languages.

3.5.2 Axiomatic Semantics

Axiomatic semantics was defined in conjunction with the development of a method to prove the correctness of programs. Such correctness proofs, when they can be constructed, show that a program performs the computation described by its specification. In a proof, each statement of a program is both preceded and followed by a logical expression that specifies constraints on program variables. These, rather than the entire state of an abstract machine (as with operational semantics), are used to specify the meaning of the statement. The notation used to describe constraints, indeed the language of axiomatic semantics, is predicate calculus. Although simple Boolean expressions are often adequate to express constraints, in some cases they are not.

3.5.2.1 Assertions

Axiomatic semantics is based on mathematical logic. The logical expressions are called predicates, or **assertions.** An assertion immediately preceding a program statement describes the constraints on the program variables at that point in the program. An assertion immediately following a statement describes the new constraints on those variables (and possibly others) after execution of the statement. These assertions are called the **precondition** and **postcondition,** respectively, of the statement. Developing an axiomatic description or proof of a given program requires that every statement in the program have both a precondition and a postcondition.

In the following sections, we examine assertions from the point of view that preconditions for statements are computed from given postconditions, although it is possible to consider these in the opposite sense. We assume all variables are integer type. As a simple example, consider the following assignment statement and postcondition:

```
sum = 2 * x + 1 {sum > 1}
```

Precondition and postcondition assertions are presented in braces to distinguish them from program statements. One possible precondition for this statement is {x > 10}.

3.5.2.2 Weakest Preconditions

The **weakest precondition** is the least restrictive precondition that will guarantee the validity of the associated postcondition. For example, in the above statement and postcondition, {x > 10}, {x > 50}, and {x > 1000} are all valid preconditions. The weakest of all preconditions in this case is {x > 0}.

If the weakest precondition can be computed from the given postcondition for each statement of a language, then correctness proofs can be constructed for programs in that language. The proof is begun by using the desired results of the program's execution as the postcondition of the last statement of the program. This postcondition, along with the last statement, is used to compute the weakest precondition for the last statement. This precondition is then used as the postcondition for the second last statement. This process continues until the beginning of the program is reached. At that point, the precondition of the first statement states the conditions under which the program will compute the desired results.

For some program statements, the computation of a weakest precondition from the statement and a postcondition is simple and can be specified by an axiom. In most cases, however, the weakest precondition can be computed only by an inference rule. An **axiom** is a logical statement that is assumed to be true; an **inference rule** is a method of inferring the truth of one assertion on the basis of the values of other assertions.

To use axiomatic semantics with a given programming language, whether for correctness proofs or for formal semantics specifications, either an axiom or an inference rule must be available for each kind of statement in the language. In the following subsections, we present an axiom for assignment statements, and inference rules for statement sequences, selection statements, and logical pretest loops. Note that we assume that neither arithmetic nor Boolean expressions have side effects.

3.5.2.3 Assignment Statements

Let x = E be a general assignment statement and Q be its postcondition. Then its precondition, P, is defined by the axiom

$$P = Q_{x \to E}$$

which means that P is computed as Q with all instances of x replaced by E. For example, if we have the assignment statement and postcondition

```
a = b / 2 - 1 {a < 10}
```

the weakest precondition is computed by substituting b / 2 - 1 in the assertion {a < 10}, as follows:

```
b / 2 - 1 < 10
b < 22
```

Thus the weakest precondition for the given assignment and postcondition is {b < 22}. Recall that the assignment axiom is guaranteed to be true only in the absence of side effects. An assignment statement has a side effect if it changes some variable other than its left side.

The usual notation for specifying the axiomatic semantics of a given statement form is

{P} S {Q}

where P is the precondition, Q is the postcondition, and S is the statement form. In the case of the assignment statement, the notation is

$\{Q_{x \to E}\}$ x = E {Q}

As another example of computing a precondition for an assignment statement, consider the following:

```
x = 2 * y - 3 {x > 25}
```

The precondition is computed as follows:

```
2 * y - 3 > 25
y > 14
```

So {y > 14} is the weakest precondition for this assignment statement and postcondition.

Note that the appearance of the left side of the assignment statement in its right side does not affect the process of computing the weakest precondition. For example, for

```
x = x + y - 3 {x > 10}
```

the weakest precondition is

```
x + y - 3 > 10
y > 13 - x
```

At the beginning of our discussion of axiomatic semantics, we stated that axiomatic semantics was developed to prove the correctness of programs. In light of that, it is natural at this point to wonder how the axiom for assignment statements can be used to prove anything. Here is how: A given assignment statement with both a precondition and a postcondition can be considered a theorem. If the assignment axiom, when applied to the postcondition and the assignment statement, produces the given precondition, the theorem is proved. For example, consider the logical statement

```
{x > 3} x = x - 3 {x > 0}
```

Using the assignment axiom on

```
x = x - 3 {x > 0}
```

produces $\{x > 3\}$, which is the given precondition. Therefore, we have proven the logical statement above.

Next, consider the logical statement

```
{x > 5} x = x - 3 {x > 0}
```

In this case, the given precondition, $\{x > 5\}$, is not the same as the assertion produced by the axiom. However, it is obvious that $\{x > 5\}$ implies $\{x > 3\}$. To use this in a proof, we need an inference rule, named the **rule of consequence.** The general form of an inference rule is

$$\frac{\text{S1, S2, ..., Sn}}{\text{S}}$$

which states that if S1, S2, ..., and Sn are true, then the truth of S can be inferred.

The form of the rule of consequence is

$$\frac{\{P\}\ S\ \{Q\}, P' => P,\ Q => Q'}{\{P'\}\ S\ \{Q\}}$$

The => symbol means "implies," and S can be any program statement. The rule can be stated as follows: If the logical statement $\{P\}\ S\ \{Q\}$ is true, the assertion P' implies the assertion P, and the assertion Q implies the assertion Q', then it can be inferred that $\{P'\}\ S\ \{Q'\}$. In other words, the rule of consequence says that a postcondition can always be weakened and a precondition can always be strengthened. This is quite useful in program proofs. For example, it allows the completion of the proof of the last logical statement example above. If we let P be $\{x > 3\}$, Q and Q' be $\{x > 0\}$, P' be $\{x > 5\}$, we have

$$\frac{\{x > 3\}\ x = x - 3\ \{x > 0\},\ (x > 5) => (x > 3),\ (x > 0) => (x > 0)}{\{x > 5\}\ x = x - 3\ \{x > 0\}}$$

This completes the proof.

3.5.2.4 Sequences

The weakest precondition for a sequence of statements cannot be described by an axiom, because the precondition depends on the particular kinds of statements in the sequence. In this case, the precondition can only be described with an inference rule. Let S1 and S2 be adjacent program statements. If S1 and S2 have the following pre- and postconditions

{P1} S1 {P2}
{P2} S2 {P3}

the inference rule for such a two-statement sequence is

$$\frac{\{P1\}\ S1\ \{P2\},\{P2\}\ S2\ \{P3\}}{\{P1\}\ S1;\ S2\ \{P3\}}$$

So, for the above example, {P1} S1; S2 {P3} describes the axiomatic semantics of the sequence S1; S2. If S1 and S2 are the assignment statements

x1 = E1

and

x2 = E2

then we have

$\{P3_{x2 \rightarrow E2}\}\ x2 = E2\ \{P3\}$
$\{(P3_{x2 \rightarrow E2})_{x1 \rightarrow E1}\}\ x1 = E1\ \{P3_{x2 \rightarrow E2}\}$

Therefore, the weakest precondition for the sequence x1 = E1; x2 = E2 with postcondition P3 is $\{(P3_{x2 \rightarrow E2})_{x1 \rightarrow E1}\}$.

For example, consider the following sequence and postcondition:

```
y = 3 * x + 1;
x = y + 3;
{x < 10}
```

The precondition for the last assignment statement is

```
y < 7
```

This is then used as the postcondition for the first. The precondition for the first assignment statement can now be computed:

```
3 * x + 1 < 7
x < 2
```

3.5.2.5 Selection

We next consider the inference rule for selection statements. We consider only selections that include **else** clauses. The inference rule is

$$\frac{\{B \text{ and } P\} \text{ S1 } \{Q\}, \{(\text{not } B) \text{ and } P\} \text{ S2 } \{Q\}}{\{P\} \text{ if } B \text{ then } S1 \text{ else } S2 \{Q\}}$$

This rule indicates that selection statements must be proven for both of their cases. The first logical statement above the line is the **then** clause; the second is the **else** clause.

Consider the following example of the computation using the selection inference rule. The example selection statement is

```
if (x > 0)
  y = y - 1
else y = y + 1
```

Suppose the postcondition for this selection statement is {y > 0}. We can use the axiom for assignment on the **then** clause

```
y = y - 1 {y > 0}
```

This produces {y - 1 > 0} or {y > 1}. Now we apply the same axiom to the **else** clause

```
y = y + 1 {y > 0}
```

This produces the precondition {y + 1 > 0} or {y > -1}. Because {y > 1} => {y > -1}, the rule of consequence allows us to use {y > 1} for the precondition of the selection statement.

3.5.2.6 Logical Pretest Loops

Another essential construct of an imperative programming language is the logical pretest, or **while** loop. Computing the weakest precondition for a **while** loop is inherently more difficult than for a sequence because the number of iterations cannot always be predetermined. In a case where the number of iterations is known, the loop can be treated as a sequence.

The problem of computing the weakest precondition for loops is similar to the problem of proving a theorem about all positive integers. In the latter case, induction is normally used, and the same inductive method can be used for loops. The principal step in induction is finding an inductive hypothesis. The corresponding step in the axiomatic semantics of a **while** loop is finding an assertion called a **loop invariant,** which is crucial to finding the weakest precondition.

The inference rule for computing the precondition for a **while** loop is

$$\frac{(I \text{ and } B) \ S \ \{I\}}{\{I\} \ \texttt{while} \ B \ \texttt{do} \ S \ \texttt{end} \ \{I \text{ and } (\text{not } B)\}}$$

where I is the loop invariant.

The axiomatic description of a **while** loop is written as

{P} **while** B **do** S **end** {Q}

The loop invariant must satisfy a number of requirements to be useful. First, the weakest precondition for the **while** must guarantee the truth of the loop invariant. In turn, the loop invariant must guarantee the truth of the postcondition upon loop termination. These constraints move us from the inference rule to the axiomatic description. During execution of the loop, the truth of the loop invariant must be unaffected by the evaluation of the loop-controlling Boolean expression and the loop body statements. Hence the name *invariant*.

Another complicating factor for **while** loops is the question of loop termination. If Q is the postcondition that holds immediately after loop exit, then a precondition P for the loop is one that guarantees Q at loop exit and also guarantees that the loop terminates.

The complete axiomatic description of a **while** construct requires all of the following to be true, in which I is the loop invariant:

P => I
{I and B} S {I}
(I and (not B)) => Q
the loop terminates

To find a loop invariant, we can use a method similar to that used for determining the inductive hypothesis in mathematical induction, which is as follows: The relationship for a few cases is computed, with the hope that a pattern emerges that will apply to the general case. It is helpful to treat the process of producing a weakest precondition as a function, wp. In general

wp(statement, postcondition) = precondition

To find I, we use the loop postcondition Q to compute preconditions for several different numbers of iterations of the loop body, starting with none. If the loop body contains a single assignment statement, the axiom for assignment statements can be used to compute these cases. Consider the example loop

while y <> x **do** y = y + 1 **end** {y = x}

Remember that the equal sign is being used for two different purposes here. In assertions, it means mathematical equality; outside assertions, it means the assignment operator.

For zero iterations, the weakest precondition is, obviously,

{y = x}

For one iteration, it is

wp (y = y + 1, {y = x}) = {y + 1 = x}, or {y = x - 1}

For two iterations, it is

wp (y = y + 1, {y = x - 1}) = {y + 1 = x - 1}, or {y = x - 2}

For three iterations, it is

wp (y = y + 1, {y = x - 2}) = {y + 1 = x - 2}, or {y = x - 3}

It is now obvious that {y < x} will suffice for cases of one or more iterations. Combining this with {y = x} for the zero iterations case, we get {y <= x}, which can be used for the loop invariant. A precondition for the **while** statement can be determined from the loop invariant. In this example, P = I can be used.

We must ensure that our choice satisfies the four criteria for I for our example loop. First, because P = I, P => I. The second requirement is that it must be true that

{I and B} S {I}

In our example, we have

{y <= x and y <> x} y = y + 1 {y <= x}

Applying the assignment axiom to

y = y + 1 {y <= x}

we get {y + 1 <= x}, which is equivalent to {y < x}, which is implied by {y <= x and y <> x}. So, the statement above is proven.

Next, we must have

{I and (not B)} => Q

In our example, we have

{(y <= x) and not (y <> x)} => {y = x}
{(y <= x) and (y = x)} => {y = x}
{y = x} => {y = x}

So this is obviously true. Next, loop termination must be considered. In this example, the question is whether the loop

{y <= x} **while** y <> x **do** y = y + 1 **end** {y = x}

terminates. Recalling that x and y are assumed to be integer variables, we can easily see that this loop does terminate. The precondition guarantees that y initially is not larger than x. The loop body increases y with each iteration, until y is equal to x. No matter how much smaller y is than x initially, it will eventually become equal to x. So the loop will terminate. Because our choice of I satisfies all four criteria, it is adequate for the loop invariant and the loop precondition.

The process used above to compute the invariant for a loop does not always produce an assertion that is the weakest precondition (although it does in the example above).

As another example of finding a loop invariant, consider the following loop statement:

while s > 1 **do** s = s / 2 **end** {s = 1}

As above, we use the assignment axiom to try to find a loop invariant and a precondition for the loop. For zero iterations, the weakest precondition is {s = 1}. For one iteration, it is

wp(s = s / 2, {s = 1}) = {s / 2 = 1}, or {s = 2}

For two iterations, it is

wp(s = s / 2, {s = 2}) = {s / 2 = 2}, or {s = 4}

For three iterations, it is

wp(s = s / 2, {s = 4}) = {s / 2 = 4}, or {s = 8}

From these cases, we can see clearly that the invariant is

{s is a nonnegative power of 2}

Once again, the computed I can serve as P, and I passes the four requirements. Unlike our earlier example of finding a loop precondition, this one clearly is not a weakest precondition. Consider using the precondition {s > 1}. The logical statement

{s > 1} **while** s > 1 **do** s = s / 2 **end** {s = 1}

can easily be proven, and this precondition is significantly broader than the one computed above. The loop and precondition are satisfied for any positive value for s, not just powers of 2 as the process indicates. Because of the rule of consequence, using a precondition that is stronger than the weakest precondition does not invalidate a proof.

Finding loop invariants is not always easy. It is helpful to understand the nature of these invariants. First, a loop invariant is a weakened version of the loop postcondition and also a precondition for the loop. So I must be weak enough to be satisfied prior to the beginning of loop execution, but when combined with the loop exit condition, it must be strong enough to force the truth of the postcondition.

Because of the difficulty of proving loop termination, that requirement is often ignored. If loop termination can be shown, the axiomatic description of the loop is called **total correctness.** If the other conditions can be met but termination is not guaranteed, it is called **partial correctness.**

In more complex loops, finding a suitable loop invariant, even for partial correctness, requires a good deal of ingenuity. Because computing the precondition for a **while** loop depends on finding a loop invariant, proving the correctness of programs with **while** loops using axiomatic semantics can be difficult.

The following is an example of a proof of correctness of a pseudocode program that computes the factorial function.

```
{n >= 0}
count = n;
fact = 1;
while count <> 0 do
    fact = fact * count;
    count = count - 1;
end
{fact = n!}
```

The method described earlier for finding the loop invariant does not work for the loop in this example. Some ingenuity is required here, which can be aided by a brief study of the code. The loop computes the factorial function in order of the last multiplication first; that is, (n - 1) * n is done first, assuming n is greater than 1. So, part of the invariant can be

fact = (count + 1) * (count + 2) * … * (n - 1) * n

But we must also ensure that count is always nonnegative, which we can do by adding that to the part above, to get

I = (fact = (count + 1) * … * n) AND (count >= 0)

Next, we must check that this I meets the requirements for invariants. We once again let I also be used for P, so P clearly implies I. The next question is

{I and B} S {I}

I and B is

((fact = (count + 1) * … * n) AND (count >= 0)) AND
    (count <> 0)

which reduces to

(fact = (count + 1) * … * n) AND (count > 0)

In our case, we must compute the precondition of the body of the loop, using the invariant for the postcondition. For

{P} count = count - 1 {I}

we compute P to be

```
{(fact = count * (count + 1) * … * n)   AND (count >= 1)}
```

Using this as the postcondition for the first assignment in the loop body,

```
{P} fact = fact * count {(fact = count * (count + 1)
                                * … * n) AND (count >= 1)}
```

In this case, P is

```
{(fact = (count + 1) * … * n) AND (count >= 1)}
```

It is clear that I and B implies this P, so by the rule of consequence,

{I AND B} S {I}

is true. Finally, the last test of I is

I AND (NOT B) => Q

For our example, this is

```
((fact = (count + 1) * … * n) AND (count >= 0)) AND
    (count = 0)) => fact = n!
```

This is clearly true, for when count = 0, the first part is precisely the defin-ition of factorial. So, our choice of I meets the requirements for a loop invari-ant. Now we can use our P (which is the same as I) from the **while** as the postcondition on the second assignment of the program

```
{P} fact = 1 {(fact = (count + 1) * … * n) AND
              (count >= 0) }
```

which yields for P

```
(1 = (count + 1) * … * n) AND (count >= 0))
```

Using this as the postcondition for the first assignment in the code

```
{P} count = n {(1 = (count + 1) * … * n) AND
              (count >= 0)) }
```

produces for P

```
{(n + 1) * … * n = 1) AND (n >= 0) }
```

The left operand of the AND operator is true (because 1 = 1) and the right operand is exactly the precondition of the whole code segment, {n >= 0}. Therefore, the program has been proven to be correct.

3.5.2.7 Evaluation

To define the semantics of a complete programming language using the axiomatic method, we must define an axiom or an inference rule for each statement type in the language. Defining axioms and inference rules for some of the statements of programming languages has proven to be a difficult task. An obvious solution to this problem is to design the language with the axiomatic method in mind, so that only statements for which axioms or inference rules can be written are included. Unfortunately, such a language would be quite small and simple, given the state of the science of axiomatic semantics.

Axiomatic semantics is a powerful tool for research into program correctness proofs, and it provides an excellent framework in which to reason about programs, both during their construction and later. Its usefulness in describing the meaning of programming languages to either language users or compiler writers is, however, highly limited.

3.5.3 Denotational Semantics

Denotational semantics is the most rigorous, widely known method for describing the meaning of programs. It is solidly based on recursive function theory. A thorough discussion of the use of denotational semantics to describe the semantics of programming languages is necessarily long and complex. It is our intent to introduce just enough to make the reader aware of how denotational semantics works.

The fundamental concept of denotational semantics is to define for each language entity both a mathematical object and a function that maps instances of that entity onto instances of the mathematical object. Because the objects are rigorously defined, they represent the exact meaning of their corresponding entities. The idea is based on the fact that there are rigorous ways of manipulating mathematical objects but not for programming language constructs. The difficulty with this method lies in creating the objects and the mapping functions. The method is named *denotational* because the mathematical objects denote the meaning of their corresponding syntactic entities.

3.5.3.1 Two Simple Examples

We use a very simple language construct, binary numbers, to introduce the denotational method. The syntax of binary numbers can be described by the following grammar rules:

```
<bin_num>  →   0
           |   1
           |   <bin_num> 0
           |   <bin_num> 1
```

A parse tree for the example binary number, 110, is shown in Figure 3.9.

Figure 3.9

A parse tree of the
binary number 110

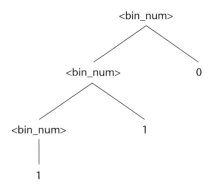

To describe the meaning of binary numbers using denotational semantics
and the grammar rules above, we associate the actual meaning with each rule
that has a single terminal symbol as its RHS. The objects in this case are simple decimal numbers. So, in this example the meaning of a binary number will
be its decimal equivalent.

In our example, meaningful objects must be associated with the first two
grammar rules. The other two grammar rules are, in a sense, computational
rules because they combine a terminal symbol, to which an object can be associated, with a nonterminal, which can be expected to represent some construct. Presuming an evaluation that progresses upward in the parse tree, the
nonterminal in the right side would already have its meaning attached. Then
such a syntax rule would require a function that computed the meaning of the
LHS, which must then represent the meaning of the complete RHS.

Let the domain of semantic values of the objects be N, the set of nonnegative decimal integer values. It is these objects that we wish to associate
with binary numbers. The semantic function, named M_{bin}, maps the syntactic
objects, as described in the grammar rules above, to the objects in N. The
function M_{bin} is defined as follows:

$$M_{bin}('0') = 0$$
$$M_{bin}('1') = 1$$
$$M_{bin}(\text{<bin\_num> } '0') = 2 * M_{bin}(\text{<bin\_num>})$$
$$M_{bin}(\text{<bin\_num> } '1') = 2 * M_{bin}(\text{<bin\_num>}) + 1$$

Notice that we put apostrophes around the syntactic digits to show they are
not mathematical digits. This is similar to the relationship between ASCII
coded digits and mathematical digits. When a program reads a number as a
string, it must be converted to a mathematical number before it can be used
as a number in the program.

The meanings, or denoted objects (which in this case are decimal numbers), can be attached to the nodes of the parse tree above, yielding the tree in

Figure 3.10. This is syntax-directed semantics. Syntactic entities are mapped to mathematical objects with concrete meaning.

In part because we need it later, we now show a similar example for describing the meaning of syntactic decimal literals.

$$\text{<dec\_num>} \rightarrow 0 \mid 1 \mid 2 \mid 3 \mid 4 \mid 5 \mid 6 \mid 7 \mid 8 \mid 9$$
$$\mid \text{<dec\_num>} (0 \mid 1 \mid 2 \mid 3 \mid 4 \mid 5 \mid 6 \mid 7 \mid 8 \mid 9)$$

The denotational mappings for these syntax rules are

$M_{dec}('0') = 0, M_{dec}('1') = 1, M_{dec}('2') = 2, ..., M_{dec}('9') = 9$
$M_{dec}(\text{<dec\_num>}\ '0') = 10 * M_{dec}(\text{<dec\_num>})$
$M_{dec}(\text{<dec\_num>}\ '1') = 10 * M_{dec}(\text{<dec\_num>}) + 1$
...
$M_{dec}(\text{<dec\_num>}\ '9') = 10 * M_{dec}(\text{<dec\_num>}) + 9$

In the following sections, we present the denotational semantics of a few simple constructs. The most important simplifying assumption made here is that both the syntax and static semantics of the constructs are correct. In addition, we assume only two scalar types are included, integer and Boolean.

3.5.3.2 The State of a Program

The denotational semantics of a program could be defined in terms of state changes in an ideal computer. Operational semantics are defined in this way, and denotational semantics nearly are, too. In a further simplification, however, they are defined in terms of only the values of all of the program's variables. The key difference between operational semantics and denotational semantics is that state changes in operational semantics are defined by coded algorithms, written in some programming language, whereas in denotational semantics, state changes are defined by rigorous mathematical functions.

Let the state s of a program be represented as a set of ordered pairs, as follows:

$$\{<i_1, v_1>, <i_2, v_2>, ..., <i_n, v_n>\}$$

Figure 3.10

A parse tree with denoted objects for 110

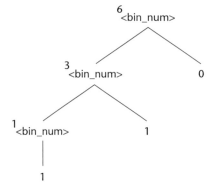

Each i is the name of a variable, and the associated v's are the current values of those variables. Any of the v's can have the special value **undef,** which indicates that its associated variable is currently undefined. Let VARMAP be a function of two parameters, a variable name and the program state. The value of VARMAP(i_j, s) is v_j (the value paired with i_j in state s). Most semantics mapping functions for programs and program constructs map states to states. These state changes are used to define the meanings of programs and program constructs. Some language constructs, such as expressions, are mapped to values, not states.

3.5.3.3 Expressions

Expressions are fundamental to most programming languages. We assume here that expressions have no side effects. Furthermore, we deal with only very simple expressions: The only operators are + and *, and an expression can have at most one operator; the only operands are scalar variables and integer literals; there are no parentheses; and the value of an expression is an integer. Following is the BNF description of these expressions:

```
<expr> → <dec_num> | <var> | <binary_expr>
<binary_expr> → <left_expr> <operator> <right_expr>
<left_expr> → <dec_num> | <var>
<right_expr> → <dec_num> | <var>
<operator> → + | *
```

The only error we consider in expressions is that a variable has an undefined value. Obviously other errors can occur, but most of them are machine dependent. Let Z be the set of integers, and let **error** be the error value. Then $Z \cup \{error\}$ is the set of values to which an expression can evaluate.

The required mapping function for a given expression E and state s follows. To distinguish between mathematical function definitions and the assignment statements of programming languages, we use the symbol $\Delta=$ to define mathematical functions.

M_e(<expr>, s) $\Delta=$
  case <expr> of
    <dec_num> => M_{dec}(<dec_num>, s)
    <var> => if VARMAP(<var>, s) = **undef**
             then **error**
             else VARMAP(<var>, s)
    <binary_expr> =>
      if (M_e(<binary_expr>.<left_expr>, s) = **undef** OR
        M_e(<binary_expr>.<right_expr>, s) = **undef**)
      then **error**
      else if (<binary_expr>.<operator> = '+' then
        M_e(<binary_expr>.<left_expr>, s) +
              M_e(<binary_expr>.<right_expr>, s)
        else M_e(<binary_expr>.<left_expr>, s) *
              M_e(<binary_expr>.<right_expr>, s)

3.5.3.4 Assignment Statements

An assignment statement is an expression evaluation plus the setting of the left-side variable to the expression's value. In this case, the meaning function maps a state to a state. This function can be described with the following:

$$M_a(x = E, s) \triangleq \text{if } M_e(E, s) = \textbf{error}$$
$$\text{then } \textbf{error}$$
$$\text{else } s' = \{<i_1', v_1'>, <i_2', v_2'>, ..., <i_n', v_n'>\}, \text{ where}$$
$$\text{for } j = 1, 2, ..., n, v_j' = \text{VARMAP}(i_j, s) \text{ if } i_j <> x;$$
$$M_e(E, s) \text{ if } i_j = x$$

Note that the two comparisons in the last two lines above, $i_j <> x$ and $i_j = x$, are of names, not values.

3.5.3.5 Logical Pretest Loops

The denotational semantics of a simple logical loop is deceptively simple. To expedite the discussion, we assume that there are two other existing mapping functions, M_{sl} and M_b, that map statement lists to states and Boolean expressions to Boolean values (or **error**), respectively. The function is

$$M_l(\textbf{while } B \textbf{ do } L, s) \triangleq \text{if } M_b(B, s) = \textbf{undef}$$
$$\text{then } \textbf{error}$$
$$\text{else if } M_b(B, s) = \text{false}$$
$$\text{then } s$$
$$\text{else if } M_{sl}(L, s) = \textbf{error}$$
$$\text{then } \textbf{error}$$
$$\text{else } M_l(\textbf{while } B \textbf{ do } L, M_{sl}(L, s))$$

The meaning of the loop is simply the value of the program variables after the statements in the loop have been executed the prescribed number of times, assuming there have been no errors. In essence, the loop has been converted from iteration to recursion, where the recursion control is mathematically defined by other recursive state mapping functions. Recursion is easier to describe with mathematical rigor than iteration.

One significant observation at this point is that this definition, like actual program loops, may compute nothing because of nontermination.

3.5.3.6 Evaluation

Objects and functions, such as those used in the statements above, can be defined for the other syntactic entities of programming languages. When a complete system has been defined for a given language, it can be used to determine the meaning of complete programs in that language. This provides a framework for thinking about programming in a highly rigorous way.

Denotational semantics can be used as an aid to language design. For example, statements for which the denotational semantic description is com-

HISTORY NOTE

A significant amount of work has been done on the possibility of using denotational language descriptions to generate compilers automatically (Jones, 1980; Milos et al., 1984; Bodwin et al., 1982). These efforts have shown that the method is feasible, but the work has never progressed to the point where it can be used to generate useful compilers.

plex and difficult may indicate to the designer that such statements may also be difficult for language users to understand and that an alternative design may be in order.

Because of the complexity of denotational descriptions, they are of little use to language users. On the other hand, they provide an excellent way to describe a language concisely.

Although the use of denotational semantics is normally attributed to Scott and Strachey (1971), the general denotational approach to language description can be traced back to the nineteenth century (Frege, 1892).

SUMMARY

Backus-Naur Form and context-free grammars are equivalent metalanguages that are almost ideally suited for the task of describing the syntax of programming languages. Not only are they concise descriptive methods, but the parse trees that can be associated with their generative actions give graphical evidence of the underlying syntactic structures. Furthermore, they are naturally related to recognition devices for the languages they generate, which leads to the relatively easy construction of syntax analyzers for compilers for these languages.

An attribute grammar is a descriptive formalism that can describe both the syntax and static semantics of a language. Attribute grammars are extensions to context-free grammars. One consists of a grammar, a set of attributes, a set of attribute computation functions, and a set of predicates, which describe static semantics rules.

There are three primary methods of semantic description: operational, axiomatic, and denotational. Operational semantics is a method of describing the meaning of language constructs in terms of their effects on an ideal machine. Axiomatic semantics, which is based on formal logic, was devised as a tool for proving the correctness of programs. In denotational semantics, mathematical objects are used to represent the meanings of language constructs. Language entities are converted to these mathematical objects with recursive functions.

BIBLIOGRAPHIC NOTES

Syntax description using context-free grammars and BNF are thoroughly discussed in Cleaveland and Uzgalis (1976).

Research in axiomatic semantics was begun by Floyd (1967) and further developed by Hoare (1969). The semantics of a large part of Pascal was described by Hoare and Wirth (1973) using this method. The parts they did not complete involved functional side effects and goto statements. These were found to be the most difficult to describe.

The technique of using preconditions and postconditions during the development of programs is described (and advocated) by Dijkstra (1976) and also discussed in detail in Gries (1981).

Good introductions to denotational semantics can be found in Gordon (1979) and Stoy (1977). Introductions to all three semantics description methods discussed in this chapter can be found in Marcotty et al., (1976). Another good reference for much of the material of this chapter is Pagan (1981). The form of the denotational semantic functions in this chapter is similar to that in Meyer (1990).

REVIEW QUESTIONS

1. Define *syntax* and *semantics*.
2. Who are language descriptions for?
3. Describe the operation of a general language generator.
4. Describe the operation of a general language recognizer.
5. What is the difference between a sentence and a sentential form?
6. Define a left recursive grammar rule.
7. What three extensions are common to most EBNFs?
8. Distinguish between static and dynamic semantics.
9. What purpose do predicates serve in an attribute grammar?
10. What is the difference between a synthesized and an inherited attribute?
11. How is the order of evaluation of attributes determined for the trees of a given attribute grammar?
12. What is the primary use of attribute grammars?
13. What is the problem with using a software pure interpreter for operational semantics?
14. Explain what the preconditions and postconditions of a given statement mean in axiomatic semantics.
15. Describe the approach of using axiomatic semantics to prove the correctness of a given program.
16. Describe the basic concept of denotational semantics.
17. In what fundamental way do operational semantics and denotational semantics differ?

PROBLEM SET

1. The two mathematical models of language description are generation and recognition. Describe how each can define the syntax of a programming language.

2. Write EBNF descriptions for the following:

   a. A Java class definition header statement

   b. A Java method call statement

   c. A C **switch** statement

   d. A C **union** definition

   e. C **float** literals

3. Rewrite the BNF of Example 3.4 to give + precedence over * and force + to be right associative.

4. Rewrite the BNF of Example 3.4 to add the ++ and -- unary operators of Java.

5. Write a BNF description of the Boolean expressions of Java, including the three operators &&, ||, and !, and the relational expressions.

6. Using the grammar in Example 3.2, show a parse tree and a leftmost derivation for each of the following statements:

   a. A = A * (B + (C * A))

   b. B = C * (A * C + B)

   c. A = A * (B + (C))

7. Using the grammar in Example 3.4, show a parse tree and a leftmost derivation for each of the following statements:

   a. A = (A + B) * C

   b. A = B + C + A

   c. A = A * (B + C)

   d. A = B * (C * (A + B))

8. Prove that the following grammar is ambiguous:

   <S> → <A>

   <A> → <A> + <A> | <id>

   <id> → a | b | c

9. Modify the grammar of Example 3.4 to add a unary minus operator that has higher precedence than either + or *.

10. Describe, in English, the language defined by the following grammar:

    <S> → <A> <B> <C>

    <A> → a <A> | a

    <B> → b <B> | b

    <C> → c <C> | c

11. Consider the following grammar:

    <S> → <A> a <B> b
    <A> → <A> b | b
    <B> → a <B> | a

    Which of the following sentences are in the language generated by this grammar?

    a. baab
    b. bbbab
    c. bbaaaaa
    d. bbaab

12. Consider the following grammar:

    <S> → a <S> c <B> | <A> | b
    <A> → c <A> | c
    <B> → d | <A>

    Which of the following sentences are in the language generated by this grammar?

    a. abcd
    b. acccbd
    c. acccbcc
    d. acd
    e. accc

13. Write a grammar for the language consisting of strings that have n copies of the letter a followed by the same number of copies of the letter b, where $n > 0$. For example, the strings ab, aaaabbbb, and aaaaaaaabbbbbbbb are in the language but a, abb, ba, and aaabb are not.

14. Draw parse trees for the sentences aabb and aaaabbbb, as derived from the grammar of Problem 13.

15. Convert the BNF of Example 3.1 to EBNF.

16. Convert the BNF of Example 3.3 to EBNF.

17. Convert the following EBNF to BNF:

    S A { bA }
    A a [b]A

18. Using the virtual machine instructions given in Section 3.5.1.1, give an operational semantic definition of the following:

    a. Pascal **repeat**
    b. Ada **for**
    c. Fortran Do of the form: Do N K = start, end, step

d. Pascal **if-then-else**

e. C **for**

f. C **switch**

19. Compute the weakest precondition for each of the following assignment statements and postconditions:

a. a = 2 * (b - 1) - 1 {a > 0}

b. b = (c + 10) / 3 {b > 6}

c. a = a + 2 * b - 1 {a > 1}

d. x = 2 * y + x - 1 {x > 11}

20. Compute the weakest precondition for each of the following sequences of assignment statements and their postconditions:

a. a = 2 * b + 1;

   b = a - 3

   {b < 0}

b. a = 3 * (2 * b + a);

   b = 2 * a - 1

   {b > 5}

21. Write a denotational semantics mapping function for the following statements:

a. Ada **for**

b. Pascal **repeat**

c. Java Boolean expressions

d. Java **for**

e. C **switch**

22. What is the difference between an intrinsic attribute and a nonintrinsic synthesized attribute?

23. Write an attribute grammar whose BNF basis is that of Example 3.6 in Section 3.4.5, but whose language rules are as follows: Data types cannot be mixed in expressions, but assignment statements need not have the same types on both sides of the assignment operator.

24. Write an attribute grammar whose base BNF is that of Example 3.2 and whose type rules are the same as for the assignment statement example of Section 3.4.5.

25. Prove the following program is correct:

{x = V$_x$ and y = V$_y$}

temp = x;

x = y;

y = temp;

{x = V$_y$ and y = V$_x$}

26. Prove the following program is correct:

```
{n > 0}
count = n;
sum = 0;
while count <> 0 do
  sum = sum + count;
  count = count - 1;
end
{sum = 1 + 2 + … + n}
```

4

Lexical and
Syntax Analysis

CHAPTER OUTLINE

A serious investigation of compiler design requires at least a semester of intensive study, including the design and implementation of a compiler for a small but realistic programming language. One half to two thirds of such a course is devoted to lexical and syntax analysis. However, a meaningful and valuable introduction can be presented in a single chapter, such as this one.

This chapter begins with an introduction to lexical analysis, including a simple example. Then the general parsing problem is discussed, including the two primary approaches to parsing and the complexity of parsing. Next, we introduce the recursive-descent implementation technique for LL parsers, including two examples of parts of a recursive-descent parser. The last section discusses bottom-up parsing and the LR parsing algorithm. This section includes an example of a small LR parsing table and the parse of a string using the LR parsing process.

4.1   Introduction

Three different approaches to implementing programming languages are introduced in Chapter 1: compilation, pure interpretation, and hybrid implementation. The compilation approach uses a translation program called a compiler, which translates programs written in a high-level programming language into machine code. Compilation is typically used to implement programming languages that are used for large industrial applications, often written in languages such as C++ and COBOL. Pure interpretation systems perform no translation; rather, programs are interpreted in their original form by a software interpreter. Pure interpretation is usually used for smaller systems in which execution efficiency is not critical, such as scripts embedded in HTML documents, written in languages such as JavaScript. Hybrid implementation systems translate programs written in high-level languages into intermediate forms, which are interpreted. These systems are now more widely used than ever, thanks in large part to the popularity of Java and Perl. Traditionally, hybrid systems have resulted in much slower program execution than compiler systems. However, in recent years the use of Just-In-Time (JIT) compilers has become widespread, particularly for Java programs. The JIT compiler, which translates intermediate code to machine code, is used just before the program is to be executed. In effect, a JIT compiler transforms a hybrid system to a compiled system.

Syntax analyzers, or parsers, are nearly always based on a formal description of the syntax of programs. The most commonly used syntax-description formalism is context-free grammars, or BNF, which are introduced in Chapter 3. Using BNF, as opposed to using some informal syntax description, has at least three compelling advantages. First, BNF descriptions of the syntax of programs are clear and concise, for both humans and for software systems that use them. Second, the BNF description can be used as the basis for the syntax analyzer. Third, implementations based on BNF are relatively easy to maintain because of their clear modularity.

Nearly all compilers separate the task of analyzing syntax into two distinct parts, lexical analysis and syntax analysis, although this terminology is confusing. The lexical analyzer deals with small-scale language constructs, such as names and numeric literals. The syntax analyzer deals with the large-scale constructs, such as expressions, statements, and program units. Section 4.2 introduces lexical analyzers. Sections 4.3, 4.4, and 4.5 discuss syntax analyzers.

There are several reasons why lexical analysis is separated from syntax analysis, as described in the following:

1. Simplicity—Techniques for lexical analysis are less complex than those required for syntax analysis, so the lexical analysis process can be simpler if it is separate. Also, removing the low-level details of lexical analysis from the syntax analyzer makes it both smaller and cleaner.

2. Efficiency—Although it pays to optimize the lexical analyzer, because lexical analysis requires a significant portion of total compilation time, it is not fruitful to optimize the syntax analyzer. Separation facilitates this selective optimization.

3. Portability—Because the lexical analyzer reads input program files and often includes buffering of that input, it is somewhat platform dependent. However, the syntax analyzer can be platform independent. It is always good to isolate machine-dependent parts of any software system.

4.2   Lexical Analysis

A lexical analyzer is essentially a pattern matcher. A pattern matcher attempts to find a substring of a given string of characters that matches a given pattern of characters. Pattern matching is a traditional part of computing. One of the earliest uses of pattern matching was with text editors, such as the ed line editor, which was introduced in an early version of UNIX. Since then, pattern matching has found its way into some programming languages, for example, Perl and JavaScript.

A lexical analyzer serves as the front end of a syntax analyzer. Technically, lexical analysis is a part of syntax analysis. A lexical analyzer performs syntax analysis at the lowest level of program structure. An input program appears to a compiler as a single string of characters. The lexical analyzer collects characters into logical groupings and assigns internal codes to the groupings according to their structure. The character groupings are called *lexemes*. The internal codes are called *tokens*. Lexemes are recognized by matching the input character string against character string patterns. Although tokens are usually coded as integer values, for the sake of readability of lexical and syntax analyzers, they are often referenced through named constants.

Consider the following example of an assignment statement:

```
sum = oldsum - value / 100;
```

Following are the tokens and lexemes of this statement:

Token	Lexeme
IDENT	sum
ASSIGN_OP	=
IDENT	oldsum
SUBTRACT_OP	-
IDENT	value
DIVISION_OP	/
INT_LIT	100
SEMICOLON	;

Lexical analyzers extract lexemes from a given input string and produce the corresponding tokens. In the early days of compilers, lexical analyzers often processed an entire program file and produced a file of tokens and lexemes. Now, however, most lexical analyzers are subprograms that produce the next lexeme and its associated token code from the input and return them to the caller, which is the syntax analyzer. The only view of the input program seen by the syntax analyzer is the output of the lexical analyzer, one lexeme at a time.

The lexical analysis process includes skipping comments and blanks outside lexemes, as they are not relevant to the meaning of the program. Also, the lexical analyzer inserts lexemes for user-defined names into the symbol table, which is used by later phases of the compiler. Finally, lexical analyzers detect syntactic errors in tokens, such as ill-formed floating-point literals, and report such errors to the user.

There are three approaches to building a lexical analyzer:

1. Write a formal description of the token patterns of the language using a descriptive language related to regular expressions and use a software tool to automatically generate a lexical analyzer. There are many such tools available for this. The oldest and most accessible of these, named lex, is commonly included as part of UNIX systems.

2. Design a state transition diagram that describes the token patterns of the language and write a program that implements the diagram.

3. Design a state transition diagram that describes the token patterns of the language and hand-construct a table-driven implementation of the state diagram.

A state transition diagram, or just state diagram, is a directed graph. The nodes of a state diagram are labeled with state names. The arcs of a state diagram are labeled with the input characters that cause the transitions. An arc may also include actions the lexical analyzer must do when the transition is taken.

State diagrams of the form used for lexical analyzers are representations of a class of mathematical machines called **finite automata**. Finite automata can be designed to recognize a class of languages called **regular languages**. **Regular expressions** and **regular grammars** are generative devices for regular languages. The tokens of a programming language are a regular language, and a lexical analyzer is a finite automaton.

We now illustrate lexical analyzer construction with a state diagram and the code that implements it. The state diagram could simply include states and transitions for each and every token pattern. However, that results in a very large and complex diagram. We therefore consider ways to simplify it. Suppose we need a lexical analyzer that only recognizes program names, reserved words, and integer literals. The names in this example consist of strings of uppercase letters, lowercase letters, and digits, but must begin with a letter. Names have no length limitation. The first thing to observe is that there are 52 different characters (any uppercase or lowercase letter) that can begin a name, which would require 52 transitions from the transition diagram's initial state. However, a lexical analyzer is only interested in determining that it is a name and is not concerned with which specific name it happens to be. Therefore, we define a character class for all 52 letters and use a single transition on the first character of any name.

Next, we observe that names and reserved words have similar patterns. Although it is possible to build a state diagram to recognize every specific reserved word of a programming language, that would result in a prohibitively large state diagram. It is much simpler and faster to have the lexical analyzer recognize names and reserved words with the same pattern and use a lookup in a table of reserved words to determine which names are reserved words.

Another opportunity for simplifying the transition diagram is with the integer literal tokens. There are 10 different characters that could begin an integer literal lexeme. This would require 10 transitions from the start state of the state diagram. Because specific digits are not a concern of the lexical analyzer, we can build a much more compact state diagram if we define a character class for digits and use a single transition on any character in this character class to a state that collects integer literals.

Next we define some utility subprograms for the common tasks inside the lexical analyzer. First, we need a subprogram, which we can name getChar, which has several duties. When called, getChar gets the next character of input from the input program and puts it in the global variable nextChar. This may require reading the next line or buffer of input. getChar must also determine the character class of the input character and put it in the global variable charClass. For our simple example language, we will have one class for letters and one for digits. The lexeme being built by the lexical analyzer, which could be implemented as a character string or an array, will be named lexeme. We implement the process of putting the character in nextChar into lexeme in a subprogram named addChar. This subprogram must be explicitly called because programs include some characters that need not be put in lexeme, just white space characters between lexemes in our language. Finally, we need a subprogram named lookup to determine whether the current contents of lexeme is a reserved word or a name. This subprogram will return zero if the lexeme is not a reserved word, but will return the token code for any reserved word. This assumes the token code for names is zero.

Token codes are numbers arbitrarily assigned to tokens by the compiler writer.

The state diagram in Figure 4.1 describes the patterns for our tokens. It includes the actions required on each transition of the state diagram.

Implementing this state diagram in code is relatively easy. The following C function is an example:

```
/* lex - a simple lexical analyzer */

        int lex() {
          getChar();
          switch (charClass) {

/* Parse identifiers and reserved words */

            case LETTER:
              addChar();
              getChar();
              while (charClass == LETTER ||
                     charClass == DIGIT) {
                addChar();
                getChar();
              }
              return lookup(lexeme);
              break;

/* Parse integer literals */
```

Figure 4.1

A state diagram to recognize names, reserved words, and integer literals

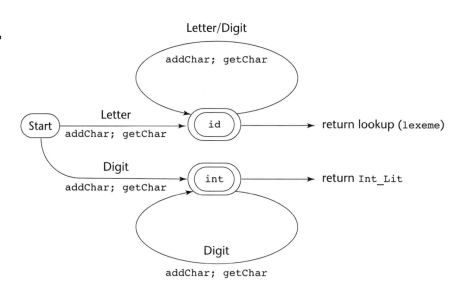

```
case DIGIT:
  addChar();
  getChar();
  while (charClass == DIGIT) {
    addChar();
    getChar();
  }
  return INT_LIT;
  break;
} /* End of switch */
} /* End of function lex */
```

This function illustrates the relative simplicity of lexical analyzers. Of course, we have left out the utility functions that perform much of the required work, as well as many of the details. Furthermore, we have dealt with a very small and simple token set.

A lexical analyzer often is responsible for the initial construction of the symbol table, which acts as a database of names for the compiler. The entries in the symbol table store information about user-defined names, as well as the attributes of the names. For example, if the name is that of a variable, the variable's type is one of it attributes that will be stored in the symbol table. Names are usually placed in the symbol table by the lexical analyzer. The attributes of a name are usually put in the symbol table by some part of the compiler that is subsequent to the actions of the lexical analyzer.

4.3 The Parsing Problem

The part of the process of analyzing syntax that is referred to as *syntax analysis* is often called *parsing*. We will use these two interchangeably.

This section discusses the general parsing problem and introduces the two main categories of parsing algorithms, top-down and bottom-up, as well as the complexity of the parsing process.

4.3.1 Introduction to Parsing

Parsers for programming languages construct parse trees for given programs. In some cases, the parse tree is only implicitly constructed, meaning that perhaps only a traversal of the tree is generated. But in all cases, the information required to build the parse tree is created during the parse. Both parse trees and derivations include all of the syntactic information needed by a language processor.

There are two distinct goals of syntax analysis: First, the syntax analyzer must check the input program to determine whether it is syntactically correct. When an error is found, the analyzer must produce a diagnostic message and recover. Recovery here means it must get back to a normal state and continue its analysis of the input program. This is required so that the compiler finds as many errors as possible during a single analysis of the input program. If this is not done well, error recovery may create more errors, or at least more error messages. The second goal of syntax analysis is to produce either a complete parse tree, or at least trace the structure of the complete parse tree. In either case, the result is used as the basis for translation.

Parsers are categorized according to the direction in which they build parse trees. The two broad classes of parsers are **top-down,** in which the tree is built from the root downward to the leaves, and **bottom-up,** in which the parse tree is built from the leaves upward to the root.

In this chapter, we will use a small set of notational conventions for grammar symbols and strings to make the discussion less cluttered. For formal languages, these are as follows:

> Terminal symbols—Lowercase letters at the beginning of the alphabet (a, b, ...)
>
> Nonterminal symbols—Uppercase letters at the beginning of the alphabet (A, B, ...)
>
> Terminals or nonterminals—Uppercase letters at the end of the alphabet (W, X, Y, Z)
>
> Strings of terminals—Lowercase letters at the end of the alphabet (w, x, y, z)
>
> Mixed strings (terminals and/or nonterminals)—Lowercase Greek letters (α, β, δ, γ)

For programming languages, terminal symbols are the small-scale syntactic constructs of the language, including the punctuation symbols and numeric literals. The nonterminal symbols of programming languages are usually connotative names or abbreviations, surrounded by pointed brackets—for example, <while_statement>, <expr>, and <function_def>. The sentences of a language (programs in the case of a programming language) are strings of terminals. Mixed strings describe right-hand sides (RHSs) of grammar rules and are used in parsing algorithms.

4.3.2   Top-Down Parsers

The derivation that is traced during a top-down parse is a leftmost derivation. A top-down parser traces or builds the parse tree in preorder. A preorder traversal of a parse tree begins with the root. Each node is visited before its branches are followed. Branches are followed in left-to-right order.

In terms of the derivation, a top-down parser can be described as follows: Given a sentential form that is part of a leftmost derivation, the parser's task is to find the next sentential form in that leftmost derivation. The general form of a left sentential form is $xA\alpha$, whereby our notational conventions x is a string of terminal symbols, A is a nonterminal, and α is a mixed string. Because x contains only terminals, A is the leftmost nonterminal in the sentential form, so it is the one that must be expanded to get the next sentential form in a leftmost derivation. Determining the next sentential form is a matter of choosing the correct grammar rule that has A as its left-hand side (LHS). For example, if the current sentential form is

xAα

and the A-rules are A → bB, A → cBb, and A → a, a top-down parser must choose among these three rules to get the next sentential form, which could be xbBα, xcBbα, or xaα. This is the parsing decision for top-down parsers.

Different top-down parsing algorithms use different information to make parsing decisions. The most common top-down parsers use the first token of input generated by the LHS being expanded. So, in the sentential form xAα, the parser would use whatever token followed the last lexeme in the string, x, to determine which A-rule should be used.

The most common top-down parsing algorithms are closely related. A recursive descent parser is a coded version of a syntax analyzer based directly on the BNF description of the language. The most common alternative to recursive descent is to use a parsing table, rather than code, to implement the BNF rules. Both of these, which are called *LL algorithms*, are equally powerful, meaning they work on the same subset of grammars. The first L in LL specifies a left-to-right scan of the input; the second L specifies that a leftmost derivation is generated. Section 4.4 introduces the recursive-descent approach to implementing an LL parser.

4.3.3 Bottom-Up Parsers

A bottom-up parser constructs a parse tree by beginning at the leaves and progressing toward the root. A bottom-up parser produces the reverse of a rightmost derivation. In terms of the derivation, a bottom-up parser can be described as follows: Given a right sentential form α, the parser must determine what substring of α is the right-hand side (RHS) of the rule in the grammar that must be reduced to its LHS to produce the previous sentential form in the rightmost derivation. For example, the first step for a bottom-up parser is to determine which substring of the initial given sentence is the RHS to be reduced to its corresponding LHS to get the second last sentential form in the derivation. The process of finding the correct RHS to reduce is complicated by the fact that a given right sentential form may include more than one RHS from the grammar of the language being parsed. The correct RHS is called the **handle**.

A bottom-up parser finds the handle of a given right sentential form by examining the symbols on one or both sides of a possible handle. Symbols to the right of the possible handle are usually tokens in the input that have not yet been analyzed.

The most common bottom-up parsing algorithms are in the LR family, where the L specifies a left-to-right scan of the input and the R specifies that a rightmost derivation is generated.

4.3.4   The Complexity of Parsing

Parsing algorithms that work for any unambiguous grammar are complex and inefficient. In fact, the complexity of such algorithms is $O(n^3)$, which means the amount of time they take is on the order of the cube of the length of the string to be parsed. This relatively large amount of time is required because these algorithms frequently must backup and reparse part of the sentence being analyzed. Such algorithms are often not useful for practical processes, such as syntax analysis for a compiler, because they are too slow. In this kind of situation, computer scientists often search for algorithms that are faster, even though they may not be as general. This means we trade generality for efficiency. In terms of parsing, faster algorithms have been found that work for only a subset of the set of all possible grammars. Algorithms that work for only subsets of the set of all grammars are acceptable as long as the subset includes grammars that describe programming languages. (Actually, as discussed in Chapter 3, the whole class of grammars is not adequate to describe all of the syntax of most programming languages.)

All algorithms used for the syntax analyzers of compilers have complexity $O(n)$, which means the time they take is linearly related to the length of the string to be parsed. This is vastly more efficient than $O(n^3)$ algorithms.

4.4   Recursive-Descent Parsing

This section introduces the top-down parser implementation process, recursive descent.

4.4.1   The Recursive-Descent Parsing Process

A recursive-descent parser is so named because it consists of a collection of subprograms, many of which are recursive, and it produces a parse tree in top-down (descending) order. This recursion is a reflection of the nature of programming languages, which include several different nested structures. The syntax of these structures is naturally described with recursive grammar rules. For example, statements are often nested in other statements. Also, parentheses in expressions must be properly nested.

EBNF is ideally suited for recursive-descent parsers. Recall from Chapter 3 that the primary EBNF extensions are braces, which specify that what they enclose can appear zero or more times, and brackets, which specify that what they enclose can appear zero or one time. Note that in both cases, the enclosed symbols are optional. For example:

<if_statement> → **if** <logic_expr> <statement> [**else** <statement>]
<ident_list> → ident {**,** ident}

In the first rule, the **else** clause of an **if** statement is optional. In the second, an <ident_list> is an identifier, followed by zero or more repetitions of a comma and an identifier.

A recursive-descent parser has a subprogram for each nonterminal in the grammar. The responsibility of the subprogram associated with a particular nonterminal is as follows: When given an input string, it traces out the parse tree that can be rooted at that nonterminal and whose leaves match the input string. In effect, a recursive-descent parsing subprogram is a parser for the language (set of strings) that can be generated by its associated nonterminal.

Consider the following EBNF description of simple arithmetic expressions:

<expr> → <term> {(+ | −) <term>}
<term> → <factor> {(* | /) <factor>}
<factor> → id | (<expr>)

Recall from Chapter 3 that an EBNF grammar for arithmetic expressions, such as this one, does not force any associativity rule. Therefore, when using such a grammar as the basis for a compiler, we must take care to ensure that the code generation process, which is normally driven by syntax analysis, produces code that adheres to the associativity rules of the language. This can easily be done when recursive descent parsing is used.

In the following example recursive-descent function, expr, the lexical analyzer is a function that is appropriately named lex. It gets the next lexeme and puts its token code in the global variable nextToken. The token codes are defined as named constants. For example, PLUS_CODE is a named constant for the token code for plus symbols.

A recursive-descent subprogram for a rule with a single RHS is relatively simple. For each terminal symbol in the RHS, that terminal symbol is compared with nextToken. If they do not match, it is a syntax error. If they match, the lexical analyzer is called to get the next input token. For each nonterminal, the parsing subprogram for that nonterminal is called.

The recursive-descent subprogram for the first rule in the example grammar above, written in C, is

```c
/* Function expr
   Parses strings in the language generated by the rule:
   <expr> -> <term> {(+ | -) <term>}
   */
void expr() {

/* Parse the first term */
```

```
      term();

/* As long as the next token is + or -, call lex to get
   the next token, and parse the next term */

  while (nextToken == PLUS_CODE ||
         nextToken == MINUS_CODE){
    lex();
    term();
  }
}
```

Recursive-descent parsing subprograms are written with the convention that each one leaves the next token of input in nextToken. So, whenever a parsing function begins, it is assured that nextToken has the leftmost token of the input that has not yet been used in the parsing process.

The part of the language that the expr function parses consists of one or more terms, separated by either plus or minus operators. This is the language generated by the nonterminal <expr>. Therefore, it first calls the function that parses terms (<term>). Then it continues to call that function as long as it finds PLUS_CODE or MINUS_CODE tokens (which it passes over by calling lex). This recursive-descent function is simpler than most, because its rule has only one RHS. Furthermore, it does not include any code for syntax error detection or recovery, because there are no detectable errors associated with the grammar rule.

A recursive-descent parsing subprogram for a nonterminal whose rule has more than one RHS begins with code to determine which RHS is to be parsed. Each RHS is examined (at compiler construction time) to determine the set of terminal symbols that can appear at the beginning of sentences it can generate. By matching these sets against the next token of input, the parser can choose the correct RHS.

The function for the <factor> nonterminal of our arithmetic expression grammar must choose between its two RHSs. It also includes error detection. In the function for <factor>, the reaction to detecting a syntax error is simply to call the error function. In a real parser, a diagnostic message must be produced when an error is detected. Furthermore, most compilers must recover from the error so that the parsing process can continue.

```
/* Function factor
   Parses strings in the language generated by the rule:
       <factor> -> id  |  (<expr>)

   */
void factor() {
```

```
/* Determine which RHS */
  if (nextToken == ID_CODE)

/* For the RHS id, just call lex */

    lex();

/* If the RHS is (<expr>) — call lex to pass over the left
   parenthesis, call expr, and check for the right
   parenthesis */

  else if (nextToken == LEFT_PAREN_CODE) {
    lex();
    expr();
    if (nextToken == RIGHT_PAREN_CODE)
      lex();
    else
      error();
  }  /* End of else if (nextToken == ...  */

/* It was neither an id nor a left parenthesis */

  else error();

}
```

The objective of this brief discussion is to convince you that a recursive-descent parser can be easily written if an appropriate grammar is available for the language. The key question now is the characteristics of an "appropriate" grammar for recursive-descent parsing.

4.4.2 The LL Grammar Class

One simple grammar characteristic that causes a catastrophic problem for LL parsers is left recursion. For example, consider the following rule:

$$A \rightarrow A + B$$

A recursive-descent parser subprogram for A immediately calls itself to parse the first symbol in its RHS. That activation of the A parser subprogram then immediately calls itself again, and again, and so forth. It is easy to see that this gets nowhere.

Indirect left recursion poses the same problem as direct left recursion. For example, suppose we have

$$A \rightarrow B\ a\ A$$
$$B \rightarrow A\ b$$

A recursive-descent parser for these rules would have the A subprogram immediately call the subprogram for B, which immediately calls the A subprogram. So, the problem is the same as for direct left recursion. The problem of left recursion is not confined to the recursive-descent approach to building top-down parsers. It is a problem for all top-down parsing algorithms. Fortunately, left recursion is not a problem for bottom-up parsing algorithms.

There is an algorithm to modify a given grammar to remove both direct and indirect left recursion (Aho et al., 1986), but we will not cover it here. When writing a grammar for a programming language, we must take care to avoid including any left recursion.

Left recursion is not the only grammar trait that disallows top-down parsing. Another is whether the parser can always choose the correct RHS on the basis of the next token of input, using only the first token generated by the leftmost nonterminal in the current sentential form. There is a relatively simple test of a non–left recursive grammar that indicates whether this can be done, called the **pairwise disjointness test**. This test requires that we be able to compute a set based on the RHSs of a given nonterminal symbol in a grammar. These sets, which are called FIRST, are defined as

$$\text{FIRST}(\alpha) = \{a \mid \alpha \Rightarrow^* a\beta\} \quad (\text{If } \alpha \Rightarrow^* \varepsilon, \varepsilon \text{ is in FIRST}(\alpha))$$

in which $\Rightarrow^*$ means 0 or more derivation steps.

An algorithm to compute FIRST for any mixed string α can be found in Aho et al. (1986). For our purposes, FIRST can usually be computed by inspection of the grammar.

The pairwise disjointness test is

> For each nonterminal, A, in the grammar that has more than one RHS, for each pair of rules, $A \rightarrow \alpha_i$ and $A \rightarrow \alpha_j$, it must be true that
>
> $$\text{FIRST}(\alpha_i) \cap \text{FIRST}(\alpha_j) = \phi$$
>
> (The intersection of the two sets, $\text{FIRST}(\alpha_i)$ and $\text{FIRST}(\alpha_j)$, must be empty.)

In other words, if a nonterminal A has more than one RHS, the first terminal symbol that can be generated in a derivation for each of them must be unique to that RHS. Consider the following rules:

$$A \rightarrow aB \mid bAb \mid c$$

The FIRST sets for the RHSs of these rules are {a}, {b}, and {c}, which are clearly disjoint. Therefore, these rules pass the pairwise disjointness test. What this means, in terms of a recursive-descent parser, is that the code of the subprogram for parsing the nonterminal A can choose which RHS it is dealing with by seeing only the first terminal symbol of input (token) that is generated by the nonterminal. Now consider the rules

A → aB | aAb

The FIRST sets for the RHSs in these rules are {a} and {a}, which are clearly not disjoint. So, these rules fail the pairwise disjointness test. In terms of the parser, the subprogram for A could not determine which RHS was being parsed by looking at the next symbol of input, because if it were an a, it could be either RHS. This issue is of course more complex if one or more of the RHSs begin with nonterminals.

In many cases, a grammar that fails the pairwise disjointness test can be modified so that it will pass the test. For example, consider the rules

<variable> → identifier | identifier [<expression>]

This states that a <variable> is either an identifier or an identifier followed by an expression in brackets (a subscript). These rules clearly do not pass the pairwise disjointness test, because both RHSs begin with the same terminal, identifier. This problem can be alleviated through a process called **left factoring**.

We now take an informal look at left factoring. Consider the rules above for <variable>. Both RHSs begin with identifier. The parts that follow identifier are ε (the empty string) and [<expression>]. The two rules can be replaced by

<variable> → identifier <new>

where <new> is defined as

<new> → ε | [<expression>]

It is not difficult to see that together, these two rules generate the same language as the two rules with which we began. However, these two pass the pairwise disjointness test.

If the grammar is being used as the basis for a recursive-descent parser, an alternative to left factoring is available. With an EBNF extension, the problem disappears in a way that is very similar to the left factoring solution. Consider the first rules above for <variable>. The subscript can be made optional by placing it in square brackets, as in

<variable> → identifier [[<expression>]]

In this rule, the outer brackets are metasymbols that indicate that what is inside is optional. The inner brackets are terminal symbols of the programming language being described. The point is that we replaced two rules with a single rule that generates the same language but passes the pairwise disjointness test.

A formal algorithm for left factoring can be found in Aho et al. (1986). Left factoring cannot solve all pairwise disjointness problems of grammars. In some cases, rules must be rewritten in other ways to eliminate the problem.

4.5   Bottom-Up Parsing

This section introduces the general process of bottom-up parsing and includes a description of the LR parsing algorithm.

4.5.1   The Parsing Problem for Bottom-Up Parsers

Consider the following grammar, which generates arithmetic expressions with addition and multiplication operators, parentheses, and the operand, id.

E → E + T | T
T → T * F | F
F → (E) | id

Notice that this grammar generates the same arithmetic expressions as the example in Section 4.4. The difference is that this grammar is left recursive, which is acceptable to bottom-up parsers. Also note that grammars for bottom-up parsers normally do not include metasymbols such as those used to specify extensions to BNF. The following rightmost derivation illustrates this grammar:

E => E + T
    => E + T * F
    => E + T * id
    => E + F * id
    => E + id * id
    => T + id * id
    => F + id * id
    => id + id * id

The underlined part of each sentential form in this derivation is the RHS that is rewritten as its corresponding LHS to get the previous sentential form. The process of bottom-up parsing produces the reverse of a rightmost derivation. So, in the derivation above, a bottom-up parser starts with the last sentential form (the input sentence) and produces the sequence of sentential forms from there until all that remains is the start symbol, which in this grammar is E. In each step, the task of the bottom-up parser is to find the specific RHS, the handle, in the sentential form that must be rewritten to get the next (previous) sentential form. As mentioned above, a right sentential form may include more than one RHS. For example, the right sentential form

E + T * id

includes three RHSs, E + T, T, and id. Only one of these is the correct one to be rewritten. For example, if the RHS E + T were chosen to be rewritten in this sentential form, the resulting sentential form would be E * id, but E * id is not a legal right sentential form for the given grammar.

The handle of a right sentential form is unique. The task of a bottom-up parser is to find the handle of any given right sentential form that can be generated by its associated grammar. Formally, handle is defined as follows:

Definition: β is the **handle** of the right sentential form γ = αβw if and only if S =>*rm αAw =>rm αβw

In this definition, =>rm specifies a rightmost derivation step, and =>*rm specifies zero or more rightmost derivation steps. Although the definition of a handle is mathematically concise, it provides little help in finding the handle of a given right sentential form. In the following, we provide the definitions of several substrings of sentential forms that are related to handles. The purpose of these is to provide some intuition about handles.

Definition: β is a **phrase** of the right sentential form γ if and only if S =>* γ = $α_1 A α_2$ =>+ $α_1 β α_2$

In this definition, =>+ means one or more derivation steps.

Definition: β is a **simple phrase** of the right sentential form γ if and only if S =>* γ = $α_1 A α_2$ => $α_1 β α_2$

If you compare these two definitions carefully, you will discover that they differ only in the last derivation specification. The definition of *phrase* uses one or more steps, while the definition of *simple phrase* uses exactly one step.

The definitions of *phrase* and *simple phrase* may appear to have the same lack of practical value as that of a *handle*, but that is not true. Consider what a phrase is relative to a parse tree. It is the string consisting of all of the leaves of the partial parse tree that is rooted at one particular internal node of the whole parse tree. A simple phrase is just a phrase that takes a single derivation step from its root nonterminal node. In terms of a parse tree, a phrase can be derived from a single nonterminal in one or more tree levels, but a simple phrase can be derived in just a single tree level. Consider the parse tree shown in Figure 4.2.

The leaves of the parse tree in Figure 4.2 comprise the sentential form, E + T * id. Because there are three internal nodes, there are three phrases. Each

Figure 4.2

A parse tree for
E + T * id

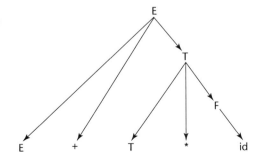

internal node is the root of a subtree, whose leaves are a phrase. The root node of the whole parse tree, E, generates all of the resulting sentential form, E + T * id, which is a phrase. The internal node, T, generates the leaves T * id, which is another phrase. Finally, the internal node, F, generates id, which is a phrase. So the phrases of the sentential form E + T * id are E + T * id, T * id, and id. Notice that phrases are not necessarily RHSs in the underlying grammar.

The simple phrases are a subset of the phrases. In the example above, the only simple phrase is id. A simple phrase is always a RHS in the grammar.

The reason for discussing phrases and simple phrases is this: The handle of any rightmost sentential form is its leftmost simple phrase. So now we have a highly intuitive way to find the handle of any right sentential form, assuming we have the grammar and can draw a parse tree. This approach to finding handles is of course not practical for a parser. (If you already have a parse tree, why do you need a parser?) Its only purpose is to provide the reader with some intuitive feel for what a handle is, relative to a parse tree, which is easier than trying to think about handles in terms of sentential forms.

We can now think of bottom-up parsing in terms of parse trees, although the purpose of a parse is to produce a parse tree. Given the parse tree for an entire sentence, you easily can find the handle, which is the first thing to rewrite in the sentence to get the previous sentential form. Then the handle can be pruned from the parse tree and the process repeated. Continuing to the root of the parse tree, the entire rightmost derivation can be constructed.

4.5.2 Shift-Reduce Algorithms

Bottom-up parsers are often called **shift-reduce algorithms**, because shift and reduce are the two most common actions they specify. The shift action moves the next input token onto the parser's stack. A reduce action replaces a RHS (the handle) on top of the parser's stack by its corresponding LHS. A parser of any kind is a **pushdown automaton** (PDA). You need not be intimate with PDAs to understand how a bottom-up parser works, although it helps. A PDA is a very simple mathematical machine that scans strings of symbols from left to right. A PDA is so named because it uses a pushdown stack as its memory. PDAs can be used as language recognizers. Given a string of symbols over some alphabet, a PDA that is designed for the purpose can determine whether the string is or is not a sentence in a language. In the process, the PDA can produce the information needed to construct a parse tree for the sentence.

With a PDA, the input string is examined, one symbol at a time, left to right. The input is treated very much as if it were stored in another stack, because the PDA never sees more than the leftmost symbol of the input.

4.5.3 LR Parsers

Many different bottom-up parsing algorithms have been devised. Most of these are variations of a process called LR, in which the L means it scans the input string left to right and the R means it produces a rightmost derivation. LR parsers use a relatively small program and a parsing table. The original LR algorithm was designed by Donald Knuth (Knuth, 1965). This algorithm, which is sometimes called **canonical LR**, was not used in the years immediately following its publication because producing the required parsing table required large amounts of computer time and memory. Subsequently, several variations on the canonical LR table constuction process were developed (DeRemer, 1971) (DeRemer & Pennello, 1982). These are characterized by two properties: (1) They require much less computer resources to produce the required parsing table, and (2) they work on smaller classes of grammars than the canonical LR algorithm.

There are several advantages to LR parsers:

1. They will work for nearly all grammars that describe programming languages.
2. They work on a larger class of grammars than other bottom-up algorithms but are as efficient as any other bottom-up parser.
3. They can detect syntax errors as soon as it is possible.
4. The LR class of grammars is a superset of the class parsable by LL parsers.

The only disadvantage of LR parsing is that it is difficult to produce by hand the parsing table for a given grammar. This is not a serious disadvantage, however, for there are many programs available that take a grammar as input and produce the parsing table (Aho et al., 1986).

Prior to the appearance of the LR parsing algorithm, there were a number of parsing algorithms that found handles of right sentential forms by looking both to the left and to the right of the substring of the sentential form that was suspected of being the handle. Knuth's insight was that you could effectively look to the left of the suspected handle all the way to the bottom of the parse stack to determine whether it was the handle. But all of the information in the parse stack that was relevant to the parsing process could be represented by a single state, which could be on the top of the stack. In other words, Knuth discovered that regardless of the length of the input string, the length of the sentential form, or the depth of the parse stack, there were only a relatively small number of different situations, as far as the parsing process is concerned. Each situation could be represented by a state and stored in the parse stack, one state symbol for each grammar symbol on the stack. At the top of the stack would always be a state symbol, which represented the relevant information from the entire history of the parse, up to the current time. We will use subscripted uppercase Ss to represent the parser states.

Figure 4.3 shows the structure of an LR parser.

The contents of the parse stack for an LR parser has the following form:

$$S_0 X_1 S_1 X_2 ... X_m S_m \text{ (top)}$$

Figure 4.3

The structure of an LR parser

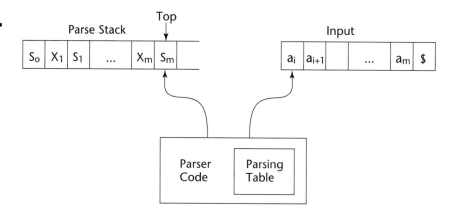

Where the Ss are state symbols and the Xs are grammar symbols. An LR parser configuration is a pair of strings (stack, input), with the detailed form

$$(S_0X_1S_1X_2S_2...X_mS_m, a_ia_{i+1}...a_n\$)$$

Notice that the input string has a dollar sign at its right end. This is put there during initialization of the parser. It is used for normal termination of the parser. Using this parser configuration, we can formally define the LR parser process, which is based on the parsing table. An LR parsing table has two parts, named ACTION and GOTO. The ACTION part of the table specifies most of what the parser does. It has state symbols as its row labels and the terminal symbols of the grammar as its column labels. Given a current parser state, which is represented by the state symbol on top of the parse stack, and the next symbol (token) of input, the parse table specifies what the parser should do. The two primary parser actions are shift and reduce. The parser either shifts the next input symbol onto the parse stack or it already has the handle on top of the stack, which it reduces to the LHS of the rule whose RHS is the same as the handle. Two other actions are possible: accept, which means the parser has successfully completed the parse of the input, and error, which means the parser has detected a syntax error.

   The rows of the GOTO part of the LR parsing table have state symbols as labels. This part of the table has nonterminals as column labels. The values in the GOTO part of the table indicate which state symbol should be pushed onto the parse stack after a reduction has been completed, which means the handle has been removed from the parse stack and the new nonterminal has been pushed onto the parse stack. The specific symbol is found at the row whose label is the state symbol on top of the parse stack after the handle and its associated state symbols have been removed. The column of the GOTO table that is used is the one with the label that is the LHS of the rule used in the reduction.

   The initial configuration of an LR parser is

$$(S_0, a_1...a_n\$)$$

The parser actions are formally defined as follows:

1. If $\text{ACTION}[S_m, a_i] = \text{Shift S}$, the next configuration is

   $(S_0 X_1 S_1 X_2 S_2 \ldots X_m S_m a_i S, a_{i+1} \ldots a_n \$)$

   The Shift process is simple: The next symbol of input is pushed onto the stack, along with the state symbol that is part of the Shift specification in the ACTION table.

2. If $\text{ACTION}[S_m, a_i] = \text{Reduce } A \rightarrow \beta$ and $S = \text{GOTO}[S_{m-r}, A]$, where r = the length of β, the next configuration is

   $(S_0 X_1 S_1 X_2 S_2 \ldots X_{m-r} S_{m-r} A S, a_i a_{i+1} \ldots a_n \$)$

   This is a much more complicated action. For a reduce action, the handle must be removed from the stack. Because for every grammar symbol on the stack there is a state symbol, the number of symbols removed from the stack is twice the number of symbols in the handle. After removing the handle and its associated state symbols, the LHS of the rule is pushed onto the stack. Finally, the GOTO table is used, with the row label being the symbol that was exposed when the handle and its state symbols were removed from the stack, and the column label being the nonterminal that is the LHS of the rule used in the reduction. So in the new configuration, the top symbol comes from the GOTO part of the table, and the topmost grammar symbol is the LHS of the rule used in the reduction.

3. If $\text{ACTION}[S_m, a_i] = \text{Accept}$, the parse is complete and no errors were found.

4. If $\text{ACTION}[S_m, a_i] = \text{Error}$, the parser calls an error-handling routine.

Although there are many parsing algorithms based on the LR concept, they only differ in the construction of the parsing table. All LR parsers use this same parsing algorithm.

Perhaps the best way to become familiar with the LR parsing process is through an example. Consider the traditional grammar for arithmetic expressions that follows:

1. $E \rightarrow E + T$
2. $E \rightarrow T$
3. $T \rightarrow T * F$
4. $T \rightarrow F$
5. $F \rightarrow (E)$
6. $F \rightarrow \text{id}$

The rules of this grammar are numbered to provide a simple way to reference them in a parsing table.

Figure 4.4 shows the LR parsing table for this grammar. Abbreviations are used for the actions, R for reduce and S for shift. R4 means reduce using

Figure 4.4

The LR parsing table
for an arithmetic
expression grammar

State	Action						Goto		
	id	+	*	(	)	$	E	T	F
0	S5			S4			1	2	3
1		S6				accept			
2		R2	S7		R2	R2			
3		R4	R4		R4	R4			
4	S5			S4			8	2	3
5		R6	R6		R6	R6			
6	S5			S4				9	3
7	S5			S4					10
8		S6			S11				
9		R1	S7		R1	R1			
10		R3	R3		R3	R3			
11		R5	R5		R5	R5			

rule 4; S6 means shift the next symbol of input onto the stack and push state 6 onto the stack. Empty positions in the ACTION table indicate syntax errors. In a complete parser, these could have calls to error-handling routines.

Initially, the parse stack has the single symbol 0, which represents state 0 of the parser. The input contains the input string with an end marker, in this case a dollar sign, attached to its right end. At each step, the parser actions are dictated by the top (rightmost in Figure 4.3) symbol of the parse stack and the next (leftmost in Figure 4.3) token of input. The correct action is chosen from the corresponding cell of the ACTION part of the parse table. The GOTO part of the parse table is used after a reduction action. Recall that GOTO is used to determine which state symbol is placed on the parse stack after a reduction.

Following is a trace of a parse of the string id + id * id, using the LR parsing algorithm and the parsing table shown in Figure 4.4.

Stack	*Input*	*Action*
0	id + id * id $	Shift 5
0id5	+ id * id $	Reduce 6 (use GOTO[0, F])
0F3	+ id * id $	Reduce 4 (use GOTO[0, T])
0T2	+ id * id $	Reduce 2 (use GOTO[0, E])
0E1	+ id * id $	Shift 6
0E1+6	id * id $	Shift 5

0E1+6id5	* id $	Reduce 6 (use GOTO[6, F])
0E1+6F3	* id $	Reduce 4 (use GOTO[6, T])
0E1+6T9	* id $	Shift 7
0E1+6T9*7	id $	Shift 5
0E1+6T9*7id5	$	Reduce 6 (use GOTO[7, F])
0E1+6T9*7F10	$	Reduce 3 (use GOTO[6, T])
0E1+6T9	$	Reduce 1 (use GOTO[0, E])
0E1	$	Accept

Algorithms to generate LR parsing tables from given grammars are described in Aho et al. (1986). There are a number of different software systems available to generate LR parsing tables. One of the earliest of these is the yacc system, which is normally part of UNIX.[1]

SUMMARY

Syntax analysis is a common part of language implementation, regardless of the implementation approach used. Syntax analysis is normally based on a formal syntax description of the language being implemented. A context-free grammar, which is also called BNF, is the most common approach for describing syntax. The task of syntax analysis is usually divided into two parts, lexical analysis and syntax analysis. There are several reasons for separating lexical analysis, namely simplicity, efficiency, and portability.

A lexical analyzer is a pattern matcher that isolates the small-scale parts of a program, which are called lexemes. Lexemes occur in categories, such as integer literals and names. These categories are called tokens. Each token is assigned a numeric code, which along with the lexeme is what the lexical analyzer produces. There are three distinct approaches to constructing a lexical analyzer: using a software tool to generate a table for a table-driven analyzer, building such a table by hand, and writing code to implement a state diagram description of the tokens of the language being implemented. The state diagram for tokens can be reasonably small if character classes are used for transitions, rather than having transitions for every possible character from every state node. Also, the state diagram can be simplified by using a table lookup to recognize reserved words.

Syntax analyzers have two goals: to detect syntax errors in a given program and to produce a parse tree, or possibly only the information required to build such a tree, for a given program. Syntax analyzers are either top-down, meaning they construct leftmost derivations and a parse tree in top-down order, or bottom-up, in which case they construct the reverse of a rightmost derivation and a parse tree in bottom-up order. Parsers that work for all unambiguous grammars have complexity $O(n^3)$. However, parsers used

---

[1] yacc is an acronym for yet another compiler compiler. It was introduced in Johnson (1975).

for implementing syntax analyzers for programming languages work on sub-classes of unambiguous grammars and have complexity O(n).

A recursive-descent parser is an LL parser that is implemented by writing code directly from the grammar of the source language. EBNF is ideal as the basis for recursive-descent parsers. A recursive-descent parser has a subprogram for each nonterminal in the grammar. The code for a given grammar rule is simple if the rule has a single RHS. The RHS is examined left to right. For each nonterminal, the code calls the associated subprogram for that nonterminal, which parses whatever the nonterminal generates. For each terminal, the code compares the terminal with the next token of input. If they match, the code simply calls the lexical analyzer to get the next token. If they do not, the subprogram reports a syntax error. If a rule has more than one RHS, the subprogram must first determine which RHS it should parse. It must be possible to make this determination on the basis of the next token of input.

Two distinct grammar characteristics prevent the construction of a recursive-descent parser based on the grammar. One of these is left recursion. Although we do not cover it, an algorithm exists to remove both direct and indirect left recursion from a grammar. The other problem is detected with the pairwise disjointness test, which tests whether a parsing subprogram can determine which RHS is being parsed on the basis of the next token of input. Some grammars that fail the pairwise disjointness test can be modified to pass it, using left factoring.

The parsing problem for bottom-up parsers is to find the substring of the current sentential form that must be reduced to its associated LHS to get the next (previous) sentential form in the rightmost derivation. This substring is called the handle of the sentential form. A parse tree can provide an intuitive basis for recognizing a handle. A bottom-up parser is a shift-reduce algorithm, because in most cases it either shifts the next lexeme of input onto the parse stack or reduces the handle that is on top of the stack.

The LR family of shift-reduce parsers is the most commonly used bottom-up parsing approach for programming languages, because parsers in this family have several advantages over alternatives. An LR parser uses a parse stack, which contains grammar symbols and state symbols to maintain the state of the parser. The top symbol on the parse stack is always a state symbol that represents all of the information in the parse stack that is relevant to the parsing process. LR parsers use two parsing tables, ACTION and GOTO. The ACTION part specifies what the parser should do, given the state symbol on top of the parse stack and the next token of input. The GOTO table is used to determine which state symbol should be placed on the parse stack after a reduction has been done.

1. What are three reasons why syntax analyzers are based on grammars?

2. Explain the three reasons why lexical analysis is separated from syntax analysis.

3. Define *lexeme* and *token*.

4. What are the primary tasks of a lexical analyzer?

5. Describe briefly the three approaches to building a lexical analyzer.

6. What is a state transition diagram?

7. Why are character classes used, rather than individual characters, for the transitions of a state diagram for a lexical analyzer?

8. What are the two distinct goals of syntax analysis?

9. Describe the differences between top-down and bottom-up parsers.

10. Describe the parsing problem for a top-down parser.

11. Describe the parsing problem for a bottom-up parser.

12. Explain why compilers use parsing algorithms that work on only a subset of all grammars.

13. Why are named constants used, rather than numbers, for token codes?

14. Describe how a recursive-descent parsing subprogram is written for a rule with a single RHS.

15. Explain the two grammar characteristics that prohibit them from being used as the basis for a top-down parser.

16. What is the FIRST set for a given grammar and sentential form?

17. Describe the pairwise disjointness test.

18. What is left factoring?

19. What is a phrase of a sentential form?

20. What is a simple phrase of a sentential form?

21. What is the handle of a sentential form?

22. What is the mathematical machine on which both top-down and bottom-up parsers are based?

23. Describe three of the advantages of LR parsers.

24. What was Knuth's insight in developing the LR parsing technique?

25. Describe the purpose of the ACTION table of an LR parser.

26. Describe the purpose of the GOTO table of an LR parser.

27. Is left recursion a problem for LR parsers?

PROBLEM SET

1. Perform the pairwise disjointness test for the following grammar rules.
   a. A → aB | b | cBB
   b. B → aB | bA | aBb
   c. C → aaA | b | caB

2. Perform the pairwise disjointness test for the following grammar rules.
   a. S → aSb | bAA
   b. A → b{aB} | a
   c. B → aB | a

3. Given the following grammar and the right sentential form, draw a parse tree and show the phrases and simple phrases, as well as the handle.

   S → aAb | bBA   A → ab | aAB   B → aB | b
   a. aaAbb
   b. bBab
   c. aaAbBb

4. Given the following grammar and the right sentential form, draw a parse tree and show the phrases and simple phrases, as well as the handle.

   S → AbB | bAc   A → Ab | aBB   B → Ac | cBb | c
   a. aAcccbbc
   b. AbcaBccb
   c. baBcBbbc

5. Show a complete parse, including the parse stack contents, input string, and action for the string id * (id + id), using the grammar and parse table in Section 4.5.3.

6. Show a complete parse, including the parse stack contents, input string, and action for the string (id + id) * id, using the grammar and parse table in Section 4.5.3.

PROGRAMMING EXERCISES

1. Design a state diagram to recognize one form of the comments of the C-based programming languages, those that begin with /* and end with */.

2. Design a state diagram to recognize the floating-point literals of your favorite programming language.

3. Write and test the code to implement the state diagram of Problem 1.

4. Write and test the code to implement the state diagram of Problem 2.

5. For those rules that pass the test in Problem 1, write a recursive-descent parsing subprogram that parses the language generated by the rules. Assume you have a lexical analyzer named `lex` and an error-handling subprogram named `error`, which is called whenever a syntax error is detected.

6. For those rules that pass the test in Problem 2, write a recursive-descent parsing subprogram that parses the language generated by the rules. Assume you have a lexical analyzer named `lex` and an error-handling subprogram named `error`, which is called whenever a syntax error is detected.

7. Implement and test the LR parsing algorithm given in Section 4.5.3.

5

Names, Bindings, Type Checking, and Scopes

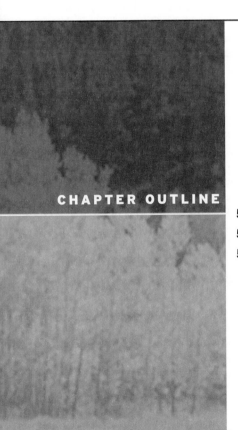

CHAPTER OUTLINE

his chapter introduces the fundamental semantic issues of variables. The most basic of these topics is covered first, the nature of names and special words in programming languages. The attributes of variables, including type, address, and value, are then discussed. The issue of aliases is included in that discussion. The important concepts of binding and binding times are then introduced. The different possible binding times for variable attributes define four different categories of variables. Their descriptions are followed by a thorough investigation of type checking, strong typing, and type compatibility rules. The two very different scoping rules for names, static and dynamic, are then described, along with the concept of a referencing environment of a statement. Finally, named constants and variable initialization are discussed.

5.1   Introduction

Imperative programming languages are, to varying degrees, abstractions of the underlying von Neumann computer architecture. The architecture's two primary components are its memory, which stores both instructions and data, and its processor, which provides operations for modifying the contents of the memory. The abstractions in a language for the memory cells of the machine are variables. In some cases, the characteristics of the abstractions are very close to the characteristics of the cells; an example of this is an integer variable, which is usually represented exactly as in an individual hardware memory word. In other cases, the abstractions are far removed from the cells, as with a three-dimensional array, which requires a software mapping function to support the abstraction.

A variable can be characterized by a collection of properties, or attributes, the most important of which is type, a fundamental concept in programming languages. The design of the data types of a language requires that a variety of issues be considered. (Data types are discussed in Chapter 6.) Among the most important of these are the scope and lifetime of variables. Related to these are the issues of type checking and initialization. A knowledge of all these concepts is requisite to understanding the imperative languages. Type compatibility is another important part of the data type design of a language.

In the remainder of this book, we will often refer to families of languages as if they were a single language. For example, when we refer to Fortran, we mean all of the versions of Fortran. This is also the case for Ada. References to C include the original version of C, as well as C89 and C99. We use the phrase **C-based languages** to refer to C, C++, Java, and C#. When we refer to a specific version of a language, it is because it is different from the other family members within the topic being discussed.

5.2   Names

Before we can begin our discussion of variables, we must discuss one of the fundamental attributes of variables—names, which have broader use than simply for variables. Names are also associated with labels, subprograms, formal parameters, and other program constructs. The term *identifier* is often used interchangeably with *name*.

5.2.1 Design Issues

The following are the primary design issues for names:

- Are names case sensitive?
- Are the special words reserved words or keywords?

These issues are discussed in the following two sections, which also include examples of several design choices.

5.2.2 Name Forms

A **name** is a string of characters used to identify some entity in a program.

Fortran 95 allows up to 31 characters in its names. C89 had no length limitation on its internal names, but only the first 31 were significant. C99 is like C89, except the first 63 characters are significant. External names (those defined outside functions, which must be handled by the linker) in C89 were restricted to six characters; in C99, this was increased to 31. Names in Java and Ada have no length limit, and all characters in them are significant. However, Ada implementations are allowed to impose a length limitation, though it must be at least 200 characters, obviously not a severe restriction. C++ does not specify a length limit on names, although implementors sometimes do. They do this so the symbol table in which identifiers are stored during compilation need not be too large, and also to simplify the maintenance of that table.

Names in most programming languages have the same form: a letter followed by a string consisting of letters, digits, and underscore characters (_). Although the use of underscore characters to form names was widely used in the 1970s and 1980s, that practice is now far less popular. In the C-based languages, it has to a large extent been replaced by the so-called "camel" notation, in which the second word of a multiple-word name is capitalized, as in `myStack`.

In versions of Fortran prior to Fortran 90, names could have embedded spaces, which were ignored. For example, the following two names were equivalent:

```
Sum Of Salaries
SumOfSalaries
```

In some languages, notably the C-based languages, uppercase and lowercase letters in names are distinct; that is, names in these languages are **case**

> **HISTORY NOTE**
>
> The earliest programming languages used single-character names. This was natural because early programming was primarily mathematical, and mathematicians have long used single-character names for unknowns in their formal notations.
>
> Fortran I broke with the tradition of the single-character name, allowing up to six characters in its names. Fortran 77 still restricted names to six characters.

sensitive. For example, the following three names are distinct in C++: rose, ROSE, and Rose. To some, this is a serious detriment to readability because names that look very similar in fact denote different entities. In that sense, case sensitivity violates the design principle that language constructs that look similar should have similar meanings. But in languages whose variable names are case sensitive, although Rose and rose look similar, there is no connection between them.

Obviously, not everyone agrees that case sensitivity is bad for names. In C, the problems of case sensitivity can be avoided by exclusive use of lowercase for names. In Java and C#, however, the problem cannot be escaped because many of the predefined names include both uppercase and lowercase letters. For example, the Java method for converting a string to an integer value is parseInt, and spellings such as ParseInt and parseint are not recognized. This is a problem of writability rather than readability, because the need to remember odd spellings makes it more difficult to write correct programs. It is a kind of intolerance on the part of the language designer, which is enforced by the compiler.

In versions of Fortran prior to 90, only uppercase letters could be used in names, a needless restriction. The origin of this was the fact that card punches had only uppercase letters. Like Fortran 90, many implementations of Fortran 77 allow lowercase letters; they simply translate them to uppercase for internal use during compilation.

5.2.3   Special Words

Special words in programming languages are used to make programs more readable by naming actions to be performed. They also are used to separate the syntactic entities of programs. In most languages, these words are classified as reserved words, but in some they are only keywords.

A **keyword** is a word of a programming language that is special only in certain contexts. Fortran is one of the languages whose special words are keywords. In Fortran, the word Real, when found at the beginning of a statement and followed by a name, is considered a keyword that indicates the statement is a declarative statement. However, if the word Real is followed by the assignment operator, it is considered a variable name. These two uses are illustrated in the following:

```
Real Apple
Real = 3.4
```

Fortran compilers and Fortran program readers must recognize the difference between names and special words by context.

A **reserved word** is a special word of a programming language that cannot be used as a name. As a language design choice, reserved words are better than keywords because the ability to redefine keywords can lead to readability problems. For example, in Fortran, one could have the statements

```
Integer Real
Real Integer
```

which declare the program variable `Real` to be of `Integer` type and the variable `Integer` to be of `Real` type. In addition to the strange appearance of these declaration statements, the appearance of `Real` and `Integer` as variable names elsewhere in the program could be misleading to program readers.

In program code examples in this book, special words are presented in boldface.

Some languages include predefined names, which are in a sense between special words and user-defined names. They have predefined meanings but can be redefined by the user. For example, the built-in data type names in Ada, such as `Integer` and `Float`, are predefined. These names are not reserved; they can be redefined by any Ada program.

In most languages, names that are defined in other program units, such as Ada and Java packages and C and C++ libraries, can be made visible to a program. These names are predefined, but only visible if explicitly imported. Once imported, they cannot be redefined.

5.3   Variables

A program variable is an abstraction of a computer memory cell or collection of cells. Programmers often think of variables as names for memory locations, but there is much more to a variable than just a name. The move from machine languages to assembly languages was largely one of replacing absolute numeric memory addresses with names, making programs far more readable and therefore easier to write and maintain. That step also provided an escape from the problem of absolute addressing, because the translator that converted the names to actual addresses also chose those addresses.

A variable can be characterized as a sextuple of attributes: (name, address, value, type, lifetime, scope). Although this may seem too complicated for such an apparently simple concept, it provides the clearest way to explain the various aspects of variables.

Our discussion of variable attributes will lead to examinations of the important related concepts of aliases, binding, binding times, declarations, type checking, strong typing, scoping rules, and referencing environments.

The name, address, type, and value attributes of variables are discussed in the following subsections. The lifetime and scope attributes are discussed in Sections 5.4.3 and 5.8, respectively.

5.3.1   Name

Variable names are the most common names in programs. They were discussed at length in Section 5.2 in the general context of entity names in programs. Most variables have names. The ones that do not are discussed in Section 5.4.3.3.

5.3.2 Address

The **address** of a variable is the memory address with which it is associated. This association is not as simple as it may at first appear. In many languages, it is possible for the same name to be associated with different addresses at different places and at different times in the program. For example, a program can have two subprograms, `sub1` and `sub2`, each of which defines a local variable that uses the same name, say `sum`. Because these two variables are independent of each other, a reference to `sum` in `sub1` is unrelated to a reference to `sum` in `sub2`. Similarly, most languages allow the same variable to be associated with different addresses at different times during program execution. For example, if a subprogram has a local variable that is allocated from the run-time stack when the subprogram is called, different calls may result in that variable having different addresses.

The process of associating variables with addresses is further discussed in Section 5.4.3. An implementation model for subprograms and their activations is discussed in Chapter 10.

The address of a variable is sometimes called its *l*-value, because that is what is required when a variable appears in the left side of an assignment statement.

5.3.2.1 Aliases

It is possible to have multiple variables that have the same address. When more than one variable can be used to access the same memory location, the names are called **aliases.** Aliasing is a hindrance to readability because it allows a variable to have its value changed by an assignment to a different variable. For example, if variables `total` and `sum` are aliases, any change to `total` also changes `sum` and vice versa. A reader of the program must always remember that `total` and `sum` are different names for the same memory cell. Because there can be any number of aliases in a program, this is very difficult in practice. Aliasing also makes program verification more difficult.

Aliases can be created in programs in several different ways. Aliases can be created using the data structures in some programming languages, for example, the union types of C and C++. Unions are discussed at length in Chapter 6.

Two pointer variables are aliases when they point to the same memory location. The same is true for reference variables. This kind of aliasing is simply a side effect of the nature of pointers and references. When a C++ pointer is set to point at a named variable, the pointer, when dereferenced, and the variable's name

HISTORY NOTE

Fortran's `Equivalence` statement was designed solely to create aliases. One of the motivations for the `Equivalence` statement was to conserve storage. Because Fortran now has dynamic storage, and also because memory is now relatively plentiful, there is no longer any reason to use `Equivalence`. As a result, `Equivalence` was deprecated in Fortran 90.

are aliases. This and other characteristics of pointers and references are discussed in Chapter 6.

Aliasing can be created in many languages through subprogram parameters. These kinds of aliases are discussed in Chapter 9.

The time when a variable becomes associated with an address is very important to an understanding of programming languages. This subject is discussed in Section 5.4.3.

5.3.3 Type

The **type** of a variable determines the range of values the variable can have and the set of operations that are defined for values of the type. For example, the **int** type in Java specifies a value range of –2147483648 to 2147483647, and arithmetic operations for addition, subtraction, multiplication, division, and modulus.

5.3.4 Value

The value of a variable is the contents of the memory cell or cells associated with the variable. It is convenient to think of computer memory in terms of *abstract* cells, rather than physical cells. The physical cells, or individually addressable units, of most contemporary computer memories are byte-sized, with a byte usually being 8 bits in length. This size is too small for most program variables. We define an abstract memory cell to have the size required by the variable with which it is associated. For example, although floating-point values may occupy four physical bytes in a particular implementation of a particular language, we think of a floating-point value as occupying a single abstract memory cell. We consider the value of each simple nonstructured type to occupy a single abstract cell. Henceforth, when we use the term *memory cell*, we mean abstract memory cell.

A variable's value is sometimes called its *r*-**value** because it is what is required when the variable is used on the right side of an assignment statement. To access the *r*-value, the *l*-value must be determined first. Such determinations are not always simple. For example, scoping rules can greatly complicate matters, as is discussed in Section 5.8.

5.4   The Concept of Binding

In a general sense, a **binding** is an association, such as between an attribute and an entity or between an operation and a symbol. The time at which a binding takes place is called **binding time.** Binding and binding times are prominent concepts in the semantics of programming languages. Bindings can take place at language design time, language implementation time, compile time, load time, link time, or run time. For example, the asterisk symbol

(∗) is usually bound to the multiplication operation at language design time. A data type, such as **int** in C, is bound to a range of possible values at language implementation time. At compile time, a variable in a Java program is bound to a particular data type. A variable may be bound to a storage cell when the program is loaded into memory. That same binding does not happen until run time in some cases, as with variables declared in Java methods. A call to a library subprogram is bound to the subprogram code at link time.

Consider the following C assignment statement, whose variable count has been defined as shown:

```
int count;
...
count = count + 5;
```

Some of the bindings and their binding times for the parts of this assignment statement are as follows:

- The type of count is bound at compile time.
- The set of possible values of count is bound at compiler design time.
- The meaning of the operator symbol + is bound at compile time, when the types of its operands have been determined.
- The internal representation of the literal 5 is bound at compiler design time.
- The value of count is bound at execution time with this statement.

A complete understanding of the binding times for the attributes of program entities is a prerequisite for understanding the semantics of a programming language. For example, to understand what a subprogram does, one must understand how the actual parameters in a call are bound to the formal parameters in its definition. To determine the current value of a variable, you may need to know when the variable was bound to storage.

5.4.1 Binding of Attributes to Variables

A binding is **static** if it first occurs before run time and remains unchanged throughout program execution. If the binding first occurs during run time or can change in the course of program execution, it is called **dynamic.** The physical binding of a variable to a storage cell in a virtual memory environment is complex, because the page or segment of the address space in which the cell resides may be moved in and out of memory many times during program execution. In a sense, such variables are bound and unbound repeatedly. These bindings, however, are maintained by computer hardware, and the changes are invisible to the program and the user. Because they are not important to the discussion, we are not concerned with these hardware bindings. The essential point is to distinguish between static and dynamic bindings.

5.4.2 Type Bindings

Before a variable can be referenced in a program, it must be bound to a data type. The two important aspects of this binding are how the type is specified and when the binding takes place. Types can be specified statically through some form of explicit or implicit declaration.

5.4.2.1 Variable Declarations

An **explicit declaration** is a statement in a program that lists variable names and specifies that they are a particular type. An **implicit declaration** is a means of associating variables with types through default conventions instead of declaration statements. In this case, the first appearance of a variable name in a program constitutes its implicit declaration. Both explicit and implicit declarations create static bindings to types.

Most programming languages designed since the mid-1960s require explicit declarations of all variables (Perl, JavaScript, and ML are three exceptions). Several widely used languages whose initial designs were done before the late 1960s, notably Fortran, PL/I, and BASIC, have implicit declarations. For example, in Fortran, an identifier that appears in a program that is not explicitly declared is implicitly declared according to the following convention: If the identifier begins with one of the letters I, J, K, L, M, or N, or their lowercase versions, it is implicitly declared to be Integer type; otherwise, it is implicitly declared to be Real type.

Although they are a minor convenience to programmers, implicit declarations can be detrimental to reliability because they prevent the compilation process from detecting some typographical and programmer errors. In Fortran, variables that are accidentally left undeclared by the programmer are given default types and unexpected attributes, which could cause subtle errors that are difficult to diagnose.

Some of the problems with implicit declarations can be avoided by requiring names for specific types to begin with particular special characters. For example, in Perl any name that begins with $ is a scalar, which can store either a string or a numeric value. If a name begins with @, it is an array; if it begins with a %, it is a hash structure. This creates different namespaces for different type variables. In this scenario, the names @apple and %apple are unrelated, because each is from a different namespace. Furthermore, a program reader always knows the type of a variable when reading its name. Note that this is different from Fortran, because Fortran has both implicit and explicit declarations, so the type of a variable cannot necessarily be determined from the spelling of its name.

In C and C++, one must sometimes distinguish between declarations and definitions. Declarations specify types and other attributes but do not cause allocation of storage. Definitions specify attributes *and* cause storage allocation. For a specific name, a C program can have any number of compatible declarations, but only a single definition. One purpose of variable declarations in C is to provide the type of a variable defined external to a function that is used in the function. It tells the compiler the type of a variable and that it is defined elsewhere. This idea carries over to the functions in C and C++, where prototypes declare names and interfaces, but not the code of functions. Function definitions, on the other hand, are complete.

5.4.2.2 Dynamic Type Binding

With dynamic type binding, the type is not specified by a declaration statement, nor can it be determined by the spelling of its name. Instead, the variable is bound to a type when it is assigned a value in an assignment statement. When the assignment statement is executed, the variable being assigned is bound to the type of the value of the expression on the right side of the assignment.

Languages in which types are dynamically bound are dramatically different from those in which types are statically bound. The primary advantage of dynamic binding of variables to types is that it provides a great deal of programming flexibility. For example, a program to process a list of numeric data in a language that uses dynamic type binding can be written as a generic program, meaning that it is capable of dealing with data of any numeric type. Whatever type data is input will be acceptable, because the variables in which the data is to be stored can be bound to the correct type when the data is assigned to the variables after input. By contrast, because of static binding of types, one cannot write a Java program to process a list of data without knowing the type of that data.

In JavaScript and PHP, the binding of a variable to a type is dynamic. For example, a JavaScript script may contain the following statement:

```
list = [10.2, 3.5]
```

Regardless of the previous type of the variable named list, this assignment causes it to become a single-dimensioned array of length 2. If the statement

```
list = 47
```

followed the assignment above, list would become a scalar variable.

There are two disadvantages to dynamic type binding. First, the error detection capability of the compiler is diminished relative to a compiler for a language with static type bindings, because any variable can be assigned a value of any type. Incorrect types of right sides of assignments are not detected as errors; rather, the type of the left side is simply changed to the incorrect type. For example, suppose that in a particular program, i and x are integer variables, and y is a floating-point array. Further suppose that the program needs the assignment statement

```
i = x
```

but because of a keying error, it has the assignment statement

```
i = y
```

In a language with dynamic type binding, no error is detected by the compiler or run-time system. i is simply changed to a floating-point array type. But because y was used instead of the correct variable x, the results are erroneous. In a language with static type binding, the compiler would detect the error and the program would not get to execution.

Note that this disadvantage is also present to some extent in some languages that use static type binding, such as Fortran, C, and C++, which in many cases automatically convert the type of the RHS of an assignment to the type of the LHS.

Perhaps the greatest disadvantage of dynamic type binding is cost. The cost of implementing dynamic attribute binding is considerable, particularly in execution time. Type checking must be done at run time. Furthermore, every variable must have a descriptor associated with it to maintain the current type. The storage used for the value of a variable must be of varying size, because different type values require different amounts of storage.

Finally, languages that have dynamic type binding for variables must be implemented using pure interpreters rather than compilers. It is not possible to create machine code instructions whose operand types are not known at compile time. Pure interpretation typically takes at least ten times as long as to execute equivalent machine code. Of course, if a language is implemented with a pure interpreter, the time to do dynamic type binding is hidden by the overall time of interpretation, so it seems less costly in that environment. On the other hand, languages with static type bindings are seldom implemented by pure interpretation, because programs in these languages can be easily translated to very efficient machine code versions.

5.4.2.3 Type Inference

ML is a programming language that supports both functional and imperative programming (Ullman, 1998). ML employs an interesting type inference mechanism, in which the types of most expressions can be determined without requiring the programmer to specify the types of the variables. For example, the function declaration

```
fun circumf(r) = 3.14159 * r * r;
```

specifies a function that takes a floating-point (**real** in ML) argument and produces a floating-point result. The types are inferred from the type of the constant in the expression. Likewise, in the function

```
fun times10(x) = 10 * x;
```

the argument and functional value are inferred to be of type **int**.

Consider the following ML function:

```
fun square(x) = x * x;
```

ML determines the type of both the parameter and the return value from the * operator in the function definition. Because this is an arithmetic operator, the

INTERVIEW

Scripting Languages and Other Examples of Slick Solutions

RASMUS LERDORF

After graduating with a degree in engineering, Rasmus Lerdorf held a number of consulting jobs. Then, in an effort to track those viewing his online resume, he created the first iteration of PHP. These days he is an advocate for the open source movement and an employee at Yahoo! in Sunnyvale, California.

SOME BACKGROUND

What was your earliest experience with computing? My father and I built a pong game together from a kit he ordered from the United States, circa 1976. I also remember getting a Texas Instruments "Speak & Spell" thing around 1978 that had the first-ever single-chip speech synthesizer in it . My first computer I got in 1983 or so. It was a Commodore Vic20 with 5k of ram and a 1MHz 6502 CPU. I spent hours typing in code snippets from magazines. In high school I played with Commodore PET and UNISYS 80186 boxes running QNX. QNX was by far the coolest operating system I had ever seen and it was somewhat anticlimactic when I later got an MS-DOS box. I think that early experience biased me toward UNIX and UNIX-like operating systems.

Do you have a favorite past job? I really enjoyed my time in Brazil and they also gave me my first introduction to Silicon Valley when they opened an office in Mountain View and I moved there in 1993. I also really liked working at the University of Toronto after that, helping them build a dialup system. A big chunk of PHP was created during that job.

> " My official title is 'Technical Yahoo!' and I am on the infrastructure team that maintains and supports the various tools used across all of Yahoo! My particular focus is PHP and Apache. "

ON SCRIPTING LANGUAGES

What's your definition of a scripting language? A higher-level language that hides the tedium and complexity of whatever traditional programming technique was used to solve a particular class of problem.

When you were working on that personal home page, then later on the system for the University of Toronto, and wanted to track the visitors to your site, then to track students, what available tools did you consider using? I don't recall really considering any existing solutions for this. Back then you would normally just read the raw access logs from your Web server. There were of course some log analysis tools mostly written in Perl that would summarize things, but I wanted to get an e-mail every time someone read my resume, and I wanted to know where that person came from. There were no tools that specifically did that.

How did you come to decide that spending the time to devise your own solution was bette than using the tools out there? The main alternative was always Perl. And despite what some have attributed to me over the years, I don't actually hate Perl. I like it and use it quite a bit, but back then my needs were simple. I was running my home page on a shared server that did not have very much RAM or CPU and forking and execing a Perl CGI for every request was too resource-intensive. I needed a simple parser I could embed directly into my Web server, and Perl was way too hard and way too big to embed, and I didn't need any of the power of Perl for what I was doing back then. So I wrote a simple little parser that I understood and could easily embed. Then, of course, it started to grow, and once you start to add any sort of logical flow it is a slippery slope toward a full programming language. The original intent was never to write a full language.

What does PHP offer today that other scripting languages (Perl, Tcl, Python, Ruby) do not? PHP
is targeted specifically at the Web problem. Everything you read about PHP is geared toward the Web, so if you are trying to solve the Web problem it is very obvious how you apply PHP. This is not as clear with other, more general-purpose languages. You first pick the language, and then you have to scramble around looking for the best way to apply that particular language.

The future of PHP: What's the next kink in the code, or the next functionality you would like to see worked out or added? We need a quality repository of PHP code and extensions because our previous trend of bundling everything with PHP itself just doesn't scale very well.

> **Coming up with solutions to problems is all about being able to approach them from many angles. Sometimes formal training and conventional wisdom can get in the way and limit what people will try. You also have to be prepared to fail repeatedly.**

ON SLICK SOLUTIONS

Here's something you said in a previous interview: "I definitely appreciate and respect a slick solution to a tough problem." What thought process, what activities, lead to finding that slick solution? Coming up with solutions to problems is all about being able to approach them from many angles. Sometimes formal training and conventional wisdom can get in the way and limit what people will try. You also have to be prepared to fail repeatedly.

A problem is only tough because you haven't found the slick solution yet. It is a bit like those scrambled word puzzles you see in the newspaper. You look at the jumbled word and it makes no sense. You try and you try to come up with the right combination of letters but you can't see it. Then someone whispers the word to you and suddenly it is obvious. Now when you look at the letters the word is right there and you can't figure out why you didn't see it right away. That's exactly the same feeling I get when I come up with, or see someone else's slick solution to a problem.

What are some of your favorite slick solutions?
The world is full of slick solutions. Paperclips, Velcro, the ballpoint pen. But I guess you are asking for things within PHP. I think one of the slick solutions was tying HTML get, post, and cookie data directly to PHP variables. It seems like an obvious thing, but at the time nobody was doing that and it made PHP a very approachable solution to Web problems. The feature has since taken some criticism because of how it might be used improperly, but I still stand by it and deem it to be slick.

type of the parameter and the function are assumed to be numeric. In ML, the default numeric type to be **int**. So, it is inferred that the type of the parameter and the return value of square is **int**.

If square were called with a floating-point value, as in

```
square(2.75);
```

it would cause an error, because ML does not coerce **real** values to **int** type. If we wanted square to accept **real** parameters, it could be rewritten as

```
fun square(x) : real = x * x;
```

Because ML does not allow overloaded functions, this version could not coexist with the earlier **int** version.

The fact that the functional value is typed **real** is sufficient to infer that the parameter is also **real** type. The following definitions are also legal:

```
fun square(x : real) = x * x;
fun square(x) = (x : real) * x;
fun square(x) = x * (x : real);
```

Type inference is also used in the purely functional languages Miranda and Haskell.

5.4.3 Storage Bindings and Lifetime

The fundamental character of an imperative programming language is in large part determined by the design of the storage bindings for its variables. It is therefore important to have a clear understanding of these bindings.

The memory cell to which a variable is bound somehow must be taken from a pool of available memory. This process is called **allocation.** **Deallocation** is the process of placing a memory cell that has been unbound from a variable back into the pool of available memory.

The **lifetime** of a variable is the time during which the variable is bound to a specific memory location. So the lifetime of a variable begins when it is bound to a specific cell and ends when it is unbound from that cell. To investigate storage bindings of variables, it is convenient to separate scalar (unstructured) variables into four categories, according to their lifetimes. We call these categories static, stack-dynamic, explicit heap-dynamic, and implicit heap-dynamic. In the following sections, we discuss the meanings of these four categories, along with their purposes, advantages, and disadvantages.

5.4.3.1 Static Variables

Static variables are those that are bound to memory cells before program execution begins and remain bound to those same memory cells until program execution terminates. Variables that are statically bound to storage have several valuable applications in programming. Obviously, globally accessible variables are often used throughout the execution of a program, thus making it necessary to have them bound to the same storage during that execution. Sometimes it is convenient to have variables that are declared in subprograms be **history sensitive,** that is, have them retain values between separate executions of the subprogram. This is a characteristic of a variable that is statically bound to storage.

Another advantage of static variables is efficiency. All addressing of static variables can be direct; other kinds of variables often require indirect addressing, which is slower. Furthermore, no run-time overhead is incurred for allocation and deallocation of static variables.

One disadvantage of static binding to storage is reduced flexibility; in particular, in a language that has only variables that are statically bound to storage, recursive subprograms cannot be supported. Another disadvantage is that storage cannot be shared among variables. For example, suppose a program has two subprograms, both of which require large arrays. Further suppose that the two subprograms are never active at the same time. If the arrays are static, they cannot share the same storage for their arrays.

C and C++ allow programmers to include the `static` specifier on a variable definition in a function, making the variables it defines static. Note that when the `static` modifier appears in the declaration of a variable in a class definition in C++, Java, and C#, it has nothing to do with the lifetime of the variable. In this context, it means the variable is a class variable, rather than an instance variable.

5.4.3.2 Stack-dynamic Variables

Stack-dynamic variables are those whose storage bindings are created when their declaration statements are elaborated, but whose types are statically bound. **Elaboration** of such a declaration refers to the storage allocation and binding process indicated by the declaration, which takes place when execution reaches the code to which the declaration is attached. Therefore, elaboration occurs during run time. For example, the variable declarations that appear at the beginning of a Java method are elaborated when the method is called and the variables defined by those declarations are deallocated when the method completes its execution.

As their name indicates, stack-dynamic variables are allocated from the run-time stack.

Some languages, for example C and Java, allow variable declarations to occur anywhere a statement can appear. In some implementations of these languages, all of the stack-dynamic variables declared in a function or method (not including those declared in nested blocks) may be bound to storage at the beginning of execution of the function or method, even though the declarations of some of these variables do not appear at the beginning. In such cases, the variable becomes visible at the declaration, but the storage binding (and initialization, if it is specified in the declaration) occurs when the function or method begins execution. The fact that storage binding of a variable takes place before it becomes visible does not affect the semantics of the language.

To be useful, at least in most cases, recursive subprograms require some form of dynamic local storage so that each active copy of the recursive subprogram has its own version of the local variables. These needs are conveniently met by stack-dynamic variables. Even in the absence of recursion, having stack-dynamic local storage for subprograms is not without merit, because all subprograms share the same memory space for their locals. The disadvantages are the run-time overhead of allocation and deallocation, slower accesses because indirect addressing is required, and the fact that subprograms cannot be history sensitive.

Fortran 95 allows implementors to use stack-dynamic variables for locals, but includes a statement

Save list

that allows the programmer to specify that some or all of the variables (those in list) in the subprogram in which Save is placed will be static.

In Java, C++, and C#, variables defined in methods are by default stack-dynamic. In Ada, all non-heap variables defined in subprograms are stack-dynamic.

All attributes other than storage are statically bound to stack-dynamic scalar variables. That is not the case for some structured types, as is discussed in Chapter 6. Implementation of allocation/deallocation processes for stack-dynamic variables is discussed in Chapter 10.

5.4.3.3 Explicit Heap-dynamic Variables

Explicit heap-dynamic variables are nameless (abstract) memory cells that are allocated and deallocated by explicit run-time instructions specified by the programmer. These variables, which are allocated from and deallocated to the heap, can only be referenced through pointer or reference variables. The heap is a collection of storage cells whose organization is highly disorganized because of the unpredictability of its use. An explicit heap-dynamic variable is created either by an operator (for example, in Ada and C++) or a call to a system subprogram provided for that purpose (for example, in C).

In C++, the allocation operator, named **new**, uses a type name as its operand. When executed, an explicit heap-dynamic variable of the operand type is created and a pointer to it is returned. Because an explicit heap-dynamic variable is bound to a type at compile time, that binding is static. However, such variables are bound to storage at the time they are created, which is during run time.

In addition to a subprogram or operator for creating explicit heap-dynamic variables, some languages include a means of destroying them.

As an example of explicit heap-dynamic variables, consider the following C++ code segment:

```
int *intnode;
...
intnode = new int;  /* allocates an int cell */
...
delete intnode;     /* deallocates the cell to which
                       intnode points */
```

In this example, an explicit heap-dynamic variable of **int** type is created by the **new** operator. This variable can then be referenced through the pointer, intnode. Later, the variable is deallocated by the **delete** operator.

In Java, all data except the primitive scalars are objects. Java objects are explicitly heap-dynamic and are accessed through reference variables. Java has no way of explicitly destroying a heap-dynamic variable; rather, implicit garbage collection is used.

C# has both explicit heap-dynamic and stack-dynamic objects, all of which are implicitly deallocated.

Explicit heap-dynamic variables are often used for dynamic structures, such as linked lists and trees, that need to grow and/or shrink during execution. Such structures can be built conveniently using pointers or references and explicit heap-dynamic variables.

The disadvantages of explicit heap-dynamic variables are the difficulty of using pointer and reference variables correctly, along with the cost of references to the variables, allocations, and deallocations. These considerations, pointer and reference data types, and implementation methods for explicit heap-dynamic variables are discussed at length in Chapter 6.

5.4.3.4 Implicit Heap-dynamic Variables

Implicit heap-dynamic variables are bound to heap storage only when they are assigned values. In fact, all their attributes are bound every time they are assigned. In a sense, they are just names that adapt to whatever use they are asked to serve. The advantage of such variables is that they have the highest degree of flexibility, allowing highly generic code to be written. The disadvantage is the run-time overhead of maintaining all the dynamic attributes, which could include array subscript types and ranges, among others. Another disadvantage is the loss of some error detection by the compiler, as discussed in Section 5.4.2.2. Examples of implicit heap-dynamic variables in JavaScript appear in Section 5.4.2.2.

5.5   Type Checking

For our discussion of type checking, we generalize the concept of operands and operators to include subprograms and assignment statements. We will think of subprograms as operators whose operands are their parameters. The assignment symbol will be thought of as a binary operator, with its target variable and its expression being the operands.

Type checking is the activity of ensuring that the operands of an operator are of compatible types. A **compatible** type is one that is either legal for the operator or is allowed under language rules to be implicitly converted by compiler-generated code to a legal type. This automatic conversion is called a **coercion.** For example, if an **int** variable and a **float** variable are added in Java, the value of the **int** variable is coerced to **float** and a floating-point add is done.

A **type error** is the application of an operator to an operand of an inappropriate type. For example, in the original version of C, if an **int** value was passed to a function that expected a **float** value, a type error would occur (because compilers for that language did not check the types of parameters).

If all bindings of variables to types are static in a language, then type checking can nearly always be done statically. Dynamic type binding requires type checking at run time, which is called dynamic type checking.

Some languages, such as JavaScript and APL, because of their dynamic type binding, allow only dynamic type checking. It is much better to detect errors at compile time than at run time because the earlier correction is usually less costly. The penalty for static checking is reduced programmer flexibility. Fewer shortcuts and tricks are possible. Such techniques, though, are now generally held in low esteem.

Type checking is complicated when a language allows a memory cell to store values of different types at different times during execution. This can be done with Ada variant records, Fortran **Equivalence**, and C and C++ unions. In these cases, type checking, if done, must be dynamic and requires the run-time system to maintain the type of the current value of such memory cells. So even though all variables are statically bound to types in languages such as C++, not all type errors can be detected by static type checking.

5.6   Strong Typing

One of the new ideas in language design that became prominent in the so-called structured programming revolution of the 1970s is **strong typing.** Strong typing is widely acknowledged as being a highly valuable concept. Unfortunately, it is often loosely defined, and it is sometimes used in computing literature without being defined at all.

The following is one simple *but incomplete* definition of a strongly typed language: A strongly typed language is one in which each name in a program in the language has a single type associated with it, and that type is known at compile time. The essence of this definition is that all types are statically bound. The weakness of this definition is that it ignores the possibility that, although a variable's type may be known, the storage location to which it is bound may store values of different types at different times. To take this possibility into account, we define a programming language to be **strongly typed** if type errors are always detected. This requires that the types of all operands can be determined, either at compile time or at run time. The importance of strong typing lies in its ability to detect all misuses of variables that result in type errors. A strongly typed language also allows the detection, at run time, of uses of the incorrect type values in variables that can store values of more than one type.

Fortran 95 is not strongly typed because the use of `Equivalence` between variables of different types allows a variable of one type to refer to a value of a different type, without the system being able to check the type of the value when one of the `Equivalenced` variables is referenced or assigned. In fact, type checking of `Equivalenced` variables would eliminate most of their usefulness.

Ada is nearly strongly typed. It is only *nearly* strongly typed because it allows programmers to breach the type-checking rules by specifically requesting that type checking be suspended for a particular type conversion. This temporary suspension of type checking can be done only when the library function `Unchecked_Conversion` is used. This function, of which there can be a version for every data type, takes a variable of its type as its parameter and returns the bit string that is the current value of that variable. No actual conversion takes place; it is merely a means of extracting the value of a variable of one type and using it as if it were of a different type. This can be useful for user-defined storage allocation and deallocation operations, in which addresses are manipulated as integers but must be used as pointers. Because no checking is done in `Unchecked_Conversion`, it is the programmer's responsibility to ensure that the use of a value gotten from it is meaningful.

C and C++ are not strongly typed languages because both include union types, which are not type checked.

ML is strongly typed but in a slightly different sense than that of the imperative languages. ML has variables whose types are all statically known, either from declarations or from its type inference rules, as discussed in Section 5.4.2.3.

Java and C#, although they are based on C++, are strongly typed in the same sense as Ada. Types can be explicitly cast, which could result in a type error. However, there are no implicit ways type errors can go undetected.

The coercion rules of a language have an important effect on the value of type checking. For example, expressions are strongly typed in Java. However, an arithmetic operator with one floating-point operand and one integer operand is legal. The value of the integer operand is coerced to floating-point, and a floating-point operation takes place. This is what is usually intended by the programmer. However, the coercion also results in a loss of part of the reason for strong typing—error detection. For example, suppose a program had the `int` variables a and b and the **float** variable d. Now, if a programmer meant to type a + b, but mistakenly typed a + d, the error would not be detected by the compiler. The value of a would simply be coerced to **float**. So, the value of strong typing is weakened by coercion. Languages with a great deal of coercion, like Fortran, C, and C++, are significantly less reliable than those with little coercion, such as Ada. Java and C# have half as many assignment type coercions as C++, so their error detection is better than that of C++, but still not nearly as effective as that of Ada. The issue of coercion is examined in detail in Chapter 7.

5.7   Type Compatibility

The idea of type compatibility was defined when the issue of type checking was introduced. In this section, we investigate the various kinds of type compatibility rules of languages. The design of the type compatibility rules of a language is important, because it influences the design of the data types and the operations provided for values of those types. Perhaps the most important result of two variables being of compatible types is that either one can have its value assigned to the other.

There are two different types of compatibility methods: name compatibility and structure compatibility. **Name type compatibility** means that two variables have compatible types only if they are defined in either the same declaration or in declarations that use the same type name. **Structure type compatibility** means that two variables have compatible types if their types have identical structures. There are some variations of these two approaches, and many languages use combinations of them.

Name type compatibility is easy to implement but is highly restrictive. Under a strict interpretation, a variable whose type is a subrange of the integers would not be compatible with an integer type variable. For example, supposing Ada used strict name type compatibility, consider the following Ada code:

```
type Indextype is 1..100;
count : Integer;
index : Indextype;
```

The variables count and index would not be compatible; count could not be assigned to index or vice versa.

Another problem with name type compatibility arises when a structured type is passed among subprograms through parameters. Such a type must be defined only once, globally. A subprogram cannot state the type of such formal parameters in local terms. This is the case with the original version of Pascal.

Structure type compatibility is more flexible than name type compatibility, but it is more difficult to implement. Under name type compatibility, only the two type names must be compared to determine compatibility. Under structure type compatibility, however, the entire structures of the two types must be compared. This comparison is not always simple. (Consider a data structure that refers to its own type, such as a linked list.) Other questions can also arise. For example, are two record or structure types compatible if they have the same structure but different field names? Are two single-dimensioned array types in an Ada program compatible if they have the same element type but have subscript ranges of 0..10 and 1..11? Are two enumeration types compatible if they have the same number of components but spell the literals differently?

Another difficulty with structure type compatibility is that it disallows differentiating between types with the same structure. For example, consider the following declarations:

```
type celsius = Float;
     fahrenheit = Float;
```

Variables of these two types are considered compatible under structure type compatibility, allowing them to be mixed in expressions, which is surely undesirable in this case. In general, types with different names are likely to be abstractions of different categories of problem values and should not be considered equivalent.

Ada generally uses name type compatibility but provides two type constructs, subtypes and derived types, that avoid the problems associated with that method. A **derived type** is a new type that is based on some previously defined type with which it is incompatible, although it may have identical structure. Derived types inherit all the properties of their parent types. Consider the following example:

```
type celsius is new Float;
type fahrenheit is new Float;
```

Variables of these two derived types are not compatible, although their structures are identical. Furthermore, variables of neither type are compatible with any other floating-point type. Literals are exempt from the rule. A literal such as 3.0 has the type universal real and is compatible with any floating-point type. Derived types can also include range constraints on the parent type, while still inheriting all of the parent's operations.

An Ada **subtype** is a possibly range-constrained version of an existing type. A subtype is compatible with its parent type. For example, consider the following declaration:

```
subtype Small_type is Integer range 0..99;
```

Variables of type Small_type are compatible with Integer variables.

For variables of an Ada unconstrained array type, structure compatibility is used. For example, consider the following type declaration and two object declarations:

```
type Vector is array (Integer range <>) of Integer;
Vector 1: Vector (1..10);
Vector 2: Vector (11..20);
```

HISTORY NOTE

The original definition of Pascal (Wirth, 1971) does not specify clearly when name or structure type compatibility is to be used. This is highly detrimental to portability, because a program that is correct in one implementation could be illegal in another. The ISO Standard Pascal (ISO, 1982) clearly states the type compatibility rules of the language, which are neither completely by name nor completely by structure. Structure is used in most cases, while name is used for formal parameters and a few other situations.

These two objects are compatible, even though they have different names and different subscript ranges. This is because for objects of unconstrained array types, structure compatibility, rather than name compatibility is used. Because both types have ten elements and the elements of both are of type Integer, they are compatible.

Consider the following Ada declarations of constrained anonymous types:

```
A : array (1..10) of Integer;
```

In this case, A has an anonymous but unique type. If we also had

```
B : array (1..10) of Integer;
```

A and B would be of anonymous but distinct and incompatible types, though they are structurally identical. The multiple declaration

```
C, D : array (1..10) of Integer;
```

creates two anonymous types, one for C and one for D, which are incompatible. This declaration is actually treated as if it were the following two declarations:

```
C : array (1..10) of Integer;
D : array (1..10) of Integer;
```

The result of this is that C and D are not compatible. If we had written instead

```
type List_10 is array (1..10) of Integer;
C, D : List_10;
```

then C and D would be compatible.

Type compatibility rules for Ada are more important than those for languages that have many coercions among types. For example, the two operands of an addition operator in Java can have virtually any combination of numeric types in the language. One of the operands will simply be coerced to the type of the other. But in Ada, there are no coercions of the operands of an arithmetic operator.

C uses structure type compatibility for all types except structures (C's records) and unions. Every **struct** and **union** declaration creates a new type that is not compatible with any other type. Note that **typedef** in C and C++ does not introduce a new type, it simply defines a new name for an existing type. So, any type defined with **typedef** is equivalent to its parent type. If two structures or unions are defined in two different files, structural type equivalence is used.

C++ uses name equivalence.

Variables can be declared in many languages without using type names, creating anonymous types.

In languages that do not allow users to define and name types, such as Fortran and COBOL, name equivalence obviously cannot be used.

Object-oriented languages such as Java and C++ bring another kind of type compatibility issue with them. The issue is object compatibility and its relationship to the inheritance hierarchy. This is discussed in Chapter 12.

Type compatibility in expressions is discussed in Chapter 7; type compatibility for subprogram parameters is discussed in Chapter 9.

5.8   Scope

One of the most important factors having an effect on the understanding of variables is scope. The **scope** of a variable is the range of statements in which the variable is visible. A variable is **visible** in a statement if it can be referenced in that statement.

The scope rules of a language determine how a particular occurrence of a name is associated with a variable. In particular, scope rules determine how references to variables declared outside the currently executing subprogram or block are associated with their declarations and thus their attributes (blocks are discussed in Section 5.8.2). A complete knowledge of these rules for a language is therefore essential to our ability to write or read programs in that language.

As defined in Section 5.4.3.2, a variable is local in a program unit or block if it is declared there. The **nonlocal variables** of a program unit or block are those that are visible within the program unit or block but are not declared there.

Scoping issues of classes, packages, and namespaces are discussed in Chapter 11.

5.8.1   Static Scope

ALGOL 60 introduced the method of binding names to nonlocal variables, called **static scoping,** which has been copied by many subsequent imperative languages, and many nonimperative languages as well. Static scoping is thus named because the scope of a variable can be statically determined, that is, prior to execution.

There are two categories of static-scoped languages: those in which subprograms can be nested, which creates nested static scopes, and those in which subprograms cannot be nested. In this latter category, static scopes are also created by subprograms but nested scopes are created only by nested class definitions and blocks (see Section 5.8.2).

Ada, and JavaScript allow nested subprograms, but the C-based languages do not.

Our discussion of static scoping in this chapter focuses on those languages that allow nested subprograms. So, for now we assume that *all* scopes are associated with program units. In this chapter, we also assume that scoping is the only method of accessing nonlocal variables in the languages under discussion. This is not true for all languages. It is not even true for all languages that use static scoping, but the assumption simplifies the discussion here.

When a reference to a variable is found by a compiler for a static-scoped language, the attributes of the variable are determined by finding the statement in which it is declared. In static-scoped languages with nested subprograms, this process can be thought of in the following way. Suppose a reference is made to a variable x in subprogram Sub1. The correct declaration is found by first searching the declarations of subprogram Sub1. If no declaration is found for the variable there, the search continues in the declarations of the subprogram that declared subprogram Sub1, which is called its **static parent**. If a declaration of x is not found there, the search continues to the next larger enclosing unit (the unit that declared Sub1's parent), and so forth, until a declaration for x is found or the largest unit's declarations have been searched without success. In that case, an undeclared variable error has been detected. The static parent of subprogram Sub1, and its static parent, and so forth up to and including the main program, are called the **static ancestors** of Sub1. Note that implementation techniques for static scoping, which are discussed in Chapter 10, are much more efficient than the process just described.

Consider the following Ada procedure:

```
procedure Big is
  X : Integer;
  procedure Sub1 is
    begin   -- of Sub1
    ...X...
    end;   -- of Sub1
  procedure Sub2 is
    X : Integer;
    begin   -- of Sub2
    ...
    end;   -- of Sub2
  begin   -- of Big
  ...
  end;   -- of Big
```

Under static scoping, the reference to the variable X in Sub1 is to the X declared in the procedure Big. This is true because the search for X begins in the procedure in which the reference occurs, Sub1, but no declaration for X is found there. The search thus continues in the static parent of Sub1, Big, where the declaration of X is found.

The presence of predefined names, which are discussed in Section 5.2.3, complicates this process somewhat. In some cases, a predefined name is like a keyword and can be redefined by the user. In such cases, a predefined name is used only if the user program does not contain a redefinition. In other cases, a predefined name may be reserved, which means the search for the meaning of a given name begins with the list of predefined names, even before the local scope declarations are checked.

In languages that use static scoping, regardless of whether nested subprograms are allowed, some variable declarations can be hidden from some other code segments. For example, consider the following skeletal C# method:

```
void sub() {
  int count;
  ...
  while ( ... ) {
    int count;
    count++;
    ...
  }
  ...
}
```

The reference to `count` in the **while** loop is to that loop's local `count`. In this case, the `count` of `sub` is hidden from the code inside the **while** loop. In general, a declaration for a variable effectively hides any declaration of a variable with the same name in a larger enclosing scope.

In Ada, hidden variables from ancestor scopes can be accessed with selective references, which include the ancestor scope's name. For example, in the preceding program, the `x` declared in the main program can be accessed in `Sub1` by the reference `Main.X`.

Although the C-based languages do not allow subprograms to be nested inside other subprogram definitions, they do have global variables. These variables are declared outside any subprogram definition. Local variables can hide these globals, as in Ada. In C++, such hidden globals can be accessed using the scope operator (`::`). For example, if `x` is a global that is hidden in a subprogram by a local named `x`, the global could be referenced as `::x`.

5.8.2 Blocks

Many languages allow new static scopes to be defined in the midst of executable code. This powerful concept, introduced in ALGOL 60, allows a section of code to have its own local variables whose scope is minimized. Such variables are typically stack dynamic, so they have their storage allocated when the section is entered and deallocated when the section is exited. Such a section of code is called a **block**.

In Ada, blocks are specified with **declare** clauses, as in

```
...
declare Temp : Integer;
begin
Temp := First;
First := Second;
```

```
Second := Temp;
end;
...
```

Note that if an Ada compound statement (delimited by **begin** and **end**) does not include declarations, the **declare** clause is not included. Blocks provide the origin of the phrase **block-structured language.**

The C-based languages allow any compound statement (a statement sequence surrounded by matched braces) to have declarations and thus define a new scope. Such compound statements are blocks. For example, if `list` were an integer array, one could write

```
if (list[i] < list[j]) {
  int temp;
  temp = list[i];
  list[i] = list[j];
  list[j] = temp;
}
```

The scopes created by blocks are treated exactly like those created by subprograms. References to variables in a block that are not declared there are connected to declarations by searching enclosing scopes in order of increasing size.

The C-based languages allow variable definitions to appear anywhere in functions. When a definition appears at a position other than at the beginning of a function, that variable's scope is from its definition statement to the end of the function.

The **for** statements of C++, Java, and C# allow variable definitions in their initialization expressions. In early versions of C++, the scope of such a variable was from its definition to the end of the smallest enclosing block. In the standard version, however, the scope is restricted to the **for** construct, as is the case with Java and C#.

The classes of C++, Java, and C# treat their instance variables different from the variables defined in their methods. The scope of a variable defined in a method starts at the definition. However, regardless of where a variable is defined in a class, its scope is the whole class.

The class and method definitions in object-oriented languages also create nested static scopes. This is discussed in Chapter 12.

5.8.3   Evaluation of Static Scoping

Static scoping provides a method of nonlocal access that works well in many situations. However, it is not without its problems. Consider the program whose skeletal structure is shown in Figure 5.1. For this example, assume that all scopes are created by the definitions of the main program and the procedures.

This program contains an overall scope for main, with two procedures that define scopes inside main, A and B. Inside A are scopes for the procedures C and D. Inside B is the scope of procedure E. We assume that the necessary data and procedure access determined the structure of this program. The required procedure access is as follows: main can call A and B, A can call C and D, and B can call A and E.

It is convenient to view the structure of the program as a tree in which each node represents a procedure and thus a scope. A tree representation of the program of Figure 5.1 is shown in Figure 5.2. The structure of this program may appear to be a very natural program organization that clearly reflects the design needs. However, a graph of the potential procedure calls of this system, shown in Figure 5.3, shows that a great deal of calling opportunity beyond that required is possible. In some languages, there are even more possibilities than are shown in this figure. For example, if forward subprogram calls are allowed, the C and D subprograms could also call B.

Figure 5.4 shows the desired calls of the example program. The difference between Figures 5.3 and 5.4 illustrates the number of possible calls that are not necessary in this specific application.

A programmer could mistakenly call a subprogram that should not have been callable, which would not be detected as an error by the compiler. That delays detection of the error until run time, which may make its correction

Figure 5.1

The structure of a program

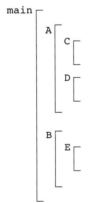

Figure 5.2

The tree structure of the program in Figure 5.1

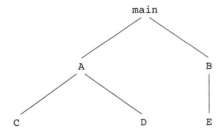

Figure 5.3

The potential call
graph of the program
in Figure 5.1

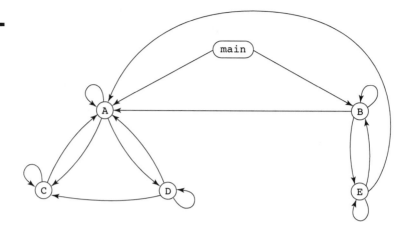

Figure 5.4

The graph of the desir-
able calls in the pro-
gram in Figure 5.1

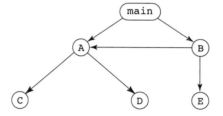

more costly. Therefore, access to procedures should be restricted to those that are necessary.

Too much data access is a closely related problem. For example, all variables declared in the main program are visible to all of the procedures, whether or not that is desired, and there is no way to avoid it.

To illustrate another kind of problem with static scoping, consider the following scenario. Suppose that after the program has been developed and tested, a modification of its specification is required. In particular, suppose that procedure E must now gain access to some variables of the scope of D. One way to provide that access is to move E inside the scope of D. But then E can no longer access the scope of B, which it presumably needs (otherwise, why was it there?). Another solution is to move the variables defined in D that are needed by E into main. This would allow access by all the procedures, which would be more than is needed and thus creates the possibility of incorrect accesses. For example, a misspelled identifier in a procedure can be taken as a reference to an identifier in some enclosing scope, instead of being detected as an error. Furthermore, suppose the variable that is moved to main is named x, and x is needed by D and E. But suppose that there is a variable named x declared in A. That would hide the correct x from its original owner, D.

One final problem with moving the declaration of x to main is that it is harmful to readability to have the declaration of variables so far from their uses.

The problems associated with variable visibility with static scoping are also present for subprogram access. In the tree of Figure 5.2, suppose that, due to some specification change, procedure E needed to call procedure D. This could only be accomplished by moving D to nest directly in main, assuming that it was also needed by either A or C. It would then also lose access to the variables defined in A. This solution, when used repeatedly, results in programs that begin with long lists of low-level utility procedures.

Thus getting around the restrictions of static scoping can lead to program designs that bear little resemblance to the original, even in areas of the program in which changes have not been made. Designers are encouraged to use far more globals than are necessary. All procedures can end up being nested at the same level, in the main program, using globals instead of deeper levels of nesting. Moreover, the final design may be awkward and contrived, and it may not reflect the underlying conceptual design. These and other defects of static scoping are discussed in detail in Clarke, Wileden, and Wolf (1980). One solution to the problems of static scoping is an encapsulation construct, discussed in Chapter 11, which is included in many newer languages.

5.8.4 Dynamic Scope

The scope of variables in APL, SNOBOL4, and the early versions of LISP is dynamic. Perl and COMMON LISP also allow variables to be declared to have dynamic scope, although these languages also use static scoping. **Dynamic scoping** is based on the calling sequence of subprograms, not on their spatial relationship to each other. Thus the scope can be determined only at run time.

Consider again the procedure Big from Section 5.8.1, which is shown again here:

```
procedure Big is
  X : Integer;
  procedure Sub1 is
    begin  -- of Sub1
    ...X...
    end;  -- of Sub1
  procedure Sub2 is
    X : Integer;
    begin  -- of Sub2
    ...
    end;  -- of Sub2
  begin  -- of Big
  ...
  end;  -- of Big
```

Assume that dynamic scoping rules apply to nonlocal references. The meaning of the identifier x referenced in Sub1 is dynamic—it cannot be determined at compile time. It may reference the variable from either declaration of x, depending on the calling sequence.

One way the correct meaning of x can be determined at run time is to begin the search with the local declarations. This is also the way the process begins with static scoping, but that is where the similarity between the two techniques ends. When the search of local declarations fails, the declarations of the dynamic parent, or calling procedure, are searched. If a declaration for x is not found there, the search continues in that procedure's dynamic parent, and so forth, until a declaration for x is found. If none is found in any dynamic ancestor, it is a run-time error.

Consider the two different call sequences for Sub1 in the example above. First, Big calls Sub2, which calls Sub1. In this case, the search proceeds from the local procedure, Sub1, to its caller, Sub2, where a declaration for x is found. So the reference to x in Sub1 in this case is to the x declared in Sub2. Next, Sub1 is called directly from Big. In this case, the dynamic parent of Sub1 is Big, and the reference is to the x declared in Big.

Note that if static scoping were used, in either calling sequence discussed above the reference to x in Sub1 would be to Big's x.

Perl's dynamic scoping is unusual—in fact it is not exactly like that discussed in this section, although the semantics are often that of traditional dynamic scoping (see Programming Exercise 1).

5.8.5 Evaluation of Dynamic Scoping

The effect of dynamic scoping on programming is profound. The correct attributes of nonlocal variables visible to a program statement cannot be determined statically. Furthermore, such variables are not always the same. A statement in a subprogram that contains a reference to a nonlocal variable can refer to different nonlocal variables during different executions of the subprogam. Several kinds of programming problems follow directly from dynamic scoping.

First, during the time span beginning when a subprogram begins its execution and ending when that execution ends, the local variables of the subprogram are all visible to any other executing subprogram, regardless of its textual proximity or how execution got to the currently executing subprogram. There is no way to protect local variables from this accessibility. Subprograms are *always* executed in the environment of all previously called subprograms that have not yet completed their executions. As a result, dynamic scoping results in less reliable programs than static scoping.

A second problem with dynamic scoping is the inability to statically type check references to nonlocals. This results from the inability to statically determine the declaration for a variable referenced as a nonlocal.

Dynamic scoping also makes programs much more difficult to read, because the calling sequence of subprograms must be known to determine the meaning of references to nonlocal variables. This can be virtually impossible for a human reader.

Finally, accesses to nonlocal variables in dynamic-scoped languages take far longer than accesses to nonlocals when static scoping is used. The reason for this is explained in Chapter 10.

On the other hand, dynamic scoping is not without merit. In some cases, the parameters passed from one subprogram to another are simply variables that are defined in the caller. None of these need to be passed in a dynamically scoped language, because they are implicitly visible in the called subprogram.

It is not difficult to understand why dynamic scoping is not as widely used as static scoping. Programs in static-scoped languages are easier to read, more reliable, and execute faster than equivalent programs in dynamic-scoped languages. It was precisely for these reasons that dynamic scoping was replaced by static scoping in most current dialects of LISP. Implementation methods for both static and dynamic scoping are discussed in Chapter 10.

5.9 Scope and Lifetime

Sometimes the scope and lifetime of a variable appear to be related. For example, consider a variable that is declared in a Java method that contains no method calls. The scope of such a variable is from its declaration to the end of the method. The lifetime of that variable is the period of time beginning when the method is entered and ending when execution of the method terminates. Although the scope and lifetime of the variable are clearly not the same because static scope is a textual, or spatial, concept whereas lifetime is a temporal concept, they at least appear to be related in this case.

This apparent relationship between scope and lifetime does not hold in other situations. In C and C++, for example, a variable that is declared in a function using the specifier **static** is statically bound to the scope of that function and is also statically bound to storage. So its scope is static and local to the function, but its lifetime extends over the entire execution of the program of which it is a part.

Scope and lifetime are also unrelated when subprogram calls are involved. Consider the following C++ functions:

```
void printheader() {
  ...
  } /* end of printheader */
void compute() {
  int sum;
  ...
  printheader();
  } /* end of compute */
```

The scope of the variable `sum` is completely contained within the `compute` function. It does not extend to the body of the function `printheader`, although `printheader` executes in the midst of the execution of `compute`. However, the lifetime of `sum` extends over the time during which `printheader` executes. Whatever storage location `sum` is bound to before the call to `printheader`, that binding will continue during and after the execution of `printheader`.

5.10   Referencing Environments

The **referencing environment** of a statement is the collection of all names that are visible in the statement. The referencing environment of a statement in a static-scoped language is the variables declared in its local scope plus the collection of all variables of its ancestor scopes that are visible. In such a language, the referencing environment of a statement is needed while that statement is being compiled, so code and data structures can be created to allow references to variables from other scopes during run time. Techniques for implementing references to nonlocal variables in both static- and dynamic-scoped languages are discussed in Chapter 10.

In Ada, scopes can be created by procedure definitions. The referencing environment of a statement includes the local variables, plus all of the variables declared in the procedures in which the statement is nested (excluding variables in nonlocal scopes that are hidden by declarations in nearer procedures). Each procedure definition creates a new scope and thus a new environment. Consider the following Ada skeletal program:

```ada
procedure Example is
  A, B : Integer;
  ...
  procedure Sub1 is
    X, Y : Integer;
    begin  -- of Sub1
    ...    ◄──────────── 1
    end;   -- of Sub1
  procedure Sub2 is
    X : Integer;
    ...
    procedure Sub3 is
      X : Integer;
      begin  -- of Sub3
      ...◄──────────── 2
      end;   -- of Sub3
    begin  -- of Sub2
    ...  ◄──────────── 3
```

```
    end;   { Sub2 }
  begin   { Example }
  ...        ◄─────────────── 4
  end.   { Example }
```

The referencing environments of the indicated program points are as follows:

Point	Referencing Environment
1	X and Y of Sub1, A and B of Example
2	X of Sub3, (X of Sub2 is hidden), A and B of Example
3	X of Sub2, A and B of Example
4	A and B of Example

Now consider the variable declarations of this skeletal program. First note that, although the scope of Sub1 is at a higher level (it is less deeply nested) than Sub3, the scope of Sub1 is not a static ancestor of Sub3, so Sub3 does not have access to the variables declared in Sub1. There is a good reason for this. The variables declared in Sub1 are stack dynamic, so they are not bound to storage if Sub1 is not in execution. Because Sub3 can be in execution when Sub1 is not, it cannot be allowed to access variables in Sub1, which would not necessarily be bound to storage during the execution of Sub3.

A subprogram is **active** if its execution has begun but has not yet terminated. The referencing environment of a statement in a dynamically scoped language is the locally declared variables, plus the variables of all other subprograms that are currently active. Once again, some variables in active subprograms can be hidden from the referencing environment. Recent subprogram activations can have declarations for variables that hide variables with the same names in previous subprogram activations.

Consider the following example program. Assume that the only function calls are the following: main calls sub2, which calls sub1.

```
void sub1() {
  int a, b;
  ... ◄─────────────── 1
}  /* end of sub1 */
void sub2() {
  int b, c;
  ... ◄───────────────2
  sub1;
}  /* end of sub2 */
void main() {
  int c, d;
  ... ◄───────────────3
  sub2();
}  /* end of main */
```

The referencing environments of the indicated program points are as follows:

Point	Referencing Environment
1	a and b of sub1, c of sub2, d of main, , (c of main and b of sub2 are hidden)
2	b and c of sub2, d of main, (c of main is hidden)
3	c and d of main

5.11   Named Constants

A **named constant** is a variable that is bound to a value only at the time it is bound to storage; its value cannot be changed by assignment or by an input statement. Named constants are useful as aids to readability and program reliability. Readability can be improved, for example, by using the name pi instead of the constant 3.14159.

Another important use of named constants is in programs that process a fixed number of data values, say 100. Such programs usually use the constant 100 in a number of locations for declaring array subscript ranges, for loop control limits, and other uses. Consider the following skeletal Java program segment:

```java
void example() {
  int[] intList = new int[100];
  String[] strList = new String[100];
  ...
  for (index = 0; index < 100; index++) {
    ...
  }
  ...
  for (index = 0; index < 100; index++) {
    ...
  }
  ...
  average = sum / 100;
  ...
}
```

When this program must be modified to deal with a different number of data values, all occurrences of 100 must be found and changed. On a large program, this can be tedious and error-prone. An easier and more reliable method is to use a named constant, as in:

```java
void example() {
  final int len = 100;
  int[] intList = new int[len];
  String[] strList = new String[len];
```

```
...
for (index = 0; index < len; index++) {
  ...
}
...
for (index = 0; index < len; index++) {
  ...
}
...
average = sum / len;
...
}
```

Now when the length must be changed, only one line must be changed, regardless of the number of times it is used in the program. This is another example of the benefits of abstraction. The name `len` is an abstraction for the number of elements in some arrays and the number of iterations in some loops. This illustrates how named constants can aid modifiability.

Fortran 95 allows only constant expressions to be used as the values of its named constants. These constant expressions can contain previously declared named constants, constant values, and operators. The reason for the restriction to constants and constant expressions in Fortran 95 is that it uses static binding of values to named constants. Named constants in languages that use static binding of values are sometimes called **manifest constants.**

Ada, C++, and Java allow dynamic binding of values to named constants. This allows expressions containing variables to be assigned to constants in the declarations. For example, the C++ statement

```
const int result = 2 * width + 1;
```

declares `result` to be an integer type named constant whose value is set to the value of the expression `2 * width + 1`, where the value of the variable `width` must be visible when `max` is allocated and bound to its value.

Ada allows named constants of enumeration and structured types, which are discussed in Chapter 6.

5.12   Variable Initialization

The discussion of binding values to named constants naturally leads to the topic of initialization of variables, because binding a value to a named constant is the same process, except it is permanent.

In many instances, it is convenient for variables to have values before the code of the program or subprogram in which they are declared begins executing. The binding of a variable to a value at the time it is bound to storage is called **initialization.** If the variable is statically bound to storage, binding and initialization occur before run time. If the storage binding is dynamic, initialization is also dynamic.

In Fortran, initial values of variables can be specified in a `Data` statement, as in

```
Real Pi
Integer Sum
Data Sum /0/, Pi /3.14159/
```

which initializes `Sum` to 0 and `PI` to `3.14159`. The actual initializations take place at compile time, in this case. Once execution begins, `Sum` and `Pi` are like any other variables.

In many languages, initial values of variables can be specified in the declaration statement, as in the Java declaration

```
int sum = 0;
```

In general, initialization occurs only once for static variables, but it occurs with every allocation for dynamically allocated variables, such as the local variables in a Java method.

SUMMARY

Case sensitivity and the relationship of names to special words, which are either reserved words or keywords, are the design issues for names.

Variables can be characterized by the sextuple of attributes: name, address, value, type, lifetime, scope.

Aliases are two or more names bound to the same storage address. They are regarded as detrimental to reliability, but are difficult to eliminate entirely from a language.

Binding is the association of attributes with program entities. Knowledge of the binding times of attributes to entities is essential to understanding the semantics of programming languages. Binding can be static or dynamic. Declarations, either explicit or implicit, provide a means of specifying the static binding of variables to types. In general, dynamic binding allows greater flexibility but at the expense of readability, efficiency, and reliability.

Scalar variables can be separated into four categories by considering their lifetimes. These are static, stack dynamic, explicit heap dynamic, and implicit heap dynamic.

Strong typing is the concept of requiring that all type errors be detected. The advantage of strong typing is increased reliability.

The type compatibility rules of a language have an important effect on the operations provided for the values in the language. Type compatibility is generally defined in terms of name compatibility or structure compatibility.

Static scoping is a central feature of ALGOL 60 and some of its descendants. It provides an efficient method of allowing visibility of nonlocal variables in subprograms. Dynamic scoping provides more flexibility than static scoping but, again, at the expense of readability, reliability, and efficiency.

The referencing environment of a statement is the collection of all of the variables that are visible to that statement.

Named constants are simply variables that are bound to values only when they are bound to storage. Initialization is the binding of a variable to a value at the time the variable is bound to storage.

REVIEW QUESTIONS

1. What are the design issues for names?
2. What is the potential danger of case-sensitive names?
3. In what way are reserved words better than keywords?
4. What is an alias?
5. Which category of C++ reference variables are always aliases?
6. What is the *l*-value of a variable? What is the *r*-value?
7. Define *binding* and *binding time*.
8. After language design and implementation, what are the four times bindings can take place in a program?
9. Define *static binding* and *dynamic binding*.
10. What are the advantages and disadvantage of implicit declarations?
11. What are the advantages and disadvantages of dynamic type binding?
12. Define *static, stack-dynamic, explicit heap-dynamic,* and *implicit heap-dynamic variables*. What are the advantages and disadvantages of these?
13. Define *coercion, type error, type checking,* and *strong typing*.
14. Define *name type compatibility* and *structure type compatibility*. What are the relative merits of these two?
15. What is the difference between an Ada derived type and an Ada subtype?
16. Define *lifetime, scope, static scope,* and *dynamic scope*.
17. How is a reference to a nonlocal variable in a static-scoped program connected to its definition?
18. What is the general problem with static scoping?
19. What is the referencing environment of a statement?
20. What is a static ancestor of a subprogram? What is a dynamic ancestor of a subprogram?
21. What is a block?
22. What are the advantages and disadvantages of dynamic scoping?
23. What are the advantages of named constants?

PROBLEM SET

1. Decide which of the following identifier forms is most readable, and then support that decision.

   ```
   SumOfSales
   sum_of_sales
   SUMOFSALES
   ```

2. Some programming languages are typeless. What are the obvious advantages and disadvantages of having no types in a language?

3. One common use of Fortran's `Equivalence` is the following: A large array of numeric values is made available to a subprogram as a parameter. The array contains many different unrelated variables, rather than a collection of repetitions of the same variable. It is represented as an array to reduce the number of names that need to be passed as parameters. Within the subprogram, a lengthy `Equivalence` statement is used to create connotative names as aliases to the various array elements, which increases the readability of the code of the subprogram. Is this a good idea or not? What alternatives to aliasing are available?

4. Write a simple assignment statement with one arithmetic operator in some language you know. For each component of the statement, list the various bindings that are required to determine the semantics when the statement is executed. For each binding, indicate the binding time used for the language.

5. Dynamic type binding is closely related to implicit heap-dynamic variables. Explain this relationship.

6. Describe a situation when a history-sensitive variable in a subprogram is useful.

7. Look up the definition of *strongly typed* as given in Gehani (1983) and compare it with the definition given in this chapter. How do they differ?

8. Consider the following Ada skeletal program:

   ```
   procedure Main is
     X : Integer;
     procedure Sub3;   -- This is a declaration of Sub3
                       -- It allows Sub1 to call it
     procedure Sub1 is
       X : Integer;
       procedure Sub2 is
         begin  -- of Sub2
         ...
         end;  -- of Sub2
       begin  -- of Sub1
       ...
   ```

```
    end;   -- of Sub1
procedure Sub3 is
  begin   -- of Sub3
    ...
    end;   -- of Sub3
  begin   -- of Main
    ...
    end;   -- of Main
```

Assume that the execution of this program is in the following unit order:

```
Main calls Sub1
Sub1 calls Sub2
Sub2 calls Sub3
```

a. Assuming static scoping, which declaration of x is the correct one for a reference to x in the following:

    i. Sub1

    ii. Sub2

    iii. Sub3

b. Repeat part a, but assume dynamic scoping.

9. Assume the following Ada program was compiled and executed using static scoping rules. What value of x is printed in procedure Sub1? Under dynamic scoping rules, what value of x is printed in procedure Sub1?

```
procedure Main is
  X : Integer;
  procedure Sub1 is
    begin   -- of Sub1
    Put(X);
    end;   -- of Sub1
  procedure Sub2 is
    X : Integer;
    begin   -- of Sub2
    X := 10;
    Sub1
    end;   -- of Sub2
  begin   -- of Main
  X := 5;
  Sub2
  end;   -- of Main
```

10. Consider the following program:

```
procedure Main is
  X, Y, Z : Integer;
  procedure Sub1 is
    A, Y, Z : Integer;
    procedure Sub2 is
    A, B, Z : Integer;
    begin  -- of Sub2
    . . .
      end;  -- of Sub2
    begin  -- of Sub1
    . . .
    end;  -- of Sub1
  procedure Sub3 is
    A, X, W : Integer;
    begin  -- of Sub3
    . . .
    end;  -- of Sub3
  begin  -- of Main
  . . .
  end;  -- of Main
```

List all the variables, along with the program units where they are declared, that are visible in the bodies of Sub1, Sub2, and Sub3, assuming static scoping is used.

11. Consider the following program:

```
procedure Main is
  X, Y, Z : Integer;
  procedure Sub1 is
    A, Y, Z : Integer;
    begin  -- of Sub1
    . . .
    end;  -- of Sub1
  procedure Sub2 is
    A, X, W : Integer;
    procedure Sub3 is
      A, B, Z : Integer;
      begin  -- of Sub3
      . . .
      end;  -- of Sub3
    begin  -- op Sub2
    . . .
```

```
      end;  -- of Sub2
   begin  -- of Main
    ...
   end;  -- of Main
```

List all the variables, along with the program units where they are declared, that are visible in the bodies of Sub1, Sub2, and Sub3, assuming static scoping is used.

12. Consider the following C program:

```c
void fun(void) {
  int a, b, c; /* definition 1 */
  ...
  while (...) {
    int b, c, d; /*definition 2 */
    ... <-----------------1
    while (...) {
      int c, d, e; /* definition 3 */
      ...<-----------------2
    }
    ... <-----------------3
  }
  ... <-----------------4
}
```

For each of the four marked points in this function, list each visible variable, along with the number of the definition statement that defines it.

13. Consider the following skeletal C program:

```c
void fun1(void);   /* prototype */
void fun2(void);   /* prototype */
void fun3(void);   /* prototype */
void main() {
  int a, b, c;
  ...
}
void fun1(void) {
  int b, c, d;
  ...
}
void fun2(void) {
  int c, d, e;
  ...
}
void fun3(void) {
  int d, e, f;
  ...
}
```

Given the following calling sequences and assuming that dynamic scoping is used, what variables are visible during execution of the last function called? Include with each visible variable the name of the function in which it was defined.

a. main calls fun1; fun1 calls fun2; fun2 calls fun3.

b. main calls fun1; fun1 calls fun3.

c. main calls fun2; fun2 calls fun3; fun3 calls fun1.

d. main calls fun3; fun3 calls fun1.

e. main calls fun1; fun1 calls fun3; fun3 calls fun2.

f. main calls fun3; fun3 calls fun2; fun2 calls fun1.

14. Consider the following program:

```
procedure Main is
   X, Y, Z : Integer;
   procedure Sub1 is
      A, Y, Z : Integer;
      begin   -- of Sub1
      ...
      end;   -- of Sub1
   procedure Sub2 is
      A, B, Z : Integer;
      begin   -- of Sub2
      ...
      end;   -- of Sub2
   procedure Sub3 is
      A, X, W : Integer;
      begin   -- of Sub3
      ...
      end;   -- of Sub3
   begin   -- of Main
   ...
   end;   -- of Main
```

Given the following calling sequences and assuming that dynamic scoping is used, what variables are visible during execution of the last subprogram activated? Include with each visible variable the name of the unit where it is declared.

a. Main calls Sub1; Sub1 calls Sub2; Sub2 calls Sub3.

b. Main calls Sub1; Sub1 calls Sub3.

c. Main calls Sub2; Sub2 calls Sub3; Sub3 calls Sub1.

d. Main calls Sub3; Sub3 calls Sub1.

e. Main calls Sub1; Sub1 calls Sub3; Sub3 calls Sub2.

f. Main calls Sub3; Sub3 calls Sub2; Sub2 calls Sub1.

PROGRAMMING EXERCISES

1. Perl allows both static and a kind of dynamic scoping. Write a Perl program that uses both and clearly shows the difference in effect of the two. Explain clearly the difference between the dynamic scoping described in this chapter and that implemented in Perl.

2. Write a COMMON LISP program that clearly shows the difference between static and dynamic scoping.

3. Write a JavaScript script that has subprograms nested three deep and in which each nested subprogram references variables defined in all of its enclosing subprograms.

4. Write a C function that includes the following sequence of statements:

```
x = 21;
int x;
x = 42;
```

Run the program and explain the results. Rewrite the same code in C++ and Java and compare the results.

6

Data Types

This chapter first introduces the concept of a data type and the characteristics of the common primitive data types. Then the designs of enumeration and subrange types are discussed. Next, structured data types, specifically arrays, records, and unions, are investigated. Set types are then discussed, followed by an in-depth look at pointers.

For each of the various categories of data types, the design issues are stated and the design choices made by the designers of some common languages are explained. These designs are then evaluated.

Implementation methods for data types often have a significant impact on their design. Therefore, implementation of the various data types is another important part of this chapter, especially for the implementation of arrays.

6.1   Introduction

A **data type** defines a collection of data objects and a set of predefined operations on those objects. Computer programs produce results by manipulating data. An important factor in determining the ease with which they can perform this task is how well the data types match the real-world problem space. It is therefore crucial that a language support an appropriate variety of data types and structures.

The contemporary concepts of data typing have evolved over the last 45 years. In the earliest languages, all problem space data structures had to be modeled with only a few basic language-supported data structures. For example, in pre-90 Fortrans, linked lists and binary trees were commonly modeled with arrays.

The data structures of COBOL took the first step away from the Fortran I model by allowing programmers to specify the accuracy of decimal data values, and also by providing a structured data type for records of information. PL/I extended the capability of accuracy specification to integer and floating-point types. This has since been incorporated in Ada and Fortran. The designers of PL/I included many data types, with the intent of supporting a large range of applications. A better approach, introduced in ALGOL 68, is to provide a few basic types and a few flexible structure-defining operators that allow a programmer to design a data structure for each need. This was clearly one of the most important advances in the evolution of data type design. User-defined types provide improved readability through the use of meaningful names for types. They allow type checking of the variables of a special category of use, which would otherwise not be possible. User-defined types also aid modifiability: A programmer can change the type of a category of variables in a program by changing only a type declaration statement.

Ada 83 embodied the contemporary concepts in data type design of the late 1970s, which resulted from a natural extension to the idea of user-defined types. The philosophy of user-defined data types is that the user should be allowed to create a unique type for each unique class of variables in the problem space. Moreover, the language must enforce the uniqueness of the types, which are in fact abstractions of problem space variables. This is a powerful concept, and it has a significant impact on the overall process of software design. Taking this concept a step farther, we arrive at abstract data types, which can be simulated in Ada 83 and are part of most subsequent programming languages. The fundamental idea of an abstract data type is that the use of a type is separated from the representation and set of operations on values of that type. All of the types provided by a high-level programming language are abstract data types. User-defined abstract data types are discussed in detail in Chapter 11.

The two most common structured (nonscalar) data types are arrays and records. These and a few other data types are specified by type operators, or constructors, which are used to form type expressions. For example, in C the type operators are brackets, parentheses, and asterisks, which are used to specify arrays, functions, and pointers.

It is convenient, both logically and concretely, to think of variables in terms of descriptors. A **descriptor** is the collection of attributes of a variable. In an implementation, a descriptor is a collection of memory cells that store variable attributes. If the attributes are all static, descriptors are required only at compile time. They are built by the compiler, usually as a part of the symbol table, and are used during compilation. For dynamic attributes, however, part or all of the descriptor must be maintained during execution. In this case, the descriptor is used by the run-time system. In all cases, descriptors are used for type checking and by allocation and deallocation operations.

The word *object* is often associated with the value of a variable and the space it occupies. In this book, however, we reserve *object* exclusively for instances of user-defined abstract data types, rather than also using it for the values of variables of predefined types. In object-oriented languages, every instance of every class, whether predefined or user-defined, is called an object. Objects are discussed in detail in Chapters 11 and 12.

In the following sections all common data types are discussed. For most, design issues particular to the type are stated. For all, one or more example designs are described. One design issue is fundamental to all data types: What operations are provided for variables of the type and how are they specified?

6.2 Primitive Data Types

Data types that are not defined in terms of other types are called **primitive data types.** Nearly all programming languages provide a set of primitive data types. Some of the primitive types are merely reflections of the hardware, for example, integer types. Others require only a little nonhardware support for their implementation.

The primitive data types of a language are used, along with one or more type constructors, to provide the structured types.

6.2.1 Numeric Types

Many early programming languages had only numeric primitive types. These types still play a central role among the types supported by contemporary languages.

6.2.1.1 Integer

The most common primitive numeric data type is **integer.** Many computers now support several sizes of integers, and these capabilities are reflected in some programming languages. For example, Java includes four signed integer sizes: **byte**, **short**, **int**, and **long**. Some languages, such as C++ and C#, include unsigned integer types, which are simply types for integer values without signs. Unsigned types are often used for binary data.

A signed integer value is represented in a computer by a string of bits, with one of the bits, typically the leftmost, representing the sign. Integer types are supported directly by the hardware.

A negative integer could be stored in sign-magnitude notation, in which the sign bit is set to indicate negative and the remainder of the bit string represents the absolute value of the number. Sign-magnitude notation, however, does not lend itself to computer arithmetic. Most computers now use a notation called **twos complement** to store negative integers, which is convenient for addition and subtraction. In twos-complement notation, the representation of a negative integer is formed by taking the logical complement of the positive version of the number and adding one. Ones-complement notation is still used by some computers. In ones-complement notation, the negative of an integer is stored as the logical complement of its absolute value. Ones-complement notation has the disadvantage that it has two representations of zero. See any book on assembly language programming for details of integer representations.

6.2.1.2 Floating-point

Floating-point data types model real numbers, but the representations are only approximations for most real values. For example, neither of the fundamental numbers π or e (the base for the natural logarithms) can be correctly represented in floating-point notation. Of course, neither of these numbers can be accurately represented in any finite space. On most computers, floating-point numbers are stored in binary, which exacerbates the problem. For example, even the value 0.1 in decimal cannot be represented by a finite number of binary digits. Another problem with floating-point types is the loss of accuracy through arithmetic operations. For more information on the problems of floating-point notation, see Knuth (1981).

Floating-point values are represented as fractions and exponents, a form that is borrowed from scientific notation. Older computers used a variety of different representations for floating-point values. However, most newer machines use the IEEE Floating-Point Standard 754 format. Language implementers use whatever representation is supported by the hardware. Most languages include two floating-point types, often called **float** and **double.** The float type is the standard size, usually being stored in 4 bytes of memory. The double type is provided for situations where larger fractional parts are needed. Double-precision variables usually occupy twice as much storage as float variables and provide at least twice the number of bits of fraction.

The collection of values that can be represented by a floating-point type is defined in terms of precision and range. **Precision** is the accuracy of the fractional part of a value, measured as the number of bits. **Range** is a combination of the range of fractions, and, more importantly, the range of exponents.

Figure 6.1 shows the IEEE Floating-Point Standard 754 format for single- and double-precision representation (IEEE, 1985). Details of the IEEE formats can be found in Tanenbaum (1998).

6.2.1.3 Decimal

Most larger computers that are designed to support business systems applications have hardware support for **decimal** data types. Decimal data types store a fixed number of decimal digits, with the decimal point at a fixed position in the value. These are the primary data types for business data processing and are therefore essential to COBOL. C# also has a decimal data type.

Decimal types have the advantage of being capable of precisely storing decimal values, at least those within a restricted range, which cannot be done in floating-point. The disadvantages of decimal types are that the range of values is restricted because no exponents are allowed, and their representation in memory is wasteful.

Decimal types are stored very much like character strings, using binary codes for the decimal digits. These representations are called **binary coded**

Figure 6.1

IEEE floating-point formats: (a) Single precision, (b) Double precision decimal (BCD). In some cases, they are stored one digit per byte, but in others they are packed two digits per byte. Either way, they take more storage than binary representations. It takes at least four bits to code a decimal digit. Therefore, to store a six-digit coded decimal number requires 24 bits of memory. However, it takes only 20 bits to store the same number in binary. The operations on decimal values are done in hardware on machines that have such capabilities; otherwise, they are simulated in software.

6.2.2   Boolean Types

Boolean types are perhaps the simplest of all types. Their range of values has only two elements, one for true and one for false. They were introduced in ALGOL 60 and have been included in most general-purpose languages designed since 1960. One popular exception is C89, in which numeric expressions are used as conditionals. In such expressions, all operands with nonzero values are considered true, and zero is considered false. Although C99 and C++ have a Boolean type, they also allow numeric expressions to be used as if they were Boolean.

Boolean types are often used to represent switches or flags in programs. Although other types, such as integers, can be used for these purposes, the use of Boolean types is more readable.

A Boolean value could be represented by a single bit, but because a single bit of memory is difficult to access efficiently on many machines, they are often stored in the smallest efficiently addressable cell of memory, typically a byte.

6.2.3   Character Types

Character data are stored in computers as numeric codings. Traditionally, the most commonly used coding was the 8-bit code ASCII (American Standard Code for Information Interchange), which uses the values 0 to 127 to code 128 different characters. ISO 8859-1 is another 8-bit character code, but it allows 256 different characters. Ada 95 uses ISO 8859-1.

Because of the globalization of business and the need for computers to communicate with other computers around the world, the ASCII character set is rapidly becoming inadequate. A 16-bit character set named Unicode has been developed as an alternative. Unicode includes the characters from most of the world's natural languages. For example, Unicode includes the Cyrillic alphabet, as used in Serbia, and the Thai digits. The first 128 characters of Unicode are identical to those of ASCII. Java was the first widely used language to use the Unicode character set. Since then, it has found its way into JavaScript and C#.

To provide the means of processing codings of single characters, many programming languages include a primitive type for them.

6.3 Character String Types

A **character string type** is one in which the values consist of sequences of characters. Character string constants are used to label output, and input and output of all kinds of data are often done in terms of strings. Of course, character strings also are an essential type for all programs that do character manipulation.

6.3.1 Design Issues

The two most important design issues that are specific to character string types are the following:

- Should strings be simply a special kind of character array or a primitive type (with no array-style subscripting operations)?
- Should strings have static or dynamic length?

6.3.2 Strings and Their Operations

If strings are not defined as a primitive type, string data is usually stored in arrays of single characters and referenced as such in the language. This is the approach taken by C and C++.

C and C++ use **char** arrays to store character strings and provide a collection of string operations through a standard library whose header file is `string.h`. Most uses of strings and most of the library functions use the convention that character strings are terminated with a special character, null, which is represented with zero. This is an alternative to maintaining the length of string variables. The library operations simply carry out their operations until the null character appears in the string being operated on. Library functions that construct strings often supply the null character. The character string literals that are built by the compiler have the null character. For example, consider the following declaration:

```
char *str = "apples";
```

In this example, `str` is a **char** pointer set to point at the string of characters, `apples0`, where `0` is the null character. This initialization of `str` is legal because character string literals are represented by **char** pointers, rather than the string itself.

Some of the most commonly used library functions for character strings in C and C++ are `strcpy`, which moves strings; `strcat`, which catenates one given string onto another; `strcmp`, which lexicographically compares (by the order of their codes) two given strings; and `strlen`, which returns the number of characters, not counting the null, in the given string. The parameters and return values for most of the string manipulation functions are **char** pointers that point to arrays of **char**. Parameters can also be string literals.

In Java, strings are supported as a primitive type by the `String` class, whose values are constant strings, and the `StringBuffer` class, whose values are changeable and are more like arrays of single characters. Subscripting is allowed on `StringBuffer` variables. C# includes string classes that are similar to those of Java. In addition to C-style strings, C++ also supports strings through its standard class library, which is also similar to that of Java.

Fortran 95 treats strings as a primitive type and provides assignment, relational operators, catenation, and substring reference operations for them. A **substring reference** is a reference to a substring of a given string. Substring references are discussed in the more general context of arrays, where the substring references are called slices.

In general, both assignment and comparison operations on character strings are complicated by the possibility of assigning and comparing operands of different lengths. For example, what happens when a longer string is assigned to a shorter string, or vice versa? Usually, simple and sensible choices are made for these situations, although users often have trouble remembering them.

Pattern matching is another fundamental character string operation. In some languages, pattern matching is supported directly in the language. In others, it is provided by a function or class library.

Perl, JavaScript, and PHP include built-in pattern matching operations. In these languages, the pattern-matching expressions are somewhat loosely based on mathematical regular expressions. In fact, they are often called regular expressions. They evolved from the early UNIX line editor, `ed`, to become part of the UNIX shell languages. Eventually, they grew to their most complex form. There is now a complete book on this kind of pattern-matching expressions (Friedl, 1997). In this section, we provide only a brief look at the style of these expressions through two relatively simple examples.

HISTORY NOTE

SNOBOL 4 was the first widely known language to support pattern matching.

Consider the following pattern expression:

```
/[A-Za-z][A-Za-z\d]+/
```

This pattern matches (or describes) the typical name form in programming languages. The brackets enclose character classes. The first class specifies all letters; the second specifies all letters and digits (a digit is specified with the abbreviation \d). If only the second class were included, we could not prevent a name from beginning with a digit. The plus operator following the second category specifies that there must be one or more of what is in the category. So, the whole pattern matches strings that begin with a letter, followed by one or more letters or digits.

Next consider the following pattern expression:

```
/\d+\.?\d*|\.\d+/
```

This pattern matches numeric literals. The \. specifies a literal decimal point. The question mark quantifies what it follows to have zero or one appearance.

The vertical bar (|) separates two alternatives in the whole pattern. The first alternative matches strings of one or more digits, possibly followed by a decimal point, followed by zero or more digits; the second alternative matches strings that begin with a decimal point, followed by one or more digits.

Pattern-matching capabililties are included in the class libraries of C++, Java, and C#.

6.3.3   String Length Options

There are several design choices regarding the length of string values. First, the length can be static and set when the string is created. Such a string is called a **static length string.** This is the choice for the immutable objects of Java's `string` class, as well as similar classes in the C++ standard class library and the .NET class library available to C#.

The second option is to allow strings to have varying length up to a declared and fixed maximum set by the variable's definition, as exemplified by the strings in C and the C-style strings of C++. These are called **limited dynamic length strings.** Such string variables can store any number of characters between zero and the maximum. Recall that strings in C use a special character to indicate the end of the string's characters, rather than maintaining the string length.

The third option is to allow strings to have varying length with no maximum, as in JavaScript and Perl. These are called **dynamic length strings.** This option requires the overhead of dynamic storage allocation and deallocation but provides maximum flexibility.

Ada 95 supports all three string length options. Type `string` from the `Standard` package provides static length strings. Type `Bounded_String`, from the `Ada.Strings.Bounded` package, supports limited dynamic length strings. Type `Unbounded_String`, from the `Ada.Strings.Unbounded` package, supports dynamic length strings.

6.3.4   Evaluation

String types are important to the writability of a language. Dealing with strings as arrays can be more cumbersome than dealing with a primitive string type. The addition of strings as a primitive type to a language is not costly in terms of either language or compiler complexity. Therefore, it is difficult to justify the omission of primitive string types in some contemporary languages. Of course, the availability of standard libraries of string manipulation subprograms can remove this deficiency when strings are not included as a primitive type.

String operations such as simple pattern matching and catenation are essential and should be included for string type values. Although dynamic length strings are obviously the most flexible, the overhead of their implementation must be weighed against that additional flexibility. They are usually only included in languages that are interpreted.

6.3.5   Implementation of Character String Types

Character string types could be supported directly in hardware, but in most cases software is used to implement string storage, retrieval, and manipulation. When character string types are represented as character arrays, the language often supplies few operations.

A descriptor for a static character string type, which is only required during compilation, has three fields. The first field of every descriptor is the name of the type. In the case of static character strings, the second field is the type's length (in characters). The third field is the address of the first character. This descriptor is shown in Figure 6.2. Limited dynamic strings require a run-time descriptor to store both the fixed maximum length and the current length, as shown in Figure 6.3. Dynamic length strings require a simpler run-time descriptor because only the current length needs to be stored.

The limited dynamic strings of C and C++ do not require run-time descriptors because the end of a string is marked with the null character. They do not need the maximum length because index values in array references are not range-checked in these languages.

Static length and limited dynamic length strings require no special dynamic storage allocation. In the case of limited dynamic length strings, sufficient storage for the maximum length is allocated when the string variable is bound to storage, so only a single allocation process is involved.

Dynamic length strings require more complex storage management. The length of a string, and therefore the storage to which it is bound, must grow and shrink dynamically.

There are two approaches to supporting the dynamic allocation and deallocation that is required for dynamic length strings. First, strings can be stored in a linked list, so that when a string grows, the newly required cells can come from anywhere in the heap. The drawbacks to this method are the extra storage occu-

Figure 6.2

Compile-time descriptor for static strings

Static string
Length
Address

Figure 6.3

Run-time descriptor for limited dynamic strings

Limited dynamic string
Maximum length
Current length
Address

pied by the links in the list representation and the necessary complexity of string operations. The alternative is to store complete strings in adjacent storage cells. The problem with this method occurs when a string grows: How can storage that is adjacent to the existing cells continue to be allocated for the string variable? Frequently, such storage is not available. Instead, a new area of memory is found that can store the complete new string, and the old part is moved to this area. Then the memory cells used for the old string are deallocated. This latter approach is the one typically used. The general problem of managing allocation and deallocation of variable-size segments is discussed in Section 6.9.9.3.

Although the linked-list method requires more storage, the associated allocation and deallocation processes are simple. However, some string operations are slowed by the required pointer chasing. On the other hand, using adjacent memory for complete strings results in faster string operations and requires significantly less storage, but the allocation and deallocation processes are slower.

6.4   User-Defined Ordinal Types

An **ordinal type** is one in which the range of possible values can be easily associated with the set of positive integers. In Java, for example, the primitive ordinal types are **integer**, **char**, and **boolean**. In some languages, users can define two kinds of ordinal types: enumeration and subrange.

6.4.1   Enumeration Types

An **enumeration type** is one in which all of the possible values, which are named constants, are provided in the definition. Enumeration types provide a way of defining and grouping collections of named constants, which are called **enumeration constants**. A typical enumeration type is shown in the following C# example:

```
enum days {Mon, Tue, Wed, Thu, Fri, Sat, Sun};
```

The enumeration constants are typically implicitly assigned the integer values, 0, 1, ..., but can be explicitly assigned any integer literal.

The design issues for enumeration types are

- Is an enumeration constant allowed to appear in more than one type definition, and if so, how is the type of an occurrence of that constant in the program checked?
- Are enumeration values coerced to integer?
- Are any other types coerced to an enumeration type?

All of these design issues are related to type checking. If an enumeration variable is coerced to a numeric type, there is little control over its range of legal operations or its range of values. If an **int** type value is coerced to an enumeration type, an enumeration type variable could be assigned any integer value whether it represented an enumeration constant or not.

6.4.1.1 Designs

In languages that do not have enumeration types, they are usually implemented directly as integer values. For example, suppose we needed to represent colors in a Fortran 77 program. We might use 0 to represent blue, 1 to represent red, and so forth. These values could be defined, as in

```
Integer red, blue
Data red, blue/0, 1/
```

Now, in the program we can use `red` and `blue` as if they were of a color type. The problem with this is that because we have not defined a type for our colors, there is no type checking when they are used. For example, it would be legal to add the two together, although that would rarely be an intended operation. They could also be combined with any other numeric type operand with any arithmetic operator, which would also rarely be a useful activity. Furthermore, because they are just variables, they could be assigned any integer value, thereby destroying the relationship with the colors. This latter problem could be prevented by making them named constants.

C and Pascal were the first widely used languages to include an enumeration data type. C++ includes C's enumeration types. In C++, we could have

```
enum colors {red, blue, green, yellow, black};
colors myColor = blue, yourColor = red;
```

The `colors` type uses the default internal values for the enumeration constants, 0, 1, ..., although the constants could have been assigned any integer literal (or even any constant-valued expression). The enumeration values are coerced to **int** when they are put in integer context. This allows their use in any numeric expression. For example, if the current value of `myColor` is `blue`, the expression

```
myColor++
```

would assign `green` to `myColor`.

C++ also allows enumeration constants to be assigned to variables of any numeric type, though that would most often be an error. However, no other type value is coerced to an enumeration type in C++. For example,

```
myColor = 4;
```

is illegal. This assignment would be legal if the right side had been cast to `colors` type. This prevents some potential errors.

C++ enumeration constants can appear in only one enumeration type in the same referencing environment.

Java does not include an enumeration type, presumably because they can be represented as data classes. For example,

```
class colors {
  public final int red = 0;
  public final int blue = 1;
  ...
}
```

Because the enumeration constants are actually type int, they can be used in any numeric expression, again allowing silly operations on them. It also allows enumeration variables to be assigned to any numeric type variable. Because they are constants, they of course cannot be assigned.

In Ada, enumeration literals are allowed to appear in more than one declaration in the same referencing environment. These are called **overloaded literals.** The rule for resolving the overloading—that is, deciding the type of an occurrence of such a literal—is that it must be determinable from the context of its appearance. For example, if an overloaded literal and an enumeration variable are compared, the literal's type is resolved to be that of the variable. In some cases, the programmer must indicate some type specification for an occurrence of an overloaded literal.

Because neither the enumeration literals nor the enumeration variables in Ada are coerced to integers, both the range of operations and the range of values of enumeration types are restricted, allowing many programmer errors to be compiler detected.

C# enumeration types are like those of C++, except that they are never coerced to integer. So, operations on enumeration types are restricted to those that make sense. Also, the range of values is restricted to that of the particular enumeration type.

6.4.1.2 Evaluation

Enumeration types can provide advantages in both readability and reliability. Readability is enhanced in a very direct way: Named values are easily recognized, whereas coded values are not.

In the area of reliability, the enumeration types of Ada and C# provide two advantages. First, no arithmetic operations are legal on enumeration types. This prevents adding days of the week, for example. Second, no enumeration variable can be assigned a value outside its defined range. If the colors enumeration type has 10 enumeration constants and uses 0..9 as its internal values, no number greater than 9 can be assigned to a colors type variable.

Because C treats enumeration variables like integer variables, it does not provide either of the two advantages.

C++ is a little better. Numeric values can be assigned to enumeration type variables only if they are cast to the type of the assigned variable. Numeric values assigned to enumeration type variables are checked to determine whether they are in the range of the internal values of the enumeration type. Unfortunately, if the user uses a wide range of explicitly assigned values, this checking is not effective. For example,

```
enum colors {red = 1, blue = 1000, green = 100000}
```

In this example, a value assigned to a variable of colors type will only be checked to determine whether it is in the range of 1..100000.

The enumeration types in C# are better than those of C++, because enumeration type variables are never coerced to integer types.

6.4.2   Subrange Types

A **subrange type** is a contiguous subsequence of an ordinal type. For example, 12..14 is a subrange of integer type. Subrange types were introduced by Pascal and are included in Ada. There are no design issues that are specific to subrange types.

6.4.2.1 Designs

In Ada, subranges are included in the category of types called *subtypes*. As was stated in Chapter 5, subtypes are not new types at all but rather only new names for possibly restricted, or constrained, versions of existing types. For example, consider the following declarations:

```
type Days is (Mon, Tue, Wed, Thu, Fri, Sat, Sun);

subtype Weekdays is Days range Mon..Fri;
subtype Index is Integer range 1..100;
```

In these examples, the restriction on the existing types is in the range of possible values. All of the operations defined for the parent type are also defined for the subtype, except assignment of values outside the specified range. For example, in the following

```
Day1 : Days;
Day2 : Weekdays;
...
Day2 := Day1;
```

the assignment is legal unless the value of Day1 is Sat or Sun.

Subrange types require the compiler to generate range-checking code for every assignment to a subrange variable. While types are checked for compatibility at compile time, subranges require run-time range checking.

One of the most common uses of user-defined ordinal types is for the indexes of arrays, as will be discussed in Section 6.5. They can also be used for loop variables. In fact, subranges of ordinal types are the only way the range of Ada **for** loop variables can be specified.

Note that subrange types are very different from Ada's derived types, which were discussed in Chapter 5. For example, consider the following type declarations:

```
type Derived_Small_Int is new Integer range 1..100;
subtype Subrange_Small_Int is Integer range 1..100;
```

Variables of both types, `Derived_Small_Int` and `Subrange_Small_Int`, inherit the value range and operations of `Integer`. However, variables of type `Derived_Small_Int` are not compatible with any `Integer` type. On the other hand, variables of type `Subrange_Small_Int` are compatible with variables and constants of `Integer` type and any subtype of `Integer`.

6.4.2.2 Evaluation

Subrange types enhance readability by making it clear to readers that variables of subtypes can store only certain ranges of values. Reliability is increased with subrange types, because assigning a value to a subrange variable that is outside the specified range is detected as an error, either by the compiler (in the case of the assigned value being a literal value) or by the run-time system (in the case of a variable or expression). It is odd that no contemporary language except Ada 95 has subrange types.

6.4.3   Implementation of User-Defined Ordinal Types

As discussed earlier, enumeration types are usually implemented as integers. Without restrictions on ranges of values and opeartions, this provides no increase in reliability.

Subrange types are implemented in exactly the same way as their parent types, except that range checks must be implicitly included by the compiler in every assignment of a variable or expression to a subrange variable. This increases code size and execution time but is usually considered well worth the cost. Also, a good optimizing compiler can optimize away some of the checking.

6.5   Array Types

An **array** is a homogeneous aggregate of data elements in which an individual element is identified by its position in the aggregate, relative to the first element. A reference to an array element in a program often includes one or more nonconstant subscripts. Such references require a run-time calculation to determine the memory location being referenced. The individual data elements of an array are of some previously defined type, either primitive or otherwise. A majority of computer programs need to model collections of values in which the values are of the same type and must be processed in the same way. Thus, the universal need for arrays is obvious.

6.5.1   Design Issues

The primary design issues specific to arrays are the following:

- What types are legal for subscripts?
- Are subscripting expressions in element references range-checked?
- When are subscript ranges bound?
- When does array allocation take place?
- Are ragged or rectangular multidimensioned arrays allowed, or both?
- Can arrays be initialized when they have their storage allocated?
- What kinds of slices are allowed, if any?

In the following sections, examples of the design choices made for the arrays of the most common programming languages are discussed.

6.5.2   Arrays and Indexes

Specific elements of an array are referenced by means of a two-level syntactic mechanism, where the first part is the aggregate name, and the second part is a possibly dynamic selector consisting of one or more items known as **subscripts** or **indexes.** If all of the indexes in a reference are constants, the selector is static; otherwise, it is dynamic. The selection operation can be thought of as a mapping from the array name and the set of index values to an element in the aggregate. Indeed, arrays are sometimes called *finite mappings*. Symbolically, this mapping can be shown as

array_name(index_value_list) → element

The syntax of array references is fairly universal: The array name is followed by the list of indexes, which is surrounded by either parentheses or brackets. A problem with using parentheses is that they often are also used to enclose the parameters in subprogram calls; this makes references to arrays appear exactly like those calls. For example, consider the following Ada assignment statement:

```
Sum := Sum + B(I);
```

Because parentheses are used for both subprogram parameters and array subscripts in Ada, both program readers and compilers are forced to use other information to determine whether B(I) in this assignment is a function call or a reference to an array element. This results in reduced readability.

The designers of Ada specifically chose parentheses to enclose subscripts so there would be uniformity between array references and function calls in expressions, in spite of potential readability problems. They made this choice in part because both array element references and function calls are mappings. Array element references map the subscripts to a particular element of the array. Function calls map the actual parameters to the function definition and, eventually, a functional value. For example, List(27) could be a direct reference to the List array's element with the subscript 27. It could also be a call to a function named List, which when passed 27 fetches the specified value from some nonarray data structure.

The C-based languages use brackets to delimit their array indices.

Two distinct types are involved in an array type: the element type and the type of the subscripts. The type of the subscripts is often a subrange of integers, but Ada allows some other types to be used as subscripts, such as Boolean, character, and enumeration.

Early programming languages did not specify that subscript ranges be implicitly checked. Range errors in subscripts are common in programs, so requiring range checking is an important factor in the reliability of languages. Among contemporary languages, C, C++, Perl, and Fortran do not specify range checking of subscripts, but Java, ML, and C# do. By default, Ada checks the range of all subscripts, but this can be disabled by the programmer.

HISTORY NOTE

The designers of pre-90 Fortrans and PL/I chose parentheses for array subscripts because no other suitable characters were available at the time. Card punches did not include bracket characters.

6.5.3   Subscript Bindings and Array Categories

The binding of the subscript type to an array variable is usually static, but the subscript value ranges are sometimes dynamically bound.

In some languages, the lower bound of the subscript range is implicit. For example, in the C-based languages, the lower bound of all index ranges is fixed at 0; in Fortran 95, it defaults to 1. In some other languages, subscript ranges must be completely specified by the programmer.

As with scalar variables, arrays occur in five categories. In this case, the category definitions are based on the binding to subscript value ranges and the binding to storage. Once again, the category names indicate where and when storage is allocated.

A **static array** is one in which the subscript ranges are statically bound and storage allocation is static (done before run time). The advantage of static arrays is efficiency: No dynamic allocation or deallocation is required.

A **fixed stack-dynamic array** is one in which the subscript ranges are statically bound, but the allocation is done at declaration elaboration time during execution. The advantage of fixed stack-dynamic arrays over static arrays is space efficiency. A large array in one subprogram can use the same space as a large array in a different subprogram, as long as both subprograms are not active at the same time.

A **stack-dynamic array** is one in which the subscript ranges are dynamically bound and the storage allocation is *dynamic* (done during run time). Once the subscript ranges are bound and the storage is allocated, however, they remain fixed during the lifetime of the variable. The advantage of stack-dynamic arrays over static and fixed stack-dynamic arrays is flexibility. The size of an array need not be known until the array is about to be used.

A **fixed heap-dynamic array** is similar to a fixed stack-dynamic array, in that the subscript ranges are dynamically bound and the storage binding is dynamic, but they are both fixed after storage is allocated. The differences are that the bindings are done when the user program requests them, rather than at elaboration time, and the storage is allocated on the heap, rather than the stack.

A **heap-dynamic array** is one in which the binding of subscript ranges and storage allocation is dynamic and can change any number of times during the array's lifetime. The advantage of heap-dynamic arrays over the others is flexibility: Arrays can grow and shrink during program execution as the need for space changes. Examples of the five categories are given in the following paragraphs.

Arrays declared in C and C++ functions that include the `static` modifier are static.

Arrays that are declared in C and C++ functions (without the `static` specifier) are examples of fixed stack-dynamic arrays.

Ada arrays can be stack dynamic, as in the following:

```
Get(List_Len);
declare
  List : array (1..List_Len) of Integer;
  begin
  ...
  end;
```

In this example, the user inputs the number of desired elements for the array `list`. The elements are then dynamically allocated when execution reaches the `declare` block. When execution reaches the end of the block, the `List` array is deallocated.

C and C++ also provide fixed heap-dynamic arrays. The standard library functions `malloc` and `free`, which are general heap allocation and deallocation operations, respectively, can be used for C arrays. C++ uses the operators `new` and `delete` to manage heap storage. Because there is no index range checking in C and C++, the length of an array is of no interest to the run-time system, so stretching or shrinking an array is easy. Arrays are treated as pointers to some collection of storage cells where the pointer can be indexed, as discussed in Section 6.9.5.

Fortran 95 also supports fixed heap-dynamic arrays.

In Java all arrays are fixed heap-dynamic arrays. Once created, these arrays keep the same subscript ranges and storage. Therefore, they are fixed heap-dynamic arrays. C# also provides fixed heap-dynamic arrays.

C# includes a second array class, `ArrayList`, that provides heap-dynamic arrays. Objects of this class are created without any elements, as in

```
ArrayList intList = new ArrayList();
```

Elements are added to this object with the `Add` method, as in

```
intArray.Add(nextOne);
```

Perl and JavaScript also support heap-dynamic arrays. They implicitly grow whenever assignments are made to elements beyond the last current element. They can be made to shrink by assigning them an empty aggregate, specified with `()`. They can be made to grow with several predefined functions, or simply by assigning a value to an element beyond the last defined element. For example, in Perl we could create an array of five numbers with

```
@list = (1, 2, 4, 7, 10);
```

Later, the array could be lengthened with the `push` function, as in

```
push(@list, 13, 17);
```

Now the array's value is `(1, 2, 4, 7, 10, 13, 17)`.

HISTORY NOTE

Fortran I limited the number of array subscripts to three, because at the time of the design, execution efficiency was a primary concern. Fortran I designers had developed a very fast method for accessing the elements of arrays of up to three dimensions, using the three index registers of the IBM 704. Fortran IV was first implemented on an IBM 7094, which had seven index registers. This allowed Fortran IV's designers to allow arrays with up to seven subscripts. Most other contemporary languages enforce no such limits.

6.5.4 Array Initialization

Some languages provide the means to initialize arrays at the time their storage is allocated. In Fortran, the `Data` statement can be used to initialize an array. For example, we could have

```
Integer List(3)
Data List /0, 5, 5/
```

The array `List` is initialized to the values from the list delimited by slashes.

C, C++, Java, and C# also allow initialization of their arrays, but with one new twist: In the C declaration

```
int list [] = {4, 5, 7, 83};
```

the compiler sets the length of the array. This is meant to be a convenience but is not without cost. It effectively removes the possibility that the system could detect some kinds of programmer errors, such as mistakenly leaving a value out of the list.

Character strings in C and C++ are implemented as arrays of **char**. These arrays can be initialized to string constants, as in

```
char name [] = "freddie";
```

The array `name` will have eight elements because all strings are terminated with a null character (zero), which is implicitly supplied by the system for string constants.

Arrays of strings in C and C++ can also be initialized with string literals. In this case, the array is one of pointers to characters. For example,

```
char *names [] = {"Bob", "Jake", "Darcie"};
```

This example illustrates the nature of character literals in C and C++. In the previous example of a string literal being used to initialize the **char** array name, the literal is taken to be a **char** array. But in the latter example (names), the literals are taken to be pointers to characters, so the array is an array of pointers to characters. For example, names[0] is a pointer to the letter 'B' in the literal character array that contains the characters 'B', 'o', 'b', and null.

In Java, similar syntax is used to define and initialize an array of references to String objects. For example,

```
String[]names = ["Bob", "Jake", "Darcie"];
```

Ada provides two mechanisms for initializing arrays in the declaration statement: by listing them in the order in which they are to be stored, or by directly assigning them to an index position using the => operator, which in Ada is called an **arrow**. For example, consider the following:

```
List : array (1..5) of Integer := (1, 3, 5, 7, 9);
Bunch : array (1..5) of Integer := (1 => 3, 3 => 4,
                                          others => 0);
```

In the first statement, all the elements of the array `List` have initializing values, which are assigned to the array element locations in the order in which they appear. In the second, the first and third array elements are initialized using direct assignment, and the **others** clause is used to initialize the remaining elements. These collections of values, delimited by parentheses, are called **aggregate values.**

6.5.5 Array Operations

An array operation is one that operates on an array as a unit. Ada allows array assignments, including those where the right side is an aggregate value rather than an array name. Ada also provides catenation, specified by the ampersand (&). Catenation is defined between two single-dimensioned arrays and between a single-dimensioned array and a scalar. Nearly all types in Ada have the built-in relational operators for equality and inequality.

Fortran 95 includes a number of array operations that are called **elemental** because they are operations between pairs of array elements. For example, the add operator (+) between two arrays results in an array of the sums of the element pairs of the two arrays. The assignment, arithmetic, relational, and logical operators are all overloaded for arrays of any size or shape. Fortran 95 also includes intrinsic, or library, functions for matrix multiplication, matrix transpose, and vector dot product.

Arrays and their operations are the heart of APL; it is the most powerful array-processing language ever devised. Because of its relative obscurity and its lack of effect on subsequent languages, however, we present here only a glimpse into its array operations.

In APL, the four basic arithmetic operations are defined for vectors (single-dimensioned arrays) and matrixes, as well as scalar operands. For example

```
A + B
```

is a valid expression, whether A and B are scalar variables, vectors, or matrixes.

APL includes a collection of unary operators for vectors and matrixes, some of which are as follows (where V is a vector and M is a matrix):

ɸV   reverses the elements of V
ɸM   reverses the columns of M
θM   reverses the rows of M
⍉M   transposes M (its rows become its columns and vice versa)
⊞M   inverts M

APL also includes several special operators that take other operators as operands. One of these is the inner product operator, which is specified with a period (.). It takes two operands, which are binary operators. For example

```
+.×
```

is a new operator that takes two arguments, either vectors or matrixes. It first multiplies the corresponding elements of two arguments, and then it sums the results. For example, if A and B are vectors,

```
A × B
```

is the mathematical inner product of A and B (a vector of the products of the corresponding elements of A and B). The statement

```
A +.× B
```

is the sum of the inner product of A and B. If A and B are matrixes, this expression specifies the matrix multiplication of A and B.

The special operators of APL are actually functional forms, which are described in Chapter 15.

6.5.6   Rectangular and Jagged Arrays

A **rectangular array** is a multidimensioned array in which all of the rows have the same number of elements, all of the columns have the same number of elements, and so forth. A **jagged array** is one in which the lengths of the rows need not be the same. This also applies to the columns or higher dimensions. For example, a jagged matrix may consist of three rows, one with 5 elements, one with 7 elements, and one with 12 elements.

Jagged arrays are made possible when multidimensioned arrays actually appear as arrays of arrays. For example, a matrix would appear as an array of arrays.

C, C++, and Java support jagged arrays but not rectangular arrays. In those languages, a reference to an element of a multidimensioned array uses a separate pair of brackets for each dimension. For example,

```
myArray[3][7]
```

Fortran, Ada, and C# support rectangular arrays. (C# also supports jagged arrays.) In these cases, all subscript expressions in references to elements are placed in a single pair of brackets. For example,

```
myArray[3, 7]
```

6.5.7   Slices

A **slice** of an array is some substructure of that array. For example, if A is a matrix, the first row of A is one possible slice, as are the last row and the first column. It is important to realize that a slice is not a new data type. Rather, it is a mechanism for referencing part of an array as a unit. If arrays cannot be manipulated as units in a language, that language has no use for slices.

One of the design questions for slices is the syntax of specifying a reference to a particular slice. A reference to a particular element of a complete array is the array name and an expression for each subscript. Because a slice is a substructure of an array, a slice reference requires fewer subscript expressions than a reference to the whole array. Somehow, however, the missing subscript expressions must be denoted, so that the present expressions are associated with the correct subscripts. The missing subscript or subscripts of slice references are sometimes specified by asterisks. For example, consider the following Fortran 95 declarations:

```
Integer Vector(1:10), Mat(1:3, 1:3), Cube(1:3, 1:3, 1:4)
```

Vector(3:6) is a four-element array with the third through sixth elements of Vector; Mat(1:3, 2) refers to the second column of Mat; Mat(3, 1:3) refers to the third row of Mat. All of these references can be used as single-dimensioned arrays. References to all array slices are treated as if they were arrays of the remaining dimensionality. Thus a slice reference such as

Cube(1:3, 1:3, 2) could be legally assigned to Mat. Slices can also appear as the destinations of assignment statements. For example, a single-dimensioned array could be assigned to a slice of a matrix. Figure 6.4 shows several slices of Mat and Cube.

More complex slices can also be specified in Fortran 95. For example, Vector(2:10:2) is a five-element array consisting of the second, fourth, sixth, eighth, and tenth elements of Vector. Slices can also have nonregular arrangements of elements of an existing array. For example, Vector((/3, 2, 1, 8/)) is an array of the third, second, first, and eighth elements of Vector.

In Ada, only highly restricted slices are allowed: those that consist of consecutive elements of a single-dimensioned array. For example, if List is an array with index range (1..100), List(5..10) is a slice of List consisting of the six elements indexed from 5 to 10. As discussed in Section 6.3.2, a slice of a String type is a substring reference.

6.5.8 Evaluation

Arrays have been included in virtually all languages. They are simple and have been well developed. The only significant advance since their introduction in Fortran I has been the inclusion of all ordinal types as possible subscript types

Figure 6.4

Example slices in Fortran 95

Mat (1:3, 2)

Mat (2:3, 1:3)

Cube (2, 1:3, 1:4)

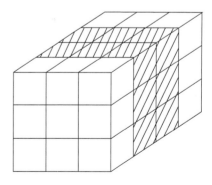

Cube (1:3, 1:3, 2:3)

and, of course, dynamic arrays. Although arrays are essential and fundamental, there is little controversy involved in their design.

Although it is sometimes convenient to allow the programmer to specify a particular substructure of a multidimensional array, the increased difficulty of implementation and readability are not necessarily worth the convenience.

6.5.9 Implementation of Array Types

Implementing arrays requires more compile-time effort than does implementing simple types, such as integer. The code to allow accessing of array elements must be generated at compile time. At run time, this code must be executed to produce element addresses. Accesses to array elements, especially in arrays with several subscripts, are more expensive than necessary if the access code is not carefully designed. This is true regardless of whether the array is statically or dynamically bound to memory. There is no way to precompute the address to be accessed by a reference such as

```
list[k]
```

A single-dimensioned array is a list of adjacent memory cells. Suppose the array `list` is defined to have a subscript range lower bound of `1`. The access function for `list` is often of the form

address(`list[k]`) = address(`list[1]`) + (k-1) * element_size

This simplifies to

address(`list[k]`) = (address(`list[1]`) - element_size) + (k * element_size)

where the first operand of the addition is the constant part of the access function, and the second is the variable part.

If the element type is statically bound and the array is statically bound to storage, then the value of the constant part can be computed before run time. Only the addition and multiplication operations remain to be done at run time. If the *base*, or beginning address, of the array is not known until run time, the subtraction must be done when the array is allocated.

The generalization of this access function for an arbitrary lower bound is

address(`list[k]`) = address(`list`[lower_bound]) + ((k - lower_bound) * element_size)

The compile-time descriptor for single-dimensioned arrays can have the form shown in Figure 6.5. The descriptor includes information required to construct the access function. If run-time checking of index ranges is not done and the attributes are all static, then only the access function is required during execution; no descriptor is needed. If run-time checking of index ranges is done, then those index ranges may need to be stored in a run-time descriptor. If the subscript ranges of a particular array type are static, the ranges may be

Figure 6.5

Compile-time description for single-dimensioned arrays

Array
Element type
Index type
Index lower bound
Index upper bound
Address

incorporated into the code that does the checking, thus eliminating the need for the run-time descriptor. If any of the descriptor entries are dynamically bound, then those parts of the descriptor must be maintained at run time.

Multidimensional arrays are more complex to implement than single-dimensioned arrays, although the extension to more dimensions is straightforward. Hardware memory is linear—it is usually a simple sequence of bytes. So values of data types that have two or more dimensions must be mapped onto the single-dimensioned memory. There are two common ways in which multidimensional arrays can be mapped to one dimension: row major order and column major order. In **row major order,** the elements of the array that have as their first subscript the lower bound value of that subscript are stored first, followed by the elements of the second value of the first subscript, and so forth. If the array is a matrix, it is stored by rows. For example, if the matrix had the values

```
3   4   7
6   2   5
1   3   8
```

it would be stored in row major order as

3, 4, 7, 6, 2, 5, 1, 3, 8

In **column major order,** the elements of an array that have as their last subscript the lower bound value of that subscript are stored first, followed by the elements of the second value of the last subscript, and so forth. If the array is a matrix, it is stored by columns. If the example matrix above were stored in column major order, it would have the following order in memory:

3, 6, 1, 4, 2, 3, 7, 5, 8

Column major order is used in Fortran, but the other languages use row major order.

It is sometimes essential to know the storage order of multidimensional arrays, for example, when such arrays are processed using pointers in C programs. In all cases, sequential access to matrix elements will be faster if they are accessed in the order in which they are stored, because that will minimize paging. (*Paging* is the movement of blocks of information between disk and main memory. The objective of paging is to keep the frequently needed parts of the program in memory and the rest on disk.)

The access function for a multidimensional array is the mapping of its base address and a set of index values to the address in memory of the element specified by the index values. The access function for two-dimensional arrays stored in row major order can be developed as follows. In general, the address of an element is the base address of the structure plus the element size times the number of elements that precede it in the structure. For a matrix in row major order, the number of elements that precedes an element is the number of rows above the element times the size of a row, plus the number of elements to the left of the element. This is illustrated in Figure 6.6, in which we make the simplifying assumption that subscript lower bounds are all 1.

To get an actual address value, the number of elements that precede the desired element must be multiplied by the element size. Now, the access function can be written as

location(a[i,j]) = address of a[1, 1] +
    ((((number of rows above the *ith* row) * (size of a row))
    + (number of elements left of the *jth* column)) *
    element size)

Because the number of rows above the *ith* row is (i - 1) and the number of elements to the left of the *jth* column is (j - 1), we have

location(a[i, j]) = address of a[1, 1] + ((((i - 1) * n) + (j - 1)) *
    element_size)

where *n* is the number of elements per row. This can be rearranged to the form

location(a[i, j]) = address of a[1, 1] - ((n + 1) * element_size) +
    ((i * n + j) * element_size)

Figure 6.6

The location of the [i,j] element in a matrix

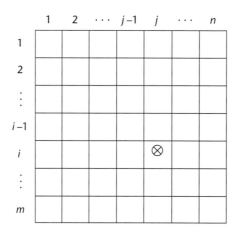

where the first two terms are the constant part and the last is the variable part.

The generalization to arbitrary lower bounds results in the following access function:

location(a[i, j]) = address of a[row_lb, col_lb] +
$$(((i - row\_lb) * n) + (j - col\_lb)) * element\_size$$

where row_lb is the lower bound of the rows and col_lb is the lower bound of the columns. This can be rearranged to the form

location(a[i, j]) = address of a[row_lb, col_lb] –
$$(((row\_lb * n) + col\_lb) * element\_size) +$$
$$(((i * n) + j) * element\_size)$$

where the first two terms are the constant part and the last is the variable part. This can be generalized relatively easily to an arbitrary number of dimensions.

For each dimension of an array, one add and one multiply instruction are required for the access function. Therefore, accesses to elements of arrays with several subscripts are costly. The compile-time descriptor for a multidimensional array is shown in Figure 6.7.

Slices add another layer of complexity to storage mapping functions. To illustrate this, consider a program in which there is a matrix and an array, and a column of the matrix is assigned to the array, as in

```
Integer Mat (1:10, 1:5), List (1:10)
...
List = Mat (1:3, 3)
```

The storage mapping function for the matrix, Mat, assuming row major order and an element size of 1, is

$$location(Mat[i, j]) = address\ of\ Mat[1,1] + ((i - 1) * 5 + (j - 1)) * 1$$
$$= (address\ of\ Mat[1,1] - 6) + ((5 * i) + j)$$

Figure 6.7

A compile-time descriptor for a multi-dimensional array

Multidimensioned array
Element type
Index type
Number of dimensions
Index range 1
⋮
Index range *n*
Address

The storage mapping function for the slice reference Mat[1:3, 3] is

$$\text{location}(\text{Mat}[i, 3]) = \text{address of Mat}[1,1] + ((i - 1) * 5 + (3 - 1)) * 1$$
$$= (\text{address of Mat}[1,1] - 3) + (5 * i)$$

Notice that this mapping has exactly the same form as any other one-dimensional array access function, although the form of the constant part is different because the basic array is two-dimensional.

The elements of Mat that are to be assigned to List are found by letting i take on the values in the subscript range of the first dimension of Mat.

6.6   Associative Arrays

An **associative array** is an unordered collection of data elements that are indexed by an equal number of values called **keys**. In the case of non-associative arrays, the indices never need to be stored (because of their regularity). In an associative array, however, the user-defined keys must be stored

INTERVIEW

The Open Source Movement and Work Life

RASMUS LERDORF

After graduating with a degree in engineering, Rasmus Lerdorf held a number of consulting jobs. Then, in an effort to track those viewing his online resume, he created the first iteration of PHP. These days he is an advocate for the open source movement and an employee at Yahoo! in Sunnyvale, California.

What are some of your thoughts on the open source community versus the commercial community? Consider your PHP solution to database connectivity to Web pages versus the corporate options: ASP, Cold Fusion, etc. What about a solution derived by way of open source versus the ideas derived from corporate led initiatives? What do you get with one that you don't with the other?

Whenever you are dealing with a commercial solution you always have to worry about the fact that you are now completely dependant on that particular commercial company. You rarely have much say in which features will be in the next version, or even,

sometimes, whether there will be a next version. They also tend to like to tie you completely to their technology, depriving you of the flexibility to switch solutions or easily integrate one solution with another. An obvious benefit of at least some commercial products is that you can buy guaranteed technical support, and there will be someone on the other end of the phone helping you out if you get stuck.

In the open source world, at least when it comes to PHP, there is a big focus on the community. I didn't write PHP—hundreds of people wrote PHP. We formed a big community of people who all share a common problem. We created a tool to help us solve that problem and we all feel a sense of ownership in it.

in the structure. So each element of an associative array is in fact a pair of entities, a key and a value. We use Perl's design of associative arrays to illustrate this data structure. Associative arrays are also supported by the standard class libraries of Java and C++.

The only design issue that is specific for associative arrays is the form of references to their elements.

6.6.1 Structure and Operations

In Perl, associative arrays are often called **hashes,** because in the implementation their elements are stored and retrieved with hash functions. The namespace for Perl hashes is distinct: Every hash variable must begin with a percent sign (%). Hashes can be set to literal values with the assignment statement, as in

```
%salaries = ("Gary" => 75000, "Perry" => 57000,
             "Mary" => 55750, "Cedric" => 47850);
```

This is also why you will often see a fanatical devotion to a certain technology in the open source world, whereas that is somewhat rare when it comes to commercial technologies. It is very easy to join this community and help, in whatever small way, with the development of PHP. People who do this get a very good sense of the technology. They can feel confident that the technology isn't going to disappear on them, that it will solve their current and likely their future problems, and that through this community they can get the technical support they need.

Think of it as going to the store to buy a shrink-wrapped solution to your problem and hoping that it is able to solve most of it, or sitting down with a thousand of your closest friends, who all have the same problem, and comparing notes and tools. The commercial solution may at times be the better solution, but that strong peer group that inevitably builds itself up around most open source projects is a very attractive alternative. Commercial companies try to create these communities around their solutions as well and some have done it quite well, but in the end the atmosphere is completely different from a healthy open source community, and you really can't compare the two. As

the tools that the community builds mature, they start to rival or surpass any already existing commercial tool. In the case of PHP, we actually preceded both ASP and Cold Fusion, so in the early days we weren't really chasing any particular commercial tool, we were simply trying to figure out how to solve the Web problem.

Can you share some thoughts on working alone to develop the solutions that you needed for your personal home page back in 1995, versus working on some sort of distributed team to take your original idea and make it into something used by over a million Web sites? I wanted to get away from having to write the same CGI code in C over and over again. Collecting common functionality in a C library and putting a simple macro-replacement parser on top of it so I could put special tags in my HTML to trigger my various routines written in C seemed like an obvious solution. So my main early requirement was speed of development and deployment of dynamic Web pages, and to get that I needed a simple framework from creating the business logic in C and accessing it from HTML. *(continues)*

INTERVIEW (continued)

I probably spent a good 18 months on the initial code before it caught anybody's attention. This was around 1994, so it was quite a bit before there was any sort of buzz around open source or free software development. I also think the barrier of entry was quite a bit lower back then. There weren't a lot of free tools that addressed the Web problem, but I still had to get PHP to the point where someone would look at it and determine that it solved enough of their problem that it was easier to use it and perhaps extend it a little bit than it was for them to start from scratch and solve the problem themselves. That is the barrier any successful open source project has had to clear at some point in its history. Taking someone else's solution, understanding it, and applying it to your own problem is a big investment in terms of time and energy, and you are never sure whether it is going to work. Before an open source project has proven itself, that barrier is a tough one, and if you ask anybody who has started a successful open source project you are likely to find that they had a period of their lives where they devoted absolutely every spare second of free time to it. That was true for me in 1994–1995 with PHP.

> **"** The [open source] community has contributed everything to PHP. Without it there would be no PHP. **"**

Do you remember the first addition you received from someone else? What was the need or requirement? I got a number of small bug fixes, but the first early large contributions were database extensions for Sybase and Oracle. I had written the original database connectivity code against a free database out of Australia called mSQL. I didn't use Sybase or Oracle, but someone out there needed to talk to those databases so they wrote the code and contributed it back.

Share what PHP looked like and what it did when you first posted it. It was a set of CGI programs loosely related that solved common problems for people's personal home pages. It had a hit counter, which also showed the IP or hostname of the person who last browsed the page. It could also log hits to an SQL database and included some tools to create pretty reports of this traffic. So the early focus was on the tools, not on the framework/language these tools were written in.

What has the open source movement contributed? What does PHP look like today in comparison? The community has contributed every-

---

Individual element values are referenced using notation that is unique to Perl. The key value is placed in braces and the hash name is replaced by a scalar variable name that is the same except for the first character. Scalar variable names begin with dollar signs ($). For example,

```
$salaries{"Perry"} = 58850;
```

A new element is added using the same statement form. An element can be removed from the hash with the delete operator, as in

```
delete $salaries{"Gary"};
```

The entire hash can be emptied by assigning the empty literal to it, as in

```
@salaries = ();
```

thing to PHP. Without it there would be no PHP. PHP has grown to be a general-purpose Web scripting language that can talk to just about anything you can imagine and is in use on about 30 percent of all the domains on the Web. It is powering the tiniest family Web page that gets hit maybe twice a month, to some of the busiest sites in the world.

ON WORKING AND YEARS IN THE BUSINESS

You've had a varied career, from big companies, to dotcoms, to personal consulting: How do you decide what you are going to do next? I look for fun and challenging projects and people I think I will enjoy working with. Sometimes you just have to take a leap of faith as well. I went to Brazil initially purely because I was working in Calgary in the winter and it was too cold. I saw some Mickey Rourke movie set in Rio and wondered what I was doing in the frozen Arctic when surely they must have computers in Brazil that needed programming.

How do you decide when to move on? When things stop being fun, I quit. If I wake up every morning dreading going to work, or if I sit each and every day watching the clock, wondering when I have put in enough hours to go home, I know it is time to quit. There will always be short periods where you would rather be elsewhere than at work, but if that feeling persists, life is too short to spend it in frustration or boredom. If you ever find yourself calculating what you make per second, or how much the company paid you to walk to the washroom and back, quit!

Do you have some sort of criteria or rules for picking your next assignment? None whatsoever. I have jumped around quite a bit, but I never have any sort of preconceived notion that I will only stay at a company for X months or years. Most often the job itself dictates how long I stay. With some jobs I was brought in to solve a particular problem. After solving the problem they would probably have preferred it if I had stuck around to help them maintain and support the solution, but by then the challenge was gone and I needed something new. Of course, now that I have a small baby at home, this may change the priorities a bit. Perhaps a cozy job without the stress that goes along with the challenges isn't such a bad idea. I'll let you know in a couple of years.

The size of a Perl hash is dynamic: It grows when a new element is added and shrinks when an element is deleted, and also when it is emptied by assignment of the empty literal. The `exists` operator returns true or false, depending on whether its operand key is an element in the hash. For example,

```
if (exists $salaries{"Shelly"}) …
```

The `keys` operator, when applied to a hash, returns an array of the keys of the hash. The `values` operator does the same for the values of the hash. The `each` operator iterates over the element pairs of a hash.

PHP's arrays are both normal arrays and associative arrays. They can be treated as either. The language provides functions that allow both indexed and hashed access to elements. An array can have elements that are created with simple numeric indices and elements that are created with string hash keys.

A hash is much better than an array if searches of the elements are required, because the implicit hashing operation used to access hash elements is very efficient. On the other hand, if every element of a list must be processed, it would be more efficient to use an array.

6.6.2 Implementing Associative Arrays

The implementation of Perl's associative arrays is optimized for fast lookups, but it also provides relatively fast reorganization when array growth requires it. A 32-bit hash value is computed for each entry and is stored with the entry, although an associative array initially uses only a small part of the hash value. When an associative array must be expanded beyond its initial size, the hash function need not be changed, rather, more bits of the hash value are used. Only half of the entries must be moved when this happens. So, although expansion of an associative array is not free, it is not as costly as you might think.

The elements in PHP's arrays are stored in a linked list, in which the nodes appear in the order in which they were created. The links are used to support iterative access to elements through the current and next functions. A hash function is used to provide access to all elements through their keys.

6.7   Record Types

A **record** is a possibly heterogeneous aggregate of data elements in which the individual elements are identified by names.

There is frequently a need in programs to model collections of data that are not homogeneous. For example, information about a college student might include name, student number, grade point average, and so forth. A data type for such a collection might use a character string for the name, an integer for the student number, a floating-point for the grade point average, and so forth. Records are designed to meet this kind of need.

Records have been part of all of the most popular programming languages, except pre-90 versions of Fortran, since the early 1960s, when they were introduced by COBOL.

In C, C++, and C#, records are supported with the **struct** data type. In C++, structures are a minor variation on classes. In C#, structures are also similar to classes, but also quite different. C# structures are stack-allocated value types, as opposed to class objects, which are heap-allocated reference types. Structures in C++ and C# are normally used as encapsulation structures, rather than data structures. They are further discussed in this capacity in Chapter 11.

The following sections describe how records are declared or defined, how references to fields within records are made, and common record operations.

The design issues that are specific to records are

- What is the syntactic form of references to fields?
- Are elliptical references allowed?

6.7.1 Definitions of Records

The fundamental difference between a record and an array is the homogeneity of elements in arrays versus the possible heterogeneity of elements in records. One result of this difference is that record elements, or *fields*, are not usually referenced by indexes. Instead, the fields are named with identifiers, and references to the fields are made using these identifiers. One more important difference between arrays and records is that records in some languages are allowed to include unions, which are discussed in Section 6.8.

The COBOL form of a record declaration, which is part of the data division of a COBOL program, is illustrated in the following example:

```
01   EMPLOYEE-RECORD.
     02   EMPLOYEE-NAME.
          05   FIRST        PICTURE IS X(20).
          05   MIDDLE       PICTURE IS X(10).
          05   LAST         PICTURE IS X(20).
     02   HOURLY-RATE       PICTURE IS 99V99.
```

The EMPLOYEE-RECORD record consists of the EMPLOYEE-NAME record and the HOURLY-RATE field. The numerals 01, 02, and 05 that begin the lines of the record declaration are **level numbers,** which indicate by their relative values the hierarchical structure of the record. Any line that is followed by a line with a higher-level number is itself a record. The PICTURE clauses show the formats of the field storage locations, with X(20) specifying 20 alphanumeric characters and 99V99 specifying four decimal digits with the decimal point in the middle.

Ada uses a different syntax for records; rather than using the level numbers of COBOL, it indicates record structures in an orthogonal way by simply nesting record declarations inside record declarations. In Ada, records cannot be anonymous—they must be named types. Consider the following Ada declaration:

```
type Employee_Name_Type is record
   First : String (1..20);
   Middle : String (1..10);
   Last : String (1..20);
end record;
type Employee_Record_Type is record
   Employee_Name: Employee_Name_Type;
   Hourly_Rate: Float;
end record;
Employee_Record: Employee_Record_Type;
```

Fortran 95 record declarations require that any nested records be previously defined as types. So, for the employee record above, the employee name record would need to be defined first, and then the employee record would simply name it as the type of its first field.

In Java, records can be defined as data classes, with nested records defined as nested classes. Data members of such classes serve as the record fields.

6.7.2   References to Record Fields

References to the individual fields of records are syntactically specified by several different methods, two of which name the desired field and its enclosing records. COBOL field references have the form

field_name OF record_name_1 OF ... OF record_name_n

where the first record named is the smallest or innermost record that contains the field. The next record name in the sequence is that of the record that contains the previous record, and so forth. For example, the MIDDLE field in the COBOL record example above can be referenced with

MIDDLE OF EMPLOYEE-NAME OF EMPLOYEE-RECORD

Most of the other languages use *dot notation* for field references, where the components of the reference are connected with periods. Names in dot notation have the opposite order of COBOL references: They use the name of the largest enclosing record first and the field name last. For example, the following is a reference to the field MIDDLE in the Ada record example above:

EMPLOYEE_RECORD.EMPLOYEE_NAME.MIDDLE

C and C++ use this same syntax for referencing the members of their structures. Fortran 95 field references also have this form, except that percent signs (%) are used instead of periods.

A **fully qualified reference** to a record field is one in which all intermediate record names, from the largest enclosing record to the specific field, are named in the reference. Both the COBOL and the Ada field references above are fully qualified. As an alternative to fully qualified references, COBOL allows **elliptical references** to record fields. In an elliptical reference, the field is named, but any or all of the enclosing record names can be omitted, as long as the resulting reference is unambiguous in the referencing environment. For example, FIRST, FIRST OF EMPLOYEE-NAME, and FIRST OF EMPLOYEE-RECORD are elliptical references to the employee's first name in the COBOL record declared above. Although elliptical references are a programmer convenience, they require a compiler to have elaborate data structures and procedures in order to correctly identify the referenced field. They are also somewhat detrimental to readability.

6.7.3   Operations on Records

Assignment is a common record operation. In most cases, the types of the two sides must be identical. Ada allows record comparisons for equality and inequality. Also, Ada records can be initialized with aggregate literals.

COBOL provides the MOVE CORRESPONDING statement for moving records. This statement copies a field of the specified source record to the destination record only if the destination record has a field with the same name. This is frequently a useful operation in data processing applications, where input records are moved to output files after some modifications. Because input records often have many fields that have the same names and purposes as fields in output records, but not necessarily in the same order, the MOVE CORRESPONDING operation can save many statements. For example, consider the following COBOL structures:

```
01   INPUT-RECORD.
     02   NAME.
          05   LAST        PICTURE IS X(20).
          05   MIDDLE      PICTURE IS X(15).
          05   FIRST       PICTURE IS X(20).
     02 EMPLOYEE-NUMBER    PICTURE IS 9(10).
     02 HOURS-WORKED       PICTURE IS 99.

01   OUTPUT-RECORD.
     02   NAME.
          05   FIRST       PICTURE IS X(20).
          05   MIDDLE      PICTURE IS X(15).
          05   LAST        PICTURE IS X(20).
     02   EMPLOYEE-NUMBER  PICTURE IS 9(10).
     02   GROSS-PAY        PICTURE IS 999V99.
     02   NET-PAY          PICTURE IS 999V99.
```

The statement

```
MOVE CORRESPONDING INPUT-RECORD TO OUTPUT-RECORD.
```

copies the FIRST, MIDDLE, LAST, and EMPLOYEE-NUMBER fields from the input record to the output record.

6.7.4 Evaluation

Records are frequently valuable data types in programming languages. The design of record types is straightforward, and their use is safe. The only aspect of records that is not clearly readable is the elliptical references allowed by COBOL.

Records and arrays are closely related structural forms, and it is therefore interesting to compare them. Arrays are used when all the data values have the same type and are processed in the same way. This processing is easily done when there is a systematic way of sequencing through the structure. Such processing is well supported by using dynamic subscripting as the addressing method.

Figure 6.8

A compile-time
descriptor for a record

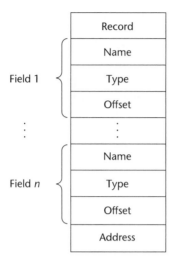

Records are used when the collection of data values is heterogeneous and
the different fields are not processed in the same way. Also, the fields of a record
often need not be processed in a particular sequential order. Field names are
like literal, or constant, subscripts. Because they are static, they provide very
efficient access to the fields. Dynamic subscripts could be used to access record
fields, but it would disallow type checking and would also be slower.

Records and arrays represent thoughtful and efficient methods of fulfill-
ing two separate but related applications of data structures.

6.7.5   Implementation of Record Types

The fields of records are stored in adjacent memory locations. But because the
sizes of the fields are not necessarily the same, the access method used for arrays
is not used for records. Instead, the offset address, relative to the beginning of the
record, is associated with each field. Field accesses are all handled using these offsets. The compile-time descriptor for a record has the general form shown in
Figure 6.8. Run-time descriptors for records are unnecessary.

6.8   Union Types

A **union** is a type that may store different type values at different times during program execution. As an example of the need for a union type, consider
a table of constants for a compiler, which is used to store the constants found
in a program being compiled. One field of each table entry is for the value of
the constant. Suppose that for a particular language being compiled, the types
of constants were integer, floating-point, and Boolean. In terms of table management, it would be convenient if the same location, a table field, could store

a value of any of these three types. Then all constant values could be addressed in the same way. The type of such a location is, in a sense, the union of the three value types it can store.

6.8.1 Design Issues

The problem of type checking union types, which was discussed in Chapter 5, leads to one major design issue. The other fundamental question is how to syntactically represent a union. In some cases, unions are confined to be parts of record structures, but in others they are not. So the primary design issues that are particular to union types are the following:

- Should type checking be required? Note that any such type checking must be dynamic.
- Should unions be embedded in records?

6.8.2 Discriminated versus Free Unions

Fortran, C, and C++ provide union constructs in which there is no language support for type checking. In Fortran, the Equivalence statement is used to specify unions; in C and C++, it is the union construct. The unions in these languages are called **free unions,** because programmers are allowed complete freedom from type checking in their use.

Type checking of unions requires that each union construct include a type indicator. Such an indicator is called a **tag,** or **discriminant,** and a union with a discriminant is called a **discriminated union.** The first language to provide discriminated unions was ALGOL 68. They are now supported by Ada.

6.8.3 Ada Union Types

The Ada design for discriminated unions, which is based on that of its predecessor language, Pascal, allows the user to specify variables of a variant record type that will store only one of the possible type values in the variant. In this way the user can tell the system when the type checking can be static. Such a restricted variable is called a **constrained variant variable.**

The tag of a constrained variant variable is treated like a named constant. Unconstrained variant records in Ada allow the values of their variants to change types during execution. However, the type of the variant can be changed only by assigning the entire record, including the discriminant. This disallows inconsistent records because if the newly assigned record is a constant data aggregate, the value of the tag and the type of the variant can be statically checked for consistency. If the assigned value is a variable, its consistency was guaranteed when it was assigned, so the new value of the variable now being assigned is sure to be consistent.

The following example shows an Ada variant record:

```ada
type Shape is (Circle, Triangle, Rectangle);
type Colors is (Red, Green, Blue);
type Figure (Form : Shape) is
  record
    Filled : Boolean;
    Color : Colors;
    case Form is
      when Circle =>
        Diameter : Float;
      when Triangle =>
        Left_Side : Integer;
        Right_Side : Integer;
        Angle : Float;
      when Rectangle =>
        Side_1 : Integer;
        Side_2 : Integer;
    end case;
  end record;
```

The structure of this variant record is shown in Figure 6.9. The following two statements declare variables of type `Figure`:

```ada
Figure_1 : Figure;
Figure_2 : Figure(Form => Triangle);
```

`Figure_1` is declared to be an unconstrained variant record that has no initial value. Its type can change by assignment of a whole record, including the discriminant, as in the following:

```ada
Figure_1 := (Filled => true,
             Color => Blue,
             Form => Rectangle,
             Side_1 => 12,
             Side_2 => 3);
```

Figure 6.9

A discriminated union of three shape variables (assume all variables are the same size)

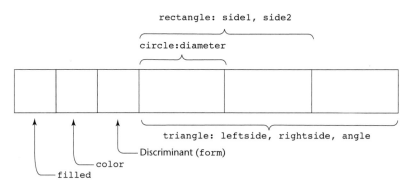

The right side of this assignment is a data aggregate.

The variable Figure_2 declared above is constrained to be a triangle and cannot be changed to another variant.

This form of discriminated union is safe, because it always allows type checking, although the references to fields in unconstrained variants must be dynamically checked.

6.8.4 Evaluation

Unions are potentially unsafe constructs in many languages. They are one of the reasons why Fortran, C, and C++ are not strongly typed: They do not allow type checking of references to their unions. On the other hand, unions can be safely used, as in their design in Ada. In most other languages, unions must be used with care.

Neither Java nor C# include unions, which may be reflective of the growing concern for safety in programming languages.

6.8.5 Implementation of Union Types

Discriminated unions are implemented by simply using the same address for every possible variant. Sufficient storage for the largest variant is allocated. In the case of constrained variants in the Ada language, the exact amount of storage can be used because there is no variation. The tag of a discriminated union is stored with the variant in a recordlike structure.

At compile time, the complete description of each variant must be stored. This can be done by associating a case table with the tag entry in the descriptor. The case table has an entry for each variant, which points to a descriptor for that particular variant. To illustrate this arrangement, consider the following Ada example:

```ada
type Node (Tag : Boolean) is
  record
  case Tag is
      when true => Count : Integer;
      when false => Sum : Float;
  end case;
 end record;
```

The descriptor for this type could have the form shown in Figure 6.10.

6.9 Pointer and Reference Types

A **pointer** type is one in which the variables have a range of values that consists of memory addresses and a special value, nil. The value nil is not a valid address and is used to indicate that a pointer cannot currently be used to reference any memory cell.

Figure 6.10

A compile-time descriptor for a discriminated union

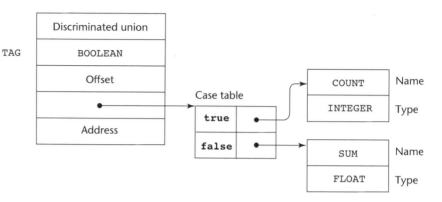

Pointers have been designed for two distinct kinds of uses. First, pointers provide some of the power of indirect addressing, which is heavily used in assembly language programming. Second, pointers provide a method of dynamic storage management. A pointer can be used to access a location in the area where storage is dynamically allocated, which is usually called a **heap.**

Variables that are dynamically allocated from the heap are called **heap-dynamic variables.** They often do not have identifiers associated with them and thus can be referenced only by pointer or reference type variables. Variables without names are called **anonymous variables.** It is in this latter application area of pointers that the most important design issues arise.

Pointers, unlike arrays and records, are not structured types, although they are defined using a type operator (* in C and C++, and **access** in Ada). Furthermore, they are also different from scalar variables because they are most often used to reference some other variable, rather than being used to store data of some sort.

Both kinds of uses of pointers add writability to a language. For example, suppose it is necessary to implement a dynamic structure like a binary tree in a language like Fortran 77, which does not have pointers. This would require the programmer to provide and maintain a pool of available tree nodes, which would probably be implemented in parallel arrays. Also, because of the lack of dynamic storage in Fortran 77, it would be necessary for the programmer to guess the maximum number of required nodes. This is clearly an awkward and cumbersome way to deal with binary trees.

Reference variables, which are discussed in Section 6.9.7, are closely related to pointers.

6.9.1 Design Issues

The primary design issues particular to pointers are the following:

- What are the scope and lifetime of a pointer variable?
- What is the lifetime of a heap-dynamic variable?

- Are pointers restricted as to the type of value to which they can point?
- Are pointers used for dynamic storage management, indirect addressing, or both?
- Should the language support pointer types, reference types, or both?

6.9.2 Pointer Operations

Languages that provide a pointer type usually include two fundamental pointer operations, assignment and dereferencing. The first operation sets a pointer variable's value to some useful address. If pointer variables are used only to manage dynamic storage, the allocation mechanism, whether by operator or built-in subprogram, serves to initialize the pointer variable. If pointers are used for indirect addressing to variables that are not heap-dynamic, then there must be an explicit operator or built-in subprogram for fetching the address of a variable, which can then be assigned to the pointer variable.

An occurrence of a pointer variable in an expression can be interpreted in two distinct ways. First, it could be interpreted as a reference to the contents of the memory cell to which the variable is bound, which in the case of a pointer is an address. This is exactly how a nonpointer variable in an expression would be interpreted, although in that case it would not be an address. However, the pointer could also be interpreted as a reference to the value in the memory cell whose address is in the memory cell to which the variable is bound. In this case, the pointer is interpreted as an indirect reference. The former case is a normal pointer reference; the latter is the result of **dereferencing** the pointer. Dereferencing, which takes a reference through one level of indirection, is the second fundamental pointer operation. To clarify dereferencing, consider a pointer variable, ptr, that is bound to a memory cell with the value 7080. Suppose that the memory cell whose address is 7080 has the value 206. A normal reference to ptr yields 7080, but a dereferenced reference to ptr yields 206.

Dereferencing of pointers can be either explicit or implicit. In Fortran 95 it is implicit, but in most other contemporary languages, it occurs only when explicitly specified. In C++, it is explicitly specified with the asterisk (*) as a prefix unary operation. For example, if ptr is a pointer variable with the value 7080, as in the above example, and the cell whose address is 7080 has the value 206, then the assignment

```
j = *ptr
```

sets j to 206. This process is shown in Figure 6.11.

When pointers point to records, the syntax of the references to the fields of these records varies among languages. In C and C++, there are two ways a pointer to a record can be used to reference a field in that record. If a pointer variable p points to a record with a field named age, (*p).age can be used to refer to that field. The operator ->, when used between a pointer to a record and a field of that record, combines dereferencing and field reference. For

Figure 6.11

The assignment operation j = *ptr

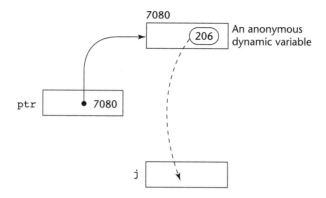

example, the expression p -> age is equivalent to (*p).age. In Ada, p.age can be used, because such uses of pointers are implicitly dereferenced.

Languages that provide pointers for the management of a heap must include an explicit allocation operation. Some also provide an explicit deallocation operation. These two operations are often in the form of built-in subprograms, although Ada, C++, and Java use an allocator operator.

6.9.3 Pointer Problems

The first high-level programming language to include pointer variables was PL/I, in which pointers can be used to refer to both heap-dynamic variables and other program variables. The pointers of PL/I are highly flexible, but their use can lead to several kinds of programming errors. Some of the problems of PL/I pointers are also present in the pointers of subsequent languages. Some recent languages, such as Java, have replaced pointers completely with reference types, which, along with implicit deallocation, eliminate the primary problems with pointers.

6.9.3.1 Dangling Pointers

A **dangling pointer,** or **dangling reference,** is a pointer that contains the address of a heap-dynamic variable that has been deallocated. Dangling pointers are dangerous for several reasons. First, the location being pointed to may have been reallocated to some new heap-dynamic variable. If the new variable is not the same type as the old one, type checks of uses of the dangling pointer are invalid. Even if the new one is the same type, its new value will bear no relationship to the old pointer's dereferenced value. Furthermore, if the dangling pointer is used to change the heap-dynamic variable, the value of the new heap-dynamic variable will be destroyed. Finally, it is possible that the location now is being temporarily used by the storage management system, possibly as a pointer in a chain of available blocks of storage, thereby allowing a change to the location to cause the storage manager to fail.

The following sequence of operations creates a dangling pointer in many languages:

1. Pointer p1 is set to point at a new heap-dynamic variable.
2. Pointer p2 is assigned p1's value.
3. The heap-dynamic variable pointed to by p1 is explicitly deallocated (setting p1 to nil), but p2 is not changed by the operation. P2 is now a dangling pointer.

6.9.3.2 Lost Heap-dynamic Variables

A **lost heap-dynamic variable** is an allocated heap-dynamic variable that is no longer accessible to the user program. Such variables are often called **garbage** because they are not useful for their original purpose, and they also cannot be reallocated for some new use by the program. Lost heap-dynamic variables are most often created by the following sequence of operations:

1. Pointer p1 is set to point to a newly created heap-dynamic variable.
2. p1 is later set to point to another newly created heap-dynamic variable.

The first heap-dynamic variable is now inaccessible, or lost.

Languages that require explicit deallocation of dynamic variables share the problem of lost heap-dynamic variables. Sometimes this problem is called **memory leakage.** In the following sections, we investigate how language designers have dealt with the problems of dangling pointers and lost heap-dynamic variables.

6.9.4   Pointers in Ada

HISTORY NOTE

Pascal included an explicit deallocate operator, **dispose**. Because of the problem of dangling pointers caused by **dispose**, some Pascal implementations simply ignored **dispose** when it appeared in a program. Although this effectively prevents dangling pointers, it also disallows the resuse of heap storage that the program no longer needs.

Ada's pointers are called **access** types. The dangling pointer problem is partially alleviated by Ada's design. A heap-dynamic variable may be (at the implementor's option) implicitly deallocated at the end of the scope of its pointer type, thus dramatically lessening the need for explicit deallocation. Because heap-dynamic variables can only be accessed by variables of one type, when the end of the scope of that type declaration is reached, no pointers can be left pointing at the object. This lessens the problem because improperly implemented explicit deallocation is the major source of dangling pointers. Unfortunately, the Ada language also has an explicit deallocator, Unchecked_Deallocation. Its name is meant to discourage its use, or at least warn the user of its potential problems.

The lost heap-dynamic variable problem is not eliminated by Ada's design of pointers.

6.9.5 Pointers in C and C++

In C and C++, pointers can be used in the same ways as addresses are used in assembly languages. This means they are extremely flexible but must be used with great care. This design offers no solutions to the dangling pointer or lost heap-dynamic variable problems. However, the fact that pointer arithmetic is possible in C and C++ makes their pointers more interesting than those of the other programming languages.

Unlike the pointers of Ada, which can only point into the heap, C and C++ pointers can point at virtually any variable anywhere in memory.

In C and C++, the asterisk (*) denotes the dereferencing operation, and the ampersand (&) denotes the operator for producing the address of a variable. For example, in the code

```
int *ptr;
int count, init;
...
ptr = &init;
count = *ptr;
```

the two assignment statements are equivalent to the single assignment

```
count = init;
```

The assignment to the variable ptr sets ptr to the address of init. The first assignment to count dereferences ptr to produce the value at init, which is then assigned to count. So the effect of the first two assignment statements is to assign the value of init to count. Notice that the declaration of a pointer specifies its domain type.

Pointers can be assigned the address value of any object of the correct domain type, or they can be assigned the constant zero, which is used for nil.

Pointer arithmetic is also possible in some restricted forms. For example, if ptr is a pointer variable that is declared to point at some object of some data type, then

```
ptr + index
```

is a legal expression. The semantics of such an expression is as follows. Instead of simply adding the value of index to ptr, the value of index is first scaled by the size of the memory cell (in memory units) to which ptr is pointing. For example, if ptr points to a memory cell for a type that is four memory units in size, then index is multiplied by 4, and the result is added to ptr. The primary purpose of this sort of address arithmetic is array manipulation. The following discussion is related to single-dimensioned arrays only.

In C and C++, all arrays use zero as the lower bound of their subscript ranges, and array names without subscripts always refer to the address of the first element. In fact, an array name without a subscript is treated exactly like a pointer, except that it is a constant and therefore cannot be assigned. Consider the following declarations:

```
int list [10];
int *ptr;
```

Consider the initializing assignment

```
ptr = list;
```

which assigns the address of list[0] to ptr, because an array name without a subscript is interpreted as the base address of the array. Given this assignment, the following are true:

- *(ptr + 1) is equivalent to list[1]
- *(ptr + index) is equivalent to list[index]
- ptr[index] is equivalent to list[index]

It is clear from these statements that the pointer operations include the same scaling that is used in indexing operations. Furthermore, pointers to arrays can be indexed as if they were array names.

Pointers can point to functions. This feature is used to pass functions as parameters to other functions. Pointers are also used for parameter passing, as discussed in Chapter 9.

C and C++ include pointers of type **void** *, which means they can point at values of any type. They are in effect generic pointers. However, type checking is not a problem with **void** * pointers, because they cannot be dereferenced. One common use of **void** * pointers is as parameters of functions that operate on memory. For example, suppose we wanted a function to move a sequence of bytes of data from one place in memory to another. It would be most general if it could be passed two pointers of any type. This would be legal if the corresponding formal parameters in the function were **void** * type. The function could then convert them to **char** * type and do the operation, regardless of what type pointers were sent as actual parameters.

6.9.6 Pointers in Fortran 95

Pointers in Fortran 95 are used to point to both heap-dynamic variables and static variables. For example, in

```
Integer, Pointer :: Int_Ptr
Integer, Pointer, Dimension (:) :: Int_List_Ptr
```

Int_Ptr can point at any value of type Integer, and Int_List_Ptr can point at any single-dimensioned array of Integer elements.

Fortran 95 pointers are implicitly dereferenced in most uses. For example, when a pointer appears in a normal expression, it is always implicitly dereferenced. A special assignment statement form pointer => target

is used when dereferencing is not desired. This assignment is used both to set pointer variables to point at particular variables and to set them to have the address values of other pointer variables. Any variable that is to be pointed to by a pointer variable must have the `Target` attribute, which is set in its declaration. For example, in the following

```
Integer, Target :: Apple
Integer Orange
```

`Apple` can be pointed to by `Int_Ptr`, but `Orange` cannot.

Fortran 95 pointers can easily become dangling, because the `Deallocate` statement, which takes a pointer as an argument, makes no attempt to determine if other pointers are pointing at a heap-dynamic variable that is being deallocated.

6.9.7   Reference Types

C++ includes a special kind of pointer type, called a **reference type,** that is used primarily for the formal parameters in function definitions. A C++ reference type variable is a constant pointer that is always implicitly dereferenced. Because a C++ reference type variable is a constant, it must be initialized with the address of some variable in its definition, and after initialization a reference type variable can never be set to reference any other variable. The implicit dereference of course prevents assignment to the address value of a reference variable.

Reference type variables are specified in definitions by preceding their names with ampersands (`&`). For example,

```
int result = 0;
int &ref_result = result;
...
ref_result = 100;
```

In this code segment, `result` and `ref_result` are aliases.

When used as formal parameters in function definitions, reference types provide for two-way communication between the caller function and the called function. This is not possible with nonpointer primitive parameter types, because C++ parameters are passed by value. Passing a pointer as a parameter accomplishes the same two-way communication, but pointer formal parameters require explicit dereferencing, making the code less readable and less safe. Reference parameters are referenced in the called function exactly as are other parameters. The calling function need not specify that a parameter whose corresponding formal parameter is a reference type is anything unusual. The compiler passes addresses, rather than values, to reference parameters.

In Java, reference variables are extended from their C++ form to one that allows them to replace pointers entirely. In their quest for increased safety over C++, the designers of Java removed C and C++ style pointers altogether. The fundamental difference between C++ pointers and Java references is that C++ pointers refer to memory addresses, whereas Java references refer to class instances. This immediately prevents arithmetic on references from being sensible. On the other hand, it does not disallow assignment. So unlike C++ reference variables, Java reference variables can be assigned to refer to different class instances. All Java class instances are referenced by reference variables. That is in fact the only use of reference variables in Java. These issues are further discussed in Chapter 12. In the following, `String` is a standard Java class:

```
String str1;
...
str1 = "This is a Java literal string";
```

In this code, `str1` is defined to be a reference to a `String` class instance or object, but is initially set to null. The subsequent assignment sets `str1` to reference the `String` object, `"This is a Java literal string"`.

Because Java class instances are implicitly deallocated (there is no explicit deallocation operator), there cannot be a dangling reference.

C# includes both the references of Java and the pointers of C++. However, the use of pointers is strongly discouraged. In fact, any method that uses pointers must include the **unsafe** modifier. Pointers were included in C# primarily to allow C# programs to have interoperability with C and C++ code.

6.9.8 Evaluation

The problems of dangling pointers and garbage have already been discussed at length. The problems of heap management are discussed in Section 6.9.9.3.

Pointers have been compared with the goto. The goto statement widens the range of statements that can be executed next. Pointer variables widen the range of memory cells that can be referenced by a variable. Perhaps the most damning statement about pointers was made by Hoare (1973): "Their introduction into high-level languages has been a step backward from which we may never recover."

The references of Java and C# provide some of the flexibility and the capabilities of pointers, without the hazards. It remains to be seen if programmers will be willing to trade the full power of C and C++ pointers for the greater safety of references.

6.9.9 Implementation of Pointer and Reference Types

In most languages, pointers are used in heap management. The same is true for Java and C# references, so we cannot treat pointers and references separately.

First we briefly describe how pointers and references are represented internally. We then discuss two possible solutions to the dangling pointer problem. Finally, we describe the major problems with heap management techniques.

6.9.9.1 Representations of Pointers and References

In most larger computers, pointers and references are single values stored in either 2- or 4-byte memory cells, depending on the size of the address space of the machine. However, most microcomputers are based on Intel microprocessors, which use addresses with two parts, a segment and an offset. So pointers and references are implemented in these systems as pairs of 16-bit words, one for each of the two parts of an address.

6.9.9.2 Solutions to the Dangling Pointer Problem

There have been several proposed solutions to the dangling pointer problem. Among these are **tombstones** (Lomet, 1975), in which every heap-dynamic variable includes a special cell, called a tombstone, that is itself a pointer to the heap-dynamic variable. The actual pointer variable points only at tombstones and never to heap-dynamic variables. When a heap-dynamic variable is deallocated, the tombstone remains but is set to nil, indicating that the heap-dynamic variable no longer exists. This prevents a pointer from ever pointing to a deallocated variable. Any reference to any pointer that points to a nil tombstone can be detected as an error.

Tombstones are costly in both time and space. Because tombstones are never deallocated, their storage is never reclaimed. Every access to a heap-dynamic variable through a tombstone requires one more level of indirection, which requires an additional machine cycle on most computers. Apparently none of the designers of the more popular languages have found the additional safety to be worth this additional cost, because no widely used language uses tombstones.

An alternative to tombstones is the **locks-and-keys approach** used in the implementation of UW-Pascal (Fischer and LeBlanc, 1977, 1980). In this compiler, pointer values are represented as ordered pairs (key, address), where the key is an integer value. Heap-dynamic variables are represented as the storage for the variable plus a header cell that stores an integer lock value. When a heap-dynamic variable is allocated, a lock value is created and placed both in the lock cell of the heap-dynamic variable and in the key cell of the pointer that is specified in the call to new. Every access to the dereferenced pointer compares the key value of the pointer to the lock value in the heap-dynamic variable. If they match, the access is legal; otherwise the access is treated as a run-time error. Any copies of the pointer value to other pointers must copy the key value. Therefore, any number of pointers can reference a given heap-dynamic variable. When a heap-dynamic variable is deallocated with dispose, its lock value is cleared to an illegal lock value. Then, if a pointer other than the one specified in the dispose is dereferenced, its address value will still be intact, but its key value will no longer match the lock, so the access will not be allowed.

Of course, the best solution to the dangling pointer problem is to take deallocation of heap-dynamic variables out of the hands of programmers. If programs cannot explicitly deallocate heap-dynamic variables, there will be no dangling pointers. To do this, the run-time system must implicitly deallocate heap-dynamic variables when they are no longer useful. LISP systems have always done this. Both Java and C# also use this approach for their reference variables. Note that C#'s pointers do not include implicit deallocation.

6.9.9.3 Heap Management

Heap management can be a very complex run-time process. We examine the process in two separate situations: one in which all heap storage is allocated and deallocated in units of a single size, and one in which variable-size segments are allocated and deallocated. Note that for deallocation, we discuss only implicit approaches. Our discussion will be brief and far from comprehensive, since a thorough analysis of these processes and their associated problems is not so much a language design issue as it is an implementation issue.

Single-Size Cells The simplest situation is when all allocation and deallocation is of a single-size cell. It is further simplified when every cell contains a pointer. This is the scenario of many implementations of LISP, where the problems of dynamic storage allocation were first encountered on a large scale. All LISP programs and most LISP data consist of cells connected into linked lists. Some string management processes are also involved, but we will ignore them here.

In a single-size allocation heap, all available cells are linked together using the pointers in the cells, forming a list of available space. Allocation is a simple matter of taking the required number of cells from this list when they are needed. Deallocation is a much more complex process. A heap-dynamic variable can be pointed to by more than one pointer, making it difficult to determine when the variable is no longer useful to the program. Simply because one pointer is disconnected from a cell obviously does not make it garbage; there could be several other pointers still pointing to the cell.

In LISP, several of the most frequent operations in programs create collections of cells that are no longer accessible to the program and therefore should be deallocated (put back on the list of available space). One of the fundamental design goals of LISP was to ensure that reclamation of unused cells would not be the task of the programmer but rather that of the run-time system. This left LISP implementors with the fundamental design question: When should deallocation be performed?

There are two distinct and in some ways opposite processes for reclaiming garbage: reference counters, in which reclamation is incremental and is done when inaccessible cells are created; and garbage collection, in which reclamation only occurs when the list of available space becomes empty.

These two methods are sometimes called the **eager approach** and the **lazy approach,** respectively.

The **reference counter** method of storage reclamation accomplishes its goal by maintaining a counter in every cell, which stores the number of pointers that are currently pointing at the cell. Embedded in the decrement operation for the reference counters, which occurs when a pointer is disconnected from the cell, is a check for a zero value. If the reference counter reaches zero, it means that no program pointers are pointing at the cell, and it has thus become garbage and can be returned to the list of available space.

There are three distinct problems with the reference counter method. First, if storage cells are relatively small, the space required for the counters is significant. Second, some execution time is obviously required to maintain the counter values. Every time a pointer value is changed, the cell to which it was pointing must have its counter decremented, and the cell to which it is now pointing must have its counter incremented. In a language like LISP, in which nearly every action involves changing pointers, that can be a significant portion of the total execution time of a program. Of course, if pointer changes are not too frequent, this is obviously not a problem. Third, complications arise when a collection of cells is connected circularly. The problem here is that each cell in the circular list has a reference counter value of at least 1, which prevents it from being collected and placed back on the list of available space. A solution to this problem can be found in Friedman and Wise (1979).

The primary alternative to reference counters is called **garbage collection.** With this method, the run-time system allocates storage cells as requested and disconnects pointers from cells as necessary, without regard for storage reclamation (allowing garbage to accumulate), until it has allocated all available cells. At this point, a garbage collection process is begun to gather all the garbage left floating around in the heap. To facilitate the garbage collection process, every heap cell has an extra indicator bit or field that is used by the collection algorithm.

The collection process consists of three distinct phases. First, all cells in the heap have their indicators set to indicate they are garbage. This is, of course, a correct assumption for only some of the cells. The second part of the process is the most difficult. Every pointer in the program is traced into the heap, and all reachable cells are marked as not being garbage. After this, the third phase is executed: All cells in the heap that have not been specifically marked as still being used are returned to the list of available space.

To illustrate the flavor of algorithms used to mark the cells that are currently in use, we provide the following simple version of a marking algorithm. We assume that all heap-dynamic variables, or heap cells, consist of an information part; a part for the mark, named `tag`; and two pointers named `llink` and `rlink`. These cells are used to build directed graphs with at most two edges leading from any node. The marking algorithm traverses all spanning trees of the graphs, marking all cells that are found. Like other graph traversals, the marking algorithm uses recursion.

```
for every pointer r do
  mark(r)

void mark(void * ptr) {
 if (ptr != 0)
   if (*ptr.tag is not marked) {
     set *ptr.tag
     mark(*ptr.llink)
     mark(*ptr.rlink)
   }
}
```

An example of the actions of this procedure on a given graph is shown in Figure 6.12. This simple marking algorithm suffers the problem of using a great deal of storage (for stack space to support recursion). A marking process that does not require additional stack space was developed by Schorr and Waite (1967). Their method reverses pointers as it traces out linked structures. Then, when the end of a list is reached, the process can follow the pointers back out of the structure.

The most serious problem with garbage collection can be summed up as follows: When you need it most, it works the worst. You need it most when the program actually needs most of the cells in the heap. Garbage collection in that situation takes a good deal of time, because most of the cells must be traced and marked as being useful. But in that case, the process yields only a small number

Figure 6.12

An example of the actions of the marking algorithm

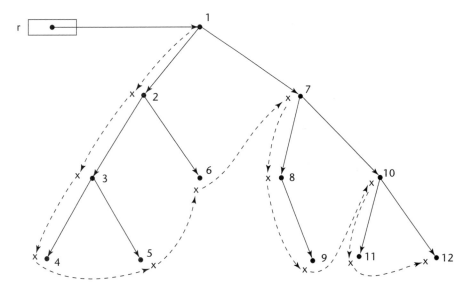

Dashed lines show the order of node_marking

of cells that can be placed on the list of available space. In addition to this problem, there is the cost of the additional space of the cell marks, which need be only a bit, and the execution time required to execute the collection process. However, these problems are not as serious as they sound, for two related reasons. First, memory is plentiful on most contemporary computers. Second, all larger computers use virtual memory, which makes their large memories appear much larger than they actually are.

Both the marking algorithms for the garbage collection method and the processes required by the reference counter method can be made more efficient by use of the pointer rotation and slide operations that are described by Suzuki (1982).

Variable-Size Cells   Managing a heap from which variable-size cells are allocated has all the difficulties of managing one for single-size cells, but also has additional problems. Unfortunately, variable-size cells are required by most programming languages. The additional problems posed by variable-size cell management depend on the method used. If garbage collection is used, the following additional problems occur:

- The initial setting of the indicators of all cells in the heap to indicate that they are garbage is difficult. Because the cells are different sizes, scanning them becomes a problem. One solution to this is to require each cell to have the cell size as its first field. Then the scanning can be done, although it takes slightly more space and somewhat more time than its counterpart for fixed-size cells.
- The marking process is nontrivial. How can a chain be followed from a pointer if there is no predefined location for the pointer in the pointed-to cell? Cells that do not contain pointers at all are also a problem. Adding a system pointer to each cell will work, but it must be maintained in parallel with the user-defined pointers. This adds both space and execution time overhead to the cost of running the program.
- Maintaining the list of available space is another source of overhead. The list can begin with a single cell consisting of all available space. Requests for segments simply reduce the size of this block. Reclaimed cells are added to the list. The problem is that before long, the list becomes a long list of various-size segments, or blocks. This slows allocation because requests cause the list to be searched for sufficiently large blocks. Eventually, the list may consist of a large number of very small blocks, which are not large enough for most requests. At this point, adjacent blocks may need to be collapsed into larger blocks. Alternatives to using the first sufficiently large block on the list can shorten the search but require the list to be ordered by block size. In either case, maintaining the list is additional overhead.

If reference counters are used, the first two problems are avoided, but the available-space list-maintenance problem remains.

SUMMARY

The data types of a language are a large part of what determines that language's style and use. Along with control structures, they form the heart of a language.

The primitive data types of most imperative languages include numeric, character, and Boolean types. The numeric types are often directly supported by hardware.

The user-defined enumeration and subrange types are convenient and add to the readability and reliability of programs.

Arrays are part of most programming languages. The relationship between a reference to an array element and the address of that element is given in an access function, which is an implementation of a mapping. Arrays can be either static, as in Fortran 77; fixed stack-dynamic, as in C functions; stack-dynamic, as in Ada blocks; fixed heap-dynamic, as with Java's objects; or heap-dynamic, as in Perl's arrays. Most languages allow only a few operations on complete arrays.

Records are now included in most languages. Fields of records are specified in a variety of ways. In the case of COBOL, they can be referenced without naming all of the enclosing records, although this is messy to implement and harmful to readability. In Java, records are supported in the class construct.

Unions are locations that can store different type values at different times. Discriminated unions include a tag to record the current type value. A free union is one without the tag. Most languages with unions do not have safe designs for them, the exception being Ada.

Pointers are used for addressing flexibility and to control dynamic storage management. Pointers have some inherent dangers: Dangling pointers are difficult to avoid, and garbage is difficult to collect.

Reference types, such as those in Java, provide heap management without the dangers of pointers.

The level of difficulty in implementing a data type has a strong influence on whether the type will be included in a language. Enumeration types, subrange types, and record types are all relatively easy to implement. Arrays are also straightforward, although array element access is an expensive process when the array has several subscripts. The access function requires one addition and one multiplication for each subscript.

Pointers are costly to implement if they are used for dynamic storage management and if steps are taken to avoid dangling pointers. Heap management is relatively easy if all cells have the same size, but becomes more complicated with variable-size cell allocation and deallocation.

BIBLIOGRAPHIC NOTES

A wealth of computer science literature exists that is concerned with data type design, use, and implementation. Hoare gives one of the earliest systematic definitions of structured types in Dahl et al. (1972). Tenenbaum compares the type design of ALGOL 68 and Pascal (Tenenbaum, 1978). Feuer and Gehani (1982) compare C and Pascal, including their type structures. A discussion of the insecurities of the Pascal data type design is included in Welsh et al. (1977). A general discussion of a wide variety of data types is given in Cleaveland (1986).

Implementing run-time checks on the possible insecurities of Pascal data types is discussed in Fischer and LeBlanc (1980). Most compiler design books, such as Fischer and LeBlanc (1988) and Aho et al. (1986), describe implementation methods for data types, as do the other programming language texts, such as Pratt and Zelkowitz (2001) and Scott (2000). A detailed discussion of the problems of heap management can be found in Tenenbaum et al. (1990). Garbage collection methods are developed by Schorr and Waite (1967) and Deutsch and Bobrow (1976). A comprehensive discussion of garbage collection algorithms can be found in Cohen (1981).

REVIEW QUESTIONS

1. What is a descriptor?
2. What are the advantages and disadvantages of decimal data types?
3. What are the design issues for character string types?
4. Describe the three string length options.
5. Define *ordinal*, *enumeration*, and *subrange types*.
6. What are the advantages of user-defined enumeration types?
7. In what ways are the user-defined enumeration types of C# more reliable than those of C++?
8. What are the design issues for arrays?
9. Define *static*, *fixed stack-dynamic*, *stack-dynamic*, *fixed heap-dynamic*, and *heap-dynamic arrays*. What are the advantages of each?
10. What array initialization feature is available in Ada that is not available in other common imperative languages?
11. What is an aggregate constant?
12. What array operations are provided specifically for single-dimensioned arrays in Ada?
13. What are the differences between the slices of Fortran 95 and those of Ada?

14. Define *row major order* and *column major order*.

15 What is an access function for an array?

16. What are the required entries in a Java array descriptor, and when must they be stored (at compile time or run time)?

17. What is the purpose of level numbers in COBOL records?

18. Define *fully qualified* and *elliptical references* to fields in records.

19. Define *union*, *free union*, and *discriminated union*.

20. What are the design issues for unions?

21. Are the unions of Ada always type checked?

22. What are the design issues for pointer types?

23. What are the two common problems with pointers?

24. Why are the pointers of most languages restricted to pointing at a single type object?

25. What is a C++ reference type and what is its common use?

26. Why are reference variables in C++ better than pointers for formal parameters?

27. What advantages do Java and C# reference type variables have over the pointers in other languages?

28. Describe the lazy and eager approaches to reclaiming garbage.

29. Why wouldn't arithmetic on Java and C# references make sense?

PROBLEM SET

1. What are the arguments for and against representing Boolean values as single bits in memory?

2. Why does a decimal value waste memory space?

3. COBOL uses several different methods of storing decimal numbers. Explain the format and purpose of each.

4. VAX minicomputers use a format for floating-point numbers that is not the same as the IEEE standard. What is this format, and why was it chosen by the designers of the VAX computers? A reference for VAX floating-point representations is Sebesta (1991).

5. Compare the tombstones and locks-and-keys methods of avoiding dangling pointers, from the points of view of safety and implementation cost.

6. What disadvantages are there in implicit dereferencing of pointers, but only in certain contexts? For example, consider the implicit dereference of a pointer to a record in Ada when it is used to reference a record field.

7. What significant justification is there for the -> operator in C and C++?

8. The unions in C and C++ are separate from the records of those languages, rather than combined as they are in Ada. What are the advantages and disadvantages to these two choices?

9. Multidimensional arrays can be stored in row major order, as in C++, or in column major order, as in Fortran. Develop the access functions for both of these arrangements for three-dimensional arrays.

10. In the Burroughs Extended ALGOL language, matrixes are stored as a single-dimensioned array of pointers to the rows of the matrix, which are treated as single-dimensioned arrays of values. What are the advantages and disadvantages of such a scheme?

11. Analyze and write a comparison of C's `malloc` and `free` functions with C++'s **new** and **delete** operators. Use safety as the primary consideration in the comparison.

12. Analyze and write a comparison of using C++ pointers and Java reference variables to refer to fixed heap-dynamic variables. Use safety and convenience as the primary considerations in the comparison.

13. Write a short discussion of what was lost and what was gained in Java's designers' decision to not include the pointers of C++.

14. What are the arguments for and against Java's implicit heap storage recovery, when compared with the explicit heap storage recovery required in C++?

15. What are the arguments for the inclusion of enumeration types in C#, although they are not in Java?

16. What would you expect to be the level of use of pointers in C#? How often will they be used when it is not absolutely necessary?

17. Make two lists of applications of matrices, one for those that require jagged matrices and one for those that require rectangular matrices. Now, argue whether just jagged, just rectangular, or both should be included in a programming language.

18. Compare the string manipulation capabilities of the class libraries of C++, Java, and C#.

PROGRAMMING EXERCISES

1. Design a set of simple test programs to determine the type compatibility rules of a C compiler to which you have access. Write a report of your findings.

2. Determine whether some C compiler to which you have access implements the `free` function.

3. Write a program that does matrix multiplication in some language that does subscript range checking and for which you can obtain an assembly language or machine language version from the compiler. Determine the number of instructions required for the subscript range checking and compare it with the total number of instructions for the matrix multiplication process.

4. If you have access to a compiler in which the user can specify whether subscript range checking is desired, write a program that does a large number of matrix accesses and times their execution. Run the program with subscript range checking and without it, and compare the times.

5. Write a simple program in C++ to investigate the safety of its enumeration types. Include at least 10 different operations on enumeration types to determine what incorrect or just silly things are legal. Now, write a C# program that does the same things and run it to determine how many of the incorrect or silly things are legal. Compare your results.

6. Write a program in C++ or C# that includes two different enumeration types and has a significant number of operations using the enumeration types. Also write the same program using only integer variables. Compare the readability and predict the reliability differences between the two programs.

7. Write a C program that does a large number of references to elements of two-dimensional arrays, using only subscripting. Write a second program that does the same operations but uses pointers and pointer arithmetic for the storage mapping function to do the array references. Compare the time efficiency of the two programs. Which of the two programs is likely to be more reliable? Why?

8. Write a Perl program that uses a hash and a large number of operations on the hash. For example, the hash could store people's names and their ages. A random number generator could be used to create three-character names and ages, which could be added to the hash. When a duplicate name was generated, it would cause an access to the hash, but not add a new element. Rewrite the same program without using hashes. Compare the execution efficiency of the two. Compare the ease of programming and readability of the two.

7

Expressions and Assignment Statements

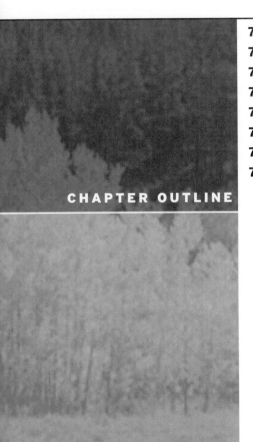

CHAPTER OUTLINE

A s the title indicates, the topic of this chapter is expressions and assignment statements. The semantic rules that determine the order of evaluation of operators in expressions are discussed first. This is followed by the potential problems of implementation-defined operand evaluation order when expressions can have side effects. Overloaded operators, both predefined and user-defined, are then discussed, along with their effects on the expressions in programs. Next, mixed-mode expressions are discussed and evaluated. This leads to the definition and evaluation of widening and narrowing type conversions, both implicit and explicit. Relational and Boolean expressions are then discussed, including the idea of short-circuit evaluation.

Finally, the assignment statement, from its simplest form to all of its variations, is covered, including assignments as expressions and mixed-mode assignments.

The chapter is focused on the expressions and assignment statements of the imperative languages. Issues of expression specification and evaluation in functional and logic languages are discussed in Chapters 15 and 16, respectively.

Character string pattern-matching expressions were discussed as a part of the material on character strings in Chapter 6, so they are not mentioned in this chapter.

7.1   Introduction

Expressions are the fundamental means of specifying computations in a programming language. It is crucial for a programmer to understand both the syntax and semantics of expressions. A formal mechanism (BNF) for describing the syntax of expressions was introduced in Chapter 3. In this chapter, we focus on the semantics of expressions—that is, what they mean—which is determined by how they are evaluated.

To understand expression evaluation, it is necessary to be familiar with the orders of operator and operand evaluation. The operator evaluation order of expressions is governed by the associativity and precedence rules of the language. Although the value of an expression sometimes depends on it, the order of operand evaluation in expressions is often unstated by language designers, a situation that allows programs to produce different results in different implementations. Other issues in expression semantics are type mismatches, coercions, and short-circuit evaluation.

The essence of the imperative programming languages is the dominant role of assignment statements. The purpose of an assignment statement is to change the value of a variable. So an integral part of all imperative languages is the concept of variables whose values change during program execution. (Nonimperative languages sometimes include variables of a different sort, such as the parameters of functions in functional languages.)

An assignment statement can simply cause a value to be copied from one memory cell to another. But in many cases, assignment statements include expressions with operators, which cause values to be copied to the processor and to be operated on, and the results to be copied back to memory.

Simple assignment statements specify an expression to be evaluated and a target location in which to place the result of the expression evaluation. As we shall see in this chapter, there are a number of variations on this basic form.

7.2   Arithmetic Expressions

Automatic evaluation of arithmetic expressions similar to those found in mathematics was one of the primary goals of the first high-level programming languages. Most of the characteristics of arithmetic expressions in programming languages were inherited from conventions that had evolved in mathematics. In programming languages, arithmetic expressions consist of operators, operands, parentheses, and function calls. The operators can be **unary,** meaning they have a single operand, or **binary,** meaning they have two operands. The C-based languages include a **ternary** operator, which has three operands, as discussed in Section 7.2.1.4.

In most imperative programming languages, binary operators are *infix*, which means they appear between their operands. One exception is Perl, which has some operators that are *prefix*, which means they precede their operands.

The purpose of an arithmetic expression is to specify an arithmetic computation. An implementation of such a computation must cause two actions: fetching the operands, usually from memory, and executing the arithmetic operations on those operands. In the following sections, we investigate the common design details of arithmetic expressions in the imperative languages.

Following are the primary design issues for arithmetic expressions, all of which are discussed in this section:

- What are the operator precedence rules?
- What are the operator associativity rules?
- What is the order of operand evaluation?
- Are there restrictions on operand evaluation side effects?
- Does the language allow user-defined operator overloading?
- What type mixing is allowed in expressions?

7.2.1   Operator Evaluation Order

We first investigate the language rules that specify the order of evaluation of operators.

7.2.1.1 Precedence

The value of an expression depends, at least in part, on the order of evaluation of the operators in the expression. Consider the following expression:

```
a + b * c
```

Suppose the variables a, b, and c have the values 3, 4, and 5, respectively. If evaluated left to right (the addition first and then the multiplication), the result is 35. If evaluated right to left, the result is 23.

Instead of simply evaluating the order from left to right or right to left, mathematicians have developed the concept of placing operators in a hierarchy of evaluation priorities and basing the evaluation order of expressions partly on this hierarchy. For example, in mathematics, multiplication is considered to be of higher priority than addition. If we follow that convention in our example expression, the multiplication would be evaluated first.

The **operator precedence** rules for expression evaluation define the order in which the operators of different precedence levels are evaluated. The operator precedence rules for expressions are based on the hierarchy of operator priorities, as seen by the language designer. The operator precedence rules of the common imperative languages are nearly all the same, because they are all based on those of mathematics. In these languages, exponentiation has the highest precedence (when it is provided by the language), followed by multiplication and division on the same level, followed by binary addition and subtraction on the same level.

Many languages also include unary versions of addition and subtraction. Unary addition is called the **identity operator** because it usually has no associated operation and thus has no effect on its operand. Ellis and Stroustrup, speaking about C++, call it a historical accident and correctly label it useless (Ellis and Stroustrup, 1990, p. 56). In Java, unary plus actually does have an effect when its operand is **short** or **byte**—it causes an implicit conversion of that operand to **int** type. Unary minus, of course, always changes the sign of its operand. In Java, unary minus also causes the implicit conversion of **short** and **byte** operands to **int** type.

In all of the common imperative languages, the unary minus operator can appear in an expression either at the beginning or anywhere inside the expression, as long as it is parenthesized to prevent it from being adjacent to another operator. For example,

```
A + (- B) * C
```

is legal, but

```
A + - B * C
```

usually is not.

As we shall see in Section 7.2.1.2, the precedence of the unary operators is rarely relevant.

The precedences of the arithmetic operators of a few common programming languages are as follows:

	Fortran	*C-based Languages*	*Ada*
Highest	**	postfix ++, --	**, **abs**
	*, /	prefix ++, --, unary +, -	*, /, **mod**, **rem**
	all +, -	*, /, %	unary +, -
Lowest	binary +, -		binary +,-

The ** operator is exponentiation. The % operator of C is exactly like the **rem** operator of Ada: It takes two integer operands and yields the remainder of the first after division by the second.[1] The Ada **mod** operator is identical to **rem** when both operands are positive, but can be different when one or both are negative. The ++ and -- operators of C are described in Section 7.7.4. The **abs** operator of Ada is a unary operator that yields the absolute value of its operand.

APL is odd among languages because it has a single level of precedence, as illustrated in the next section.

Precedence accounts for only some of the rules for the order of operator evaluation; associativity rules also affect it.

7.2.1.2 Associativity

Consider the following expression:

```
a - b + c - d
```

If the addition and subtraction operators have the same level of precedence, the precedence rules say nothing about the order of evaluation of the operators in this expression.

When an expression contains two adjacent occurrences of operators with the same level of precedence, the question of which operator is evaluated first is answered by the **associativity** rules of the language. An operator can either have left or right associativity, meaning that the leftmost occurrence is evaluated first or the rightmost occurrence is evaluated first, respectively.

Associativity in common imperative languages is left to right, except that the exponentiation operator (when provided) associates right to left. In the Java expression

```
a - b + c
```

---

[1] In versions of C before C99, the % operator was implementation dependent in some situations, because division was also implementation dependent.

the left operator is evaluated first. But exponentiation in Fortran is right associative, so in the expression

```
A ** B ** C
```

the right operator is evaluated first.

In Ada, exponentiation is nonassociative, which means that the expression

```
A ** B ** C
```

is illegal in Ada. Such an expression must be parenthesized to show the desired order, as in either

```
(A ** B) ** C
```

or

```
A ** (B ** C)
```

Now we can explain why the precedence of unary operators is often not important. Fortran unary and binary minus operations have the same precedence, but in Ada (and most other common languages) unary minus has precedence over binary minus. However, consider the expression

```
- A - B
```

Because Fortran uses left associativity for both unary and binary minus, and because Ada gives precedence to unary minus over binary minus, this expression is equivalent to

```
(-A) - B
```

in both languages. Next consider the following expressions:

```
- A / B
- A * B
- A ** B
```

In the first two cases, the relative precedence of the unary minus operator and the binary operator is irrelevant—the order of evaluation of the two operators has no effect on the value of the expression. In the last case, however, it does matter. Of the common programming languages, only Fortran and Ada have the exponentiation operator. In both cases, exponentiation has higher precedence than unary minus, so

```
- A ** B
```

is equivalent to

```
- (A ** B)
```

When unary operators appear at positions other than at the left end of expressions, they must be parenthesized in both languages, so in those situations those operators are forced to have the highest precedence (parentheses are discussed in Section 7.2.1.3).

There is one situation where the precedence of a unary operator can be confusing. In Ada, the precedence of unary minus is lower than that of **mod**, so the expression

```
- 17 mod 5
```

is equivalent to

```
- (17 mod 5)
```

which evaluates to –2, rather than 3, which would be the result if unary minus had higher precedence than **mod**, as it does in the C-based languages.

The associativity rules for a few of the most common imperative languages are given below:

Language	*Associativity Rule*
Fortran	Left: *, /, +, –
	Right: **
C-based languages	Left: *, /, %, binary +, binary –
	Right: ++, --, unary –, unary +
Ada	Left: all except **
	Nonassociative: **

As stated in Section 7.2.1.1, in APL, all operators have the same level of precedence. Thus the order of evaluation of operators in APL expressions is determined entirely by the associativity rule, which is right to left for all operators. For example, in the expression

```
A × B + C
```

the addition operator is evaluated first, followed by the multiplication operator (× is the APL multiplication operator). If A was 3, B was 4, and C was 5, the value of this APL expression would be 27.

Many compilers make use of the fact that some arithmetic operators are mathematically associative, meaning that the associativity rules have no impact on the value of an expression containing only those operators. For example, addition is mathematically associative, so in mathematics the value of the expression

```
A + B + C
```

does not depend on the order of operator evaluation. If floating-point operations for mathematically associative operations were also associative, the compiler could use this fact to perform some simple optimizations. Specifically, if the compiler is allowed to reorder the evaluation of operators, it may be able to produce slightly faster code for expression evaluation. Compilers actually do these kinds of optimizations.

Unfortunately, both floating-point representations and floating-point arithmetic operations are only approximations of their mathematical counterparts (because of size limitiations). The fact that a mathematical operator is associative does not necessarily imply that the corresponding floating-point operation is associative. In fact, only if all the operands and intermediate results can be exactly represented in floating-point notation will the process be precisely associative. For example, there are pathological situations in which integer addition on a computer is *not* associative. For example, suppose that a program must evaluate the expression

```
A + B + C + D
```

and that A and C are very large positive numbers, and B and D are negative numbers with very large absolute values. In this situation, adding B to A does not cause an overflow, but adding C to A does. Likewise, adding C to B does not cause overflow, but adding D to B does. Because of the limitations of computer arithmetic, addition is catastrophically unassociative in this case. Therefore, if the compiler reorders these addition operations, it affects the value of the expression. This is, of course, a problem that can be avoided by the programmer, assuming the approximate values of the variables are known. The programmer can simply parenthesize the expression (see Section 7.2.1.3) to ensure that only the safe order of evaluation is possible. However, this situation can arise in far more subtle ways, in which the programmer is less likely to notice the order dependence.

7.2.1.3 Parentheses

Programmers can alter the precedence and associativity rules by placing parentheses in expressions. A parenthesized part of an expression has precedence over its adjacent unparenthesized parts. For example, although multiplication has precedence over addition, in the expression

```
(A + B) * C
```

the addition will be evaluated first. Mathematically, this is perfectly natural. In this expression, the first operand of the multiplication operator is not available until the addition in the parenthesized subexpression is evaluated.

Languages that allow parentheses in arithmetic expressions could dispense with all precedence rules and simply associate all operators left to right or right to left. The programmer would specify the desired order of evaluation with parentheses. This would be simple because neither the author nor the readers of programs would need to remember any precedence or associativity rules. The disadvantage of this scheme is that it makes writing expressions more tedious, and it also seriously compromises the readability of the code. Yet this was the choice made by Ken Iverson, the designer of APL.

7.2.1.4 Conditional Expressions

We now look at the ternary operator, ?:, which is part of the C-based languages. This operator is used to form conditional expressions.

Sometimes **if-then-else** statements are used to perform a conditional expression assignment. For example, consider

```
if (count == 0)
  average = 0;
else
  average = sum / count;
```

In the C-based languages, this can be specified more conveniently in an assignment statement using a conditional expression, which has the form

expression_1 ? expression_2 : expression_3

where expression_1 is interpreted as a Boolean expression. If expression_1 evaluates to true, the value of the whole expression is the value of expression_2; otherwise, it is the value of expression_3. For example, the effect of the **if-then-else** above can be achieved with the following assignment statement, using a conditional expression:

```
average = (count == 0) ? 0 : sum / count;
```

In effect, the question mark denotes the beginning of the **then** clause, and the colon marks the beginning of the **else** clause. Both clauses are mandatory. Note that ? is used in conditional expressions as a ternary operator.

Conditional expressions can be used anywhere in a program (in a C-based language) where any other expression can be used.

7.2.2 Operand Evaluation Order

A less commonly discussed design characteristic of expressions is the order of evaluation of operands. Variables in expressions are evaluated by fetching their values from memory. Constants are sometimes evaluated the same way. In other cases, a constant may be part of the machine language instruction and not require a memory fetch. If an operand is a parenthesized expression, then all operators it contains must be evaluated before its value can be used as an operand.

If neither of the operands of an operator has side effects, then operand evaluation order is irrelevant. Therefore, the only interesting case arises when the evaluation of an operand does have side effects.

7.2.2.1 Side Effects

A **side effect** of a function, called a **functional side effect,** occurs when the function changes either one of its parameters or a global variable. (A global variable is declared outside the function but is accessible in the function.)

Consider the expression

```
a + fun(a)
```

If fun does not have the side effect of changing a, then the order of evaluation of the two operands, a and fun(a), has no effect on the value of the expression. However, if fun changes a, there is an effect. Consider the following situation: fun returns the value of its argument divided by 2 and changes its parameter to have the value 20. Suppose we have the following:

```
a = 10;
b = a + fun(a);
```

Then, if the value of a is fetched first (in the expression evaluation process), its value is 10 and the value of the expression is 15. But if the second operand is evaluated first, then the value of the first operand is 20 and the value of the expression is 25.

The following C program illustrates the same problem when a function changes a global variable that appears in an expression:

```
int a = 5;
int fun1() {
  a = 17;
  return 3;
}   /* of fun1 */
void fun2() {
  a = a + fun1();
}   /* of fun2 */
void main() {
  fun2();
}   /* of main */
```

The value computed for a in fun2 depends on the order of evaluation of the operands in the expression a + fun1(). The value of a will be either 8 or 20.

There are two solutions to the problem of operand evaluation order. First, the language designer could disallow function evaluation from affecting the value of expressions by simply disallowing functional side effects. The second method of avoiding the problem is to state in the language definition that operands in expressions are to be evaluated in a particular order and demand that implementors guarantee that order.

Disallowing functional side effects is difficult, and it eliminates some flexibility for the programmer. Consider the case of C and C++, which have only functions, meaning all subprograms return one value. To eliminate the side effects of two-way parameters and still provide subprograms that return more than one value, a new subprogram type that is similar to the procedures of the other imperative languages would be required. Access to globals in functions would also have to be disallowed. However, when efficiency is important, using access to global variables to avoid

HISTORY NOTE

The designers of Fortran 77 envisioned a third solution. The Fortran 77 definition states that expressions that have function calls are legal only if the functions do not change the values of other operands in the expression. Unfortunately, it is not easy for the compiler to determine the exact effect a function can have on variables outside the function, especially in the presence of global variables provided by Common and the aliasing provided by Equivalence. This is a case where the language definition specifies the conditions under which a construct is legal but leaves it to the programmer to ensure that such constructs are legally specified in programs.

parameter passing is an important method of increasing execution speed. In compilers, for example, global access to data such as the symbol table is commonplace.

The problem with having a strict evaluation order is that some code optimization techniques used by compilers involve reordering operand evaluations. A guaranteed order disallows those optimization methods when function calls are involved. There is, therefore, no perfect solution, as is borne out by actual language designs.

The Java language definition guarantees that operands appear to be evaluated in left-to-right order, eliminating the problem discussed in this section.

7.3 Overloaded Operators

Arithmetic operators are often used for more than one purpose. For example, + is used to specify integer addition and floating-point addition. Some languages, Java for example, also use it for string catenation. This multiple use of an operator is called **operator overloading** and is generally thought to be acceptable, as long as readability and/or reliability do not suffer.

As an example of the possible dangers of overloading, consider the use of the ampersand (&) in C. As a binary operator, it specifies a bitwise logical AND operation. As a unary operator, however, its meaning is totally different. As a unary operator with a variable as its operand, the expression value is the address of that variable. In this case, the ampersand is called the address-of operator. For example, the execution of

```
x = &y;
```

causes the address of y to be placed in x. There are two problems with this multiple use of the ampersand. First, using the same symbol for two completely unrelated operations is detrimental to readability. Second, the simple keying error of leaving out the first operand for a bitwise AND operation can go undetected by the compiler, because it is interpreted as an address-of operator. Such an error may be difficult to diagnose.

Virtually all programming languages have a less serious but similar problem, which is often due to the overloading of the minus operator. The problem is only that the compiler cannot tell if the operator is meant to be binary or unary. So once again, failure to include the first operand when the operator is meant to be binary cannot be detected as an error by the compiler. However, the meanings of the two operations, unary and binary, are at least closely related, so readability is not adversely affected.

Distinct operator symbols not only increase readability, but they are sometimes convenient to use for common operations as well. The division operator is an example. Consider the problem of finding the floating-point average of a list of integers. Normally the sum of those integers is computed as an integer. Suppose this has been done in the variable sum, and the number of values is in `count`. Now, if the floating-point average is to be computed and placed in the floating-point variable `avg`, this computation could be specified in C++ as

```
avg = sum / count;
```

But this assignment produces an incorrect result in most cases. Because both operands of the division operator are integer type, an integer division operation takes place in which the result is truncated to an integer. Then, in spite of the fact that the destination (`avg`) is floating-point type, its value from this assignment cannot have a fractional part. The integer result of division is converted to floating-point for the assignment *after* the truncation from the integer division.

One solution to the problem is to include two different division operators, one for integer division and one for floating-point division. This was done in Pascal, in which **div** specifies integer division and / specifies floating-point division. So, the following assignment can be used to get the correct floating-point quotient of the two integer values in `sum` and `count`:

```
avg := sum / count
```

where `avg` is floating-point type. Both operands of the division operator will be implicitly converted to floating-point, and a floating-point division operation is used. This kind of implicit conversion operation is further discussed in Section 7.4.1.

JavaScript avoids this problem by not having any integer arithmetic.

Another alternative solution is included in PHP. In PHP, if two integers are divided and the result is not an integer (a number with no fractional part), a floating-point value is produced.

Outside of JavaScript and PHP, explicit conversions must be used on the integer operands. Such conversions are discussed in Section 7.4.2.

Some languages that support abstract data types (see Chapter 11), for example, Ada, C++, Fortran 95, and C# allow the programmer to further overload operator symbols. For example, suppose a user wants to define the * operator between a scalar integer and an integer array to mean that each element of the array is to be multiplied by the scalar. This could be done by writing a function subprogram named * that performs this new operation. The compiler will choose the correct meaning when an overloaded operator is specified, based on the types of the operands, as with language-defined overloaded operators. For example, if this new definition for * is defined in a C# program, a C# compiler will use the new definition for * whenever the * operator appears with a simple integer as the left operand and an integer array as the right operand.

When sensibly used, user-defined operator overloading can aid readability. For example, if + and * are overloaded for a matrix abstract data type and `A`, `B`, `C`, and `D` are variables of that type, then

```
A * B + C * D
```

can be used instead of

```
MatrixAdd(MatrixMult(A, B), MatrixMult(C, D))
```

On the other hand, user-defined overloading can be harmful to readability. For one thing, nothing prevents a user from defining + to mean multiplication. Furthermore, seeing an * operator in a program, the reader must find both the types of the operands and the definition of the operator to determine its meaning. Any or all of these definitions could be in other files.

C++ has a few operators that cannot be overloaded. Among these are the class or structure member operator (.) and the scope resolution operator (::). Interestingly, operator overloading was one of the C++ features that was not copied into Java. However, it did reappear in C#.

7.4 Type Conversions

Type conversions are either narrowing or widening. A **narrowing conversion** converts a value to a type that cannot store even approximations of all of the values of the original type, for example, converting a **double** to a **float** in Java (the range of **double** is much larger than that of **float**). A **widening conversion** converts a value to a type that can include at least approximations of all of the values of the original type, for example, converting an **int** to a **float** in Java. Widening conversions are nearly always safe, whereas narrowing conversions are not.

Narrowing conversion obviously can cause problems. For example, if the floating-point value 1.3E25 is converted to an integer, the result will be only distantly related to the original value.

Although widening conversions are usually safe, they can result in reduced accuracy. In many language implementations, although integer to floating-point conversions are widening conversions, some accuracy may be lost. For example, in many cases, integers are stored in 32 bits, which allows at least nine decimal digits of precision. But floating-point values are also stored in 32 bits, with only about seven decimal digits of precision (because of the space used for the exponent). So, integer to floating-point widening can result in the loss of two digits of precision.

Type conversions can be either explicit or implicit. The following two subsections discuss these two kinds of type conversions.

7.4.1 Coercion in Expressions

One of the design decisions concerning arithmetic expressions is whether an operator can have operands of different types. Languages that do allow such expressions, which are called **mixed-mode expressions,** must define conventions for implicit operand type conversions, called **coercions,** because computers usually do not have binary operations that take operands of different types.

Recall that in Chapter 5 we defined coercion to be an implicit type conversion that is initiated by the compiler. We refer to type conversions explicitly requested by the programmer as explicit conversions, or casts, not coercions.

Although some operator symbols may be overloaded, we assume that a computer system, either in hardware or in some level of software simulation, has an operation for each operand type and operator defined in the language. For overloaded operators in a language that uses static type binding, the compiler chooses the correct type of operation on the basis of the types of the operands. When the two operands of an operator are not of the same type and that is legal in the language, the compiler must choose one of them to be coerced and supply the code for that coercion. In the following discussion, we examine the coercion design choices of several common languages.

Language designers are not in agreement on the issue of coercions in arithmetic expressions. Those against a broad range of coercions are concerned with the reliability problems that can result from such coercions, because they eliminate the benefits of type checking. Those who would rather include a wide range of coercions are more concerned with the loss in flexibility that results from restrictions. The issue is whether programmers should be concerned with this category of errors or whether the compiler should detect them.

As a simple illustration of the problem, consider the following skeletal Java method:

```
void myMethod() {
  int a, b, c;
  float d;
  ...
  a = b * d;
  ...
}
```

HISTORY NOTE

As a more extreme example of the dangers and costs of too much coercion, consider PL/I's efforts to achieve flexibility in expressions. In PL/I, a character string variable can be combined with an integer in an expression. At run time, the string is scanned for a numeric value. If the value happens to contain a decimal point, the value is assumed to be of floating-point type, the other operand is coerced to floating-point, and the resulting operation is floating-point. This coercion policy is very expensive because both the type check and the conversion must be done at run time. It also eliminates the possibility of detecting programmer errors in expressions, because a binary operator can combine an operand of any type with an operand of virtually any other type.

Assume that the second operand of the multiplication operator was supposed to be c, but because of a keying error it was typed as d. Because mixed-mode expressions are legal in Java, the compiler would not detect this as an error. It would simply insert code to coerce the value of the other operand, b, to **float**. If mixed-mode expressions were not legal in Java, this keying error would have been detected by the compiler as a type error.

Because error detection is reduced when mixed-mode expressions are allowed, Ada allows very few mixed type operands in expressions. It does not allow mixing of integer and floating-point operands in an expression, with one exception: The exponentiation operator, ******, can take either a floating-point or an integer type for the first operand and an integer type for the second operand. Ada allows a few other kinds of operand type mixing, usually related to subrange types.

In most of the other common languages, there are no restrictions on mixed-mode arithmetic expressions.

The C-based languages have integer types that are smaller than the **int** type. In Java, they are **byte** and **short**. Operands of all of these types are coerced to **int** whenever virtually any operator is applied to them. So while data can be stored in variables of these types, it cannot be manipulated before conversion to a larger type. For example, consider the following Java code:

```
byte a, b, c;
...
a = b + c;
```

The values of b and c are coerced to **int** and an **int** addition is performed. Then the sum is converted to **byte** and put in a.

7.4.2 Explicit Type Conversion

Most languages provide some capability for doing explicit conversions, both widening and narrowing. In some cases, warning messages are produced when an explicit narrowing conversion results in a significant change to the value of the object being converted.

In the C-based languages, explicit type conversions are called **casts**. To specify a cast, the desired type is placed in parentheses just before the expression to be converted, as in

```
(int) angle
```

One of the reasons for the parentheses around the type name in these conversions is that the first of these languages, C, has several two-word type names, such as **long int**.

In Ada, the casts have the syntax of function calls. For example,

```
Float(Sum)
```

7.4.3 Errors in Expressions

A number of errors can occur in expression evaluation. If the language requires type checking, then operand type errors cannot occur. We already discussed the errors that can occur because of coercions of operands in expressions. The other kinds of errors are due to the limitations of computer arithmetic and the inherent limitations of arithmetic. The most common error is created when the result of an operation cannot be represented in the memory cell where it must be stored. This is called **overflow** or **underflow**, depending on whether the result was too large or too small. One limitation of arithmetic is that division by zero is disallowed. Of course, the fact that it is not mathematically allowed does not prevent a program from attempting to do it.

Floating-point overflow and underflow, and division by zero are examples of run-time errors, which are sometimes called **exceptions**. Language facilities that allow programs to detect and deal with exceptions are discussed in Chapter 14.

7.5   Relational and Boolean Expressions

In addition to arithmetic expressions, programming languages include relational and Boolean expressions.

7.5.1   Relational Expressions

A **relational operator** is an operator that compares the values of its two operands. A **relational expression** has two operands and one relational operator. The value of a relational expression is Boolean, except when Boolean is not a type included in the language. The relational operators are often overloaded for a variety of types. The operation that determines the truth or falsehood of a relational expression depends on the operand types. It can be simple, as for integer operands, or complex, as for character string operands. Typically, the types of the operands that can be used for relational operators are numeric types, strings, and ordinal types.

HISTORY NOTE

The Fortran I designers used English abbreviations because the symbols > and < were not on the card punches at the time of Fortran I's design.

The syntax of the relational operators available in some common languages is as follows:

Operation	Ada	C-based Languages	Fortran 95
Equal	=	==	.EQ. or ==
Not equal	/=	!=	.NE. or <>
Greater than	>	>	.GT. or >
Less than	<	<	.LT. or <
Greater than or equal	>=	>=	.GE. or >=
Less than or equal	<=	<=	.LE. or >=

JavaScript and PHP have two additional relational operators, === and !==. These are similar to their relatives, == and !=, but prevent their operands from coercion. For example, the expression

"7" == 7

is true in JavaScript, because when a string and a number are the operands of a relational operator, the string is coerced to a number. However,

```
"7" === 7
```

is false, because no coercion is done with this operator.

The relational operators always have lower precedence than the arithmetic operators, so that in expressions such as

```
a + 1 > 2 * b
```

the arithmetic expressions are evaluated first.

7.5.2 Boolean Expressions

Boolean expressions consist of Boolean variables, Boolean constants, relational expressions, and Boolean operators. The operators usually include those for the AND, OR, and NOT operations, and sometimes for exclusive OR and equivalence. Boolean operators usually take only Boolean operands (Boolean variables, Boolean literals, or relational expressions) and produce Boolean values.

In the mathematics of Boolean algebras, the OR and AND operators must have equal precedence. In accordance with this, Ada's AND and OR operators have equal precedence. However, the C-based languages assign a higher precedence to AND than OR. Perhaps this resulted from the baseless correlation of multiplication with AND and of addition with OR, which would naturally assign higher precedence to AND.

Because arithmetic expressions can be the operands of relational expressions, and relational expressions can be the operands of Boolean expressions, the three categories of operators must be placed in different precedence levels, relative to each other.

The precedence of the arithmetic, relational, and Boolean opeartors in the C-based languages is

Highest	postfix ++, --
	unary +, -, prefix ++, --, !
	*, /, %
	binary +, -
	<, >, <=, >=
	=, !=
	&&
Lowest	||

Versions of C prior to C99 are odd among the popular imperative languages in that they have no Boolean type and thus no Boolean values. Instead, numeric values are used to represent Boolean values. In place of Boolean operands, numeric variables and constants are used, with zero considered false and all nonzero values considered true. The result of evaluating such an expression is an integer, with the value 0 if false and 1 if true.

One odd result of C's design is that the expression

```
a > b > c
```

is legal. The leftmost relational operator is evaluated first because the relational operators of C are left associative, producing either 0 or 1. Then this result is compared with the variable c. There is never a comparison between b and c.

When the nonarithmetic operators of the C-based languages are included, there are more than 40 operators and at least 14 different levels of precedence. This is clear evidence of the richness of the collections of operators and the complexity of expressions possible in these languages.

Readability dictates that a language should include a Boolean type, as we stated in Chapter 6, rather than simply using numeric types in Boolean expressions, as in C89. (Recall that both C99 and C++ still accept arithmetic expressions as Boolean expressions.) Some error detection is lost in C's use of numeric types, because any numeric expression, whether intended or not, is a legal operand to a Boolean operator. In the other imperative languages, any non-Boolean expression used as an operand of a Boolean operator is detected as an error.

7.6   Short-Circuit Evaluation

A **short-circuit evaluation** of an expression is one in which the result is determined without evaluating all of the operands and/or operators. For example, the value of the arithmetic expression

```
(13 * a) * (b / 13 - 1)
```

is independent of the value of (b / 13 - 1) if a is 0, because $0 * x = 0$ for any x. So when a is 0, there is no need to evaluate (b / 13 - 1) or perform the second multiplication. However, in arithmetic expressions this shortcut is not easily detected during execution, so it is never taken.

The value of the Boolean expression

```
(a >= 0) && (b < 10)
```

is independent of the second relational expression if a < 0, because (FALSE && x) is FALSE for all values of x. So when a < 0, there is no need to evaluate b, the constant 10, the second relational expression, or the && operation. Unlike the case of arithmetic expressions, this shortcut can be easily discovered during execution.

To illustrate a potential problem with non-short-circuit evaluation of Boolean expressions, suppose Java did not do short-circuit evaluation. Now suppose we write a table lookup loop using the **while** statement. One simple version of Java code for such a lookup, assuming that `list`, which has `listlen` elements, is the array to be searched and `key` is the searched-for value, is

```
index = 1;
while ((index < listlen) && (list[index] <> key))
  index = index + 1;
```

If evaluation is not short circuit, both relational expressions in the Boolean expression of the **while** statement are evaluated, regardless of the value of the first. Thus, if `key` is not in `list`, the program will terminate with a subscript out-of-range error. The same iteration that has `index == listlen` will reference `list[listlen]`, which causes the indexing error because `list` is declared to have `listlen-1` as an upper-bound subscript value.

If a language provides short-circuit evaluation of Boolean expressions and it is used, this is not a problem. In the preceding example, a short-circuit evaluation scheme would evaluate the first operand of the AND operator, but it would skip the second operand if the first operand is false.

Short-circuit evaluation of expressions exposes the problem of allowing side effects in expressions. Suppose that short-circuit evaluation is used on an expression and part of the expression that contains a side effect is not evaluated; then the side effect will only occur in complete evaluations of the whole expression. If program correctness depends on the side effect, short-circuit evaluation can result in a serious error. For example, consider the Java expression

```
(a > b) || ((b++) / 3)
```

In this expression, `b` is changed (in the second arithmetic expression) only when `a <= b`. If the programmer assumed `b` would be changed every time this expression is evaluated during execution, the program will fail.

Ada allows the programmer to specify short-circuit evaluation of the Boolean operators AND and OR by using the two-word operators **and then** and **or else**. For example, again assuming that `List` is declared to have a subscript range of `1..Listlen`, the Ada code

```
Index := 1;
while (Index <= Listlen) and then (List (Index) /= Key)
  loop
  Index := Index + 1;
  end loop;
```

will not cause an error when `Key` is not in `List` and `Index` becomes larger than `Listlen`.

In the C-based languages, the usual AND and OR operators, `&&` and `||`, respectively, are short circuit. However, these languages also have bitwise AND and OR operators, `&` and `|`, respectively, that can be used on Boolean-valued operands and are not short circuit. Of course, the bitwise operators are only equivalent to the usual Boolean operators if all operands are restricted to being either 0 (for true) or 1 (for false).

The inclusion of both short-circuit and ordinary operators in Ada is clearly the best design because it provides the programmer the flexibility of choosing short-circuit evaluation for any or all Boolean expressions.

7.7   Assignment Statements

As we have previously stated, the assignment statement is one of the central constructs in imperative languages. It provides the mechanism by which the user can dynamically change the bindings of values to variables. In the following section, the simplest form of assignment is discussed. Subsequent sections describe a variety of alternatives.

7.7.1   Simple Assignments

The general syntax of the simple assignment statement is

<target_variable> <assignment_operator> <expression>

Fortran, BASIC, and the C-based languages use the equal sign for the assignment operator.

The C-based languages use == as the equality relational operator to avoid confusion with their assignment operator.

ALGOL 60 pioneered the use of := as the assignment operator, which avoids the confusion of assignment with equality. Pascal, Modula-2, and Ada also use this assignment operator.

The assignment operator in the C-based languages is treated much like a binary operator, and as such it can appear embedded in expressions. This operator is discussed in Section 7.7.5.

The design choices of how assignments are used in a language have varied widely. In some languages, such as Fortran and Ada, an assignment can only appear as a stand-alone statement, and the destination is restricted to a single variable. There are, however, many alternatives.

7.7.2   Conditional Targets

C++, Java, and C# allow conditional targets on assignment statements. For example, consider

```
flag ? count1 : count2 = 0;
```

This is equivalent to

```
if (flag)

  count1 = 0;

else

  count2 = 0;
```

7.7.3 Compound Assignment Operators

A **compound assignment operator** is a shorthand method of specifying a commonly needed form of assignment. The form of assignment that can be abbreviated with this technique has the destination variable also appearing as the first operand in the expression on the right side, as in

```
a = a + b
```

Compound assignment operators were introduced by ALGOL 68, were later adopted in a slightly different form by C, and are part of the other C-based languages. The syntax of these assignment operators is the catenation of the desired binary operator to the = operator. For example,

```
sum += value;
```

is equivalent to

```
sum = sum + value;
```

The C-based languages have versions of the compound assignment operators for most of their binary operators.

7.7.4 Unary Assignment Operators

The C-based languages include two special unary arithmetic operators that are actually abbreviated assignments. They combine increment and decrement operations with assignment. The operators ++ for increment, and -- for decrement, can be used either in expressions or to form stand-alone single-operator assignment statements. They can appear as either prefix operators, meaning they precede the operands, or as postfix operators, meaning they follow the operands. In the assignment statement

```
sum = ++ count;
```

the value of count is incremented by 1 and then assigned to sum. This could also be stated as

```
count = count + 1;
sum = count;
```

If the same operator is used as a postfix operator, as in

```
sum = count ++;
```

the assignment of the value of `count` to `sum` occurs first; then `count` is incremented. The effect is the same as that of the two statements

```
sum = count;
count = count + 1;
```

An example of the use of the unary increment operator to form a complete assignment statement is

```
count ++;
```

which simply increments `count`. It does not look like an assignment, but it certainly is one. It is equivalent to the statement

```
count = count + 1;
```

When two unary operators apply to the same operand, the association is right to left. For example, in

```
- count ++
```

count is first incremented and then negated. So it is

```
- (count ++)
```

not

```
(- count) ++
```

7.7.5   Assignment as an Expression

In the C-based languages, the assignment statement produces a result, which is the same as the value assigned to the target. It can therefore be used as an expression and as an operand in other expressions. This design treats the assignment operator much like any other binary operator, except that it has the side effect of changing its left operand. For example, in C, it is common to write statements such as

```
while ((ch = getchar()) != EOF) { ... }
```

In this statement, the next character from the standard input file, usually the keyboard, is gotten with `getchar` and assigned to the variable `ch`. The result, or value assigned, is then compared with the constant `EOF`. If `ch` is not equal to `EOF`, the compound statement `{ ... }` is executed. Note that the assignment must be parenthesized—in these languages the precedence of the assignment operator is lower than that of the relational operators. Without the parentheses, the new character would be compared with `EOF` first. Then the result of that comparison, either 0 or 1, would be assigned to `ch`.

The disadvantage of allowing assignment statements to be operands in expressions is that it provides yet another kind of expression side effect. This type of side effect can lead to expressions that are difficult to read and understand. An expression with any kind of side effect has this disadvantage. Such an expression cannot be read as an expression, which in mathematics is a denotation of a value, but only as a list of instructions with an odd order of execution. For example, the expression

```
a = b + (c = d / b++) - 1
```

denotes the instructions

Assign b to `temp`
Assign b + 1 to b
Assign d / `temp` to c
Assign b + c to `temp`
Assign `temp` - 1 to a

Note that C's use of the assignment operator allows the effect of multiple-target assignments, such as

```
sum = count = 0;
```

in which `count` is first assigned the zero, and then `count`'s value is assigned to `sum`.

There is a loss of error detection in the C design of the assignment operation that frequently leads to program errors. In particular, if we type

if (x = y) ...

instead of

if (x == y) ...

which is an easy mistake to make, it is not detectable as an error by the compiler. Rather than testing a relational expression, the value that is assigned to x is tested (in this case, it is the value of y that reaches this statement). This is actually a result of three design decisions: allowing assignment to behave like an ordinary binary operator, using arithmetic expressions as Boolean operands, and using two very similar operators, = and ==, to have completely different meanings. This is another example of the safety deficiencies of C and C++ programs. Note that Java and C# allow only **boolean** expressions in their **if** statements, disallowing this problem.

7.8 Mixed-mode Assignment

We discussed mixed-mode expressions in Section 7.4.1. Frequently, assignment statements also are mixed-mode. The design question is, Does the type of the expression have to be the same as the type of the variable being assigned, or can coercion be used in some cases of type mismatch?

Fortran and the C-based languages use coercion rules for mixed-mode assignment that are similar to those they use for mixed-mode expressions; that is, many of the possible type mixes are legal, with coercion freely applied. Ada does not allow mixed-mode assignment.

In a clear departure from C and C++, Java and C# allow mixed-mode assignment only if the required coercion is widening. So, an **int** value can be assigned to a **float** variable, but not vice versa. Disallowing half of the possible mixed-mode assignments is a simple but effective way to increase the reliability of Java and C#, relative to C and C++.

In all languages that allow mixed-mode assignment, the coercion takes place only after the right side expression has been evaluated. One alternative would be to coerce all operands in the right side to the type of the target before evaluation. For example, consider the following code:

```
int a, b;
float c;
...
c = a / b;
```

Because c is **float**, the values of a and b could be coerced to **float** before the division, which could produce a different value for c than if the coercion were delayed (for example, if a were 2 and b were 3).

SUMMARY

Expressions consist of constants, variables, parentheses, function calls, and operators. Assignment statements include target variables, assignment operators, and expressions.

The semantics of an expression is determined in large part by the order of evaluation of operators. The associativity and precedence rules for operators in the expressions of a language determine the order of operator evaluation in those expressions. Operand evaluation order is important if functional side effects are possible. Type conversions can be widening or narrowing. Some narrowing conversions produce erroneous values. Implicit type conversions, or coercions, in expressions are common, although they eliminate the error-detection benefit of type checking, thus lowering reliability.

Assignment statements have appeared in a wide variety of forms, including conditional targets and assigning operators.

REVIEW QUESTIONS

1. Define *operator precedence* and *operator associativity*.
2. Define *functional side effect*.
3. What is a coercion?
4. What is a conditional expression?

5. What is an overloaded operator?

6. Define *narrowing* and *widening conversions*.

7. What is a mixed-mode expression?

8. How does operand evaluation order interact with functional side effects?

9. What is short-circuit evaluation?

10. Name a language that always does short-circuit evaluation of Boolean expressions. Name one that never does it. Name one in which the programmer is allowed to choose.

11. How does C support relational and Boolean expressions?

12. What is the purpose of a compound assignment operator?

13. What is the associativity of C's unary arithmetic operators?

14. What is one possible disadvantage of treating the assignment operator as if it were an arithmetic operator?

15. What mixed-mode assignments are allowed in Ada?

16. What mixed-mode assignments are allowed in Java?

PROBLEM SET

1. When might you want the compiler to ignore type differences in an expression?

2. State your own arguments for and against allowing mixed-mode arithmetic expressions.

3. Do you think the elimination of overloaded operators in your favorite language would be beneficial? Why or why not?

4. Would it be a good idea to eliminate all operator precedence rules and require parentheses to show the desired precedence in expressions? Why or why not?

5. Should C's assigning operations (for example, +=) be included in other languages? Why or why not?

6. Should C's single-operand assignment forms (for example, ++count) be included in other languages? Why or why not?

7. Describe a situation in which the add operator in a programming language would not be commutative.

8. Describe a situation in which the add operator in a programming language would not be associative.

9. Assume the following rules of associativity and precedence for expressions:

Precedence:	*Highest*	$*$, $/$, **not**
		$+$, $-$, $\&$, **mod**
		$-$ (unary)
		$=$, $/=$, $<$, $<=$, $>=$, $>$
		and
	Lowest	**or**, **xor**
Associativity:	*Left to right*	

Show the order of evaluation of the following expressions by parenthesizing all subexpressions and placing a superscript on the right parenthesis to indicate order. For example, for the expression

```
a + b * c + d
```

the order of evaluation would be represented as

$((a + (b * c)^1)^2 + d)^3$

a. `a * b - 1 + c`

b. `a * (b - 1) / c mod d`

c. `(a - b) / c & (d * e / a - 3)`

d. `-a or c = d and e`

e. `a > b xor c or d <= 17`

f. `-a + b`

10. Show the order of evaluation of the expressions of Problem 9, assuming that there are no precedence rules and all operators associate right to left.

11. Write a BNF description of the precedence and associativity rules defined for the expressions in Problem 9. Assume the only operands are the names a, b, c, d, and e.

12. Using the grammar of Problem 11, draw parse trees for the expressions of Problem 9.

13. Let the function fun be defined as

```
int fun(int *k) {
  *k += 4;
  return 3 * (*k) - 1;
}
```

Suppose fun is used in a program as follows:

```
void main() {
  int i = 10, j = 10, sum1, sum2;
  sum1 = (i / 2) + fun(&i);
  sum2 = fun(&j) + (j / 2);
}
```

What are the values of sum1 and sum2

a. if the operands in the expressions are evaluated left to right?

b. if the operands in the expressions are evaluated right to left?

14. What is your primary argument against (or for) the operator precedence rules of APL?

15. For some language of your choice, make up a list of operator symbols that could be used to eliminate all operator overloading.

16. Determine whether the narrowing explicit type conversions in two languages you know provide error messages when a converted value loses its usefulness.

17. Should an optimizing compiler for C or C++ be allowed to change the order of subexpressions in a Boolean expression? Why or why not?

18. Answer the question in Problem 18 for Ada.

19. Consider the following C program:

```
int fun(int *i) {
  *i += 5;
  return 4;
}
void main() {
  int x = 3;
  x = x + fun(&x);
}
```

What is the value of x after the assignment statement in main, assuming

a. operands are evaluated left to right.

b. operands are evaluated right to left.

PROGRAMMING EXERCISES

1. Run the code given in Problem 13 (in the Problem Set) on some system that supports C to determine the values of sum1 and sum2. Explain the results.

2. Rewrite the program of Exercise 1 in C++, Java, and C#, run them, and compare the results.

3. Write a test program in your favorite language that determines and outputs the precedence and associativity of its arithmetic and Boolean operators.

4. Write an Ada program that illustrates the difference between **mod** and **rem** using a variety of positive and negative integer operands.

5. Write a Java program that exposes Java's rule for operand evaluation order when one of the operands is a method call.

6. Repeat Exercise 5 with C++.

7. Repeat Exercise 6 with C#.

8

Statement-Level Control Structures

CHAPTER OUTLINE

The flow of control, or execution sequence, in a program can be examined at several levels. In Chapter 7 we discussed the flow of control within expressions, which is governed by operator associativity and precedence rules. At the highest level is the flow of control among program units, which is discussed in Chapters 9 and 13. Between these two extremes is the important issue of the flow of control among statements, which is the subject of this chapter.

We begin by giving an overview of the evolution of control statements in the imperative programming languages. This is followed by a thorough examination of selection constructs, including those for two-way and multiple selection. We then discuss the variety of looping constructs that have been developed and used in programming languages. Then we take a close look at the controversial unconditional branch statement. Finally, we describe the guarded command control constructs.

8.1   Introduction

Computations in imperative language programs are accomplished by evaluating expressions and assigning the resulting values to variables. There are, however, few useful programs that consist entirely of assignment statements. At least two additional linguistic mechanisms are necessary to make the computations in programs flexible and powerful: some means of selecting among alternative control flow paths (of statement execution) and some means of causing the repeated execution of certain collections of statements. Statements that provide these kinds of capabilities are called **control statements.**

The control statements of the first successful programming language, Fortran, were, in effect, designed by the architects of the IBM 704. All were directly related to machine language instructions, so their capabilities had more to do with instruction design than language design. At the time, little was known about the difficulty of programming, and, as a result, the control statements of Fortran in the late 1950s were thought to be entirely acceptable. By today's standards, however, they are considered wholly inadequate.

A great deal of research and discussion was devoted to control statements in the 10 years between the mid-1960s and the mid-1970s. One of the primary conclusions of these efforts was that, although a single control statement (a selectable goto) is obviously sufficient, a language that is designed *not* to include a goto needs only a small number of different control statements. In fact, it was proven that all algorithms that can be expressed by flowcharts can be coded in a programming language with only two control statements: one for choosing between two control flow paths and one for logically controlled iterations (Böhm and Jacopini, 1966). An important result of this is that unconditional branch statements are superfluous—potentially useful but nonessential. This fact, combined with the practical problems of using unconditional branches, or gotos, led to a great deal of debate about the goto, as will be discussed in Section 8.4.1.

Programmers care less about the results of theoretical research on control statements than they do about writability and readability. All languages that have become widely used include more control statements than the two that are minimally required, because writability is enhanced by a larger number of control statements. For example, rather than requiring the use of a **while** for all loops, it is easier to write programs when a **for** can be used to build loops that are naturally controlled by a counter. The primary factor that restricts the number of control statements in a language is readability, because the presence of a large number of statement forms demands that program readers learn a larger language. Recall that few people learn all of the constructs of a very large language; instead, they learn the subset they choose to use, which is often a different subset from that used by the programmer who wrote the program they are trying to read. On the other hand, too few control statements can require the use of lower-level statements, such as the goto, which makes programs less readable.

The question as to the best collection of control statements to provide the required capabilities and the desired writability has been widely debated. It is essentially a question of how much a language should be expanded to increase its writability at the expense of its simplicity, size, and readability.

A **control structure** is a control statement and the collection of statements whose execution it controls.

There is one design issue that is relevant to all of the selection and iteration control statements: whether the control structure can have multiple entries. All selection and iteration statements control the execution of code segments, and the question is whether the execution of those code segments always begins with the first statement in the segment. It is now generally believed that multiple entries add little to the flexibility of a control construct, relative to the decrease in readability caused by the increased complexity. Note that multiple entries are possible only in languages that include gotos and statement labels.

At this point the reader may wonder why multiple exits from control structures is not listed as a design issue here. Because there is no danger in multiple exits, they are included in all languages. Thus, they are not a serious issue.

8.2   Selection Statements

A **selection statement** provides the means of choosing between two or more execution paths in a program. Such statements are fundamental and essential parts of all programming languages, as was proven by Böhm and Jacopini.

Selection statements fall into two general categories, two-way and *n*-way, or multiple selection. Two-way selectors are discussed in Section 8.2.1; multiple-way selectors are covered in Section 8.2.2.

8.2.1   Two-Way Selection Statements

Although the two-way selection statements of contemporary imperative languages are quite similar, the variations in the evolution of them has been based on a collection of design considerations. The general form of a two-way selector is as follows:

if control_expression
  then clause
  else clause

8.2.1.1 Design Issues

The design issues for two-way selectors can be summarized as follows:

- What is the form and type of the expression that controls the selection?
- How are the then and else clauses specified?
- How should the meaning of nested selectors be specified?

8.2.1.2 The Control Expression

Control expressions are specified in parentheses if the **then** reserved word is not used to introduce the then clause, as in the C-based languages. In those cases where the **then** reserved word is used, there is less need for the parentheses, so they are often omitted, as in Ada.

In C89, which did not have a Boolean data type, arithmetic expressions were used as control expressions. This can also be done in C99 and C++. However, in those languages either arithmetic or Boolean expressions can be used. In other contemporary languages, such as Ada, Java, and C#, only Boolean expressions can be used for control expressions.

8.3.1.3 Clause Form

In most contemporary languages, the then and else clauses either appear as single statements or compound statements. One exception is Perl, in which all then and else clauses must be compound statements, even if they contain single statements. The C-based languages, as well as Perl, JavaScript, and PHP, use braces to form compound statements. In Fortran 95 and Ada, the then and else clauses are statement sequences. The last clause in a selection construct in these languages is terminated with two special words (**end** and **if** in Ada). This has implications for the specification of the meaning of nested selectors, as is discussed in Section 8.2.1.4.

8.2.1.4 Nesting Selectors

An interesting problem arises when two-way selection constructs can be nested. Consider the following Java-like code:

```
if (sum == 0)
  if (count == 0)
    result = 0;
else
    result = 1;
```

This construct can be interpreted in two different ways, depending on whether the else clause is matched with the first then clause or the second. Notice that the indentation seems to indicate that the else clause belongs with the first then clause. However, indentation has no effect on semantics in contemporary languages and is therefore ignored by their compilers.

The crux of the problem in this example is that the else clause follows two then clauses with no intervening else clause, and there is no syntactic indicator to specify a matching of the else clause to one of the then clauses. In Java, as in many other imperative languages, the static semantics of the language specify that the else clause is always paired with the nearest unpaired then clause (above the else clause). A rule, rather than a syntactic entity, is used to provide the disambiguation. So, in the above example, the else clause would be the alternative to the second then clause. The disadvantage of using a rule rather than some syntactic entity is that although the programmer may have meant the else clause to be the alternative to the first then clause and the compiler found the structure syntactically correct, its semantics is the opposite. To force the alternative semantics in Java, a different syntactic form is required, in which the inner **if** is put in a compound, as in

```
if (sum == 0) {
  if (count == 0)
    result = 0;
}
else
  result = 1;
```

C, C++, and C# have the same problem as Java with selection statement nesting. Because Perl requires that all then and else clauses be compound, it does not have the problem.

One way to avoid the issue of nested selection statements is to use an alternative means of forming compound statements. Consider the syntactic structure of the Java **if** statement. The then clause follows the control expression and the else clause is introduced by the reserved word **else**. When the then clause is a single statement and the else clause is present, although there is no need to mark the end, the **else** reserved word in fact marks the end of the then clause. When the then clause is a compound, it is terminated by a right brace. However, if the last clause in an **if**, whether then or else, is not a compound, there is no syntactic entity to mark the end of the whole selection construct. The use

HISTORY NOTE

The designers of ALGOL 60 chose to use syntax, rather than a rule, to connect else clauses to then clauses. Specifically, an **if** statement is not allowed to be nested directly in a then clause. If an **if** must be nested in a then clause, it must be placed in a compound statement, as in the latter Java example above.

The difference between the two designs is that the Java version allows one to write the nested selector that looks like it pairs the else clause with the first then clause but does not, whereas this same form is syntactically illegal in ALGOL 60, thereby disallowing Java's subtle problem.

of a special word for this purpose resolves the question of the semantics of nested selectors and also adds to the readability of the construct. This is the design of the selection construct in Fortran 95 and Ada. For example, consider the following Ada construct:

```
if A > B then
  Sum := Sum + A;
  Acount := Acount + 1;
else
  Sum := Sum + B;
  Bcount := Bcount + 1;
end if;
```

The design of this construct is more regular than that of the selection constructs of the C-based languages, because the form is the same regardless of the number of statements in the then and else clauses. (This is also true for Perl.) In Ada, the then and else clauses consist of statement sequences rather than compound statements. The first interpretation of the selector example at the beginning of Section 8.2.1.4 can be written in Ada as follows:

```
if Sum = 0 then
  if Count = 0 then
    Result := 0;
  else
    Result := 1;
  end if;
end if;
```

Because the **end if** reserved words close the nested **if**, it is clear that the else clause is matched to the inner then clause.

The second interpretation of the selection construct in Section 8.2.1.4 can be written in Ada as follows:

```
if Sum = 0 then
  if Count = 0 then
    Result := 0;
  end if;
else
  Result := 1;
end if;
```

8.2.2   Multiple Selection Constructs

The **multiple selection** construct allows the selection of one of any number of statements or statement groups. It is, therefore, a generalization of a selector. In fact, two-way selectors can be built with a multiple selector.

The need to choose among more than two control paths in a program is common. Although a multiple selector can be built from two-way selectors and gotos, the resulting structures are cumbersome, difficult to write and read, and unreliable. Therefore, the need for a special structure is clear.

8.2.2.1 Design Issues

Some of the design issues for multiple selectors are similar to some of those for two-way selectors. For example, one issue is the question of the type of expression on which the selector is based. In this case, the range of possibilities is larger, in part because the number of possible selections is larger. A two-way selector needs an expression with only two possible values. Another issue is whether single statements, compound statements, or statement sequences may be selected. Next, there is the question of whether only a single selectable segment can be executed when the construct is executed. This is not an issue for two-way selectors because they allow only one of the clauses to be on a control path during one execution. As we shall see, the resolution of this issue for multiple selectors is a trade-off between reliability and flexibility. Finally, there is the issue of what should result from the selector expression evaluating to a value that does not select one of the segments. (Such a value would be unrepresented among the selectable segments.) The choice here is between simply disallowing the situation from arising and having the construct do nothing at all when it does arise.

The following is a summary of these design issues:

- What is the form and type of the expression that controls the selection?
- How are the selectable segments specified?
- Is execution flow through the structure restricted to include just a single selectable segment?
- How should unrepresented selector expression values be handled, if at all?

8.2.2.2 Examples of Multiple Selectors

The C multiple selector construct, **switch**, which is also part of C++ and Java, is a relatively primitive design. Its general form is

```
switch (expression) {
  case constant_expression_1: statement_1;
  . . .
  case constant_expression_n: statement_n;
  [default: statement_n+1 ]
}
```

where the control expression and the constant expressions are integer type. The selectable statements can be statement sequences, compound statements, or blocks. The optional **default** segment is for unrepresented values of the control expression. If the value of the control expression is not represented, the construct does nothing.

The **switch** construct does not provide implicit branches at the end of those code segments. This allows control to flow through more than one selectable code segment on a single execution. Consider the following example:

```
switch (index) {
  case 1:
  case 3: odd += 1;
          sumodd += index;
  case 2:
  case 4: even += 1;
          sumeven += index;
  default: printf("Error in switch, index = %d\n", index);
  }
```

This code prints the error message on every execution. Likewise, the code for the 2 and 4 constants is executed every time the code at the 1 or 3 constants is executed. To logically separate these segments, an explicit branch must be included. The **break** statement, which is actually a restricted goto, is normally used for exiting **switch** constructs

The following **switch** construct uses **break** to restrict each execution to a single selectable segment:

```
switch (index) {
  case 1:
  case 3: odd += 1;
          sumodd += index;
          break;
  case 2:
  case 4: even += 1;
          sumeven += index;
          break;
  default: printf("Error in switch, index = %d\n", index);
}
```

Occasionally, it is convenient to allow control to flow from one selectable code segment to another. This is obviously the reason why there are no implicit branches in the **switch** construct. The reliability problem with this design arises when the mistaken absence of a **break** statement in a segment allows control to incorrectly flow to the next segment. The designers of C's **switch** chose to trade some decrease in reliability for some increase in flexibility. Studies have shown, however, that the ability to have control flow from one selectable segment to another is rarely used. C's **switch** is modeled on the multiple selection statement in ALGOL 68, which also does not have implicit branches from selectable segments.

The C# switch statement differs from that of its C-based predecessors in that a static semantics rule disallows the implicit execution of more than one segment. The rule is that every selectable segment must end with an explicit unconditional branch statement, either a **break**, which transfers control out of the **switch** construct, or a goto, which can transfer control to one of the slectable segments (or virtually anywhere else). For example,

```
switch (value) {
   case -1:
      Negatives++;
      break;
   case 0:
      Positives++;
      goto case 1;
   case 1:
      Positives++;
   default:
      Console.WriteLine("Error in switch \n");
}
```

Note that `Console.WriteLine` is the method for displaying strings in C#.

The Ada **case** statement is a descendant of the multiple-selector statement that appeared in ALGOL W in 1966. The general form of this construct is as follows:

```
case expression is
   when choice list => statement_sequence;
   . . .
   when choice list => statement_sequence;
   [when others => statement_sequence;]
end case;
```

where the expression is of ordinal type (integer, Boolean, character, or enumeration type) and the **when others** clause is optional.

The choice lists of Ada **case** statements are often single constants, but they can also be subranges, such as `10..15`. They can also use OR operators, specified by the symbol |, to create lists of constants. For example, the following could appear as a choice list: `10|15|20`. The **when others** clause is used for unrepresented values. Ada requires the choice lists to be exhaustive, which provides a bit more reliability because it disallows the error of inadvertent omission of one or more choice values. Most Ada **case** statements include a **when others** clause to ensure that the choice list is exhaustive. Because the choice lists must be exhaustive, there is never a question of what happens when the control expression has an unrepresented value.

The choice lists must be of the same type as the expression, of course. They must be mutually exclusive; that is, a constant may not appear in more than one choice list.

The semantics of the Ada **case** is as follows: The expression is evaluated, and the value is compared with the constants in the choice lists. If a match is found, control transfers to the statement attached to the matched constant. When statement execution is completed, control transfers to the first statement following the whole **case** construct. So, the Ada **case** statement is more reliable than the **switch** statments of C, C++, and Java, which do not have implicit exits after the selectable segments.

8.2.2.3 Multiple Selection Using `if`

In many situations, a **switch** or **case** construct is inadequate for multiple selection. For example, when selections must be made on the basis of a Boolean expression rather than some ordinal type, nested two-way selectors can be used to simulate a multiple selector. To alleviate the poor readability of deeply nested two-way selectors, some languages, such as Perl and Ada, have been extended specifically for this use. The extension allows some of the special words to be left out. In particular, **else-if** sequences are replaced with a single special word, and the closing special word on the nested **if** is dropped. The nested selector is then called an **elsif clause**. Consider the following Ada selector construct:

```
if Count < 10 then Bag1 := True;
elsif Count < 100 then Bag2 := True;
elsif Count < 1000 then Bag3 := True;
end if;
```

which is equivalent to the following:

```
if Count < 10 then
  Bag1 := True;
else
  if Count < 100 then
    Bag2 := True;
  else
    if Count < 1000 then
      Bag3 := True;
    end if;
  end if;
end if;
```

The **elsif** version is the more readable of the two. Notice that this example is not easily simulated with a **case** statement, because each selectable statement is chosen on the basis of a Boolean expression. Therefore, the **elsif** construct is not a redundant form of **case**. In fact, none of the multiple selectors in contemporary languages are as general as the **if-then-elsif** construct. An operational semantics description of a general selector statement with **elsif** clauses, in which the E's are logic expressions and the S's are statements, is given below:

```
if E1 goto 1
if E2 goto 2
     ...
1: S1
      goto out
2: S2
      goto out
...
out: ...
```

From this description, we can see the difference between multiple selection structures and **elsif** constructs: In a multiple selection construct, all the E's would be restricted to comparisons between the value of a single expression and some other values.

Languages that do not include the **elsif** construct can use the same control structure, with only slightly more typing.

elsif constructs are based on the common mathematics construct, the conditional expression. Functional programming languages, which will be discussed in Chapter 15, often use conditional expressions as one of their basic control constructs.

8.3 Iterative Statements

An **iterative statement** is one that causes a statement or collection of statements to be executed zero, one, or more times. Every programming language from Plankalkül on has included some method of repeating the execution of segments of code. Iteration is the very essence of the power of the computer. If iteration were not possible, programmers would be required to state every action in sequence; useful programs would be huge and inflexible, and take unacceptably large amounts of time to write and mammoth amounts of memory to store.

The repeated execution of a statement is often accomplished in a functional language by recursion rather than by iterative constructs. Recursion in functional languages will be discussed in Chapter 15.

The first iterative constructs in programming languages were directly related to arrays. This resulted from the fact that in the earliest years of the computer era, computing was overwhelmingly numerical in nature, frequently using loops to process data in arrays.

Several categories of iteration control statements have been developed. The primary categories are defined by how designers answered two basic design questions:

- How is the iteration controlled?
- Where should the control mechanism appear in the loop?

The primary possibilities for iteration control are logical, counting, or a combination of the two. The main choices for the location of the control mechanism are the top of the loop or the bottom of the loop. Top and bottom here are logical, rather than physical, denotations. The issue is not the physical placement of the control mechanism; rather, it is whether the mechanism is executed and affects control before or after execution of the loop's body. A third option, which allows the user to decide where to put the control, is discussed in Section 8.3.3.

The **body** of a loop is the collection of statements whose execution is controlled by the iteration statement. We use the term **pretest** to mean that the test for loop completion occurs before the loop body is executed and **posttest** to mean that it occurs after the loop body is executed. The iteration statement and the associated loop body together form an **iteration construct.**

In addition to the primary iteration statements, we discuss an alternative form that is in a class by itself: user-defined iteration control.

8.3.1   Counter-Controlled Loops

A counting iterative control statement has a variable, called the **loop variable,** in which the count value is maintained. It also includes some means of specifying the **initial** and **terminal** values of the loop variable, and the difference between sequential loop variable values, often called the **stepsize.** The initial, terminal, and stepsize specifications of a loop are called the **loop parameters.**

Although logically controlled loops are more general than counter-controlled loops, they are not necessarily more commonly used. Because counter-controlled loops are more complex, their design is more demanding.

Counter-controlled loops are sometimes supported by machine instructions designed for that purpose. Unfortunately, machine architecture might outlive the prevailing approaches to programming at the time of the architecture design. For example, VAX computers have an instruction that is very convenient for the implementation of posttest counter-controlled loops, which Fortran had at the time of the design of the VAX (mid-1970s). But Fortran no longer had such a loop by the time VAX computers became widely used.

It is, of course, also true that language constructs outlive machine architecture. For example, the author knows of no contemporary machine that has a three-way branch instruction to implement Fortran's arithmetic If statement, although that statement was included in Fortran I because the IBM 704 had such an instruction.

8.3.1.1   Design Issues

There are many design issues for iterative counter-controlled statements. The nature of the loop variable and the loop parameters provide a number of design issues. The type of the loop variable and that of the loop parameters obviously should be the same or at least compatible, but what types should be allowed? One apparent choice is integer, but what about enumeration, character, and floating-point types? Another question is whether the loop variable is a normal variable, in terms of scope, or whether it should have some special scope. Related to the scope issue is the question of the value of the loop variable after loop termination. Allowing the user to change the loop variable or the loop parameters within the loop can lead to code that is very difficult to understand, so another question is whether the additional flexibility that might be gained by allowing such changes is worth that additional complexity. A similar question arises about the number of times and the specific time when the loop parameters are evaluated: If they are evaluated just once, it results in simple but less flexible loops.

The following is a summary of these design issues:

- What are the type and scope of the loop variable?
- What value does the loop variable have at loop termination?
- Should it be legal for the loop variable or loop parameters to be changed in the loop, and if so, does the change affect loop control?
- Should the loop parameters be evaluated only once, or once for every iteration?

8.3.1.2 The Do Statement of Fortran 95

The general form of the Fortran 95 Do statement is

Do label variable = initial, terminal [, stepsize]

where the label is that of the last statement in the loop body, and the stepsize, when absent, defaults to 1. The loop variable must be Integer type; the loop parameters are allowed to be expressions and can have positive or negative values. They are evaluated at the beginning of the execution of the Do statement, and the value is used to compute an **iteration count,** which then has the number of times the loop is to be executed. The loop is controlled by the iteration count, not the loop parameters, so even if the parameters are changed in the loop, which is legal, those changes cannot affect loop control. The iteration count is an internal variable that is inaccessible to the user code.

Do constructs can only be entered through the Do statement, thereby making the statement a single-entry structure. When a Do terminates—regardless of how it terminates—the loop variable has its most recently assigned value. Thus the usefulness of the loop variable is independent of the method by which the loop terminates. An operational semantics description of the Fortran 95 Do statement is given below:

```
init_value = init_expression
terminal_value = terminal_expression
step_value = step_expression
```

```
        do_var = init_value
        iteration_count =
          max(int((terminal_value - init_value + step_value) / step_value) , 0)
loop:
    if iteration_count ≤ 0 goto out
    [loop body]
    do_var = do_var + step_value
    iteration_count = iteration_count - 1
    goto loop
out: . . .
```

Fortran 95 also has a second form of Do:

```
[name:]  Do variable = initial, terminal [, stepsize]
        . . .
        End  Do [name]
```

This Do uses a specific closing special word (or phrase), End Do, instead of a labeled statement.

8.3.1.3 The Ada `for` Statement

The Ada **for** statement has the following form:

```
for variable in [reverse] discrete_range loop
  . . .
end loop;
```

A discrete range is a subrange of an integer or enumeration type, such as 1..10 or Monday..Friday. The **reverse** reserved word, when present, indicates the values of the discrete range are assigned to the loop variable in reverse order. Note that Ada's **for** is simpler than Fortran's Do, because the stepsize is always one (or the next element of the discrete range).

The most interesting new feature of the Ada **for** statement is the scope of the loop variable, which is the range of the loop. The variable is implicitly declared at the **for** statement and implicitly undeclared after loop termination. For example, in

```
Count : Float := 1.35;
for Count in 1..10 loop
  Sum := Sum + Count;
end loop;
```

the Float variable Count is unaffected by the **for** loop. Upon loop termination, the variable Count is still Float type with the value of 1.35. Also, the Float-type variable Count is hidden from the code in the body of the loop, being masked by the loop counter Count, which is implicitly declared to be the type of the discrete range, Integer.

The Ada loop variable cannot be assigned a value in the loop body. Variables used to specify the discrete range can be changed in the loop, but because the range is evaluated only once, these changes do not affect loop control. It is not legal to branch into the Ada **for** loop body. Below is an operational semantics description of the Ada **for** loop:

```
     [define for_var (its type is that of the discrete range)]
     [evaluate discrete range]
loop:
     if [there are no elements left in the discrete range] goto out
     for_var = [next element of discrete range]
     [loop body]
     goto loop
out:
     [undefine for_var]
```

Because the scope of the loop variable is the loop body, loop variables are not defined after loop termination, so their values there are not relevant.

8.3.1.4 The `for` Statement of the C-Based Languages

The general form of C's **for** statement is

```
for (expression_1; expression_2; expression_3)
  loop body
```

The loop body can be a single statement, a compound statement, or a null statement.

Because statements in C produce results and thus can be considered expressions, the expressions in a **for** statement are often statements. The first expression is for initialization and is evaluated only once, when the **for** statement execution begins. The second expression is the loop control and is evaluated before each execution of the loop body. As is usual in C, a zero value means false and all nonzero values mean true. Therefore, if the value of the second expression is zero, the **for** is terminated; otherwise the loop statements are executed. In C99, the expression could be a Boolean type. A C99 Boolean type stores only the values 0 or 1. The last expression in the **for** is executed after each execution of the loop body. It is often used to increment the loop counter. An operational semantics description of the C **for** statement is shown below. Because C expressions are also statements, we show expression evaluations as statements.

```
     expression_1
loop:
     if expression_2 = 0 goto out
     [loop body]
     expression_3
     goto loop
out: ...
```

A typical C counting loop is

```
for (index = 0; index <= 10; index++)
  sum = sum + list[index];
```

All of the expressions of C's **for** are optional. An absent second expression is considered true, so a **for** without one is potentially an infinite loop. If the first and/or third expressions are absent, no assumptions are made. For example, if the first expression is absent, it simply means that no initialization takes place.

Note that C's **for** need not count. It can easily model counting *and* logical loop structures, as demonstrated in the next section.

The C **for** design choices are the following: There are no explicit loop variable or loop parameters. All involved variables can be changed in the loop body. The expressions are evaluated in the order stated above. Despite the fact that it can create havoc, it is legal to branch into a C **for** loop body.

C's **for** is more flexible than the counting loop statements of Fortran and Ada, because each of the expressions can comprise multiple statements, which in turn allow multiple loop variables that can be of any type. When multiple statements are used in a single expression of a **for** statement, they are separated by commas. All C statements have values, and this form of multiple statement is no exception. The value of such a multiple statement is the value of the last component.

Consider the following **for** statement:

```
for (count1 = 0, count2 = 1.0;
     count1 <= 10 && count2 <= 100.0;
     sum = ++count1 + count2, count2 *= 2.5);
```

The operational semantics description of this is

```
    count1 = 0
    count2 = 1.0
loop:
    if count1 > 10 goto out
    if count2 > 100.0 goto out
    count1 = count1 + 1
    sum = count1 + count2
    count2 = count2 * 2.5
    goto loop
out: ...
```

The C **for** statement above does not need and thus does not have a loop body. All the desired actions happen to be part of the **for** statement itself, rather than in its body. The first and third expressions are multiple statements. In both of these cases, the whole expression is evaluated, but the resulting value is not used in the loop control.

The **for** statement of C99 and C++ differs from that of earlier versions of C in two ways. First, in addition to an arithmetic expression, it can use a

Boolean expression for loop control. Second, the first expression can include variable definitions. For example,

```
for (int count = 0; count < len; count++) { ... }
```

The scope of a variable defined in the **for** statement is from its definition to the end of the loop body.

The **for** statement of Java and C# is like that of C++, except that the loop control expression is restricted to **boolean**.

In all of the C-based languages, the loop parameters are evaluated with every iteration. Furthermore, variables that appear in the loop parameter expression can be changed in the loop body. Therefore, these loops can be far more complex and are often less reliable than the counting loops of Fortran and Ada.

8.3.2 Logically Controlled Loops

In many cases, collections of statements must be repeatedly executed, but the repetition control is based on a Boolean expression rather than a counter. For these situations, a logically controlled loop is convenient. In fact, logically controlled loops are more general than counter-controlled loops. Every counting loop can be built with a logical loop, but the reverse is not true. Also, recall that only selection and logical loops are essential to express the control structure of any flowchart.

8.3.2.1 Design Issues

Because they are much simpler than counter-controlled loops, logically controlled loops have fewer design issues.

- Should the control be pretest or posttest?
- Should the logically controlled loop be a special form of a counting loop or a separate statement?

8.3.2.2 Examples

The C-based programming languages include both pretest and posttest logically controlled loops that are not special forms of their counter-controlled iterative statements. The pretest and posttest logical loops have the following forms:

```
while (control_expression)
    loop body
```

and

```
do
    loop body
while (control_expression)
```

These two statement forms are exemplified by the following C# code segments:

```
sum = 0;
indat = Console.ReadLine();
while (indat >= 0) {
  sum += indat;
  indat = Console.ReadLine();
}

value = Console.ReadLine();
do {
  value /= 10;
  digits ++;
} while (value > 0);
```

Note that all variables in these examples are integer type. The ReadLine method of the Console object gets a line of text from the keyboard.

In the pretest version (**while**), the statement is executed as long as the expression evaluates to true. In the C, C++, and Java posttest statement (**do**), the loop body is executed until the expression evaluates to false. The only real difference between the **do** and the **while** is that the **do** always causes the loop body to be executed at least once. In both cases, the statement can be compound. The operational semantics descriptions of those two statements are given below:

while

```
loop:
  if control_expression is false goto out
  [loop body]
  goto loop
out: ...
```

do-while

```
loop:
  [loop body]
  if control_expression is true goto loop
```

It is legal in both C and C++ to branch into both **while** and **do** loop bodies. The C89 version uses an arithmetic expression for control; in C99 and C++, it may be either arithmetic or Boolean.

Java's **while** and **do** statements are similar to those of C and C++, except the control expression must be **boolean** type, and because Java does not have a goto, the loop bodies cannot be entered anywhere but at their beginnings.

Fortran 95 has neither a pretest nor a posttest logical loop. Ada has a pretest logical loop but no posttest version of the logical loop.

Perl has two pretest logical loops, **while** and **until**, but no posttest loop. The **until** is similar to **while**, but uses the inverse of the value of the control expression.

Posttest loops are infrequently useful and also can be somewhat dangerous in the sense that programmers sometimes forget that the loop body will *always* be executed at least once. The syntactic design of placing a posttest control after the loop body, where it has its semantic effect, helps avoid such problems by making the logic clear.

8.3.3 User-Located Loop Control Mechanisms

In some situations, it is convenient for a programmer to choose a location for loop control other than the top or bottom of the loop. As a result, some languages provide this capability. A syntactic mechanism for user-located loop control, or exit, can be relatively simple, so its design is not difficult. Perhaps the most interesting question is whether a single loop or several nested loops can be exited. The design issues for such a mechanism are the following:

- Should the conditional mechanism be an integral part of the exit?
- Should only one loop body be exited, or can enclosing loops also be exited?

C and C++ have unconditional unlabeled exits (**break**). Java, Perl, and C# have unconditional labeled exits (**break** in Java and C#, **last** in Perl).

Following is an example of nested loops in C#, in which there is a break out of the outer loop from the nested loop.

```
outerLoop:
  for (row = 0; row < numRows; row++)
    for (col = 0; col < numCols; col++) {
      sum += mat[row][col];
      if (sum > 1000.0)
        break outerLoop;
    }
```

C and C++ include an unlabeled control statement, **continue**, that transfers control to the control mechanism of the smallest enclosing loop. This is not an exit but rather a way to skip the rest of the loop statements on the current iteration without terminating the loop structure. For example, consider the following:

```
while (sum < 1000) {
  getnext(value);
  if (value < 0) continue;
  sum += value;
}
```

Part 1: Linguistics and the Birth of Perl

LARRY WALL

Larry Wall wears many hats—he is involved in book publishing, language publishing, software publishing, child rearing (he has four kids). He has spent time studying at Seattle Pacific University, at Berkeley, and at UCLA. He has also worked at Unisys, Jet Propulsion Laboratories, and Seagate. Language publishing has brought him the most fame ("and the least money" he adds): Larry is the author of the Perl scripting language.

FIRST, A BIT ABOUT YOUR PROFESSIONAL BACKGROUND

What was your best job? Working at JPL [Jet Propulsion Laboratories] was a lot of fun. I did both system administration and software development there. The sysadmin job was particularly nice because it was one of those 90 percent boredom, 10 percent panic jobs, so I had plenty of time to work on Perl.

What was your weirdest job? That's a hard one. Most of my jobs turn out weird, one way or another, so it's hard to pick. Let's see...I've been a camp counselor called "Crazy Horse." I've written business software in BASIC on a Wang system that could only be manipulated via menus. I was the concertmaster for several years at MusiComedy Northwest. Perhaps my weirdest gig is the recording session at which I was the only one who could play the violin part, so they recorded me eight or ten times so I'd sound like the whole violin section.

What's your current job? My current job is to design Perl 6. Unfortunately nobody is paying me for that at the moment. Of course, nobody was officially paying me for the first five versions either. But it would be nice if someone were at least unofficially paying me for it this time. Perhaps by the time you read this someone will have hired me to be a waiter/actor in Hollywood.

LINGUISTICS AND COMPUTING LANGUAGES

You studied linguistics. At the time you were engaged in these studies, what career paths were you considering? My wife and I were going to be field linguists in Africa and were for a time associated with Wycliffe Bible Translators, until my (newly developed) food allergies put the kibosh on that. In any event, I don't know that I'd have made a very good field linguist—I've probably done linguists more good by staying out of the field and writing Perl. Nevertheless, I still love linguistics and have been teaching myself Japanese for the last few years just to keep the synapses from coagulating, or curdling, or whatever it is they most naturally do.

How did your interest in spoken languages translate to program languages? [Before] I wrote Perl, I have to admit that my linguistics and my computer science were pretty much compartmentalized. On the computer side, I wrote several compilers without asking myself why most computer languages seem so unnatural. On the linguistics side, I wrote a few natural language programs in Lisp, but generally didn't consider natural languages amenable to analysis by computer. (Anyone who has used Babblefish will discover this is still the case.) But it wasn't until I started working on Perl that I realized there are many principles that make a natural language feel natural, and some of those principles can be taught to computers without driving them nuts.

THE BIRTH OF PERL

What were you working on at Unisys in the days leading up to the creation of Perl? I was a system administrator and systems programmer in support of a secret project for the NSA [National Security Agency]. If I told you about it, you'd have to kill me. Er, that seems wrong.... Anyway, I spent a lot of time locked in "copper rooms," as they call them, playing with computers that didn't officially exist.

How did the idea for a new language come about? We were trying to do configuration management across the country over a low-speed encrypted link. This was producing mounds of textual data but little useful information. So Perl was initially designed to sift through scattered files containing text, find the important bits, and print out reports. Both of the official glosses for Perl reflect this: "Practical Extraction and Report Language" and "Pathologically Eclectic Rubbish Lister."

What business need was not being met? Essentially, the need for flexibility. We were using UNIX for its flexibility, but the toolkit UNIX provided for shell scripting was too unwieldy to navigate around inside text files the way we needed. The awk programming language was a step in the right direction, but just didn't do it for me. And I figured I could do better. The UNIX tools were all really good at what they were good at, and made it next to impossible to do the

> **"** It wasn't until I started working on Perl that I realized there are many principles that make a natural language feel natural, and some of those principles can be taught to computers without driving them nuts. **"**

things they weren't good at. The problem was ...that the basic toolbox approach was trying to act like an extensible language without actually succeeding. I thought if I could distill the good bits of UNIX into a real language with fine enough granularity to get at the fiddly bits when you needed to, people might find it useful. And that's why Perl 1 was born.

Which is your first love: designing a language or designing a program? Did one lead to the other? To answer the second part first, I don't think anyone can design a language without first using language. We naturally learn languages [from the] bottom up, first imitating the various pieces of language, and only later abstracting out the principles that hold the language together. Computer scientists like to think that they can design things [from the] top down, but that only works when you already know what kind of answer you're looking for. In general, languages designed to solve particular kinds of problems aren't terribly interesting—at least not to me.

So I had to learn to program first. That being said, I don't think you could call it a "first love." It's more like a "first love/hate." People who truly love programming don't design new computer languages. They aren't motivated. You only design a new language when you find your current language frustrating you in some way. So it follows that if you want to pursue a career in computer language design, you'd better be prepared for a life of continual frustration. That just goes with the territory. If you ever find yourself satisfied with your new language, you're an arrogant idiot. Not that that precludes being a good language designer. Of course, you can be an arrogant idiot like me and still be properly frustrated. So there's certainly some hope for you.

A negative value causes the assignment statement to be skipped, and control is transferred instead to the conditional at the top of the loop. On the other hand, in

```
while (sum < 1000) {
  getnext(value);
  if (value < 0) break;
  sum += value;
}
```

a negative value terminates the loop.

Java, Perl, and C# have statements similar to **continue**, except they can include labels that specify which loop is to be continued.

Both **last** and **break** provide for multiple exits from loops, which is somewhat of a hindrance to readability. However, unusual conditions that require loop termination are so common that such a construct is justified. Furthermore, readability is not seriously harmed, because the target of all such loop exits is the first statement after the loop (or an enclosing loop) rather than just anywhere in the program.

The motivation for user-located loop exits is simple: They fulfill a common need for goto statements through a highly restricted branch statement. The target of a goto can be many places in the program, both above and below the goto itself. However, the targets of user-located loop exits must be below the exit and can only follow immediately the end of a compound statement.

8.3.4   Iteration Based on Data Structures

Only one additional kind of looping structure remains to be considered here: iteration that depends on data structures. Rather than have a counter or Boolean expression control the iterations, these loops are controlled by the number of elements in a data structure. Perl, JavaScript, PHP, and C# have such statements.

C#'s `foreach` statement iterates on the elements of arrays and other collections. For example,

```
String[] strList = {"Bob", "Carol", "Ted", "Beelzebub"};
...
foreach (String name in strList)
  Console.WriteLine("Name: {0}", name);
```

The notation `{0}` in the parameter to `Console.WriteLine` above indicates the position in the string to be displayed where the value of the first named variable, `name` in this example, is to be placed.

A more general data-based iteration statement uses a user-defined data structure and a user-defined function to go through the structure's elements.

This function is called an **iterator.** The iterator is called at the beginning of each iteration, and each time it is called, the iterator returns an element from a particular data structure in some specific order. For example, suppose a program has a user-defined binary tree of data nodes, and the data in each node must be processed in some particular order. A user-defined iteration statement for the tree would successively set the loop variable to point to the nodes in the tree, one for each iteration. The initial execution of the user-defined iteration statement needs to issue a special call to the iterator to get the first tree element. The iterator must always remember which node it presented last so that it visits all nodes without visiting any node more than once. So an iterator must be history sensitive. A user-defined iteration statement terminates when the iterator fails to find more elements.

The **for** construct of the C-based languages, because of its great flexibility, can be used to simulate a user-defined iteration statement. Once again, suppose the nodes of a binary tree are to be processed. If the tree root is pointed to by a variable named root, and if traverse is a function that sets its parameter to point to the next element of a tree in the desired order, the following could be used:

```
for (ptr = root; ptr == null; traverse(ptr)) {
  ...
}
```

In this statement, traverse is the iterator.

Predefined iterators are used to provide iterative access to PHP's unique arrays. The **current** pointer points at the element last accessed through iteration. The **next** iterator moves **current**t to the next element in the array. The **prev** iterator moves **current** to the previous element. **current** can be set or reset to the array's first element with the **reset** operator. The following code displays all of the elements of an array of numbers, $list:

```
reset $list
print ("First number: " + current($list) + "<br />");
while ($current_value = next($list))
  print ("Next number: " + $current_value + "<br \>");
```

User-defined iteration statements are more important in object-oriented programming than they were in earlier software development paradigms, because users now routinely construct abstract data types for data structures, especially collections. In such cases, a user-defined iteration statement and its iterator must be provided by the author of the data abstraction because the representation of the objects of the type is not known to the user.

In C++, iterators for user-defined types, or classes, are often implemented either as friend functions to the class or as separate iterator classes.

In Java, the elements of a user-defined collection that implements the Collection interface can be iteratively visited with an implementation of the

Iterator interface. The Iterator interface has three fundamental methods, next, hasNext, and remove. The next method is the actual iterator. It throws the NoSuchElementException when there are no more elements in the collection being iterated. The hasNext method, which is often called before next is called, returns **true** if there is at least one more element.

As stated earlier, the **foreach** statement of C# is used to iterate the elements of any collection that implements the IEnumerable interface.

8.4   Unconditional Branching

An **unconditional branch statement** transfers execution control to a specified place in the program.

8.4.1   Problems with Unconditional Branching

The most heated debate in language design of the late 1960s was over the issue of whether unconditional branching should be part of any high-level language, and if so, whether its use should be restricted.

The unconditional branch, or goto, is the most powerful statement for controlling the flow of execution of a program's statements. However, using the goto carelessly can lead to serious problems. The goto has stunning power and great flexibility (all other control structures can be built with goto and a selector), but this very power makes its use dangerous. Without restrictions on use, imposed either by language design or programming standards, goto statements can make programs virtually unreadable, and as a result, highly unreliable and difficult to maintain.

These problems follow directly from a goto's capability of forcing any program statement to follow any other in execution sequence, regardless of whether that statement precedes or follows the first in textual order. Readability is best when the execution order of statements is nearly the same as the order in which they appear—in our case, this would mean top to bottom, which is the order to which we are accustomed. Thus restricting gotos so they can transfer control only downward in a program partially alleviates the problem. It allows gotos to transfer control around code sections in response to errors or unusual conditions, but disallows their use to build any sort of loop.

A few languages have been designed without a goto—for example, Modula-2 and Java. However, most currently popular languages include a goto statement. Kernighan and Ritchie (1978) call the goto infinitely abusable, but it is nevertheless included in Ritchie's language, C. The languages that have eliminated the goto have provided additional control statements,

HISTORY NOTE

Although several thoughtful people had suggested them earlier, it was Edsger Dijkstra who gave the computing world the first widely read exposé on the dangers of the goto. In his letter he noted, "The goto statement as it stands is just too primitive; it is too much an invitation to make a mess of one's program" (Dijkstra, 1968a). During the first few years after publication of Dijkstra's views on the goto, a large number of people argued publicly for either outright banishment or at least restrictions on the use of the goto. Among those who did not favor complete elimination was Donald Knuth, who argued that there were occasions when the efficiency of the goto outweighed its harm to readability (Knuth, 1974).

usually in the form of loop exits, to replace many of the typical applications of the goto.

The relatively new language, C#, includes a goto, even though one of the languages on which it is based, Java, does not have one. One legitimate use of C#'s goto is in the **switch** statement, as discussed in Section 8.2.2.2.

All of the loop exit statements discussed in Section 8.4.3 are actually camouflaged goto statements. They are, however, severely restricted gotos and are not harmful to readability. In fact, it can be argued that they improve readability because to avoid their use results in convoluted and unnatural code that would be much harder to understand.

8.5 Guarded Commands

Alternative and different forms of selection and loop structures were suggested by Dijkstra (1975). His motivation was to provide control statements that would support a program design methodology that ensured correctness during development rather than relying on verification or testing of completed programs to ensure their correctness. This methodology is described in Dijkstra (1976).

Guarded commands are covered in this chapter because they are the basis for two linguistic mechanisms developed later for concurrent programming in two languages, CSP (Hoare, 1978) and Ada. Concurrency in Ada is discussed in Chapter 13. They are also used to define functions in Haskell, as discussed in Chapter 15.

Dijkstra's selection construct has the form

```
if   <Boolean expression>  ->  <statement>
[]   <Boolean expression>  ->  <statement>
[]   ...
[]   <Boolean expression>  ->  <statement>
fi
```

The closing reserved word, **fi**, is the opening reserved word spelled backward. This form of closing reserved word is taken from ALGOL 68. The small blocks, called *fatbars*, are used to separate the guarded clauses and allow the clauses to be statement sequences.

This selection construct has the appearance of a multiple selection, but its semantics is different. All of the Boolean expressions are evaluated each time the construct is reached during execution. If more than one expression is true, one of the corresponding statements can be nondeterministically chosen for execution. An implementation may always choose the statement associated with the first Boolean expression that evaluates to true. But it may choose any statement associated with a true Boolean expression. So, the correctness of the program cannot depend on which statement is chosen (among those associated with true Boolean expressions). If none of the Boolean expressions are true, a run-time error occurs that causes program termination. This forces the programmer to consider and list all possibilities, as with Ada's **case** statement. Consider the following example:

```
if i = 0 -> sum := sum + i
[] i > j -> sum := sum + j
[] j > i -> sum := sum + i
fi
```

If i = 0 and j > i, this construct chooses nondeterministically between the first and third assignment statements. If i is equal to j and is not zero, a run-time error occurs because none of the conditions is true.

This construct can be an elegant way of allowing the programmer to state that the order of execution, in some cases, is irrelevant. For example, to find the largest of two numbers, we can use

```
if x >= y -> max := x
[] y >= x -> max := y
fi
```

This computes the desired result without overspecifying the solution. In particular, if x and y are equal, it does not matter which we assign to max. This is a form of abstraction provided by the nondeterministic semantics of the statement.

The semantics of the guarded commands are difficult to describe precisely. Although flow diagrams are not good tools for program design, they are sometimes useful for semantics descriptions. Figure 8.1 is a flowgraph describing the approach used by Dijkstra's selector statement. Note that this flowgraph is relatively imprecise, reflecting the difficulty in capturing the semantics of the guarded commands.

The loop structure proposed by Dijkstra has the form

```
do <Boolean expression> -> <statement>
[] <Boolean expression> -> <statement>
[] ...
[] <Boolean expression> -> <statement>
od
```

The semantics of this construct is that all Boolean expressions are evaluated on each iteration. If more than one are true, one of the associated statements is nondeterministically (perhaps randomly) chosen for execution, after which the expressions are again evaluated. When all expressions are simultaneously false, the loop terminates.

Consider the following code, which appears in slightly different form in Dijkstra (1975). The four variables q1, q2, q3, and q4 are to have their values rearranged so that $q1 \leq q2 \leq q3 \leq q4$.

```
do q1 > q2 -> temp := q1; q1 := q2; q2 := temp;
[] q2 > q3 -> temp := q2; q2 := q3; q3 := temp;
```

Figure 8.1

Flowgraph of the
approach used with
Dijkstra's selector
statement

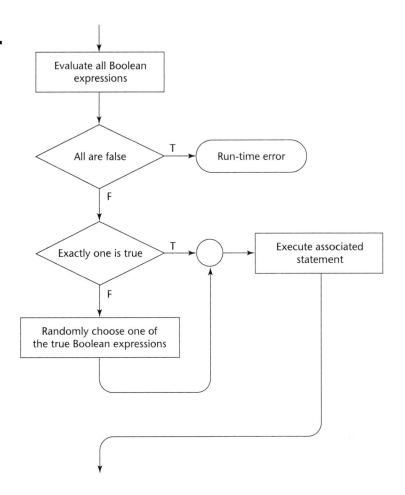

```
[ ] q3 > q4 -> temp := q3; q3 := q4; q4 := temp;
od
```

A flowgraph describing the approach used by Dijkstra's loop statement is
shown in Figure 8.2. Once again, note that the control-flow semantics of this
construct cannot be completely depicted in a flowgraph.

Dijkstra's *guarded commands*, as these two constructs are known, are interesting in part because they illustrate how the syntax and semantics of statements
can have an impact on program verification, and vice versa. Program verification is virtually impossible when goto statements are used. Verification is
greatly simplified if either only logical loops and selections are used, or only
guarded commands are used. The axiomatic semantics of guarded commands is
conveniently specified (Gries, 1981). It should be obvious, however, that there
is considerably increased complexity in the implementation of the guarded
commands over their conventional deterministic counterparts.

Figure 8.2

Flowgraph of the
approach used with
Dijkstra's loop
statement

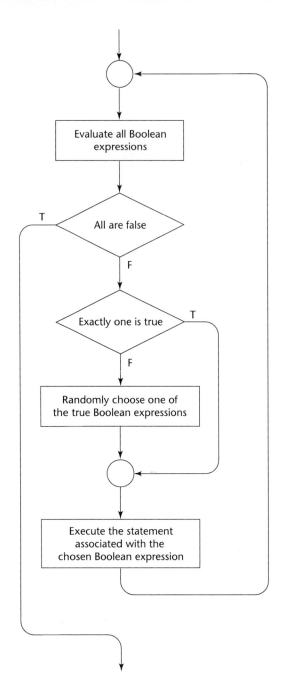

8.6   Conclusions

We have described and discussed a variety of statement-level control structures. A brief evaluation now seems to be in order.

First, we have the theoretical result that only sequence, selection, and pretest logical loops are absolutely required to express computations (Böhm and Jacopini, 1966). This result has been used by those who wish to ban unconditional branching altogether. Of course, there are already sufficient practical problems with the goto to condemn it without also finding a theoretical reason. One of the main legitimate needs for gotos, premature exits from loops, can be met with hightly restricted branch statements, such as **break**.

One obvious misuse of the Böhm and Jacopini result is to argue against the inclusion of *any* control structures beyond selection and pretest logical loops. No widely used language has yet taken that step; further, we doubt that any ever will because of the effect on writability and readability. Programs written with only selection and pretest logical loops are generally less natural in structure, more complex, and therefore harder to write and more difficult to read. For example, the C# multiple selection structure is a great boost to C# writability, with no clear negatives. Another example is the counting loop structure of many languages, especially when the statement is simple, as in Ada.

It is not so clear that the utility of many of the other control structures that have been proposed is worth their inclusion in languages (Ledgard and Marcotty, 1975). This question rests to a large degree on the fundamental question of whether the size of languages must be minimized. Both Wirth (1975) and Hoare (1973) strongly endorse simplicity in language design. In the case of control structures, simplicity means that only a few control statements should be in a language, and they should all be simple.

The rich variety of statement-level control structures that have been invented shows the diversity of opinion among language designers. After all the invention, discussion, and evaluation, there is still no unanimity of opinion on the precise set of control statements that should be in a language. Most contemporary languages do, of course, have similar control statements, but there is still some variation in the details of their syntax and semantics. Furthermore, there is still disagreement on whether a language should include a goto; C++ and C# do, but Java does not.

One final note: The control structures of functional and logic programming languages are all quite different from those described in this chapter. These mechanisms are discussed in some detail in Chapters 15 and 16, respectively.

SUMMARY

The control statements of the imperative languages occur in several categories: selection, multiple selection, iterative, and unconditional branching.

The **switch** statement of the C-based languages is representative of multiple selection statements. The C# version eliminates the reliability problem of its predecessors by disallowing the implicit fall through from a selected segment to the following selectable segment.

A large number of different loop statements have been invented for high-level languages, starting with Fortran's counting Do. Ada's **for** statement is, in terms of complexity, the opposite. It elegantly implements only the most commonly needed counting loop forms. C's **for** statement is the most flexible iteration construct, although its flexibility leads to some reliability problems.

The C-based languages have exit statements for their loops; these statements take the place of one of the most common uses of goto statements.

Data-based iterators are loop constructs for processing data structures, such as linked lists, hashes, and trees. The **for** statement of the C-based languages allows the user to create iterators for user-defined data. The **foreach** statement of Perl and C# is a predefined iterator for standard data structures. In the contemporary object-oriented languages, iterators for collections are specified with standard interfaces, which are implemented by the designers of the collections.

The unconditional branch, or goto, has been part of most imperative languages. Its problems have been widely discussed and debated. The current consensus is that it should remain in most languages but that its dangers should be minimized through programming discipline.

Dijkstra's guarded commands are alternative control constructs with positive theoretical characteristics. Although they have not been adopted as the control constructs of a language, part of the semantics appear in the concurrency mechanisms of CSP and Ada and the function definitions of Haskell.

REVIEW QUESTIONS

1. What is the definition of *control structure*?
2. What is the definition of *block*?
3. What are the design issues for selection structures?
4. What are the common solutions to the nesting problem for two-way selectors?
5. What are the design issues for multiple selection statements?
6. What is unusual about C's multiple selection statement? What design trade-off was made in this design?
7. Explain how C#'s switch statement is safer than that of Java.

8. What are the design issues for counter-controlled loop statements?

9. What is a pretest loop statement? What is a posttest loop statement?

10. What is the difference between the **for** statement of C++ and that of Java?

11. What are the design issues for logically controlled loop statements?

12. What is the main reason user-located loop control statements were invented?

13. What advantage does C#'s **break** statement have over C's **break** statement?

14. What are the differences between the **break** statement of C++ and that of Java?

15. What is a user-defined iteration control?

16. What common programming language borrows part of its design from Dijkstra's guarded commands?

PROBLEM SET

1. Describe three situations where a combined counting and logical looping construct is needed.

2. Study the iterator feature of CLU in Liskov et al. (1984) and determine its advantages and disadvantages.

3. Compare the set of Ada control statements with those of C# and decide which are better and why.

4. What are the pros and cons of using unique closing reserved words on compound statements?

5. Analyze the potential readability problems with using closure reserved words for control statements that are the reverse of the corresponding initial reserved words, such as the **case-esac** reserved words of ALGOL 68. For example, consider common typing errors such as the reversal of two adjacent characters.

6. Use the *Science Citation Index* to find an article that refers to Knuth (1974). Read the article and Knuth's paper and write a paper that summarizes both sides of the goto argument.

7. In his paper on the goto issue, Knuth (1974) suggests a loop control construct that allows multiple exits. Read the paper and write an operational semantics description of the construct.

8. What are the arguments both for and against the exclusive use of Boolean expressions in the control statements in Java (as opposed to also allowing arithmetic expressions, as in C and C++)?

PROGRAMMING EXERCISES

1. Rewrite the following pseudocode segment using a loop structure in the specified languages:

```
k ← (j + 13) / 27
loop:
  if k > 10 then goto out
  k ← k + 1
  i ← 3 * k - 1
  goto loop
out: ...
```

   a. Fortran 95
   b. Ada
   c. C, C++, Java, or C#

   Assume all variables are integer type. Discuss which language, for this code, has the best writability, the best readability, and the best combination of the two.

2. Redo Problem 1, except this time make all the variables and constants floating-point type, and change the statement

```
k ← k + 1
```

   to

```
k ← k + 1.2
```

3. Rewrite the following code segment using a multiple selection statement in the following languages:

```
if (k = 1) or (k = 2) then j := 2 * k - 1
if (k = 3) or (k = 5) then j := 3 * k + 1
if (k = 4) then j := 4 * k - 1
if (k = 6) or (k = 7) or (k = 8) then j := k - 2
```

   a. Fortran 95 (you'll have to look this one up)
   b. Ada
   c. C, C++, Java, or C#

   Assume all variables are integer type. Discuss the relative merits of the use of these languages for this particular code.

4. Consider the following C program segment. Rewrite it using no gotos or **break**s.

```
j = -3;
for (i = 0; i < 3; i++) {
  switch (j + 2) {
    case 3:
    case 2: j--; break;
    case 0: j += 2; break;
```

```
      default: j = 0;
    }
  if (j > 0) break;
  j = 3 - i
}
```

5. In a letter to the editor of *CACM*, Rubin (1987) uses the following code segment as evidence that the readability of some code with gotos is better than the equivalent code without gotos. This code finds the first row of an $n \times n$ integer matrix named x that has nothing but zero values.

```
for (i = 1; i <= n; i++) {
  for (j = 1; j <= n; j++)
    if (x[i][j] != 0)
      goto reject;
  println ('First all-zero row is:', i);
  break;
reject:
  }
```

Rewrite this code without gotos in one of the following languages: C, C++, Java, C#, or Ada. Compare the readability of your code to that of the code above.

6. Consider the following programming problem: The values of three integer variables, first, second, and third, must be placed in the three variables max, mid, and min, with the obvious meanings, without using arrays or user-defined or predefined subprograms. Write two solutions to this problem, one that uses nested selections and one that does not. Compare the complexity and expected reliability of the two.

9

Subprograms

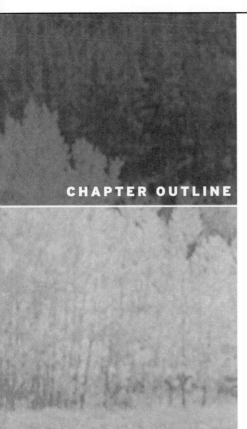

CHAPTER OUTLINE

Subprograms are the fundamental building blocks of programs and are therefore among the most important concepts in programming language design. We now explore the design of subprograms, including parameter-passing methods, local referencing environments, overloaded subprograms, generic subprograms, and the aliasing and side effects problems that are associated with subprograms. We also include a brief discussion of coroutines, which provide symmetric unit control.

Implementation methods for subprograms are discussed in Chapter 10.

9.1 Introduction

Two fundamental abstraction facilities can be included in a programming language: process abstraction and data abstraction. In the early history of high-level programming languages, only process abstraction was recognized and included. Process abstraction has been a central concept in all programming languages. In the 1980s, however, many people began to believe that data abstraction was equally important. Data abstraction is discussed in detail in Chapter 11.

The first programmable computer, Babbage's Analytical Engine, built in the 1840s, had the capability of reusing collections of instruction cards at several different places in a program when that was convenient. In a modern programming language, such a collection of statements is written as a subprogram. This reuse results in several different kinds of savings, including memory space and coding time. Such reuse is also an abstraction, for the details of the subprogram's computation are replaced in a program by a statement that calls the subprogram. Instead of explaining how some computation is to be done in a program, that explanation (the collection of statements in the subprogram) is enacted by a call statement, effectively abstracting away the details. This increases the readability of a program by exposing its logical structure while hiding the small-scale details.

The methods of object-oriented languages are closely related to the subprograms discussed in this chapter. The primary ways methods differ from subprograms is the way they are called and their association with classes and objects. Although these special characteristics of methods are discussed in Chapter 12, the features they share with subprograms, such as parameters and local variables, are included in this chapter.

9.2 Fundamentals of Subprograms

9.2.1 General Subprogram Characteristics

All subprograms discussed in this chapter, except the coroutines described in Section 9.11, have the following characteristics:

- Each subprogram has a single entry point.

- The calling program unit is suspended during the execution of the called subprogram, which implies that there is only one subprogram in execution at any given time.
- Control always returns to the caller when the subprogram execution terminates.

Although Fortran subprograms can have multiple entries, that particular kind of entry is relatively unimportant because it does not provide any fundamentally different capabilities. Therefore, in this chapter, we will ignore the possibility of multiple entries in Fortran subprograms.

Alternatives to the above assumptions result in coroutines (Section 9.11) and concurrent units, which are explored in Chapter 13.

9.2.2   Basic Definitions

A **subprogram definition** describes the interface to and the actions of the subprogram abstraction. A **subprogram call** is the explicit request that the called subprogram be executed. A subprogram is said to be **active** if, after having been called, it has begun execution but has not yet completed that execution. The two fundamental kinds of subprograms, procedures and functions, are defined and discussed in Section 9.2.4.

A **subprogram header,** which is the first part of the definition, serves several purposes. First, it specifies that the following syntactic unit is a subprogram definition of some particular kind. The specification of the subprogram's kind is often accomplished with a special word. Second, the header provides a name for the subprogram. Third, it may optionally specify a list of parameters. They are optional because not all subprograms have parameters.

Consider the following header examples:

```
Subroutine Adder(parameters)
```

This is the header of a Fortran subroutine subprogram named `Adder`. In Ada, the header for this subprogram would be

procedure `Adder(parameters)`

No special word appears in the header of a C subprogram to specify its kind. C has only one kind of subprogram, the function, and the header of a function is recognized by context rather than by a special word. For example,

void `adder(parameters)`

would serve as the header of a function named `adder`, where **void** indicates that it does not return a value.

The **parameter profile** (sometimes called the *signature*) of a subprogram is the number, order, and types of its formal parameters. The **protocol** of a subprogram is its parameter profile plus, if it is a function, its return type. In languages in which subprograms have types, those types are defined by the subprogram's protocol.

Subprograms can have declarations as well as definitions. This parallels the variable declarations and definitions in C, in which the declarations can be used to provide type information but not to define variables. A variable declaration in C is used only outside function definitions. A declaration is necessary when a variable must be referenced before the compiler has seen its definition. Subprogram declarations provide the subprogram's protocol, but do not include their bodies. They are necessary when the compiler must translate a call to a subprogram before it has seen that subprogram's definition. In both the cases of variables and subprograms, declarations are needed for static type checking. In the case of subprograms, it is the type of the parameters that must be checked. Function declarations are common in C and C++ programs, where they are called **prototypes.**

Java and C# do not need declarations of their methods, because there is no requirement that methods be defined before they are called in those languages.

9.2.3 Parameters

Subprograms typically describe computations. There are two ways that a non-method subprogram can gain access to the data that it is to process: through direct access to nonlocal variables (declared elsewhere but visible in the subprogram) or through parameter passing. Data passed through parameters are accessed through names that are local to the subprogram. Parameter passing is more flexible than direct access to nonlocal variables. In essence, a subprogram with parameter access to the data it is to process is a parameterized computation. It can perform its computation on whatever data it receives through its parameters (presuming the types of the parameters are as expected by the subprogram). If data access is through nonlocal variables, the only way the computation can proceed on different data is to assign new values to those nonlocal variables between calls to the subprogram. Extensive access to nonlocals can reduce reliability. Variables that are visible to the subprogram where access is desired often end up also being visible where access to them is not needed. This problem was discussed in Chapter 5.

Although methods also access external data through nonlocal references and parameters, the primary data to be processed by a method is the object through which the method is called. However, when a method does access nonlocal data, the reliability problems are the same as with non-object-oriented languages. Also, in an object-oriented language, method access to class variables (those associated with the class, rather than an object) is related to the concept of nonlocal data and should be avoided whenever possible. In this case, as well as the case of a C function accessing nonlocal data, the method can have the side effect of changing something other than its parameters or local data. Such changes complicate the semantics of the method, making it less reliable.

In some situations, it is convenient to be able to transmit computations, rather than data, as parameters to subprograms. In these cases, the name of the subprogram that implements that computation may be used as a parameter. This form of parameter is discussed in Section 9.6. Data parameters are discussed in Section 9.5.

The parameters in the subprogram header are called **formal parameters.** They are sometimes thought of as dummy variables because they are not variables in the usual sense: In most cases, they are bound to storage only when the subprogram is called, and that binding is often through some other program variables.

Subprogram call statements must include the name of the subprogram and a list of parameters to be bound to the formal parameters of the subprogram. These parameters are called **actual parameters.** They must be distinguished from formal parameters because the two can have different restrictions on their forms, and of course their uses are quite different.

In nearly all programming languages, the correspondence between actual and formal parameters—or the binding of actual parameters to formal parameters—is done by simple position: The first actual parameter is bound to the first formal parameter and so forth. Such parameters are called **positional parameters.** This is a good method of relating actual parameters to their corresponding formal parameters, as long as the parameter lists are relatively short.

When lists are long, however, it is easy for the programmer to make mistakes in the order of actual parameters in the list. One solution to this problem is to provide **keyword parameters,** in which the name of the formal parameter to which an actual parameter is to be bound is specified with the actual parameter. The advantage of keyword parameters is that they can appear in any order in the actual parameter list. Ada procedures can be called using this method, as in

```
Sumer(Length => My_Length,
      List => My_Array,
      Sum => My_Sum);
```

where the definition of Sumer has the formal parameters Length, List, and Sum.

The disadvantage to keyword parameters is that the user of the subprogram must know the names of formal parameters.

In addition to keyword parameters, Ada and Fortran 95 allow positional parameters. The two can be mixed in a call, as in

```
Sumer(My_Length,
      Sum => My_Sum,
      List => My_Array);
```

The only restriction with this is that after a keyword parameter appears in the list, all remaining parameters must be keyworded. This is necessary because position may no longer be well defined after a keyword parameter has appeared.

In C++, Fortran 95, Ada, and PHP, formal parameters can have default values. A default value is used if no actual parameter is passed to the formal parameter in the subprogram header. Consider the following Ada function header:

```
function Compute_Pay(Income : Float;
                     Exemptions : Integer := 1;
                     Tax_Rate : Float) return Float;
```

The `Exemptions` formal parameter can be absent in a call to `Compute_Pay`; when it is, the value 1 is used. No comma is included for an absent actual parameter in an Ada call because the only value of such a comma would be to indicate the position of the next parameter, which in this case is not necessary because all actual parameters after an absent actual parameter must be key-worded. For example, consider the following call:

```
Pay := Compute_Pay(20000.0, Tax_Rate => 0.15);
```

In C++, which has no keyword parameters, the rules for default parameters are necessarily different. The default parameters must appear last, for parameters are positionally associated. Once a default parameter is omitted in a call, all remaining formal parameters must have default values. A C++ function header for `Compute_Pay` can be written as follows:

```
float compute_pay(float income, float tax_rate,
                  int exemptions = 1)
```

Notice that the parameters are rearranged so that the one with the default value is last. An example call to the C++ `compute_pay` function is

```
pay = compute_pay(20000.0, 0.15);
```

In most languages that do not have default values for formal parameters, the number of actual parameters in a call must match the number of formal parameters in the subprogram definition header. However, in C, C++, Perl, and JavaScript this is not required. When there are fewer actual parameters in a call than formal parameters in a function definition, it is the programmer's responsibility to ensure that the parameter correspondence, which is always positional, and the subprogram execution are sensible.

Although this design, which allows a variable number of parameters, is clearly prone to error, it is also sometimes convenient. For example, the `printf` function of C can print any number of items (data values and/or literal strings). Ada subprograms must have a fixed number of parameters, so a predefined Ada output procedure prints only a single value. Such output subprograms are more cumbersome to use.

C# allows methods to accept a variable number of parameters, as long as they are of the same type. The method specifies its formal parameter with the **params** modifier. The call can send either an array or a list of expressions, whose values are placed in an array by the compiler and provided to the called method. For example, consider the following method:

```
public void DisplayList(params int[] list) {
   foreach (int next in list) {
      Console.WriteLine("Next value {0}", next);
   }
}
```

If `DisplayList` is defined for the class `MyClass` and we have the following declarations,

```
Myclass myObject = new Myclass;
int[] myList = new int[6] {2, 4, 6, 8, 10, 12};
```

`DisplayList` could be called with both of the following:

```
myObject.DisplayList(myList);
myObject.DisplayList(2, 4, 3 * x - 1, 17);
```

9.2.4 Procedures and Functions

There are two distinct categories of subprograms, procedures and functions, both of which can be viewed as approaches to extending the language. Procedures are collections of statements that define parameterized computations. These computations are enacted by single call statements. In effect, procedures define new statements. For example, because Ada does not have a sort statement, a user can build a procedure to sort arrays of data and use a call to that procedure in place of the unavailable sort statement.

Procedures can produce results in the calling program unit by two methods. First, if there are variables that are not formal parameters but are still visible in both the procedure and the calling program unit, the procedure can change them. Second, if the subprogram has formal parameters that allow the transfer of data to the caller, those parameters can be changed.

Functions structurally resemble procedures but are semantically modeled on mathematical functions. If a function is a faithful model, it produces no side effects; that is, it modifies neither its parameters nor any variables defined outside the function. In practice, many functions in programs have side effects.

Functions are called by appearances of their names in expressions, along with the required actual parameters. The value produced by a function's execution is returned to the calling code, effectively replacing the call itself. For example, the value of the expression `f(x)` is whatever value `f` produces when called with the parameter `x`. For a function that does not produce side effects, the returned value is its only effect.

Functions define new user-defined operators. For example, if a language does not have an exponentiation operator, a function can be written that returns the value of one of its parameters raised to the power of another parameter. Its header in C++ could be

```
float power(float base, float exp)
```

which could be called with

```
result = 3.4 * power(10.0, x)
```

The standard C++ libraries already include a similar function named pow. Compare this with the same operation in Perl, in which exponentiation is a built-in operation:

```
result = 3.4 * 10.0 ** x
```

In Ada, C++, and C#, users are permitted to overload operators by defining new functions. In these languages, the user could define an exponentiation operator that could be used much like the built-in exponentiation operator in Perl. User-defined operator overloading is discussed in Section 9.10.

Some imperative languages provide both functions and procedures. The C-based languages have only functions (and/or methods). However, these functions can behave like procedures. They can be defined to return no value if their return type is **void**. Because expressions in these languages can be used as statements, a stand-alone call to a **void** function is legal. For example, consider the following function header and call:

```
void sort(int list[], int listlen);
...
sort(scores, 100);
```

The methods of Java, C++, and C# are syntactically similar to the functions of C.

9.3   Design Issues for Subprograms

Subprograms are complex structures in programming languages, and it follows from this that a lengthy list of issues is involved in their design. One obvious issue is the choice of one or more parameter-passing methods that will be used. The wide variety of approaches that have been used in various languages is a reflection of the diversity of opinion on the subject. A closely related issue is whether the types of actual parameters will be type-checked against the types of the corresponding formal parameters.

The nature of the local environment of a subprogram dictates to some degree the nature of the subprogram. The most important question here is whether local variables are statically or dynamically allocated.

Next, there is the question of whether subprogram definitions can be nested. Another issue is whether subprogram names can be passed as parameters. If subprogram names can be passed as parameters and the language allows subprograms to be nested, there is the question of the correct referencing environment of a subprogram that has been passed as a parameter.

Finally, there are the questions of whether subprograms can be overloaded or generic. An **overloaded subprogram** is one that has the same name as another subprogram in the same referencing environment. A **generic subprogram** is one whose computation can be done on data of different types with different calls.

The following is a summary of these design issues for subprograms in general. Additional issues that are specifically associated with functions are discussed in Section 9.9.

- What parameter-passing method or methods are used?
- Are the types of the actual parameters checked against the types of the formal parameters?
- Are local variables statically or dynamically allocated?
- Can subprogram definitions appear in other subprogram definitions?
- If subprograms can be passed as parameters and subprograms can be nested, what is the referencing environment of a passed subprogram?
- Can subprograms be overloaded?
- Can subprograms be generic?

These issues and example designs are discussed in the following sections.

9.4 Local Referencing Environments

Subprograms can define their own variables, thereby defining local referencing environments. Variables that are defined inside subprograms are called **local variables** because their scope is usually the body of the subprogram in which they are defined.

In the terminology of Chapter 5, local variables can be either static or stack dynamic. If local variables are stack dynamic, they are bound to storage when the subprogram begins execution and are unbound from storage when that execution terminates. There are several advantages of stack-dynamic local variables, the primary one being the flexibility they provide the subprogram. It is essential that recursive subprograms have stack-dynamic local variables. Another advantage of stack-dynamic locals is that the storage for local variables in an active subprogram can be shared with the local variables in all inactive subprograms. This is not as great an advantage as it was when computers had smaller memories.

The main disadvantages of stack-dynamic local variables are the following: First there is the cost of the time required to allocate, initialize (when necessary), and deallocate such variables for each activation. Second, accesses to stack-dynamic local variables must be indirect, whereas accesses to static variables can be direct. This indirectness is required because the place in the stack where a particular local variable will reside can only be determined during execution (see Chapter 10). On most computers, indirect addressing is slower than direct addressing. Finally, with stack-dynamic local variables, subprograms cannot be history sensitive; that is, they cannot retain data values of local variables between calls. It is sometimes convenient to be able to write history-sensitive subprograms. A common example of a need for a history-sensitive subprogram is one whose task is to generate pseudorandom numbers. Each call to such a subprogram computes one pseudorandom number, using the last one it computed. It must, therefore, store the last one in a static local variable. Coroutines and the subprograms used in iterator loop constructs (discussed in Chapter 8) are other examples that need to be history sensitive.

The primary advantage of static local variables over stack-dynamic local variables is that they are more efficient—they usually can be accessed faster because there is no indirection. Furthermore, they require no run-time overhead for allocation and deallocation. And, of course, they allow subprograms to be history sensitive. The greatest disadvantage of static local variables is their inability to support recursion. Also, their storage cannot be shared with the local variables of other inactive subprograms.

In most comtemporary imperative languages, local variables in a subprogram are by default stack dynamic. In C and C++ functions, locals are stack dynamic unless specifically declared to be **static**. For example, in the following C (or C++) function, the variable sum is static and count is stack dynamic.

```
int adder(int list[], int listlen) {
  static int sum = 0;
  int count;
  for (count = 0; count < listlen; count ++)
    sum += list [count];
  return sum;
}
```

Ada subprograms and the methods of C++, Java, and C# have only stack-dynamic local variables.

As discussed in Chapter 5, Fortran 95 implementors can choose whether local variables are to be static or stack dynamic. Actually, because pre-90 Fortrans do not allow recursion, there is really no compelling reason to make them stack dynamic. The savings in storage is not usually thought to be worth the loss in efficiency. Fortran 95 users can force one or more local variables to be static regardless of the implementation by listing their names on a Save statement.

In Fortran 95, a subprogram can be explicitly specified to be recursive, in which case its local variables are stack dynamic. This idea of specifying that a particular subprogram can be recursively called originated with PL/I. The purpose of this explicit specification is to allow nonrecursive subprograms to be implemented in a more efficient way.

9.5   Parameter-Passing Methods

Parameter-passing methods are the ways in which parameters are transmitted to and/or from called subprograms. We first focus on the different semantics models of parameter-passing methods. Then we discuss the various implementation models invented by language designers for these semantics models. Next we survey the design choices of the various imperative languages and discuss the actual methods used to implement the implementation models. We finally consider the design considerations that face a language designer in choosing among the methods.

9.5.1   Semantics Models of Parameter Passing

Formal parameters are characterized by one of three distinct semantics models: (1) They can receive data from the corresponding actual parameter; (2) they can transmit data to the actual parameter; or (3) they can do both. These three semantics models are called **in mode**, **out mode**, and **inout mode**, respectively.

There are two conceptual models of how data transfers take place in parameter transmission: Either an actual value is copied (to the caller, to the callee, or both ways), or an access path is transmitted. Most commonly, the access path is a simple pointer or reference. Figure 9.1 illustrates the three semantics models of parameter passing when values are copied.

Figure 9.1

The three semantics models of parameter passing when physical moves are used

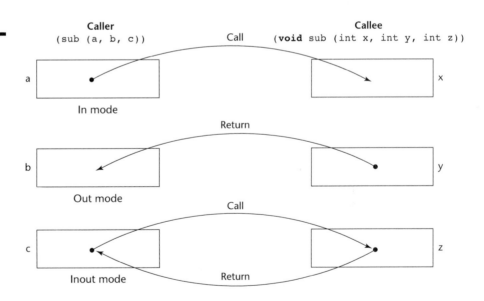

9.5.2 Implementation Models of Parameter Passing

A variety of models has been developed by language designers to guide the implementation of the three basic parameter transmission modes. In the following sections, we discuss several of these, along with their relative strengths and weaknesses.

9.5.2.1 Pass-by-Value

When a parameter is **passed by value,** the value of the actual parameter is used to initialize the corresponding formal parameter, which then acts as a local variable in the subprogram, thus implementing in-mode semantics.

Pass-by-value is normally implemented by copy, because accesses are more efficient with this approach. It could be implemented by transmitting an access path to the value of the actual parameter in the caller, but that would require that the value be in a write-protected cell (one that can only be read). Enforcing the write protection is not always a simple matter. For example, suppose the subprogram to which the parameter was passed passes it in turn to another subprogram. This is another reason to use copy transfer. As we will see in Section 9.5.3, C++ provides a convenient and effective method for enforcing write protection on pass-by-value parameters that are transmitted by access path.

The main disadvantage of the pass-by-value method if copies are used is that additional storage is required for the formal parameter, either in the called subprogram or in some area outside both the caller and the called subprogram. In addition, the actual parameter must be copied to the storage area for the corresponding formal parameter. The storage and the copy operations can be costly if the parameter is large, such as a array with many elements.

9.5.2.2 Pass-by-Result

Pass-by-result is an implementation model for out-mode parameters. When a parameter is passed by result, no value is transmitted to the subprogram. The corresponding formal parameter acts as a local variable, but just before control is transferred back to the caller, its value is transmitted back to the caller's actual parameter, which obviously must be a variable. (How would the caller reference the computed result if it were a literal or an expression?) If values are returned by copy (as opposed to access paths), as they typically are, pass-by-result also requires the extra storage and the copy operations that are required by pass-by-value. As with pass-by-value, the difficulty of implementing pass-by-result by transmitting an access path usually results in it being implemented by data copy. In this case, the problem is in ensuring that the initial value of the actual parameter is not used in the called subprogram.

One problem with the pass-by-result model is that there can be an actual parameter collision, such as the one created with the call

```
sub(p1, p1)
```

In sub, assuming the two formal parameters have different names, the two can obviously be assigned different values. Then whichever of the two is copied to their corresponding actual parameter last becomes the value of p1. Thus the order in which the actual parameters are copied determines their value. Because the order is sometimes implementation dependent, portability problems can occur that are difficult to diagnose.

Calling a procedure with two identical actual parameters can also lead to different kinds of problems when other parameter-passing methods are used, as discussed in Section 9.5.2.4.

Another problem that can occur with pass-by-result is that the implementor may be able to choose between two different times to evaluate the addresses of the actual parameters: at the time of the call or at the time of the return. For example, suppose a subprogram has the parameter list[index]. If index is changed by the subprogram, either through global access or as a formal parameter, then the address of list[index] will change between the call and the return. The implementor must choose the time at which the address to which to return the value will be determined, at the time of the call or at the time of the return. This makes programs unportable between implementations that choose differently in this issue.

9.5.2.3 Pass-by-Value-Result

Pass-by-value-result is an implementation model for inout-mode parameters in which actual values are copied. It is in effect a combination of pass-by-value and pass-by-result. The value of the actual parameter is used to initialize the corresponding formal parameter, which then acts as a local variable. In fact, pass-by-value-result formal parameters must have local storage associated with the called subprogram. At subprogram termination, the value of the formal parameter is transmitted back to the actual parameter.

Pass-by-value-result is sometimes called **pass-by-copy** because the actual parameter is copied to the formal parameter at subprogram entry and then copied back at subprogram termination.

Pass-by-value-result shares with pass-by-value and pass-by-result the disadvantages of requiring multiple storage for parameters and time for copying values. It shares with pass-by-result the problems associated with the order in which actual parameters are assigned.

9.5.2.4 Pass-by-Reference

Pass-by-reference is a second implementation model for inout-mode parameters. Rather than copying data values back and forth, however, as in pass-by-value-result, the pass-by-reference method transmits an access path, sometimes just an address, to the called subprogram. This provides the access path to the cell storing the actual parameter. Thus the called subprogram is allowed to access the actual parameter in the calling program unit. In effect, the actual parameter is shared with the called subprogram.

The advantage of pass-by-reference is that the passing process itself is efficient, in terms of both time and space. Duplicate space is not required, nor is any copying.

There are, however, several disadvantages to the pass-by-reference method. First, access to the formal parameters will be slower than pass-by-value parameters, because of the additional level of indirect addressing that is required. Second, if only one-way communication to the called subprogram is required, inadvertent and erroneous changes may be made to the actual parameter.

Another serious problem of pass-by-reference is that aliases can be created. This should be expected because pass-by-reference makes access paths available to the called subprograms, thereby broadening their access to non-local variables. There are several ways aliases can be created when parameters are passed by reference.

First, collisions can occur between actual parameters. Consider a C++ function that has two parameters that are to be passed by reference (see Section 9.5.3), as in

```
void fun(int &first, int &second)
```

If the call to fun happens to pass the same variable twice, as in

```
fun(total, total)
```

then first and second in fun will be aliases.

Collisions between array elements can also cause aliases. For example, suppose the function fun is called with two array elements that are specified with variable subscripts, as in

```
fun(list[i], list[j])
```

If these two parameters are passed by reference and i happens to be equal to j, then first and second are again aliases.

Collisions between array-element parameters and elements of arrays passed as array-name parameters are another possible cause of aliases. If two of the formal parameters of a subprogram are an element of an array and the other is the whole array, and both are passed by reference, then a call such as

```
fun1(list[i], list)
```

could result in aliasing in fun1, because fun1 can access all elements of list through the second parameter and access a single element through its first parameter.

Still another way to get aliasing with pass-by-reference parameters is through collisions between formal parameters and nonlocal variables that are visible. For example, consider the following C code:

```
int * global;
void main() {
    extern int * global;
    ...
    sub(global);
    ...
}
void sub(int * param) {
    extern int * global;
    ...
}
```

Inside sub, param, and global are aliases.

The problem with these kinds of aliasing is the same as in other circumstances: It is harmful to readability and thus to reliability. It also makes program verification extremely difficult.

All these possible aliasing situations are eliminated if pass-by-value-result is used instead of pass-by-reference. However, in place of aliasing, other problems sometimes arise, as discussed in Section 9.5.2.3.

9.5.2.5 Pass-by-Name

Pass-by-name is an inout-mode parameter transmission method that does not correspond to a single implementation model. When parameters are passed by name, the actual parameter is, in effect, textually substituted for the corresponding formal parameter in all its occurrences in the subprogram. This is quite different from the methods discussed thus far, in which cases formal parameters are bound to actual values or addresses at the time of the subprogram call. A pass-by-name formal parameter is bound to an access method at the time of the subprogram call, but the actual binding to a value or an address is delayed until the formal parameter is assigned or referenced.

The concept of late binding, on which pass-by-name is based, is by no means an odd or discredited one. The powerful mechanism of dynamic binding and polymorphism, which is an integral part of object-oriented programming, is simply a late binding of method calls to methods. (However, while pass-by-name is very expensive, relative to other methods of parameter passing, dynamic binding in object-oriented languages has little additional overhead.) Lazy evaluation is another useful mechanism that is a form of late binding. It is, briefly, the process of only evaluating parts of functional code when it becomes certain that the evaluation of that code is necessary. In the imperative languages, short-circuit evaluation of Boolean expressions is an example of lazy evaluation. All expression evaluation in the functional language Haskell is lazy, as is discussed in Chapter 15.

Because pass-by-name is not used in any widely used language, it is not discussed further here. However, it is used at compile time by the macros in assembly languages and for the generic parameters of the generic subprograms in C++ and Ada, as discussed in Section 9.7.

9.5.3   Parameter-Passing Methods of the Major Languages

Fortran has always used the inout-mode semantics model of parameter passing, but the language does not specify whether pass-by-reference or pass-by-value-result should be used. In most Fortran implementations before Fortran 77, parameters were passed by reference. In later implementations, however, pass-by-value-result has been frequently used for simple variable parameters.

C uses pass-by-value. Pass-by-reference (inout mode) semantics is achieved by using pointers as parameters. The value of the pointer is copied to the called function and nothing is copied back. However, because what was passed is an access path to the data of the caller, the called function can change the caller's data. C copied this use of the pass-by-value method from ALGOL 68. In both C and C++, formal parameters can be typed as pointers to constants. The corresponding actual parameters need not be constants, for in such cases they are coerced to constants. This allows pointer parameters to provide the efficiency of pass-by-reference with the one-way semantics of pass-by-value. Write protection of those parameters in the called function is implicit.

C++ includes a special pointer type, called a *reference type*, as discussed in Chapter 6, that is often used for parameters. Reference parameters are implicitly dereferenced in the function or method, and their semantics are pass-by-reference. C++ also allows reference parameters to be defined to be constants. For example, we could have

```
void fun(const int &p1, int p2, int &p3) { ... }
```

where p1 is pass-by-reference but cannot be changed in the function fun, parameter p2 is pass-by-value, and p3 is pass-by-reference. Neither p1 nor p3 need be explicitly dereferenced in fun.

Constant parameters and in-mode parameters are not exactly alike. Constant parameters clearly implement in-mode parameters. However, in all of the common imperative languages except Ada, in-mode parameters can be assigned in the subprogram even though those changes are never reflected in the values of the corresponding actual parameters. Constant parameters can never be assigned.

As with C and C++, all Java parameters are passed by value. However, because objects can only be accessed through reference variables, object parameters are in effect passed by reference. Although an object reference passed as a parameter cannot itself be changed in the called subprogram, the referenced object can be changed if a method is available to cause the change. Because reference variables cannot point to scalar variables directly and Java does not have pointers, scalars cannot be passed by reference in Java (although a reference to an object that contains a scalar can).

The designers of Ada defined versions of the three semantics modes of parameter transmission: in, out, and inout. The three modes are appropriately named with the reserved words **in**, **out**, and **in out**, where **in** is the default method. For example, consider the following Ada subprogram header:

```
procedure Adder(A : in out Integer;
                B : in Integer;
                C : out Float)
```

Ada formal parameters declared to be **out** mode can be assigned but not referenced. Parameters that are **in** mode can be referenced but not assigned. Quite naturally, **in out** mode parameters can be both referenced and assigned.

Fortran 95 is very similar to Ada in that its formal parameters can be declared to be in, out, or in out mode, using the Intent attribute. For example, consider the following beginning of a Fortran 95 subprogram:

```
Subroutine Adder(A, B, C)
   Integer, Intent(Inout) :: A
   Integer, Intent(In) :: B
   Integer, Intent(Out) :: C
```

The semantics modes of the parameters of this subprogram are the same as the Ada example above.

The default parameter-passing method of C# is pass-by-value. Pass-by-reference can be specified by preceding both a formal parameter and its corresponding actual parameter with **ref**. For example, consider the following C# skeletal method and call:

```
void sumer(ref int oldSum, int newOne) { ... }
...
summer(ref sum, newValue);
```

The first parameter to sumer is passed by reference; the second is passed by value.

C# supports out-mode parameters, which are pass-by-reference parameters that do not need initial values. Such parameters are specified in the formal parameter list with the **out** modifier.

PHP's parameter passing is similar to that of C#, except that either the actual parameter or the formal parameter can specify pass-by-reference. Pass-by-reference is specified by preceding one or both of the parameters with an ampersand.

INTERVIEW

Part 2: Scripting Languages in General and Perl in Particular

LARRY WALL

SOME SPECIFICS ON SCRIPTING LANGUAGES

Can you share your definition of a scripting language? People often argue over the difference between a scripting language and a programming language. If you ask me, I'll tell you that a script is what you hand the actors, and a program is what you hand the audience. The idea being that a script is something that is being molded into shape by the writer, the director, and the actors, while a program denotes a relatively fixed sequence of predetermined events.

There's no hard and fast distinction between scripting and programming, and scripts have a way of turning into programs over time. But to run with our metaphor, while you're writing your program, it's behaving more like a script, and when you're finished developing your script, it's acting more like a program.

Certain kinds of language make it a little easier to whip things up on the spur of the moment, so those languages tend to be classified as "scripting" languages. Other languages try to make it easier to manipulate complex data precisely and efficiently, at the expense of having to specify a lot of things in advance before you can say what you really want to say. These languages tend to be called "programming" languages. Perl is generally presented to people as a scripting language, but that's an oversimplification, or maybe an undercomplexification....

What should the reader understand about a scripting language? The most important thing to understand is that, while people usually plan to "throw away the prototype," they rarely in fact do. What you intended to be one-shot code often turns out to be "good enough" to stay in production far longer than you might have guessed. So it's generally better to plan for that in the first place, with the expectation that your quick-and-dirty prototype will in fact grow into a clean, modular design over time. That's all assuming your language will let you evolve your program, of course. Not all languages will.

MORE ON PERL AND HOW IT CAME TO BE

What distinguishes Perl from the other scripting languages? I think a good scripting language should support the evolution of your script into a "Real Program." To that end, Perl gives you complete multi-paradigm programming support to back up its scripting support. In other words, Perl acts like a grownup computer language when you're ready for it to.

Scripts are like on ramps to a freeway. Most programming languages try to provide either the on ramps without the freeway or the freeway without

Perl employs a primitive means of passing parameters. All actual parameters are implicitly placed in a predefined array named @_ (of all things!). The subprogram retrieves the actual parameter values (or addresses) from this array. The most peculiar thing about this array is its magical nature, exposed by the fact that its elements are in effect aliases for the actual parameters. Therefore, if an element of @_ is changed in the called subprogram, that change is reflected in the corresponding actual parameter in the call, assuming there is a corresponding actual parameter and it is a variable.

the on ramps. Perl tries to give you both, because Perl is a eat-your-cake-and-have-it-too language. That's why the Perl slogan is "There's More Than One Way To Do It." Perl doesn't try to enforce a particular style; some problems might be better solved by pipes and pattern matching, while others might be better solved by functional programming, or by event-driven programming, or by object-oriented programming.

In contrast, other languages often try to lock you into a particular way of thinking, or make it difficult to interface to the outside world. Perl isn't trying to be a perfect language, but a useful language, which often involves cooperating with other languages and systems in a humble sort of way. Natural languages are not utopias, nor do they try to lock you into a monastery. Computer languages shouldn't either.

When you created Perl did you think it would be what it is now? What is it about Perl that makes it so useful for the Internet? And, because marketing is so important, what was going on in industry/the computing realm that helped Perl take off, in your opinion? Hmm. Well, I knew Perl would be big, but I didn't know it would be this big. I figured from the start that Perl would make awk and sed obsolete for text processing, and (to a lesser extent) shell programming obsolete for gluing random interfaces together. Once I added in all the system administration operations, I was not at

all surprised that it became the language of choice for most UNIX system administrators.

What I did not anticipate was the Web, nor that much of the Web would be prototyped in Perl. Given that the HTTP is a text-based protocol, however, and given that Web servers needed glue code to translate between that text and backend database servers, Perl was in the right place at the right time with the right capabilities.

But this is just another example of how a good tool is used for purposes not envisioned by its creator. But that's not entirely an accident—a good creator will try to build in capabilities that could be used serendipitously when the opportunity arises.

> **"** People often argue over the difference between a scripting language and a programming language. If you ask me, I'll tell you that a script is what you hand the actors, and a program is what you hand the audience. **"**

What part of the language do you like the most? The part I like the best is that I'm allowed to change the parts I like the least. Seriously, the parts I like the best are the ones that are being conserved in the design of Perl 6. For instance, Perl has always been pretty good at evolving, and at cooperating humbly with other programs and languages in its environment. This should only continue to get better. Perl will remain good at rapid prototyping and text processing. It will get even better at pattern matching. (All assuming we ever finish Perl 6....)

On a closing note, if you weren't doing all this, how would you be spending your days? Probably driving the people around me crazy. Oh, wait...

9.5.4 Type-Checking Parameters

It is now widely accepted that software reliability demands that the types of actual parameters be checked for consistency with the types of the corresponding formal parameters. Without such type checking, small typographical errors can lead to program errors that may be difficult to diagnose because they are not detected by the compiler or the run-time system. For example, in the function call

```
result = sub1(1)
```

the actual parameter is an integer constant. If the formal parameter of `sub1` is a floating-point type, no error will be detected without parameter type checking. Although an integer 1 and a floating-point 1 have the same value, the representations of these two are very different. `sub1` cannot produce a correct result given an integer actual parameter value when it expects a floating-point value.

Early programming languages, such as Fortran 77 and the original version of C, did not require parameter type checking; most later languages require it. However, the relatively recent languages, Perl, JavaScript, and PHP do not.

C and C++ require some special discussion in the matter of parameter type checking. In the original C, neither the number of parameters nor their types were checked. In C89, the formal parameters of functions can be defined in two ways. First, they can be as in the original C; that is, the names of the parameters are listed in parentheses and the type declarations for them follow, as in

```
double sin(x)
  double x;
  { ... }
```

Using this method avoids type checking, thereby allowing calls such as

```
double value;
int count;
...
value = sin(count);
```

to be legal but nonsense.

The alternative is called the **prototype** method, in which the formal parameter types are included in the list, as in

```
double sin(double x)
  { ... }
```

If this version of `sin` is called with the same call as above, that is

```
value = sin(count);
```

it is also legal. The type of the actual parameter (**int**) is checked against that of the formal parameter (**double**). Although they do not match, **int** is coercible to **double**, so the conversion is done. If the conversion is not possible (for example, if the actual parameter had been an array) or if the number of parameters is wrong, then a syntax error is detected. So in C89, the user chooses whether he or she wants parameters to be type checked.

In C99 and C++, all functions must have their formal parameters in prototype form. However, type checking can be avoided for some of the parameters by replacing the last part of the parameter list with an ellipsis, as in

```
int printf(const char* format_string, ...);
```

A call to `printf` must include at least one parameter, a pointer to a constant character string. Beyond that, anything (including nothing) is legal. The way `printf` determines whether there are additional parameters is by the presence of special symbols in the string parameter. For example, the format code for integer output is `%d`. This appears as part of the string, as in

```
printf("The sum is %d\n", sum);
```

The `%` tells the `printf` library function there is one more parameter.

9.5.5 Implementing Parameter-Passing Methods

We now address the question of how the various implementation models of parameter passing are actually implemented.

In most contemporary languages, parameter communication takes place through the run-time stack. The run-time stack is initialized and maintained by the run-time system, which is a system program that manages the execution of programs. The run-time stack is used extensively for subprogram control linkage and parameter passing, as is discussed in Chapter 10. In the following discussion, we assume that the stack is used for all parameter transmission.

Pass-by-value parameters have their values copied into stack locations. The stack locations then serve as storage for the corresponding formal parameters. Pass-by-result parameters are implemented as the opposite of pass-by-value. The values assigned to the pass-by-result actual parameters are placed in the stack, where they can be retrieved by the calling program unit upon termination of the called subprogram. Pass-by-value-result parameters can be implemented directly from their semantics as a combination of pass-by-value and pass-by-result. The stack location for the parameters is initialized by the call and is then used like a local variable in the called subprogram.

Pass-by-reference parameters are perhaps the simplest to implement. Regardless of the type of the actual parameter, only its address must be placed in the stack. In the case of literals, the address of the literal is put in the stack. In the case of an expression, the compiler must build code to evaluate the expression just before the transfer of control to the called subprogram. The address of the memory cell in which the code places the result of its evaluation is then put in the stack. The compiler must be sure to prevent the called subprogram from changing parameters that are literals or expressions, as discussed below. Access to the formal parameters in the called subprogram is by indirect addressing from the stack location of the address. The implementation of pass-by-value, -result, -value-result, and -reference, where the run-time stack is used, is shown in Figure 9.2. Subprogram `sub` is called from

Figure 9.2

One possible stack implementation of the common parameter-passing methods

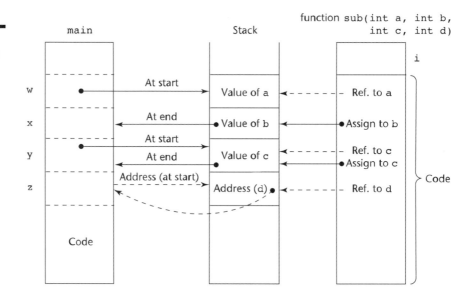

main with the call sub(w, x, y, z), where w is passed by value, x is passed by result, y is passed by value-result, and z is passed by reference.

A subtle but fatal error can occur with pass-by-reference and pass-by-value-result parameters if care is not taken in their implementation. Suppose a program contains two references to the constant 10, the first as an actual parameter in a call to a subprogram. Further suppose that the subprogram mistakenly changes the formal parameter that corresponds to the 10 to the value 5. The compiler for this program may have built a single location for the value 10 during compilation, as compilers often do, and use that location for all references to the constant 10 in the program. But after the return from the subprogram, all subsequent occurrences of 10 will actually be references to the value 5. If this is allowed to happen, it creates a programming problem that is very difficult to diagnose. This did in fact happen with many implementations of Fortran IV.

In Ada 95, all scalars are passed by copy and all structured parameters are passed by reference.

9.5.6   Multidimensional Arrays as Parameters

The storage-mapping functions that are used to map the index values of references to elements of multidimensional arrays to addresses in memory were discussed at length in Chapter 6. In some languages, such as C and C++, when a multidimensional array is passed as a parameter to a subprogram, the compiler must be able to build the mapping function for that array while seeing only the text of the subprogram (not the calling subprogram). This is true because the subprograms can be compiled separately from the programs that

HISTORY NOTE

The Ada 83 language definition specifies that scalar (non-structured) parameters are to be passed by copy; that is, **in** and **in out** mode parameters are to be local variables that are initialized by copying the value of the corresponding actual parameter. Simple parameters that are **out** or **in out** mode are to have their values copied back to the corresponding actual parameter at subprogram termination. The order of these copies, when there are more than one, is not defined by the language definition. The evaluation of **out** and **in out** mode parameters is done before the transfer of control to the called subprogram occurs. For example, suppose an **out** mode actual parameter has the form

`List(Index)`

The address value of this parameter is computed at the time of the call. If `Index` happened to be visible in the called subprogram and the subprogram changed it, the parameter address would not be affected.

In the case of formal parameters that are arrays or records, Ada 83 implementors were given the choice between pass-by-value-result and pass-by-reference. By failing to specify the implementation method for passing structured parameters, the Ada 83 designers left open the possibility of a subtle problem. The problem is that

(continues)

call them. Consider the problem of passing a matrix to a function in C. Multidimensional arrays in C are really arrays of arrays, and they are stored in row major order. Following is a storage mapping function for row-major order for matrices when the lower bound of all indices is zero and the element size is 1:

$$\text{address}(\texttt{mat[i, j]}) = \text{address}(\texttt{mat[0,0]}) + i * \text{number\_of\_columns} + j$$

Notice that this mapping function needs the number of columns but not the number of rows. Therefore, in C and C++, when a matrix is passed as a parameter, the formal parameter must include the number of columns in the second pair of brackets. This is illustrated in the following skeletal C program:

```
void fun(int matrix[][10]) {
  ... }
void main() {
  int mat[5][10];
  ...
  fun(mat);
  ...
}
```

The problem with this method of passing matrixes as parameters is that it does not allow the programmer to write a function that can accept matrixes with different numbers of columns; a new function must be written for every matrix with a different number of columns. This, in effect, disallows writing flexible functions that may be effectively reusable if the functions deal with multidimensional arrays. In C and C++, there is a way around the problem because of their inclusion of pointer arithmetic. The matrix can be passed as a pointer, and the actual dimensions of the matrix can be included as parameters. Then the function can evaluate the user-written storage-mapping function using pointer arithmetic each time an element of the matrix must be referenced. For example, consider the following function prototype:

```
void fun(float *mat_ptr, int num_rows,
         int num_cols);
```

The following statement can be used to move the value of the variable x to the `[row][col]` element of the parameter matrix in fun:

```
*(mat_ptr + (row * num_cols) + col) = x;
```

Although this works, it is obviously difficult to read, and because of its complexity it is error prone. The difficulty with reading this

(continued)
the two implementation methods can lead to different program results for certain programs. This difference can occur because the pass-by-reference method provides access to a location in the calling program that can also be provided if the actual parameter is also visible as a global, thereby creating an alias. If pass-by-value-result is used in place of pass-by-reference, this dual access to the actual parameter is not possible.

An additional problem is the following: Suppose the subprogram terminates abnormally (via an exception); the actual parameter in the pass-by-value-result implementation will be unchanged, whereas the pass-by-reference implementation may have changed the corresponding actual parameter before the error occurred. Once again, there can be a difference between the two implementation methods.

Ada 83 programs that produce different results depending on how the **in out** method is implemented are termed **erroneous**. Despite this label, however, there is no way the compiler can detect the erroneous condition. So the error is usually detected only when the user moves the program from one implementation to another and realizes that it no longer behaves the same way. The Ada 83 design philosophy in this situation is that programmers must guard against aliasing: If they create aliases, they must contend with the potential problems.

can be alleviated by using a macro to define the storage-mapping function, such as

```
#define mat_ptr(r,c)
            (*(mat_ptr + ((r) * num_cols) + (c)))
```

With this, the assignment above can be written as

```
mat_ptr(row,col) = x;
```

Other languages deal differently with the problem of passing multidimensional arrays. Ada compilers are able to determine the defined size of dimensions of all arrays that are used as parameters at the time subprograms are compiled. In Ada, unconstrained array types can be formal parameters. An unconstrained array type is one in which the index ranges are not given in the array type definition. Definitions of variables of unconstrained array types must include index ranges. The code in a subprogram that is passed an unconstrained array can obtain the index range information of the actual parameter associated with such parameters. For example, consider the following definitions:

```
type Mat_Type is array (Integer range <>,
                        Integer range <>) of Float;
Mat_1 : Mat_Type(1..100, 1..20);
```

A function that returns the sum of the elements of arrays of Mat_Type type follows:

```
function Sumer(Mat : in Mat_Type) return Float is
  Sum : Float := 0.0;
  begin
  for Row in Mat'range(1) loop
    for Col in Mat'range(2) loop
      Sum := Sum + Mat(Row, Col);
    end loop;  — for Col ...
  end loop;  — for Row ...
  return Sum;
  end Sumer;
```

The **range** attribute returns the subscript range of the named subscript of the actual parameter array, so this works regardless of the size or index ranges of the parameter.

In Fortran, the problem is addressed in the following way. Formal parameters that are arrays must have a declaration after the header. For single-dimensioned arrays, the subscripts in such declarations are irrelevant. But for multidimensional arrays, the subscripts in such declarations allow the compiler to build the storage-mapping function. Consider the following example skeletal Fortran subroutine:

```
Subroutine Sub(Matrix, Rows, Cols, Result)
  Integer, Intent(In) :: Rows, Cols
  Real, Dimension(Rows, Cols), Intent(In) :: Matrix
  Real, Intent(In) :: Result
  ...
  End Subroutine Sub
```

This works perfectly as long as the Rows actual parameter has the value used for the number of rows in the definition of the passed matrix. The number of rows is needed because Fortran stores arrays in column major order. If the array to be passed is not currently filled with useful data to the defined size, then both the defined index sizes and the filled index sizes can be passed to the subprogram. Then the defined sizes are used in the local declaration of the array, and the filled index sizes are used to control the computation in which the array elements are referenced. For example, consider the following Fortran subprogram:

```
Subroutine Matsum(Matrix, Rows, Cols, Filled_Rows,
                   Filled_Cols, Sum)
  Real, Dimension(Rows, Cols), Intent(In) :: Matrix
  Integer, Intent(In) :: Rows, Cols, Filled_Rows,
                          Filled_Cols
  Real, Intent(Out) :: Sum
  Integer :: Row_Index, Col_Index
  Sum = 0.0
  Do Row_Index = 1, Filled_Rows
    Do Col_Index = 1, Filled_Cols
      Sum = Sum + Matrix(Row_Index, Col_Index)
    End Do
  End Do
  End Subroutine Matsum
```

Java and C# use a technique for passing multidimensional arrays as parameters that is similar to that of Ada. In Java and C#, arrays are objects. They are all single-dimensioned, but the elements can be arrays. Each array inherits a named constant (length in Java and Length in C#) that is set to the length of the array when the array object is created. The formal parameter for a matrix appears with two sets of empty brackets, as in the Java method below that does what the Ada example function Sumer does:

```
float sumer(float mat[][]) {
  float sum = 0.0f;
  for (int row = 0; row < mat.length; row++) {
```

```
    for (int col = 0; col < mat[row].length; col++) {
      sum += mat[row][col];
    } //** for (int row ~
  } //** for (int col ~
  return sum;
}
```

Because each array has its own length value, in a matrix the rows can have different lengths.

9.5.7 Design Considerations

Two important considerations are involved in choosing parameter-passing methods: efficiency and whether one-way or two-way data transfer is needed.

Contemporary software engineering principles dictate that access by subprogram code to data outside the subprogram should be minimized. With this goal in mind, in-mode parameters should be used whenever no data are to be returned through parameters to the caller. Out-mode parameters should be used when no data are transferred to the called subprogram but the subprogram must transmit data back to the caller. Finally, inout-mode parameters should be used only when data must move in both directions between the caller and the called subprogram.

There is a practical consideration that is in conflict with this principle. Sometimes it is justifiable to pass access paths for one-way parameter transmission. For example, when a large array is to be passed to a subprogram that does not modify it, a one-way method may be preferred. However, pass-by-value would require that the entire array be moved to a local storage area of the subprogram. This would be costly in both time and space. Because of this, large arrays are often passed by reference. This is precisely the reason why the Ada 83 definition allowed implementors to choose between the two methods for structured parameters. C++ constant reference parameters offer another solution. Another alternative approach would be to allow the user to choose between the methods.

The choice of a parameter-passing method for functions is related to another design issue: functional side effects. This issue is discussed in Section 9.9.

9.5.8 Examples of Parameter Passing

Consider the following C function:

```
void swap1(int a, int b) {
  int temp = a;
  a = b;
  b = temp;
}
```

Suppose this function is called with

```
swap1(c, d);
```

Recall that C uses pass-by-value. The actions of `swap1` can be described by the following pseudocode:

```
a = c          — Move first parameter value in
b = d          — Move second parameter value in
temp = a
a = b
b = temp
```

Although `a` ends up with `d`'s value and `b` ends up with `c`'s value, the values of `c` and `d` are unchanged because nothing is transmitted back to the caller.

We can modify the C swap function to deal with pointer parameters to achieve the effect of pass-by-reference:

```
void swap2(int *a, int *b) {
  int temp = *a;
  *a = *b;
  *b = temp;
}
```

`swap2` can be called with

```
swap2(&c, &d);
```

The actions of `swap2` can be described with

```
a = &c          — Move first parameter address in
b = &d          — Move second parameter address in
temp = *a
*a = *b
*b = temp
```

In this case, the swap operation is successful: The values of `c` and `d` are in fact interchanged.

`swap2` can be written in C++ using reference parameters as follows:

```
void swap2(int &a, int &b) {
  int temp = a;
  a = b;
  b = temp;
}
```

This simple swap operation is not possible in Java, because it has neither pointers nor C++'s kind of references. In Java, a reference variable can only point to an object, not a scalar value.

The semantics of pass-by-value-result is identical to those of pass-by-reference, except when aliasing is involved. Recall that Ada uses pass-by-value-result for inout-mode scalar parameters. To explore pass-by-value-result, consider the following function, swap3, which we assume uses pass-by-value-result parameters. It is written in a syntax similar to that of Ada.

```
procedure swap3(a : in out integer, b : in out integer) is
  temp : integer;
  begin
  temp := a;
  a := b;
  b := temp;
  end swap3;
```

Suppose swap3 is called with

```
swap3(c, d);
```

The actions of swap3 with this call are

```
addr_c = &c          — Move first parameter address in
addr_d = &d          — Move second parameter address in
a = *addr_c          — Move first parameter value in
b = *addr_d          — Move second parameter value in
temp = a
a = b
b = temp
*addr_c = a          — Move first parameter value out
*addr_d = b          — Move second parameter value out
```

So once again, this swap subprogram operates correctly. Next, consider the call

```
swap3(i, list[i]);
```

In this case, the actions are

```
addr_i = &i            — Move first parameter address in
addr_listi = &list[i]  — Move second parameter address in
a = *addr_i            — Move first parameter value in
b = *addr_listi        — Move second parameter value in
temp = a
a = b
b = temp
*addr_i = a            — Move first parameter value out
*addr_listi = b        — Move second parameter value out
```

Again, the subprogram operates correctly, in this case because the addresses to which to return the values of the parameters are computed at the time of the call rather than at the time of the return. If the addresses of the actual parameters were computed at the time of the return, the results would be wrong.

Finally, we must explore what happens when aliasing is involved with pass-by-value-result and pass-by-reference. Consider the following skeletal program written in C-like syntax:

```
int i = 3;   /* i is a global variable */
void fun(int a, int b) {
  i = b;
}
void main() {
  int list[10];
  list[i] = 5;
  fun(i, list[i]);
}
```

In fun, if pass-by-reference is used, i and a are aliases. If pass-by-value-result is used, i and a are not aliases. The actions of fun, assuming pass-by-value-result, are

```
addr_i = &i              — Move first parameter address in
addr_listi = &list[i]    — Move second parameter address in
a = *addr_i              — Move first parameter value in
b = *addr_listi          — Move second parameter value in
i = b                    — Sets i to 5
*addr_i = a              — Move first parameter value out
*addr_listi = b          — Move second parameter value out
```

In this case, the assignment to the global i in fun changes its value from 3 to 5, but the copy back of the first formal parameter (the second last line above) sets it back to 3. The important observation here is that if pass-by-reference is used, the result is that the copy back is not part of the semantics, and i remains 5. Also note that because the address of the second parameter is computed at the beginning of fun, any change to the global i has no effect on the address used at the end to return the value of list[i].

9.6   Parameters That Are Subprogram Names

A number of situations occur in programming that are most conveniently handled if subprogram names can be sent as parameters to other subprograms. One of the more common of these occurs when a subprogram must sample some mathematical function. For example, a subprogram that does numerical integration estimates the area under the graph of a function by sampling the function at a number of different points. When such a subprogram is written, it should be usable for any given function; it should not need to be rewritten for every function that must be integrated. It is therefore natural that the name of a program function that evaluates the mathematical function to be integrated be sent to the integrating subprogram as a parameter.

Although the idea is natural and seemingly simple, the details of how it works can be confusing. If only the transmission of the subprogram code was necessary, it could be done by passing a single pointer. However, two complications arise.

First, there is the matter of type checking the parameters of the activations of the subprogram that was passed as a parameter.

In C and C++, functions cannot be passed as parameters, but pointers to functions can. The type of a pointer to a function is the function's protocol. Because the protocol includes all parameter types, such parameters can be completely type checked.

Fortran 95 has a mechanism for providing types of parameters for subprograms that are passed as parameters, and they must be checked. Ada does not allow subprograms to be passed as parameters. The functionality of passing subprograms as parameters is instead provided by Ada's generic facility, which is discussed in Section 9.8.

In languages that allow nested subprograms, such as JavaScript, there is another issue related to subprogram names that are passed as parameters. The question is what referencing environment for executing the passed subprogram should be used. The three choices are:

1. The environment of the call statement that enacts the passed subprogram (**shallow binding**)

2. The environment of the definition of the passed subprogram (**deep binding**)

3. The environment of the call statement that passed the subprogram as an actual parameter (**ad hoc binding**)

The following example program, written with the syntax of JavaScript, illustrates these choices.

```javascript
function sub1() {
  var x;
  function sub2() {
    alert(x);  // Creates a dialog box with the value of x
    };
  function sub3() {
    var x;
    x = 3;
    sub4(sub2);
    };
  function sub4(subx) {
    var x;
```

```
    x = 4;
    subx( );
    };
x = 1;
sub3( );
};
```

HISTORY NOTE

The original definition of Pascal (Jensen and Wirth, 1974) allowed subprograms to be passed as parameters without including their parameter type information. If independent compilation is possible (which it was not in the original Pascal), the compiler is not even allowed to check for the correct number of parameters. In the absence of independent compilation, checking for parameter consistency is possible but is a very complex task, and it usually is not done. Fortran 77 suffered the same problem, but because parameter type consistency is never checked in Fortran 77, it was not an additional problem.

Consider the execution of sub2 when it is called in sub4. For shallow binding, the referencing environment of that execution is that of sub4, so the reference to x in sub2 is bound to the local x in sub4, and the output of the program is 4. For deep binding, the referencing environment of sub2's execution is that of sub1, so the reference to x in sub2 is bound to the local x in sub1, and the output is 1. For ad hoc binding, the binding is to the local x in sub3, and the output is 3.

In some cases, the subprogram that declares a subprogram also passes that subprogram as a parameter. In those cases, deep binding and ad hoc binding are the same. Ad hoc binding has never been used because, one can assume, the environment in which the procedure appears as a parameter has no natural connection to the passed subprogram.

Shallow binding is not appropriate for static-scoped languages with nested subprograms. For example, suppose the procedure Sender passes the procedure Sent as a parameter to the procedure Receiver. The problem is that Receiver may not be in the static environment of Sent, thereby making it very unnatural for Sent to have access to Receiver's variables. On the other hand, it is perfectly normal in such a language for any subprogram, including one sent as a parameter, to have its referencing environment determined by the lexical position of its definition. It is therefore more logical for these languages to use deep binding. Some dynamic-scoped languages use shallow binding.

9.7 Overloaded Subprograms

An overloaded operator is one that has multiple meanings. The meaning of a particular instance of an overloaded operator is determined by the types of its operands. For example, if the * operator has two floating-point operands in a Java program, it specifies floating-point multiplication. But if the same operator has two integer operands, it specifies integer multiplication.

An **overloaded subprogram** is a subprogram that has the same name as another subprogram in the same referencing environment. Every version of an overloaded subprogram must have a unique protocol; that is, it must be different from the others in the number, order, or types of its parameters, or in its return type if it is a function. The meaning of a call to an overloaded subprogram is determined by the actual parameter list (and/or possibly the type of the returned value, in the case of a function).

C++, Java, Ada, and C# include predefined overloaded subprograms. For example, many classes in C++, Java, and C# have overloaded constructors. Because each version of an overloaded subprogram has a unique parameter profile, the compiler can disambiguate occurrences of calls to them by the different type parameters.

In Ada, the return type of an overloaded function can used to disambiguate calls. Therefore, two overloaded functions can have the same parameter profile and differ only in their return types. This works because Ada does not allow mixed-mode expressions, so the context of a function call can specify the type that is returned from the function. C++, Java, and C# allow mixed-mode expressions, and the return type is irrelevant to disambiguation of overloaded functions (or methods).

Users are also allowed to write multiple versions of subprograms with the same name in Ada, Java, C++, and C#. Once again in C++, Java, and C#, the most common user-defined overloaded methods are constructors.

Overloaded subprograms that have default parameters can lead to ambiguous subprogram calls. For example, consider the following C++ code:

```
void fun(float b = 0.0);
void fun();
...
fun();
```

The call is ambiguous and will cause a compilation error.

9.8   Generic Subprograms

Software reuse can be an important contributor to software productivity increases. One way to increase the reusability of software is to lessen the need to create different subprograms that implement the same algorithm on different types of data. For example, a programmer should not need to write four different sort subprograms to sort four arrays that differ only in element type.

A **generic** or **polymorphic subprogram** takes parameters of different types on different activations. Overloaded subprograms provide a particular kind of polymorphism called **ad hoc polymorphism.** A more general kind of polymorphism is provided by the functions of APL. Because of the dynamic type binding of APL, the types of parameters can be left unspecified; they are simply bound to the type of the corresponding actual parameters.

Parametric polymorphism is provided by a subprogram that takes a generic parameter that is used in a type expression that describes the types of the parameters of the subprogram. Both Ada and C++ provide a kind of compile-time parametric polymorphism.

9.8.1 Generic Subprograms in Ada

Ada provides parametric polymorphism through a construct that supports the construction of multiple versions of program units to accept parameters of different data types. The different versions of the subprogram are instantiated, or constructed, by the compiler on request from the user program. Because the versions of the subprogram all have the same name, this provides the illusion that a single subprogram can process data of different types on different calls. Because program units of this sort are generic in nature, they are sometimes called **generic units.**

The same mechanism can be used to allow different executions of a subprogram to call different instantiations of a generic subprogram. This is useful in providing the functionality of subprograms passed as parameters.

The following example illustrates a procedure that has three generic parameters, allowing the subprogram to take as a parameter a generic array. It is an exchange sort procedure that is designed to work on any array with elementary numeric type elements, using any ordinal type subscript range:

```ada
generic
  type Index_Type is (<>);
  type Element_Type is private;
  type Vector is array (Index_Type range <>) of
        Element_Type;
  procedure Generic_Sort(List : in out Vector);
  procedure Generic_Sort(List : in out Vector) is
    Temp : Element_Type;
    begin
    for Top in List'First..Index_Type'Pred(List'Last) loop
      for Bottom in Index_Type'Succ(Top)..List'Last loop
        if List(Top) > List(Bottom) then
          Temp := List(Top);
          List(Top) := List(Bottom);
          List(Bottom) := Temp;
        end if;
        end loop; — for Bottom ...
      end loop; — for Top ...
    end Generic_Sort;
```

Parts of this generic procedure may appear rather odd if you are not familiar with Ada. However, it is not important to understand all the details of the syntax. The array type and the type of its elements are the two generic parameters of this procedure. The array is declared to have any type subscript (that is, any type that is legal as a subscript) with any range.

This generic sort is nothing more than a template for a procedure; no code is generated for it by the compiler, and it has no effect on a program unless it is instantiated for some type. Instantiation is accomplished with a statement such as the following:

```
procedure Integer_Sort is new Generic_Sort(
                              Index_Type => Integer;
                              Element_Type => Integer;
                              Vector => Int_Array);
```

The compiler reacts to this statement by building a version of `Generic_Sort` named `Integer_Sort` that sorts arrays of type `Int_Array` with `Integer` type elements and `Integer` type subscripts.

`Generic_Sort`, as written, assumes that the operator > is defined for the elements of the array to be sorted. The genericity of `Generic_Sort` can be increased by including a comparison function among its generic parameters.

Recall that Ada does not allow subprograms to be passed as parameters to other subprograms. To provide that functionality, Ada uses generic formal subprograms. In a language such as Fortran, subprograms are passed as parameters so that a particular call of a subprogram can execute using the specific passed subprogram to compute its result. In Ada, the same result is achieved by allowing the user to instantiate a generic subprogram any number of times, each with a different subprogram that can be used. For example, consider the following Ada generic procedure:

```
generic
  with function Fun(X : Float) return Float;
  procedure Integrate (Lowerbd : in Float;
                       Upperbd : in Float;
                       Result : out Float);
  procedure Integrate (Lowerbd : in Float;
                       Upperbd : in Float;
                       Result : out Float) is
    Funval : Float;
    begin
    ...
    Funval := Fun(Lowerbd);
    ...
    end Integrate;
```

This could be instantiated for a user-defined function `Fun1` with

```
procedure Integrate_Fun1 is new Integrate(Fun => Fun1);
```

Now, `Integrate_Fun1` is a procedure for integrating the function `Fun1`.

9.8.2 Generic Functions in C++

Generic functions in C++ have the descriptive name of template functions. The definition of a template function has the general form

template <**template** parameters>
— a function definition that may include the template parameters

A template parameter (there must be at least one) has one of the forms

class identifier
typename identifier

Template parameters can also be another template declaration, but we do not consider that option here.
    As an example, consider the template function

```
template <class Type>
Type max(Type first, Type second) {
  return first > second ? first : second;
}
```

where `Type` is the parameter that specifies the type of data on which the function will operate. This template function can be instantiated for any type for which the operator > is defined. For example, if it were instantiated with **int** as the parameter, it would be

```
int max(int first, int second) {
  return first > second ? first : second;
}
```

Although this process could be defined as a macro, a macro would have the disadvantage of not operating correctly if the parameters were expressions with side effects. For example, suppose the macro were defined as

```
#define max(a, b) ((a) > (b)) ? (a) : (b)
```

This is generic in the sense that it works for any numeric type. However, it does not always work correctly if called with a parameter that has a side effect, such as

```
max(x++, y)
```

This produces

```
((x++) > (y) ? (x++) : (y))
```

Whenever the value of x is greater than that of y, x will be incremented twice.
    C++ template functions are instantiated implicitly either when the function is named in a call or when its address is taken with the & operator. For

example, the template function defined above would be instantiated twice by the following code segment, once for **int** type parameters and once for **char** type parameters:

```
int a, b, c;
char d, e, f;
...
c = max(a, b);
f = max(d, e);
```

The following is the C++ version of the generic sort subprogram given in Section 9.8.1. It is somewhat different because C++ array subscripts are restricted to being integers with the lower bound fixed at zero.

```
template <class Type>
void generic_sort(Type list[], int len) {
  int top, bottom;
  Type temp;
  for (top = 0; top < len - 2; top++)
    for (bottom = top + 1; bottom < len - 1; bottom++)
      if (list[top] > list[bottom]) {
        temp = list[top];
        list[top] = list[bottom];
        list[bottom] = temp;
      }  //** end of for (bottom = ...
}  //** end of generic_sort
```

An example instantiation of this template function is

```
float flt_list[100];
...
generic_sort(flt_list, 100);
```

The generic subprograms of Ada and the templated functions of C++ are a kind of poor cousins to a subprogram in which the types of the formal parameters are dynamically bound to the types of the actual parameters in a call. In this case, only a single copy of the code is needed, whereas with the Ada and C++ approaches, a copy must be created at compile time for each different type that is required and the binding of subprogram calls to subprograms is static.

9.8.3   Generic Subprograms in Other Languages

Neither Java nor C# currently supports generic methods. However, a design of generic classes and methods for Java named GJ will be included in the next major release of Java, 1.5. Furthermore, C# also will soon acquire generic methods and classes.

Smalltalk, Java, Ada 95, and C++ support methods in which the calls are dynamically bound to the correct version of the method, according to the types of the actual parameters. This is discussed in Chapter 12.

9.9   Design Issues for Functions

The following two design issues are specific to functions:

- Are side effects allowed?
- What types of values can be returned?

9.9.1   Functional Side Effects

Because of the problems of side effects of functions that are called in expressions, as described in Chapter 5, parameters to functions should always be in-mode parameters. Some languages, in fact, require this; for example, Ada functions can have only in-mode formal parameters. This effectively prevents a function from causing side effects through its parameters or through aliasing of parameters and globals. In most other languages, however, functions can have either pass-by-value or pass-by-reference parameters, thus allowing functions that cause side effects and aliasing.

9.9.2   Types of Returned Values

Most imperative programming languages restrict the types that can be returned by their functions. C allows any type to be returned by its functions except arrays and functions. Both of these can be handled by pointer type return values. C++ is like C but also allows user-defined types, or classes, to be returned from its functions. The Ada language is alone among current imperative languages in that its functions can return values of any type. Because functions are not types in Ada, they cannot be returned from functions.

In some programming languages, subprograms are first-class objects, which means thay can be treated much like data objects. In JavaScript, for example, functions can be passed as parameters and returned from functions. The same is true for many functional languages (see Chapter 15).

Neither Java nor C# can have functions, although their methods are similar to functions. In both, any type or class can be returned by methods. Because methods are not types, they cannot be returned.

9.10   User-Defined Overloaded Operators

Operators can be overloaded by the user in Ada and C++ programs. As an example of this, consider the following Ada function that overloads the multiplication operator (*) to compute the dot product of two arrays. The dot product of two arrays of equal length is the sum of the products of each of the corresponding pairs of elements of the two arrays. Suppose Vector_Type has been defined to be an array type with Integer elements:

```
function "*"(A, B : in Vector_Type) return Integer is
  Sum : Integer := 0;
  begin
  for Index in A'range loop
    Sum := Sum + A(Index) * B(Index);
  end loop;  -- for Index ...
  return Sum;
  end "*";
```

The dot product, as specified in this function definition, will be computed whenever the asterisk appears with two operands of Vector_Type type. The asterisk can be further overloaded any number of times, as long as the defining functions have unique protocols.

The dot product function above could also be written in C++. The prototype of such a function could be

```
int operator *(const vector &a, const vector &b, int len);
```

The question naturally arises: How much operator overloading is good, or can you have too much? The answer is, to a large degree, a matter of taste. The argument against too much operator overloading is mainly one of readability. In many cases, it is more readable to call a function to carry out an operation than to use an operator that is more frequently used for other type operands. Even in the case of the dot product, it may be too easy to forget what is involved when a simple assignment statement, such as

```
c = a * b
```

is found in a program. It is easy to assume a, b, and c are simple scalars.

Another consideration is the process of building a software system from modules created by different groups. If the different groups overloaded the same operators in different ways, these differences would obviously need to be eliminated before putting the system together.

9.11   Coroutines

A coroutine is a special kind of subprogram. Rather than the master–slave relationship between a caller and a called subprogram that exists with conventional subprograms, caller and called coroutines are on a more equal basis. In fact, the coroutine control mechanism is often called the **symmetric unit control model**.

Coroutines have multiple entry points, which are controlled by the coroutines themselves. They also have the means to maintain their status

HISTORY NOTE

The actual origin of the concept of symmetric unit control is difficult to determine. One of the earliest published applications of coroutines was in the area of syntax analysis (Conway, 1963). The first high-level programming language to include facilities for coroutines was SIMULA 67. Recall that the original purpose of SIMULA was system simulation, which often requires the modeling of independent processes. This need was the motivation for the development of SIMULA 67's coroutines. Other languages that support coroutines are BLISS (Wulf et al., 1971), INTERLISP (Teitelman, 1975), and Modula-2 (Wirth, 1985).

between activations. This means that coroutines must be history sensitive and thus have static local variables. Secondary executions of a coroutine often begin at points other than its beginning. Because of this, the invocation of a coroutine is called a **resume** rather than a call.

One of the usual characteristics of subprograms is maintained in coroutines: Only one coroutine actually executes at a given time. Rather than executing to their ends, however, coroutines often partially execute and then transfer control to some other coroutine. When restarted, a coroutine resumes execution just after the statement it used to transfer control elsewhere. This sort of execution sequence is related to the way multiprogramming operating systems work. Although there may be only one processor, all of the executing programs in such a system appear to run concurrently while sharing the processor. In the case of coroutines, this is sometimes called **quasi-concurrency**.

Typically, coroutines are created in an application by a program unit called the **master unit,** which is not a coroutine. When created, coroutines execute their initialization code and then return control to that master unit. When all of a family of coroutines are constructed, the master program resumes one of the coroutines, and the members of the family of coroutines then resume each other in some order until their work is completed, if in fact it can be completed. If the execution of a coroutine reaches the end of its code section, control is transferred to the master unit that created it. This is the mechanism for ending execution of the collection of coroutines, when that is desirable. In some programs, the coroutines run whenever the computer is running.

One example of a problem that can be solved with this sort of collection of coroutines is the simulation of a card game. Suppose the game has four players who all use the same strategy for playing. Such a game can be simulated by having a master program unit create a family of coroutines, each with a collection, or hand, of cards. The master program could then start the simulation by resuming one of the player coroutines, which, after it had played its turn, could resume the next player coroutine, and so forth until the game ended.

The same form of resume statement can be used both to start and to restart the execution of a coroutine.

Suppose program units A and B are coroutines. Figure 9.3 shows two ways an execution sequence involving A and B might proceed.

In Figure 9.3a, the execution of coroutine A is started by the master unit. After some execution, A starts B. When coroutine B in Figure 9.3a first causes control to return to coroutine A, the semantics is that A continues from where it ended its last execution. In particular, its local variables have the values left them by the previous activation. Figure 9.3b shows an alternative execution sequence of coroutines A and B. In this case, B is started by the master unit.

Rather than have the patterns shown in Figure 9.3, a coroutine often has a loop containing a resume. Figure 9.4 shows the execution sequence of this

Figure 9.3

Two possible execution
control sequences for
two coroutines without
loops

(a)

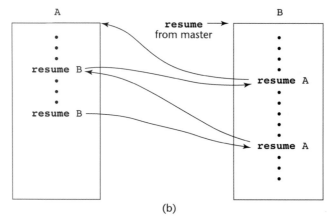

(b)

Figure 9.4

Coroutine execution
sequence with loops

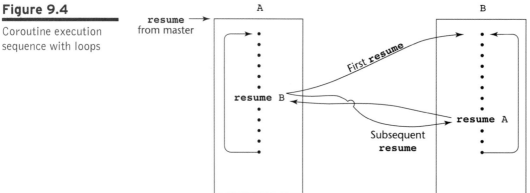

scenario. In this case, A is started by the master unit. Inside its main loop, A resumes B, which in turn resumes A in its main loop.

SUMMARY

Process abstractions are represented in programming languages by subprograms. A subprogram definition describes the actions represented by the subprogram. A subprogram call enacts those actions.

Formal parameters are the names that subprograms use to refer to the actual parameters given in subprogram calls.

Subprograms can be either functions, which model mathematical functions and are used to define new operations, or procedures, which define new statements.

Local variables in subprograms can be stack dynamic, providing support for recursion, or static, providing efficiency and history-sensitive local variables.

There are three fundamental semantics models of parameter passing—in mode, out mode, and inout mode—and a number of approaches to implementation.

Aliasing can occur when pass-by-reference parameters are used, both among two or more parameters and between a parameter and an accessible nonlocal variable.

Parameters that are subprogram names provide a necessary service but are sometimes difficult to understand. The opaqueness lies in the referencing environment that is available when a subprogram that has been passed as a parameter is executing.

Ada, C++, and C# allow both subprogram and operator overloading. Subprograms can be overloaded as long as the various versions can be disambiguated by the types of their parameters or returned values. Function definitions can be used to build additional meanings for operators.

Subprograms in Ada and C++ can be generic, using parametric polymorphism, so the desired types of their data objects can be passed to the compiler, which then can construct units for the requested types.

A coroutine is a special subprogram that has multiple entries. They can be used to provide interleaved execution of subprograms.

REVIEW QUESTIONS

1. What are the three general characteristics of subprograms?
2. What does it mean for a subprogram to be active?
3. What is a parameter profile? What is a subprogram protocol?
4. What are formal parameters? What are actual parameters?
5. What are the advantages and disadvantages of keyword parameters?

6. What are the design issues for subprograms?

7. What are the advantages and disadvantages of dynamic local variables?

8. What are the three semantic models of parameter passing?

9. What are the modes, the conceptual models of transfer, the advantages, and the disadvantages of pass-by-value, pass-by-result, pass-by-value-result, and pass-by-reference parameter-passing methods?

10. In what ways can aliases occur with pass-by-reference parameters?

11. What is the difference between the way original C and C89 deal with an actual parameter whose type is not identical to that of the corresponding formal parameter?

12. What is the problem with Ada's policy of allowing implementors to decide which parameters to pass by reference and which to pass by value-result?

13. What are two fundamental design considerations for parameter-passing methods?

14. What are the two issues that arise when subprogram names are parameters?

15. Define *shallow* and *deep binding* for referencing environments of subprograms that have been passed as parameters.

16. What is an overloaded subprogram?

17. What is parametric polymorphism?

18. What causes a C++ template function to be instantiated?

19. What are the design issues for functions?

20. In what ways are coroutines different from conventional subprograms?

PROBLEM SET

1. What are arguments for and against a user program building additional definitions for existing operators, as can be done in Ada and C++? Do you believe such user-defined operator overloading is good or bad? Support your answer.

2. In most Fortran IV implementations, parameters were passed by reference, using access path transmission only. State both the advantages and disadvantages of this design choice.

3. Argue in support of the Ada 83 designers' decision to allow the implementor to choose between implementing **in out** mode parameters by copy or by reference.

4. Suppose you wish to write a method that prints a heading on a new output page, along with a page number that is 1 in the first activation and that increases by 1 with each subsequent activation. Can this be done without parameters and without reference to nonlocal variables in Java? Can it be done in C#?

5. Consider the following program written in C syntax:

```
void main() {
  int value = 2, list[5] = {1, 3, 5, 7, 9};
  swap(value, list[0]);
  swap(list[0], list[1]);
  swap(value, list[value]);

  }
void swap(int a, int b) {
  int temp;
  temp = a;
  a = b;
  b = temp;
  }
```

For each of the following parameter-passing methods, what are all of the values of the variables value and list after each of the three calls to swap?

a. Passed by value

b. Passed by reference

c. Passed by value-result

6. Present one argument against providing both static and dynamic local variables in subprograms.

7. Argue against the C design of providing only function subprograms.

8. From a textbook on Fortran, learn the syntax and semantics of statement functions. Justify their existence in Fortran.

9. Study the methods of user-defined operator overloading in C++ and Ada, and write a report comparing the two using our criteria for evaluating languages.

10. C# supports out-mode parameters, but neither Java nor C++ does. Give an explanation of this difference.

PROGRAMMING EXERCISES

1. Write a Fortran program that determines whether a Fortran compiler to which you have access implements local variables as static or stack dynamic. *Hint:* The easiest way to check this is to have your program test the history sensitivity of a subprogram.

2. Write a program in a language that you know to determine the ratio of the time required to pass a large array by reference and the time required to pass the same array by value. Make the array as large as possible on the machine and implementation you use. Pass the array as many times as necessary to get reasonably accurate timings of the passing operations.

3. Write a C# or Ada program that determines when the address of an out-mode parameter is computed (at the time of the call or at the time execution of the subprogram finishes).

4. Write a Perl program that passes by reference a literal to a subprogram, which attempts to change the parameter. Given the overall design philosopy of Perl, explain the results.

5. Repeat Exercise 4 in C#.

6. Write a program in some language that has both static and stack-dynamic local variables in subprograms. Create six large (at least 100 × 100) matrices in the subprogram, three static and three stack dynamic. Fill two of the static matrices and two of the stack-dynamic matrices with random numbers in the range of 1 to 100. The code in the subprogram must perform a large number of matrix multiplication operations on the static matrices and time the process. Then it must repeat this with the stack-dynamic matrices. Compare and explain the results.

10

Implementing Subprograms

CHAPTER OUTLINE

T he purpose of this chapter is to explore the implementation of subprograms. The discussion will provide the reader with some insight into how subprogram linkage works, and also why ALGOL 60 was a challenge to the unsuspecting compiler writers of the early 1960s. We begin with the simplest situation, non-nestable subprograms with static local variables, and progress to more complicated subprograms with stack-dynamic local variables, and finally to nested subprograms with stack-dynamic local variables. The increased difficulty of implementing subprograms in languages with nested subprograms is caused by the need to include mechanisms to access nonlocal variables.

The static chain method of accessing nonlocals in static-scoped languages is discussed in detail. Techniques for implementing blocks are covered briefly. Several methods of implementing nonlocal variable access in a dynamic-scoped language are discussed.

Sections 10.1 to 10.5 deal exclusively with static-scoped languages; Section 10.6 discusses the implementation of subprograms in dynamic-scoped languages.

10.1   The General Semantics of Calls and Returns

The subprogram call and return operations of a language are together called its **subprogram linkage.** The implementation of subprograms must be based on the semantics of subprogram linkage.

A subprogram call in a typical language has numerous actions associated with it. The call must include the mechanism for whatever parameter-passing method is used. If local variables are not static, the call must cause storage to be allocated for the locals declared in the called subprogram and bind those variables to that storage. It must save the execution status of the calling program unit. It must arrange to transfer control to the code of the subprogram and ensure that control can return to the proper place when the subprogram execution is completed. Finally, if the language supports nested subprograms, the call must cause some mechanism to be created to provide access to nonlocal variables that are visible to the called subprogram.

The required actions of a subprogram return are also complicated. If the subprogram has parameters that are out mode and are implemented by copy, the first action of the return process is to move the local values of the associated formal parameters to the actual parameters. Next, it must deallocate the storage used for local variables and restore the execution status of the calling program unit. If the language supports nested subprograms, some action must then be taken to return the mechanism used for nonlocal references to the configuration it had before the call. Finally, control must be returned to the calling program unit.

10.2   Implementing "Simple" Subprograms

We begin with the task of implementing "simple" subprograms, where by simple we mean that subprograms cannot be nested and all local variables are static. Early versions of Fortran were examples of languages that had this kind of simple subprograms.

The semantics of a call to a "simple" subprogram requires the following actions:

1. Save the execution status of the current program unit.
2. Carry out the parameter-passing process.
3. Pass the return address to the callee.
4. Transfer control to the callee.

The semantics of a return from a "simple" subprogram requires the following actions:

1. If there are pass-by-value-result or out-mode parameters, the current values of those parameters are moved to the corresponding actual parameters.
2. If the subprogram is a function, the functional value is moved to a place accessible to the caller.
3. The execution status of the caller is restored.
4. Control is transferred back to the caller.

The call and return actions require storage for the following:

- Status information about the caller
- Parameters
- Return address
- Functional value for function subprograms

These, along with the local variables and the subprogram code, form the complete set of information a subprogram needs to execute and then return control to the caller.

A "simple" subprogram consists of two separate parts: the actual code of the subprogram, which is constant, and the local variables and data listed above, which can change when the subprogram is executed. Both of these parts have fixed sizes.

The format, or layout, of the noncode part of a subprogram is called an **activation record,** because the data it describes are only relevant during the activation of the subprogram. The form of an activation record is static. An **activation record instance** is a concrete example of an activation record, a collection of data in the form of an activation record.

Because languages with "simple" subprograms do not support recursion, there can be only one active version of a given subprogram at a time. Therefore, there can be only a single instance of the activation record for a subprogram. One possible layout for activation records is shown in Figure 10.1. The saved execution status of the caller is omitted here and in the remainder of this chapter simply because it is not relevant to the discussion.

Because an activation record instance for a "simple" subprogram has fixed size, it can be statically allocated. In fact, it could be attached to the code part of the subprogram.

Figure 10.2 shows a program consisting of a main program and three subprograms: A, B, and C. Although the figure shows all the code segments separated from all the activation record instances, in some cases the activation record instances are attached to their associated code segments.

The construction of the complete program shown in Figure 10.2 is not done entirely by the compiler. In fact, because of independent compilation, the four program units—MAIN, A, B, and C—may have been compiled on different days, or even in different years. At the time each unit is compiled, the

Figure 10.1

An activation record for "simple" subprograms

Figure 10.2

The code and activation records of a program with "simple" subprograms

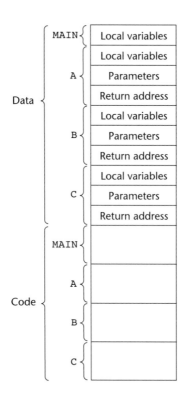

machine code for it, along with a list of references to external subprograms is written to a file. The executable program shown in Figure 10.2 is put together by the **linker,** which is part of the operating system. (Sometimes linkers are called *loaders, linker/loaders,* or *link editors.*) When the linker is called for a main program, its first task is to find the files that contain the translated subprograms referenced in that program, along with their activation record instances, and load them into memory. Then the linker must set the target addresses of all calls to those subprograms in the main program to the entry addresses of those subprograms. The same must be done for all calls to subprograms in the loaded subprograms and all calls to library subprograms. In the example above, the linker was called for MAIN. The linker had to find the machine code programs for A, B, and C, along with their activation record instances, and load them into memory with the code for MAIN. Then it had to patch in the target addresses for all calls to A, B, C, and any library subprograms in A, B, C, and MAIN.

10.3 Implementing Subprograms with Stack-Dynamic Local Variables

We now examine the implementation of the subprogram linkage in languages in which locals are stack dynamic, again focusing on the call and return operations.

One of the most important advantages of stack-dynamic local variables is support for recursion. Therefore, languages that use stack-dynamic local variables also support recursion.

For now, we do not discuss the additional complexity required when subprograms can be nested.

10.3.1 More Complex Activation Records

Subprogram linkage in languages that use stack-dynamic local variables are more complex than the linkage of "simple" subprograms for the following reasons:

- The compiler must generate code to cause the implicit allocation and deallocation of local variables.
- Recursion adds the possibility of multiple simultaneous activations of a subprogram, which means there can be more than one instance (incomplete execution) of a subprogram at a given time, with one call from outside the subprogram and one or more recursive calls. Recursion, therefore, requires multiple instances of activation records, one for each subprogram activation that can exist at the same time. Each activation requires its own copy of the formal parameters and the dynamically allocated local variables, along with the return address.

The format of an activation record for a given subprogram in most languages is known at compile time. In many cases, the size is also known for activation records because all local data is of fixed size. That is not the case in some other languages, such as Ada, in which the size of a local array can depend on the value of an actual parameter. In those cases, the format is static, but the size can be dynamic. In languages with stack-dynamic local variables, activation record instances must be created dynamically. The typical activation record for such a language is shown in Figure 10.3.

Figure 10.3

A typical activation record for a language with stack-dynamic local variables

Because the return address, dynamic link, and parameters are placed in the activation record instance by the caller, these entries must appear first. We assume for this chapter that the stack grows upward. Therefore, the return address will be at the bottom of an activation record.

The return address often consists of a pointer to the code segment of the caller and an offset address in that code segment of the instruction following the call. The **dynamic link** is a pointer to the top of the activation record instance of the caller. In static-scoped languages, this link is used in the destruction of the current activation record instance when the procedure completes its execution. The stack top is set to the value of the old dynamic link. The dynamic link is required because in some cases there are other allocations from the stack by a subprogram beyond its activation record. For example, temporaries needed by the machine language version of the subprogram may be allocated there. So, although the size of the activation record may be known, the size cannot simply be subtracted from the stack top pointer to remove the activation record. The actual parameters in the activation record are the values or addresses provided by the caller.

Local scalar variables are bound to storage within an activation record instance. Local variables that are structures are sometimes allocated elsewhere, and only their descriptors and a pointer to that storage are part of the activation record. Local variables are allocated and possibly initialized in the called subprogram, so they appear last.

Consider the following skeletal C function:

```
void sub(float total, int part) {
  int list[5];
  float sum;
  ...
}
```

The activation record for sub is shown in Figure 10.4.

Figure 10.4

The activation record for function **sub**

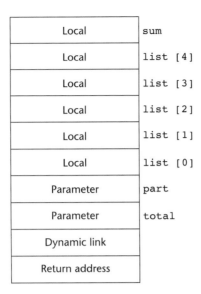

Local	sum
Local	list [4]
Local	list [3]
Local	list [2]
Local	list [1]
Local	list [0]
Parameter	part
Parameter	total
Dynamic link	
Return address	

Activating a subprogram requires the dynamic creation of an instance of the activation record for the subprogram. As stated earlier, the format of the activation record is fixed at compile time, although its size may depend on the call in some languages. Because the call and return semantics specify that the subprogram last called is the first to complete, it is reasonable to create instances of these activation records on a stack. This stack is part of the run-time system, and therefore is called the **run-time stack,** although we will usually just refer to it as the stack. Every subprogram activation, whether recursive or nonrecursive, creates a new instance of an activation record on the stack. This provides the required separate copies of the parameters, local variables, and return address.

Recall from Chapter 9 that a subprogram is **active** from the time it is called until the time that execution is completed. At the time it becomes inactive, its local scope ceases to exist and its referencing environment is no longer meaningful. So at that time, its activation record instance is destroyed.

10.3.2 An Example Without Recursion

Consider the following skeletal C program:

```c
void fun1(int x) {
  int y;
  ...          <————————2
  fun3(y);
  ...
}
```

```
void fun2(float r) {
  int s, t;
  ...        <———————————1
  fun1(s);
  ...
}

void fun3(int q) {
  ...      <———————————3
}

void main() {
  float p;
  ...
  fun2(p);
  ...
}
```

The sequence of procedure calls in this program is

main calls fun2
fun2 calls fun1
fun1 calls fun3

The stack contents for the points labeled 1, 2, and 3 are shown in Figure 10.5.

At point 1, only the activation record instances for function main and function fun2 are on the stack. When fun2 calls fun1, an instance of fun1's activation record is created on the stack. When fun1 calls fun3, an instance of fun3's activation record is created on the stack. When fun3's execution ends, the instance of its activation record is removed from the stack, and the dynamic link is used to reset the stack top pointer. A similar process takes place when functions fun1 and fun2 terminate. After the return from the call to fun2 from main, the stack has only the instance of the activation record of main. Note that some implementations do not actually use an activation record instance on the stack for main functions, such as the one shown in the figure. However, it can be done this way, and it simplifies both the implementation and our discussion. In this example and in all others in this chapter, we assume that the stack grows from lower addresses to higher addresses.

The collection of dynamic links present in the stack at a given time is called the **dynamic chain,** or **call chain.** It represents the dynamic history of how execution got to its current position, which is always in the subprogram code whose activation record instance is on top of the stack. References to

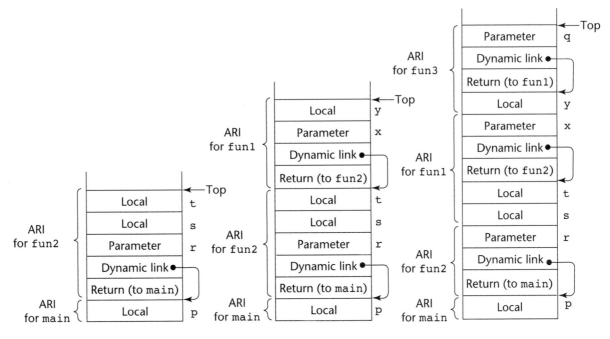

ARI = activation record instance

Figure 10.5

Stack contents for three points in a program

local variables can be represented in the code as offsets from the beginning of the activation record of the local scope. Such an offset is called a **local_offset.**

The local_offset of a variable in an activation record can be determined at compile time, using the order, types, and sizes of variables declared in the subprogram associated with the activation record. To simplify the discussion, assume that all variables take one position in the activation record. The first local variable declared in a subprogram would be allocated in the activation record two positions plus the number of parameters from the bottom (the first two positions are for the return address and the dynamic link). The second local variable declared would be one position nearer the stack top and so forth. For example, consider the preceding example program. In fun1, the local_offset of y is 3. Likewise, in fun2, the local_offset of s is 3; for t it is 4.

10.3.3   Recursion

Consider the following example C program, which uses recursion to compute the factorial function:

```c
int factorial(int n) {
    <————————————1
  if (n <= 1)
    return 1;
  else return (n * factorial(n - 1));
      <————————————2
}
void main() {
  int value;
  value = factorial(3);
      <————————————3
}
```

The activation record format for the function `factorial` is shown in Figure 10.6. Notice that it has an additional entry for the returned value of the function.

Figure 10.7 shows the contents of the stack for the three times that execution reaches position 1 in the function `factorial`. Each shows one more activation of the function, with its functional value undefined. The first activation record instance has the return address to the calling function, `main`. The others have a return address to the function itself; these are for the recursive calls.

Figure 10.8 shows the stack contents for the three times that execution reaches position 2 in the function `factorial`. Position 2 is meant to be the time after the **return** is executed but before the activation record has been removed from the stack. Recall that the code for the function multiplies the current value of the parameter n by the value returned by the recursive call to the function. The first return from `factorial` returns the value 1. The activation record instance for that activation has a value of 1 for its version of the parameter n. The result from that multiplication, 1, is returned to the second activation of `factorial` to be multiplied by its parameter value for n, which is 2. This returns the value 2 to the first activation of `factorial` to be multiplied by its parameter value for n, which is 3, yielding the final functional value of 6, which is then returned to the first call to `factorial` in `main`.

Figure 10.6

The activation record for `factorial`

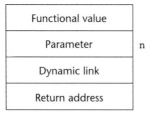

Functional value	
Parameter	n
Dynamic link	
Return address	

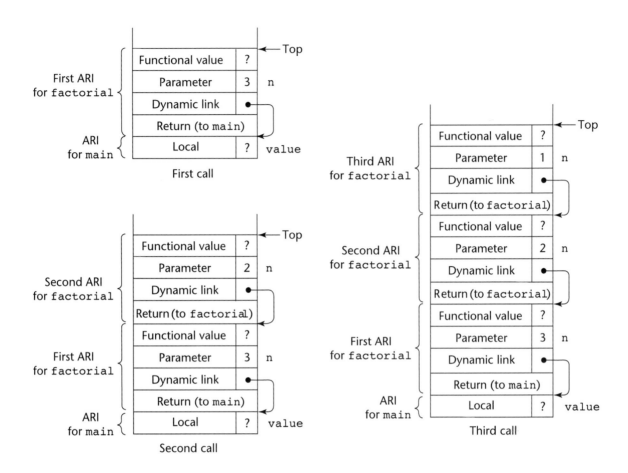

ARI = activation record instance

Figure 10.7

Stack contents at position 1 in `factorial`

10.4   Nested Subprograms

Some of the non-C-based static-scoped programming languages use stack-dynamic local variables and allow subprograms to be nested. Among these are Fortran 95, Ada, and JavaScript. In this section, we examine the most commonly used approach to implementing subprograms in this environment.

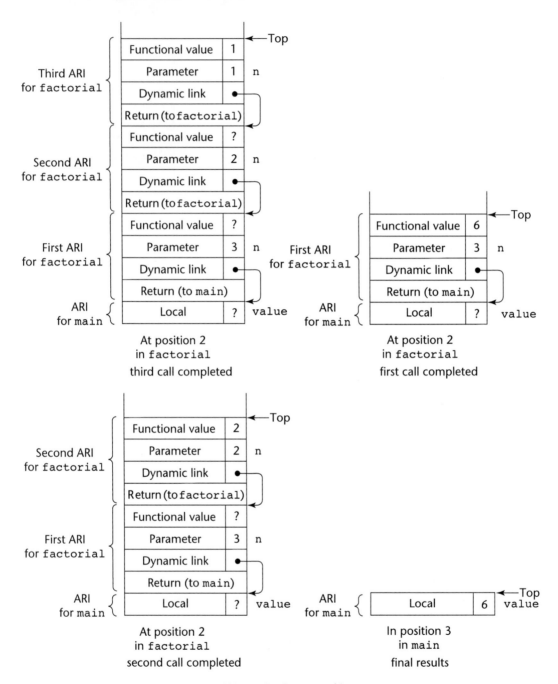

Figure 10.8

Stack contents during execution of main
and factorial

10.4.1 The Basics

A reference to a nonlocal variable in a static-scoped language with nested subprograms requires a two-step access process. All variables that can be nonlocally accessed are in existing activation record instances and therefore are somewhere in the stack. The first step of the access process is to find the instance of the activation record in the stack in which the variable was allocated. The second part is to use the local_offset of the variable (within the activation record instance) to access it.

Finding the correct activation record instance is the more interesting and more difficult of the two steps. First note that in a given subprogram, only variables that are declared in static ancestor scopes are visible and can be accessed. Also, activation record instances of all of the static ancestors are guaranteed to exist on the stack when variables in them are referenced by a nested subprogram. This is guaranteed by the static semantic rules of the static-scoped languages: A subprogram is callable only when all of its static ancestor subprograms are active. If a particular static ancestor were not active, its local variables would not be bound to storage, so it would be nonsense to allow access to them.

The semantics of nonlocal references dictates that the correct declaration is the first one found when looking through the enclosing scopes, most closely nested first. So to support nonlocal references, it must be possible to find all of the instances of activation records in the stack that correspond to those static ancestors. This observation leads to the implementation approach described in the following.

We do not address the issue of blocks until Section 10.5, so in the remainder of Section 10.4, all scopes are defined by subprograms. Because functions cannot be nested in the C-based languages (the only static scopes are created with blocks), the discussions of this section do not apply to those languages directly.

10.4.2 Static Chains

The most common way to implement static scoping in languages that allow nested subprograms is static chaining. In this approach, a new pointer, called a static link, is added to the activation record. The **static link,** which is sometimes called a *static scope pointer*, points to the bottom of the activation record instance of an activation of the static parent. It is used for accesses to nonlocal variables. Typically, the static link appears in the activation record below the parameters. The addition of the static link to the activation record requires that local offsets are different than when the static link is not included. Instead of having two activation record elements before the parameters, there are now three: the return address, the static link, and the dynamic link.

A **static chain** is a chain of static links that connect certain activation record instances in the stack. During the execution of a procedure P, the

INTERVIEW

Keeping It Simple

NIKLAUS WIRTH

Niklaus Wirth began his career in engineering at the Swiss Federal Institute of Technology (ETH) in Zurich. He then studied in Canada and went on to receive a Ph.D. from the University of California at Berkeley in 1963. Throughout his career he has held positions such as assistant professor of computer science (at Stanford University and then at the University of Zürich), professor of informatics at ETH Zürich, and researcher at Xerox PARC in California. Professor Wirth won a Computer Pioneer award from the IEEE and received ACM's Turing Award "for developing a sequence of innovative computer languages, EULER, ALGOL-W, PASCAL and MODULA."

ON DESIGNS AND SOLUTIONS

The clear and uniform structure of Pascal set a new standard. What was it about Pascal that improved so significantly on these tools? Mainly the fact that Pascal expresses the most basic elements of programming and lets them be composed and combined in a free and general way. It is a structured language both for statements and data.

You've spent a lot of time thinking about solutions that marry hardware and software: The Lilith Computer and Oberon and Modula. What about considering programming tool solutions within the larger framework of the hardware draws

> **"**Concentrating on the essentials and leaving off bells and whistles would lead to simpler systems that would be more economical, simpler to understand and operate, and which might therefore be less susceptible to mistakes.**"**

you to considering both when designing solutions? If computer architecture and software are built properly and fit together harmoniously, both parts become simpler and more economical. Most importantly, they become easier to understand.

I read this quote in an interview you gave: "A good designer must rely on experience, on precise, logical thinking, and on pedantic exactness. No magic will do." How is one able to distinguish between the magic and the best solution, and dismiss the former for the latter? I guess mostly through experience. Good teachers who have this ability to distinguish help enormously.

In another interview you mentioned the state of design today and what drove it: "The wishes of

static link of its activation record instance points to an activation record instance of P's static parent program unit. That instance's static link points, in turn, to P's static grandparent program unit's activation record instance, if there is one. So the static chain links all the static ancestors of an executing subprogram, in order of static parent first. This chain can obviously be used to implement the accesses to nonlocal variables in static-scoped languages.

the users count more than their needs, and people are more easily sold by cool features—even if rarely used—than by the goal of reliable and transparent programs." If the opposite had been true what do you think today's operating system or today's Web interfaces would look like to the average user? How would they be better? Very often, clients specifying a software system do not know exactly what they require. Hence their "wishes" may not truly reflect their actual needs. The results are specifications with many items that on closer inspection are quite superfluous, or at least unimportant. Concentrating on the essentials and leaving off bells and whistles would lead to simpler systems that would be more economical, simpler to understand and operate, and which might therefore be less susceptible to mistakes.

You've expressed this idea that what technology makes possible is most commonly exaggerated—for example, leading artificial intelligence on a mission to try and create machines that "think." Can you elaborate some on why you think this exaggerated belief in technology leads scientists down a fruitless path? The hype about many items of modern IT—not only artificial intelligence—misleads not so much scientists, but rather customers (and funding agencies). It is one thing to support long-term research with calculated risk, and another to sell products with exaggerated promises that cannot be substantiated.

ABOUT THE STATE OF THE ART AND ITS TOOLS

Thinking about the past 10 years, what are a couple of advancements in language features that have most contributed to better programming? Program and data structures, and the associated idea of assertions and loop invariants. Modular design and separate compilation of modules. Hierarchies of data types (in OOP called subclasses with inheritance).

In this comparative languages course, students study functional languages, logic languages, procedural languages, and OOP. How should students consider procedural programming in their studies and work? Is it an historical style? One soon to become a niche style? It is important that CS students know the various programming paradigms: procedural, functional, logic, and object-oriented. But obviously the procedural style remains closest to the computer on which programs are interpreted ("run"). The computer's characteristic feature is memory with individually updated cells. Their correspondence in programming languages is the variable. The object-oriented style is based on the procedural style; it is a variant of it, not really different, even if procedures are now called "methods," and calling a procedure is termed "sending a message." I consider functional and logic programming "niche styles" much rather than procedural programming.

Finding the correct activation record instance of a nonlocal variable using static links is relatively straightforward. When a reference is made to a nonlocal variable, the activation record instance containing the variable can be found by searching the static chain until a static ancestor activation record instance is found that contains the variable. However, it is much easier than that. Because the nesting of scopes is known at compile time, the compiler can determine not only that a reference is nonlocal but also the length of the static chain that must be followed to reach the activation record instance that contains the nonlocal object.

Let **static_depth** be an integer associated with a static scope that indicates how deeply it is nested in the outermost scope. An Ada main procedure has a static_depth of 0. If procedure A is defined in a main procedure, its static_depth is 1. If procedure A contains the definition of a nested procedure B, then B's static_depth is 2.

The length of the static chain needed to reach the correct activation record instance for a nonlocal reference to a variable X is exactly the difference between the static_depth of the procedure containing the reference to X and the static_depth of the procedure containing the declaration for X. This difference is called the **nesting_depth,** or **chain_offset,** of the reference. The actual reference can be represented by an ordered pair of integers (chain_offset, local_offset), where chain_offset is the number of links to the correct activation record instance (local_offset is described in Section 10.3.2). For example, consider the following skeletal program:

```
procedure A is
  procedure B is
    procedure C is
      ...
    end;   -- of C
    ...
  end;   -- of B
  ...
end;   -- of A
```

The static_depths of A, B, and C are 0, 1, and 2, respectively. If procedure C references a variable declared in A, the chain_offset of that reference would be 2 (static_depth of C minus the static_depth of A). If procedure C references a variable declared in B, the chain_offset of that reference would be 1. References to locals can be handled using the same mechanism, with a chain_offset of 0.

To illustrate the complete process of nonlocal accesses, consider the following skeletal Ada program:

```
procedure Main_2 is
  X : Integer;
  procedure Bigsub is
    A, B, C : Integer;
    procedure Sub1 is
      A, D : Integer;
      begin   -- of Sub1
        A := B + C;    <───────────────1
```

```
      . . .
      end;   -- of Sub1
   procedure Sub2(X : Integer) is
     B, E : Integer;
     procedure Sub3 is
        C, E : Integer;
        begin   -- of Sub3
        . . .
        Sub1;
        . . .
        E := B + A;   <————————2
        end;   -- of Sub3
      begin   -- of Sub2
      . . .
      Sub3;
      . . .
      A := D + E;    <————————3
      end;   -- of Sub2
   begin   -- of Bigsub
   . . .
   Sub2(7);
   . . .
   end;   -- of Bigsub
 begin   -- of Main_2
 . . .
 Bigsub;
 . . .
 end;   -- of Main_2
```

The sequence of procedure calls is

Main_2 calls Bigsub
Bigsub calls Sub2
Sub2 calls Sub3
Sub3 calls Sub1

The stack situation when execution first arrives at point 1 in this program is shown in Figure 10.9.

At position 1 in procedure Sub1, the reference is to the local variable, A, not to the nonlocal variable A from Bigsub. This reference to A has the chain_offset/local_offset pair (0, 3). The reference to B is to the nonlocal B from Bigsub. It can be represented by the pair (1, 4). The local_offset is 4, because a 3 offset would be the first local variable (Bigsub has no parameters). Notice that if the dynamic link were used to do a simple search for an activation record instance with a declaration for the variable B, it would find the variable B declared in Sub2, which would be incorrect. If the (1, 4) pair were used

Figure 10.9

Stack contents at
position 1 in the
program Main_2

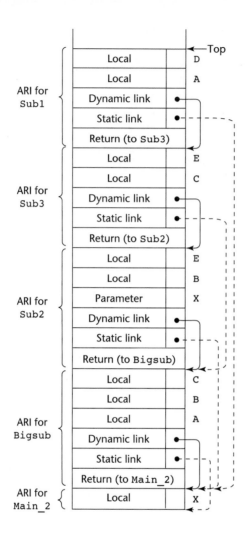

ARI = activation record instance

with the dynamic chain, the variable E from Sub3 would be used. The static link, however, points to the activation record for Bigsub, which has the correct version of B. The variable B in Sub2 is not in the referencing environment at this point and is (correctly) not accessible. The reference to C at point 1 is to the C defined in Bigsub, which is represented by the pair (1, 5).

After Sub1 completes its execution, the activation record instance for Sub1 is removed from the stack, and control returns to Sub3. The reference to the variable E at position 2 in Sub3 is local and uses the pair (0, 4) for access. The reference to the variable B is to the one declared in Sub2, because that is the nearest static ancestor that contains such a declaration. It is accessed with the pair (1, 4). The local_offset is 4 because B is the first variable declared in Sub1, and Sub2 has one parameter. The reference to the variable A is to the A declared in Bigsub, because neither Sub3 nor its static parent Sub2 has a declaration for a variable named A. It is referenced with the pair (2, 3).

After Sub3 completes its execution, the activation record instance for Sub3 is removed from the stack, leaving only the activation record instances for Main_2, Bigsub, and Sub2. At position 3 in Sub2, the reference to the variable A is to the A in Bigsub, which has the only declaration of A among the active routines. This access is made with the pair (1, 3). At this position, there is no visible scope containing a declaration for the variable D, so this reference to D is a static semantics error. The error would be detected when the compiler attempted to compute the chain_offset/local_offset pair. The reference to E is to the local E in Sub2, which can be accessed with the pair (0, 5).

In summary, the references to the variable A at points 1, 2, and 3, would be represented by the following points:

(0, 3) (local)
(2, 3) (two levels away)
(1, 3) (one level away)

It is reasonable at this point to ask how the static chain is maintained during program execution. If its maintenance is too complex, the fact that it is simple and effective will be unimportant. We assume here that parameters that are subprogram names are not implemented.

The static chain must be modified for each subprogram call and return. The return part is trivial: When the subprogram terminates, its activation record instance is removed from the stack. After this removal, the new top activation record instance is that of the unit that called the subprogram whose execution just terminated. Because the static chain from this activation record instance was never changed, it works correctly just as it did before the call to the other subprogram. Therefore, no other action is required.

The action required at a subprogram call is more complex. Although the correct parent scope is easily determined at compile time, the most recent activation record instance of the parent scope must be found at the time of the call. This can be done by looking at activation record instances on the dynamic chain until the first one of the parent scope is found. However, this search can be avoided by treating procedure declarations and references exactly like variable declarations and references. When the compiler encounters a subprogram call, among other things, it determines the subprogram that declared the called subprogram, which must be a static ancestor of the calling routine. It then computes the nesting_depth, or number of enclosing scopes between the caller and the subprogram that declared the called subprogram. This information is stored and can be accessed by the subprogram call during execution. At the time of the call, the static link of the called subprogram 's activation record instance is determined by moving down the static chain of the caller the number of links equal to the nesting_depth computed at compile time.

Consider again the program Main_2 and the stack situation shown in Figure 10.9. At the call to Sub1 in Sub3, the compiler determines the nesting_depth of Sub3 (the caller) to be two levels inside the procedure that declared the called procedure Sub1, which is Bigsub. When the call to Sub1 in Sub3 is executed, this information is used to set the static link of the activation record instance for Sub1. This static link is set to point to the activation record instance that is pointed to by the second static link in the static chain from the caller's activation record instance. In this case, the caller is Sub3, whose static link points to its parent's activation record instance (that of Sub2). The static link of the activation record instance for Sub2 points to the activation record instance for Bigsub. So the static link for the new activation record instance for Sub1 is set to point to the activation record instance for Bigsub.

This method works for all subprogram linkage, except when parameters that are subprogram names are involved.

One criticism of using the static chain to access nonlocal variables is that references to variables in scopes beyond the static parent cost more than references to locals. The static chain must be followed, one link per enclosing scope from the reference to the declaration. Fortunately, in practice references to distant nonlocal variables are rare, so this is not a serious problem. Another criticism of the static chain approach is that it is difficult for a programmer working on a time-critical program to estimate the costs of nonlocal references, because the cost of each reference depends on the depth of nesting between the reference and the scope of declaration. Further complicating this problem is that subsequent code modifications may change nesting depths, thereby changing the timing of some references, both in the changed code and possibly in code far from the changes.

10.4.3   Displays

One alternative to static chains is to use a display. For this approach, the static links are collected in a single array called a **display,** rather than being stored in the activation records. The contents of the display at any specific time is a list of addresses of the accessible activation record instances in the stack—one for each active scope—in the order in which they are nested.

Accesses to nonlocals using a display require exactly two steps for every access, regardless of the number of scope levels between the reference and the declaration of the variable being accessed. These two steps are accomplished as follows: The link to the correct activation record, which resides in the display, is found using a statically computed value called the display_offset, which is closely related to the static chain chain_offset. The local_offset within the activation record instance is computed and used exactly as with static chain implementations. A nonlocal reference is represented by an ordered pair of integers, (display_offset, local_offset). A nonlocal variable can be addressed conveniently and quickly with two applications of an offset-indirect addressing mode, which many contemporary computers have.

Although displays have some advantages over static chains, they are weak advantages. If the display can be stored in registers, the advantages are magnified, but the alternative uses of registers are worth more than the gain obtained by using them for a display. Therefore, displays are not widely used in contemporary implementations.

10.5 Blocks

Recall from Chapter 5 that a number of languages, including the C-based languages, provide for user-specified local scopes for variables called **blocks**. As an example of a block, consider the following code segment:

```
{ int temp;
  temp = list[upper];
  list[upper] = list[lower];
  list[lower] = temp;
}
```

A block is specified in the C-based languages as a segment of code that begins with one or more data definitions and is enclosed in braces. The lifetime of the variable temp in the block above begins when control enters the block and ends when control exits the block. The advantage of using such a local is that it cannot interfere with any other variable with the same name that is declared elsewhere in the program.

Blocks can be implemented by using the static chain process we described for implementing nested subprograms. Blocks are treated as parameterless subprograms that are always called from the same place in the program. So, every block has an activation record. An instance of its activation record is created every time the block is executed.

Blocks can also be implemented in a different and somewhat simpler and more efficient way. The maximum amount of storage required for block variables at any time during the execution of a program can be statically determined, because blocks are entered and exited in strictly textual order. This amount of space can be allocated after the local variables in the activation record. Offsets for all block variables can be statically computed, so block variables can be addressed exactly as if they were local variables.

For example, consider the following skeletal program:

```
void main() {
  int x, y, z;
  while ( ... ) {
```

```
int a, b, c;
...
while ( ... ) {
  int d, e;
  ...
}
}
while ( ... ) {
  int f, g;
  ...
}
...
}
```

For this program, the static memory layout shown in Figure 10.10 could be used. Note that f and g occupy the same memory locations as a and b, because a and b are popped off the stack when their block is exited (before f and g are allocated).

Figure 10.10

Block variable storage when blocks are not treated as parameter-less procedures

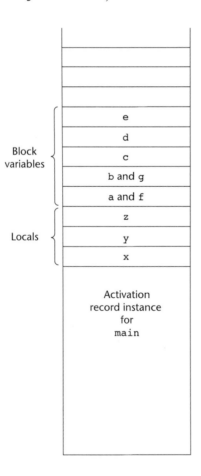

10.6   Implementing Dynamic Scoping

There are at least two distinct ways in which local variables and nonlocal references to them can be implemented in a dynamic-scoped language: deep access and shallow access. Note that deep access and shallow access are not concepts related to deep and shallow binding. The primary difference between binding and access here is that deep and shallow bindings result in different semantics; deep and shallow accesses do not.

10.6.1   Deep Access

If local variables are stack-dynamic and are part of the activation records in a dynamic-scoped language, references to nonlocal variables can be resolved by searching through the activation record instances of the other subprograms that are currently active, beginning with the one most recently activated. This concept is similar to that of accessing nonlocal variables in a static-scoped language with nested subprograms, except that the dynamic—rather than the static—chain is followed. The dynamic chain links together all subprogram activation record instances in the reverse of the order in which they were activated. Therefore, the dynamic chain is exactly what is needed to reference nonlocal variables in a dynamic-scoped language. This method is called **deep access** because access may require searches deep in the stack.

Consider the following example program:

```
void sub3() {
  int x, z;
  x = u + v;
  ...
}

void sub2() {
  int w, x;
  ...
}

void sub1() {
  int v, w;
  ...
}

void main() {
  int v, u;
  ...
}
```

This program is written in a syntax that gives it the appearance of a program in a C-based language, but it is not meant to be in any particular language. Suppose the following sequence of function calls occurs:

```
main calls sub1
sub1 calls sub1
sub1 calls sub2
sub2 calls sub3
```

Figure 10.11 shows the stack during the execution of function sub3 after this calling sequence. Notice that the activation record instances do not have static links, which would serve no purpose in a dynamic-scoped language.

Consider the references to the variables x, u, and v in function sub3. The reference to x is found in the activation record instance for sub3. The reference to u is found by searching *all* of the activation record instances on the stack, because the only existing variable with that name is in main. This involves following four dynamic links and examining ten variable names. The reference to v is found in the most recent (nearest on the dynamic chain) activation record instance for the procedure sub1.

There are two important differences between the deep access method for nonlocal access in a dynamic-scoped language and the static chain method for static-scoped languages. First, in a dynamic-scoped language, there is no way to determine at compile time the length of the chain that must be searched. Every activation record instance in the chain must be searched until the first instance of the variable is found. This is one reason why dynamic-scoped languages typically have slower execution speeds than static-scoped languages. Second, activation records must store the names of variables for the search process, whereas in static-scoped language implementations only the values are required. (Names are not required for static scoping because all variables are represented by the chain_offset/local_offset pairs.)

10.6.2 Shallow Access

Shallow access is an alternative implementation method, not an alternative semantics. As stated above, the semantics of deep access and shallow access are identical. In the shallow access method, variables declared in subprograms are not stored in the activation records of those subprograms. Because with dynamic scoping there is at most one visible version of a variable of any specific name at a given time, a very different approach can be taken. One variation of shallow access is to have a separate stack for each variable name in a complete program. Every time a new variable with a particular name is created by a declaration at the beginning of a subprogram activation, the variable is given a cell on the stack for its name. Every reference to the name is to the variable on top of the stack associated with that name, because the top one is the most recently created. When a subprogram terminates, the lifetime of its local variables ends, and the stacks for those variable names are popped. This

Figure 10.11

Stack contents for
a dynamic-scoped
program

ARI = activation record instance

method allows very fast references to variables, but maintaining the stacks at
the entrances and exits of subprograms is costly.

Figure 10.12 shows the variable stacks for the above example program in
the same situation as shown with the stack in Figure 10.11.

Another option for implementing shallow access is to use a central table
that has a location for each different variable name in a program. Along with
each entry, a bit called **active** is maintained that indicates whether the name
has a current binding or variable association. Any access to any variable can
then be to an offset into the central table. The offset is static, so the access can
be fast. SNOBOL implementations use the central table implementation
technique.

Maintenance of a central table is straightforward. A subprogram call
requires that all of its local variables be logically placed in the central table. If
the position of the new variable in the central table is already active—that is,
if it contains a variable whose lifetime has not yet ended (which is indicated by
the active bit), that value must be saved somewhere during the lifetime of the
new variable. Whenever a variable begins its lifetime, the active bit in its central table position must be set.

Figure 10.12

One method of using
shallow access to
implement dynamic
scoping

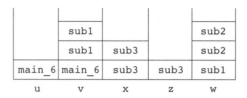

u	v	x	z	w
	sub1			sub2
	sub1	sub3		sub2
main_6	main_6	sub3	sub3	sub1

(The names in the stack cells indicate the
program units of the variable declaration.)

There have been several variations in the design of the central table and in the way values are stored when they are temporarily replaced. One variation is to have a "hidden" stack on which all saved objects are stored. Because subprogram calls and returns, and thus the lifetimes of local variables, are nested, this works well.

The second variation is perhaps the cleanest and least expensive to implement. A central table of single cells is used, storing only the current version of each variable name. Replaced variables are stored in the activation record of the subprogram that created the replacement variable. This is a stack mechanism, but one that already exists, so the new overhead is minimal.

The choice between shallow and deep access to nonlocal variables depends on the relative frequencies of subprogram calls and nonlocal references. The deep access method provides fast subprogram linkage, but references to nonlocals, especially references to distant nonlocals (in terms of the call chain), are costly. The shallow access method provides much faster references to nonlocals, especially distant nonlocals, but is more costly in terms of subprogram linkage.

SUMMARY

Subprogram linkage semantics requires many actions by the implementation. In the case of "simple" subprograms, these actions are relatively easy. In languages with stack-dynamic local variables and nested subprograms, subprogram linkage is more complex.

Subprograms in languages with stack-dynamic local variables and nested subprograms have two components: the actual code, which is static, and the activation record, which is stack-dynamic. Activation record instances contain the formal parameters and local variables, among other things.

Static chains are the primary method of implementing accesses to nonlocal variables in static-scoped languages with nested subprograms.

Access to nonlocal variables in a dynamic-scoped language can be implemented by use of the dynamic chain or through some central variable table method. Dynamic chains provide slow accesses but fast calls and returns. The central table methods provide fast accesses but slow calls and returns.

REVIEW QUESTIONS

1. What are the two reasons why implementing subprograms with stack-dynamic local variables is more difficult than implementing "simple" subprograms?
2. What is the difference between an activation record and an activation record instance?
3. Why are the return address, dynamic link, and parameters placed in the bottom of the activation record?
4. What are the two steps in locating a nonlocal variable in a static-scoped language with stack-dynamic local variables and nested subprograms?
5. Define *static chain*, *static_depth*, *nesting_depth*, and *chain_offset*.
6. Explain how a reference to a nonlocal variable is found when static chains are used.
7. What are the two potential problems with the static chain method?
8. What is a display?
9. Explain how a reference to a nonlocal variable is found when a display is used.
10. How are references to variables represented in the static chain method?
11. Explain the two methods of implementing blocks.
12. Describe the deep access method of implementing dynamic scoping.
13. Describe the shallow access method of implementing dynamic scoping.
14. What are the two differences between the deep access method for non-local access in dynamic-scoped languages and the static chain method for static-scoped languages?
15. Compare the efficiency of the deep access method to that of the shallow access method, in terms of both calls and nonlocal accesses.

PROBLEM SET

1. Show the stack with all activation record instances, including static and dynamic chains, when execution reaches position 1 in the following skeletal program. Assume `Bigsub` is at level 1.

```
procedure Bigsub is
   procedure A is
      procedure B is
         begin   -- of B
         ...  <───────────────1
         end;   -- of B
```

```
      procedure C is
        begin   -- of C
        ...
        B;
        ...
        end;   -- of C
      begin   -- of A
      ...
      C;
      ...
      end;   -- of A
    begin   -- of Bigsub
    ...
    A;
    ...
    end;   -- of Bigsub
```

2. Show the stack with all activation record instances, including static and dynamic chains, when execution reaches position 1 in the following skeletal program. Assume Bigsub is at level 1.

```
procedure Bigsub is
  procedure A(Flag : Boolean) is
    procedure B is
      ...
      A(false);
      end;   -- of B
    begin   -- of A
    if flag
      then B;
      else C;
    ...
    end;   -- of A
  procedure C is
    procedure D is
      ... <———————————1
      end;   -- of D
    ...
    D;
    end;   -- of C
  begin   -- of Bigsub
  ...
  A(true);
  ...
  end;   -- of Bigsub
```

The calling sequence for this program for execution to reach D is

Bigsub calls A
A calls B
B calls A
A calls C
C calls D

3. Although local variables in Java methods are dynamically allocated at the beginning of each activation, under what circumstances could the value of a local in a particular activation retain the value of the previous activation?

4. It is stated in this chapter that when nonlocal variables are accessed in a dynamic-scoped language using the dynamic chain, variable names must be stored in the activation records with the values. If this were actually done, every nonlocal access would require a sequence of costly string comparisons on names. Design an alternative to these string comparisons that would be faster.

5. Pascal allows gotos with nonlocal targets. How could such statements be handled if static chains were used for nonlocal variable access? *Hint:* Consider the way the correct activation record instance of the static parent of a newly enacted procedure is found (see Section 10.4.2).

6. The static chain method could be expanded slightly by using two static links in each activation record instance where the second points to the static grandparent activation record instance. How would this affect the time required for subprogram linkage and nonlocal references?

11

Abstract Data Types and Encapsulation Constructs

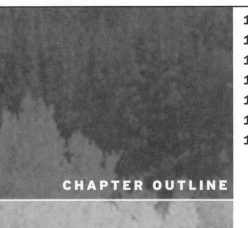

CHAPTER OUTLINE

n this chapter, we explore programming language constructs for data abstraction. We begin with Ada, one of the first languages to support abstract data types, and then discuss the C-based languages that support data abstraction. Among the new ideas of the last 45 years in programming methodologies and programming language design, data abstraction is one of the most profound.

We begin by discussing the general concept of abstraction in programming and programming languages. Data abstraction is then defined and illustrated with an example. This is followed by descriptions of the support for data abstraction in Ada, C++, Java, and C#. Implementations of the same example data abstraction are given in Ada, C++, and Java. This illuminates the similarities and differences in the design of the language facilities that support data abstraction. Next, the capabilities in Ada and C++ to build parameterized abstract data types are discussed.

Constructs that support abstract data types are encapsulations of the data and operations on objects of the type. Encapsulations that contain multiple types are required for the construction of larger programs. These encapsulations and the associated namespace issues are also discussed in this chapter.

11.1 The Concept of Abstraction

An abstraction is a view or representation of an entity that includes only the attributes of significance in a particular context. Abstraction allows one to collect instances of entities into groups in which their common attributes need not be considered. These common attributes are abstracted away. Within the groups, only the attributes that distinguish the individual elements need be considered. This results in significant simplification of the elements in the group. Less abstract views of these entities may be considered when it is necessary to see a higher level of detail. Abstraction is a weapon against the complexity of programming; its purpose is to simplify the programming process. It is an effective weapon because it allows programmers to focus on essential attributes and ignore subordinate attributes.

The two fundamental kinds of abstraction in contemporary programming languages are process abstraction and data abstraction.

The concept of **process abstraction** is among the oldest in programming language design. Even Plankalkül supported process abstraction. All subprograms are process abstractions because they provide a way for a program to specify that some process is to be done without providing the details of how it is to be done (at least in the calling program). For example, when a program needs to sort an array of numeric data objects of some type, it usually uses a subprogram for the sorting process. At the point where the sorting process is required, a statement such as

```
sortInt(list, listLen)
```

is placed in the program. This call is an abstraction of the actual sorting process, whose algorithm is not specified. The call is independent of the algorithm implemented in the called subprogram.

In the case of the subprogram `sortInt`, the only essential attributes are the name of the array to be sorted, the type of its elements, the array's length, and the fact that the call to `sortInt` will result in the array being sorted. The particular algorithm that `sortInt` implements is an attribute that is not essential to the user. The user needs to see only the name and protocol of the sorting subprogram to be able to use it.

The evolution of data abstraction necessarily followed that of process abstraction because an integral and central part of every data abstraction is its operations, which are defined as process abstractions.

11.2   Introduction to Data Abstraction

An abstract data type, simply put, is an encapsulation that includes only the data representation of one specific data type and the subprograms that provide the operations for that type. Through access control, unnecessary details of the type can be hidden from units outside the encapsulation that use the type. Program units that use an abstract data type can declare variables of that type, even though the actual representation is hidden from them. An instance of an abstract data type is called an **object.**

One of the motivations for data abstraction is similar to that of process abstraction. It is a weapon against complexity, a means of making large and/or complicated programs more manageable. Other motivations for and advantages of abstract data types are discussed later in this section.

Object-oriented programming, which is described in Chapter 12, is an outgrowth of the use of data abstraction in software development, and data abstraction is one of its most important components.

11.2.1   Floating-Point as an Abstract Data Type

The concept of abstract data types, at least in terms of built-in types, is not a recent development. All built-in data types, even those of Fortran I, are abstract data types, although they are rarely called that. For example, consider a floating-point data type. Most languages include at least one of these, which provides a means of creating variables for floating-point data, and also provides a set of arithmetic operations for manipulating objects of the type.

Floating-point types in high-level languages employ a key concept in data abstraction: information hiding. The actual format of the data value in a floating-point memory cell is hidden from the user. The only operations available are those provided by the language. The user is not allowed to create new operations on data of the type, except those that can be constructed using the built-in operations. The user cannot directly manipulate the parts of the actual representation of objects because that representation is hidden. It is this feature that allows program portability between implementations of a particular language, even though the implementations may use different representations for particular data types. For example, before the IEEE 754 standard floating-point representations appeared in the mid-1980s, there were several different representations being used by different computer architectures. However, this did not prevent programs from being portable to the various architectures.

11.2.2 User-Defined Abstract Data Types

A user-defined abstract data type should provide the same characteristics provided by language-defined types, such as a floating-point type: (1) a type definition that allows program units to declare variables of the type but hides the representation of these variables; and (2) a set of operations for manipulating objects of the type.

We now formally define an abstract data type in the context of user-defined types. An **abstract data type** is a data type that satisfies the following two conditions:

- The declarations of the type and the operations on objects of the type, which provide the type's interface, are contained in a single syntactic unit. The implementation of the type and its operations may be in the same unit, or may be given in a separate syntactic unit. Also, other program units are allowed to create variables of the defined type.
- The representation of objects of the type is hidden from the program units that use the type, so the only direct operations possible on those objects are those provided in the type's definition.

Program units that use a specific abstract data type are called **clients** of that type.

The primary advantage of packaging the declarations of the type and its operations in a single syntactic unit is it provides a method of organizing a program into logical units that can be compiled separately. The advantage of having the implementation of the type and its operations in a different syntactic unit is that it is good to keep specifications and implementation separate. Clients need to see the specification, but cannot be allowed to see the implementation. If both the declarations and the definitions of types and operations are in the same syntactic unit, there must be some means of hiding the definitions from clients.

There are several advantages to hiding representation details. The most important of these is clients are not able to "see" the representation details, and thus their code cannot depend on that representation. This results in representations that can be changed without requiring changes to the clients. The interface for the abstraction represents some, but not all, of its attributes.

Another distinct and important benefit of information hiding is increased reliability. Clients cannot change the underlying representations of objects directly, either intentionally or by accident, thus increasing the integrity of such objects. Objects can be changed only through the provided operations. It is difficult to overstate the importance of hiding the representation details of an abstract data type.

11.2.3 An Example

Suppose an abstract data type is to be constructed for a stack that has the following abstract operations:

create(stack)	Creates and possibly initializes a stack object
destroy(stack)	Deallocates the storage for the stack
empty(stack)	A predicate (or Boolean) function that returns true if the specified stack is empty and false if otherwise
push(stack, element)	Pushes the specified element on the specified stack
pop(stack)	Removes the top element from the specified stack
top(stack)	Returns a copy of the top element from the specified stack

Note that some implementation designs of abstract data types do not require the create and destroy operations. For example, simply defining a variable to be of an abstract data type may implicitly create the underlying data structure and initialize it.

A client of the stack type could have a code sequence such as the following:

```
...
create(stk1);
push(stk1, color1);
push(stk1, color2);
if(! empty(stk1))
  temp = top(stk1);
...
```

Suppose that the original implementation of the stack abstraction uses an adjacency representation (one that implements stacks in arrays). At a later time, because of memory management problems with the adjacency representation, it is changed to a linked list representation. Because data abstraction was used, this change can be made in the code that defines the stack type, but no changes will be required in any of the clients of the stack abstraction. In particular, the code sequence above does not need to be changed. Of course, a change in protocol of any of the operations would require changes in the clients.

In summary, the goal of data abstraction is to allow programs to define data types that have the characteristics and behavior of built-in types.

11.3   Design Issues for Abstract Data Types

A facility for defining abstract data types in a language must provide a syntactic unit that can encapsulate the type definition and subprogram definitions of the abstraction operations. It must be possible to make the type name and subprogram headers visible to clients of the abstraction. This allows clients to declare variables of the abstract type and manipulate their values. Although the type name must have external visibility, the type definition must be hidden. The same is often true for subprogram definitions—the headers must be visible but the bodies may be hidden.

Few, if any, general built-in operations should be provided for objects of abstract data types, other than those provided with the type definition. There simply are not many operations that apply to a broad range of possible abstract data types. Among these are assignment and comparisons for equality and inequality. If the language does not allow users to overload assignment, it must be built in. Comparisons for equality and inequality should be predefined in some cases but not in others. For example, if the type is implemented as a pointer, equality may mean pointer equality, but the user may want it to mean equality of the structures pointed to by the pointers.

Some operations are required by most abstract data types, but because they are not universal they must be provided by the designer of the type. Among these are iterators, accessors, constructors, and destructors. Iterators were discussed in Chapter 8. Accessors are used to provide a form of access to data that is hidden to direct access from clients. Constructors are used to initialize parts of newly created objects. Destructors are used to reclaim heap storage that may be used by parts of abstract data type objects.

As stated earlier, an abstract data type encapsulates a single data type and its operations. Many contemporary languages, including C++, Java, and C#, directly support abstract data types. The alternative to this is to provide a more generalized encapsulation construct that can define any number of entities, any of which can be selectively specified to be visible outside the enclosing unit. This is the approach of Ada. Encapsulations are not abstract data types, but rather are generalizations of abstract data types. As such, they can be used to define abstract data types. Although we discuss Ada's encapsulation construct in this section, we treat it as a minimal encapsulation for single data types. Generalized encapsulations are the topic of Section 11.6.

The first design issue for abstract data types is whether they can be parameterized. For example, if the language supports parameterized abstract data types, one could design an abstract data type for queues that could store elements of any scalar type. Parameterized abstract data types are discussed in Section 11.5. Another design issue is what access controls are provided and how such controls are specified.

11.4   Language Examples

The concept of data abstraction had its origins in SIMULA 67, although that language provided only partial support for abstract data types. In this section, we describe the support for data abstraction provided by Ada, C++, Java, and C#.

11.4.1   Abstract Data Types in Ada

Ada provides an encapsulation construct that can be used to define a single abstract data type, including the ability to hide its representation. Ada was one of the first languages to offer full suport for abstract data types.

11.4.1.1   Encapsulation

The encapsulating constructs in Ada are called **packages.** Packages can have two parts, each of which is also called a package. These are called the **specification package,** which provides the interface of the encapsulation, and the **body package,** which provides the implementation of the entities named in the specification. Not all packages have a body part (packages that encapsulate only types and constants do not have or need bodies).

A specification package and its associated body package share the same name. The reserved word **body** in a package header identifies it as being a body package. Specification and body packages may be compiled separately, provided the specification package is compiled first.

11.4.1.2   Information Hiding

The user can choose to make an entity entirely visible to clients or provide only the interface information. Of course, if the representation is not hidden, then the defined type is not an abstract data type. Hiding the representation from clients is accomplished by providing two sections of the specification package—one in which entities are visible to clients and one that hides its contents. For an abstract data type, an abbreviated declaration appears in the visible part of the specification, providing only the name of the type and the fact that its representation is hidden. The representation of the type appears in a part of the specification called the **private** part, which is introduced by the reserved word **private**. The private clause is always at the end of the specification.

INTERVIEW

C++: Its Birth, Its Ubiquitousness, and Common Criticisms

BJARNE STROUSTRUP

Bjarne Stroustrup is the designer and original implementer of C++ and the author of *The C++ Programming Language* and *The Design and Evolution of C++*. His research interests include distributed systems, simulation, design, programming, and programming languages. Dr. Stroustrup is the College of Engineering Professor in Computer Science at Texas A&M University. He is actively involved in the ANSI/ISO standardization of C++. After more than two decades at AT&T he retains a link with AT&T Labs—doing research as a member of the Information and Software Systems Research Lab. He is an ACM Fellow, an AT&T Bell Laboratories Fellow, and an AT&T Fellow. In 1993, Stroustrup received the ACM Grace Murray Hopper award "for his early work laying the foundations for the C++ programming language. Based on the foundations and Dr. Stroustrup's continuing efforts, C++ has become one of the most influential programming languages in the history of computing."

I. A BRIEF HISTORY OF YOU AND COMPUTING

What were you working on, and where before you joined Bell Labs in the early 1980s? At Bell Labs, I was doing research in the general area of distributed systems. I joined in 1979. Before that, I was finishing my Ph.D. in that field in Cambridge University.

Did you immediately start on 'C with Classes' (which would later become C++)? I worked on a few projects related to distributed computing before starting on C with Classes and during the development of that and of C++. For example, I was trying to find a way to distribute the UNIX kernel across several computers and helped a lot of projects build simulators.

Was it an interest in mathematics that got you into this profession? I signed up for a degree in "mathematics with computer science" and my master's degree is officially a math degree. I—wrongly— thought that computing was some kind of applied math. I did a couple of years of math and rate myself a poor mathematician, but that's still much better than not knowing math. At the time I signed up, I had never even seen a computer. What I love about computing is the programming rather than the more mathematical fields.

II. DISSECTING A SUCCESSFUL LANGUAGE

I'd like to work backward, listing some items I think make C++ ubiquitous, and get your reaction; It's 'open source,', nonproprietary, and standardized by ANSI/ISO. The ISO C++ standard is important. There are many independently developed and evolving C++ implementations. Without a standard for them to adhere to and a standards process to help coordinate the evolution of C++, a chaos of dialects would erupt.

It is also important that there are both open-source and commercial implementations available. In addition, for many users, it is crucial that the standard provides a measure of protection from manipulation by implementation providers.

The ISO standards process is open and democratic. The C++ committee rarely meets with fewer than 50 people present and typically more than eight nations are represented at each meeting. It is not just a vendors' forum.

It's ideal for systems programming (which, at the time C++ was born was the largest sector of the market developing code).

Yes, C++ is a strong contender for any systems programming project. It is also effective for embedded systems programming, which is currently the fastest growing sector. Yet another growth area for C++ is high-performance numeric/engineering/scientific programming.

Its object-oriented nature and inclusion of classes/libraries make programming more efficient and transparent.
C++ is a multiparadigm programming language. That is, it supports several fundamental styles of programming (including object-oriented programming) and combinations of those styles. When used well, this leads to cleaner, more flexible and more efficient libraries than can be provided using just one paradigm. The C++ standard library containers and algorithms, which is basically a generic programming framework, is an example. When used together with (object-oriented) class hierarchies, the result is an unsurpassed combination of type safety, efficiency, and flexibility.

Its incubation in the AT&T development environment.
AT&T Bell Labs provided an environment that was crucial for C++'s development. The labs were an exceptionally rich source of challenging problems and a uniquely supportive environment for practical research. C++ emerged from the same research lab as C did and benefited from the same intellectual tradition, experience, and exceptional people. Throughout, AT&T supported the standardization of C++. However, C++ was not the beneficiary of a massive marketing campaign, like many modern languages. That's simply not the way the labs work.

Did I miss anything on your top list?
Undoubtedly.

Now, let me paraphrase from the C++ critiques and get your reactions: It's huge/unwieldy. The "hello world" problem is ten times larger in C++ than in C.
C++ is certainly not a small language, but then few modern languages are. If a language is small, you tend to need huge libraries to get work done and often have to rely on conventions and extensions. I prefer to have key parts of the inevitable complexity in the language where it can be seen, taught, and effectively standardized rather than hidden elsewhere in a system. For most purposes, I don't consider C++ unwieldy.

The C++ "hello world" program isn't larger than its C equivalent on my machine, and it shouldn't be on yours. In fact, the object code for the C++ version of the "hello world" program is smaller than the C version on my machine. There is no language reason why the one version should be larger than the other. It is all an issue of how the implementor organized the libraries. If one version is significantly larger than the other, report the problem to the implementor of the larger version.

It's tougher to program in C++ (compared with C). Something the critics say. Even you once admitted it, saying something about shooting yourself in the foot with C versus C++.
Yes, I did say something along the lines of "C makes it easy to shoot yourself in the foot; C++ makes it harder, but when you do, C++ blows your whole leg off." What people tend to miss is that what I said about C++ is to a varying extent true for all powerful languages. As you protect people from simple dangers, they get themselves into new and less obvious problems. Someone who avoids the simple problems may simply be heading for a not-so-simple one. One problem with very supporting and protective environments is that the hard problems may be discovered too late or be too hard to remedy once discovered. Also, a rare problem is harder to find than a frequent one because you don't suspect it.

It's appropriate for embedded systems of today but not for the Internet software of today.
C++ is suitable for embedded systems today. It is also suitable—and widely used—for "Internet software" today. For example, have a look at my "C++ applications" Web page. You'll notice that some of the major Web service providers, such as Amazon, Adobe, Google, Quicken, and Microsoft, critically rely on C++. Gaming is a related area in which you find heavy C++ use.

Did I miss another one you get a lot?
Sure.

Suppose an abstract data type named `Node_Type` is to be defined in a package. `Node_Type` is declared in the visible part of the specification package without its representation details, as in

```
type Node_Type is private;
```

In the private clause, the declaration of `Node_Type` is repeated, but this time with the complete type definition, as in

```
package Linked_List_Type is
  type Node_Type is private;
  ...
  private
    type Node_Type;
    type Ptr is access Node_Type;
    type Node_Type is
      record
      Info : Integer;
      Link : Ptr;
      end record;
  end Linked_List_Type;
```

If none of the entities in a package are to be hidden, there is no purpose or need for the private part of the specification. Of course, such a package could not define an abstract data type.

The reason why a type's representation appears in the specification package at all has to do with compilation issues. A client can only see the specification package (not the body package), but the compiler must be able to allocate objects of the exported type when compiling the client. Furthermore, the client is compilable when only the specification package for the abstract data type is present. Therefore, the compiler must be able to determine the size of an object from the specification package. So the representation of the type must be visible to the compiler but not to the client code. This is exactly the situation specified by the private clause in a specification package.

Types that are declared to be private are called **private types.** Private data types have built-in operations for assignment and comparisons for equality and inequality. Any other operation must be declared in the specification package that defined the type.

An alternative to private types is a more restricted form, **limited private types.** Limited private types are described in the private section of a specification package, as are private types. The only syntactic difference is that limited private types are declared to be **limited private** in the visible part of the package specification. Objects of a type that is declared limited private have no built-in operations. Such a type is useful when the usual predefined operations of assignment and comparison are not meaningful or useful. For example, assignment and comparison are rarely used for stacks. If assignment or equality comparisons are required but the built-in versions are not useful, these operations must be provided by the specification package. The assignment operation must be in the form of a normal procedure, whereas the equal and not-equal operators can be provided by overloading those operators for the new type.

11.4.1.3 An Example

The following is the specification package for a stack abstract data type:

```
package Stack_Pack is
-- The visible entities, or public interface
  type Stack_Type is limited private;
  Max_Size : constant := 100;
  function Empty(Stk : in Stack_Type) return Boolean;
  procedure Push(Stk : in out Stack_Type;
                     Element : in Integer);
  procedure Pop(Stk : in out Stack_Type);
  function Top(Stk : in Stack_Type) return Integer;
-- The part that is hidden from clients
  private
    type List_Type is array (1..Max_Size) of Integer;
    type Stack_Type is
      record
      List  : List_Type;
      Topsub : Integer range 0..Max_Size := 0;
      end record;
  end Stack_Pack;
```

Notice that no create or destroy operations are included, because they are not necessary.

The body package for Stack_Pack is

```
with Ada.Text_IO; use Ada.Text_IO;
package body Stack_Pack is
  function Empty(Stk: in Stack_Type) return Boolean is
    begin
    return Stk.Topsum = 0;
    end Empty;

  procedure Push(Stk : in out Stack_Type;
                     Element : in Integer) is
    begin
    if Stk.Topsum >= Max_Size then
      Put_Line("ERROR - Stack overflow");
    else
      Stk.Topsub := Stk.Topsub + 1;
```

```
        Stk.List(Topsub) := Element;
      end if;
    end Push;

    procedure Pop(Stk : in out Stack_Type) is
      begin
      if Stk.Topsub = 0
        then Put_Line("ERROR - Stack underflow");
        else Stk.Topsub := Stk.Topsub - 1;
      end if;
      end Pop;

    function Top(Stk : in Stack_Type) return Integer is
      begin
      if Stk.Topsub = 0
        then Put_Line("ERROR - Stack is empty");
        else return Stk.List(Stk.Tosub);
      end if;
      end Top;
    end Stack_Pack;
```

The first line of the code of this body package contains two clauses: a **with** and a **use**. The **with** clause makes the names defined in external packages visible, in this case Ada.Text_IO, which provides functions for input and output of text. The **use** clause eliminates the need for explicit qualification of the references to entities from the named package. The issues of access to external encapsulations and name qualifications are further discussed in Section 11.6.

The body package must have subprogram definitions with headings that match the subprogram headings in the associated specification package. The specification package promises that these subprograms will be defined in the associated body package.

The following procedure, Use_Stacks, is a client of package Stack_Pack. It illustrates how the package might be used.

```
with Stack_Pack, Ada.Text_IO;
use Stack_Pack, Ada.Text_IO;
procedure Use_Stacks is
  Topone : Integer;
  Stack : Stack_Type;    -- Creates a Stack_Type object
  begin
  Push(Stack, 42);
  Push(Stack, 17);
  Topone := Top(Stack);
  Pop(Stack);
  ...
  end Use_Stacks;
```

11.4.2   Abstract Data Types in C++

C++ was created by adding features to C. The first important additions were those to support object-oriented programming. Because one of the primary components of object-oriented programming is abstract data types, C++ obviously must support them.

While Ada provides encapsulation that can be used to simulate abstract data types, C++ provides two constructs that are very similar to each other, the class and the struct, which more directly support abstract data types. Because structs are most commonly used when only data is included, we do not discuss them further here.

C++ classes are types; as stated previously, Ada packages are more generalized encapsulations that can define any number of abstract data types. A program unit that gains visibility to an Ada package can access any of its public entities directly by their names. A C++ program unit that declares an instance of a class can also access any of the public entities in that class, but only through an instance of the class.

11.4.2.1   Encapsulation

The data defined in a C++ class are called **data members;** the functions (methods) defined in a class are called **member functions.** All of the instances of a class share a single set of member functions, but each instance gets its own set of the class's data members. Class instances can be either stack dynamic or heap dynamic. If stack dynamic, they are referenced directly with value variables. If heap dynamic, they are referenced through pointers. In this section, we consider only stack-dynamic classes. Stack-dynamic instances of classes are always created by elaboration of an object declaration. Furthermore, the lifetime of such a class instance ends when the end of the scope of its declaration is reached. Classes can have heap-dynamic data members, so that even though a class instance is stack-dynamic, it can include data members that are heap-dynamic and allocated from the heap. C++ provides the **new** and **delete** operators to manage the heap.

A member function of a class can be defined in two distinct ways: The complete definition can appear in the class, or only its header. When both the header and the body of a member function appear in the class definition, the member function is implicitly inlined. Recall that this means that its code is placed in the caller's code, rather than requiring the usual call and return linkage process. If only the header of a member function appears in the class definition, its complete definition appears outside the class and is separately compiled. It is a good idea to have small member functions inlined, because linkage time will be saved at a cost of only a small amount of space.

11.4.2.2   Information Hiding

A C++ class can contain both hidden and visible entities (meaning they are either hidden from or visible to clients of the class). Entities that are to be hidden are placed in a **private** clause, and visible, or public, entities are written in a **public** clause. The **public** clause therefore describes the interface to class objects. There is also a third category of visibility, **protected**, which is discussed in the context of inheritance in Chapter 12.

C++ allows the user to include **constructor** functions in class definitions, which are used to initialize the data members of newly created objects. A constructor may also allocate the heap-dynamic data members of the new object. Constructors are implicitly called when an object of the class type is created. A constructor has the same name as the class whose objects it initializes. There can be more than one constructor for a class, in which case they are obviously overloaded. Each constructor of a class must have a unique parameter profile.

A C++ class can also include a function called a **destructor,** which is implicitly called when the lifetime of an instance of the class ends. All heap-dynamic objects live until explicitly deallocated with the **delete** operator. As stated above, stack-dynamic class instances can contain heap-dynamic data members. The destructor function for such an instance can include a **delete** operator on the heap-dynamic members to deallocate their heap space. Destructors are often used as a debugging aid, in which case they simply display or print the values of some or all of the object's data members before those members are deallocated. The name of a destructor is the class's name, preceded by a tilde (~).

Neither constructors nor destructors have return types, and neither use **return** statements. Both constructors and destructors can be explicitly called.

11.4.2.3 An Example

Our example of a C++ abstract data type is, once again, a stack:

```cpp
#include <iostream.h>
class stack {
  private:  //** These members are visible only to other
            //** members and friends (see Section 11.6.4)
    int *stackPtr;
    int maxLen;
    int topPtr;
  public:   //** These members are visible to clients
    stack() {   //** A constructor
      stackPtr = new int [100];
      maxLen = 99;
      topPtr = -1;
    }
    ~stack() {delete [] stackPtr;};  //** A destructor
    void push(int number) {
      if (topPtr == max_len)
```

```
              cerr << "Error in push—stack is full\n";
          else stackPtr[++topPtr] = number;
      }
      void pop() {
        if (topPtr == -1)
          cerr << "Error in pop—stack is empty\n";
        else topPtr--;
      }
      int top() {return (stackPtr[topPtr]);}
      int empty() {return (topPtr == -1);}
}
```

We will discuss only a few of the aspects of this class definition, because it is not necessary to understand all of the details of the code. The #include is used to provide visibility to a standard input and output package, iostream, which includes the simple error output stream used by the code, cerr. The stack class has three data members—stackPtr, maxLen, and topPtr—all of which are private. It also has four public member functions—push, pop, top, and empty—a constructor, and a destructor. The constructor uses the allocator operator **new** to allocate an array of 100 **int** elements from the heap. It also initializes maxLen and topPtr. The purpose of the destructor function is to deallocate the storage for the array used to implement the stack when the lifetime of a stack object ends. This array was allocated by the constructor. Because the bodies of the member functions are included, they are all implicitly inlined.

An example program that uses the C++ stack abstract data type is

```
void main() {
  int topOne;
  stack stk;  //** Creates an instance of the stack class
  stk.push(42);
  stk.push(17);
  topOne = stk.top();
  stk.pop();
  ...
}
```

When the end of this function is reached during execution, the lifetimes of the variables topOne and stk end, which results in the destructor for stk being implicitly called. This causes the array part of stack to be deallocated.

A stack is a silly example for most contemporary languages, because support for stacks is included in their standard class libraries. However, stacks provide a simple example we can use to allow comparison of the languages discussed in this section.

11.4.2.4 Evaluation

C++ support for abstract data types, through its class construct, is similar in expressive power to that of Ada, through its packages. Both provide effective mechanisms for encapsulation and information hiding of abstract data types. The primary difference is that classes are types, whereas Ada packages are more general encapsulations. Furthermore, the class was designed for more than data abstraction, as discussed in Chapter 12.

11.4.3   Abstract Data Types in Java

Java support for abstract data types is similar to that of C++. There are, however, a few important differences. All user-defined data types in Java are classes (Java does not include structs), and all objects are allocated from the heap and accessed through reference variables. Although C++ abstract data types can be generic (see Section 11.5.2), Java's cannot (at least not yet). Another difference between the support for abstract data types in Java and that of C++ is that subprograms (methods) in Java can *only* be defined in classes. So one cannot have just function headers in Java classes with the corresponding function definitions stored elsewhere. Therefore, a Java abstract data type is both declared and defined in a single syntactic unit. Definitions are hidden from clients by making them private.

Rather than having private and public clauses in its class definitions, in Java access modifiers that can be attached to method and variable definitions.

The following is a Java class definition for our stack example:

```java
import java.io.*;
class StackClass {
  private int [] stackRef;
  private int maxLen,
              topIndex;
  public StackClass() {  // A constructor
    stackRef = new int [100];
    maxLen = 99;
    topIndex = -1;
  }
  public void push(int number) {
    if (topIndex == maxLen)
      System.out.println("Error in push—stack is full");
    else stackRef[++topIndex] = number;
  }
  public void pop() {
    if (topIndex == -1)
      System.out.println("Error in pop—stack is empty");
    else --topIndex;
  }
```

```
  public int top() {return (stackRef[topIndex]);}
  public boolean empty() {return (topIndex == -1);}
}
```

An example class that uses `StackClass` follows:

```
public class TstStack {
  public static void main(String[] args) {
    StackClass myStack = new StackClass();
    myStack.push(42);
    myStack.push(29);
    System.out.println("29 is: " + myStack.top());
    myStack.pop();
    System.out.println("42 is: " + myStack.top());
    myStack.pop();
    myStack.pop();  // Produces an error message
  }
}
```

One obvious difference is the lack of a destructor in the Java version, obviated by Java's implicit garbage collection.

Our example does not illustrate many important differences between the support for abstract data types of C++ and that of Java. However, as will be discussed in Section 11.6, there are more differences between the multiple type encapsulations of C++ and those of Java. Furthermore, when considering the other aspects of object-oriented programming, as is done in Chapter 12, there are many more differences between Java's classes and those of C++.

11.4.4 Abstract Data Types in C#

Recall that C# is based on both C++ and Java, although it adds some new constructs of its own.

C# uses the access modifiers, **private**, **public**, and **protected**, exactly as they are used in Java. However, it includes two additional modifiers, **internal** and **protected internal**. The **internal** modifier is described in Section 11.6, where generalized encapsulations are discussed.

Also like Java, all C# class instances are heap dynamic. Default constructors, which provide initial values for instance data, are available for all classes. These constructors provide typical initial values, such as 0 for **int** types and **false** for **boolean** type. A user can furnish a constructor for any class he or she defines. Such a constructor can assign initial values to some or all of the instance data of the class. Any instance variable that is not initialized in a user-defined constructor is assigned a value by the default constructor.

Because C# uses garbage collection for most of its heap objects, destructors are rarely used.

Although the principles of abstract data types dictate that data members of objects should be hidden from clients, many situations arise in which clients must access these data members. The common solution is to provide accessor methods, getters and setters, that allow indirect access to the so-called hidden data. Although clients have access through the getters and setters, it is still better than simply making the data public, which would provide direct access. The reasons accessors are better are as follows:

1. Read-only access can be provided, by having a getter method but no corresponding setter method.

2. Constraints can be included in setters. For example, if the data value should be restricted to a particular range, the setter can enforce that.

3. The actual implementation of the data member can be changed without affecting the clients if getters and setters are the only access.

C# provides properties, which it borrowed from Delphi, as a way of implementing getters and setters without requiring explicit method calls. Properties provide implicit access to specific private instance data. For example, consider the following simple class and client code:

```
public class Weather {
  public int DegreeDays {  //** DegreeDays is a property
    get {
      return degreeDays;
    }
    set {
      degreeDays = value;
    }
  }
  private int degreeDays;
    ...
  }
...
Weather w = new Weather();
int degreeDaysToday, oldDegreeDays;
...
w.DegreeDays = degreeDaysToday;
...
oldDegreeDays = w.DegreeDays;
```

In the class Weather, the property DegreeDays is defined. This property provides a getter method and a setter method for access to the private data member, degreeDays. In the client code following the class definition, degreeDays is treated as if it were a public member variable, although access to it is only available through the property. Notice the use of the implicit variable, **value**, in the setter method. This is the mechanism by which the new value of the property is referenced.

As discussed in Section 11.4.2, C++ includes both classes and structs, which are nearly identical constructs. The only difference is that the default access modifier for class is **private**, whereas for structs it is **public**. C# also has structs, but they are very different from those of C++. In C#, structs are in a sense lightweight classes. They can have constructors, properties, methods, and data fields, and can implement interfaces, but do not support inheritance. One other fundamental difference between structs and classes in C# is that structs are value types, as opposed to reference types. They are allocated on the run-time stack, rather than the heap. If they are passed as parameters, they are passed by value. All C# value types, which includes all of its primitive types, are actually structs. Although it seems odd, struct objects are created with the same **new** operator used to create class objects. (C#'s **new** is like that of C++ and Java.)

Structs are used in C# primarily to implement relatively small simple types that need never be base types for inheritance and/or it is convenient for the objects of the type to be stack, as opposed to heap allocated.

11.5   Parameterized Abstract Data Types

It is often convenient to parameterize abstract data types. For example, we should be able to design a stack abstract data type that can store any scalar type elements rather than be required to write a separate stack abstraction for every different scalar type. In the following two subsections, the capabilities of Ada and C++ to construct parameterized abstract data types are discussed.

Neither Java nor C# currently support parameterized abstract data types, although that may change in the near future.

11.5.1   Ada

Generic procedures in Ada were discussed and illustrated in Chapter 9. Packages can also be generic, so we can also construct generic, or parameterized, abstract data types.

The Ada stack abstract data type example shown in Section 11.4.1 suffers two restrictions: (1) Stacks of its type can store only integer type elements, and (2) the stacks can have only up to 100 elements. Both of these restrictions can be eliminated by using a generic package, which can be instantiated for other element types and any desirable size. (This is a generic instantiation, which is very different from the instantiation of a class to create an object.) The following specification package describes the interface of a generic stack abstract data type with these features:

```
generic
  Max_Size : Positive;  -- A generic parameter for stack size
  type Element_Type is private;  -- A generic parameter for
                                 -- element type
```

```
package Generic_Stack is
-- The visible entities, or public interface
  type Stack_Type is limited private;
  function Empty(Stk : in Stack_Type) return Boolean;
  procedure Push(Stk : in out Stack_Type;
                 Element : in Element_Type);
  procedure Pop(Stk : in out Stack_Type);
  function Top(Stk : in Stack_Type) return Element_Type;
-- The hidden part
private
  type List_Type is array (1..Max_Size) of Element_Type;
  type Stack_Type is
    record
    List : List_Type;
    Topsub : Integer range 0..Max_Size := 0;
    end record;
  end Generic_Stack;
```

The body package for `Generic_Stack` is the same as the body package for `Stack_Pack` in the previous section except that the type of the `Element` formal parameter in `Push` and `Top` is `Element_Type` instead of `Integer`.

The following statement instantiates `Generic_Stack` for a stack of 100 elements of `Integer` type:

```
package Integer_Stack is new Generic_Stack(100, Integer);
```

One could also build an abstract data type for a stack of length 500 for `Float` elements, as in

```
package Float_Stack is new Generic_Stack(500, Float);
```

These instantiations build two different source code versions of `Generic_Stack` at compile time.

11.5.2   C++

C++ also supports parameterized, or generic, abstract data types. To make the example C++ stack class of Section 11.4.2 generic in the stack size, only the constructor function needs to be changed, as in

```
stack(int size) {
  stkPtr = new int [size];
  maxLen = size - 1;
  top = -1;
}
```

The declaration for a stack object now may appear as

```
stack stk(150);
```

The class definition for stack can include both constructors, so users can use the default size stack or specify some other size.

The element type of the stack can be made a parameter by making the class a templated class. Then the element type can be a template parameter. The definition of the templated class for a stack type is

```cpp
#include <iostream.h>
template <class Type>  // Type is the template parameter
class stack {
  private:
    Type *stackPtr;
    const int maxLen;
    int topPtr;
  public:
// A constructor for 100 element stacks
    stack()
      :stackPtr   new Type [100];
      maxLen   99,
      topPtr   -1
    {}
// A constructor for a given number of elements
    stack(int size) {
      stackPtr = new Type [size];
      maxLen = size - 1;
      top = -1;
    }
    ~stack() {delete stackPtr;};  // A destructor
    void push(Type number) {
      if (top_ptr == maxLen)
        cout << "Error in push—stack is full\n";
      else stackPtr[++ topPtr] = number;
    }
    void pop() {
      if (topPtr == -1)
        cout << "Error in pop—stack is empty\n";
      else topPtr --;
    }
    Type top() {return (stackPtr[ topPtr]);}
    int empty() {return (topPtr == -1);}
}
```

As in Ada, C++ templated classes are instantiated at compile time. The difference is that in C++ the instantiations are implicit: A new instantiation is created whenever an object is created that requires a version of the templated class that does not yet exist.

11.6 Encapsulation Constructs

The first part of this chapter discusses abstract data types, which are minimal encapsulations.[1] This section describes the multiple-type encapsulations that are needed for larger programs.

11.6.1 Introduction

When the size of a program reaches beyond a few thousand lines, two practical problems become evident. From the programmer's point of view, having such a program appear as a single collection of subprograms or abstract data type definitions does not impose an adequate level of organization on the program to keep it intellectually manageable. The second practical problem for larger programs is recompilation. For relatively small programs, recompiling the whole program after each modification is not costly. But for larger programs, the cost of recompilation ceases to be insignificant. So there is an obvious need to find ways to avoid recompilation of the parts of a program that are not affected by a change. The obvious solution to both of these problems is to organize programs into collections of logically related code and data, each of which can be compiled without recompilation of the rest of the program. An **encapsulation** is such a collection.

Encapsulations are often placed in libraries and made available for reuse in programs other than those for which they were written. People have been writing programs with more than a few thousand lines for over 40 years, so techniques for providing encapsulations have been evolving for some time.

11.6.2 Nested Subprograms

In languages that allow nested subprograms, programs can be organized by nesting subprogram definitions inside the logically larger subprograms that use them. This can be done in Ada and Fortran 95. As discussed in Chapter 5, however, this method of organizing programs, which uses static scoping, is far from ideal. Therefore, even in languages that allow nested subprograms, they are not used as a primary organizing encapsulation construct.

11.6.3 Encapsulation in C

C does not provide strong support for abstract data types, although both abstract data types and multiple-type encapsulations can be simulated.

In C, a collection of related functions and data definitions can be placed in a file, which can be independently compiled. Such a file, which acts as a library, has an implementation of its entities. The interface to such a file, including data, type, and function declarations, is placed in a separate file called a **header**

---

[1]In the case of Ada, the package encapsulation can be used for single types, but also for multiple types.

file. Type representations can be hidden by defining them as pointers to struct types in the header file. The complete definitions of such struct types need only appear in the implementation file. The header file, in source form, and the compiled version of the implementation file are furnished to clients. The header file is included in the client code, using an `#include` preprocessor specification, so that references to functions and data in the client code can be type checked. The `#include` specification also documents the fact that the client program depends on the library implementation file. This approach effectively separates the specification and implementation of an encapsulation.

Although these encapsulations work, they are not completely safe. For example, a user could simply cut and paste the definitions from the header file into the client program, rather than using `#include`. This would work, because `#include` simply copies the contents of its operand file into the file in which the `#include` appears. However, there are two problems with this. First, the documentation of the dependence of the client program on the library (and its header file) is lost. Second, the author of the library could change the header file and the implementation file, but the client could attempt to use the new implementation file (without ever knowing it had changed) but the old header file, which could result in failure of the user's program.

Another fundamental problem with C's approach to abstract data types is that the C linker does not check types between a header file and its associated implementation file. Once again, it is the user's responsibility to be sure both the header and implementation files are up to date. This is usually done with a `make` utility.

11.6.4 Encapsulation in C++

Encapsulation in C++ is similar to that of C. Header files are used to provide the interface to the resources of the encapsulation. In fact, because of the complex interplay of C++ templates and separate compilation, the header files of C++ template libraries often include complete definitions of resources, rather than just data declarations and subprogram protocols. This is due in part to the use of the C linker for C++ programs. This linker does not type check declarations in header files against definitions in implementation files.

One language design problem that results from having classes but no generalized encapsulation construct is that it is not always natural to associate object operations with single objects. For example, suppose we have an abstract data type for matrices and one for vectors, and need a multiplication operation between a vector and a matrix. In which class should this operation appear, considering that it must have access to the data members of both the vector and the matrix classes? In the case of C++, these kinds of situations can be handled by allowing nonmember functions to be "friends" of a class. Friend functions have access to the private entities of the class where they are declared to be friends. For the matrix/vector multiplication operation, one C++ solution is to define the operation outside both the matrix and the vector classes, but define it to be a friend of both. The following skeletal code illustrates this scenario:

```
class Matrix;  //** A class declaration
class Vector {
  friend Vector multiply(const Matrix&, const Vector&);
  ...
};
class Matrix {  //** The class definition
  friend Vector multiply(const Matrix&, const Vector&);
  ...
};
//** The function that uses both Matrix and Vector objects
Vector multiply(const Matrix& m1, const Vector& v1) {
  ...
}
```

In addition to functions, whole classes can be defined to be friends of a class; then all the private members of the class are visible to all of the members of the friend class.

11.6.5 Ada Packages

Ada specification packages can include any number of data and subprogram declarations in their public and private sections. Therefore, they can include interfaces for any number of abstract data types, as well as any other program resources. So, the package is Ada's multiple-type encapsulation construct.

Ada packages can be compiled separately. The two package parts, specification and body, and also be compiled separately if the specification package is compiled first. An entire program that uses any number of external packages can be compiled separately, as long as the specifications of all of the used packages have been compiled. The bodies of the used packages can be compiled after the client program.

Consider the situation described in Section 11.6.4 of the vector and matrix types and the need for methods with access to the private parts of both, which is handled in C++ with friend functions. In Ada, both the matrix and the vector types could be defined in an Ada package, which obviates the need for friend functions.

11.6.6 C# Assemblies

C# includes a larger encapsulation construct than the class. In this case, the construct is the one used by all of the .NET programming languages, the assembly. An **assembly** is a collection of files that appears to application programs to be a single dynamic link library or an executable (EXE). A **dynamic** link library (DLL) is a collection of classes and methods that are individually linked to an executing program when needed. Therefore, although a program has access to all of the resources in a particular DLL, only the parts that are actually used are ever loaded and linked to the program. DLLs have been part of the Windows programming environment since the beginnings of Windows. In addition to the object code for its resources, an assembly includes type definitions for every class it contains, as well as metadata about the code resources. The metadata includes a manifest, which is a list of all types defined in the assembly, as well as a version number for the assembly.

As mentioned previously, C# has an access modifier, **internal**. An **internal** member of a class is visible to all classes in the assembly in which it appears.

Because an assembly is a self-contained executable unit, it can have only one entry point.

11.7 Naming Encapsulations

We have considered encapsulations to be syntactic containers for logically related software resources, in particular, abstract data types. There is another kind of encapsulation that is highly useful for constructing large programs, a naming encapsulation. A naming encapsulation is used to create a new scope for names. Because large programs define large numbers of global names, there must be some way of subdividing these names into logical groupings, which is what a naming encapsulation does. Without such a mechanism, the global namespace becomes very large, making it difficult to invent new names that do not already appear in the complete program. Naming encapsulations are logical encapsulations, in the sense that they are not contiguous. Several different collections of code can be placed in the same namespace, even though they are stored in different places. In the following, we briefly describe the uses of naming encapsulations in C++, Java, and Ada.

11.7.1 C++ Namespaces

C++ includes a specification, **namespace**, that helps programs manage the problem of global namespaces. One can place each library in its own namespace and qualify the names in the program with the name of the namespace when they are used outside that namespace. For example, suppose there is an abstract data type header file that implements stacks. If there is concern that some other library file may define a name that is used in the stack abstract data type, we would place the file that defines the stack in its own namespace. This is done by placing all of the declarations for the stack in a namespace block, as in

```
namespace MyStack {
  // Declarations
}
```

The implementation file for the stack abstract data type could reference the names declared in the header file with the scope resolution operator, `::`, as in

```
MyStack::topPtr
```

The implementation file could also appear in a namespace block specification identical to the one used on the header file, which would make all of the names declared in the header file directly available. This is definitely simpler, but slightly less readable, because it is less obvious where a specific name in the implementation file is declared.

Client code can gain access to the names in the namespace of the header file by qualifying those names with with the name of the namespace, as discussed above for the implementation file.

C++ has a directive, **using**, that can be used to qualify names from other namespaces. The **using** directive is not discussed here, because it was designed to be a transition tool for using C++ libraries that were created before namespaces were added to the language.

Be aware that namespaces are a complicated feature of C++, and we have mentioned only the simplest part of the story here.

C# includes namespaces that are much like those of C++.

11.7.2 Java Packages

Java includes a naming encapsulation construct, the package. Packages can contain more than one class definition, and the classes in a package are partial friends of one another. *Partial* here means that the entities defined in a class in a package that either are public or protected (see Chapter 12) or have no access specifier are visible to all other classes in the package. A package can have only one public class definition.

Entities without access modifiers are said to have **package scope**, because they are visible throughout the package. Java therefore has less need for explicit friend declarations and does not include the friend functions or friend classes of C++.

The resources defined in a file are specified to be in a particular package with the package declaration, as in

package myStack;

The package declaration must appear as the first line of the file. The resources of every file that does not include a package declaration are implicitly placed in the same unnamed package.

The clients of a package can reference the names defined in the package using fully qualified names. For example, if the package myStack defines a variable named topPtr, that variable can be referenced in a client of myStack as myStack.topPtr. Because this can quickly become cumbersome when packages are nested, Java provides the **import** declaration, which allows shorter references to names defined in a package. For example, suppose the client includes the following:

```
import myStack.*;
```

Now, the variable `topPtr`, as well as other names defined in the `myStack` package, can be referenced by just their names. To access only one name from the package, the specific name can be given on the import declaration, as in

```
import myStack.topPtr;
```

11.7.3 Ada Packages

Packages, which often contain libraries, are defined in hierarchies, which correspond to file hierarchies. For example, if `subPack` is a package defined as a child of the package `pack`, the `subPack` code file would appear in a subdirectory of the directory that stored the `pack` package. The standard class libraries of Java are also defined in a hierarchy of packages, stored in a hierarchy of directories.

As discussed in Section 11.4.1, packages also define namespaces. Visibility to a package from a program unit is gained with the **with** clause. For example,

```
with Ada.Text_IO;
```

This makes the resources and namespace of the package `Ada.Text_IO` available. Access to the names defined in the namespace of `Ada.Text_IO` must be qualified. For example, the `Put` procedure from `Ada.Text_IO` must be accessed as

```
Ada.Text_IO.Put
```

To access the names in `Ada.Text_IO` without qualification, the **use** clause can be used, as in

```
use Ada.Text_IO;
```

With this clause, the `Put` procedure from `Ada.Text_IO` can be accessed simply as `Put`.

SUMMARY

The concept of abstract data types and their use in program design was a milestone in the development of programming as an engineering discipline. Although the concept is relatively simple, its use did not become convenient and safe until languages were designed to support it.

The two primary features of abstract data types are the packaging of data objects with their associated operations and information hiding. A language may support abstract data types directly or simulate them with more general encapsulations.

Ada provides encapsulations—packages—that can be used to simulate abstract data types. Packages normally have two parts, a specification, which presents the client interface, and a body, which supplies the implementation of the abstract data type. Data type representations can appear in the specification package but be hidden from clients by putting them in the private clause of the package. The abstract type itself is defined to be private in the public part of the specification package. Private types have built-in operations for assignment and comparison for equality and inequality.

C++ data abstraction is provided by classes. Classes are types, and instances can be either stack or heap dynamic. A member function (method) can have its complete definition appear in the class, or only the protocol is given in the class and the definition is placed in another file, which can be separately compiled. C++ classes can have three clauses, each prefixed with an access modifier: private, public, or protected. Both constructors and destructors can be given in class definitions. Heap-allocated objects must be explicitly deallocated with **delete** or a destructor.

Java data abstractions are similar to those of C++, except all Java objects are allocated from the heap and are accessed through reference variables. Also, all objects are garbage collected. Rather than having access modifiers attached to clauses, in Java the modifiers appear on individual declarations (or definitions).

C# supports abstract data types with both classes and structs. Its structs are value types and do not support inheritance. Otherwise, C# classes are similar to those of Java.

Both Ada and C++ allow their abstract data types to be parameterized, Ada through its generic packages and C++ through its templated classes.

To support the construction of large programs, most contemporary languages include multiple-type encapsulation constructs, which can contain a collection of logically related types. An encapsulation may also provide access control to its entities. Encapsulations provide the programmer with a method of organizing programs that also facilitates recompilation.

C++, C#, Java, and Ada include naming encapsulations. For Java, they are named packages; for C++ and C#, they are namespaces. Partially because of the availability of packages, Java does not have friend functions or friend classes. In Ada, packages can be used as naming encapsulations.

REVIEW QUESTIONS

1. Define *abstract data type*.

2. What are the advantages of the two parts of the definition of *abstract data type*?

3. What are the language design requirements for a language that supports abstract data types?

4. What are the language design issues for abstract data types?

5. Explain how information hiding is provided in an Ada package.

6. What is the difference between **private** and **limited private** types in Ada?

7. What is in an Ada specification package? What about a body package?

8. What is the fundamental difference between a C++ class and an Ada package?

9. In what different places can the definition of a C++ member function appear?

10. What is the purpose of a C++ constructor?

11. Where are all Java methods defined?

12. How are C++ class objects created?

13. Where are Java class objects created?

14. Why does Java not have destructors?

15. What is a friend function? What is a friend class?

16. What is one reason Java does not have friend functions or friend classes?

17. Describe the fundamental differences between C#'s structs and its classes.

18. How is a struct object in C# created?

19. How are instances of Ada generic classes created?

20. How are instances of C++ template classes created?

21. Describe the two problems that appear in the construction of large programs that led to the development of encapsulation constructs.

22. What problems can occur using C to define abstract data types?

23. What is a C++ namespace and what is its purpose?

24. Describe the purposes of the **with** and **use** clauses.

25. What is a Java package and what is its purpose?

26. Describe a .NET assembly.

PROBLEM SET

1. Some software engineers believe that all imported entities should be qualified by the name of the exporting program unit. Do you agree? Support your answer.

2. Suppose someone designed a stack abstract data type in which the function, **top**, returned an access path (or pointer) rather than returning a copy of the top element. This is not a true data abstraction. Why? Give an example that illustrates the problem.

3. Write an analysis of the similarities of and differences between Java packages and C++ namespaces.

PROGRAMMING EXERCISES

1. Design the example abstract stack type in Fortran using a single subprogram with multiple entries for the type definition and the operations.

2. How does the Fortran implementation of Problem 1 compare with the Ada implementation in this chapter in terms of reliability and flexibility?

3. Design an abstract data type for a matrix abstraction in a language that you know, including operations for addition, subtraction, and matrix multiplication.

4. Design a queue abstract data type in a language you know, including operations for enqueue, dequeue, and empty.

5. Modify the C++ class for the abstract stack type to use a linked list representation and test it with the same code that appears in this chapter.

6. Write an abstract data type for complex numbers, including operations for addition, subtraction, multiplication, division, extraction of each of the parts of a complex number, and construction of a complex number from two floating-point constants, variables, or expressions. Use Ada, C++, Java, or C#.

7. Write an abstract data type for queues whose elements store 10-character names. The queue elements must be dynamically allocated from the heap. Queue operations are enqueue, dequeue, and empty. Use either Ada, C++, Java, or C#.

12

Support for Object-Oriented Programming

This chapter begins with a brief introduction to object-oriented programming. This is followed by an extended discussion of the primary design issues for inheritance and dynamic binding. Next, we discuss the support for object-oriented programming in Smalltalk, C++, Java, C#, and Ada 95. Then the object model of JavaScript is briefly described. The chapter concludes with a short overview of the implementation of dynamic bindings of method calls to methods in object-oriented languages.

12.1   Introduction

Languages that support object-oriented programming now are firmly entrenched in the mainstream. From COBOL to LISP, including virtually every language in between, dialects that support object-oriented programming have appeared. C++ and Ada 95 support procedural and data-oriented programming, in addition to object-oriented programming. CLOS, an object-oriented version of LISP (Bobrow et al., 1988), also supports functional programming. Some of the newer languages that were designed to support object-oriented programming do not support other programming paradigms, but still employ some of the basic structures and have the appearance of the older imperative languages. Among these are Java and C#. Finally, there is one purely object-oriented language that is quite unconventional, Smalltalk. Smalltalk was the first language to offer complete support for object-oriented programming. The specific support for object-oriented programming varies widely among languages, and that is an important topic of this chapter.

This chapter relies heavily on Chapter 11. It is in fact a continuation of that chapter. This reflects the reality that object-oriented programming is in essence an application of the principle of abstraction to abstract data types. Specifically, in object-oriented programming the commonality of a collection of similar abstract data types is factored out and put in a new type. The members of the collection inherit the common parts from that new type. This is inheritance, which is at the center of object-oriented programming and the languages that support it.

12.2   Object-Oriented Programming

12.2.1   Introduction

The concept of **object-oriented programming** has its roots in SIMULA 67 but was not fully developed until the evolution of Smalltalk resulted in Smalltalk 80 (in 1980, of course). Indeed, some consider Smalltalk to be the only purely object-oriented programming language. A language that is object oriented must provide support for three key language features: abstract data types, inheritance, and dynamic binding of method calls to methods.

12.2.2 Inheritance

By the middle to late 1980s, it became apparent to many software developers that one of the best opportunities for increased productivity in their profession was in software reuse. Abstract data types, with their encapsulation and access controls, were obviously the units to be reused. The problem with the reuse of abstract data types is that, in nearly all cases, the features and capabilities of the existing type are not quite right for the new use. The old type requires at least some minor modification. Such modifications can be difficult, for they require the person doing the modification to understand part, if not all, of the existing code. Furthermore, in many cases the modifications require changes to all client programs.

A second problem with programming with abstract data types is that their definitions are all independent and are at the same level. This often makes it impossible to organize a program to match the problem space being addressed by the program. In many cases, the underlying problem has categories of objects that are related, both as siblings (being similar to each other) and as parents and children (having a kind of descendant relationship).

Inheritance offers a solution to both the modification problem posed by abstract data type reuse and the program organization problem. If a new abstract data type can inherit the data and functionality of some existing type, and is also allowed to modify some of those entities and add new entities, reuse is greatly facilitated without requiring changes to the reused abstract data type. Programmers can take an existing abstract data type and mold it to fit a new problem requirement. Furthermore, inheritance provides a framework for the definition of hierarchies of related classes that can reflect the descendant relationships in the problem space.

The abstract data types in object-oriented languages, following the lead of SIMULA 67, are usually called **classes.** As with instances of abstract data types, class instances are called **objects.** A class that is defined through inheritance from another class is a **derived class** or **subclass.** A class from which the new class is derived is its **parent class** or **superclass.** The subprograms that define the operations on objects of a class are called **methods.** The calls to methods are sometimes called **messages.** The entire collection of methods of an object is called the **message protocol,** or **message interface,** of the object. Computations in an object-oriented program are specified by messages sent from objects to other objects.

In the simplest case, a class inherits all of the entities (variables and methods) of its parent class. This can be complicated by access controls on the entities in a parent class. For example, as we saw in the abstract data type definitions in Chapter 11, some of the entities are classified as being public and others are private. These access controls allow the program designer to hide parts of the abstract data type from clients. Derived classes are another kind of client to which access may be granted or withheld. To take this into account, some object-oriented languages include a third category of access control, often called **protected,** that is used to provide access to derived classes while withholding it from clients. The issue of whether a subclass includes all of the entities of its parent class is addressed in more detail in Section 12.3.2.

In addition to inheriting entities from its parent class, a derived class can add new entities and modify inherited methods. A modified method has the same name, and often the same protocol, as the one of which it is a modification. The new method is said to **override** the inherited version, which is then called an **overriden method.** The most common purpose of an overriding method is to provide an operation that is specific for objects of the derived class but is not appropriate for objects of the parent class.

Classes can have two kinds of methods and two kinds of variables. The most commonly used methods and variables are called **instance methods** and **instance variables.** Every object of a class has its own set of instance variables, which store the object's state. The only difference between two objects of the same class is the state of their instance variables. Instance methods operate only on the objects of the class. **Class variables** belong to the class, rather than its object, so there is only one copy for the class. **Class methods** can perform operations on the class, and possibly also on the objects of the class. In most of the remainder of this chapter, we will ignore class methods and class variables.

If a new class is a subclass of a single parent class, then the derivation process is called **single inheritance.** If a class has more than one parent class, the process is called **multiple inheritance.** When a number of classes are related through single inheritance, their relationships to each other can be shown in a derivation tree. The class relationships in a multiple inheritance can be shown in a derivation graph.

One disadvantage of inheritance as a means of increasing the possibility of reuse is that it creates a dependency among the classes in an inheritance hierarchy. This works against one of the advantages of abstract data types, which is that they are independent of each other. Of course, not all abstract data types must be completely independent. But in general the independence of abstract data types is one of their strongest positive characteristics. However, it may be difficult, if not impossible, to increase the reusability of abstract data types without creating dependencies among some of them. Furthermore, in many cases the dependencies naturally mirror dependencies in the problem space.

12.2.3 Polymorphism and Dynamic Binding

The third characteristic of object-oriented programming languages is a kind of polymorphism provided by the dynamic binding of messages to method definitions. This is supported by allowing one to define variables of the type of the parent class that are also able to reference objects of any of the subclasses of that class. The parent class can define a method that is overriden by its subclasses. The operations defined by these methods are similar, but must be customized for each class in the hierarchy. When such a method is called through the base class reference variable, that call is bound to the method in the proper class dynamically. One purpose of this dynamic binding is to allow software systems to be more easily extended during both development and maintenance. Such programs can be written to perform operations on generic class objects. These operations are generic in that they can apply to objects of any class related through derivation from the same base class.

In many cases the design of an inheritance hierarchy results in one or more classes that are so high in the hierarchy that an instantiation of them does not make sense. For example, suppose that there was a `building` class as the parent or ancestor class of a `French_Gothic` class. It probably would not make sense to have an implemented `draw` method in `building`. But because all of its descendant classes should have such an implemented method, the protocol (but not the body) of that method is included in `building`. This method is often called an **abstract method** (*pure virtual method* in C++). A class that includes at least one abstract method is called an **abstract class** (*abstract base class* in C++). Such a class cannot be instantiated because not all of its methods have bodies. Any subclass of an abstract class that is to be instantiated must provide implementations of all of the inherited abstract methods.

12.3 Design Issues for Object-Oriented Languages

A number of issues must be considered when designing the programming language features to support inheritance and dynamic binding. Those that we consider most important are discussed in this section.

12.3.1 The Exclusivity of Objects

A language designer who is totally committed to the object model of computation designs an object system that absorbs all other concepts of type. Everything, from the smallest integer to a complete software system, is an object in this mind set. The advantage of this choice is the elegance and pure uniformity of the language and its use. The primary disadvantage is that simple operations must be done through the message-passing process, which often makes them slower than similar operations in an imperative model, where machine instructions implement such simple operations.

In this purest model of object-oriented computation, all types are classes. There is no distinction between predefined and user-defined classes. In fact, all classes are treated the same way and all computation is accomplished through message passing.

One alternative to the exclusive use of objects that is common in imperative languages to which support for object-oriented programming has been added is to retain a complete imperative typing model and simply add the object model. This results in a larger language whose type structure is confusing to all but expert users.

Another alternative to the exclusive use of objects is to have an imperative-style type structure for the primitive scalar types. This provides the speed of operations on primitive values that is comparable to those expected in the imperative model. Unfortunately, this alternative also leads to complications in the language. Invariably, nonobject values must be mixed with objects. This creates a need for so-called *wrapper classes* for the nonobject types, so that some commonly needed operations can be sent to objects with nonobject type values. In Section 12.6.1, we will discuss an example of this in Java.

12.3.2   Are Subclasses Subtypes?

The issue here is relatively simple: Does an "is-a" relationship hold between a derived class and its parent class? From a purely semantics point of view, if a derived class is-a parent class, then objects of the derived class must be behaviorly equivalent to objects of the parent class. At a less abstract level, an is-a relationship guarantees that a variable of the derived class type could appear anywhere a variable of the parent class type was legal, without causing a type error.

The subtypes of Ada are examples of this simple form of inheritance. For example,

```
subtype Small_Int is Integer range -100..100;
```

Variables of Small_Int type have all of the operations of Integer variables but can store only a subset of the values possible in Integer. Furthermore, every Small_Int variable can be used anywhere an Integer variable can be used. That is, every Small_Int variable is, in a sense, an Integer variable.

A derived class is called a **subtype** if it has an is-a relationship with its parent class. The characteristics of a subclass that ensure that it is a subtype are as follows: The subclass can only add variables and methods and override inherited methods in "compatible" ways. *Compatible* here means that the overriding method can replace the overridden method without causing type errors. Having an identical number of parameters and identical parameter types and return type would, of course, guarantee compliance. Less severe restrictions are possible, depending on the type compatibility rules of the language.

Our definition of subtype clearly disallows having entities in the parent class that are not inherited to the subclass.

It may appear that subtype relationships and inheritance relationships are nearly identical. However, this is far from correct. An explanation of this, along with a C++ example, is given in Section 12.5.2.

12.3.3   Type Checking and Polymorphism

In Section 12.2, polymorphism in the object-oriented realm is defined to be the use of a polymorphic pointer or reference to access a method whose name is overridden in the class hierarchy that defines the object to which the pointer or reference is defined to point. The polymorphic variable is the type of the parent class, and the parent class defines at least the protocol of a method that is overridden by the derived classes. The polymorphic variable can reference objects of the parent class and the derived classes, so the class of the object to which it points cannot always be statically determined. The binding of messages to methods that are sent through polymorphic variables must be dynamic. The issue here is when the type checking of this binding takes place.

This issue is an important one, for it aligns with the fundamental nature of the programming language. If the language design has strong typing as one of its basic goals, as many contemporary languages do, then this type checking should be statically done. This forces some serious restrictions on the relationship between polymorphic messages and methods.

There are two kinds of type checking that must be done between a message and a method in a strongly typed language: The message's parameter types must be checked against the method's formal parameters, and the return type of the method must be checked against the message's expected type. If these types must match exactly, then an overriding method must have the same number and types of parameters and return type as the overridden method. One relaxation of this rule could be to allow assignment compatibility between actual and formal parameters and between the returned type and the type expected by the message.

The obvious alternative to static type checking is to delay type checking until the polymorphic variable is used to call a method. As in other situations, this kind of dynamic type checking is more expensive and delays type error detection.

12.3.4   Single and Multiple Inheritance

Another simple issue is: Does the language allow multiple inheritance (in addition to single inheritance)? Well, maybe it's not so simple. The purpose of multiple inheritance is to allow a new class to inherit from two or more classes.

Because multiple inheritance is sometimes highly useful, why would a language designer not include it? The reasons fall in two categories: complexity and efficiency. The additional complexity is illustrated by several problems. First, note that if a class has two unrelated parent classes and neither defines a name that is defined in the other, there is no problem. However, suppose a subclass named C inherits from both class A and class B and both A and B define an inheritable method named display. If C needs to reference both versions of display, how can that be done? In C++, the scope resolution operator (::) can be used to specify which version of display is being called, as in A::display() or B::display(). If the scope resolution operator is not included in a call to display, the compiler will flag it as a static semantics error. This ambiguity problem is further complicated when the two parent classes both define identically named methods and one or both of them must be overrriden in the subclass.

Another issue arises if both A and B are derived from a common parent, Z, and C has both A and B as parent classes. This situation is called **diamond** or **shared** inheritance. In this case, both A and B should include Z's inheritable variables. Suppose Z includes an inheritable variable named sum. The question is whether C should inherit both versions of sum or just one, and if just one, which one? There may be programming situations in which just one of the two should be inherited, and others in which both should be inherited. Section 12.10 includes a brief look at the implementation of these situations. Diamond inheritance is shown in Figure 12.1.

The question of efficiency may be more perceived than real. In C++, for example, supporting multiple inheritance requires just one extra addition operation for each dynamically bound method call, at least with some machine architectures (Stroustrup, 1994, p. 270). Although this is required even if the program does not use multiple inheritance, it is a small additional cost.

The use of multiple inheritance can easily lead to complex program organizations. Many who have attempted to use multiple inheritance have found that designing the classes to be used as multiple parents is difficult. Maintenance of systems that use multiple inheritance can be a more serious problem, for multiple inheritance leads to more complex dependencies among classes. It is not clear to some that the benefits of multiple inheritance are worth the added effort to design and maintain a system that uses it.

12.3.5 Allocation and Deallocation of Objects

There are two design questions concerning the allocation and deallocation of objects. The first of these is the place from which objects are allocated. If they behave like the abstract data types, then perhaps they can be allocated from anywhere. This means they could be allocated from the run-time stack, or explicitly created on the heap with an operator or function, such as **new**. If they are all heap dynamic, there is the advantage of having a uniform method of creation and access through pointer or reference variables. This simplifies the assignment operation for objects, making it in all cases only a pointer or

Figure 12.1

An example of
diamond inheritance

reference value change. It also allows references to objects to be implicitly dereferenced, simplifying the access syntax.

If objects are stack dynamic, there is a problem with regard to subtypes. If class B is a child of class A and B is a subtype of A, then an object of B type can be assigned to a variable of A type. For example, if b1 is a variable of B type and a1 is a variable of A type, then

```
b1 = a1;
```

is a legal statement. If a1 and b1 are references to heap-dynamic objects, there is no problem—the assignment is a simple pointer assignment. However, if a1 and b1 are stack-dynamic, then they are value variables in which the value of the object must be copied to the space of the target object. If B adds a data field to what it inherited from A, then a1 will not have sufficient space on the stack for all of b1. The excess will simply be truncated, which could be confusing to programmers who write or use the code.

The second question here is concerned with those cases where objects are allocated from the heap. The question is whether deallocation is implicit or explicit or both. If deallocation is implicit, some implicit method of storage reclamation is required, such as reference counters or garbage collection. If allocation can be explicit, that raises the issue of whether dangling pointers or references can be created.

12.3.6 Dynamic and Static Binding

As we have already discussed, dynamic binding of messages to methods in an inheritance hierarchy is an essential part of object-oriented programming. The question here is whether all binding of messages to methods is dynamic. The alternative is to allow the user to specify whether a specific binding is to be dynamic or static. The advantage of this is that static bindings are faster. So if a binding need not be dynamic, why pay the price?

This completes our discussion of the design issues for object-oriented programming languages.

12.4 Support for Object-Oriented Programming in Smalltalk

Many think of Smalltalk as being the definitive object-oriented programming language. It was the first language to include complete support for that paradigm. Therefore, it is natural to begin a survey of language support for object-oriented programming with Smalltalk.

12.4.1 General Characteristics

A program in Smalltalk consists entirely of objects, and the concept of an object therefore is truly universal. Virtually everything, from items as simple as the integer constant 2 to a complex file-handling system, is an object. As objects, they are treated uniformly. They all have local memory, inherent processing ability, the capability to communicate with other objects, and the possibility of inheriting methods and instance variables from ancestors.

Messages can be parameterized with variables that reference objects. Replies to messages have the form of objects and are used to return requested information or only to confirm that the requested service has been completed.

All Smalltalk objects are allocated from the heap and are referenced through reference variables, which are implicitly dereferenced. There is no explicit deallocation statement or operation. All deallocation is implicit, using a garbage collection process for storage reclamation.

Unlike hybrid languages such as C++ and Ada 95, Smalltalk was designed for just one software development paradigm, object oriented. Furthermore, it adopts none of the appearance of the imperative languages. Its purity of purpose is reflected in its simple elegance and uniformity of design.

12.4.2   Type Checking and Polymorphism

The dynamic binding of messages to methods in Smalltalk operates as follows: A message to an object causes the class to which the object belongs to be searched for a corresponding method. If the search fails, it is continued in the superclass of that class, and so forth, up to the system class, Object, which has no superclass. Object is the root of the class derivation tree on which every class is a node. If no method is found anywhere in that chain, an error occurs. It is important to remember that this method search is dynamic—it takes place when the message is sent. Smalltalk does not, under any circumstances, bind messages to methods statically.

The only type checking in Smalltalk is dynamic, and the only type error occurs when a message is sent to an object that has no matching method, either locally or through inheritance. This is a different concept of type checking than that of most other languages. Smalltalk type checking has the simple goal of ensuring that a message matches a method.

Smalltalk variables are not typed; any name can be bound to any object. As a direct result, Smalltalk supports dynamic polymorphism. All Smalltalk code is generic in the sense that the types of the variables are irrelevant, as long as they are consistent. The meaning of an operation (method or operator) on a variable is determined by the class of the variable to which the variable is currently bound.

The point of this discussion is that as long as the objects referenced in an expression have methods for the messages of the expression, the types of the objects are irrelevant. This means that all code is generic; none is tied to a particular type.

12.4.3   Inheritance

A Smalltalk subclass inherits all of the instance variables, instance methods, and class methods of its superclass. The subclass can also have its own instance variables, which must have names that are distinct from the variable names in its ancestor classes. Finally, the subclass can define new methods and redefine methods that already exist in an ancestor class. When a subclass has a method whose name and protocol are the same as an ancestor class, the subclass method hides that of the ancestor class. Access to such a hidden method is provided by prefixing the message with the pseudovariable **super**. This causes the method search to begin in the superclass rather than locally.

Because entities in a parent class cannot be hidden from subclasses, all subclasses are subtypes.

Smalltalk supports single inheritance; it does not allow multiple inheritance.

12.4.4 Evaluation of Smalltalk

Smalltalk is a small language, although the Smalltalk system is large. The syntax of the language is simple and very regular. It is a good example of the power that can be provided by a small language if that language is built around a simple but powerful concept. In the case of Smalltalk, that concept is that all programming can be done using only a class hierarchy built using inheritance, objects, and message passing.

In comparison with conventional compiled imperative language programs, equivalent Smalltalk programs are significantly slower. Although it is theoretically interesting that array indexing and loops can be provided within the message-passing model, efficiency is an important factor in the evaluation of programming languages. Therefore, efficiency will clearly be an issue in most discussions of the practical applicability of Smalltalk.

Smalltalk's dynamic binding allows type errors to go undetected until run time. A program can be written and compiled that includes messages to nonexistent methods. This causes a great deal more error repair later in the development than would occur in a static-typed language.

Overall, the design of Smalltalk consistently came down on the side of language elegance and strict adherence to the principles of object-oriented programming support, often without regard for practical matters, especially execution efficiency. This is most obvious in the exclusive use of objects and the typeless variables.

The Smalltalk user interface has had an important impact on computing: The integrated use of windows, mouse-pointing devices, and pop-up or pull-down menus dominate contemporary software systems.

Perhaps the greatest impact of Smalltalk is the advancement of object-oriented programming, now the most widely used design and coding methodology.

12.5 Support for Object-Oriented Programming in C++

Chapter 2 describes how C++ evolved from C and SIMULA 67, with the design goal of support for object-oriented programming. C++ classes, as they are used to support abstract data types, are discussed in Chapter 11. C++

On Paradigms and Better Programming

BJARNE STROUSTRUP

I. PROGRAMMING PARADIGMS

Your thoughts on the object-oriented paradigm: Its pluses and minuses.   Let me first say what I mean by OOP—too many people think that "object-oriented" is simply a synonym for "good." If so, there would be no need for other paradigms. The key to OO is the use of class hierarchies providing polymorphic behavior through some rough equivalent of virtual functions. For proper OO, it is important to avoid directly accessing the data in such a hierarchy and use only a well-designed functional interface.

In addition to its well-documented strengths, object-oriented programming also has obvious weaknesses. In particular, not every concept naturally fits into a class hierarchy, and the mechanisms supporting object-oriented programming can impose significant overheads compared to alternatives. For many simple abstractions, classes that do not rely on hierarchies and runtime binding provide a simpler and more efficient alternative. Furthermore, where no runtime resolution is needed, generic programming relying on (compile-time) parametric polymorphism is a better behaved and more efficient approach.

So, C++: Is it OO or other?   C++ supports several paradigms—including OOP, generic programming, and procedural programming—and combinations of these paradigms define multiparadigm programming as supporting more than one programming style ("paradigm") and combinations of those styles.

Do you have a mini example of multiparadigm programming?   Consider this variant of the classic "collection of shapes" examples (originating from the early days of the first language to support object-oriented programming: Simula67):

```
void draw_all(const vector<Shape*>& vs)
{
    for (int i = 0; i<vs.size(); ++i)
        vs[i]->draw();
}
```

Here, I use the generic container, `vector`, together with the polymorphic type, `Shape`. The `vector` provides static type safety and optimal run-time performance. The `Shape` provides the ability to handle a `Shape` (i.e., any object of a class derived from `Shape`) without recompilation.

We can easily generalize this to any container that meets the C++ standard library requirements:

support for the other essentials of object-oriented programming is explored in this section. The whole collection of details of C++ classes, inheritance, and dynamic binding is large and complex. This section discusses only the most important among these topics, specifically those directly related to the design issues discussed in Section 12.3.

C++ is still the most widely used object-oriented programming language. So, naturally, it is the one with which other languages are often compared. For both of these reasons, our coverage of C++ here is more detailed than that of the other example languages discussed in this chapter.

```
template<class C> void draw_all(const C& c)

{

    typedef typename C::const_iterator CI;
    for (CP p = c.begin(); p!=c.end(); ++p)
        (*p)->draw();

}
```

Using iterators allows us to apply this `draw_all()` to containers that do not support subscripts, such as a standard library list:

```
    vector<Shape*> vs;
    list<Shape*> ls;
    // ...
    draw_all(vs);
    draw_all(ls);
```

We can even generalize this further to handle any sequence of elements defined by a pair of iterators:

```
template<class Iterator> void draw_all(Iterator b, Iterator e)
{

    for_each(b,e,mem_fun(Shape::Draw));

}
```

To simplify the implementation, I used the standard library algorithm `for_each`.

We might call this last version of `draw_all()` for a standard library list and an array:

```
list<Shape*> ls;
```

```
Shape* as[100];
// ...
draw_all(ls.begin(),ls.end());
draw_all(as,as+100);
```

II. SELECTING THE 'RIGHT' LANGUAGE FOR THE JOB

How useful is it to have this background in numerous paradigms? Or would it be better to invest time in becoming even more familiar with OO languages rather than learning these other paradigms? It is essential for anyone who wants to be considered a professional in the areas of software to know several languages and several programming paradigms. Currently, C++ is the best language for multiparadigm programming and a good language for learning various forms of programming. However, it's not a good idea know just C++, let alone to know just a single-paradigm language. That would be a bit like being colorblind or monoglot: You would hardly know what you were missing. Much of the inspiration to good programming comes from having learned and appreciated several programming styles and seen how they can be used in different languages.

Furthermore, I consider programming of any nontrivial program a job for professionals with a solid and broad education, rather than for people with a hurried and narrow "training."

12.5.1 General Characteristics

Because one of the primary design considerations of C++ was that it be almost completely backward compatible with C, it retains the type system of C and adds classes to it. Therefore, C++ has both traditional imperative language types and the class structure of an object-oriented language. It also supports both methods and functions (not related to specific classes). This makes it a hybrid language, supporting both procedural programming and object-oriented programming.

The objects of C++ can either be stack dynamic or heap dynamic. Explicit deallocation is required for heap-dynamic objects using the **delete** operator, because C++ does not include implicit storage reclamation.

All C++ classes include at least one constructor method, which is used to initialize the data members of the new object. Constructor methods are implicitly called when an object is created. If any of the data members are heap allocated, the constructor does that allocation. If no constructor is included in a class definition, the compiler includes a trivial constructor. This default constructor calls the constructor of the parent class, if there is a parent class (see Section 12.5.2).

Many class definitions include a destructor method, which is implicitly called when an object of the class ceases to exist. The destructor is used to delete heap-allocated data members. It may also be used to record part or all of the state of the object just before it dies, usually for debugging purposes.

12.5.2   Inheritance

A C++ class can be derived from an existing class, which is then its parent, or base, class. Unlike Smalltalk, a C++ class can also be stand-alone, without a superclass.

Recall that the data defined in a class definition are called *data member functions* of that class, and the functions defined in a class definition are called *member functions* of that class. Some or all of the data member functions and member functions of the base class may be inherited by the derived class, which can also add new data members and member functions and modify inherited member functions. Because private member functions of the base class are not visible in subclasses, derived classes in C++ can be prevented from being subtypes.

Recall from Chapter 11 that class members can be private, protected, or public. Private members are accessible only by member functions and friends of the class. Both functions and classes can be declared to be friends of a class and thereby be given access to its private members. Public members are visible everywhere. Protected members are like private members, except in derived classes, whose access is described below. Derived classes can modify accessibility for their inherited members. The syntactic form of a derived class is

```
class derived_class_name : access_mode  base_class_name
   {data member and member function declarations};
```

The access_mode can be either **public** or **private**. The public and protected members of a base class are also public and protected, respectively, in a public derived class. In a private derived class, both the public and protected members of the base class are private. So in a class hierarchy, a private derived class cuts off access to all members of all ancestor classes to all successor classes, and protected members may or may not be accessible to subsequent subclasses (past the first). Private members of a base class are inherited by a derived class, but they are not visible to the members of that derived class and are therefore of no use there. Consider the following example:

```
class base_class {
  private:
    int a;
    float x;
  protected:
    int b;
    float y;
  public:
    int c;
    float z;
};

class subclass_1 : public base_class { ... };
class subclass_2 : private base_class { ... };
```

In `subclass_1`, `b` and `y` are protected, and `c` and `z` are public. In `subclass_2`, `b`, `y`, `c`, and `z` are private. No derived class of `subclass_2` can have members with access to any member of `base_class`. The data members `a` and `x` in `base_class` are not accessible in either `subclass_1` or `subclass_2`.

Under private class derivation, no member of the parent class is implicitly visible to the instances of the derived class. Any member that must be made visible must be reexported in the derived class. This reexportation in effect exempts a member from being hidden even though the derivation was private. For example, consider the following class definition:

```
class subclass_3 : private base_class {
  base_class :: c;
  ...
}
```

Now, instances of `subclass_3` can access `c`. As far as `c` is concerned, it is as if the derivation had been public. The double colon (`::`) in this class definition is a scope resolution operator. It specifies the class where its following entity is defined.

Consider the following example of C++ inheritance, in which a general linked list class is defined and then used to define two useful subclasses:

```
class single_linked_list {
  class node {
    friend class single_linked_list;
    private:
      node *link;
      int contents;
```

```
    };
    private:
      node *head;
    public:
      single_linked_list() {head = 0};
      void insert_at_head(int);
      void insert_at_tail(int);
      int remove_at_head();
      int empty();
};
```

The nested class, node, defines a cell of the linked list to consist of an integer location and a pointer to a cell. It lists single_linked_list as a **friend**, thus granting objects of class single_linked_list access to its two data members, link and contents. This is necessary because enclosing classes have no access rights to members of their nested classes.

The enclosing class, single_linked_list, has just a single data member, a pointer to act as the list's header. It contains a constructor function, which simply sets head to the null pointer value. The four member functions allow nodes to be inserted at either end of a list object, nodes to be removed from one end of a list, and lists to be tested for empty.

The following definitions provide stack and queue classes, both based on the single_linked_list class:

```
class stack : public single_linked_list {
  public:
    stack() {}
    void push(int value) {
      single_linked_list :: insert_at_head(int value);
    }
    int pop() {
      return single_linked_list :: remove_at_head();
    }
};
class queue : public single_linked_list {
  public:
    queue() {}
    void enqueue(int value) {
      single_linked_list :: insert_at_tail(int value);
    }
    int dequeue() {
      single_linked_list :: remove_at_head();
    }
};
```

Note that objects of both the `stack` and `queue` subclasses can access the `empty` function defined in the base class, `single_linked_list` (because it is a public derivation). Both subclasses define constructor functions that do nothing. When an object of a subclass is created, the proper constructor in the subclass is implicitly called. Then any applicable constructor in the base class is called. So in our example, when an object of type `stack` is created, the `stack` constructor is called, which does nothing. Then the constructor in `single_linked_list` is called, which does the necessary initialization.

The classes `stack` and `queue` both suffer from the same serious problem: Objects of both can access all of the public members of the parent class, `single_linked_list`. Therefore, a `stack` object could call `insert_at_tail`, thereby destroying the integrity of its stack. Likewise, a `queue` object could call `insert_at_head`. These unwanted accesses are allowed because both `stack` and `queue` are subtypes of `single_linked_list`. These two derived classes can be written to make them not subtypes of their parent class by using **private**, rather than **public**, derivation. Then both will also need to reexport `empty`, because it will become hidden to their instances. The new definitions of the stack and queue types, named `stack_2` and `queue_2`, are shown in the following:

```
class stack_2 : private single_linked_list {
  public:
    stack_2() {}
    void push(int value) {
      single_linked_list :: insert_at_head(int value);
    }
    int pop() {
      return single_linked_list :: remove_at_head();
    }
    single_linked_list:: empty;
};
class queue_2 : private single_linked_list {
  public:
    queue_2() {}
    void enqueue(int value) {
      single_linked_list :: insert_at_tail(int value);
    }
    int dequeue() {
      single_linked_list :: remove_at_head();
    }
    single_linked_list:: empty;
};
```

The two versions of stack and queue illustrate the difference between subtypes and derived types that are not subtypes. The linked list is a generalization of both stacks and queues, because both can be implemented as linked lists. So, it is natural to inherit from a linked-list class to define stack and queue classes. However, neither is a subtype of the linked-list class. Rather, the linked list is actually a subtype of the other two.

One of the reasons why friends are necessary is that sometimes a subprogram must be written that can access the members of two different classes. For example, suppose a program uses a class for vectors and one for matrices, and a subprogram is needed to multiply objects of these two classes. In C++, the multiply function is simply made a friend of both classes.

C++ provides multiple inheritance, which allows more than one class to be named as the parent of a new class. For example,

```
class A { ... };
class B { ... };
class C : public A, public B { ... };
```

Class C inherits all of the members of both A and B. If both A and B happen to include members with the same name, they can be unambiguously referenced in objects of class C by using the scope resolution operator. Some problems with the C++ implementation of multiple inheritance are discussed in Section 12.10.

Overriding methods in C++ must have exactly the same protocol as the overridden method. If there is any difference in the protocols, the method in the subclass is considered a new method that is unrelated to the method with the same name in the ancestor class.

12.5.3   Dynamic Binding

All of the member functions we have defined thus far are statically bound; that is, a call to one of them is statically bound to a function definition. A C++ object could be manipulated through a value variable, rather than a pointer or a reference. (Such an object would be stack dynamic.) However, in that case the object's type is known and static, so dynamic binding is not needed. On the other hand, a pointer or reference variable that has the type of a base class can be used to point to any heap-dynamic objects of any class derived from that base class, making it a polymorphic variable. C++ does not allow value variables (as opposed to pointers or references) to be polymorphic. When a polymorphic variable is used to call a function defined in one of the derived classes, the call must be dynamically bound to the correct function definition. Member functions that must be dynamically bound must be declared to be virtual functions by preceding their headers with the reserved word **virtual**, which can only appear in a class body.

Consider the situation of having a base class named shape, along with a collection of derived classes for different kinds of shapes, such as circles, rectangles, and so forth. If these shapes need to be displayed, then the displaying member function, draw, must be unique for each subclass, or kind of shape.

These versions of draw must be defined to be virtual. When a call to draw is made with a pointer to the base class of the derived classes, that call must be dynamically bound to the member function of the correct derived class. The following has the definitions of the example situation just described:

```
public class shape {
  public:
    virtual void draw() = 0;
  ...
}
public class circle : public shape {
  public:
    virtual void draw() { ... }
  ...
}
public class rectangle : public shape {
  public:
    virtual void draw() { ... }
  ...
}
public class square : public rectangle {
  public:
    virtual void draw() { ... }
  ...
}
```

Given these definitions, the following has examples of both statically and dynamically bound calls:

```
square s;
rectangle r;
shape &ref_shape = s;   // a reference to the square s
ref_shape.draw();       // dynamically bound to draw in
                        // square
r.draw();               // statically bound to draw in
                        // rectangle
```

Notice that the draw function in the definition of the base class shape above is set to 0. This peculiar syntax is used to indicate that this member function is a **pure virtual function,** meaning it has no body and it cannot be called. It must be redefined in derived classes. The purpose of a pure virtual function is to provide the interface of a function without giving any of its implementation. This allows every subclass to define its own version of the function.

Any class that includes a pure virtual function is an **abstract class.** No object of an abstract class can be created. In a strict sense, an abstract class is one that cannot have concrete objects but rather is used only to represent the concepts of a type. Subclasses of such a type can, of course, have objects. C++ provides abstract classes to model these truly abstract classes. If a subclass of an abstract class does not redefine a pure virtual function of its parent class, that function remains as a pure virtual function.

Abstract classes and inheritance together support a powerful technique for software development. They allow types to be hierarchically defined so that related types can be subclasses of truly abstract types that define their common abstract characteristics.

Dynamic binding allows the code that uses members like `draw` to be written before all or even any of the versions of `draw` are written. New derived classes could be added years later, without requiring any change to the code that uses such dynamically bound members. This is a powerful feature of object-oriented languages.

12.5.4 Evaluation

It is natural to compare the object-oriented features of C++ with those of Smalltalk, which is what is done in this section.

The inheritance of C++ is more intricate than that of Smalltalk in terms of access control. By using both the access controls within the class definition and the derivation access controls, and also the possibility of friend functions and classes, the C++ programmer has highly detailed control over the access to class members. Furthermore, although there is some debate over its real value, C++ provides multiple inheritance, whereas Smalltalk allows only single inheritance.

In C++, the programmer can specify whether static binding or dynamic binding is to be used. Because static binding is faster, this is an advantage for those situations where dynamic binding is not necessary. Furthermore, even the dynamic binding in C++ is fast when compared with that of Smalltalk. Binding a virtual member function call in C++ to a function definition has a fixed cost, regardless of how distant in the inheritance hierarchy the definition appears. Calls to virtual functions require only five more memory references than statically bound calls (Stroustrup, 1988). In Smalltalk, however, messages are always dynamically bound to methods, and the farther away in the inheritance hierarchy the correct method is, the longer it takes. The disadvantage of allowing the user to decide which bindings are static and which are dynamic is that the original design must include these decisions, which may have to be changed later.

The static type checking of C++ is an advantage over Smalltalk, where all type checking is dynamic. A Smalltalk program can be compiled with messages to nonexistent methods, which are discovered when the program is executed. A C++ compiler finds such errors. Compiler-detected errors are less expensive to repair than those found in testing.

Smalltalk is essentially typeless, meaning that all code is effectively generic. This provides a great deal of flexibility, but static type checking is sacrificed. C++ provides generic classes through its template facility (as described in Chapter 11), which retains the benefits of static type checking.

The primary advantage of Smalltalk lies in the elegance and simplicity of the language that results from the single philosophy of its design. It is purely and completely devoted to the object-oriented paradigm, devoid of compromises necessitated by the whims of an entrenched user base. C++, on the other hand, is a large and complex language with no single philosophy as its foundation, except to support object-oriented programming and include the C user base. One of its most significant goals was to preserve the efficiency and flavor of C while providing the advantages of object-oriented programming. Some people feel that the features of this language do not always fit well together and that much of the complexity is unnecessary.

According to Chambers and Ungar (1991), Smalltalk ran a particular set of small C-style benchmarks at only 10 percent of the speed of optimized C. C++ programs require only slightly more time than equivalent C programs (Stroustrup, 1988). Given the great efficiency gap between Smalltalk and C++, it is little wonder that the commercial use of C++ is far more widespread than that of Smalltalk. Of course, there are other factors in this difference, but efficiency is clearly a strong argument in favor of C++.

12.6 Support for Object-Oriented Programming in Java

Because Java's design of classes, inheritance, and methods is similar to that of C++, we focus in this section only on those areas in which Java differs from C++.

12.6.1 General Characteristics

As with C++, Java does not use objects exclusively. However, in Java only values of the primitive scalar types (Boolean, character, and the numeric types) are not objects. Java has no enumeration or record types, and its arrays are objects. The reason to have nonobjects is efficiency. However, as discussed in Section 12.3.1, having two type systems leads to some cumbersome situations. One of these in Java is that the predefined data structure Vector can only contain objects. So if you want to put a primitive type value into a Vector object, the value must first be placed in an object. This can be done by creating a new object of the wrapper class for the primitive type. Such a class has an instance variable of that primitive type and a constructor that takes a value of the primitive type as a parameter and assigns it to its instance variable. For example, to put 10 into the Vector object referenced by the variable myVector, we could use the following statement:

```
myVector.addElement(new Integer(10));
```

where addElement is a method of Vector that inserts a new element and Integer is the wrapper class for **int**.

Whereas C++ classes can be defined to have no parent, that is not possible in Java. All Java classes must be subclasses of the root class, Object, or some class that is a descendant of Object. One reason to have a single root class is that there are some operations that are universally needed. Among these is a method for comparing objects for equality.

All Java objects are explicit heap dynamic. Most are allocated with the **new** operator, but there is no explicit deallocation operator. Garbage collection is used for storage reclamation. Like many other language features, although garbage collection avoids some serious problems, such as dangling pointers, it can cause other problems. One such difficulty arises because the garbage collector deallocates, or reclaims the storage occupied by an object, but it does no more. For example, if an object has access to some resource other than heap memory, such as a file or a lock on a shared resource, the garbage collector does not reclaim these. For these situations, Java allows the inclusion of a special method, **finalize**, which is related to a C++ destructor function.

A **finalize** method is implicitly called when the garbage collector is about to reclaim the storage occupied by the object.[1] The problem with **finalize** is that the time it will run cannot be forced or even predicted. The alternative to using **finalize** to reclaim resources held by an object about to be garbage collected is to include a method that does the reclamation. The only problem with this is that all clients of the objects must be aware of this method and remember to call it.

12.6.2 Inheritance

Java directly supports only single inheritance. However, it includes a kind of abstract class, called an **interface,** which provides a version of multiple inheritance. An interface definition is similar to a class definition, except that it can contain only named constants and method declarations (not definitions). So an interface is no more than what its name indicates—it defines only the specification of a class. (Recall that a C++ abstract class can have instance variables and all but one of the methods can be completely defined.) The typical use of an interface is to define a class that inherits both some of the methods and variables from its parent class, and also implements a parent interface.

As an example of an interface, consider the sort method of the standard Java class, Arrays. Any class that uses this method must provide an implementation of a method to compare the elements to be sorted. The Comparable interface provides the protocol for this comparing method, which is named compareTo. The code for the Comparable interface is as follows:

---

[1] One common use of finalize is similar to a common use of C++ destructors, to output some information about an object just before it is destroyed, primarily for debugging purposes.

```
public interface Comparable {
    public int compareTo(Object b);
}
```

The compareTo method must return a negative integer if the object through which it is called belongs before the parameter object, zero if they are equal, and a positive integer if the parameter belongs before the object through which compareTo was called. A class that implements the Comparable interface can sort the contents of any array, as long as the implemented compareTo method provides the appropriate value.

Chapter 14 illustrates the use of interfaces in Java event handling.

In Java, a method can be defined to be **final**, which means that it cannot be overridden in any descendant class. When the **final** reserved word is specified on a class definition, it means the class cannot be the parent of any subclass.

12.6.3 Dynamic Binding

In C++, a method must be defined to be virtual to allow dynamic binding. In Java, all method calls are dynamically bound unless the called method has been defined to be **final**, in which case it cannot be overridden and all bindings are static.

12.6.4 Evaluation

Java's design for supporting object-oriented programming is similar to that of C++, but employs more consistent adherence to object-oriented principles. Because of its lack of functions, Java does not support procedural programming. Also, Java does not allow parentless classes and uses dynamic binding as the "normal" approach to bind method calls to method definitions. Access control for the contents of a class definition are rather simple when compared with the jungle of access controls of C++, ranging from derivation controls to friend functions. Finally, Java uses interfaces to provide a simple form of support for multiple inheritance, whereas C++ includes complete but complex support for it.

12.7 Support for Object-Oriented Programming in C#

C#'s support for object-oriented programming is similar to that of Java.

12.7.1 General Characteristics

As discussed in Chapter 11, C# includes both classes and structs, with the classes being very similar to Java's classes and the structs being somewhat less powerful stack-dynamic constructs.

12.7.2 Inheritance

C# uses the syntax of C++ for defining classes. For example,

```
public class NewClass : ParentClass { ... }
```

A method inherited from the parent class can be replaced in the derived class by marking its definition in the subclass with **new**. The **new** method hides the method of the same name in the parent class to normal access. However, the parent class version can still be called by prefixing the call with **base**. For example,

```
base.Draw();
```

12.7.3 Dynamic Binding

To allow dynamic binding of method calls to methods in C#, both the base method and its corresponding methods in derived classes must be specially marked. The base class method must be marked with **virtual**, as in C++. To avoid accidental overriding, the corresponding methods in derived classes must be marked **override**. The inclusion of **override** makes it clear that the method is a new version of an inherited method. For example, the C# version of the C++ shape class that appears in Section 12.5.3 is

```
public class Shape {
  public virtual void Draw() { ... }
  ...
}
public class Circle : Shape {
  public override void Draw() { ... }
  ...
}
public class Rectangle : Shape {
  public override void Draw() { ... }
  ...
}
public class Square : Rectangle {
  public override void Draw() { ... }
  ...
}
```

C# includes abstract methods, similar to those of C++, except that they are specified with different syntax. For example, the following is a C# abstract method:

```
abstract public void Draw();
```

As in C++, a C# abstract method must be implemented in all subclasses of the class in which it appears. Any class that includes an abstract method must also be marked **abstract**. An abstract class cannot be instantiated.

As with Java, all C# classes are ultimately derived from a single root class, `Object`. The `Object` class defines a collection of methods, including `ToString`, `Finalize`, and `Equals`, which are inherited by all C# types.

12.7.4 Evaluation

Because C# is the most recently designed C-based object-oriented language, one should expect that its designers learned from their predecessors and duplicated the successes of the past and remedied some of the problems. The result of this is that the differences between C#'s support for object-oriented programming and that of Java are relatively minor.

12.8 Support for Object-Oriented Programming in Ada 95

Ada 95 was derived from Ada 83, with some significant extensions. This section presents a brief look at the extensions that were designed to support object-oriented programming. Because Ada 83 already included constructs for building abstract data types, which are discussed in Chapter 11, the necessary additional features were those for supporting inheritance and dynamic binding. The design objectives for these features included the goals of requiring minimal changes to the type and package structures of Ada 83 and retaining as much static type checking as possible.

12.8.1 General Characteristics

Ada 95 classes are a new category of types called **tagged types,** which can be either records or private types. They are defined in packages, which allows them to be separately compiled. Tagged types are so named because each object of a tagged type implicitly includes a system-maintained tag that indicates its type. The subprograms that define the operations on a tagged type appear in the same declaration list as the type declaration. Consider the following example:

```
package Person_Pkg is
  type Person is tagged private;
  procedure Display(P : in Person);
  private
    type Person is tagged
      record
        Name : String(1..30);
        AddressS : String(1..30);
        Age : Integer;
      end record;
end Person_Pkg;
```

This package defines the type Person that can be used on its own and as the parent class of other derived classes.

Unlike C++, there is no implicit calling of constructor or destructor subprograms in Ada 95. These subprograms can be written, but they must be explicitly called by the programmer.

12.8.2 Inheritance

Ada 83 has a restricted form of inheritance in its derived types and subtypes. In both of these, a new type can be defined on the basis of an existing type. But the only modification allowed is to restrict the range of values of the new type. Derived classes in Ada 95 are based on tagged types. New entities are added to the inherited entities by including a record definition. Consider the following example:

```
with Person_Pkg; use Person_Pkg;
package Student_Pkg is
  type Student is new Person with
    record
      Grade_Point_Average : Float;
      Grade_Level : Integer;
    end record;
  procedure Display(St : in Student);
end Student_Pkg;
```

In this example, the derived type Student is defined to have the entities of its parent class, Person, along with the new entities Grade_Point_Average and Grade_Level. It also redefines the procedure Display. This new class is defined in a separate package to allow it to be changed without requiring recompilation of the package containing the definition of the parent type.

Through this inheritance mechanism, there is no way to prevent entities of the parent class from being included in the derived class. Consequently, derived classes can only extend parent classes, and are therefore subtypes.

Suppose we have the following definitions:

```
P1 : Person;
S1 : Student;
Fred : Person:= ("Fred", "321 Mulberry Lane", 35);
Freddie : Student:= ("Freddie", "725 Main St.", 20, 3.25,
                          3);
```

Because Student is a subtype of Person, the assignment

```
P1 := Freddie;
```

should be legal, and it is. The Grade_Point_Average and Grade_Level entities of Freddie are simply ignored in the required coercion.

The obvious question now is whether an assignment in the opposite direction is legal; that is, can we assign a `Person` to a `Student`? In Ada 95, this is legal in a form that includes the entities in the subclass. In our example, the following is legal:

```
S1 := (Fred, 3.05, 2);
```

To derive a class that does not include all of the parent class's entities, child library packages are used. A child library package is simply a package whose name is prefixed with that of a parent package. Child library packages can also be used in place of the friend definitions in C++. For example, if a subprogram must be written that can access the members of two different classes, the parent package can define one of the classes, and the child package can define the other. Then a subprogram in the child package can access the members of both.

Ada 95 does not provide multiple inheritance. Although generic classes and multiple inheritance are only distantly related concepts, there is a way to achieve an effect similar to multiple inheritance using generics. However, it is not as elegant as the C++ approach, and it is not discussed here.

12.8.3 Dynamic Binding

Ada 95 provides both static binding and dynamic binding of procedure calls to procedure definitions in tagged types. Dynamic binding is forced by using a classwide type, which represents all of the types in a class hierarchy rooted at a particular type. Every tagged type implicitly has a classwide type. For a tagged type T, the classwide type is specified with `T'class`. If T is a tagged type, a variable of type `T'class` can be of type T or any type derived from T.

Consider again the `Person` and `Student` classes defined in Section 12.8.2. Suppose we have a variable of type `Person'class`, Pcw, which sometimes references a `Person` object an sometimes references a `Student` object. Further suppose we want to display the object referenced by Pcw, regardless of whether it is referencing a `Person` object or a `Student` object. This requires the call to `Display` to be dynamically bound to the correct version of `Display`. We could use a new procedure that takes the `Person` type parameter and sends it to `Display`. Following is such a procedure:

```
procedure Display_Any_Person(P: in Person) is
  begin
  Display(P);
  end Display_Any_Person;
```

This procedure can be called with both of the following calls:

```
with Person_Pkg; use Person_Pkg;
with Student_Pkg; use Student_Pkg;
P : Person;
```

```
S : Student;
Pcw : Person'class;
...
Pcw := P;
Display_Any_Person(Pcw);  — call the Display in Person
Pcw := S;
Display_Any_Person(Pcw);  — call the Display in Student
```

Ada 95 also supports polymorphic pointers. They are defined to have the classwide type, as in

```
type Any_Person_Ptr is access Person'class;
```

Purely abstract base types can be defined in Ada 95 by including the reserved word **abstract** in the type definitions and the subprogram definitions. Furthermore, the subprogram definitions cannot have bodies. Consider this example:

```
package Base_Pkg is
  type T is abstract tagged null record;
  procedure Do_It (A : T) is abstract;
end Base_Pkg;
```

12.8.4 Evaluation

Ada offers complete support for object-oriented programming, although users of other object-oriented languages may find that support to be weak. Although packages can be used to build abstract data types, they are actually more generalized encapsulation constructs. Unless child library packages are used, there no way to restrict inheritance, in which case all subclasses are subtypes. This form of access restriction is highly limited, compared to that offered by C++, Java, and C#.

C++ clearly offers a better form of multiple inheritance than Ada 95. However, the use of child library units to control access to the entities of the parent class seems to be a cleaner solution than the friend functions and classes of C++. For example, if the need for a friend is not known when a class is defined, it will need to be changed and recompiled when such a need is discovered. In Ada 95, new classes in new child packages are defined without disturbing the parent package, because every name defined in the parent package is visible in the child package.

The inclusion in C++ of constructors and destructors for initialization of objects is good, but Ada 95 includes no such capabilities.

Another difference between these two languages is that the designer of a C++ root class must decide whether a particular member function will be statically or dynamically bound. If the choice is made in favor of static binding, but a later change in the system requires dynamic binding, the root class must be changed. In Ada 95, this design decision need not be made with the design of the root class. Each call can itself specify whether it will be statically or dynamically bound, regardless of the design of the root class.

A more subtle difference is that dynamic binding in the C-based object-oriented languages is restricted to pointers and/or references to objects, rather than the objects themselves. Ada 95 has no such restriction, so in this case Ada 95 is more orthogonal.

12.9 The Object Model of JavaScript

Although JavaScript does not have classes and supports neither inheritance nor dynamic binding, it uses an object model that is loosely based on the objects of C++ and Java. The design of JavaScript is therefore an interesting alternative to the traditional concepts of language support for objects.

12.9.1 General Characteristics

JavaScript was originally designed by Netscape as a scripting language for use in programming Web servers. It has since grown and evolved to a prominent position as a language for augmenting HTML documents, in which it is used to provide computational capability to those documents. Recently, with the development of the Document Object Model, JavaScript has become a powerful tool for making HTML documents dynamic. Because of this, JavaScript has become a popular language.

In spite of the first part of its name, JavaScript has little in common with Java. It is, however, true to the last part of its name—it is a scripting language. Snippets of JavaScript code can be scattered in various parts of an HTML document. When a browser encounters JavaScript code in a document it is reading and displaying, the code is immediately interpreted.

JavaScript is similar to Java only in that it uses a similar syntax. There are many fundamental differences. Java is a statically typed object-oriented language; JavaScript is dynamically typed. JavaScript does not have classes. Its objects serve both as objects and models of objects. Without classes, JavaScript cannot support class-based inheritance. Without class-based inheritance, JavaScript cannot support polymorphism. Although JavaScript has objects, they are quite different from those of the object-oriented languages.

As is the case with most languages that support object-oriented programming, JavaScript has two categories of variables, those that reference objects and those that directly store values of primitive types. Variables can be declared, but no type is implied by the declaration. The type of a variable can change every time a value is assigned to it. The new type is the type of the assigned value. Any variable can be used to store any primitive type value or refer to any object.

12.9.2   JavaScript Objects

In JavaScript, objects have collections of properties, which correspond to the members of classes in Java and C++. Each property is either a data property or a method property.

JavaScript objects appear as Perl hashes (see Chapter 6), both internally and externally. Each object is a list of property-value pairs. The properties are names; the values are data values or references to objects, some of which are methods. All functions and methods are objects and are referenced through variables. The only difference between a function and a method is that a method is referenced through an object property.

As is the case with a Perl hash, the collection of properties of a JavaScript object is dynamic—properties can be added or deleted at any time. This makes JavaScript objects very different from the objects of languages such as C++ and Java. Every object is characterized by its collection of properties, although objects do not have types in any formal sense. JavaScript includes a **typeof** operator, but it returns the string "object" for every object.

12.9.3   Object Creation and Modification

Objects are often created with a **new** expression, which must include a call to a constructor method. The constructor that is called in the **new** expression creates the properties that characterize the new object. In an object-oriented language, the **new** operator creates a particular object, meaning an object with a type and a specific collection of members. Constructors in such languages initialize members but do not create them. In JavaScript, the **new** operator creates a blank object, or one with no properties. The constructor both creates and initializes the properties.

The following statement creates an object using the constructor for the predefined Object object, which creates no properties:

```
var my_object = new Object();
```

The variable my_object now references the new object. Constructors are further discussed below.

The properties of an object are accessed using dot notation, in which the first word is the object name and the second is the property name. Properties are not actually variables. They are keys into a hash, so as with Perl hash keys, they have no values of their own. They are used with object variables to access property values. Because they are not variables, properties are never declared.

As stated above, at any time during interpretation, properties can be added to or deleted from an object. A property for an object is created by assigning a value to that property. Consider the following example:

```
var my_car = new Object();  // Create a blank object
my_car.make = "Ford";  // Create and initialize the make property
my_car.model = "Contour SVT";  // Create and initialize model
```

This code creates a new object, `my_car`, with two properties, `make` and `model`. Because objects can be nested, we can create a new object that is a property of `my_car` with properties of its own. For example,

```
my_car.engine = new Object();
my_car.engine.config = "V6";
my_car.engine.hp = 200;
```

If an attempt is made to access a property of an object that does not exist, the value **undefined** is used. A property can be deleted with **delete**. For example,

delete `my_car.model;`

JavaScript constructors are special methods that create and initialize the properties for newly created objects. Every **new** expression must include a call to a constructor. Constructors are actually called by the **new** operator, which immediately precedes their names in the **new** expression.

A constructor obviously must be able to reference the object on which it is to operate. JavaScript has a predefined reference variable for this purpose, named **this**. When the constructor is called, **this** is a reference to the newly created object. The **this** variable is used to create and initialize the properties of the object. For example, consider the following constructor:

```
function car(new_make, new_model, new_year) {
    this.make = new_make;
    this.model = new_model;
    this.year = new_year;
}
```

This constructor could be used as in the following:

```
my_car = new car("Ford", "Contour SVT", "2000");
```

If a method is to be included in the object, it is initialized the same way as if it were a data property. For example, suppose we created a method for `car` objects that displayed the property values, named `display_car`.

The `display_car` method is added to the object being created with **new** and the call to the constructor by adding the following line to the constructor:

```
this.display = display_car;
```

The only concept of categories of objects in JavaScript that is related to the concept of class in an object-oriented programming language is the collection of objects created by use of the same constructor. All such objects would have the same set of properties and methods, at least initially. However, there is no convenient way to determine in the script whether two objects have the same set of properties and methods.

12.9.4   Evaluation

JavaScript is effective at what it is designed to be, a scripting language. If it were meant for large-scale software systems, its object model would be wholly inadequate. Without the encapsulation capability of classes, large programs in JavaScript could not be effectively organized. Without inheritance, reuse would be much more difficult. So, although the object model of JavaScript is interesting, it does not address the needs that motivated the development of object-oriented programming languages.

12.10   Implementation of Object-Oriented Constructs

There are at least two parts of language support for object-oriented programming that pose interesting questions for language implementers, storage structures for instance variables and the dynamic bindings of messages to methods. In this section we take a brief look at these two.

12.10.1   Instance Data Storage

In C++, classes are defined as extensions of C's record structures, structs. This similarity suggests a storage structure for the instance variables of class instances—that of a record. We call this form of this structure a **class instance record** (CIR). The structure of a CIR is static, so it is built at compile time and used as a template for the creation of the data of class instances. Subclasses of a class can simply extend the CIR of the parent class by adding the new instance variables.

Because the structure of the CIR is static, access to all instance variables can be done as it is in records, using constant offsets from the beginning of the CIR instance. This makes these accesses as efficient as those for the fields of records.

The CIR for a class that has a parent simply adds its new data to the parent CIR.

12.10.2   Dynamic Binding of Method Calls to Methods

Methods in a class that are statically bound need not be involved in the CIR for the class. However, methods that will be dynamically bound must have entries in this structure. Such entries could simply have a pointer to the code of the method, which must be set at object creation time. Calls to a method could then be connected to the corresponding code through this pointer in the CIR. The drawback to this technique is that every instance would need to store pointers to all dynamically bound methods that could be called from the instance.

Notice that the list of dynamically bound methods that can be called from an instance of a class is the same for all instances of that class. Therefore, the list of such methods must only be stored once. So the CIR for an instance needs only a single pointer to that list to enable it to find called methods. The storage structure for the list is sometimes called a **virtual method table** (vtable). Method calls can be represented as offsets from the beginning of the vtable. Polymorphic variables of an ancestor class always reference the CIR of the correct type object, so getting to the correct version of a dynamically bound method is assured. Consider the following Java example, in which all methods are dynamically bound:

```java
public class A {
  public int a, b;
  public void draw() { ... }
  public int area() { ... }
}
public class B extends A {
  public int c, d;
  public void draw() { ... }
  public void sift() { ... }
}
```

The CIRs for the A and B classes, along with their vtables, are shown in Figure 12.2.

Suppose a class named C creates objects of both class A and class B, with references named aObj and bObj, respectively. Further suppose that there is an assignment statement in C

```java
aObj = bObj;
```

Now, if there is a call

```java
aObj.draw();
```

and the assignment statement only copies bObj's pointer to aObj, A's draw method would be called, which would be incorrect. This illustrates that the assignment of bObj the reference to aObj, must have the side effect of changing the vtable pointer of aObj to point to the vtable of class B.

Multiple inheritance complicates the implementation of dynamic binding. Consider the following three C++ class definitions:

```cpp
class A {
  public:
    int a;
    virtual void fun() { ... }
    virtual void init() { ... }
class B {
  public:
    int b;
    virtual void sum() { ... }
```

```
};
class C : public A, public B {
  public:
    int c;
    virtual void fun() { ... }
    virtual void dud() { ... }
};
```

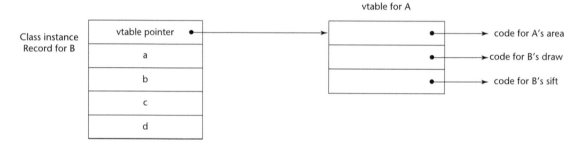

Figure 12.2

An example of the CIRs with
single inheritance

The c class inherits the variable a and the init method from the A class. It redefines the fun method, although both its fun and that of the parent class A are potentially visible through a polymorphic variable (of type A). From B, c inherits the variable b and the sum method. c defines its own variable, c, and defines an uninherited method, dud. A CIR for c must include A's data, B's data, and c's data, as well as some means of accessing all visible methods. Under single inheritance, the CIR would include a pointer to a vtable that has the addresses of the code of all visible methods. With multiple inheritance, however, it is not that simple. There must be at least two different views available in the CIR, one for each of the parent classes, one of which includes the view for the subclass, c. This inclusion of the view of the subclass in the parent class' view is just as in the implementation of single inheritance.

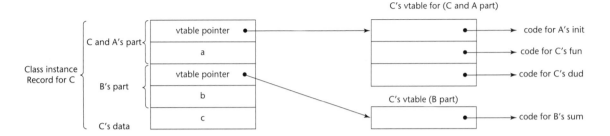

Figure 12.3

An example of a subclass
CIR with multiple parents

There must also be two vtables, one for the A and C view and one for the
B view. The first part of the CIR for C in this case can be the C and A view,
which begins with a vtable pointer for the methods of C and those inherited
from A, and includes the data inherited from A. Following this in C's CIR is
the B view part, which begins with a vtable pointer for the virtual methods of
B, which is followed by the data inherited from B and the data defined in C.
The CIR for C is shown in Figure 12.3.

SUMMARY

Object-oriented programming involves three fundamental concepts: abstract
data types, inheritance, and dynamic binding. Object-oriented programming
languages support the paradigm with classes, methods, objects, and message
passing.

The discussion of object-oriented programming languages in this chapter revolves around six design issues: exclusivity of objects, subclasses and subtypes, type checking and polymorphism, single and multiple inheritance,
dynamic binding, and explicit or implicit deallocation of objects.

Smalltalk is a pure object-oriented language—everything is an object and
all computation is accomplished through message passing. In Smalltalk all
subclasses are subtypes. All type checking and binding of messages to methods is dynamic, and all inheritance is single. Smalltalk has no explicit deallocation operation.

C++ provides support for data abstraction, inheritance, and optional
dynamic binding of messages to methods, along with all of the conventional
features of C. This means that it has two distinct type systems. While
Smalltalk's dynamic binding provides somewhat more programming flexibility than the hybrid language, C++, it is far less efficient. C++ provides multiple inheritance and explicit object deallocation. C++ includes a variety of

access controls for the entities in classes, some of which prevent subclasses from being subtypes. Both constructor and destructor methods can be included in classes; both are implicitly called.

Java is not a hybrid language like C++; it is meant to support only object-oriented programming. As with C++, Java has both primitive scalar types and classes. All objects are allocated from the heap and are accessed through reference variables. There is no explicit object deallocation operation. The only subprograms are methods, and they can only be called through objects or classes. Only single inheritance is directly supported, although a kind of multiple inheritance is possible using interfaces. All binding of messages to methods is dynamic, except in the case of methods that cannot be overridden. In addition to classes, Java includes packages as a second encapsulation construct.

Ada 95 provides support for object-oriented programming through tagged types, which can use inheritance. Dynamic binding is possible by using classwide types. Derived types are extensions to parent types, unless they are defined in child library packages, in which case entities of the parent type can be eliminated in the derived type. Outside child library packages, all subclasses are subtypes.

C#, which is based on C++ and Java, supports for object-oriented programming. Objects can be instantiated from either classes or structs. The struct objects are stack dynamic and do not support inheritance. Methods in a derived class can call the hidden methods of the parent class by including **base** on the method name. Methods that can be overridden must be marked **virtual**, and the overriding methods must be marked with **override**. All classes (and all primitives) are derived from Object.

Although JavaScript is not an object-oriented language, it includes an interesting variation on the concept of object.

Dynamic binding of method calls to methods can be implemented using class instance records and virtual tables of method addresses. This approach can be extended to include support for multiple inheritance.

REVIEW QUESTIONS

1. What are the three characteristic features of object-oriented languages?
2. What is the difference between a class variable and an instance variable?
3. What is an overriding method?
4. Describe a situation where dynamic binding is a great advantage over its absence.
5. What is a virtual method?
6. Describe briefly the seven design issues used in this chapter for object-oriented languages.
7. What is the message protocol of a method?

8. Why is it that classes of Smalltalk can respond to messages?

9. Explain how Smalltalk messages are bound to methods. When does this take place?

10. What type checking is done in Smalltalk? When does it take place?

11. What kind of inheritance does Smalltalk support?

12. What are the two primary effects that Smalltalk has had on computing?

13. In essence, all Smalltalk variables are of a single type. What is that type?

14. From where can C++ objects be allocated?

15. How are C++ heap-allocated objects deallocated?

16. Are all C++ subclasses subtypes?

17. Under what circumstances is a C++ method call statically bound to a method?

18. What drawback is there to allowing designers to specify which methods can be statically bound?

19. Explain the difference between the two uses of **private** in C++.

20. What is a **friend** function in C++?

21. How is the type system of Java different from that of C++?

22. From where can Java objects be allocated?

23. How are Java objects deallocated?

24. Are all Java subclasses subtypes?

25. Under what circumstances is a Java method call statically bound to a method?

26. In what way do overriding methods in C# syntactically differ from their counterparts in C++?

27. How can the parent version of an inherited method that is overridden in a subclass be called in that subclass in C#?

28. Are all Ada 95 subclasses subtypes?

29. How is a call to a subprogram in Ada 95 specified to be dynamically bound to a subprogram definition? When is this decision made?

30. In what fundamental ways do JavaScript objects differ from Java objects?

31. What is the primary difference between a JavaScript constructor and one in Java?

PROBLEM SET

1. Compare the dynamic binding of C++ and Java.

2. Compare the class entity access controls of C++ and Java.

3. Compare the class entity access controls of C++ and Ada 95.

4. Compare the multiple inheritance of C++ with that provided by interfaces in Java.

5. Compare the generic capabilities of GJ (generic Java) with those of C++.

6. What is one programming situation where multiple inheritance has a significant advantage over interfaces?

PROGRAMMING EXERCISES

1. Rewrite the `single_linked_list`, `stack_2`, and `queue_2` classses in Section 12.5.2 in Java and compare the result with the C++ version in terms of readability and ease of programming.

2. Repeat Exercise 1 using Ada 95.

13

Concurrency

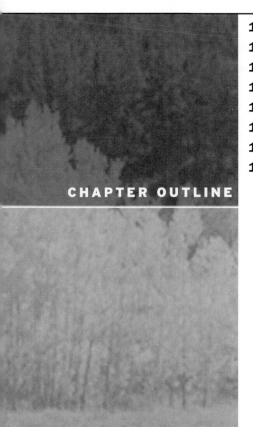

CHAPTER OUTLINE

This chapter begins with descriptions of the various kinds of concurrency at the subprogram, or unit level, and at the statement level. Included in this introduction is a brief description of some common kinds of multiprocessor computer architectures. Next, we present a lengthy discussion on unit-level concurrency. We begin by describing the fundamental concepts that must be understood before discussing unit-level concurrency, including competition and cooperation synchronization. Next, the design issues for providing language support for concurrency are described. Then we present a detailed discussion, including program examples, of the three major approaches to language support for concurrency: semaphores, monitors, and message passing. A pseudocode example program is used to demonstrate how semaphores can be used. An example program in Concurrent Pascal is used to illustrate the use of monitors; for message passing, an Ada program is used. The Ada features that support concurrency are described in some detail. These include tasks, protected objects, and asynchronous message passing. Support for unit-level concurrency in Java and C# is then discussed. The last section of the chapter has a discussion of statement-level concurrency, including a short description of part of the language support provided for it in High-Performance Fortran.

13.1   Introduction

Concurrency is naturally divided into instruction level (executing two or more machine instructions simultaneously), statement level (executing two or more statements simultaneously), unit level (executing two or more subprogram units simultaneously), and program level (executing two or more programs simultaneously). Because no language issues are involved with them, we do not discuss instruction-level and program-level concurrency in this chapter. Concurrency at both the subprogram and the statement levels are discussed, with most of the discussion focused on the subprogram level.

Concurrent execution of subprograms can occur either physically on separate processors or logically by sharing a single processor. At first glance, this may appear to be a simple concept, but it presents a significant challenge to the programming language designer.

Concurrent control methods increase programming flexibility. They were originally invented to be used for particular problems faced in operating systems, but they are required for a variety of other programming applications. For example, many software systems are designed to simulate actual physical systems, and many of these physical systems consist of multiple concurrent subsystems. For these applications, the traditional but more restricted form of subprogram control is inadequate.

Statement-level concurrency is quite different from concurrency at the unit level. From a language designer's point of view, statement-level concurrency is largely a matter of specifying how data should be distributed over multiple memories and which statements can be executed concurrently.

The intention of this chapter is to discuss the aspects of concurrency that are most relevant to language design issues rather than to present a definitive study of all of the issues of concurrency. That would clearly be inappropriate for a book on programming languages.

13.1.1 Multiprocessor Architectures

A large number of different computer architectures have more than one processor and can support some form of concurrent execution. Before beginning to discuss kinds of concurrent execution of programs and statements, we briefly describe some of these architectures.

The first computers that had multiple processors actually had one general-purpose processor and one or more other processors that were used only for input and output operations. This allowed these computers, which appeared in the late 1950s, to concurrently execute one program while performing input or output for other programs. Because this kind of concurrency does not require language support, we will not consider it further.

By the early 1960s, there were machines that had multiple complete processors. These processors were used by the job scheduler of the operating system, which distributed separate jobs from a batch-job queue to the separate processors. Systems with this structure supported program-level concurrency.

In the mid-1960s, multiprocessor computers appeared that had several identical partial processors that were fed certain instructions from a single instruction stream. For example, some machines had two or more floating-point multipliers, while others had two or more complete floating-point arithmetic units. The compilers for these machines were required to determine which instructions could be executed concurrently and to schedule these instructions accordingly. Systems with this structure supported instruction-level concurrency.

There are now many different kinds of multiprocessor computers, the most common two categories of which are described in the following two paragraphs.

Computers that have multiple processors that execute the same instruction simultaneously, each on different data, are called Single-Instruction Multiple-Data (SIMD) architecture computers. In an SIMD computer, each processor has its own local memory. One processor controls the operation of the other processors. Because all of the processors, except the controller, execute the same instruction at the same time, no synchronization is required in the software. Perhaps the most widely used SIMD machines are a category of machines called **vector processors**. They have groups of registers that store the operands of a vector operation in which the same instruction is executed on the whole group of operands simultaneously. The kinds of programs that can most benefit from this architecture are common in scientific computation, an area of computing that is often the target of multiprocessor machines.

Computers that have multiple processors that operate independently but whose operations can be synchronized are called Multiple-Instruction Multiple-Data (MIMD) computers. Each processor in an MIMD computer executes its own instruction stream. MIMD computers can appear in two distinct configurations: distributed and shared memory systems. The distributed MIMD machines, in which each processor has its own memory, can be either built in a single box or distributed, perhaps over a large area. The shared memory MIMD machines obviously must provide some means of synchronization to prevent memory access clashes. Even distributed MIMD machines require synchronization to operate together on single programs. MIMD computers, which are more expensive and more general than SIMD computers, clearly support unit-level concurrency.

13.1.2 Categories of Concurrency

There are two distinct categories of concurrent unit control. The most general category of concurrency is that in which, assuming that more than one processor is available, several program units from the same program literally execute simultaneously. This is **physical concurrency.** A slight relaxation of this concept of concurrency allows the programmer and the application software to assume that there are multiple processors providing actual concurrency when, in fact, the actual execution of programs is taking place in interleaved fashion on a single processor. This is **logical concurrency.** It is similar to the illusion of simultaneous execution that is provided to different users of a multiprogramming computer system. From the programmer's and language designer's points of view, logical concurrency is the same as physical concurrency. It is the language implementor's task to map the logical concurrency to the underlying hardware. Both logical and physical concurrency allow the concept of concurrency to be used as a program design methodology. For the remainder of this chapter, we will mean logical concurrency whenever we use the word *concurrency* without qualification.

One useful technique for visualizing the flow of execution through a program is to imagine a thread laid on the statements of the source text of the program. Every statement reached on a particular execution is covered by the thread representing that execution. Visually following the thread through the source program traces the execution flow through the executable version of the program. Of course, in all but the simplest of programs, the thread follows a highly complex path. A **thread of control** in a program is the sequence of program points reached as control flows through the program.

Programs that have coroutines (see Chapter 9), though they are sometimes called **quasi-concurrent,** have a single thread of control. Programs executed with physical concurrency can have multiple threads of control. Each processor can execute one of the threads. Although logically concurrent program execution may actually have only a single thread of control, such programs can only be designed and analyzed by imagining them as having multiple threads of control. When a multithreaded program executes on a single processor machine, its threads are mapped onto a single thread. It becomes, in this case, a virtually multithreaded program.

Statement-level concurrency is a relatively simple concept. Loops that include statements that operate on array elements are unwound so the processing can be distributed over multiple processors. For example, a loop that executes 500 repetitions and includes a statement that operates on one of 500 array elements may be unwound so that each of ten different processors can simultaneously process 50 of the array elements.

13.1.3 Motivations for Studying Concurrency

The primary reason to study concurrency is that it provides a method of conceptualizing program solutions to problems. Many problem domains lend themselves naturally to concurrency in much the same way that recursion is a natural way to design the solution to some problems. Many programs are written to simulate physical entities and activities. In many cases, the system being simulated includes more than one entity, and the entities do whatever they do simultaneously—for example, aircraft flying in a control area, relay stations in a communications network, and the various machines in a manufacturing facility. To simulate such systems accurately with software, software that can deal with concurrency is required.

The second reason to discuss concurrency is that multiple processor computers currently are being used, although that use is not widespread. This creates the need for software to make effective use of that hardware capability. Because of the importance of both statement-level and unit-level concurrency, facilities to provide them must be developed and included in contemporary programming languages.

13.2 Introduction to Subprogram-Level Concurrency

Before we can discuss language support for concurrency, we must introduce the underlying concepts of concurrency and the requirements for it to be useful. Then we can discuss the language design issues for languages that support concurrency.

13.2.1 Fundamental Concepts

A **task** is a unit of a program, similar to a subprogram, that can be in concurrent execution with other units of the same program. Each task in a program can provide one thread of control. Tasks are sometimes called **processes**.

There are three characteristics of tasks that distinguish them from subprograms. First, a task may be implicitly started, whereas a subprogram must be explicitly called. Second, when a program unit invokes a task, it need not wait for the task to complete its execution before continuing its own. Lastly, when the execution of a task is completed, control may or may not return to the unit that started that execution.

Tasks fall into two general categories, heavyweight and lightweight. Simply stated, **heavyweight tasks** execute in their own address space and have their own run-time stacks. **Lightweight tasks** all run in the same address space and use the same run-time stack.

A task can communicate with other tasks through shared nonlocal variables, through message passing, or through parameters. If a task does not communicate with or affect the execution of any other task in the program in any way, it is said to be **disjoint.** Because tasks often work together to create simulations or solve problems and therefore are not disjoint, they must use some form of communication to either synchronize their executions or share data or both.

Synchronization is a mechanism that controls the order in which tasks execute. Two kinds of synchronization are required when tasks share data: cooperation and competition. **Cooperation synchronization** is required between task A and task B when task A must wait for task B to complete some specific activity before task A can continue its execution. **Competition synchronization** is required between two tasks when both require the use of some resource that cannot be simultaneously used. Specifically, if task A needs to access shared data location x while task B is accessing x, task A must wait for task B to complete its processing of x, regardless of what that processing is. So, for cooperation synchronization, tasks may need to wait for the completion of specific processing upon which their correct operation depends, whereas for competition synchronization, tasks may need to wait for the completion of any other processing by any task currently occurring on specific shared data.

A simple form of cooperation synchronization can be illustrated by a common problem called the **producer-consumer problem**. This problem originated in the development of operating systems, in which one program unit produces some data value or resource and another uses it. Produced data are usually placed in a storage buffer by the producing unit and removed from that buffer by the consuming unit. The sequence of stores to and removals from the buffer must be synchronized. The consumer unit must not be allowed to take data from the buffer if the buffer is empty. Likewise, the producer unit cannot be allowed to place new data in the buffer if the buffer is full. This is called the **problem of cooperation synchronization** because the users of the shared data structure must cooperate if the buffer is to be used correctly.

Competition synchronization prevents two tasks from accessing a shared data structure at exactly the same time—a situation that could destroy the integrity of that shared data. To provide competition synchronization, mutually exclusive access to the shared data must be guaranteed.

To clarify the competition problem, consider the following scenario: Suppose task A must add 1 to the shared integer variable TOTAL, which has an initial value of 3. Furthermore, suppose task B must multiply the value of TOTAL by 2. Each task accomplishes its operation on TOTAL by fetching the value of TOTAL, performing an arithmetic operation, and putting the new value back in TOTAL. Without competition synchronization, three different values could result from these operations. If task A completes its operation before task B begins, the value will be 8, which is assumed here to be correct. But if both A and B fetch the value of TOTAL before either task puts its new value back, the result will be incorrect. If A puts its value back first, the value of TOTAL will be 6. This case is shown in Figure 13.1. If B puts its value back first, the value of TOTAL will be 4. A situation that leads to these problems is sometimes called a **race condition**, because two or more tasks are racing to use the shared resource and the behavior of the program depends on which task arrives first. The importance of competition synchronization should now be clear.

One general method for providing mutually exclusive access to a shared resource is to consider the resource to be something that a task can possess and then allow only a single task to possess it at a time. To gain possession of a shared resource, a task must request it. When a task is finished with a shared resource that it possesses, it must relinquish that resource so that the resource can be made available to other tasks.

Three methods of providing for mutually exclusive access to a shared resource are semaphores, which are discussed in Section 13.3; monitors, which are discussed in Section 13.4; and message passing, which is discussed in Section 13.5.

Mechanisms for synchronization must be able to delay task execution. Synchronization imposes an order of execution on tasks that is enforced with these delays. To understand what happens to tasks through their lifetimes, we must consider how task execution is controlled. Regardless of whether a machine has a single processor or more than one, there is always the possibility of there being more tasks than there are processors. A program called a **scheduler** manages the sharing of processors among the tasks. If there were never any interruptions and tasks all had the same priority, the scheduler could

Figure 13.1

The need for competition synchronization

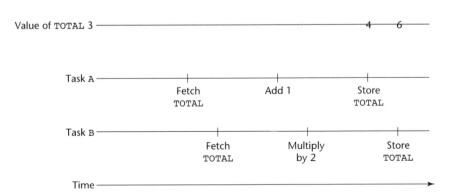

simply give each task a time slice, such as 0.1 seconds, and when a task's turn came, the scheduler could let it execute on a processor for that amount of time. Of course, there are several events that complicate this, for example, delays for synchronization and waits for input or output operations.

Tasks can be in several different states, which are

1. New: A task is in the new state when it has been created but has not yet begun its execution.

2. Runnable or ready: A runnable task is ready to run but is not currently running. It either has not been given processor time by the scheduler, or it had run previously but was blocked in one of the ways described in paragraph 4. Tasks that are runnable are stored in a queue that is often called the **task ready queue.**

3. Running: A running task is one that is currently executing; that is, it has a processor and its code is being executed.

4. Blocked: A task that is blocked has been running, but that execution was interrupted by one of several different events, the most common of which is an input or output operation. Because input and output operations are much slower than program execution, a task that starts an input or output operation is blocked from using the processor while it waits until the input or output operation is completed. In addition to these kinds of blocking, some languages provide operations for the user program to specify that a task be blocked.

5. Dead: A dead task is no longer active in any sense. A task dies when its execution is completed or it is explicitly killed by the program.

One important issue in task execution is the following: How is a ready task chosen to move to the running state when the task currently running has become blocked or whose time slice has expired? Several different algorithms have been used for this choice, some based on specifiable priority levels. The algorithm that does the choosing is implemented in the scheduler.

Associated with the concurrent execution of tasks and the use of shared resources is the concept of liveness. In the environment of sequential programs, a program has the characteristic of **liveness** if it continues to execute, eventually leading to completion. In more general terms, liveness means that if some event—say, program completion—is supposed to occur, it will occur, eventually. That is, progress is continually made. In the environment of concurrency and the use of shared resources, the liveness of a task can cease to exist, meaning that the program cannot continue and thus will never terminate.

For example, suppose task A and task B both need the shared resources X and Y to complete their work. Further suppose that task A gains possession of X and task B gains possession of Y. After some execution, task A needs resource Y to continue, so it requests Y but must wait until B releases it. Likewise, task B requests X but must wait until A releases it. Neither relinquishes the resource it possesses, and as a result, both lose their liveness, guaranteeing that execution of the program will never complete normally. This particular kind of loss of liveness is called **deadlock.** Deadlock is a serious threat to the reliability of a program, and therefore its avoidance demands serious consideration in both language and program design.

We are now ready to discuss some of the linguistic mechanisms for providing concurrent unit control.

13.2.2 Language Design for Concurrency

A number of languages have been designed to support concurrency, beginning with PL/I in the middle 1960s and including the contemporary languages, Ada 95, Java, and C#.

13.2.3 Design Issues

The most important design issues for language support for concurrency have already been discussed at length: competition and cooperation synchronization. In addition to these, there are several design issues of secondary importance. Prominent among them is how to control task scheduling. Also, there are the issues of how and when tasks start and end executions, and how and when they are created.

Keep in mind that our discussion of concurrency is intentionally incomplete, and only the most important of the language design issues related to support for concurrency are discussed.

The following sections discuss three alternative answers to the design issues for concurrency: semaphores, monitors, and message passing.

13.3   Semaphores

A semaphore is a very simple mechanism that can be used to provide synchronization of tasks. In the following paragraphs we describe semaphores and discuss how they can be used for this purpose.

13.3.1 Introduction

In an effort to provide competition synchronization through mutually exclusive access to shared data structures, Edsger Dijkstra devised semaphores in 1965 (Dijkstra, 1968b). Semaphores can also be used to provide cooperation synchronization.

A **semaphore** is a data structure consisting of an integer and a queue that stores task descriptors. A **task descriptor** is a data structure that stores all of the relevant information about the execution state of a task. The concept of a semaphore is that, to provide limited access to a data structure, guards are placed around the code that accesses the structure. A **guard** is a linguistic device that allows the guarded code to be executed only when a specified condition is true. A guard can be used to allow only one task to access a shared data structure at a time. A semaphore is an implementation of a guard. An integral part of a guard mechanism is a technique for ensuring that all attempted executions of the guarded code eventually take place. This is accomplished by having requests for access that occur when access cannot be granted be stored in the task descriptor queue, from which they are later allowed to leave and execute the guarded code. This is the reason a semaphore must have both a counter and a task descriptor queue.

The only two operations provided for semaphores were originally named P and V by Dijkstra, after the two Dutch words *passeren* (to pass) and *vrygeren* (to release) (Andrews and Schneider, 1983). We will refer to these as *wait* and *release* in the following discussion.

13.3.2　Cooperation Synchronization

Through much of this chapter, we use the example of a shared buffer to illustrate the different approaches to providing cooperation and competition synchronization. For cooperation synchronization, such a buffer must have some way of recording both the number of empty positions and the number of filled positions in the buffer (to prevent buffer underflow and overflow). The counter component of a semaphore variable can be used for this purpose. One semaphore variable, say `emptyspots`, can be used to store the number of empty locations in a shared buffer, and another, say `fullspots`, can be used to store the number of filled locations in the buffer. The task queues of these two semaphores store tasks that have been blocked by the delay operation of the semaphore.

Our example buffer is designed as an abstract data type in which all data enters the buffer through the subprogram `DEPOSIT`, and all data leaves the buffer through the subprogram `FETCH`. Then the `DEPOSIT` subprogram only needs to check with the `emptyspots` semaphore to see if there are any empty positions. If there is at least one, it can go ahead with the `DEPOSIT`, which must include decrementing the counter of `emptyspots`. If the buffer is full, the caller to `DEPOSIT` must be made to wait in the `emptyspots` queue for an empty spot to become available. When the `DEPOSIT` is complete, the `DEPOSIT` subprogram increments the counter of the `fullspots` semaphore to indicate there is one more filled location in the buffer.

The `FETCH` subprogram has the opposite sequence of `DEPOSIT`. It checks the `fullspots` semaphore to see if the buffer contains at least one item. If it does, an item is removed and the `emptyspots` semaphore has its counter incremented by 1. If the buffer is empty, the calling process is put in the `fullspots` queue to wait until an item appears. When `FETCH` is finished, it must increment the counter of `emptyspots`.

The operations on semaphore types often are not direct—they are done through the wait and release subprograms. Therefore, the DEPOSIT operation just described is actually accomplished in part by calls to wait and release. Note that wait and release must be able to access the task-ready queue.

The wait subprogram is used to test the counter of a given semaphore variable. If the value is greater than zero, the caller can carry out its operation. In this case, the counter value of the semaphore variable is decremented to indicate there are now one fewer of whatever it counts. If the value of the counter is zero, the caller must be placed on the waiting queue of the semaphore variable, and the processor must be given to some other ready task.

The release operation is used by a task to allow some other task to have one of whatever the counter of the specified semaphore variable counts. If the queue of the specified semaphore variable is empty, which means no task is waiting, release increments its counter (to indicate there is one more of whatever is being controlled that is now available). If one or more tasks are waiting, release moves one of them from the semaphore queue to the ready queue.

The following are concise descriptions of wait and release:

wait(aSemaphore)
if aSemaphore's counter > 0 **then**
    decrement aSemaphore's counter
else
    put the caller in aSemaphore's queue
    attempt to transfer control to some ready task
      (if the task ready queue is empty, deadlock occurs)
end

release(aSemaphore)
if aSemaphore's queue is empty (no task is waiting) **then**
    increment aSemaphore's counter
else
    put the calling task in the task-ready queue
    transfer control to a task from aSemaphore's queue
end

We can now present an example program that implements cooperation synchronization for a shared buffer. In this case, the shared buffer stores integer values and is structured as a logically circular structure. It is designed for use by possibly multiple producer and consumer tasks.

The following code shows the definition of such producer and consumer tasks. Two semaphores are used to ensure against buffer underflow or overflow, thus providing cooperation synchronization. Assume that the buffer has length BUFLEN, and the routines that actually manipulate it already exist as FETCH and DEPOSIT. Accesses to the counter of a semaphore are specified by dot notation. For example, if `fullspots` is a semaphore, its counter is referenced by `fullspots.count`.

```
semaphore fullspots, emptyspots;
fullspots.count := 0;
emptyspots.count := BUFLEN;
task producer;
  loop
  -- produce VALUE --
  wait(emptyspots);     { wait for a space }
  DEPOSIT(VALUE);
  release(fullspots);   { increase filled spaces }
  end loop;
end producer;

task consumer;
  loop
  wait(fullspots);      { make sure it is not empty }
  FETCH(VALUE);
  release(emptyspots); { increase empty spaces }
  -- consume VALUE --
  end loop
end consumer;
```

The semaphore `fullspots` causes the `consumer` task to be queued to wait for a buffer entry if it is currently empty. The semaphore `emptyspots` causes the `producer` task to be queued to wait for an empty space in the buffer if it is currently full.

13.3.3 Competition Synchronization

Our buffer example does not provide competition synchronization. Access to the structure can be controlled with an additional semaphore. This semaphore need not count anything, but simply indicate with its counter whether the buffer is currently being used. The `wait` statement allows the access only if the semaphore's counter has the value 1, which indicates that shared buffer is not currently being accessed. If the semaphore's counter has a value of 0, there is a current access taking place, and the task is placed on the queue of the semaphore. Notice that the semaphore's counter must be initialized to 1. The queues of semaphores must always be initialized to empty.

A semaphore that only requires a binary-valued counter, like the one we use to provide competition synchronization, is called a **binary semaphore.**

The example code that follows illustrates the use of semaphores to provide both competition and cooperation synchronization for a concurrently accessed shared buffer.

The access semaphore is used to ensure mutually exclusive access to the buffer. Note again that there may be more than one producer and more than one consumer.

```
semaphore access, fullspots, emptyspots;
access.count := 1;
fullspots.count := 0;
emptyspots.count := BUFLEN;


task producer;
  loop
  -- produce VALUE --
  wait(emptyspots);      { wait for a space }
  wait(access);          { wait for access }
  DEPOSIT(VALUE);
  release(access);       { relinquish access }
  release(fullspots);    { increase filled spaces }
  end loop;
end producer;

task consumer;
  loop
  wait(fullspots);       { make sure it is not empty }
  wait(access);          { wait for access }
  FETCH(VALUE);
  release(access);       { relinquish access }
  release(emptyspots);   { increase empty spaces }
  -- consume VALUE --
  end loop
end consumer;
```

A brief look at this example may lead one to believe there is a problem with it. Specifically, suppose that while a task is waiting at the wait(access) call in consumer another task takes the last value from the shared buffer. Fortunately, this cannot happen, because the wait(fullspots) reserves a value in the buffer for the task that calls it by decrementing the fullspots counter.

There is one crucial aspect of semaphores that thus far has not been discussed. Recall the earlier description of the problem of competition synchronization: Operations on shared data must not be overlapped. If a second operation can be begun while an earlier operation is still in progress, the shared data can become corrupted. A semaphore is itself a shared data object, so the operations on semaphores are also susceptible to the same problem. It is therefore essential that semaphore operations be uninterruptible. Many

HISTORY NOTE

PL/I was the first programming language to include concurrent tasks. It allowed user programs to execute any subprogram concurrently with the unit that called it. The mechanism for synchronization of these concurrent executions was, however, wholly inadequate. It consisted of only binary semaphores, which were called *events*, and the ability to detect when a task had completed its execution.

ALGOL 68, which allowed compound statement-level concurrency, included a semaphore data type named **sema**.

computers have uninterruptible instructions that were designed specifically for semaphore operations. If such instructions are not available, then using semaphores to provide competition synchronization is a serious problem with no simple solution.

13.3.4 Evaluation

Using semaphores to provide cooperation synchronization creates an unsafe programming environment. There is no way to statically check for the correctness of their use, which depends on the semantics of the program in which they appear. In the buffer example, leaving the `wait(emptyspots)` statement out of the `producer` task would result in buffer overflow. Leaving the `wait(fullspots)` statement out of the `consumer` task would result in buffer underflow. Leaving out either of the releases would result in deadlock. These are cooperation synchronization failures.

The reliability problems that semaphores cause in providing cooperation synchronization also arise when using them for competition synchronization. Leaving out the `wait(access)` statement in either task can cause insecure access to the buffer. Leaving out the `release(access)` statement in either task results in deadlock. These are competition synchronization failures. Noting the danger in using semaphores, Per Brinch Hansen wrote "The semaphore is an elegant synchronization tool for an ideal programmer who never makes mistakes" (Brinch Hansen, 1973). Unfortunately, programmers of that kind are rare.

13.4 Monitors

One solution to some of the problems of semaphores in a concurrent environment is to encapsulate shared data structures with their operations and hide their representations—that is, make shared data structures abstract data types. This solution can provide competition synchronization without semaphores by transferring responsibility for synchronization to the run-time system.

13.4.1 Introduction

When the concepts of data abstraction were being formulated, the people involved in that effort applied the same concepts to shared data in concurrent programming environments to produce monitors. According to Per Brinch Hansen (Brinch Hansen, 1977, p. xvi), Edsger Dijkstra suggested in 1971 that all synchronization operations on shared data be gathered into a single program unit. Brinch Hansen formalized this concept in the environment of operating systems (Brinch Hansen, 1973). The following year, Hoare named these structures *monitors* (Hoare, 1974).

The first programming language to incorporate monitors was Concurrent Pascal (Brinch Hansen, 1975). Modula (Wirth, 1977), CSP/k (Holt et al., 1978), and Mesa (Mitchell et al., 1979) also provide monitors. The following discussion of monitors is based on their incarnation in Concurrent Pascal.

Concurrent Pascal is Wirth's Pascal with three important kinds of constructs added: classes from SIMULA 67, processes (the Concurrent Pascal name for tasks), and monitors. Our concern here is with the features that support concurrent programming: processes and monitors.

A Concurrent Pascal process has a syntactic form similar to that of a procedure, but the semantics is quite different. All processes are types, so they are defined in **type** statements of the form

```
type process_name = process (formal parameters)
         -- local declarations --
         -- process body --
end
```

Because they are types, process definitions are merely templates for actual processes. Because variable declarations are used to create processes, processes can be created either statically or dynamically. Declaring a variable to be of a process type creates the code for the process but does nothing else. To cause the allocation of its local data and to begin its execution, an **init** statement with actual parameters must be used, such as

```
init process_variable_name (actual parameters)
```

After execution of the **init**, the process remains in the running state for the duration of the program, except when it is blocked.

The general form of Concurrent Pascal monitors is

```
type monitor_name = monitor (formal parameters)
         ---- declarations of shared variables ----
         ---- definitions of local procedures ----
         ---- definitions of exported procedures ----
         ---- initialization code ----
end
```

The exported procedures of a monitor are syntactically different from local procedures only in that they contain the reserved word **entry** in their **procedure** statements.

The **init** statement, with actual parameters, is used to create instances of monitors. This causes dynamic allocation of storage for the variables of the process and execution of the initialization code. The lifetime of monitor variables, except those in monitor procedures, begins with the **init** and terminates with the program. Their scope is restricted to the monitor itself. The exported procedures of a monitor can be called by either processes or procedures in other monitors.

13.4.2 Competition Synchronization

One of the most important features of monitors is that shared data is resident in the monitor rather than in any of the client units. Thus the programmer does not synchronize mutually exclusive access to shared data through the use of semaphores or other mechanisms. Because all accesses are resident in the monitor, the monitor implementation can be made to guarantee synchronized access by simply allowing only one access at a time. Calls to monitor procedures are implicitly queued if the monitor is busy at the time of the call.

13.4.3 Cooperation Synchronization

Although mutually exclusive access to shared data is intrinsic with a monitor, cooperation between processes is still the task of the programmer. In particular, the programmer must guarantee that a shared buffer does not experience underflow or overflow. For this purpose, Concurrent Pascal has a special data type, **queue**, and two operations on it, `delay` and `continue`. The **queue** type is a form of semaphore, and the two operations are related to the send and release semaphore operations. A variable of **queue** type stores processes that are waiting to use a shared data structure.

The `delay` operation takes a **queue** type variable as a parameter. Its action is to place the process that calls it in the specified queue and remove its exclusive access rights to monitor data structures. Thus the process that executes `delay` has its execution suspended. The monitor is then available to other processes. So `delay` differs from the wait semaphore operation because `delay` always blocks the caller.

The `continue` operation also takes a **queue** type parameter. Its action is to disconnect the process that calls it from the monitor, thus freeing the monitor to access by other processes; `continue` then examines the specified queue. If the queue contains a process, that process is removed and its execution, which had been suspended by a `delay` operation, is restarted. The `continue` operation differs from the release operation for semaphores because release always has some effect, whereas `continue` does nothing if the queue is empty.

A program containing four processes and a monitor that provides synchronized access to a concurrently shared buffer is shown in Figure 13.2.

Using the **queue** data type and the `delay` and `continue` operations, a monitor can be constructed that controls a shared buffer, thus providing both competition and cooperation synchronization. In the following example, a shared buffer is implemented as a logically circular list of 100 integers.

```
type databuf =
  monitor
    const bufsize = 100;
    var buf : array [1..bufsize] of integer;
        next_in,
        next_out    : 1..bufsize;
```

Figure 13.2

A program using a
monitor to control
access to a shared
buffer

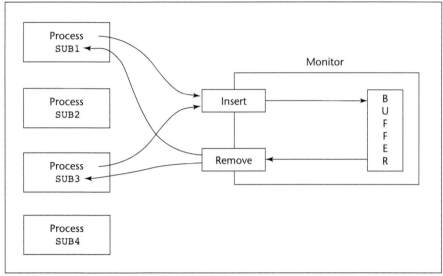

```
            filled        : 0..bufsize;
            sender_q,
            receiver_q : queue;

procedure entry deposit(item : integer);
  begin
  if filled = bufsize
    then delay(sender_q);
  buf[next_in] := item;
  next_in := (next_in mod bufsize) + 1;
  filled := filled + 1;
  continue(receiver_q)
  end;

procedure entry fetch(var item : integer);
  begin
  if filled = 0
    then delay(receiver_q);
  item := buf[next_out];
  next_out := (next_out mod bufsize) + 1;
  filled := filled - 1;
  continue(sender_q)
  end;

begin
filled := 0;
next_in := 1;
next_out := 1
end;
```

An instance of type `databuf` is an abstraction of a particular kind of buffer for storing integers. Besides storing integers, a `databuf` type buffer coordinates the activities of adding and removing its values by concurrent processes. The integrity of this buffer is guaranteed by the mechanisms used to construct it. It is protected against underflow and overflow, and concurrent processes using it cannot destructively interfere with each other.

An example of declarations for the processes that can use the `databuf` monitor is as follows:

```
type producer = process(buffer : databuf);
  var newvalue : integer;
  begin
  cycle
    -- produce newvalue --
    buffer.deposit(newvalue);
  end
  end;

type consumer = process(buffer : databuf);
  var stored_value : integer;
  begin
  cycle
    buffer.fetch(stored_value);
    -- consume stored_value --
  end
  end;
```

The **type** declarations of the monitor `databuf` and the two processes `producer` and `consumer` can be included in the declaration section of a program in which they are to be used, as in

```
-- type declarations --

var new_producer : producer;
    new_consumer : consumer;
    new_buffer   : databuf;
begin
init new_buffer, new_producer(new_buffer),
    new_consumer(new_buffer);
end;
```

This may appear a bit odd to the reader not familiar with concurrent programs, because it is not obvious how the program either begins or terminates. Our example program begins when the **init** is executed, creating a buffer and two processes, at which time the processes begin execution. Note that the **cycle .. end** in both the consumer and producer are infinite loops. They never end.

13.4.4 Evaluation

Monitors are a better way to provide competition synchronization than sema-phores, primarily because of the problems of semaphores, as discussed in Section 13.3. The use of **queue** type variables to provide cooperation syn-chronization through delay and continue is, however, subject to the same problems as semaphores used in other languages for this purpose.

13.5 Message Passing

The monitor construct is a dependable and safe method for providing com-petition synchronization for shared data access in concurrent units that share a single memory. However, consider the problem of synchronizing the units in a distributed system, in which each processor has its own memory, rather than a single shared memory. Obviously, the monitor construct does not model this situation very naturally. However, synchronization in a distributed system can be achieved quite naturally with message passing.

13.5.1 Introduction

The first efforts to design languages that provide the capability for message passing among concurrent tasks were those of Brinch Hansen (1978) and Hoare (1978). The pioneer developers of message passing also developed a technique for handling the problem of what to do when multiple simultane-ous requests were made by other tasks to communicate with a given task. It was decided that some form of nondeterminism was required to provide fair-ness in choosing which among those requests would be taken first. This fairness can be defined in various ways, but in general it means that all requesters are provided an equal chance of communicating with a given task (assuming every requester has the same priority). Nondeterministic constructs for statement-level control, called *guarded commands*, were introduced by Dijkstra (1975). (Guarded commands are discussed in Chapter 8.) Guarded commands are the basis of the construct designed for controlling message passing.

13.5.2 The Concept of Synchronous Message Passing

Message passing can be either synchronous or asynchronous. The asyn-chronous message passing of Ada 95 is described in Section 13.5.9. Here we describe synchronous message passing. The basic concept of synchronous message passing is that tasks are often busy and, when busy, are unwilling to be interrupted by other units. Suppose task A and task B are both in execu-tion, and A wishes to send a message to B. Clearly, if B is busy, it is not desir-able to allow another task to interrupt it. That would disrupt B's current processing. Furthermore, messages usually cause associated processing in the receiver, which may not be sensible if other processing is incomplete. The alternative is to provide a linguistic mechanism that allows a task to specify to other tasks when it is ready to receive messages. This is somewhat like an executive who instructs his or her secretary to hold all incoming calls until another activity, perhaps an important meeting, is completed. Later, the executive tells the secretary he or she is now willing to receive one of the callers who has been placed on hold.

A task can be designed so it can suspend its execution at some point, either because it is idle or because it needs information from another unit before it can continue. This is like a person who is waiting for an important call. In some cases, there is nothing else to do but sit and wait. In this situation, if task A wants to send a message to B, and B is willing to receive a message, the message can be transmitted. This actual transmission is called a **rendezvous.** Note that a rendezvous can occur only if both the sender and receiver want it to happen. The information of the message can be transmitted in either or both directions.

Both cooperation and competition synchronization of tasks can be conveniently handled with the message-passing model, as described in the following subsections.

13.5.3   The Ada Synchronous Message-Passing Model

The Ada design for tasks is partially based on the work of Brinch Hansen and Hoare in that message passing is the design basis and nondeterminism is used to choose among competing message-sending tasks.

The full Ada tasking model is complex, and the following discussion of it must be limited. The focus here will be on the Ada version of the synchronous message-passing mechanism.

Ada tasks can be more active than monitors. Monitors are passive entities that provide management services for the shared data they store. They provide their services, however, only when those services are requested. When used to manage shared data, Ada tasks can be thought of as managers that can reside with the resource they manage. They have several mechanisms, some deterministic and some nondeterministic, that allow them to choose among competing requests for access to their resources.

The form of Ada tasks is similar to that of Ada packages. There are two parts, a specification part and a body part, both with the same name. The interface of a task is its entry points, or locations where it can accept messages from other tasks. It is natural that these be listed in the specification part of a task. Because a rendezvous can involve an exchange of information, messages can have parameters; therefore, task entry points must also allow parameters, which must also be described in the specification part. In appearance, a task specification is very similar to the package specification for an abstract data type.

As an example of an Ada task specification, consider the following, which includes a single entry point named `Entry_1`, which has an in-mode parameter:

```
task Task_Example is
  entry Entry_1(Item : in Integer);
end Task_Example;
```

A task body must include some syntactic form of entry points that correspond to the **entry** clauses in that task's specification part. In Ada, these are specified by **accept** clauses, which are introduced by the **accept** reserved word. An **accept clause** is defined as the range of statements beginning with the **accept** reserved word and ending with the matching **end** reserved word. **accept** clauses are themselves relatively simple, but other constructs in which they can be embedded can make their semantics quite complex. A simple **accept** clause has the form

```
accept entry_name (formal parameters) do
  . . .
end entry_name;
```

The **accept** name matches the name in an **entry** clause in the associated task specification part. The optional parameters provide the means of communicating data between the caller and the called task. The statements between the **do** and the **end** define the operations that take place during the rendezvous. These statements are together called the **accept clause body.** During the actual rendezvous, the sender task is suspended.

Ada tasks communicate with other tasks using the rendezvous mechanism. Whenever a task entry point, or **accept** clause, receives a message that it is not ready to accept, for whatever reason, the sender task must be suspended until the entry point in the receiver task is ready to accept the message. Of course, the entry point must also remember the sender tasks that have sent messages that were not accepted. For this purpose, each **entry** clause in a task has a queue associated with it. The queue records a list of other tasks that have attempted to communicate with the associated entry point.

The following is the skeletal body of the task whose specification was given above:

```
task body Task_Example is
  begin
  loop
    accept Entry_1(Item : in Integer) do
      . . .
    end Entry_1;
  end loop;
  end Task_Example;
```

The **accept** clause of this task body is the implementation of the **entry** named Entry_1 in the task specification. If the execution of Task_Example begins and reaches the Entry_1 **accept** clause before any other task sends a message to Entry_1, Task_Example is suspended. If another task sends a message to Entry_1 while Task_Example is suspended at its **accept**, a rendezvous occurs and the **accept** clause body is executed. Then, because of the loop, execution proceeds to the **accept** again. If no additional calling task has sent a message to Entry_1, execution is again suspended to wait for the next message.

A rendezvous can occur in two basic ways in this simple example. First, the receiver task, Task_Example, can be waiting for another task to send a message to the Entry_1 entry. When the message is sent, the rendezvous occurs. This is the situation described above. Second, the receiver task can be busy with one rendezvous, or with some other processing not associated with a rendezvous, when another task attempts to send a message to the same entry. In that case, the sender is suspended until the receiver is free to accept that message in a rendezvous. If several messages arrive while the receiver is busy, the senders are queued to wait their turn for a rendezvous.

The two rendezvous just described are illustrated with the time line diagrams in Figure 13.3.

Tasks need not have entry points. Such tasks are called **actor tasks** because they do not wait for a rendezvous in order to do their work. Actor tasks can rendezvous with other tasks by sending them messages. In contrast to actor tasks, a task can have entry points but little or no code other than that associated with accepting messages, so it can only react to other tasks. Such a task is called a **server task.**

An Ada task that sends a message to another task must know the entry name in that task. However, the opposite is not true: A task entry need not know the name of the task from which it will accept messages. This asymmetry is in contrast to the design of the language known as CSP (Communicating Sequential Processes) (Hoare, 1978). In CSP, which also uses the message-passing model of concurrency, tasks accept messages only from explicitly named tasks. The disadvantage of this is that libraries of tasks cannot be built for general use.

The usual graphical method of describing a rendezvous in which task A sends a message to task B is shown in Figure 13.4.

Ada tasks are types, and as such they can be either anonymous or named. An Ada task with a named type can be dynamically created using the **new** operator and referenced through a pointer. For example, consider the following:

```
task type Buffer is
  entry Deposit(Value : in Integer);
  entry Fetch(Value : out Integer);
end;
```

Figure 13.3

Two ways a rendezvous with TASK_EXAMPLE can occur

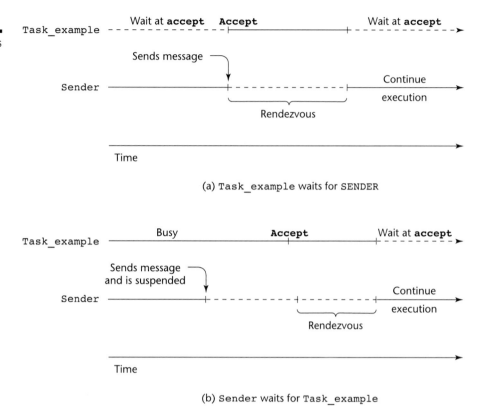

(a) Task_example waits for SENDER

(b) Sender waits for Task_example

Figure 13.4

Graphical representation of a rendezvous caused by a message sent from task **A** to task **B**

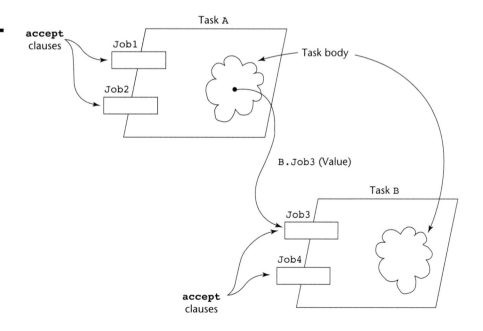

```
type Buf_Ptr is access Buffer;
...
Buf : Buf_Ptr;
Buf := new Buffer;
```

Tasks are declared in the declaration part of a package, subprogram, or block. Statically created tasks begin executing at the same time as the statements in the code to which that declarative part is attached. For example, a task declared in a main program begins execution at the same time as the first statement in the code body of the main program. Tasks created with **new** begin executing immediately. Task termination, which is a complex issue, is discussed later in this section.

Tasks may have any number of entries. The order in which the associated **accept** clauses appear in the task dictates the order in which messages can be accepted. If a task has more than one entry point and requires them to be able to receive messages in any order, the task uses a **select** statement to enclose the entries, as in the following:

```
task body Task_Example is
  loop
    select
      accept Entry_1(formal parameters) do
        ...
      end Entry_1;
      ...
    or
      accept Entry_2(formal parameters) do
        ...
      end Entry_2;
      ...
    end select;
  end loop;
end Task_Example;
```

In this task, there are two **accept** clauses, each of which has an associated queue. The action of the **select**, when it is executed, is to examine the queues associated with the two **accept** clauses. If one of the queues is empty but the other contains at least one waiting message, the **accept** clause associated with the waiting message has a rendezvous with the task that sent the first message that was received. If both **accept** clauses have empty queues, the **select** waits until one of the entries is called. If both **accept** clauses have nonempty queues, one of the **accept** clauses is nondeterministically chosen to have a rendezvous with one of its callers. The loop forces the **select** statement to be executed repeatedly, forever.

The **end** of the **accept** clause marks the end of the code that assigns or references the formal parameters of the **accept** clause. The code, if there is any, between an **accept** clause and the next **or** (or the **end select**, if the **accept** clause is the last one) is called the **extended accept clause**. The extended **accept** clause is executed only after the associated (immediately preceding) **accept** clause is executed. This execution of the extended **accept** clause is not part of the rendezvous and can take place in parallel with the calling task. The sender is suspended during the rendezvous, but it is restarted (put back in the ready queue) when the end of the **accept** clause is reached. If an **accept** clause has no formal parameters, the **do-end** is not required, and the **accept** clause can consist entirely of an extended **accept** clause. Such an **accept** clause would be used exclusively for synchronization.

13.5.4 Cooperation Synchronization

Each **accept** clause can have a guard attached, in the form of a **when** clause, that can delay rendezvous. For example,

```
when not Full(Buffer) =>
  accept Deposit(New_Value) do
```

An **accept** clause with a **when** clause can be either open or closed. If the Boolean expression of the **when** clause is currently true, that **accept** clause is called **open**; if the Boolean expression is false, the **accept** clause is called **closed**. An **accept** clause that does not have a guard is always open. An open **accept** clause is available for rendezvous; a closed **accept** clause cannot rendezvous.

Suppose there are several guarded **accept** clauses in a **select** clause. Such a **select** clause is usually placed in an infinite loop. The loop causes the **select** clause to be executed repeatedly, with each **when** clause evaluated on each repetition. Each repetition causes a list of open **accept** clauses to be constructed. If exactly one of the open clauses has a nonempty queue, a message from that queue is taken and a rendezvous takes place. If more than one of the open **accept** clauses have nonempty queues, one queue is chosen nondeterministically, a message is taken from that queue, and a rendezvous takes place. If the queues of all open clauses are empty, the task waits for a message to arrive at one of those **accept** clauses, at which time a rendezvous will occur. If a **select** is executed and every **accept** clause is closed, a run-time exception, or error, results. This possibility can be avoided either by making sure one of the **when** clauses is always true or by adding an **else** clause in the **select**. An **else** clause can include any sequence of statements, except an **accept** clause.

A **select** clause may have a special statement, **terminate**, that is selected only when it is open and no other **accept** clause is open. A **terminate** clause, when selected, means that the task is finished with its job but is not yet terminated. Task termination is discussed later in this section.

13.5.5   Competition Synchronization

The features described so far provide for cooperation synchronization and communication among tasks. We next discuss how mutually exclusive access to shared data structures can be enforced.

If access to a data structure is to be controlled by a task, then mutually exclusive access can be achieved by declaring the data structure within a task. The semantics of task execution usually guarantees mutually exclusive access to the structure, because only one **accept** clause in the task can be active at a given time. The only exceptions to this occur when tasks are nested in procedures or other tasks. For example, if a task that defines a shared data structure has a nested task, that nested task can also access the shared structure, which could destroy the integrity of the data. Thus, tasks that are meant to control access to a shared data structure should not define tasks.

The following is an example of an Ada task to provide synchronized access to a buffer. It is very similar in effect to our monitor example.

```ada
task Buf_Task is
  entry Deposit(Item : in Integer);
  entry Fetch(Item : out Integer);
end Buf_Task;


task body Buf_Task is
  Bufsize : constant Integer := 100;
  Buf    : array (1..Bufsize) of Integer;
  Filled : Integer range 0..Bufsize := 0;
  Next_In,
  Next_Out : Integer range 1..Bufsize := 1;
  begin
  loop
    select
      when Filled < Bufsize =>
        accept Deposit(Item : in Integer) do
          Buf(Next_In) := Item;
        end Deposit;
        Next_In := (Next_In mod Bufsize) + 1;
        Filled := Filled + 1;
    or
      when Filled > 0 =>
        accept Fetch(Item : out Integer) do
          Item := Buf(Next_Out);
        end Fetch;
        Next_Out := (Next_Out mod Bufsize) + 1;
        Filled := Filled - 1;
    end select;
  end loop;
end Buf_Task;
```

In this example, both **accept** clauses are extended. These allow concurrent execution of Buf_Task with the calling tasks.

The tasks for the producer and consumer that could use Buf_Task have the following form:

```
task Producer;
task Consumer;
task body Producer is
  New_Value : Integer;
  begin
    loop
      -- produce New_Value --
      Buf_Task.Deposit(New_Value);
    end loop;
  end Producer;

task body Consumer is
  Stored_Value : Integer;
  begin
    loop
      Buf_Task.Fetch(Stored_Value);
      -- consume Stored_Value --
    end loop;
  end Consumer;
```

13.5.6 Task Termination

We now address the issue of task termination. We must first define task completion. The execution of a task is **completed** if control has reached the end of its code body. This may occur because an exception is raised for which there is no handler (Ada exception handling is described in Chapter 14). If a task has not created any other tasks, called *dependents*, it is terminated when its execution is completed. A task that has created dependent tasks is terminated when the execution of its code is completed and all of its dependents are terminated. A task may end its execution by waiting at an open **terminate** clause. In this case, the task is terminated only when its master (the block, subprogram, or task that created it) and all of the tasks that depend on that master have either completed or are waiting at an open **terminate** clause. In that case, all of these tasks are terminated simultaneously. A block or subprogram is not exited until all of its dependent tasks are terminated.

13.5.7 Priorities

Both named and anonymous types can be assigned priorities. This is done with a pragma, as in

```
pragma Priority(expression);
```

The value of the expression specifies the relative priority for the task or task type definition in which it appears. The possible range of priority values is implementation dependent. The highest priority possible can be specified with the Last attribute the priority type, which is defined in System (System is a predefined package). For example, the following specifies the highest priority in any implementation:

```ada
pragma Priority(System.Priority'Last);
```

13.5.8 Binary Semaphores

If access to a data structure is to be controlled and the data structure is not encapsulated in a task, another means must be used to provide mutually exclusive access. One way is to build a binary semaphore task to use with the task that references the data structure. Such a binary semaphore task could be defined as follows:

```ada
task Binary_Semaphore is
  entry Wait;
  entry Release;
end Binary_Semaphore;

task body Binary_Semaphore is
  begin
  loop
    accept Wait;
    accept Release;
  end loop;
  end Binary_Semaphore;
```

The purpose of this task is to guarantee that the Wait and Release operations occur in alternating fashion.

The Binary_Semaphore task illustrates the simplifications that are possible when Ada messages are passed only for synchronization, rather than to also pass data. Specifically, notice the simple form of **accept** clauses that do not need bodies.

Use of the Binary_Semaphore task to provide mutually exclusive access to a shared data structure would take place exactly as with the use of semaphores in the example program in Section 13.3. Of course, this use of semaphores suffers all of the potential problems discussed there.

Like semaphores, monitors can be simulated with the Ada tasking capability. Tasks provide implicit mutually exclusive access, exactly as do monitors. So the Ada tasking model supports both semaphores and monitors.

13.5.9 Protected Objects

As we have seen, access to shared data can be controlled by enclosing the data in a task and allowing access only through task entries, which implicitly provide for competition synchronization. One problem with this method is that it is difficult to implement the rendezvous mechanism efficiently. Ada 95 protected objects provide an alternative method of providing competition synchronization that need not involve rendezvous.

A protected object is not a task; it is more like a monitor. Protected objects can be accessed by either protected subprograms or by entries similar to those in tasks. The protected subprograms can either be protected procedures, which provide mutually exclusive read-write access to the data of the protected object, or protected functions, which provide concurrent read-only access to that data. Within the body of a protected procedure, the current instance of the enclosing protected unit is defined to be a variable; within the body of a protected function, the current instance of the enclosing protected unit is defined to be a constant, which allows concurrent read-only access.

Entry calls to a protected object provide synchronous communication with one or more tasks using the same protected object. These entry calls provide access similar to that provided to the data enclosed in a task.

The buffer problem that is solved with a task in the previous subsection can be more simply solved with a protected object.

```ada
protected Buffer is
  entry Deposit(Item : in Integer);
  entry Fetch(Item : out Integer);
private
  Bufsize : constant Integer := 100;
  Buf     : array (1..Bufsize) of Integer;
  Filled : Integer range 0..Bufsize := 0;
  Next_In,
  Next_Out : Integer range 1..Bufsize := 1;
end Buffer;

protected body Buffer is
  entry Deposit(Item : in Integer)
                  when Filled < Bufsize is
    begin
    Buf(Next_In) := Item;
    Next_In := (Next_In mod Bufsize) + 1;
    Filled := Filled + 1;
    end Deposit;
  entry Fetch(Item : out Integer) when Filled > 0 is
    begin
    Item := Buf(Next_Out);
    Next_Out := (Next_Out mod Bufsize) + 1;
    Filled := Filled - 1;
    end Fetch;
end Buffer;
```

13.5.10   Asynchronous Message Passing

The rendezvous mechanism we have described so far in this section is strictly synchronous; both the sender and the receiver must be ready for communication before they actually communicate through the rendezvous.

A task can have a special **select** clause, called an **asynchronous select**, which can react immediately to messages from other tasks. Such a clause can have either of two different triggering alternatives, an entry call or a **delay** statement. In addition to the triggering part, the asynchronous select clause has an abortable part, which could contain any sequence of Ada statements. The semantics of an asynchronous select clause is that it executes just one of its two parts. If the triggering event occurs (either the **entry** call is received or the **delay** timer terminates), it executes that part. Otherwise, it executes the abortable clause. The following two examples of asynchronous **select** clauses appear in the Ada 95 reference manual (ARM, 1995). In the first code segment, the abortable clause is executed repeatedly (because of the loop) until the call to `Terminal.Wait_For_Interrupt` is received. In the second code segment, the function called in the abortable clause executes for at least five seconds. If it is not finished by then, the **select** is exited.

```
-- Main command loop for a command interpreter
loop
  select
    Terminal.Wait_For_Interrupt;
    Put_Line("Interrupted");
  then abort
    -- This will be abandoned upon terminal interrupt
    Put_Line("-> ");
    Get_Line(Command, Last);
    Process_Command(Command (1..Last));
  end select;
end loop;
-- A time-limited calculation
select
  delay 5.0;
  Put_Line("Calculation does not converge");
then abort
  -- This calculation should finish in 5.0 seconds;
  --  if not, it is assumed to diverge.
  Horribly_Complicated_Recursive_Function(X, Y);
end select;
```

13.5.11   Evaluation

In the absence of distributed processors with independent memories, the choice between monitors and message passing as a means of providing competition synchronization is somewhat a matter of taste. Cooperation synchronization in message passing is less dependent than semaphores (which are required with monitors for cooperation synchronization) on correct usage. Overall, therefore, message passing is slightly better, even in a shared memory environment.

For distributed systems, however, message passing is a better model for concurrency, because it naturally supports the concept of separate processes executing in parallel on separate processors.

13.6 Java Threads

The concurrent units in Java are methods named run, whose code can be in concurrent execution with other such methods (of other objects) and with the main method. The process in which the run methods run is called a **thread**. Javas threads are lightweight tasks, which means they all run in the same address space. This is different from Ada tasks, which are heavyweight threads (they run in their own address spaces).

There are two ways to define a class with a run method. One of these is to define a subclass of the predefined class, Thread, and override its run method. However, if the new subclass has a necessary natural parent, then defining it as a subclass of Thread obviously will not work. In these situations, a subclass that inherits from its natural parent and implements the Runnable interface is defined. Runnable provides the run method protocol. This approach still requires a Thread object, as will be seen in Section 13.6.4.

13.6.1 The Thread Class

The Thread class is not the natural parent of any other classes. It provides some services for its subclasses, but it is not related in any natural way to their computational purposes. Nevertheless, Thread is the only *class* available to the programmer for creating concurrent Java programs. As previously stated, Section 13.6.4 will briefly discuss the use of the Runnable interface.

The bare essentials of Thread are two methods named run and start. The run method is always overridden by subclasses of Thread. The code of the run method describes the actions of the thread. The start method of Thread starts its thread as a concurrent unit by calling its run method. The call to start is unusual in that control returns immediately to the caller, which then continues its execution, in parallel with the newly started run method.

Following is a skeletal subclass of Thread and a code fragment that creates an object of the subclass and starts the run method's execution in the new thread:

```
class MyThread extends Thread {
  public void run() { ... }
}
...
```

```
Thread myTh = new MyThread();
myTh.start();
```

When a Java application program (as opposed to an applet) begins execution, a new thread is created (in which the **main** method will run) and **main** is called. Applets also run in their own threads. Therefore, all Java programs run in threads.

When a program has multiple threads, a scheduler must manage which thread or threads will run at any given time. In most cases, there is only a single processor, so only one thread actually runs at a time. It is difficult to give a precise description of how the Java scheduler works, because the different implementations (Solaris, Windows, etc.) currently do not schedule threads in exactly the same way. Typically, however, the scheduler gives equal-size time slices to each runnable thread in round-robin fashion as long as all of these threads have the same priority. Section 13.6.2 describes how different priorities can be given to different threads.

The Thread class provides several methods for controlling the execution of threads. The yield method, which takes no parameters, is a request from the running thread to voluntarily surrender the processor. The thread is immediately put in the task-ready queue, making it runnable. The scheduler then chooses the highest priority thread from the task-ready queue. If there are no other runnable threads with priority higher than the one that just yielded the processor, it may also be the next thread to get the processor. yield is a static method, so it must be called with the name of the class, rather than the name of an object, as a prefix.

The sleep method has a single parameter, which is the integer number of milliseconds that the caller of sleep wants the thread to be blocked. After the specified number of milliseconds has passed, the thread will be put in the task-ready queue. Because there is no way to know how long a thread will be in the task-ready queue before it runs, the parameter to sleep is the minimum amount of time the thread will *not* be in execution. The sleep method can throw InterruptedException, which must be handled in the method that calls sleep. Exceptions are described in detail in Chapter 14.

The join method is used to force a method to delay its execution until the run method of another thread has completed its execution. join is used when the processing of a method cannot continue until the work of the other thread is complete. For example, we might have the following run method:

```
public void run() {
  ...
  Thread myTh = new Thread();
  myTh.start();
  // do part of the computation of this thread
  myTh.join();  // Wait for myTh to complete
  // do the rest of the computation of this thread
}
```

The `join` method puts the thread that calls it in the blocked state, which can only be ended by the completion of the thread on which `join` was called. If that thread happens to be blocked, there is the possibility of deadlock. To prevent this, `join` can be called with a parameter, which is the time limit in milliseconds of how long the calling thread will wait for the called thread to complete. For example,

```
myTh.join(2000);
```

will cause the calling thread to wait 2 seconds for `myTh` to complete. If it has not completed its execution after 2 seconds have passed, the calling thread is put back in the ready queue, which means it will continue its execution as soon as it is scheduled.

Early versions of Java included three more `Thread` methods: `stop`, `suspend`, and `resume`. All three of these have been deprecated because of safety problems. The `stop` method is sometimes overridden with a simple method that destroys the thread by setting its reference variable to **null**.

The normal way a `run` method ends its execution is by reaching the end of its code. However, in many cases threads run until told to terminate. Regarding this, there is the question of how a thread can determine whether it should continue or end. The `interrupt` method is one way to communicate to a thread that it should stop. This method does not stop the thread; rather, it sends the thread a message that actually just sets a bit in the thread, which can be checked by the thread. The bit is checked with the predicate method, `isInterrupted`. This is not a complete solution, because the thread you are attempting to interrupt may be sleeping or waiting at the time the `interrupt` method is called, which means it will not be checking to see if it has been interrupted. For these situations, the `interrupt` method also throws an exception, `InterruptedException`, which also causes the thread to awaken (from sleeping or waiting). So, a thread can periodically check to see if it has been interrupted and if so, it can terminate. The thread cannot miss the interrupt, because if it was asleep or waiting when the interrupt occured, it will be awakened by the interrupt. Actually, there are more details to the actions and uses of `interrupt`, but they are not covered here.

13.6.2 Priorities

The priorities of threads need not all be the same. A thread's default priority is the same as the thread that created it. If `main` creates a thread, its default priority is the constant `NORM_PRIORITY`, which is usually 5. Thread defines two other priority constants, `MAX_PRIORITY` and `MIN_PRIORITY`, whose values are usually 10 and 1, respectively.[1] The priority of a thread can be changed with the method

---

[1]The number of priorities is implementation dependent, so there may be fewer or more than 10 levels in some implementations.

setPriority. The new priority can be any of the predefined constants or any other number between MIN_PRIORITY and MAX_PRIORITY. The getPriority method returns the current priority of a thread.

When there are threads with different priorities, the scheduler's behavior is controlled by those priorities. When the executing thread is blocked or killed or the time slice for it expires, the scheduler chooses the thread from the task-ready queue that has the highest priority. A thread with lower priority will run only if one of higher priority is not in the task-ready queue when the opportunity arises.

13.6.3   Competition Synchronization

In Java, competition synchronization is implemented by specifying that the methods that access shared data are run completely before another method is executed on the same object. In other words, we can specify that once a particular method begins its execution, that execution will be completed before any other method begins its execution on the same object. Such methods place a lock on the object, which prevents other synchronized methods from executing on the object. This is specified on a method by adding the **synchronized** modifier to the method's definition, as in the following skeletal class definition:

```
class ManageBuf {
  private int [100] buf;
  ...
  public synchronized void deposit(int item) { ... }
  public synchronized int fetch() { ... }
  ...
}
```

The two methods defined in ManageBuf are both defined to be **synchronized**, which prevents them from interfering with each other while executing on the same object, even if they are called by separate threads.

In some cases, the number of statements that deal with the shared data structure is significantly less than the number of other statements in the method in which it resides. In these cases, it is better to synchronize the code segment that accesses or changes the shared data structure rather than the whole method. This can be done with a so-called *synchronized statement*, whose general form is

```
synchronized(expression)
  statement
```

where the expression must evaluate to an object and the statement can be a single statement or a compound statement. The object is locked during execution of the statement or compound statement. So the statement or compound statement is executed exactly as if it were the body of a synchronized method.

An object that has synchronized methods defined for it must have a queue associated with it that stores the synchronized methods that have attempted to execute on it while it was being operated upon by another synchronized method. When a synchronized method completes its execution on an object, a method that is waiting in the object's waiting queue, if there is such a method, is put in the task-ready queue.

13.6.4 Cooperation Synchronization

Cooperation synchronization in Java is accomplished by using the `wait`, `notify`, and `notifyAll` methods that are defined in `Object`, the root class of all Java classes. All classes except `Object` inherit these methods. Every object has a wait list of all of the threads that have called `wait` on the object. The `notify` method is called to tell one waiting thread that the event it was waiting for has happened. The specific thread that is awakened by `notify` cannot be determined, because the Java Virtual Machine (JVM) chooses one from the wait list of the thread object at random. Because of this, along with the fact that the waiting threads may all be waiting for different conditions, the `notifyAll` method is often used, rather than `notify`. The `notifyAll` method awakens all of the threads on the object's wait list, starting their execution just after their call to `wait`.

`wait`, `notify`, and `notifyAll` can only be called from within a synchronized method because they use the lock placed on an object by such a method. The call to `wait` is usually put in a **while** loop that is controlled by the condition for which the method is waiting. Because of the use of `notifyAll`, some other thread may have changed the condition to false since it was last tested.

The `wait` method can throw `InterruptedException`, which is a descendant of `Exception` (Java's exception handling is discussed Chapter 14). Therefore, any code that calls `wait` must also catch `InterruptedException`. Assuming the condition for which we wait is called `theCondition`, the conventional way to use `wait` is as follows:

```
try {
  while (!theCondition)
    wait();
  -- Do whatever is needed after theCondition comes true
}
catch(InterruptedException myProblem) { ... }
```

The following program implements a circular queue for storing **int** values. It illustrates both cooperation and competition synchronization.

```
// Queue
// This class implements a circular queue for storing int
// values. It includes a constructor for allocating and
// initializing the queue to a specified size. It has
// synchronized methods for inserting values into and
// removing values from the queue.

class Queue {
  private int [] que;
  private int nextIn,
              nextOut,
              filled,
              queSize;

  public Queue(int size) {
    que = new int [size];
    filled = 0;
    nextIn = 1;
    nextOut = 1;
    queSize = size;
  }  //** end of Queue constructor

  public synchronized void deposit (int item) {
    try {
      while (filled == queSize)
        wait();
      que [nextIn] = item;
      nextIn = (nextIn % queSize) + 1;
      filled++;
      notifyAll();
    }  //** end of try clause
    catch(InterruptedException e) {}
  }  //** end of deposit method

  public synchronized int fetch() {
    int item = 0;
    try {
      while (filled == 0)
        wait();
      item = que [nextOut];
      nextOut = (nextOut % queSize) + 1;
      filled--;
      notifyAll();
    }  //** end of try clause
    catch(InterruptedException e) {}
```

```
      return item;
  } //** end of fetch method
} //** end of Queue class
```

Notice that the exception handler (**catch**) does nothing here.

Classes to define producer and consumer objects that could use the Queue class can be defined as

```
class Producer extends Thread {
  private Queue buffer;
  public Producer(Queue que) {
    buffer = que;
  }
  public void run() {
    int new_item;
    while (true) {
      //-- Create a new_item
      buffer.deposit(new_item);
    }
  }
}

class Consumer extends Thread {
  private Queue buffer;
  public Consumer(Queue que) {
    buffer = que;
  }
  public void run() {
    int stored_item;
    while (true) {
      buffer.fetch(stored_item);
      //-- Consume the stored_item
    }
  }
}
```

The following code creates a Queue object, and a Producer and a Consumer object, both attached to the Queue object, and starts their execution:

```
Queue buff1 = new Queue(100);
Producer producer1 = new Producer(buff1);
Consumer consumer1 = new Consumer(buff1);
producer1.start();
consumer1.start();
```

We could define one or both of the `Producer` and the `Consumer` as implementations of the `Runnable` interface rather than as subclasses of `Thread`. The only difference is in the first line, which would now appear as

```
class Producer implements Runnable {
```

To create and run an object of such a class, it is still necessary to create a `Thread` object that is connected to the object. This is illustrated in the following code:

```
Producer producer1 = new Producer(buff1);
Thread producerThread = new Thread(producer1);
producerThread.start();
```

13.6.5   Evaluation

Java's support for concurrency is relatively simple but effective. Because they are heavyweight threads, Ada's tasks easily can be distributed to different processors, in particular different processors with different memories, which could be on different computers in different places. These kinds of systems are not possible with Java's lightweight threads. Both monitors and semaphores can be constructed easily using the threads of Java.

13.7   C# Threads

Although C#'s threads are loosely based on those of Java, there are significant differences. Following is a brief overview of C#'s threads.

13.7.1   Basic Thread Operations

Rather than just methods named `run`, as in Java, any C# method can run in its own thread. A C# thread is created by creating a `Thread` object. The `Thread` constructor must be sent an instantiation of a predefined delegate class, `ThreadStart`,[2] to which must be sent the method that implements the actions of the thread. For example, we might have

```
public void MyRun1() { ... }
...
Thread myThread = new Thread(new ThreadStart(MyRun1));
```

---

[2]A C# delegate is an object-oriented version of a function pointer. In this case, it literally points to the method we want to run in the new thread.

As with Java, creating a thread does not start its concurrent execution. Once again, that must be requested through a method, in this case named `Start`, as in

```
myThread.Start();
```

As in Java, a thread can be made to wait for another thread to finish its execution before continuing, using the similarly named method, `Join`.

A thread can be suspended for a specified amount of time with `Sleep`, which is a public static method of `Thread`. The parameter to `Sleep` is an integer number of milliseconds. Unlike its Java relative, C#'s `Sleep` does not raise any exceptions, so it need not be called in a **try** block.

A thread can be terminated with the `Abort` method, although it does not literally kill the thread. Instead, it throws the `ThreadAbortException`, which the thread can catch. When the thread catches this exception, it usually deallocates any resources it allocated, and then ends (by getting to the end of its code).

13.7.2 Synchronizing Threads

There are three different ways that C# threads can be synchronized, the `Interlock` class, the `lock` statement, and the `Monitor` class. The `Interlock` class is used when the only operations that need to be synchronized are the incrementing and decrementing of an integer. These operations are done atomically with the two methods of `Interlock`, `Increment` and `Decrement`, which take a reference to an integer as the parameter. For example, to increment a shared counter named `counter` in a thread, we could use

```
Interlocked.Increment(ref counter);
```

The `lock` statement is used to mark a critical section of code in a thread. The syntax of this is as follows:

```
lock(expression) {
    // The critical section
}
```

The expression, which looks like a parameter to `lock`, is usually a reference to the object on which the thread is running, **this**.

The `Monitor` class has four methods, `Enter`, `Wait`, `Pulse`, and `Exit`, that can be used to provide more sophisticated synchronization of threads. The `Enter` method, which takes an object reference as its parameter, marks the beginning of synchronization of the thread on that object. The `Wait` method suspends execution of the thread and instructs the Common Language Runtime (CLR) of .NET that this thread wants to resume its execution the next time there is an opportunity. The `Pulse` method, which also takes an object reference as its parameter, notifies waiting threads they now have a chance to run again. `Pulse` is similar to Java's `notifyAll`. Threads that have been waiting are run in the order in which they called the `Wait` method. The `Exit` method ends the critical section of the thread.

13.7.3 Evaluation

C#'s threads are an advance over those of its predecessor, Java. For one thing, any method can be run it its own thread. Thread termination is also cleaner with C#. Synchronization of thread execution is more sophisticated in C#. C# threads, like those of Java, are lightweight, so they cannot be as versitile as Ada's tasks.

13.8   Statement-Level Concurrency

In this section, we take a brief look at language design for statement-level concurrency. From the language design point of view, the objective of such designs is to provide a mechanism that the programmer can use to inform the compiler of ways it can map the program onto a multiprocessor architecture.[3]

In this section, we discuss only one collection of linguistic constructs from one language for statement-level concurrency. Furthermore, we will describe the constructs and their objectives in terms of SIMD architecture machines (see Section 13.1.1), although they were designed to be useful for a variety of architecture configurations.

The problem addressed by the language constructs we discuss is that of minimizing the communication required among processors and the memories of other processors. The assumption is that it is faster for a processor to access data in its own memory than that of some other processor. Well-designed compilers can do a great deal in this process, but much more can be done if the programmer is able to provide information to the compiler about the possible concurrency that could be used.

13.8.1   High-Performance Fortran

High-Performance Fortran (HPF) (ACM, 1993b) is a collection of extensions to Fortran 90 that are meant to allow programmers to specify information to the compiler to help it optimize the execution of programs on multiprocessor computers. HPF includes both new specification statements and intrinsic, or built-in, subprograms. This section discusses only some of the new statements.

The primary specification statements of HPF are for specifying the number of processors, the distribution of data over the memories of those proces-

---

[3]Although ALGOL 68 included a semaphore type that was meant to deal with statement-level concurrency, we do not discuss that application of semaphores here.

sors, and the alignment of data with other data in terms of memory placement. The HPF specification statements appear as special comments in a Fortran program. Each of them is introduced by the prefix !HPF$, where the ! is the character used to begin lines of comments in Fortran 90. This prefix makes them invisible to Fortran 90 compilers but easy for HPF compilers to recognize.

The PROCESSORS specification has the form

```
!HPF$ PROCESSORS procs (n)
```

This statement is used to specify to the compiler the number of processors that can be used by the code generated for this program. This information is used in conjunction with other specifications to tell the compiler how data is to be distributed to the memories associated with the processors.

The DISTRIBUTE statement specifies what data is to be distributed and the kind of distribution that is to be used. Its form is

```
!HPF$ DISTRIBUTE (kind) ONTO procs :: identifier_list
```

In this statement, the kind can be either BLOCK or CYCLIC. The identifier list is the names of the array variables that are to be distributed. A variable that is specified to be BLOCK distributed is divided into n equal groups, where each group consists of contiguous collections of array elements evenly distributed over the memories of all the processors. For example, if an array with 500 elements named LIST is BLOCK distributed over five processors, the first 100 elements of LIST will be stored in the memory of the first processor, and so forth. A CYCLIC distribution specifies that individual elements of the array are cyclically stored in the memories of the processors. For example, if LIST is CYCLIC distributed, again over five processors, the first element of LIST will be stored in the memory of the first processor, the second element in the memory of the second processor, and so forth.

The form of the ALIGN statement is

```
ALIGN array1_element WITH array2_element
```

ALIGN is used to relate the distribution of one array with that of another. For example,

```
ALIGN list1(index) WITH list2(index+1)
```

specifies that the index element of list1 is to be stored in the memory of the same processor as the index+1 element of list2, for all values of index. The two array references in an ALIGN appear together in some statement of the program. Putting them in the same memory (which means the same processor) ensures that the references to them will be as close as possible.

Consider the following example code segment:

```
      REAL list_1 (1000), list_2 (1000)
      INTEGER list_3 (500), list_4 (501)
!HPF$ PROCESSORS proc (10)
```

```
!HPF$ DISTRIBUTE (BLOCK) ONTO procs :: list_1, list_2
!HPF$ ALIGN list_3 (index) WITH list_4 (index+1)
    ...
      list_1 (index) = list_2 (index)
      list_3 (index) = list_4 (index+1)
```

In each execution of the above assignment statements, the two referenced array elements will be stored in the memory of the same processor.

The HPF specification statements actually only provide information for the compiler that it may or may not use to optimize the code it produces. What the compiler actually does depends on its level of sophistication and the particular architecture of the target machine.

The FORALL statement specifies a collection of statements that may be executed concurrently. For example,

```
FORALL (index = 1:1000) list_1 (index) = list_2 (index)
```

specifies the assignment of the elements of list_2 to the corresponding elements of list_1. Conceptually, it specifies that the right side of all 1,000 assignments can be evaluated first, before any assignments take place. This is what permits concurrent execution of all of the assignment statements. The HPF FORALL statement is included in Fortran 95.

We have briefly discussed only a part of the capabilities of HPF. However, it should be enough to provide the reader with an idea of the kinds of language extensions that are useful for programming computers with possibly large numbers of processors.

SUMMARY

Concurrent execution can be at the instruction, statement, or subprogram level. We use the phrase *physical concurrency* when multiple processors are actually used to execute concurrent units. If concurrent units are executed on a single processor, we use the term *logical concurrency*. The underlying conceptual model of all concurrency can be referred to as *logical concurrency*.

Most multiprocessor computers fall into one of two categories, SIMD or MIMD. MIMD computers can be distributed.

Two of the primary facilities that languages that support subprogram-level concurrency must provide are mutually exclusive access to shared data structures (competition synchronization) and cooperation among tasks (cooperation synchronization).

Tasks can be in any one of five different states: new, ready, running, blocked, or dead.

A semaphore is a data structure consisting of an integer and a task description queue. Semaphores can be used to provide both competition and cooperation synchronization among concurrent tasks. It is easy to use semaphores incorrectly, resulting in errors that cannot be detected by the compiler, linker, or run-time system.

Monitors are data abstractions that provide a natural way of allowing mutually exclusive access to data shared among tasks. They are included in several programming languages, none of which is widely used. Cooperation synchronization in languages with monitors must be provided with some form of semaphores.

Ada provides complex but effective constructs, based on the message-passing model, for concurrency. Ada's tasks are heavyweight tasks. The basic concurrent units are tasks that communicate with each other through the rendezvous mechanism, which is synchronous message passing. A rendezvous is the action of a task accepting a message sent by another task. Ada includes both simple and complicated methods of controlling the occurrences of rendezvous among tasks.

Ada 95 includes additional capabilities for the support of concurrency, primarily protected objects, and asynchronous message passing.

Java provides lightweight concurrent units in a rather simple but effective way. Any class that either inherits from `Thread` or implements `Runnable` can override an inherited method named `run` and have that method's code executed concurrently with other such methods and with the main program. Competition synchronization is specified by defining methods that access shared data to be synchronized. Small sections of code can also be synchronized. Cooperation synchronization is accomplished by using the methods `wait`, `notify`, and `notifyAll`. The `Thread` class also provides the `sleep`, `yield`, `join`, and `interrupt` methods.

C#'s support for concurrency is based on that of Java, but is more sophisticated. Any method can be run in a thread. Three kinds of thread synchronization are supported with the `Interlock` and `Monitor` classses and the `lock` statement.

High-Performance Fortran includes statements for specifying how data is to be distributed over the memory units connected to multiple processors. Also included are statements for specifying collections of statements that can be executed concurrently.

BIBLIOGRAPHIC NOTES

The general subject of concurrency is discussed at great length in Andrews and Schneider (1983), Holt et al. (1978), and Ben-Ari (1982).

The monitor concept is developed and its implementation in Concurrent Pascal is described by Brinch Hansen (1977).

The early development of the message-passing model of concurrent unit control is discussed by Hoare (1978) and Brinch Hansen (1978). An in-depth discussion of the development of the Ada tasking model can be found in

Ichbiah et al. (1979). Ada 95 is described in detail in ARM (1995). High-Performance Fortran is described in ACM (1993b).

REVIEW QUESTIONS

1. What are the three possible levels of concurrency in programs?
2. Describe the logical architecture of an SIMD computer.
3. Describe the logical architecture of an MIMD computer.
4. What level of program concurrency is best supported by SIMD computers?
5. What level of program concurrency is best supported by MIMD computers?
6. What is the difference between physical and logical concurrency?
7. What is a thread of control in a program?
8. Define *task*, *disjoint task*, *synchronization*, *competition* and *cooperation synchronization*, *liveness*, *race condition*, and *deadlock*.
9. What kind of tasks do not require any kind of synchronization?
10. Describe the five different states in which a task can be.
11. What is the purpose of a task ready queue?
12. What are the design issues for language support for concurrency?
13. Describe the actions of the wait and release operations for semaphores.
14. What is a binary semaphore? What is a counting semaphore?
15. What are the primary problems with using semaphores to provide synchronization?
16. What advantage do monitors have over semaphores?
17. Define *rendezvous*, **accept** *clause*, **entry** *clause*, *actor task*, *server task*, *extended* **accept** *clause*, *open* **accept** *clause*, *closed* **accept** *clause*, and *completed task*.
18. Which is more general, concurrency through monitors or concurrency through message passing?
19. Are Ada tasks created statically or dynamically?
20. What purpose does an extended **accept** clause serve?
21. How is cooperation synchronization provided for Ada tasks?
22. What is the advantage of protected objects in Ada 95 over tasks for providing access to shared data objects?
23. Describe the Ada 95 asynchronous **select** clause.
24. Specifically, what Java program unit can run concurrently with the main method in an application program?

25. What does the Java `sleep` method do?
26. What does the Java `yield` method do?
27. What does the Java `join` method do?
28. What does the Java `interrupt` method do?
29. What are the two Java constructs that can be synchronized?
30. Describe the actions of the three Java methods that are used to support cooperation synchronization?
31. Explain why Java includes the `Runnable` interface.
32. What kinds of methods can run in a C# thread?
33. What is different about C#'s `Sleep` method, relative to Java's `sleep`?
34. What exactly does C#'s `Abort` method do?
35. What is the purpose of the `Interlock` class?
36. What does the C# `lock` statement do?
37. What is the objective of the specification statements of High-Performance Fortran?
38. What is the purpose of the `FORALL` statement of High-Performance Fortran?

PROBLEM SET

1. Explain clearly why competition synchronization is not a problem in a programming environment that supports coroutines but not concurrency.
2. What is the best action a system can take when deadlock is detected?
3. Busy waiting is a method whereby a task waits for a given event by continuously checking for that event to occur. What is the main problem with this approach?
4. In the producer-consumer example of Section 13.3, suppose that we incorrectly replaced the `release(access)` in the consumer process with `wait(access)`. What would be the result of this error on execution of the system?
5. From a book on assembly language programming for a computer that uses an Intel Pentium processor, determine what instructions are provided to support the construction of semaphores.
6. Suppose two tasks A and B must use the shared variable `Buf_Size`. Task A adds 2 to `Buf_Size`, and task B subtracts 1 from it. Assume that such arithmetic operations are done by the three-step process of fetching the current value, performing the arithmetic, and putting the new value back. In the

absence of competition synchronization, what sequences of events are possible and what values result from these operations? Assume the initial value of `Buf_Size` is 6.

7. Compare the Java competition synchronization mechanism with that of Ada.

8. Compare the Java cooperation synchronization mechanism with that of Ada.

9. What happens if a monitor procedure calls another procedure in the same monitor?

10. Explain the relative safety of cooperation synchronization using semaphores and using Ada's when clauses in tasks?

11. What is the relationship of monitors to Ada tasks for competition synchronization?

PROGRAMMING EXERCISES

1. Write an Ada task to implement general semaphores.

2. Write an Ada task to manage a shared buffer such as the one in our example, but use the semaphore task from Programming Exercise 1.

3. Define semaphores in Ada and use them to provide both cooperation and competition synchronization in the shared buffer example.

4. Repeat Programming Exercise 3 with Java.

5. Write the shared buffer example of the chapter in C#.

6. The reader-writer problem can be simply stated as follows: A shared memory location can be concurrently read by any number of tasks, but when a task must write to the shared memory location, it must have exclusive access. Write a Java program for the reader-writer problem.

7. Repeat Programming Exercise 6 with Ada.

8. Repeat Programming Exercise 6 with C#.

14

Exception Handling
and Event Handling

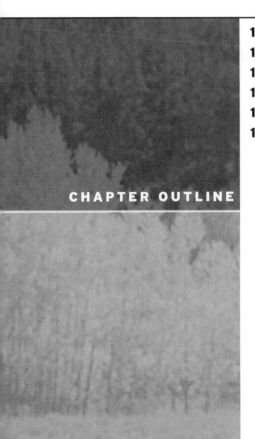

CHAPTER OUTLINE

This chapter discusses programming language support for two related parts of many contemporary programs, exception handling and event handling. Both exceptions and events can occur at times that cannot be predetermined, and both require special language constructs. Furthermore, some of the language concepts—for example, propagation—are similar for exception handling and event handling.

We first describe the fundamental concepts of exception handling, including hardware- and software-detectable exceptions, exception handlers, and the raising of exceptions. Then the design issues for exception handling are introduced and discussed, including the binding of exceptions to exception handlers, continuation, default handlers, and exception disabling. This is followed by a description and an evaluation of the exception-handling facilities of three programming languages: Ada, C++, and Java.

The latter part of this chapter is about event handling. We first present an introduction to the basic concepts of event handling. This is followed by a brief discussion of the event-handling approach of Java for its GUI components.

14.1   Introduction to Exception Handling

Most computer hardware systems are capable of detecting certain run-time error conditions, such as floating-point overflow. Many programming languages were designed and implemented in such a way that the user program can neither detect nor attempt to deal with such errors. In these languages, the occurrence of such an error simply causes the program to be terminated and control to be transferred to the operating system. The typical operating system reaction to a run-time error is to print a diagnostic message, which may be very meaningful or highly cryptic, and then terminate the program.

In the case of input and output operations, however, the situation is somewhat different. For example, a Fortran Read statement can intercept input errors and end-of-file conditions, both of which are detected by the input device hardware. In both cases, the Read statement can specify the label of some statement in the user program that deals with the condition. In the case of the end-of-file, it is clear that the condition is not always to be considered an error. In most cases, it is nothing more than a signal that one kind of processing is completed and a new kind should begin. In spite of the obvious difference between end-of-file and events that are always errors, such as a failed input process, Fortran handles both situations with the same mechanism. Consider the following Fortran Read statement:

```
Read(Unit=5, Fmt=1000, Err=100, End=999) Weight
```

The Err clause specifies that control is to be transferred to the statement labeled 100 if an error occurs in the read operation. The End clause specifies that control is to be transferred to the statement labeled 999 if the read operation encounters the end of the file. So Fortran uses simple branches for both input errors and end-of-file.

There is a category of serious errors that are not detectable by hardware but could be detected by code generated by the compiler. For example, array subscript range errors are almost never detected by hardware (there were a few computers that *did* detect subscript range errors in hardware), but they lead to fatal errors that often are noticed only later in the program execution.

Detection of subscript range errors is sometimes required by the language design. For example, Java compilers usually generate code to check the correctness of every subscript expression (they do not generate such code when it can be determined at compile time that a subscript expression cannot have an out-of-range value, for example, if the subscript is a literal). In C, subscript ranges are not checked because the cost of such checking was (and is) not believed to be worth the benefit of detecting such errors. In some compilers for some languages, subscript range checking can be selected (if not turned on by default) or turned off (if it is on by default) as desired in the program or in the command that executes the compiler.

Many contemporary languages include mechanisms that allow programs to react in a standard way to program-detected unusual events. Programs may also be notified when certain events are detected by hardware or system software, so that they also can react to these events. These mechanisms are collectively called exception handling.

Perhaps the most important reason some languages do not include exception handling is the complexity it adds to the language.

14.1.1 Basic Concepts

We term both the errors detected by hardware, such as disk read errors, and unusual conditions, such as end-of-file (which are also detected by hardware), as exceptions. We further extend the concept of an exception to include errors or unusual conditions that are software-detectable (either by a software interpreter or the user code itself). Accordingly, we define **exception** to be any unusual event, erroneous or not, that is detectable either by hardware or software and that may require special processing.

The special processing that may be required when an exception is detected is called **exception handling.** This processing is done by a code unit or segment called an **exception handler.** An exception is **raised** when its associated event occurs. In many recent C-based languages, exceptions are said to be *thrown*, rather than *raised*.[1] Exception handlers are usually different for different exception types. Detection of end-of-file nearly always requires some specific program action. But, clearly, that action would not also be appropriate for an array index range error exception. In some cases, the only action could be the generation of an error message and an orderly termination of the program.

---

[1] C++ was the first C-based language that included exception handling. The word *throw* was used, rather than *raise*, because the standard C library includes function named raise.

In some situations, it may be desirable to ignore certain hardware-detectable exceptions—for example, division by zero—for a time. This would be done by disabling the exception. A disabled exception could be enabled again at a later time.

The absence of separate or specific exception-handling facilities in a language does not preclude the handling of user-defined, software-detected exceptions. Such an exception detected within a program unit is often handled by the unit's caller, or invoker. One possible design is to send an auxiliary parameter, which is used as a status variable. The status variable is assigned a value in the called unit according to the correctness and/or normalness of its computation. Immediately upon return from the called unit, the caller tests the status variable. If the value indicates that an exception has occurred, the handler, which may reside in the calling unit, can be enacted. Many of the C standard library functions use a variant of this approach: The return values are used as error indicators.

Another possibility is to pass a label parameter to the subprogram. Of course, this is only possible in languages that allow labels to be used as parameters. Passing a label allows the called unit to return to a different point in the caller if an exception has occurred. As in the first alternative, the handler is often a segment of the calling unit's code. This is a common use of label parameters in Fortran.

A third possibility is to have the handler as a separate subprogram whose name is passed as a parameter to the called unit. In this case, the handler subprogram is provided by the caller, but the called unit calls the handler when an exception is raised. One problem with this approach is that one is required to send a handler subprogram with *every* call, whether it is needed or not. Furthermore, to deal with several different kinds of exceptions, several different handler routines would need to be passed, complicating the code.

If it is desirable to handle an exception in the unit in which it is detected, the handler is included as a segment of code in that unit.

There are some definite advantages to having exception handling built into a language. First, without exception handling the code required to detect error conditions can considerably clutter a program. For example, suppose a subprogram includes expressions that contain 10 references to array elements, and any one of them could have an index out-of-range error. Further suppose that the language does not require index range checking. Without built-in exception handling, every one of these operations would need to be preceded by code to detect the possible index range error. The presence of exception handling in the language could permit the compiler to insert such checks in the code when requested by the program.

Another advantage of language support for exception handling results from exception propagation. Exception propagation allows an exception raised in one program unit to be handled in some other unit in its dynamic or static ancestry. This allows a single exception handler to be used for any number of different program units. This reuse can result in significant savings in development cost, program size, and program complexity.

A language that supports exception handling encourages its users to consider all of the events that could occur during program execution and how they can be handled. This is far better than not considering such possibilities and simply hoping nothing will go wrong. This advantage is related to requiring a multiple selector construct to include actions for all possible values of the control expression, as is required by Ada.

Finally, there are programs in which dealing with nonerroneous but unusual situations can be simplified with exception handling, and that without it program structure can become overly convoluted.

14.1.2 Design Issues

We now explore some of the design issues for an exception-handling system when it is part of a programming language. Such a system might allow both predefined and user-defined exceptions and exception handlers. Note that predefined exceptions are implicitly raised, whereas user-defined exceptions are explicitly raised by user code. Consider the following skeletal subprogram that includes an exception-handling mechanism:

```
void example() {
  ...
  average = sum / total;
  ...
  return;
/* Exception handlers */
  when zero_divide {
    average = 0;
    printf("Error—divisor (total) is zero\n");
  }
  ...
}
```

The exception of division by zero is intercepted in the function, which transfers control to the appropriate handler, which is then executed.

The first design issue for exception handling is how an exception occurrence is bound to an exception handler. This issue occurs on two different levels. On the unit level, there is the question of how the same exception being raised at different points in a unit can be bound to different handlers within the unit. For example, in the subprogram above, there is a handler for a division-by-zero exception that appears to be written to deal with an occurrence of division by zero in a particular statement (the one shown). But suppose the function includes several other expressions with division operators. For those operators, this handler would probably not be appropriate. So, it should be possible to bind the exceptions that can be raised by particular statements to particular handlers, even though the same exception can be raised by many different statements.

At a higher level, the binding question arises when there is no exception handler local to the unit in which the exception is raised. In this case, the designer must decide whether to propagate the exception to some other unit and, if so, where. How this propagation takes place and how far it goes have an important impact on the writability of exception handlers. For example, if handlers must be local, then many handlers must be written, which complicates both the writing and reading of the program. On the other hand, if exceptions are propagated, a single handler might handle the same exception raised in several program units, which may require the handler to be more general than one would prefer.

After an exception handler executes, either control can transfer to somewhere in the program outside of the handler code, or program execution can simply terminate. We term this the question of control continuation after handler execution, or simply **continuation.** Termination is obviously the simplest choice, and in many error exception conditions, it is the best. However, in other situations, particularly those associated with unusual but not erroneous events, the choice of continuing execution is best. In these cases, some conventions must be chosen to determine where execution should continue. It might be the statement that raised the exception, the statement after the statement that raised the exception, or possibly some other unit. The choice to return to the statement that raised the exception may seem like a good one, but in the case of an error exception, it is only useful if the handler somehow is able to modify the values or operations that caused the exception to be raised. Otherwise the exception will simply be reraised. The required modification for an error exception is often very difficult. Even when possible, however, it may not be a sound practice. It allows the program to remove the symptom of a problem without removing the cause.

The two issues of binding of exceptions to handlers and continuation are illustrated in Figure 14.1.

Another design issue is the following: If users are allowed to define exceptions, how are these exceptions specified? The usual answer is to require that they be declared in the specification parts of the program units in which they can be raised. The scope of a declared exception is usually the scope of the program unit that contains the declaration.

In the case where a language provides predefined exceptions, several other design issues follow. For example, should the language run-time system provide default handlers for the built-in exceptions, or should the user be required to write handlers for all exceptions? Another question is whether predefined exceptions can be raised explicitly by the user program. This can be convenient if there are software-detectable situations in which the user would like to use a predefined handler.

HISTORY NOTE

PL/I (ANSI, 1976) pioneered the concept of allowing user programs to be directly involved in exception handling. The language allowed the user to write exception handlers for a long list of language-defined exceptions. Furthermore, PL/I introduced the concept of user-defined exceptions, which allow programs to create software-detected exceptions. These exceptions use the same mechanisms that are used for the built-in exceptions.

Since PL/I was designed, a substantial amount of work has been done to design alternative methods of exception handling. In particular, CLU (Liskov et al., 1984), Mesa (Mitchell et al., 1979), Ada, COMMON LISP (Steele, 1984), ML (Milner et al., 1990), C++, Modula-3 (Cardelli et al., 1989), Eiffel, Java, and C# include exception-handling facilities.

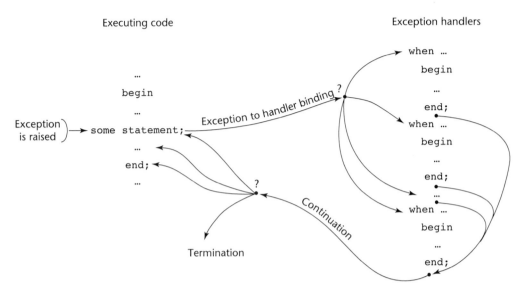

Figure 14.1

Exception-handling control flow

Another issue is whether hardware-detectable errors should be treated as exceptions that could be handled by user programs. If not, all exceptions obviously are software-detectable. A related question is whether there should be any predefined exceptions. Predefined exceptions are implicitly raised by either hardware or system software.

Finally, there is the question of whether exceptions, either predefined or user-defined, can be temporarily or permanently disabled. This question is somewhat philosophical, particularly in the case of predefined error conditions. For example, suppose a language has a predefined exception that is raised when a subscript range error occurs. Many believe that subscript range errors should always be detected, and therefore it should not be possible for the program to disable detection of these errors. Others argue that subscript range checking is too costly for production software, where, presumably, the code is sufficiently error-free that range errors should not occur.

The exception-handling design issues can be summarized as follows:

- How and where are exception handlers specified, and what is their scope?
- How is an exception occurrence bound to an exception handler?
- Where does execution continue, if at all, after an exception handler completes its execution? (This is the question of continuation.)
- How are user-defined exceptions specified?
- If there are predefined exceptions, should there be default exception handlers for programs that do not provide their own?
- Can predefined exceptions be explicitly raised?

- Are hardware-detectable errors treated as exceptions that may be handled?
- Are there any predefined exceptions?
- Should it be possible to disable predefined exceptions?

We are now prepared to examine the exception-handling facilities of three contemporary programming languages.

14.2   Exception Handling in Ada

Exception handling in Ada is a powerful tool for constructing more reliable software systems. It includes the good parts of the exception-handling design of two earlier languages with exception handling, PL/I and CLU.

14.2.1   Exception Handlers

Ada exception handlers are usually local to the code in which the exception can be raised. Because this provides them with the same referencing environment, parameters for handlers are not necessary and are not allowed.

Exception handlers have the general form

when exception_choice {| exception_choice} => statement_sequence

where the braces are metasymbols that mean that what they contain may be left out or repeated any number of times. The exception_choice has the form

exception_name | **others**

The exception_name indicates the particular exception or exceptions that this handler is meant to handle. The statement sequence is the handler body. The reserved word **others** indicates that the handler is meant to handle any exceptions not named in any other local handler.

Exception handlers can be included in blocks or in the bodies of subprograms, packages, or tasks. Regardless of the block or unit in which they appear, handlers are gathered together in an **exception** clause, which must be placed at the end of the block or unit. For example, the usual form of an exception clause is shown in the following:

```
begin
-- the block or unit body --
exception
    when exception_name_1 =>
      -- first handler --
    when exception_name_2 =>
      -- second handler --
      -- other handlers --
end;
```

Any statement that is legitimate in the block or unit in which the handler appears is also legal in the handler.

14.2.2 Binding Exceptions to Handlers

When the block or unit that raises an exception includes a handler for that exception, the exception is statically bound to that handler. If an exception is raised in a block or unit that does not have a handler for that particular exception, the exception is propagated to some other block or unit. The way in which exceptions are propagated depends on the program entity in which the exception occurs.

When an exception is raised in a procedure, whether in the elaboration of its declarations or in the execution of its body, and the procedure has no handler for it, the exception is implicitly propagated to the calling program unit at the point of the call. This policy is reflective of the design philosophy that exception propagation from subprograms should trace back through the control path (dynamic ancestors), not through static ancestors.

If the calling unit to which an exception has been propagated also has no handler for the exception, it is again propagated to that unit's caller. This continues, if necessary, to the main procedure. If an exception is propagated to the main procedure and a handler is still not found, the program is terminated.

In the realm of exception handling, an Ada block is considered to be a parameterless procedure that is "called" by its parent block when execution control reaches the block's first statement. When an exception is raised in a block, in either its declarations or executable statements, and the block has no handler for it, the exception is propagated to the next larger enclosing scope, which is the code that "called" it. The point to which the exception is propagated is just after the end of the block in which it occurred, which is its "return" point.

When an exception is raised in a package body and the package body has no handler for the exception, the exception is propagated to the declaration section of the unit containing the package declaration. If the package happens to be a library unit (which is separately compiled), the program is terminated.

If an exception occurs at the outermost level in a task body and the task contains a handler for the exception, that handler is executed and the task is marked as being completed. If the task does not have a handler for the exception, the task is simply marked as being completed; the exception is not propagated. The control mechanism of a task is too complex to lend itself to a reasonable and simple answer to the question of where its unhandled exceptions should be propagated.

Exceptions can also occur during the elaboration of the declarative sections of subprograms, blocks, packages, and tasks. For example, suppose that a function is called to initialize a variable in its declaration statement, as in the following:

```
procedure River is
  Current_Flow : Float := Get_Flow;
```

```
...
begin
  ...
end River;
```

Assume that Get_Flow is a function with no parameters. If Get_Flow raises and propagates an exception to its caller, the exception is reraised in this declaration. Storage allocation during declaration elaboration can also raise an exception.

When exceptions are raised during the declaration elaborations of procedures, packages, and blocks, those exceptions are propagated exactly as if the exception were raised in the associated code section. In the case of a task, the task is marked as being completed, no further elaboration takes place, and the built-in exception Tasking_Error is raised at the point of activation for the task.

14.2.3   Continuation

The block or unit that raises an exception, along with all units to which the exception was propagated but that did not handle it, is always terminated. Control never returns implicitly to the raising block or unit after the exception is handled. Control simply continues after the exception clause, which is always at the end of a block or unit. This causes an immediate return to a higher level of control.

When deciding where execution would continue after exception handler execution was completed in a program unit, the Ada design team had little choice, because the requirements specification for Ada (Department of Defense, 1980a) clearly states that program units that raise exceptions cannot be continued or resumed. However, in the case of a block, a statement can be retried after it raises an exception and that exception is handled. For example, suppose a statement that can raise an exception and a handler for that exception are both enclosed in a block, which is itself enclosed in a loop. The following example code segment, which gets four integer values in the desired range from the keyboard, illustrates this kind of structure:

```
...
type Age_Type is range 0..125;
type Age_List_Type is array (1..4) of Age_Type;
package Age_IO is new Integer_IO (Age_Type);
use Age_IO;
Age_List : Age_List_Type;
...
begin
for Age_Count in 1..4 loop
  loop  -- loop for repetition when exceptions occur
  Except_Blk:
```

```
      begin   -- compound to encapsulate exception handling
      Put_Line("Enter an integer in the range 0..125");
      Get(Age_List(Age_Count));
      exit;
      exception
        when Data_Error =>   -- Input string is not a number
          Put_Line("Illegal numeric value");
          Put_Line("Please try again");
        when Constraint_Error =>   -- Input is < 0 or > 125
          Put_Line("Input number is out of range");
          Put_Line("Please try again");
      end Except_Blk;
    end loop;   -- end of the infinite loop to repeat input
               -- when there is an exception
end loop;   -- end of for Age_Count in 1..4 loop
...
```

Control stays in the inner loop, which contains only the block, until a valid input number is received.

14.2.4 Other Design Choices

There are four exceptions that are defined in the default package, `Standard`:

```
Constraint_Error
Program_Error
Storage_Error
Tasking_Error
```

Each of these is actually a category of exceptions. For example, the exception `Constraint_Error` is raised when an array subscript is out of range, when there is a range error in a numeric variable that has a range restriction, when a reference is made to a record field that is not present in a discriminated union, and in many additional situations.

In addition to the exceptions defined in `Standard`, other predefined packages define other exceptions. For example, `Ada.Text_IO` defines the `End_Error` exception.

User-defined exceptions are defined with the following declaration form:

exception_name_list : **exception**

Such exceptions are treated exactly as predefined exceptions, except that they must be raised explicitly.

There are default handlers for the predefined exceptions, all of which result in program termination.

Exceptions are explicitly raised with the **raise** statement, which has the general form

raise [exception_name]

The only place a **raise** statement can appear without naming an exception is within an exception handler. In that case, it reraises the same exception that caused execution of the handler. This has the effect of propagating the exception according to the propagation rules stated previously. A **raise** in an exception handler is useful when one wishes to print an error message where an exception is raised but handle the exception elsewhere.

An Ada **pragma** is a directive to the compiler. Certain run-time checks that are parts of the built-in exceptions can be disabled in Ada programs by use of the `Suppress` **pragma**, the simple form of which is

pragma `Suppress(check_name)`

The `Suppress` **pragma** can appear only in declaration sections. When it appears, the specified check may be suspended in the associated block or program unit of which the declaration section is a part. Explicit raises are not affected by `Suppress`. Although it is not required, most Ada compilers implement the `Suppress` **pragma**.

Examples of checks that can be suppressed are the following: `Index_Check` and `Range_Check` specify two of the checks that are normally done in an Ada program; `Index_Check` refers to array subscript range checking; `Range_Check` refers to checking such things as the range of a value being assigned to a subtype variable. If either `Index_Check` or `Range_Check` is violated, `Constraint_Error` is raised. `Division_Check` and `Overflow_Check` are suppressible checks associated with `Numeric_Error`. The following **pragma** disables array subscript range checking:

pragma `Suppress(Index_Check);`

There is an option of `Suppress` that allows the named check to be further restricted to particular objects, types, subtypes, and program units.

14.2.5 An Example

The following example program illustrates some simple but common uses of exception handlers in Ada. The program computes and prints a distribution of input grades by using an array of counters. There are 10 categories of grades (0–9, 10–19, ..., 90–100). The grades themselves are used to compute indexes into an array of counters, one for each grade category. Invalid input grades are detected by trapping indexing errors in the counter array. A grade of 100 is special in the computation of the grade distribution because the categories all have 10 possible grade values, except the highest, which has 11 (90, 91, ..., 100). (The fact that there are more possible A grades than Bs or Cs is conclusive evidence of the generosity of teachers.) The grade of 100 is also handled in the same exception handler that is used for invalid input data.

```ada
with Ada.Text_IO, Ada.Integer.Text_IO;
use Ada.Text_IO, Ada.Integer.Text_IO;
procedure Grade_Distribution is
  Freq: array (1..10) of Integer := (others => 0);
  New_Grade,
  Index,
  Limit_1,
  Limit_2 : Integer;
  begin
    loop
    Get(New_Grade);
    Index := New_Grade / 10 + 1;
      begin  -- A block for the Constraint_Error handler
      Freq(Index) := Freq(Index) + 1;
      exception
        when Constraint_Error =>
          if New_Grade = 100 then
            Freq(10) := Freq(10) + 1;
          else
            Put("ERROR -- new grade: ");
            Put(New_Grade);
            Put(" is out of range");
            New_Line;
          end if;
      end;  -- end of block for the Constraint_Error
handler
    end loop;
  exception  -- This handler includes all final
computations
    when End_Error =>
      Put("Limits  Frequency");
      New_Line; New_Line;
      for Index in 0..9 loop
        Limit_1 := 10 * Index;
        Limit_2 := Limit_1 + 9;
        if Index = 9 then
          Limit_2 := 100;
        end if;
        Put(Limit_1);
        Put(Limit_2);
        Put(Freq(Index + 1));
        New_Line;
      end loop;  -- for Index in 0..9 ...
  end Grade_Distribution;
```

Notice that the code to handle invalid input grades is in its own local block. This allows the program to continue after such exceptions are handled, as in our earlier example that reads values from the keyboard.

14.2.6   Evaluation

As is the case in some other language constructs, Ada's design of exception handling represents something of a consensus, at least at the time of its design (the late 1970s and early 1980s), of ideas on the subject. It is clearly a significant advance over the exception handling of PL/I (see the history sidebar in Section 14.1.2). For some time, Ada was the only widely used language that included exception handling. Exception handling is part of most recently defined languages.

14.3   Exception Handling in C++

The exception handling of C++ was accepted by the ANSI C++ standardization committee in 1990 and subsequently found its way into C++ implementations. The design is based in part on the exception handling of CLU, Ada, and ML. One major difference between the exception handling of C++ and that of Ada is the absence of predefined exceptions in C++. Thus, in C++, all exceptions are user-defined and explicitly raised.

14.3.1   Exception Handlers

In Section 14.2, we saw that Ada uses program units or blocks to specify the scope for exception handlers. C++ uses a special construct that is introduced with the reserved word **try** for this purpose. A **try** construct includes a compound statement called the **try** clause and a list of exception handlers. The compound statement defines the scope of the following handlers. The general form of this construct is

```
try {
//** Code that is expected to raise an exception
}
catch (formal parameter) {
//** A handler body
}
...
catch (formal parameter) {
//** A handler body
}
```

Each of the **catch** functions are exception handlers. A **catch** function can have only a single formal parameter, which is similar to a formal parameter in a function definition in C++, including the possibility of it being an ellipsis (...). A handler with an ellipsis formal parameter is the catch-all handler; it is enacted for any raised exception if no appropriate handler has been found. The formal parameter also can be a naked type specifier, such as **float**, as in a function prototype. In such a case, the only purpose of the formal parameter is to make the handler uniquely identifiable. When information about the exception is to be passed to the handler, the parameter includes a variable name that is used for that purpose. Because the class of the parameter can be any user-defined class, the parameter can include as many data members as are necessary. The process by which thrown exceptions are connected to handlers is discussed in Section 14.3.2.

In C++, exception handlers can include any C++ code.

14.3.2 Binding Exceptions to Handlers

C++ exceptions are raised only by the explicit statement **throw**, whose general form is

throw [expression];

The brackets here are metasymbols used to specify that the expression is optional. A **throw** without an operand can only appear in a handler. When it appears there, it reraises the exception, which is then handled elsewhere. This is exactly like the Ada use of a **raise** statement without an exception name.

The type of the **throw** expression selects the particular handler, which of course must have a "matching" type formal parameter. In this case, *matching* means the following: A handler with a formal parameter of type T, **const** T, T& (a reference to an object of type T), or **const** T& matches a **throw** with an expression of type T. In the case where T is a class, a handler whose parameter is type T or any class that is an ancestor of T matches. There are more complicated situations in which a **throw** expression matches a formal parameter, but they will not be described here.

An exception raised in a **try** construct causes an immediate end to the execution of the code in that **try** construct. The search for a matching handler begins with the handlers that immediately follow the **try** construct. The matching process is done sequentially on the handlers until a match is found. This means that if any other match precedes an exactly matching handler, the exactly matching handler will not be used. If there is a **catch** with an ellipsis formal parameter, it will match any **throw**, so it is not useful to place such a **catch** anywhere but at the end of the list of handlers.

If an exception is raised in a **try** clause and there is no matching handler associated with that **try** clause, the exception is propagated. If the **try** clause is nested inside another **try** clause, the exception is propagated to the handlers associated with the outer **try** clause. If none of the enclosing **try** clauses yields a matching handler, the exception is propagated to the caller of the function in which it was raised. If the call to the function was not in a **try** clause, the exception is propagated to that function's caller. If no matching handler is found in the program through this propagation process, the program is terminated.

14.3.3   Continuation

After a handler has completed its execution, control flows to the first statement following the **try** construct (the statement immediately after the last handler in the sequence of handlers of which it is an element). A handler may reraise an exception, using a **throw** without an expression, in which case that exception is propagated.

14.3.4   Other Design Choices

In terms of the design issues summarized in Section 14.1.2, the exception handling of C++ is simple. There are *only* user-defined exceptions, and they are not specified (though they might be declared as new classes). There are no default handlers, for system-detected exceptions cannot be handled. Exceptions cannot be disabled.

A C++ function can list the types of the exceptions (the types of the **throw** expressions) that it could raise, but not handle. This is done by attaching the reserved word **throw**, followed by a parenthesized list of these types, to the function header. For example,

```
int fun() throw (int, char *) { ... }
```

specifies that the function `fun` could raise but not handle exceptions of type **int** and **char** `*` but no others. The **throw** clause must list all exceptions that could be propagated from the function. The purpose of the **throw** clause is to specify to users of the function what exceptions might be propagated from the function. If the types in the **throw** clause are classes, then the function can propagate any exception that is derived from the listed classes. If a function header has a **throw** clause and propagates an exception that is not listed in the **throw** clause and is not derived from a class listed there, it causes a fatal error. Note that this error cannot be detected at compile time. The list of types in the list may be empty, meaning the function will not propagate any exceptions. If there is no **throw** specification on the header, the function can propagate any exception. The list is not part of the function's type.

When an exception terminates a **try** construct, all stack-dynamic and heap-dynamic variables that were allocated by code executed in the **try** construct before the exception occurred are deallocated. Therefore, the handler can never access such variables.

14.3.5   An Example

The following example has the same intent and use of exception handling as the Ada program shown in Section 14.2.5. It produces a distribution of input grades by using an array of counters for 10 categories. Illegal grades are detected by checking for invalid subscripts used in incrementing the selected counter.

```cpp
#include <iostream.h>
void main() {    //* Any exception can be raised
  int new_grade,
      index,
      limit_1,
      limit_2,
      freq[10] = {0,0,0,0,0,0,0,0,0,0};
  short int eof_condition;
  try {
    while (1) {
      if (!cin >> new_grade)   //* When cin detects eof,
        throw eof_condition;   //* raise eof_condition
      index = new_grade / 10;
      {try {
        if (index < 0 || index > 9)
          throw(new_grade);
        freq[index]++;
      }  //* end of inner try compound
       catch(int grade) {  //* Handler for index errors
        if (grade == 100)
          freq[9]++;
        else
          cout << "Error -- new grade: " << grade
               << " is out of range" << endl;
      }  //* end of catch(int grade)
     }  //* end of the block for the inner try-catch pair
    }  //* end of while (1)
  }  //* end of outer try compound
  catch(short int) {  //** Handler for eof
    cout << "Limits    Frequency" << endl;
    for (index = 0; index < 10; index++) {
      limit_1 = 10 * index;
      limit_2 = limit_1 + 9;
      if (index == 9)
        limit_2 = 100;
      cout << limit_1 << limit_2 << freq[index] << endl;
    }  //* end of for (index == 9)
  }  //* end of catch (short int)
}  //* end of main
```

This program is meant to illustrate the mechanics of C++ exception handling. However, both of the uses of exceptions in this example are better handled by other means. The end-of-file condition is easier to handle by simply controlling the **while** loop with the cin expression as the control expression. Furthermore, the index range exception is usually handled in C++ by overloading the indexing operation, which could then raise the exception, rather than the direct detection of the indexing operation with the selection construct used in our example.

14.3.6   Evaluation

In some ways the C++ exception-handling mechanism is similar to that of Ada. For example, unhandled exceptions in functions are propagated to the function's caller. But in other ways the C++ design is quite different: There are no predefined hardware-detectable exceptions that can be handled by the user, and exceptions are not named. This leads to the odd design that exceptions are connected to handlers through a parameter type in which the formal parameter could be absent. The type of the formal parameter of a handler determines the condition under which it is called but may have nothing whatever to do with the nature of the raised exception. Therefore, the use of predefined types for exceptions certainly does not promote readability. It is much better to define classes for exceptions with meaningful names in a meaningful hierarchy that can be used for defining exceptions.

14.4   Exception Handling in Java

In Chapter 13, the Java example program includes the use of exception handling with little explanation. This section describes the details of Java's exception-handling capabilities.

Java's exception handling is based on that of C++, but it is designed to be more in line with the object-oriented language paradigm. Furthermore, Java includes a collection of predefined exceptions that are implicitly raised by the Java Virtual Machine (JVM).

14.4.1   Classes of Exceptions

All Java exceptions are objects of classes that are descendants of the `Throwable` class. The Java system includes two predefined exception classes that are subclasses of `Throwable`, `Error`, and `Exception`. The `Error` class and its descendants are related to errors that are thrown by the JVM, such as running out of heap memory. These exceptions are never thrown by user programs, and they should never be handled there. There are two system-defined direct descendants of `Exception`, `RuntimeException` and `IOException`. As its name indicates, `IOException` is thrown when an error has occurred in an input or output operation, all of which are defined as methods in the various classes defined in the package `java.io`.

There are predefined classes that are descendants of `RuntimeException`. In most cases, `RuntimeException` is thrown (by the JVM) when a user program causes an error. For example, `ArrayIndexOutOfBoundsException`, which is defined in `java.util`, is a commonly thrown exception that descends from `RuntimeException`. Another commonly thrown exception that descends from `RuntimeException` is `NullPointerException`.

User programs can define their own exception classes. The convention in Java is that user-defined exceptions are subclasses of `Exception`.

14.4.2 Exception Handlers

The exception handlers of Java have the same form as those of C++, except the parameter of every **catch** must be present and its class must be a descendant of the predefined class, `Throwable`.

The syntax of the **try** construct in Java is exactly as that of C++, except for the **finally** clause described in Section 14.4.6.

14.4.3 Binding Exceptions to Handlers

Throwing an exception is quite simple. An instance of the exception class is given as the operand of the **throw** statement. For example, suppose we define an exception named `MyException` as

```
class MyException extends Exception {
  public MyException() {}
  public MyException(String message) {
    super (message);
  }
}
```

This exception can be thrown with

```
throw new MyException();
```

The creation of the instance of the exception for the **throw** could be done separately from the **throw** statement, as in

```
MyException myExceptionObject = new MyException();
...
throw myExceptionObject;
```

One of the two constructors we have included in our new class has no parameter and the other has a `String` object parameter that it sends to the superclass (`Exception`), which displays it. So our new exception could be thrown with

```
throw new MyException
    ("a message to specify the location of the error");
```

The binding of exceptions to handlers in Java is similar to that of C++. If an exception is thrown in the compound statement of a **try** construct, it is bound to the first handler (**catch** function) immediately following the **try**

INTERVIEW

The Birth of Java

JAMES GOSLING

James Gosling is a Fellow and Vice President at Sun Microsystems, the creator of the Java programming language, and he is one of the computer industry's most noted programmers. He was the 1996 recipient of Software Development's Programming Excellence Award. He developed NeWS, Sun's network-extensible window system, and was a principal in the Andrew project at Carnegie-Mellon University, from which he holds a Ph.D. in computer science.

PERSONAL HISTORY/ DOWN MEMORY LANE

How did you get involved with computing?
When I was 14 years old a friend of my dad's took me on a tour of the computing facilities at the University of Calgary. I got hooked. Simply put, it was love at first sight. I then taught myself how to program, got a job at the physics department when I was in high school, and it snowballed from there.

What was your first computing job? Writing ground software for the ISIS-II satellite for the physics department at the University of Calgary.

What was your favorite job? My first job was pretty special. But I like my current one a lot too: being a researcher at Sun's research labs. Officially, I am "VP and Fellow."

> " [Java] was originally called "oak," because that was growing outside my office window when I had to pick a name and was staring out the window. "

JAVA: THE BIRTH OF A LANGUAGE

Lots of languages were born as a sort of by-product of a separate goal. I've heard this was the case with Java and the Green Project. Can you tell us the story? A group of us were investigating future trends that might have an impact on Sun. We pretty quickly focused in on the spread of digital systems into devices not normally thought of as computers (such as cell phones, televisions, control systems), coupled with the growth of networking. We started building a prototype device to help us learn about the space. Problems were encountered that stemmed from the base programming tools we were using. My part of the project ended up being to solve the tool problem. The result was Java.

Why create a language? Nothing else worked. The first prototype was done in C++, but we thought about

clause whose parameter is the same class as the thrown object, or an ancestor of it. If a matching handler is found, the **throw** is bound to it and it is executed.

Exceptions can be handled and then rethrown by including a **throw** statement without an operand at the end of the handler. The newly thrown exception will not be handled in the same **try** where it was originally thrown, and discarded many others. They were [all] too tied to specific CPU architectures (at the binary level) with little regard for security. Not to mention, they had some reliability issues.

You've talked about Simula as Java's predecessor. Why Simula? It was the original OO language. I used Simula a lot in years past. Over C and C++ it had single inheritance and tight memory mode.

What couple of features distinguished Java from the popular languages out there? Productivity, reliability, security, portability.

How much did these features and the current development trends in hardware and software play into the immediate success of Java? A lot.

JAVA: THE NAME GAME

Why was the original project called Green? No good reason. Apple had a research project called "Pink," so colors were in. We got ours from the door to the suite of offices we worked in: It was green. [Java] was originally called "oak," because that was growing outside my office window when I had to pick a name and was staring out the window. That original name had all kinds of trademark conflicts. The lawyers made us find a name that was clear of issues.

Are you tired of the name Java? No.

If you could name Java something else today, what name would you give it? Gak! That's too hard a question. Picking names is really tough.

JAVA: PAST, PRESENT, FUTURE

If you could go back and change two features of Java, or rework them, what might they be? Lightweight objects and switch statements.

Do you think about these things? Yes.

Looking back at what you were trying to build on Project Green, do such devices exist today? Were you "barking up the right tree" at the time? Yes. Palm Pilots and modern, fancy cell phones are directly in line with what we were trying to do.

If you were assigned to a Project Green-type goal today, on what user functionality would you focus your efforts? Or better said, if the Internet and Java were the "wow" tools of the early 1990s, what will be the next "wow" tool? The next "wow" tool hasn't changed—it still is the Internet. We've hardly begun exploiting it.

Jump forward 15 years: What functionality may programming languages offer then that they do not offer now? Reasoning/verification.

If you weren't doing this, what would you be doing? Anything that involves building stuff.

so looping is not a concern. This rethrowing is usually done when some local action is useful, but further handling by an enclosing **try** clause or a caller is necessary. A **throw** statement in a handler could also throw some exception other than the one that transferred control to this handler; one particular exception could cause another to be thrown.

To ensure that exceptions that can be thrown in a **try** clause are always handled in a method, a special handler can be written that matches all exceptions that are derived from `Exception` simply by defining the handler with an `Exception` type parameter, as in

```
catch (Exception genericObject) {
  ...
}
```

Because a class name always matches itself or any ancestor class, any class derived from `Exception` matches `Exception`. Of course, such an exception handler should always be placed at the end of the list of handlers, for it will block the use of any handler that follows it in the **try** construct in which it appears. This is because the search for a matching handler is sequential, and the search ends when a match is found.

14.4.4   Other Design Choices

The object parameter to an exception handler is not entirely useless, as it may have appeared to be so far in this discussion. During program execution, the Java run-time system stores the class name of every object in the program. The method `getClass` can be used to get an object that stores the class name, which itself can be gotten with the `getName` method. So we can retrieve the name of the class of the actual parameter from the **throw** statement that caused the handler's execution. For the handler above, this is done with

```
genericObject.getClass().getName()
```

In addition, the message associated with the parameter object, which is created by the constructor, can be gotten with

```
genericObject.getMessage()
```

Furthermore, in the case of user-defined exceptions, the thrown object could include any number of data fields that might be useful in the handler.

The **throws** clause of Java has the appearance and placement (in a program) that is similar to that of the **throw** specification of C++. However, the semantics of **throws** is somewhat different from that of the C++ **throw** clause.

The appearance of an exception class name in the **throws** clause of a Java method specifies that that exception class or any of its descendant exception classes can be thrown by the method. For example, when a method specifies that it can throw `IOException`, it means it can throw an `IOException` object or an object of any of its descendant classes, such as `EOFException`.

Exceptions of class `Error` and `RuntimeException` and their descendants are called **unchecked exceptions.** All other exceptions are called **checked exceptions.** Unchecked exceptions are never a concern of the compiler. However, the compiler ensures that all checked exceptions a method can throw are either listed in its **throws** clause or are handled in the method. The reason why exceptions of the classes `Error` and `RuntimeException` and their descendants are unchecked is that any method could throw them. A program can catch unchecked exceptions, but is is not required.

A method cannot declare more exceptions in its **throws** clause than the method it overrides, though it may declare fewer. So if a method has no **throws** clause, neither can any method that overrides it. A method can throw any exception listed in its **throws** clause, along with any of its descendant classes. A method that does not directly throw a particular exception, but calls another method that could throw that exception, must list the exception in its **throws** clause. This is the reason the buildDist method (in the example below), which uses the readLine method, must specify IOException in the **throws** clause of its header.

A method that calls a method that lists a particular checked exception in its **throws** clause has three alternatives for dealing with that exception: First, it can catch the exception and handle it. Second, it can catch the exception and throw an exception that is listed in its own **throws** clause. Third, it could declare the exception in its own **throws** clause and not handle it, which effectively propagates the exception to an enclosing **try** clause, if there is one, or to the method's caller if there is no enclosing **try** clause.

There are no default exception handlers, and it is not possible to disable exceptions. Continuation in Java is exactly as in C++.

14.4.5   An Example

Following is the Java class with the capabilities of the C++ program in Section 14.4:

```java
import java.io.*;

// The exception definition to deal with the end of data
class NegativeInputException extends Exception {
  public NegativeInputException() {
    System.out.println("End of input data reached");
  }  //** end of constructor
}  //** end of NegativeInputException class

class GradeDist {
  int newGrade,
      index,
      limit_1,
      limit_2;
  int [] freq = {0, 0, 0, 0, 0, 0, 0, 0, 0, 0};

  void buildDist() throws IOException {
  //  Input: A list of integer values that represent
  //         grades, followed by a negative number
```

```
// Output: A distribution of grades, as a percentage for
//           each of the categories 0-9, 10-19, ...,
//           10-100.
  DataInputStream in = new DataInputStream(System.in);
  try {
    while (true) {
      System.out.println("Please input a grade");
      newGrade = Integer.parseInt(in.readLine());
      if (newGrade < 0)
        throw new NegativeInputException();
      index = newGrade / 10;
      try {
        freq[index]++;
      } //** end of inner try clause
      catch(ArrayIndexOutOfBoundsException) {
        if (newGrade == 100)
          freq [9]++;
        else
          System.out.println("Error - new grade: " +
                        newGrade + " is out of range");
      } //** end of catch (ArrayIndex...
    } //** end of while (true) ...
  } //** end of outer try clause
  catch(NegativeInputException) {
    System.out.println ("\nLimits    Frequency\n");
    for (index = 0; index < 10; index++) {
      limit_1 = 10 * index;
      limit_2 = limit_1 + 9;
      if (index ==9)
        limit_2 = 100;
      System.out.println("" + limit_1 + " - " +
                      limit_2 + "       " + freq [index]);
    } //** end of for (index = 0; ...
  } //** end of catch (NegativeInputException ...
} //** end of method buildDist
```

The exception for a negative input, NegativeInputException, is defined in the program. Its constructor displays a message when an object of the class is created. Its handler produces the output of the method. ArrayIndexOutOfBoundsException is a predefined unchecked exception that is thrown by the JVM. In both of these cases, the handler does not include an object name in its parameter. In neither case would a name serve any purpose. Note that all handlers get objects as parameters, but they often are not useful.

14.4.6 The `finally` Clause

There are some situations in which a process must be executed regardless of whether or not a **try** clause throws an exception and regardless of whether or not a thrown exception is caught in a method. One example of such a situation is a file that must be closed. Another is if the method has some external resource that must be freed in the method regardless of how the execution of the method terminates. The **finally** clause was designed for these kinds of needs. A **finally** clause is placed at the end of the list of handlers just after a complete **try** construct. In general, the **try** construct and its **finally** clause appears as

```
try {
  ...
}
catch (...) {
  ...
}
... //** More handlers
finally {
  ...
}
```

The semantics of this construct is as follows: If the **try** clause throws no exceptions, the **finally** clause is executed before execution continues after the **try** construct. If the **try** clause throws an exception and it is caught by a following handler, the **finally** clause is executed after the handler completes its execution. If the **try** clause throws an exception but it is not caught by a handler following the **try** construct, the **finally** clause is executed before the exception is propagated.

A **try** construct with no exception handlers can be followed by a **finally** clause. This only makes sense, of course, if the compound statement has a **break**, **continue**, or **return** statement. Its purpose in these cases is the same as when it is used with exception handling. For example, we could have something like the following:

```
try {
  for (index = 0; index < 100; index++) {
    ...
    if (... ) {
      return;
    } //** end of if
    ...
  } //** end of for
} //** end of try clause
finally {
```

```
    . . .
}   //** end of try construct
```

The **finally** clause here will be executed, regardless of whether the **return** terminates the loop or it ends normally.

14.4.7 Evaluation

The Java mechanisms for exception handling are an improvement over the C++ version on which they are based.

First, a C++ program can throw any type defined in the program or by the system. In Java, only objects that are instances of `Throwable` or some class that descends from it can be thrown. This separates the objects that can be thrown from all of the other objects (and nonobjects) that inhabit a program. What significance can be attached to an exception that causes an **int** value to be thrown?

Second, a C++ program unit that does not include a **throws** clause can throw any exception, which tells the reader nothing. A Java method that does not include a **throws** clause cannot throw any checked exception that it does not handle. Therefore, the reader of a Java method knows from its header what exceptions it could throw but does not handle.

Third, the addition of the **finally** clause is a great convenience in certain situations. It allows cleanup kinds of actions to take place regardless of how a compound statement terminated.

Finally, the JVM implicitly throws a variety of predefined exceptions, such as for array indices out of range and null reference variable accesses, which can be handled by any user program. A C++ program can handle only those exceptions that it explicitly throws.

Relative to the exception handling of Ada, Java's facilities are roughly comparable. The presence of the **throws** clause in a Java method is a good aid to readability, whereas Ada has no corresponding feature. Java is certainly closer to Ada than it is to C++ in one area, that of allowing programs to deal with system-detected exceptions.

C# includes exception handling constructs that are very much like those of Java, except that C# does not have a **throws** clause.

14.5   Introduction to Event Handling

Event handling is similar to exception handling. In both cases, the handlers are implicitly called by the occurrence of something, either an exception or an event. While exceptions either can be created explicitly by user code or implicitly by hardware or a software interpreter, events are created by external actions, such as user interactions through a graphical user interface. In this section, the fundamentals of event handling, which are substantially less complex than those of exception handling, are introduced.

14.5.1 Basic Concepts of Event Handling

In conventional (non-event-driven) programming, the code itself specifies the order in which that code is executed, although the order is usually affected by the program's input data. In event-driven programming, parts of the program are executed at completely unpredictable times, often triggered by user interactions with the executing program.

The particular kind of event handling discussed in this chapter is related to graphical user interfaces. Therefore, most of the events are caused by user interactions through graphical objects, often called *widgets*. The most common examples of widgets are buttons. Implementing reactions to user interactions with GUI components is the most common form of event handling.

An **event** is a notification that something specific has occurred, such as a mouse click on a button. Strictly speaking, an event is an object that is implicitly created by the run-time system in response to a user action, at least in the context in which event handling is being discussed here.

An **event handler** is a segment of code that is executed in response to the appearance of an event. Event handlers enable a program to be responsive to user actions.

Although event-driven programming was being used long before the graphical user interfaces (GUI) appeared, it has only become a widely used programming methodology in response to the popularity of these interfaces. As an example, consider the GUIs presented to users of Web browsers. Many Web documents presented to browsers are now dynamic. Browsers provide options to users through widgets. For example, a user may be allowed to change the foreground or background colors of the display of a document by clicking the appropriate button in a collection of radio buttons. The color changes are performed by event handlers designed to react to clicks of those radio buttons.

Another common use of event handlers is to check for simple errors and omissions in the elements of a form, either when they are changed or when the form is submitted to the Web server for processing. Forms are the primary way that Web sites can gather input from Web clients. A form is a collection of widgets. Using event handling on the browser to check the validity of form data saves the time of sending that data to the server, where its correctness then must be checked by a server-resident program or script before it can be processed. This kind of event-driven programming is often done using a client-side scripting language, such as JavaScript.

14.6 Event Handling with Java

Java supports two different approaches to presenting interactive displays to users, either from application programs or from applets. Both use the same classes to define the GUI components and the event handlers that provide the interactivity. Although we only discuss applets, the section also applies to application programs.

The initial version of Java provided a somewhat primitive form of support for GUI components. In version 1.2 of the language, a new collection of components were added. These were collectively called Swing. In this section we only discuss Swing components and handling the events they create.

Before discussing event handling for GUI components, we provide a brief introduction to some Swing components.

14.6.1   Java Swing GUI Components

The Swing package, defined in `javax.swing`, includes a collection of components, which are what we have called widgets. Because our interest here is event handling, not GUI components, we only discuss two categories of widgets, text boxes and radio buttons.

A text box is an object of class `JTextField`. The simplest `JTextField` constructor takes a single parameter, the length of the box in characters. For example,

```
JTextField name = new JTextField(32);
```

The `JTextField` constructor can also take a literal string, which is displayed as its contents. The string parameter, when present, appears as the first parameter.

Radio buttons are special buttons that are placed in a button group. A button group is an object of class `ButtonGroup`, whose constructor takes no parameters. The `JRadioButton` constructor, used for creating radio buttons, takes two parameters: the label and the initial state of the radio button (**true** or **false**). After the radio buttons are created, they are put in their button group with the `add` method of the group object. Consider the following example:

```
ButtonGroup payment = new ButtonGroup();
JRadioButton box1 = new JRadioButton("Visa", true);
JRadioButton box2 = new JRadioButton("Master Charge",
                                     false);
JRadioButton box3 = new JRadioButton("Discover", false);
payment.add(box1);
payment.add(box2);
payment.add(box3);
```

An applet's display is actually a frame, which is a multilayered structure. We are interested in just one of those layers, the content pane. The content pane is where applets put their output. User programs do not place anything directly in the content pane; rather, they place graphical objects in a panel and then add the panel to the content pane. For applications, a frame is created and the constructed panel is added to that frame's content pane.

A content pane is created as a `Container` object, using the `getContentPane` method, as in

```
Container contentPane = getContentPane();
```

Predefined graphic objects, such as GUI components, can be placed directly in a panel that is created in the applet and then added to the applet's content pane. The following creates the panel object we use in the following discussion of components.

```
JPanel myPanel = new JPanel();
```

The background color for a panel can be set with the `setBackground` method, as shown here:

```
myPanel.setBackground(Color.yellow);
```

The `setForeground` method sets the default color of everything to be drawn in the panel. For example, the following statement changes the default drawing color to blue (assuming it was not already blue):

```
myPanel.setForeground(Color.blue);
```

After the components have been created with constructors, they must be placed in the panel with the `add` method:

```
myPanel.add(button1);
```

In Java, layout manager objects are used to control the placement of components in a panel. The default layout manager for Swing is `BorderLayout`, which places components on the borders of the panel. This is fine for some situations. However, it is often convenient to have more control over where components are placed in a panel. For this, Java includes several other layout managers. One of these is `GridLayout`, which divides the panel area into rows and columns of compartments, each of which can contain a component. The parameters to the `GridLayout` constructor are the number of rows and columns, and the number of pixels between the rows and columns, respectively. The layout manager for a panel is specified with the `setLayout` method, which takes a layout manager object as its parameter. For example, consider the following code, which creates a new panel named `buttonPanel` and a `GridLayout` layout manager object for the panel:

```
JPanel buttonPanel = new JPanel();
buttonPanel.setLayout(new GridLayout(2, 3, 15, 15));
```

This also sets the panel's grid layout to have two rows of three components each, with 15 pixels between the components.

14.6.2   The Java Event Model

User interactions with GUI components create events that can be caught by event handlers, which provide the associated computations. GUI components are considered event generators; they all generate events. In Java, event handlers are called **event listeners**. Event listeners are connected to event generators through event listener registration. Listener registration is done with a method of the class that implements the listener interface, as described later in this section. The panel object into which the components are placed can be the event listener for those components. Only event listeners that are registered for a specific event are notified when that event occurs.

An event generator tells a listener of an event by sending a message to the listener (in other words, by calling one of the listener's methods). The listener method that receives the message implements an event handler. To make the event-handling methods conform to a standard protocol, an interface is used. An interface prescribes standard method protocols but does not provide implementations of those methods. This protocol could be specified by forcing the event generator to be a subclass of a class from which it would inherit the protocol. However, the JApplet class already has a superclass, and in Java, a class can have just one parent class. Therefore, the protocol must come from an interface. A class cannot be instantiated unless it provides definitions for all methods in the interfaces that it implements.

A class that needs to implement a listener must implement an interface for those listeners. There are many classes of events and listener interfaces. The event classes appear in two categories, semantic events and low-level events. A few of the most commonly used classes of events are shown in Table 14.1.

Each semantic event listener interface prescribes one method for the handler. The low-level interfaces have several different handler methods. The handler methods for the two most commonly used semantic events are shown in Table 14.2.

Table 14.1	**Class Name**	**User Actions That Create the Event Object**
Event Classes		
	SEMANTIC EVENT CLASSES	
	ActionEvent	Click a button, select from a menu or list, or press the Enter button in a text field
	ItemEvent	Select a checkbox or list item
	TextEvent	Change the contents of a text field or text area
	LOWER-LEVEL EVENT CLASSES	
	ComponentEvent	Resize, move, show, or hide a component
	KeyEvent	Press or release a key
	MouseEvent	Depress or release a mouse button, or move the cursor into or out of the component
	MouseMotionEvent	Change the position of the mouse cursor over the component
	FocusEvent	Get or lose focus for a component

Table 14.2	Interface	Handler Method
Semantic Event Listener Interfaces and Their Handler Methods	ActionListener	actionPerformed
	ItemListener	itemStateChanged

As stated previously, the connection of a component to an event listener is made with a method of the class that implements the listener interface. For example, because `ActionEvent` is the class name of event objects created by user actions on buttons, the `addActionListener` method is used to register a listener for buttons. The listener for button events created in a panel in an applet could be implemented in the panel. So, for a button named `button1` in a panel named `myPanel` that implements the `ActionEvent` event handler for buttons, we would register the listener with the following statement:

```
button1.addActionListener(this);
```

When an event handler has only a few lines, it can be implemented as an instance of an anonymous nested class. For example, suppose that we have a button whose event handler just sets the font for a text object. The registration of the handler and the handler itself can be defined with this code:

```
button.addActionListener(new ActionListener() {
  public void actionPerformed(ActionEvent e) {
    text.setFont(newFont);
  }
});
```

The embedded, or inner, anonymous class implements the `action Performed` method.

Each event handler method receives an event parameter, which provides information about the event. Event classes have methods, such as `getState`, to access that information. For example, when called through a radio button, `getState` returns true or false, depending on whether the button was on or off, respectively.

All the event-related classes are in the `java.awt.event` package, so it is usually imported to any applet class that uses events.

The following is the example applet, `RadioB`, that illustrates the use of events and event handling to display dynamic content in an applet. This applet constructs radio buttons that control the font style of the contents of a text field. It creates a `Font` object for each of four font styles. Each of these has a radio button to enable the user to select the style. The applet then creates a text string, whose font style will be controlled by the user through the radio buttons. The event handler `itemStateChanged` determines which radio button is pressed, after being informed by the `ItemEvent` object that a change has been made in the radio buttons. Then it sets the font style of the text string accordingly.

This example does not use anonymous inner classes to implement the event handlers. In this case, that approach requires more code than having a single handler because there are four required handlers.

```java
/* RadioB.java
   An applet to illustrate event handling with interactive
   radio buttons that control the font style of a
   textfield
   */
import java.awt.*;
import java.awt.event.*;
import java.applet.*;
import javax.swing.*;

public class RadioB extends JApplet implements
                                        ItemListener {

// Make most of the variables class variables, because
//   both init and the event handler must see them

    private Container contentPane = getContentPane();
    private JTextField text;
    private Font plainFont, boldFont, italicFont,
                boldItalicFont;
    private JRadioButton plain, bold, italic, boldItalic;
    private ButtonGroup radioButtons = new ButtonGroup();
    private JPanel myPanel = new JPanel();

// The init method is where the document is initially
//   built

    public void init() {

// Set the background color of the panel

        myPanel.setBackground(Color.cyan);

// Create the fonts

            plainFont = new Font("Serif", Font.PLAIN, 16);
            boldFont = new Font("Serif", Font.BOLD, 16);
            italicFont = new Font("Serif", Font.ITALIC, 16);
            boldItalicFont = new Font("Serif", Font.BOLD +
                                    Font.ITALIC, 16);
```

```
// Create the test text string, set its font, and add it
//  to the panel

        text = new JTextField(
            "In what font style should I appear?", 30);
        myPanel.add(text);
        text.setFont(plainFont);

// Create radio buttons for the fonts and add them to
//   the panel

        plain = new JRadioButton("Plain", true);
        bold = new JRadioButton("Bold");
        italic = new JRadioButton("Italic");
        boldItalic = new JRadioButton("Bold Italic");
        radioButtons.add(plain);
        radioButtons.add(bold);
        radioButtons.add(italic);
        radioButtons.add(boldItalic);

// Register the event handlers to myPanel

        plain.addItemListener(this);
        bold.addItemListener(this);
        italic.addItemListener(this);
        boldItalic.addItemListener(this);

// Now add the buttons to the panel

        myPanel.add(plain);
        myPanel.add(bold);
        myPanel.add(italic);
        myPanel.add(boldItalic);

// Now add the panel to the content pane for the applet

        contentPane.add(myPanel);

    }  // End of init()

// The event handler

    public void itemStateChanged (ItemEvent e) {
```

```
        // Determine which button is on and set the font
        //   accordingly

            if (plain.isSelected())
                text.setFont(plainFont);
            else if (bold.isSelected())
                text.setFont(boldFont);
            else if (italic.isSelected())
                text.setFont(italicFont);
            else if (boldItalic.isSelected())
                text.setFont(boldItalicFont);

        } // End of itemStateChanged

    } // End of RadioB applet
```

The RadioB applet produces the screen shown in Figure 14.2.

Figure 14.2

Output of the RadioB applet

SUMMARY

Exception handling has been incorporated into few widely used languages, although many experimental languages designed since the mid-1970s have had such facilities.

Ada provides extensive exception-handling facilities and a small but comprehensive collection of built-in exceptions. The handlers are attached to the program entities, although exceptions can be implicitly or explicitly propagated to other program entities if no local handler is available.

C++ includes no predefined exceptions. Exceptions are bound to handlers by connecting the type of the expression in the **throw** statement to that of the formal parameter of the handler. Handlers all have the same name, **catch**.

Java exceptions are objects whose ancestry must trace back to a class that descends from the Throwable class. There are two categories of exceptions, checked and unchecked. Checked exceptions are a concern for the user program and the compiler. Unchecked exceptions can occur anywhere and are often ignored by user programs.

The Java **throws** clause of a method lists the checked exceptions that it could throw and does not handle. It must include exceptions that methods it calls could raise and propagate back to its caller.

The Java **finally** clause provides a mechanism for guaranteeing that some code will be executed regardless of how the execution of a **try** compound terminates.

An event is a notification that something has occurred that requires handling. Events are often created by user interactions with a program, usually through a graphical user interface. Java event handlers are called event listeners. An event listener must be registered for an event if it is to be notified when the event occurs. Two of the most commonly used event listeners are actionPerformed and itemStateChanged, whose protocols are provided by associated interfaces.

BIBLIOGRAPHIC NOTES

One of the most important papers on exception handling that is not connected with a particular programming language is the work by Goodenough (1975). The problems with the PL/I design for exception handling are covered in MacLaren (1977). The CLU exception-handling design is clearly described by Liskov and Snyder (1979). Exception-handling facilities of the Ada language are described in ARM (1995). Exception handling in C++ is described by Stroustrup (1997). Exception handling in Java is described by Campione et al. (2001).

REVIEW QUESTIONS

1. Define *exception*, *exception handler*, *raising an exception*, *disabling an exception*, *continuation*, and *built-in exception*.
2. What are the design issues for exception handling?
3. What does it mean for an exception to be bound to an exception handler?
4. What are the possible frames for exceptions in Ada?
5. Where are unhandled exceptions propagated in Ada if raised in a subprogram? A block? A package body? A task?
6. Where does execution continue after an exception is handled in Ada?
7. How can an exception be explicitly raised in Ada?
8. How is a user-defined exception defined in Ada?
9. How can an exception be suppressed in Ada?

10. What is the name of all C++ exception handlers?

11. How can exceptions be explicitly raised in C++?

12. How are exceptions bound to handlers in C++?

13. How can an exception handler be written in C++ so that it handles any exception?

14. Where does execution control go when a C++ exception handler has completed its execution?

15. Does C++ include built-in exceptions?

16. What is the root class of all Java exception classes?

17. What is the parent class of most Java user-defined exception classes?

18. How can an exception handler be written in Java so that it handles any exception?

19. What is the difference between a C++ **throw** specification and a Java **throws** clause?

20. What is the difference between checked and unchecked exceptions in Java?

21. Can you disable a Java exception?

22. What is the purpose of the Java **finally** clause?

PROBLEM SET

1. What run-time errors or conditions, if any, can Pascal programs detect and handle?

2. From textbooks on the PL/I and Ada programming languages, look up the respective sets of built-in exceptions. Do a comparative evaluation of the two, considering both completeness and flexibility.

3. From (AARM, 1995), determine how exceptions that take place during rendezvous are handled.

4. From a textbook on COBOL, determine how exception handling is done in COBOL programs.

5. In languages without exception-handling facilities, it is common to have most subprograms include an "error" parameter, which can be set to some value representing "OK" or some other value representing "error in procedure." What advantage does a linguistic exception-handling facility like that of Ada have over this method?

6. In a language without exception-handling facilities, we could send an error-handling procedure as a parameter to each procedure that can detect errors that must be handled. What disadvantages are there to this method?

7. Compare the methods suggested in Problems 6 and 7. Which do you think is better and why?

8. Compare the exception-handling facilities of C++ with those of Ada. Which design, in your opinion, is the most flexible? Which makes it possible to write more reliable programs?

9. Consider the following Java skeletal program:

```java
class Big {
  int i;
  float f;
  void fun1() throws {int} {
    ...
    try {
      ...
      throw i;
      ...
      throw f;
      ...
    }
    catch(float) { ... }
    ...
  }
}
class Small {
  int j;
  float g;
  void fun2() throws {float} {
    ...
    try {
      ...
      try {
        Big.fun1();
        ...
        throw j;
        ...
        throw g;
        ...
      }
      catch(int) { ... }
      ...
    }
    catch(float) { ... }
  }
}
```

In each of the four **throw** statements, where is the exception handled? Note that fun1 is called from fun2 in class Small.

PROGRAMMING EXERCISES

1. Write an Ada code segment that retries a call to a procedure, Tape_Read, that reads input from a tape drive and can raise the Tape_Read_Error exception.

2. Suppose you are writing an Ada procedure that has three alternative methods for accomplishing its requirements. Write a skeletal version of this procedure so that if the first alternative raises any exception, the second is tried, and if the second alternative raises any exception, the third is executed. Write the code as if the three methods were procedures named Alt1, Alt2, and Alt3.

3. Write an Ada program that inputs a list of integer values in the range of −100 to 100 from the keyboard and computes the sum of the squares of the input values. This program must use exception handling to ensure that the input values are in range and are legal integers, to handle the error of the sum of the squares becoming larger than a standard Integer variable can store, and to detect end-of-file and use it to cause output of the result. In the case of overflow of the sum, an error message must be printed and the program terminated.

4. Write a C++ program for the specification of Problem 3.

5. Write a Java program for the specification of Problem 3.

6. Write a detailed comparison of the exception-handling capabilities of C++ and those of Java.

15

Functional Programming Languages

CHAPTER OUTLINE

This chapter introduces functional programming and some of the programming languages that have been designed for this approach to software development. Because these languages are based on mathematical functions, we begin by reviewing the fundamental ideas of these. Also included in this section is a brief discussion of functional forms and a few examples of the most common of these. Next, the idea of a functional programming language is introduced, followed by a look at the first functional language, LISP, and its list data structures and functional syntax, which is based on lambda notation. The next somewhat lengthy section is devoted to an introduction to Scheme, including some of its primitive functions, special forms, functional forms, and some examples of simple functions written in Scheme. Next, we give short introductions to COMMON LISP, ML, and Haskell to show some different (from Scheme) design ideas for functional programming languages. A section follows that describes some of the applications of functional programming languages. Finally, we present a short comparison of functional and imperative languages.

15.1   Introduction

The first 14 chapters of this book have been concerned primarily with the imperative and object-oriented programming languages. With the exception of Smalltalk, the object-oriented languages we have discussed have had forms that are similar to the imperative languages.

The high degree of similarity among the imperative languages arises in part from one of the common basis of their design: the von Neumann architecture, as discussed in Chapter 1. We can think of the imperative languages collectively as a progression of developments to improve the basic model, which was Fortran I. All have been designed to make efficient use of von Neumann architecture computers. Although the imperative style of programming has been found acceptable by most programmers, its heavy reliance on the underlying architecture is thought by some to be an unnecessary restriction on the process of software development.

Other bases for language design exist, some of them oriented more to particular programming paradigms or methodologies than to efficient execution on a particular computer architecture. Thus far, however, only a small minority of programs are written in nonimperative languages.

The functional programming paradigm, which is based on mathematical functions, is the design basis for one of the most important nonimperative styles of languages. This style of programming is supported by functional, or applicative, programming languages.

LISP began as a purely functional language but soon acquired some important imperative features that increased its execution efficiency. It is still the most important of the functional languages, at least in the sense that it is the only one that has achieved widespread use. Scheme is a small, static-scoped dialect of LISP. COMMON LISP is an amalgam of several early 1980s dialects of LISP. ML and Haskell are strongly typed functional languages with more conventional syntax than LISP and Scheme.

One objective of this chapter is to provide an introduction to functional programming using the core of Scheme, intentionally leaving out its imperative features. Sufficient material on Scheme is included to allow the reader to write some simple but interesting programs. It is difficult to acquire an actual feel for functional programming without some actual programming experience, so that is strongly encouraged.

15.2   Mathematical Functions

A mathematical function is a **mapping** of members of one set, called the **domain set,** to another set, called the **range set.** A function definition specifies the domain and range sets, either explicitly or implicitly, along with the mapping. The mapping is described by an expression or, in some cases, by a table. Functions are often applied to a particular element of the domain set. Note that the domain set may be the cross product of several sets. A function yields, or returns, an element of the range set.

One of the fundamental characteristics of mathematical functions is that the evaluation order of their mapping expressions is controlled by recursion and conditional expressions, rather than by the sequencing and iterative repetition that are common to the imperative programming languages.

Another important characteristic of mathematical functions is that, because they have no side effects, they always define the same value given the same set of arguments. Side effects in programming languages are connected to variables that model memory locations.

In mathematics, there is no such thing as a variable that models a memory location. Local variables in functions in imperative programming languages maintain the state of the function. In mathematics, there is no concept of the state of a function.

A mathematical function defines a value, rather than specifying a sequence of operations on values in memory to produce a value. There are no variables in the sense of imperative languages, so there can be no side effects.

15.2.1   Simple Functions

Function definitions are often written as a function name, followed by a list of parameters in parentheses, followed by the mapping expression. For example,

$$\text{cube}(x) \equiv x * x * x, \text{ where } x \text{ is a real number}$$

In this definition the domain and range sets are the real numbers. The symbol $\equiv$ is used to mean "is defined as." The parameter, x, can represent any member of the domain set, but it is fixed to represent one specific element during evaluation of the function expression. This is how the parameters of mathematical functions differ from the variables in imperative languages.

Function applications are specified by pairing the function name with a particular element of the domain set. The range element is obtained by evaluating the function mapping expression with the domain element substituted for the occurrences of the parameter. For example, cube(2.0) yields the value 8.0. Once again, it is important to note that during evaluation, the mapping of a function contains no unbound parameters, where a bound parameter is a name for a particular value. Every occurrence of a parameter is bound to a value from the domain set and is considered a constant during evaluation.

Early theoretical work on functions separated the task of defining a function from that of naming the function. Lambda notation, as devised by Alonzo Church (Church, 1941), provides a method for defining nameless functions. A **lambda expression** specifies the parameter and the mapping of a function. The lambda expression is the function itself. For example, consider

$$\lambda(x)x * x * x$$

As stated above, before evaluation, a parameter represents any member of the domain set, but during evaluation it is bound to a particular member. When a lambda expression is evaluated for a given parameter, the expression is said to be applied to that parameter. The mechanics of such an application are the same as for any function evaluation. Application of the lambda expression above is denoted, as in the following example:

$$(\lambda(x)x * x * x)(2)$$

which results in the value 8.

Lambda expressions, like other function definitions, can have more than one parameter.

15.2.2 Functional Forms

A higher-order function, or **functional form,** is one that either takes functions as parameters or yields a function as its result, or both. One common kind of functional form is **function composition,** which has two functional parameters and yields a function whose value is the first actual parameter function applied to the result of the second. Function composition is written as an expression, using $\circ$ as an operator, as in

$$h \equiv f \circ g$$

For example, if

$$f(x) \equiv x + 2$$
$$g(x) \equiv 3 * x$$

then h is defined as

$$h(x) \equiv f(g(x)), \text{ or } h(x) \equiv (3 * x) + 2$$

Apply-to-all is a functional form that takes a single function as a parameter. If applied to a list of arguments, apply-to-all applies its functional parameter to each of the values in the list argument and collects the results in a list or sequence. Apply-to-all is denoted by α. Consider the following example:

Let

$$h(x) \equiv x * x$$

then

$$\alpha(h, (2, 3, 4)) \text{ yields } (4, 9, 16)$$

There are many other functional forms, but these two examples should illustrate their characteristics.

15.3 Fundamentals of Functional Programming Languages

The objective of the design of a functional programming language is to mimic mathematical functions to the greatest extent possible. This results in an approach to problem solving that is fundamentally different from approaches used with imperative languages. In an imperative language, an expression is evaluated and the result is stored in a memory location, which is represented as a variable in a program. This necessary attention to memory cells results in a relatively low-level programming methodology. A program in an assembly language often must also store the results of partial evaluations of expressions. For example, to evaluate

$$(x + y)/(a - b)$$

the value of $(x + y)$ is computed first. That value must then be stored while $(a - b)$ is evaluated. The compiler handles the storage of intermediate results of expression evaluations in high-level languages. The storage of intermediate results is still required, but the details are hidden from the programmer.

A purely functional programming language does not use variables or assignment statements. This frees the programmer from concerns about the memory cells of the computer on which the program is executed. Without variables, iterative constructs are not possible, for they are controlled by variables. Repetition must be done by recursion rather than by repetition. Programs are function definitions and function application specifications, and executions consist of evaluating the function applications. Without variables, the execution of a purely functional program has no state in the sense of operational and denotational semantics. The execution of a function always produces the same result when given the same parameters. This is called **referential transparency.** It makes the semantics of purely functional languages far simpler than the semantics of the imperative languages and the functional languages that include imperative features.

A functional language provides a set of primitive functions, a set of functional forms to construct complex functions from those primitive functions, a function application operation, and some structure or structures for representing data. These structures are used to represent the parameters and values computed by functions. A well-defined functional language requires only a small number of primitive functions.

Although functional languages are often implemented with interpreters, they can also be compiled.

Imperative languages usually provide only limited support for functional programming. The most serious drawback to using an imperative language to do functional programming is that functions in imperative languages have restrictions on the types of values that can be returned. In some languages, for example Fortran, only scalar type values can be returned. More importantly, imperative languages typically cannot return a function. Such restrictions limit the kinds of functional forms that can be provided. Another serious problem with the functions of imperative languages is the possibility of functional side effects.

15.4   The First Functional Programming Language: LISP

A number of functional programming languages have been developed. The oldest and most widely used is LISP. Studying functional languages through LISP is somewhat akin to studying the imperative languages through Fortran: LISP was the first functional language, but although it has steadily evolved over the last 40 years, it no longer represents the latest design concepts for functional languages. In addition, with the exception of the first version, all LISP dialects include imperative language features, such as imperative-style variables, assignment statements, and iteration. (Imperative-style variables are used to name memory cells, whose values can change many times during program execution.) Despite this and their somewhat odd form, the descendants of the original LISP represent well the fundamental concepts of functional programming and are therefore worthy of study.

15.4.1   Data Types and Structures

There were only two types of data objects in the original LISP: atoms and lists.[1] They are not types in the sense that imperative languages have types. In fact, the original LISP was a typeless language. Atoms are either symbols, in the form of identifiers, or they are numeric literals.

---

[1] Actually, lists are the most commonly used form of a more general data structure, the dotted pair. We will ignore dotted pairs, except to explain in Section 15.5.6 how one can be accidentally created.

Recall from Chapter 2 that LISP originally used lists as its data structure because they were thought to be an essential part of list processing. As it eventually developed, however, LISP rarely requires the operations of insertion and deletion.

Lists are specified in LISP by delimiting their elements within parentheses. The elements of **simple lists** are restricted to atoms, as in

(A B C D)

Nested list structures are also specified by parentheses. For example, the list

(A (B C) D (E (F G)))

is a list of four elements. The first is the atom A; the second is the sublist (B C); the third is the atom D; the fourth is the sublist (E (F G)), which has as its second element the sublist (F G).

Internally, lists are usually stored as single-linked list structures, in which each node has two pointers and represents an element. A node for an atom has its first pointer pointing to some representation of the atom, such as its symbol or numeric value. A node for a sublist element has its first pointer pointing to the first node of the sublist. In both cases, the second pointer of a node points to the next element of the list. A list is referenced by a pointer to its first element.

The internal representations of our two example lists are shown in Figure 15.1. Note that the elements of a list are shown horizontally. The last

Figure 15.1

Internal representation
of two LISP lists

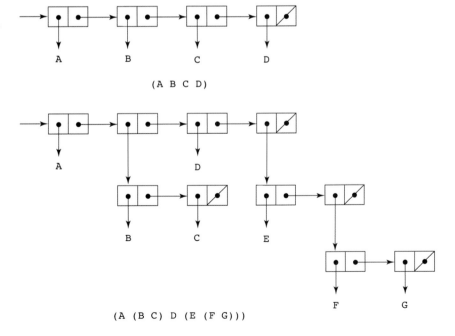

(A B C D)

(A (B C) D (E (F G)))

element of a list has no successor, so its link is NIL. Sublists are shown with the same structure.

15.4.2   The First LISP Interpreter

The original intent was to have a notation for LISP programs that would be as close to Fortran's as possible, with additions when necessary. This notation was called M-notation, for meta-notation. There was to be a compiler that would translate programs written in M-notation into semantically equivalent machine code programs for the IBM 704.

Early in the development of LISP, McCarthy decided to write a paper that would promote list processing as an approach to general symbolic processing. Among others, McCarthy believed that list processing could be used to study computability, which at the time was usually studied using Turing machines. McCarthy thought that the processing of symbolic lists was a more natural model of computation than Turing machines. One of the common requirements of the study of computation is that one must be able to prove certain computability characteristics of the whole class of whatever model of computation is being used. In the case of the Turing machine model, one can construct a universal Turing machine that can mimic the operations of any other Turing machine. From this concept came the idea of constructing a universal LISP function that could evaluate any other function in LISP.

The first requirement for the universal LISP function was a notation that allowed functions to be expressed in the same way data was expressed. The parenthesized list notation described in Section 15.4.1 had already been adopted for LISP data, so it was decided to invent conventions for function definitions and function calls that could also be expressed in list notation. Function calls were specified in a prefix list form called Cambridge Polish, as in the following:

(function_name   argument_1 ... argument_n)

For example, if + is a function that takes two numeric parameters,

(+ 5 7)

evaluates to 12.

The lambda notation described in Section 15.2.1 was chosen to specify function definitions. It had to be modified, however, to allow the binding of functions to names so that functions could be referenced by other functions and by themselves. This name binding was specified by a list consisting of the function name and a list containing the lambda expression, as in

(function_name (LAMBDA (arg_1 ... arg_n) expression))

If you have had no prior exposure to functional programming, it may seem odd to even consider a nameless function. However, nameless functions are sometimes useful in functional programming (as well as in mathematics). For example, consider a function whose action is to produce a function for immediate application to a parameter list. The produced function has no need for a name, for it is applied only at the point of its construction. Such an example is given in Section 15.5.6.

LISP functions specified in this new notation were called S-expressions, for symbolic expressions. Eventually, all LISP structures, both data and code, were called S-expressions. An S-expression can be either a list or an atom. We will often refer to S-expressions simply as expressions.

McCarthy successfully developed a universal function that could evaluate any other function. This function was named EVAL and was itself in the form of an expression. Two of the people in the AI Project, Stephen B. Russell and Daniel J. Edwards, noticed that an implementation of EVAL could serve as a LISP interpreter, and they promptly constructed such an implementation (McCarthy et al., 1965).

There were several important results of this quick, easy, and unexpected implementation. First, all early LISP systems copied EVAL and were therefore interpretive. Second, the definition of M-notation, which was the planned programming notation for LISP, was never completed or implemented, so S-expressions became LISP's only notation. The use of the same notation for data and code has important consequences, one of which will be discussed in Section 15.5.12. Third, much of the original language design was effectively frozen, keeping certain odd features in the language, such as the conditional expression form and the use of ( ) for both the empty list and logical false.

Another feature of early LISP systems that was apparently accidental was the use of dynamic scoping. Functions were evaluated in the environments of their callers. No one at the time knew much about scoping, and it is doubtful that much thought was given to the choice. Dynamic scoping was used for most dialects of LISP before 1975. Contemporary dialects either use static scoping or allow the programmer to choose between static and dynamic scoping.

15.5   An Introduction to Scheme

In this section, we describe a part of Scheme (Dybvig, 1996). We have chosen Scheme because it is relatively simple, it is popular in colleges and universities, and Scheme interpreters are readily available for a wide variety of computers. The version of Scheme described in this section is Scheme 4. Note that this section covers only a small part of Scheme, and that it includes none of Scheme's imperative features.

15.5.1   Origins of Scheme

The Scheme language, which is a dialect of LISP, emerged from MIT in the mid-1970s (Sussman and Steele, 1975). It is characterized by its small size, its exclusive use of static scoping, and its treatment of functions as first-class entities. As first-class entities, Scheme functions can be the values of expressions and elements of lists, and they can be assigned to variables and passed as parameters. Early versions of LISP did not provide all of these capabilities.

As a small language with simple syntax and semantics, Scheme is well-suited to educational applications, such as courses in functional programming, and also general introductions to programming.

Note that most of the functions in the following sections that are written in Scheme would require only minor modifications to be rewritten as LISP functions.

15.5.2   The Scheme Interpreter

The Scheme interpreter is a read-evaluate-write infinite loop. It repeatedly reads an expression typed by the user (in the form of a list), interprets the expression, and displays the resulting value. Expressions are interpreted by the function, EVAL. Literals evaluate to themselves. So, if you type a number to the interpreter, it simply displays the number. Expressions that are calls to primitive functions are evaluated in the following way: First, each of the parameter expressions is evaluated, in no particular order. Then the primitive function is applied to the parameter values, and the resulting value is displayed.

15.5.3   Primitive Numeric Functions

This subsection introduces Scheme by discussing its primitive functions that deal only with numeric atoms, as opposed to symbolic atoms and lists.

Scheme includes primitive functions for the basic arithmetic operations. These are +, -, *, and /, for add, subtract, multiply, and divide. * and + can have zero or more parameters. If * is given no parameters, it returns 1; if + is given no parameters, it returns 0. + adds all of its parameters together. * multiplies all its parameters together. / and - can have two or more parameters. In the case of subtraction, all but the first parameter are subtracted from the first. Division is similar to subtraction. Some examples are:

Expression	Value
42	42
(* 3 7)	21
(+ 5 7 8)	20
(- 5 6)	-1
(- 15 7 2)	6
(- 24 (* 4 3))	12

SQRT returns the square root of its numeric parameter, if the parameter's value is not negative.

15.5.4 Defining Functions

A Scheme program is a collection of function definitions. Obviously, the means to define these functions is a prerequisite to writing the simplest program. Recall from Section 15.2.1 that the form of Scheme functions is based on lambda notation. In Scheme, a nameless function actually includes the word, LAMBDA, and is called a **lambda expression.** For example,

```
(LAMBDA (x) (* x x))
```

is a nameless function that returns the square of its given parameter. This function can be applied in the same way that named functions are: by placing it in the beginning of a list that contains the actual parameters. For example, we could have

```
((LAMBDA (x) (* x x)) 7)
```

which yields 49. x is called a **bound variable** within the lambda expression. A bound variable never changes in the expression after being bound to an actual parameter value at the time the lambda expression is first called for evaluation.

The Scheme special form function DEFINE serves two fundamental needs of Scheme programming: to bind a name to a value and to bind a name to a lambda expression. The former use may sound like DEFINE can be used to create imperative language style variables. However, these name bindings create named constants, not variables.

DEFINE is called a special form because it is interpreted (by EVAL) in a different way than the normal primitives like the arithmetic functions, as we shall soon see.

The simplest form of DEFINE is one used to bind a name to the value of an expression. This form is

```
(DEFINE symbol expression)
```

For example,

```
(DEFINE pi 3.14159)
(DEFINE two_pi (* 2 pi))
```

If these two expressions have been typed to the Scheme interpreter and then pi is typed, the number 3.14159 will be displayed; when two_pi is typed, 6.28318 will be displayed. In both cases, the numbers may have more digits than are shown here.

Names in Scheme can consist of letters, digits, and special characters except parentheses; they are case insensitive but must not begin with a digit.

The DEFINE function can also be used to bind a lambda expression to a name. In this case, the lambda expression is abbreviated to remove the word *lambda*. To bind a name to a lambda expression, DEFINE takes two lists as parameters. The first parameter is the prototype of a function call, with the function name followed by the formal parameters, together in a list. The second list includes one or more expressions to which the name is to be bound. The general form of such a DEFINE is

```
(DEFINE (function_name parameters)
    expression {expression}
)
```

The following example call to DEFINE binds the name square to the expression that follows it, which takes one parameter:

```
(DEFINE (square number) (* number number))
```

Once the interpreter evaluates this function, it can be used, as in

```
(square 5)
```

which displays 25.

To illustrate the difference between primitive functions and the DEFINE special form, consider

```
(DEFINE x 10)
```

If DEFINE were a primitive function, EVAL's first action on this expression would be to evaluate the two parameters of DEFINE. If x were not already bound to a value, this would be an error. Furthermore, if x were already defined, it would also be an error, because this DEFINE would attempt to redefine x, which is illegal.

Following is another example of a simple function. This one computes the length of the hypotenuse of a right triangle, given the lengths of the two other sides.

```
(DEFINE (hypotenuse side1 side2)
    (SQRT(+(square side1)(square side2)))
)
```

Notice that hypotenuse uses square, which we defined earlier.

Scheme parameters are passed by value, so regardless of what a function does to its parameters, the actual parameters are not affected.

15.5.5 Output Functions

Scheme includes a few simple output functions, such as

```
(DISPLAY expression)
```

and

```
(NEWLINE)
```

with the obvious semantics. Most output from Scheme programs, however, is the normal output from the interpreter, displaying results of applying EVAL to top-level functions.

15.5.6 Numeric Predicate Functions

A predicate function is one that returns a Boolean value (either true or false). Scheme includes a collection of predicate functions for numeric data. Among them are the following:

Function	Meaning
=	Equal
<>	Not equal
>	Greater than
<	Less than
>=	Greater than or equal to
<=	Less than or equal to
EVEN?	Is it an even number?
ODD?	Is it an odd number?
ZERO?	Is it zero?

Notice that all predefined predicate functions that have words for names, have names that end with question marks. In Scheme, the two Boolean values are #T and #F. The Scheme interpreter returns the empty list, ( ), instead of #F. Any non-null list returned by a predicate function is interpreted as #T.

15.5.7 Control Flow

The control flow mechanisms of Scheme are modeled after those of mathematical functions. Control flow in mathematical function definitions is quite different from that in programs in imperative programming languages. Whereas functions in imperative languages are defined as collections of statements that may include several kinds of sequence control flow, mathematical functions do not have multiple statements and use only recursion and conditional expressions for evaluation flow. For example, the factorial function can be defined with these two operations as

$$f(n) \equiv \begin{cases} 1 \text{ if } n = 0 \\ n * f(n-1) \text{ if } n > 0 \end{cases}$$

Note that a mathematical conditional expression is in the form of a list of pairs, each of which is a guarded expression. Each guarded expression consists of a predicate guard and an expression. The value of such a conditional expression is the value of the expression associated with the predicate that is true. Only one of the predicates is true for a given parameter or parameter list.

Scheme has two control structures, one for two-way selection and one for multiple selection. Both of these are special forms. The two-way selector, named IF, has three parameters: a predicate expression, a then expression, and an else expression. A call to IF has the form

```
(IF predicate then_expression else_expression)
```

For example,

```
(DEFINE (factorial n)
  (IF (= n 0)
    1
    (* n (factorial (- n 1)))
))
```

Notice how closely the form of this function relates to that of the mathematical definition of factorial given above.

The Scheme multiple selector special form is named COND. COND is a slightly generalized version of the mathematical conditional expression; it allows more than one predicate to be true at the same time. Because different mathematical conditional expressions have different numbers of parameters, COND does not require a fixed number of actual parameters. Each parameter to COND is a pair of expressions in which the first is a predicate.

The general form of COND is

```
(COND
          (predicate_1 expression {expression})
          (predicate_2 expression {expression})
          ...
          (predicate_n expression {expression})
          (ELSE expression {expression})
)
```

In some implementations, ELSE is optional.

The semantics of COND is as follows: The predicates of the parameters are evaluated one at a time, in order from the first, until one evaluates to #T. The expressions that follow the first predicate that is found to be #T are then evaluated, and the value of the last is returned as the value of COND. Note that the atom #T could be used as a constant predicate in a COND, in which case #T's expressions are always evaluated and the value of the last is returned as COND's value. Of course, it only makes sense to use #T as the predicate of the last parameter of COND. The special predicate constant ELSE, which means the same as #T, is usually used in these situations.

If no parameter to COND has a predicate that evaluates to #T, COND returns ( ) (the empty list). Notice the similarity between a COND and the multiple selection statement with an "otherwise" clause at the end, such as an Ada **case** statement.

Following is an example of a simple function that uses COND.

```
(DEFINE (compare x y)
    (COND
        ((> x y) (DISPLAY "x is greater than y"))
        ((< x y) (DISPLAY "y is greater than x"))
        (ELSE    (DISPLAY "x and y are equal"))
)
```

The following subsections contain additional examples of the use of COND.

15.5.8 List Functions

The most common use of the LISP-based programming languages, indeed the most common use of functional languages, is list processing. This subsection introduces the Scheme functions for dealing with lists.

The first Scheme primitive we describe is a utility function required by the nature of the Scheme function application operation, EVAL. It is called to handle the evaluate part of the read-evaluate-write action of the Scheme interpreter. When applied to a primitive function, EVAL first evaluates the parameters of the given function. This action is necessary when the actual parameters in a function call are themselves function calls, which is frequently the case. In some calls, however, the parameters are data elements rather than function references. When a parameter is not a function reference, it obviously should not be evaluated. We were not concerned with this earlier, because numeric literals cannot be mistaken for function names.

Suppose we have a function that has two parameters, an atom and a list, whose purpose is to determine whether the given atom is in the given list. Neither the atom nor the list should be evaluated; they are literal data to be examined. To avoid evaluating a parameter, it is first given as a parameter to the primitive function QUOTE, which simply returns it without change. The following examples illustrate QUOTE:

```
(QUOTE A) returns A
(QUOTE (A B C)) returns (A B C)
```

In the remainder of this chapter, we will use the common abbreviation of the call to QUOTE, which is done simply by preceding the expressions to be quoted by an apostrophe ('). Thus, instead of (QUOTE (A B)), we will use '(A B).

A programming language for list processing must include primitives for manipulating lists. In particular, it must provide operations for selecting parts of a list, which in a sense dismantle the list, and at least one operation for constructing lists. There are two primitive list selectors in Scheme: CAR and CDR (pronounced "could-er"). The CAR function returns the first element of a given list. The following examples illustrate CAR:

```
(CAR '(A B C)) returns A
(CAR '((A B) C D)) returns (A B)
(CAR 'A) is an error because A is not a list
(CAR '(A)) returns A
(CAR '()) is an error
```

The CDR function returns the remainder of a given list after its CAR is removed:

```
(CDR '(A B C)) returns (B C)
(CDR '((A B) C D)) returns (C D)
(CDR 'A) is an error
(CDR '(A)) returns ()
```

The names of the CAR and CDR functions are peculiar at best. The origin of these names lies in the first implementation of LISP, which was on an IBM 704 computer. The 704's memory words had two fields, named *decrement* and *address*, that were used in various operand addressing strategies. Each of these fields could store a machine memory address. The 704 also included two machine instructions, named CAR (contents of address register) and CDR (contents of decrement register), that extracted the associated fields. It was natural to use the two fields to store the two pointers of a list node so that a memory word could neatly store a node. Using these conventions, the CAR and CDR instructions of the 704 provided efficient list selectors. The names carried over into the primitives of all dialects of LISP.

As another example of a simple function, consider

```
(DEFINE (second lst) (CAR (CDR lst)))
```

Once this function is evaluated, it can be used, as in

```
(second '(A B C))
```

which returns B.

CONS is a primitive list constructor. It builds a list from its two arguments, the first of which can be either an atom or a list; the second is usually a list. Its action is to insert its first parameter as the new CAR of its second parameter. Consider the following examples:

```
(CONS 'A '()) returns (A)
(CONS 'A '(B C)) returns (A B C)
(CONS '() '(A B)) returns (() A B)
(CONS '(A B) '(C D)) returns ((A B) C D)
```

The results of these CONS operations are shown in Figure 15.2. Note that CONS is, in a sense, the inverse of CAR and CDR. CAR and CDR take a list apart,

Figure 15.2

The result of several
CONS operations

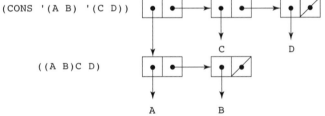

and CONS constructs a new list from given list parts. The two parameters to CONS become the CAR and CDR of the new list. Thus, if lis is a list, then

```
(CONS (CAR lis) (CDR lis))
```

returns a list identical to lis.

Dealing only with the relatively simple problems and programs discussed in this chapter, it is unlikely one would ever intentionally apply CONS to two atoms. However, that is legal and commonly happens accidentally. The result of such an application is a dotted pair, so named because of the way it is displayed by Scheme. For example, consider the following call:

```
(CONS 'A 'B)
```

If the result of this is displayed, it would appear as

```
(A . B)
```

This dotted pair indicate that instead of an atom and a pointer or a pointer and a pointer, this cell has two atoms.

LIST is a function that constructs lists from a variable number of parameters. It is a shorthand version of nested CONS functions, as illustrated in

```
(LIST 'apple 'orange 'grape) returns (apple orange grape)
```

15.5.9   Predicate Functions for Symbolic Atoms and Lists

Scheme has three essential predicate functions, EQ?, NULL?, and LIST?, for symbolic atoms and lists.

The EQ? function takes two symbolic parameters. It returns #T if both parameters are atoms and the two are the same; otherwise, it returns (). Consider the following examples:

```
(EQ? 'A 'A) returns #T
(EQ? 'A 'B) returns ()
(EQ? 'A '(A B)) returns ()
(EQ? '(A B) '(A B)) returns () or #T
```

As the last case indicates, the result of comparing lists with EQ? is implementation dependent—some yield #T and some yield (). The reason for this difference is that EQ? is often implemented as a pointer comparison (do two given pointers point to the same place?), and two lists that are exactly the same are often not duplicated in memory. At the time the Scheme system creates a list, it checks to see whether there is already such a list. If there is, the new list is nothing more than a new pointer to the existing list. In these cases, the two lists will be judged equal by EQ?. However, in some cases, it may be difficult to detect the presence of an identical list, in which case a new list is created. In this scenario, EQ? yields ().

Note that EQ? works for symbolic atoms but does not necessarily work for numeric atoms. The = predicate works for numeric atoms but not symbolic atoms. As discussed above, EQ? also does not work reliably for list parameters.

Sometimes it is convenient to be able to test two atoms for equality when it is not known whether they are symbolic or numeric. For this purpose, Scheme has a different predicate, EQV?, which works on both numeric and symbolic atoms. The primary reason to use EQ? or = rather than EQV? when it is possible is that EQ? and = are faster than EQV?.

The LIST? predicate function returns #T if its single argument is a list and () otherwise, as in the following examples:

```
(LIST? '(X Y)) returns #T
(LIST? 'X) returns ()
(LIST? '()) returns #T
```

The NULL? function tests its parameter to determine whether it is the empty list and returns #T if it is. Consider the following examples:

```
(NULL? '(A B)) returns ()
(NULL? '()) returns #T
(NULL? 'A) returns ()
(NULL? '(())) returns ()
```

The last call yields `()` because the parameter is not the empty list. Rather, it is a list containing a single element, the empty list.

15.5.10 Example Scheme Functions

This section contains several examples of function definitions in Scheme. These programs solve simple list-processing problems.

Consider the problem of membership of a given atom in a given simple list. (A simple list is one without sublists.) If the function is named `member`, it could be used as follows:

```
(member 'B '(A B C)) returns #T
(member 'B '(A C D E)) returns ()
```

Thinking in terms of iteration, the membership problem is simply to compare the given atom and the individual elements of the given list, one at a time in some order, until either a match is found or there are no more elements in the list to be compared. A similar process can be accomplished using recursion. The function can compare the given atom with the CAR of the list. If they match, the value #T is returned. If they do not match, the CAR of the list should be ignored and the search continued on the CDR of the list. This can be done by having the function call itself with the CDR of the list as the list parameter and return the result of this recursive call. This process will end if the given atom is found in the list. If the atom is not in the list, the function will eventually be called (by itself) with a null list. That must force the function to return `()`. In this process, there are two ways out of the recursion: Either the list is empty on some call and `()` is returned, or a match is found and #T is returned.

Altogether, there are three cases that must be handled in the function: an empty input list, a match between the atom and the CAR of the list, or a mismatch between the atom and the CAR of the list, which causes the recursive call. These three are the three parameters to COND, with the last being the default case that is triggered by an ELSE predicate. The complete function follows:

```
(DEFINE (member atm lis)
  (COND
    ((NULL? lis) '())
    ((EQ? atm (CAR lis)) #T)
    (ELSE (member atm (CDR lis)))
))
```

This form is typical of simple Scheme list-processing functions. In such functions, the data in lists are processed one element at a time. The individual elements may be gotten with CAR, and the process is continued using recursion on the CDR of the list.

Notice that the null test must precede the equal test, because applying CAR to an empty list is an error.

As another example, consider the problem of determining whether two given lists are equal. If the two lists are simple, the solution is relatively easy, although some unfamiliar techniques are involved. A predicate function, equalsimp, for comparing simple lists is shown here:

```
(DEFINE (equalsimp lis1 lis2)
  (COND
    ((NULL? lis1) (NULL? lis2))
    ((NULL? lis2) '())
    ((EQ? (CAR lis1) (CAR lis2))
        (equalsimp (CDR lis1) (CDR lis2)))
    (ELSE ' ())
))
```

The first case, which is handled by the first parameter to COND, is for when the first list parameter is the empty list. This can occur in an external call if the first list parameter is initially empty. Because a recursive call uses the CDRs of the two parameter lists as its parameters, the first list can be empty in such a call if the first list has had all of its elements removed by previous recursive calls. When the first list is empty, the second list must be checked to see whether it is also empty. If so, they are equal (either initially or the CARs were equal on all previous recursive calls), and NULL? correctly returns #T. If the second list is not empty, it is larger than the first list and () should be returned, as it is by NULL?. Recall that any nonempty list that is returned by a predicate function is interpreted as #T.

The next case deals with the second list being empty when the first list is not. This situation occurs only when the first list is larger than the second. Only the second list must be tested, because the first case catches all instances of the first list being empty.

The third case is the recursive step that tests for equality between two corresponding elements in the two lists. It does this by comparing the CARs of the two nonempty lists. If they are equal, then the two lists are equal up to that point, so recursion is used on the CDRs of both. This case fails when two unequal atoms are found. When this occurs, the process need not continue, so the default case, the ELSE is selected and it returns ().

Note that equalsimp expects lists as parameters and does not operate correctly if either or both parameters are atoms.

The problem of comparing general lists is slightly more complex than this, because sublists must be traced completely in the comparison process. This is a situation where the power of recursion is uniquely appropriate, because the form of sublists is the same as that of the given lists. Any time the corresponding elements of the two given lists are lists, they are separated into their two parts, CAR and CDR, and recursion is used on them. This is a perfect example of the usefulness of the divide-and-conquer approach. If the corresponding elements of the two given lists are atoms, they can simply be compared using EQ?.

The definition of the complete function follows:

```
(DEFINE (equal lis1 lis2)
  (COND
    ((NOT (LIST? lis1)) (EQ? lis1 lis2))
    ((NOT (LIST? lis2))'())
    ((NULL? lis1) (NULL? lis2))
    ((NULL? lis2)) '())
    ((equal (CAR lis1) (CAR lis2))
        (equal (CDR lis1) (CDR lis2)))
    (ELSE '())
))
```

The first two cases of the COND handle the situation where either of the parameters is an atom instead of a list. The third and fourth cases are for the situation where one or both lists are empty. These cases also prevent subsequent cases from attempting to take the CAR of an empty list. The fifth COND case is the most interesting. The predicate is a recursive call with the CARs of the lists as parameters. If this recursive call returns #T, then recursion is used again on the CDRs of the lists. This allows the two lists to include sublists to any depth.

This definition of equal works on any pair of expressions, not just lists. equal is equivalent to the system predicate function EQUAL?. Note that EQUAL? should be used only when necessary (the forms of the actual parameters are not known), because it is much slower than EQ? and EQV?.

Another commonly needed list operation is that of constructing a new list that contains all of the elements of two given list arguments. This is usually implemented as a Scheme function named append. It can be constructed by repeated use of CONS to place the elements of the first list argument into the second list argument. To clarify the action of append, consider the following examples:

```
(append '(A B) '(C D R)) returns (A B C D R)
(append '((A B) C) '(D (E F))) returns ((A B) C D (E F))
```

The definition of append is

```
(DEFINE (append lis1 lis2)
  (COND
    ((NULL? lis1) lis2)
    (ELSE (CONS (CAR lis1) (append (CDR Lis1) lis2)))
))
```

The first COND case is used to terminate the recursive process when the first argument list is empty, returning the second list. In the second case (the ELSE), the CAR of the first parameter list is CONSed onto the result returned by the recursive call, which passes the CDR of the first list as its first parameter.

Consider the following Scheme function, named guess, which uses the member function described in this section. Try to determine what it does before reading the description that follows it. Assume the parameters are simple lists.

```
(DEFINE (guess lis1 lis2)
  (COND
    ((NULL? lis1) '())
    ((member (CAR lis1) lis2)
            (CONS (CAR lis1) (guess (CDR lis1) lis2)))
    (ELSE (guess (CDR lis1) lis2))
))
```

guess yields a simple list that contains the common elements of its two parameter lists. So if the parameter lists represent sets, guess computes a list that represents the intersection of those two sets.

LET is a function that allows names to be temporarily bound to the values of subexpressions. It is often used to factor out the common subexpressions from more complicated expressions. These names can then be used in the evaluation of another expression. Its general form is

```
(LET (
          (name_1 expression_1)
          (name_2 expression_2)
          ...
          (name_n expression_n))
          expression {expression}
)
```

The semantics of LET is that the first n expressions are evaluated and the resulting values are bound to their associated names. Then the expressions in the body are evaluated. The result of LET is the value of the last expression in its body. The following example illustrates the use of LET. It computes the roots of a given quadratic equation, assuming the roots are real.[2]

```
(DEFINE (quadratic_roots a b c)
  (LET (
    (root_part_over_2a
            (/ (SQRT (- (* b b) (* 4 a c))) (* 2 a)))
```

---

[2]Some versions of Scheme include complex as a data type and will compute the roots of the equation, regardless of whether they are real or complex.

```
      (minus_b_over_2a (/ (- 0 b) (* 2 a)))
        )
    (DISPLAY (+ minus_b_over_2a root_part_over_2a))
    (NEWLINE)
    (DISPLAY (- minus_b_over_2a root_part_over_2a))
))
```

The DISPLAY function is convenient in quadratic_roots because we want this function to display its two results.

LET creates a new local static scope in much the same way as Ada's **declare**. New variables can be created, used, and then discarded when the end of the new scope is reached. The named components of LET are like assignment statements, but they can be used only in LET's new scope. Furthermore, they cannot be rebound to new values in LET.

LET is actually just shorthand for a LAMBDA expression. The following two expressions are equivalent:

```
(LET ((alpha 7))(* 5 alpha))
((LAMBDA (alpha) (* 5 alpha)) 7)
```

In the first expression, 7 is bound to alpha with LET; in the second, 7 is bound to alpha through the parameter of the LAMBDA expression

15.5.11 Functional Forms

This section describes two common mathematical functional forms that are provided by Scheme, composition and apply-to-all. Both of these are mathematically defined in Section 15.2.2.

15.5.11.1 Functional Composition

Functional composition is the only primitive functional form provided by the original LISP. All subsequent LISP dialects, including Scheme, also provide it. Functional composition is the essence of how EVAL works. All non-quoted lists are assumed to be function calls, which requires their parameters to be evaluated first. This applies recursively to the smallest list in any expression, which is precisely what functional composition means. The following examples illustrate function composition:

```
(CDR (CDR '(A B C))) returns (C)
(CAR (CAR '((A B) B C))) returns A
(CDR (CAR '((A B C) D))) returns (B C)
(NULL? (CAR '(() B C))) returns #T
(CONS (CAR '(A B)) (CDR '(A B))) returns (A B)
```

Notice that the function names in inner calls are not quoted because they must be evaluated rather than treated as literal data.

15.5.11.2 An Apply-to-All Functional Form

The most common functional forms provided in common functional programming languages are variations of mathematical apply-to-all functional forms. The simplest of these is mapcar, which has two parameters, a function and a list. mapcar applies the given function to each element of the given list, and it returns a list of the results of these applications. A Scheme definition of mapcar follows:

```
(DEFINE (mapcar fun lis)
  (COND
    ((NULL? lis) '())
    (ELSE (CONS (fun (CAR lis)) (mapcar fun (CDR lis))))
))
```

Note the simple form of mapcar, which expresses a complex functional form. This is testament to the great expressive power of Scheme.

As an example of the use of mapcar, suppose we want all of the elements of a list cubed. We can accomplish this with

```
(mapcar (LAMBDA (num) (* num num num)) '(3 4 2 6))
```

This call returns (27 64 8 216).

Note that in this example the first parameter to mapcar is a LAMBDA expression. When EVAL evaluates the LAMBDA expression, it constructs a function that has the same form as any predefined function except that it is nameless. In the expression above, this nameless function is immediately applied to each element of the parameter list and the results are returned in a list.

15.5.12   Functions That Build Code

The fact that programs and data have the same structure can be exploited in constructing programs. Recall that the Scheme interpreter is a function named EVAL. The Scheme system applies EVAL to every expression typed at the Scheme prompt. The EVAL function can also be called directly by Scheme programs. This provides the possibility of a Scheme program creating expressions and calling EVAL to evaluate them.

One of the simplest examples of this process involves numeric atoms. Scheme includes a function for numeric atoms named +, which takes any number of numeric atoms as arguments and returns their sum. For example, (+ 3 7 10 2) returns 22.

Our problem is the following: Suppose that in a program we have a list of numeric atoms and need the sum. We cannot apply + directly on the list, because + can take only atomic parameters, not a list of numeric atoms. We could, of course, write a function that repeatedly adds the CAR of the list to the sum of its CDR, using recursion to go through the list. Such a function follows:

```
(DEFINE (adder lis)
  (COND
    ((NULL? lis) 0)
    (ELSE (+ (CAR lis) (adder (CDR lis))))
))
```

An alternative solution to the problem is to write a function that builds a call to + with the proper parameter forms. This can be done by using CONS to insert the atom + into the list of numbers. This new list can then be submitted to EVAL for evaluation, as in the following:

```
(DEFINE (adder lis)
  (COND
    ((NULL? lis) 0)
    (ELSE (EVAL (CONS '+ lis)))
))
```

Note that the + function's name is quoted to prevent EVAL from evaluating it in the evaluation of CONS. As an example, consider that the call

```
(adder '(3 4 6))
```

causes adder to build the list

```
(+ 3 4 6)
```

The list is then submitted to EVAL, which invokes + and returns the result, 13.

In all earlier versions of Scheme, the EVAL function evaluates its expression in the outermost scope of the program. The latest version of Scheme, Scheme 4, requires a second parameter to EVAL that specifies the scope in which the expression is to be evaluated. For simplicity's sake, we left the scope parameter out of our example, and we do not discuss scope names here.

15.6 COMMON LISP

COMMON LISP (Steele, 1984) was created in an effort to combine the features of several early 1980s dialects of LISP, including Scheme, into a single language. Being something of a union of languages, it is quite large and complex. Its basis, however, is the original LISP, so its syntax, primitive functions, and fundamental nature come from that language.

Recognizing the occasional flexibility provided by dynamic scoping, as well as the simplicity of static scoping, COMMON LISP allows both. The default scoping for variables is static, but by declaring a variable to be "special," that variable becomes dynamically scoped.

The list of features of COMMON LISP is long: a large number of data types and structures, including such things as records, arrays, complex numbers, and character strings; powerful input and output operations; a form of packages for modularizing collections of functions and data, and also providing access control.

In a sense, Scheme and COMMON LISP are opposites. Scheme is far smaller and semantically simpler, in part because of its exclusive use of static scoping. COMMON LISP was meant to be a commercial language and has succeeded in being a widely used language for AI applications. Scheme, on the other hand, is more frequently used in college courses on functional programming. It is also more likely to be studied as a functional language because of its relatively small size. An important design criterion of COMMON LISP that caused it to be a very large language was the desire to make it compatible with several earlier dialects of LISP.

15.7   ML

ML (Milner et al., 1990) is a static-scoped functional programming language, like Scheme. However, it differs from LISP and its dialects, including Scheme, in a number of significant ways. Perhaps the most important difference is that ML is a strongly typed language, whereas Scheme is essentially typeless. ML has type declarations, although because of its type inferencing, which is discussed briefly in Chapter 5, they are often not used. The type of every variable and expression can be determined at compile time. Another important difference between Scheme and ML is that ML uses a syntax that is more closely related to that of an imperative language than that of LISP. For example, arithmetic expressions are written in ML using infix notation. ML has exception handling and a module facility for implementing abstract data types. A brief history of the development and primary features of ML are given in Chapter 2.

Function declarations in ML appear in the general form

```
fun function_name (formal_parameters) = function_body_expression;
```

For example,

```
fun square (x : int) = x * x;
```

The type of the return value can be specified after the parameter list, as in

```
fun square(x : int) : int = x * x;
```

Of course, in this function the type of the return value need not be explicitly specified.

The following line,

```
fun square (x) = x * x;
```

defines the same function as the last function definition, because ML assumes the **int** type, given the operator in the expression (x * x). So functions that use arithmetic operators cannot be polymorphic. The same is true for functions that use relational operators, except = and <>, and Boolean operators. However, functions that use only list operations, =, <>, and tuple operators (those for forming tuples and for component selection), can be polymorphic.

If we wanted a `square` function for **real** type values and we had already defined `square` for **int** values, we would need to define it with a different name, because user-defined overloaded functions are not allowed. Furthermore, if we defined `square` for **real** parameters, it could not be called with an integer actual parameter, because ML, like Ada, does not coerce integer values to **real** type.

The ML selection control flow construct is actually a conditional expression with the form

if E **then** then_expression **else** else_expression

where E must evaluate to a Boolean value.

The conditional expressions of Scheme can appear at the function definition level in ML. In Scheme, the COND function is used to determine the value of the given parameter, which in turn specifies the value returned by COND. In ML, the computation performed by a function can be defined for different forms of the given parameter. This is meant to mimic the form and meaning of conditional function definitions in mathematics. In ML, the particular expression that defines the return value of a function is chosen by pattern matching against the given parameter. For example, without using this pattern matching, a function to compute factorial could be written as:

```
fun fact(n : int): int = if n = 0 then 1
                         else n * fact(n - 1);
```

Multiple definitions of a function can be written using parameter pattern matching. The different function definitions that depend on the form of the parameter are separated by an OR symbol (|). For example, using pattern matching, the factorial function could be written as

```
fun fact(0) = 1
|   fact(n: int): int = n * fact(n - 1);
```

If `fact` is called with the actual parameter 0, the first definition is used; if an **int** value that is not zero is sent, the second definition is used.

ML has lists and list operations, although their appearance is not like those of Scheme. Lists are specified in square brackets, with the elements separated by commas, as in the following list of integers:

```
[5, 7, 9]
```

[ ] is the empty list, which could also be specified with `nil`.

The Scheme CONS function is a binary infix operator in ML, represented as ::. For example,

```
3 :: [5, 5, 9]
```

evaluates to [3, 5, 7, 9].

The elements of a list must be of the same type, so the following list would be illegal:

```
[5, 7.3, 9]
```

ML has functions that correspond to Scheme's CAR and CDR, named hd (head) and tl (tail). For example,

```
hd [5, 7, 9] is 5
tl [5, 7, 9] is [7, 9]
```

Because of the availability of patterned function parameters, the hd and tl functions are much less frequently used in ML than in Scheme. For example, in a parameter, the expression

```
(h :: t)
```

is actually two formal parameters, the head and tail of given list parameter. For example, the number of elements in a given list can be computed with the following function:

```
fun length([]) = 0
|    length(h :: t) = 1 + length(t);
```

As another example of these concepts, consider the append function, which does what the Scheme APPEND function does.

```
fun append([], lis2) = lis2
|    append(h :: t, lis2) = h :: append(t, lis2);
```

The first case in this function handles the situation of the function being called with an empty list as the first parameter. This case also terminates the recursion when the initial call has a nonempty first parameter. The second case of the function breaks the first parameter list into its head and tail (CAR and CDR). The head is CONSed onto the result of the recursive call, which uses the tail as its first parameter.

In ML, names can be bound to values with value declaration statements of the form

val new_name = expression;

For example,

val distance = time * speed;

Do not get the idea that this statement is exactly like the assignment statements in the imperative languages, for it is not. The **val** statement binds a name to a value, but the name cannot be later rebound to a new value. Well, in a sense it can. Actually, if you do rebind a name with a second **val** statement, it causes a new entry in the environment that is not related to the previous version of the name.[3] In fact, after the new binding, the old environment entry (for the previous binding) is no longer visible. Also, the type of the new binding need not be the same as that of the previous binding. **val** statements do not have side effects. They simply add a name to the current environment and bind it to a value, like the LET special form of Scheme. The normal use of **val** is in a **let** expression, whose general form is

let val new_name = expression_1 **in** expression_2 **end**

For example,

```
let
  val pi = 3.14159
in
  pi * radius * radius
end;
```

There are no type coercions in ML; the types of the operands of an operator or assignment simply must match to avoid syntax errors.

ML also has enumerated types, arrays, and tuples, which are similar to records.

15.8 Haskell

Haskell (Thompson, 1996) is similar to ML in that it uses a similar syntax, is static scoped, is strongly typed, and uses the same type inferencing method. There are two characteristics of Haskell that set it apart from ML. First, it uses a different evaluation technique called **lazy evaluation,** in which no subexpression is evaluated until its value is required. This allows infinite lists to be defined. Second, Haskell includes **list comprehensions**, which allow sets to be defined using syntax that is very similar to mathematical set notation.

The code in this section is written in version 1.4 of Haskell. Consider the following definition of the factorial function, which uses pattern matching on its parameters.

```
fact 0 = 1
fact n = n * fact (n - 1)
```

---

[3]The environment can be thought of as a symbol table that stores names, and also the values to which the names are bound.

Note the differences in syntax between this definition and its ML version in Section 15.7. First, there is no reserved word to introduce the function definition (fun for ML). Second, parentheses are not used to delimit the formal parameters.[4]

Using pattern matching, we can define a function for computing the nth Fibonacci number with the following:

```
fib 0 = 1
fib 1 = 1
fib (n + 2) = fib (n + 1) + fib n
```

Guards can be added to lines of a function definition to specify the circumstances under which the definition can be applied. For example,

```
fact n
  | n == 0    = 1
  | n > 0     = n * fact(n - 1)
```

This is a more precise definition of factorial than our previous one, for it restricts the range of actual parameter values to those for which it works. Pattern matching would of course fail in this use, for the parameter pattern is n for both value expressions. This form of a function definition is called a *conditional expression*.

An **otherwise** can appear as the last condition in a conditional expression, with the obvious semantics. For example,

```
sub n
  | n < 10     = 0
  | n > 100    = 2
  | otherwise  = 1
```

As with ML, lists are written in brackets in Haskell, as in

```
colors = ["blue", "green", "red", "yellow"]
```

Haskell includes a collection of list operators. For example, lists can be catenated with ++, : serves as an infix version of CONS, and .. is used to specify arithmetic series. For example,

```
5:[2, 7, 9]   results in [5, 2, 7, 9]
[1, 3..11]   results in [1, 3, 5, 7, 9, 11]
[1, 3, 5] ++ [2, 4, 6]   results in [1, 3, 5, 2, 4, 6]
```

---

[4]The parentheses are actually optional in ML.

Notice that the : operator is just like ML's :: operator.[5] Using : and pattern matching, we can define a simple function to compute the product of a given list of numbers:

```
product [] = 1
product (a:x) = a * product x
```

Using product, we can write a factorial function in the simpler form

```
fact n = product [1..n]
```

In Haskell, a **where** clause is similar to ML's **let** and **val**, except the bindings are given after the expression that uses them. For example, we could write

```
quadratic_root a b c =
     [minus_b_over_2a - root_part_over_2a,
      minus_b_over_2a + root_part_over_2a]
     where
       minus_b_over_2a = - b / (2.0 * a)
       root_part_over_2a =
                    sqrt(b ^ 2 - 4.0 * a * c) / (2.0 * a)
```

List comprehensions provide a method of describing lists that represent sets. The syntax of a list comprehension is the same as that often used to describe sets in mathematics, the general form of which is

[body | qualifiers]

For example,

```
[n * n * n | n ← [1..50]]
```

defines a list of the cubes of the numbers from 1 to 50. It is read as "a list of all n*n*n such that n is taken from the range of 1 to 50." In this case the qualifier is in the form of a **generator.** It generates the numbers from 1 to 50. In other cases, the qualifiers are in the form of Boolean expressions, in which case they are called **tests.** This notation can be used to describe algorithms for doing many things, such as finding permutations of lists and sorting lists. For example, consider the following function, which when given a number n returns a list of all its factors:

```
factors n = [ i | i ← [1..n div 2], n mod i == 0]
```

---

[5]It is interesting that ML uses : for attaching a type name to a name and :: for cons, while Haskell uses these two operators in exactly opposite ways.

The list comprehension in `factors` creates a list of numbers, each temporarily bound to the name `i`, ranging from 1 to `n/2`, such that `n mod i` is zero. This is indeed a very exacting and short definition of the factors of a given number.

Next, consider the conciseness of Haskell shown in the following implementation of the quicksort algorithm:

```
sort [] =   []
sort (h:t) = sort [b | b <- t, b ≤ h]
  ++ [h] ++
  sort [b | b ← t, b > h]
```

This definition of quicksort is significantly shorter than the same algorithm coded in an imperative language.

We now return to the topic of lazy evaluation. Recall that in Scheme the parameters to a function are fully evaluated before the function is called. Lazy evaluation means that parameters to functions are evaluated only when it is necessary to evaluate the function. So if a function has two parameters, but on a particular execution of the function the first parameter is not used, the actual parameter passed for that execution will not be evaluated. Furthermore, if only a part of an actual parameter must be evaluated for an execution of the function, the rest is left unevaluated. Finally, actual parameters are evaluated only once, if at all.

The fact that a language uses lazy evaluation opens up some interesting possibilities. One of these is defining infinite data structures. For example, consider the following:

```
positives = [0..]
evens = [2, 4..]
squares = [n * n | n ← [0..]]
```

Of course, no computer can actually represent all of the numbers of these lists, but that does not prevent their use if lazy evaluation is used. For example, if we wanted to know if a particular number was a perfect square, we could check the squares list with a membership function. Suppose we had a predicate function named `member` that determined whether a given list contained a given atom. Then we could use it as in

```
member squares 16
```

which would return `True`. The `squares` definition would be evaluated until the 16 was found. The `member` function would need to be carefully written. Specifically, suppose it were defined as follows:

```
member [] b = False
member (a:x) b = (a == b) || member x b
```

The second line of this definition breaks the first parameter into its head and tail. Its return value is true if either the head matches the element for which it is searching (b), or if the recursive call with the tail of the list returns True.

This definition of member would work correctly with squares only if the given number was a perfect square. If not, squares would keep generating squares forever, or until some memory limitation was reached, looking for the given number in the list. The following function performs the membership test of an ordered list, abandoning the search and returning False if a number greater than the searched-for number is found.

```
member2 (m:x) n
  | m < n      = member2 x n
  | m == n     = True
  | otherwise  = False
```

Lazy evaluation is not without its costs. It would certainly be surprising if such expressive power and flexibility came free. In this case, the cost is in a far more complicated semantics, which results in much slower speed of execution.

15.9 Applications of Functional Languages

Over the past 40 years in the history of high-level programming languages only a few functional languages have gained widespread use. Most prominent among these is LISP.

LISP is a versatile and powerful language. For its first 15 years, it was thought of, mostly by nonusers, as a strange-looking and odd-behaving language that was very costly to use. Indeed, it was common in the 1960s and early 1970s to think of two categories of languages, one containing LISP and one with all of the other programming languages.

LISP was developed for symbolic computation and list-processing applications, which lie mainly in the AI realm of computing. In many AI applications, LISP and its derivatives are still the standard languages.

Within AI a number of areas have been developed, primarily through the use of LISP. Although other kinds of languages can be used—primarily, logic programming languages—most existing expert systems, for example, were developed in LISP. LISP also dominates in the areas of knowledge representation, machine learning, intelligent training systems, and the modeling of speech.

Outside AI, LISP has also been successful. For example, the EMACS text editor is written in LISP, as is the symbolic mathematics system, MACSYMA, which does symbolic differentiation and integration, among other things. The LISP machine was a personal computer whose entire systems software was written in LISP. LISP has also been successfully used to construct experimental systems in a variety of application areas.

Scheme is widely used to teach functional programming. It is also used in some universities to teach introductory programming courses. Use of ML and Haskell has been, for the most part, restricted to research laboratories and universities.

15.10   A Comparison of Functional and Imperative Languages

Functional languages can have a very simple syntactic structure. The list structure of LISP is the best example of this. The syntax of the imperative languages is much more complex. The semantics of functional languages can also be simple compared to that of the imperative languages.

Concurrent execution in the imperative languages is difficult to design and difficult to use. For example, consider the tasking model of Ada, in which cooperation among concurrent tasks is the responsibility of the programmer. Functional programs can be executed by first translating them into graphs. These graphs can then be executed through a graph reduction process, which can be done with a great deal of concurrency that was not specified by the programmer. The graph representation naturally exposes many opportunities for concurrent execution. Cooperation synchronization in this process is not the concern of the programmer. Further description of this process is beyond the scope of this book.

In an imperative language, the programmer must make a static division of the program into its concurrent parts, which are then written as tasks. This can be a complicated process. Programs in functional languages can be divided into concurrent parts dynamically by the execution system, making the process highly adaptable to the hardware on which it is running. Understanding concurrent programs in imperative languages is much more difficult.

For the first twenty five or so years of their existence, programs written in functional programming languages were far slower than equivalent programs in an imperative language, largely due to the use of interpreters for functional languages. That great difference was lessened dramatically by the appearance of compilers for functional languages. However, it is generally true that the more efficient of the imperative language, such as C and Fortran, are still faster than the functional languages, compiled or not. It now appears that it is not just the poor efficiency of functional languages that impede their rise to popularity. Perhaps imperative programming languages are somehow more natural tools.

SUMMARY

Mathematical functions are named or unnamed mappings that use only conditional expressions and recursion to control their evaluations. Complex functions can be built using functional forms, in which functions are used as parameters, returned values, or both.

Functional programming languages are modeled on mathematical functions. In their pure form, they do not use variables or assignment statements to produce results; rather they use functional applications, conditional expressions, and recursion for execution control, and functional forms to construct complex functions. LISP began as a purely functional language but soon had a number of imperative language features added in order to increase its efficiency and ease of use.

The first version of LISP grew out of the need for a list-processing language for AI applications. LISP is still the most widely used language for that area.

The first implementation of LISP was serendipitous: The original version of EVAL was developed solely to demonstrate that a universal LISP function could be written.

Because LISP data and LISP programs have the same form, it is possible to have a program build another program. The availability of EVAL allows such programs to be executed immediately.

Scheme is a relatively simple dialect of LISP that uses static scoping exclusively. Like LISP, Scheme's primary primitives include functions for constructing and dismantling lists, for conditional expressions, and simple predicates for numbers, symbols, and lists. Scheme includes some imperative operations, such as for changing an element of a given list.

COMMON LISP is a large LISP-based language that was designed to include most of the features of the LISP dialects of the early 1980s. It allows both static- and dynamic-scoped variables and includes many imperative features.

ML is a static-scoped and strongly typed functional programming language that uses a syntax that is more similar to an imperative language than to LISP. It includes a type inferencing system, exception handling, a variety of data structures, and abstract data types.

Haskell is similar to ML, except that all expressions in Haskell are evaluated using a lazy method, which allows programs to deal with infinite lists. Haskell also supports list comprehensions, which provide a convenient and familiar syntax for describing sets.

Although LISP's primary area of application is AI, it has been successfully used for a number of different areas of problem solving.

Although there may be advantages to purely functional languages over their imperative relatives, their lower efficiency of execution on von Neumann machines has prevented them from being considered by many as replacements.

BIBLIOGRAPHIC NOTES

The first published version of LISP can be found in McCarthy (1960). A widely used version from the mid-1960s until the late 1970s is described in McCarthy et al. (1965) and Weissman (1967). COMMON LISP is described in Steele (1984). The Scheme language, along with some of its innovations and advantages, is discussed in Rees and Clinger (1986). Dybvig (1996) is a good source of information on programming in Scheme. ML is defined in Milner et al. (1990). Ullman (1994) is an excellent introductory textbook for ML. Programming in Haskell is introduced in Thompson (1996).

A rigorous discussion of functional programming in general can be found in Henderson (1980). The process of implementing functional languages through graph reduction is discussed in detail in Peyton Jones (1987).

REVIEW QUESTIONS

1. Define *functional form* and *referential transparency*.
2. What data types were part of the original LISP?
3. What is the difference between EQ?, EQV?, and =?
4. What are the differences between the evaluation method used for the Scheme special form, DEFINE, and that used for its primitive functions?
5. What are the two forms of DEFINE?
6. Describe the semantics of COND.
7. Describe the semantics of LET.
8. Why were imperative features added to most dialects of LISP?
9. In what ways are COMMON LISP and Scheme opposites?
10. What scoping rule is used in Scheme? In COMMON LISP? In ML? In Haskell?
11. What are three ways that ML is very different from Scheme?
12. What is type inferencing, as used in ML? (See Chapter 5.)
13. What are three features of Haskell that make it very different from Scheme?
14. What does *lazy evaluation* mean?

PROBLEM SET

1. Read John Backus's paper on FP (Backus, 1978) and compare the features of Scheme discussed in this chapter with the corresponding features of FP.
2. Find definitions of the Scheme functions EVAL and APPLY, and explain their actions.
3. One of the most modern and complete programming environments for any language is the INTERLISP system for LISP, as described in "The

INTERLISP Programming Environment," by Teitelmen and Masinter (*IEEE Computer*, Vol. 14, No. 4, April 1981). Read this article carefully and compare the difficulty of writing LISP programs on your system with that of using INTERLISP (assuming that you do not normally use INTERLISP).

4. Refer to a book on LISP programming and determine what arguments support the inclusion of the PROG feature in LISP.

5. A functional language could use some data structure other than the list. For example, it could use sequences of symbols. What primitives would such a language have in place of the CAR, CDR, and CONS primitives of Scheme?

6. What does the following Scheme function do?

```scheme
(define (y s lis)
  (cond
    ((null? lis) '() )
    ((equal? s (car lis)) lis)
    (else (y s (cdr lis)))
))
```

7. What does the following Scheme function do?

```scheme
(define (x lis)
  (cond
    ((null? lis) 0)
    ((not (list? (car lis)))
      (cond
        ((eq? (car lis) nil) (x (cdr lis)))
        (else (+ 1 (x (cdr lis))))))
    (else (+ (x (car lis)) (x (cdr lis))))
))
```

PROGRAMMING EXERCISES

1. Write a Scheme function that computes the volume of a sphere, given its radius.

2. Write a Scheme function that computes the real roots of a given quadratic equation. If the roots are complex, the function must display a message indicating that. This function must use an IF function. The three parameters to the function are the three coefficients of the quadratic equation.

3. Repeat Exercise 2 using a COND function, rather than an IF function.

4. Write a Scheme function that returns the number of zeros in a given simple list of numbers.

5. Write a Scheme function that deletes all top-level instances of a given atom from a given list.

6. Write a Scheme function that removes the last element from a given list.

7. Repeat Exercise 5, except that the atom can be either an atom or a list.

8. Write a Scheme function that takes two atoms and a list as parameters and replaces all occurrences of the first given atom in the list with the second given atom, no matter how deeply the first atom is nested.

9. Write a Scheme function that returns the reverse of its simple list parameter.

10. Write a Scheme predicate function that tests for the structural equality of two given lists. Two lists are structurally equal if they have the same list structure, although their atoms may be different.

11. Write a Scheme function that returns the union of two simple list parameters that represent sets.

12. Write a Scheme function with two parameters, an atom and a list, that returns the list with all occurrences, no matter how deep, of the given atom deleted. The returned list cannot contain anything in place of the deleted atoms.

13. Write a Scheme function that takes a list as a parameter and returns it with the second top-level element removed. If the given list does not have two elements, the function should return ( ).

14. Write a Scheme function that takes a simple list of numbers at its parmeter and returns the list with the numbers in ascending order.

15. Write a Scheme function that takes a simple list of numbers as its parameter and returns the largest and smallest numbers in the list

16

Logic Programming Languages

CHAPTER OUTLINE

The objectives of this chapter are to introduce the concepts of logic programming and logic programming languages, including a brief description of a subset of Prolog. We begin with an introduction to predicate calculus, which is the basis for logic programming languages. This is followed by a discussion of how predicate calculus can be used for automatic theorem proving systems. We then present a general overview of logic programming. Next, a lengthy section introduces the basics of the Prolog programming language, including arithmetic, list processing, and a trace tool that can be used to help debug programs and also to illustrate how the Prolog system works. The last two sections describe some of the problems of Prolog as a logic language and some of the application areas in which Prolog has been used.

16.1   Introduction

Chapter 15 discusses the functional programming paradigm, which is significantly different from the software development methodologies used with the imperative languages. In this chapter, we describe another different programming methodology. In this case, the approach is to express programs in a form of symbolic logic and use a logical inferencing process to produce results. Logic programs are declarative rather than procedural, which means that only the specifications of the desired results are stated rather than detailed procedures for producing them.

Programming that uses a form of symbolic logic as a programming language is often called **logic programming,** and languages based on symbolic logic are called **logic programming languages,** or **declarative languages.** We have chosen to describe the logic programming language Prolog because it is the only widely used logic language.

The syntax of logic programming languages is remarkably different from that of the imperative and functional languages. The semantics of logic programs also bears little resemblance to that of imperative language programs. These observations should lead the reader to some curiosity about the nature of logic programming and declarative languages.

16.2   A Brief Introduction to Predicate Calculus

Before we can discuss logic programming, we must briefly investigate its basis, which is formal logic. This is not our first contact with formal logic in this book; it was used extensively in the axiomatic semantics described in Chapter 3.

A **proposition** can be thought of as a logical statement that may or may not be true. It consists of objects and the relationships of objects to each other. Formal logic was developed to provide a method for describing propositions, with the goal of allowing those formally stated propositions to be checked for validity.

Symbolic logic can be used for the three basic needs of formal logic: to express propositions, to express the relationships between propositions, and to describe how new propositions can be inferred from other propositions that are assumed to be true.

There is a close relationship between formal logic and mathematics. In fact, much of mathematics can be thought of in terms of logic. The fundamental axioms of number and set theory are the initial set of propositions, which are assumed to be true. Theorems are the additional propositions that can be inferred from the initial set.

The particular form of symbolic logic that is used for logic programming is called **first-order predicate calculus** (though it is a bit imprecise, we will usually refer to it as simply predicate calculus). In the following subsections, we present a brief look at predicate calculus. Our goal is to lay the groundwork for a discussion of logic programming and the logic programming language Prolog.

16.2.1   Propositions

The objects in logic programming propositions are represented by simple terms, which are either constants or variables. A constant is a symbol that represents an object. A variable is a symbol that can represent different objects at different times, although in a sense that is far closer to mathematics than the variables in an imperative programming language.

The simplest propositions, which are called **atomic propositions,** consist of compound terms. A **compound term** is one element of a mathematical relation, written in a form that has the appearance of mathematical function notation. Recall from Chapter 15 that a mathematical function is a mapping, which can be represented either as an expression or as a table or list of tuples. So compound terms are elements of the tabular definition of a function.

A compound term is composed of two parts: a **functor,** which is the function symbol that names the relation, and an ordered list of parameters. A compound term with a single parameter is a 1-tuple; one with two parameters is a 2-tuple, and so forth. For example, we might have the two propositions

    man(jake)
    like(bob, steak)

which state that {jake} is a 1-tuple in the relation named man, and that {bob, steak} is a 2-tuple in the relation named like. If we added the proposition

    man(fred)

to the two propositions above, then the relation man would have two distinct elements, {jake} and {fred}. All of the simple terms in these propositions—man, jake, like, bob, and steak—are constants. Note that these propositions have no intrinsic semantics. They mean whatever we want them to mean. For example, the second example above may mean that bob likes steak, or that steak likes bob, or that bob is in some way similar to a steak.

Propositions can be stated in two modes: one in which the proposition is defined to be true, and one in which the truth of the proposition is something that is to be determined. In other words, propositions can be stated to be facts or queries. The example propositions above could be either.

Compound propositions have two or more atomic propositions, which are connected by logical connectors, or operators, in the same way compound logic expressions are constructed in imperative languages. The names, symbols, and meanings of the predicate calculus logical connectors are as follows:

Name	Symbol	Example	Meaning
negation	$\neg$	$\neg\, a$	not a.
conjunction	$\cap$	$a \cap b$	a and b.
disjunction	$\cup$	$a \cup b$	a or b.
equivalence	$\equiv$	$a \equiv b$	a is equivalent to b.
implication	$\supset$	$a \supset b$	a implies b.
	$\subset$	$a \subset b$	b implies a.

The following are examples of compound propositions:

$a \cap b \supset c$
$a \cap \neg\, b \supset d$

The operator $\neg$ has the highest precedence. The operators $\cap$, $\cup$, and $\equiv$ all have higher precedence than $\supset$ and $\subset$. So the second example above is equivalent to

$(a \cap (\neg\, b)) \supset d$

Variables can appear in propositions but only when introduced by special symbols called *quantifiers*. Predicate calculus includes two quantifiers, as described below, where X is a variable and P is a proposition:

Name	Example	Meaning
universal	$\forall XP$	For all X, P is true.
existential	$\exists X.P$	There exists a value of X such that P is true.

The period between X and P simply separates the variable from the proposition. For example, consider the following:

$\forall X.(\mathrm{woman}(X) \supset \mathrm{human}(X))$
$\exists X.(\mathrm{mother}(\mathrm{mary}, X) \cap \mathrm{male}(X))$

The first of these propositions means that for any value of X, if X is a woman, then X is a human. The second means that there exists a value of X such that mary is the mother of X and X is a male; in other words, mary has a son. The scope of the universal and existential quantifiers is the atomic propositions to which they are attached. This scope can be extended using parentheses, as in the two compound propositions just described. So the universal and existential quantifiers have higher precedence than any of the operators.

16.2.2 Clausal Form

We are discussing predicate calculus because it is the basis for logic programming languages. As with other languages, logic languages are best in their simplest form, meaning redundancy should be minimized.

One problem with the predicate calculus as we have described it thus far is that there are too many different ways of stating propositions that have the same meaning; that is, there is a great deal of redundancy. This is not such a problem for logicians, but if predicate calculus is to be used in an automated (computerized) system, it is a serious problem. To simplify matters, a standard form for propositions is desirable. Clausal form, which is a relatively simple form of propositions, is one such standard form. Without loss of generality, all propositions can be expressed in clausal form. A proposition in clausal form has the following general syntax:

$$B_1 \cup B_2 \cup ... \cup B_n \subset A_1 \cap A_2 \cap ... \cap A_m$$

in which the As and Bs are terms. The meaning of this clausal form proposition is as follows: If all of the As are true, then at least one B is true. The primary characteristics of clausal form propositions are the following: Existential quantifiers are not required; universal quantifiers are implicit in the use of variables in the atomic propositions; and no operators other than conjunction and disjunction are required. Also, conjunction and disjunction need appear only in the order shown in the general clausal form: disjunction on the left side and conjunction on the right side. All predicate calculus propositions can be algorithmically converted to clausal form. Nilsson (1971) gives proof that this can be done, as well as a simple conversion algorithm for doing it.

The right side of a clausal form proposition is called the **antecedent.** The left side is called the **consequent** because it is the consequence of the truth of the antecedent. As examples of clausal form propositions, consider the following:

likes(bob, trout) $\subset$ likes(bob, fish) $\cap$ fish(trout)
father(louis, al) $\cup$ father(louis, violet) $\subset$ father(al, bob) $\cap$ mother(violet, bob) $\cap$ grandfather(louis, bob)

The English version of the first of these states that if bob likes fish and a trout is a fish, then bob likes trout. The second states that if al is bob's father and violet is bob's mother and louis is bob's grandfather, then louis is either al's father or violet's father.

16.3 Predicate Calculus and Proving Theorems

Predicate calculus provides a method of expressing collections of propositions. One use of collections of propositions is to determine whether any interesting or useful facts can be inferred from them. This is exactly analogous to the work of mathematicians, who strive to discover new theorems that can be inferred from known axioms and theorems.

The early days of computer science (the 1950s and early 1960s) saw a great deal of interest in automating the theorem-proving process. One of the most significant breakthroughs in automatic theorem-proving was the discovery of the resolution principle by Alan Robinson at Syracuse University (Robinson, 1965).

Resolution is an inference rule that allows inferred propositions to be computed from given propositions, thus providing a method with potential application to automatic theorem proving. Resolution was devised to be applied to propositions in clausal form. The concept of resolution is the following: Suppose there are two propositions with the forms

$$P_1 \subset P_2$$
$$Q_1 \subset Q_2$$

Their meaning is that P_2 implies P_1 and Q_2 implies Q_1. Further suppose that P_1 is identical to Q_2, so that we could rename P_1 and Q_2 as T. Then, we could rewrite the two propositions as

$$T \subset P_2$$
$$Q_1 \subset T$$

Now, because P_2 implies T and T implies Q_1, it is logically obvious that P_2 implies Q_1, which we could write as

$$Q_1 \subset P_2$$

The process of inferring this proposition from the original two propositions is resolution.

As another example, consider the two propositions:

older(joanne, jake) $\subset$ mother(joanne, jake)
wiser(joanne, jake) $\subset$ older(joanne, jake)

From these propositions, the following proposition can be constructed using resolution:

wiser(joanne, jake) $\subset$ mother(joanne, jake)

The mechanics of this resolution construction are simple: The terms of the left sides of the two propositions are ANDed together to make the left side of the new proposition. Then the same thing is done to get the right side of the new proposition. Next, any term that appears on both sides of the new proposition is removed from both sides. The process is exactly the same when the propositions have multiple terms on either or both sides. The left side of the new inferred proposition initially contains all of the terms of the left sides of the two given propositions. The new right side is similarly constructed. Then the term that appears in both sides of the new proposition is removed. For example, if we have

father(bob, jake) $\cup$ mother(bob, jake) $\subset$ parent(bob, jake)
grandfather(bob, fred) $\subset$ father(bob, jake) $\cap$ father(jake, fred)

resolution says that

mother(bob, jake) ∪ grandfather(bob, fred) ⊂
parent(bob, jake) ∩ father(jake, fred)

which has all but one of the atomic propositions of both of the original propositions. The one atomic proposition that allowed the operation father(bob, jake) in the left side of the first and in the right side of the second is left out. In English, we would say

if: bob is the parent of jake implies that bob is either the father
         or mother of jake
and: bob is the father of jake and jake is the father of fred implies
         that bob is the grandfather of fred
then: *if* bob is the parent of jake and jake is the father of fred
         then: either bob is jake's mother or bob is fred's grandfather

Resolution is actually more complex than these simple examples illustrate. In particular, the presence of variables in propositions requires resolution to find values for those variables that allow the matching process to succeed. This process of determining useful values for variables is called **unification.** The temporary assigning of values to variables to allow unification is called **instantiation.**

It is common for the resolution process to instantiate a variable with a value, fail to complete the required matching, and then be required to backtrack and instantiate the variable with a different value. We will discuss unification and backtracking more extensively in the context of Prolog.

A critically important property of resolution is its ability to detect any inconsistency in a given set of propositions. This property allows resolution to be used to prove theorems, which can be done as follows: We can envision a theorem proof in terms of predicate calculus as a given set of pertinent propositions, with the negation of the theorem itself stated as a new proposition. The theorem is negated so that resolution can be used to prove the theorem by finding an inconsistency. This is proof by contradiction. Typically, the original propositions are called the **hypotheses,** and the negation of the theorem is called the **goal.**

Theoretically, this is a valid and useful process. The time required for resolution, however, can be a problem. Although resolution is a finite process when the set of propositions is finite, the time required to find an inconsistency in a large database of propositions may be huge.

Theorem proving is the basis for logic programming. Much of what is computed can be couched in the form of a list of given facts and relationships as hypotheses, and a goal to be inferred from the hypotheses, using resolution.

When propositions are used for resolution, only a restricted kind of clausal form can be used, which further simplifies the resolution process. The special kinds of propositions, called **Horn clauses,** can be in only two forms:

They have either a single atomic proposition on the left side or an empty left side.[1] The left side of a clausal form proposition is sometimes called the *head*, and Horn clauses with left sides are called *headed Horn clauses*. Headed Horn clauses are used to state relationships, such as

likes(bob, trout) ⊂ likes(bob, fish) ∩ fish(trout)

Horn clauses with empty left sides, which are often used to state facts, are called *headless Horn clauses*. For example,

father(bob, jake)

Most, but not all, propositions can be stated as Horn clauses.

16.4   An Overview of Logic Programming

Languages used for logic programming are called *declarative languages* because programs written in them consist of declarations rather than assignments and control flow statements. These declarations are actually statements, or propositions, in symbolic logic.

One of the essential characteristics of logic programming languages is their semantics, which is called **declarative semantics.** The basic concept of this semantics is that there is a simple way to determine the meaning of each statement, and it does not depend on how the statement might be used to solve a problem. Declarative semantics is considerably simpler than the semantics of the imperative languages. For example, the meaning of a given proposition in a logic programming language can be concisely determined from the statement itself. In an imperative language, the semantics of a simple assignment statement requires examination of local declarations, knowledge of the scoping rules of the language, and possibly even examination of programs in other files just to determine the types of the variables in the assignment statement. Then, assuming the expression of the assignment contains variables, the execution of the program prior to the assignment statement must be traced to determine the values of those variables. The resulting action of the statement, then, depends on its run-time context. Comparing this with the simple examination of a single statement, with no need to consider textual context or execution sequences, it is clear that declarative semantics is far simpler than the semantics of imperative languages. Thus, declarative semantics is often stated as one of the advantages that declarative languages have over imperative languages (Hogger, 1984, pp. 240–241).

Programming in both imperative and functional languages is primarily procedural, which means that the programmer knows *what* is to be accomplished by a program and instructs the computer on exactly *how* the computation is to be done. In other words, the computer is treated as a simple device

---

[1]Horn clauses are named after Alfred Horn, who studied clauses in this form [Horn, 1951].

that obeys orders. Everything that is computed must have every detail of that computation spelled out. Some people believe that this is the essence of the difficulty of programming computers.

Programming in some kinds of nonimperative languages, and in particular in logic programming languages, is nonprocedural. Programs in such languages do not state exactly *how* a result is to be computed but rather describe the form of the result. The difference is that we assume the computer system can somehow determine *how* the result is to be gotten. What is needed to provide this capability for logic programming languages is a concise means of supplying the computer with both the relevant information and a method of inference for computing desirable results. Predicate calculus supplies the basic form of communication to the computer, and resolution provides the inference technique.

An example commonly used to illustrate the difference between procedural and nonprocedural systems is sorting. In a language like C++, sorting is done by explaining in a C++ program all of the details of some sorting algorithm to a computer that has a C++ compiler. The computer, after translating the C++ program into machine code or some interpretive intermediate code, follows the instructions and produces the sorted list.

In a nonprocedural language, it is necessary only to describe the characteristics of the sorted list: It is some permutation of the given list such that for each pair of adjacent elements, a given relationship holds between the two elements. To state this formally, suppose the list to be sorted is in an array named list that has a subscript range $1...n$. The concept of sorting the elements of the given list, named old_list, and placing them in a separate array, named new_list, can then be expressed as follows:

sort(old_list, new_list) $\subset$ permute(old_list, new_list) $\cap$ sorted(new_list)
sorted(list) $\subset$ $\forall$j such that $1 \leq j < n$, list(j) $\leq$ list(j+1)

where permute is a predicate that returns true if its second parameter array is a permutation of its first parameter array.

From this description, the nonprocedural language system could produce the sorted list. That makes nonprocedural programming sound like the mere production of concise software requirements specifications, which is a fair assessment. Unfortunately, however, it is not that simple. Logic programs that use only resolution face serious problems of machine efficiency. Furthermore, the best form of a logic language may not yet have been determined, and good methods of creating programs in logic programming languages for large problems have not yet been developed.

16.5 The Origins of Prolog

As was stated in Chapter 2, Alain Colmerauer and Phillippe Roussel at the University of Aix-Marseille, with some assistance from Robert Kowalski at the University of Edinburgh, developed the fundamental design of Prolog.

Colmerauer and Roussel were interested in natural language processing, and Kowalski was interested in automated theorem proving. The collaboration between the University of Aix-Marseille and the University of Edinburgh continued until the mid-1970s. Since then, research on the development and use of the language has progressed independently at those two locations, resulting in, among other things, two syntactically different dialects of Prolog.

The development of Prolog and other research efforts in logic programming received limited attention outside of Edinburgh and Marseille until the announcement in 1981 that the Japanese government was launching a large research project called the Fifth Generation Computing Systems (FGCS) (Fuchi, 1981; Moto-oka, 1981). One of the primary objectives of the project was to develop intelligent machines, and Prolog was chosen as the basis for this effort. The announcement of FGCS aroused in researchers and the governments of the United States and several European countries a sudden strong interest in artificial intelligence and logic programming.

After a decade of effort, the FGCS project was quietly dropped. Despite the great assumed potential of logic programming and Prolog, little of great significance had been discovered. This led to the decline in the interest in and use of Prolog, although it still has its applications and proponents.

16.6　The Basic Elements of Prolog

There are now a number of different dialects of Prolog. These can be grouped into several categories: those that grew from the Marseille group, those that came from the Edinburgh group, and a collection of dialects that have been developed for microcomputers, such as micro-Prolog, which is described by Clark and McCabe (1984). The syntactic forms of these are somewhat different. Rather than attempt to describe the syntax of several dialects of Prolog or some hybrid of them, we have chosen one particular, widely available dialect, which is the one developed at Edinburgh. This form of the language is sometimes called **Edinburgh syntax.** Its first implementation was on a DEC System-10 (Warren et al., 1979). Prolog implementations are available for virtually all popular computer platforms, for example, from the Free Software Organization (`http://www.gnu.org`).

16.6.1　Terms

As with programs in other languages, Prolog programs consist of collections of statements. There are only a few kinds of statements in Prolog, but they can be complex. All Prolog statements are constructed from terms.

A Prolog **term** is a constant, a variable, or a structure. A constant is either an **atom** or an integer. Atoms are the symbolic values of Prolog and are similar to their counterparts in LISP. In particular, an atom is either a string of letters, digits, and underscores that begins with a lowercase letter or a string of any printable ASCII characters delimited by apostrophes.

A variable is any string of letters, digits, and underscores that begins with an uppercase letter. Variables are not bound to types by declarations. The binding of a value, and thus a type, to a variable is called an **instantiation.** Instantiation occurs only in the resolution process. A variable that has not been assigned a value is called **uninstantiated.** Instantiations last only as long as it takes to satisfy one complete goal, which involves the proof or disproof of one proposition. Prolog variables are only distant relatives, in terms of both semantics and use, to the variables in the imperative languages.

The last kind of term is called a **structure.** Structures represent the atomic propositions of predicate calculus, and their general form is the same:

functor(parameter list)

The functor is any atom and is used to identify the structure. The parameter list can be any list of atoms, variables, or other structures. As discussed at length in the following section, structures are the means of specifying facts in Prolog. They can also be thought of as objects, in which case they allow facts to be stated in terms of several related atoms. In this sense, structures are relations, for they state relationships among terms. A structure is also a predicate when its context specifies it to be a query (question).

16.6.2 Fact Statements

Our discussion of Prolog statements begins with those statements used to construct the hypotheses, or database of assumed information—the statements from which new information can be inferred.

Prolog has two basic statement forms; these correspond to the headless and headed Horn clauses of predicate calculus. The simplest form of headless Horn clause in Prolog is a single structure, which is interpreted as an unconditional assertion, or fact. Logically, facts are simply propositions that are assumed to be true.

The following examples illustrate the kinds of facts one can have in a Prolog program. Notice that every Prolog statement is terminated by a period.

```
female(shelley).
male(bill).
female(mary).
male(jake).
father(bill, jake).
father(bill, shelley).
mother(mary, jake).
mother(mary, shelley).
```

These simple structures state certain facts about jake, shelley, bill, and mary. For example, the first states that shelley is a female. The last four connect their two parameters with a relationship that is named in the functor atom; for example, the fifth proposition might be interpreted to mean that `bill` is the `father` of `jake`. Note that these Prolog propositions, like those of predicate calculus, have no intrinsic semantics. They mean whatever the programmer wants them to mean. For example, the proposition

```
father(bill, jake).
```

could mean `bill` and `jake` have the same `father` or that `jake` is the `father` of `bill`. The most common and straightforward meaning, however, is that `bill` is the `father` of `jake`.

16.6.3 Rule Statements

The other basic form of Prolog statement for constructing the database corresponds to a headed Horn clause. This form can be related to a known theorem in mathematics from which a conclusion can be drawn if the set of given conditions is satisfied. The right side is the antecedent, or *if* part, and the left side is the consequent, or *then* part. If the antecedent of a Prolog statement is true, then the consequent of the statement must also be true. Because they are Horn clauses, the consequent of a Prolog statement is a single term, while the antecedent can be either a single term or a conjunction.

Conjunctions contain multiple terms that are separated by logical AND operations. In Prolog, the AND operation is implied. The structures that specify atomic propositions in a conjunction are separated by commas, so one could consider the commas to be AND operators. As an example of a conjunction, consider the following:

```
female (shelley), child (shelley).
```

The general form of the Prolog headed Horn clause statement is

```
consequence_1 :- antecedent_expression.
```

It is read as follows: "consequence_1 can be concluded if the antecedent expression is true or can be made to be true by some instantiation of its variables." For example,

```
ancestor(mary, shelley) :- mother(mary, shelley).
```

states that if `mary` is the `mother` of `shelley`, then `mary` is an `ancestor` of `shelley`. Headed Horn clauses are called **rules** because they state rules of implication between propositions.

As with clausal form propositions in predicate calculus, Prolog statements can use variables to generalize their meaning. Recall that variables in clausal form provide a kind of implied universal quantifier. The following demonstrates the use of variables in Prolog statements:

```
parent(X, Y) :- mother(X, Y).
parent(X, Y) :- father(X, Y).
```

```
grandparent(X, Z) :- parent(X, Y) , parent(Y, Z).
sibling(X, Y) :- mother(M, X) , mother(M, Y),
                 father(F, X) , father(F, Y).
```

These statements give rules of implication among some variables, or universal objects. In this case, the universal objects are X, Y, Z, M, and F. The first rule states that if there are instantiations of X and Y such that mother(X, Y) is true, then for those same instantiations of X and Y, parent(X, Y) is true.

16.6.4 Goal Statements

So far, we have described the Prolog statements for logical propositions, which are used to describe both known facts and rules that describe logical relationships among facts. These statements are the basis for the theorem-proving model. The theorem is in the form of a proposition that we want the system to either prove or disprove. In Prolog, these propositions are called **goals,** or **queries.** The syntactic form of Prolog goal statements is identical to that of headless Horn clauses. For example, we could have

```
man(fred).
```

to which the system will respond either yes or no. The answer yes means that the system has proved the goal was true under the given database of facts and relationships. The answer no means that either the goal was proved false or the system was simply unable to prove it.

Conjunctive propositions and propositions with variables are also legal goals. When variables are present, the system not only asserts the validity of the goal but also identifies the instantiations of the variables that make the goal true. For example,

```
father(X, mike).
```

can be asked. The system will then attempt, through unification, to find an instantiation of X that results in a true value for the goal.

Because goal statements and some nongoal statements have the same form (headless Horn clauses), a Prolog implementation must have some means of distinguishing between the two. Interactive Prolog implementations do this by simply having two modes, indicated by different interactive prompts: one for entering fact and rule statements and one for entering goals. The user can change the mode at any time.

16.6.5 The Inferencing Process of Prolog

This section examines Prolog resolution. Efficient use of Prolog requires that the programmer know precisely what the Prolog system does with his or her program.

Queries are called **goals.** When a goal is a compound proposition, each of the facts (structures) is called a **subgoal.** To prove that a goal is true, the inferencing process must find a chain of inference rules and/or facts in the database that connect the goal to one or more facts in the database. For example, if Q is the goal, then either Q must be found as a fact in the database or the inferencing process must find a fact P_1 and a sequence of propositions P_2, P_3, ..., P_n such that P

$$P_2 :- P_1$$
$$P_3 :- P_2$$
...
$$Q :- P_n$$

Of course, the process can and often is complicated by rules with compound right sides and rules with variables. The process of finding the Ps, when they exist, is basically a comparison, or matching, of terms with each other.

Because the process of proving a subgoal is done through a proposition-matching process, it is sometimes called **matching.** In some cases, proving a subgoal is called **satisfying** that subgoal.

Consider the following query:

```
man(bob).
```

This goal statement is the simplest kind. It is relatively easy for resolution to determine whether it is true or false: The pattern of this goal is compared with the facts and rules in the database. If the database includes the fact

```
man(bob).
```

the proof is trivial. If, however, the database contains the following fact and inference rule,

```
father(bob).
man(X) :- father(X).
```

Prolog would be required to find these two statements and use them to infer the truth of the goal. This would necessitate unification to instantiate X temporarily to bob.

Now consider the goal

```
man(X).
```

In this case, Prolog must match the goal against the propositions in the database. The first proposition that it finds that has the form of the goal, with any object as its parameter, will cause X to be instantiated with that object's value. X is then displayed as the result. If there is no proposition having the form of the goal, the system indicates, by saying no, that the goal cannot be satisfied.

There are two opposite approaches to attempting to match a given goal to a fact in the database. The system can begin with the facts and rules of the database and attempt to find a sequence of matches that lead to the goal. This approach is called **bottom-up resolution,** or **forward chaining.** The alternative is to begin with the goal and attempt to find a sequence of matching propositions that lead to some set of original facts in the database. This approach is called **top-down resolution,** or **backward chaining.** In general, backward chaining works well when there is a reasonably small set of candidate answers. The forward chaining approach is better when the number of possibly correct answers is large; in this situation, backward chaining would require a very large number of matches to get to an answer. Prolog implementations use backward chaining for resolution, presumably because its designers believed backward chaining was more suitable for a larger class of problems than forward chaining.

Consider again the example query:

```
man(bob).
```

Assume the database contains

```
father(bob).
man(X) :- father(X).
```

Forward chaining would search for and find the first proposition. The goal is then inferred by matching the first proposition with the right side of the second rule (`father(X)`) through instantiation of X to bob and then matching the left side of the second proposition to the goal. Backward chaining would first match the goal with the left side of the second proposition (`man(X)`) through the instantiation of X to bob. As its last step, it would match the right side of the second proposition (now `father(bob)`) with the first proposition.

The next design question arises whenever the goal has more than one structure, as in our example above. The question then is whether the solution search is done depth first or breadth first. A **depth-first** search finds a complete sequence of propositions—a proof—for the first subgoal before working on the others. A **breadth-first** search works on all subgoals of a given goal in parallel. Prolog's designers chose the depth-first approach primarily because it can be done with fewer computer resources. The breadth-first approach is a parallel search that can take a large amount of memory.

The last feature of Prolog's resolution mechanism that must be discussed is backtracking. When a goal with multiple subgoals is being processed and the system fails to show the truth of one of the subgoals, the system abandons the subgoal it could not prove. Instead, the system reconsiders the previous subgoal, if there is one, and attempts to find an alternative solution to it. This backing up in the goal to the reconsideration of a previously proven subgoal is called **backtracking.** A new solution is found by beginning the search where the previous search for that subgoal stopped. Multiple solutions to a subgoal result from different instantiations of its variables. Backtracking can require a great deal of time and space because it may have to find all possible proofs to every subgoal. These subgoal proofs may not be organized to minimize the time required to find the one that will result in the final complete proof, which exacerbates the problem.

To solidify your understanding of backtracking, consider the following example. Assume that there is a set of facts and rules in a database and that Prolog has been presented with the following compound goal:

```
male(X), parent(X, shelley).
```

This goal asks whether there is an instantiation of X such that X is a male and X is a parent of shelley. Prolog first finds the first fact in the database with male as its functor. It then instantiates X to the parameter of the found fact, say mike. Then it attempts to prove that parent(mike, shelley) is true. If it fails, it backtracks to the first subgoal, male(X), and attempts to resatisfy it with some alternative instantiation of X. The resolution process may have to find every male in the database before it finds the one that is a parent of shelley. It definitely must find all males to prove that the goal cannot be satisfied. Note that our example goal might be processed more efficiently if the order of the two subgoals were reversed. Then, only after resolution had found a parent of shelley would it try to match that person with the male subgoal. This is more efficient if shelley has fewer parents than there are males in the database, which seems like a fair assumption. Section 16.7.1 discusses a method of limiting the backtracking done by a Prolog system.

Database searches in Prolog always proceed in the direction of first to last.

The following two subsections describe Prolog examples that further illustrate the resolution process.

16.6.6 Simple Arithmetic

Prolog supports integer variables and integer arithmetic. Originally, the arithmetic operators were functors, so that the sum of 7 and the variable X was formed with

```
+(7, X)
```

Prolog now allows a more abbreviated syntax for arithmetic with the **is** operator. This operator takes an arithmetic expression as its right operand and a variable as its left operand. All variables in the expression must already be instantiated, but the left-side variable cannot be previously instantiated. For example, in

```
A is B / 17 + C.
```

If B and C are instantiated but A is not, then this clause will cause A to be instantiated with the value of the expression. When this happens, the clause is satisfied. If either B or C is not instantiated or A is instantiated, the clause is not satisfied and no instantiation of A can take place. The semantics of an **is** proposition is considerably different from that of an assignment statement in an imperative language. This difference can lead to an interesting scenario. Because the **is** operator makes the clause in which it appears look like an assignment statement, a beginning Prolog programmer may be tempted to write a statement such as

```
Sum is Sum + Number.
```

which is never useful, or even legal, in Prolog. If Sum is not instantiated, the reference to it in the right side is undefined and the clause fails. If Sum is already instantiated, the clause fails because the left operand cannot have a current instantiation when **is** is evaluated. In either case, the instantiation of Sum to the new value will not take place. (If the value of Sum + Number is required, it can be bound to some new name.)

Prolog does not have assignment statements in the same sense as imperative languages. They are simply not needed in most of the programming for which Prolog was designed. The usefulness of assignment statements in imperative languages depends on the capability of the programmer to control the execution control flow of the code in which the assignment statement is embedded. Because this type of control is not always possible in Prolog, such statements are far less useful.

As a simple example of the use of numeric computation in Prolog, consider the following problem: Suppose we know the average speeds of several automobiles on a particular racetrack and the amount of time they are on the track. This basic information can be coded as facts, and the relationship between speed, time, and distance can be written as a rule, as in the following:

```
speed(ford, 100).
speed(chevy, 105).
speed(dodge, 95).
speed(volvo, 80).
time(ford, 20).
time(chevy, 21).
time(dodge, 24).
time(volvo, 24).
distance(X, Y) :- speed(X, Speed),
                  time(X, Time),
                  Y is Speed * Time.
```

Now, queries can request the distance traveled by a particular car. For example, the query

```
distance(chevy, Chevy_Distance).
```

instantiates Chevy_Distance with the value 2205. The first two clauses in the right side of the distance computation statement simply instantiate the variables Speed and Time with the corresponding values of the given automobile functor. After satisfying the goal, Prolog also displays the name Chevy_Distance and its value.

At this point it is instructive to take an operational look at how a Prolog system produces results. Prolog has a built-in structure named `trace` that displays the instantiations of values to variables at each step during the attempt to satisfy a given goal. `trace` is used to understand and debug Prolog programs. To understand `trace`, it is best to introduce a different model of the execution of Prolog programs, called the **tracing model.**

The tracing model describes Prolog execution in terms of four events: (1) call, which occurs at the beginning of an attempt to satisfy a goal, (2) exit, which occurs when a goal has been satisfied, (3) redo, which occurs when backtrack causes an attempt to resatisfy a goal, and (4) fail, which occurs when a goal fails. Call and exit can be related directly to the execution model of a subprogram in an imperative language if processes like `distance` are thought of as subprograms. The other two events are unique to logic programming systems. In the following trace example, the goal requires no redo or fail events.

The following is a trace of the computation of the value for `Chevy_Distance`:

```
trace.
distance(chevy, Chevy_Distance).

(1)  1 Call: distance(chevy, _0)?
(2)  2 Call: speed(chevy, _5)?
(2)  2 Exit: speed(chevy, 105)
(3)  2 Call: time(chevy, _6)?
(3)  2 Exit: time(chevy, 21)
(4)  2 Call: _0 is 105*21?
(4)  2 Exit: 2205 is 105*21
(1)  1 Exit: distance(chevy, 2205)

Chevy_Distance = 2205
```

Symbols in the trace that begin with the underscore character (_) are internal variables used to store instantiated values. The first column of the trace indicates the subgoal whose match is currently being attempted. For example, in the trace above, the first line with the indication (3) is an attempt to instantiate the temporary variable _6 with a `time` value for `chevy`, where `time` is the second term in the right side of the statement that describes the computation of `distance`. The second column indicates the call depth of the matching process. The third column indicates the current action.

To illustrate backtracking, consider the following example database and traced compound goal:

```
likes(jake, chocolate).
likes(jake, apricots).
likes(darcie, licorice).
likes(darcie, apricots).

trace.
likes(jake, X), likes(darcie, X).
```

```
(1) 1 Call: likes(jake, _0)?
(1) 1 Exit: likes(jake, chocolate)
(2) 1 Call: likes(darcie, chocolate)?
(2) 1 Fail: likes(darcie, chocolate)
(1) 1 Redo: likes(jake, _0)?
(1) 1 Exit: likes(jake, apricots)
(3) 1 Call: likes(darcie, apricots)?
(3) 1 Exit: likes(darcie, apricots)
```

```
X = apricots
```

One can think about Prolog computations graphically as follows: Consider each goal as a box with four ports—call, fail, exit, and redo. Control enters a goal in the forward direction through its call port. Control can also enter a goal from the reverse direction through its redo port. Control can also leave a goal in two ways: If the goal succeeded, control leaves through the exit port; if the goal failed, control leaves through the fail port. A model of the example above is shown in Figure 16.1. In this example, control flows through each subgoal twice. The second subgoal fails the first time, which forces a return through redo to the first subgoal.

16.6.7 List Structures

So far, the only Prolog data structure we have discussed is the atomic proposition, which looks more like a function call than a data structure. Atomic propositions, which are also called structures, are actually a form of records. The other basic data structure supported is the list, which is similar to the list structure used by LISP. Lists are sequences of any number of elements, where the elements can be atoms, atomic propositions, or any other terms, including other lists.

Figure 16.1

Control flow model for the goal `likes (jake, X), likes (darcie, X)`

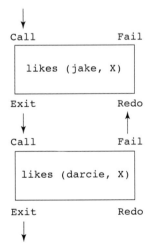

Prolog uses the syntax of ML and Haskell to specify lists. The list elements are separated by commas, and the entire list is delimited by square brackets, as in

```
[apple, prune, grape, kumquat]
```

The notation `[ ]` is used to denote the empty list. Instead of having explicit functions for constructing and dismantling lists, Prolog simply uses a special notation. `[X | Y]` denotes a list with head `X` and tail `Y`, where head and tail correspond to CAR and CDR in LISP. This is similar to the notation used in ML and Haskell.

A list can be created with a simple structure, as in

```
new_list([apple, prune, grape, kumquat]).
```

which states that the constant list `[apple, prune, grape, kumquat]` is a new element of the relation named `new_list` (a name we just made up). This statement does not bind the list to a variable named `new_list`; rather, it does the kind of thing that the proposition

```
male(jake)
```

does. That is, it states that `[apple, prune, grape, kumquat]` is a new element of `new_list`. Therefore, we could have a second proposition with a list argument, such as

```
new_list([apricot, peach, pear])
```

In query mode, one of the elements of `new_list` can be dismantled into head and tail with

```
new_list([New_List_Head | New_List_Tail]).
```

If `new_list` has been set to have the two elements as above, this statement instantiates `New_List_Head` with the head of the first list element (in this case, `apple`) and `New_List_Tail` with the tail of the list (or `[prune, grape, kumquat]`). If this were part of a compound goal and backtracking forced a new evaluation of it, `New_List_Head` and `New_List_Tail` would be reinstantiated to `apricot` and `[peach, pear]`, respectively, because `[apricot, peach, pear]` is the next element of `new_list`.

The | operator used to dismantle lists can also be used to create lists from given instantiated head and tail components, as in

```
[Element_1 | List_2]
```

If `Element_1` has been instantiated with `pickle` and `List_2` has been instantiated with `[peanut, prune, popcorn]`, the notation above will create, for this one reference, the list `[pickle, peanut, prune, popcorn]`.

As was stated above, the list notation that includes the | symbol is universal: It can specify either a list construction or a list dismantling. Note further that the following are equivalent:

```
[apricot, peach, pear | []]
[apricot, peach | [pear]]
[apricot | [peach, pear]]
```

With lists, certain basic operations are often required, such as those found in LISP, ML, and Haskell. As an example of such operations in Prolog, we examine a definition of append, which is related to such a function in LISP. In this example, the differences and similarities between functional and declarative languages can be seen. We need not specify how Prolog is to construct a new list from the given lists; rather, we need only specify the characteristics of the new list in terms of the given lists.

In appearance, the Prolog definition of append is very similar to the ML version that appears in Chapter 15, and a kind of recursion in resolution is used in a similar way to produce the new list. In the case of Prolog, the recursion is caused and controlled by the resolution process. As with ML and Haskell, a pattern-matching process is used to choose, based on the actual parameter, between two different definitions of the append process.

The first two parameters to the append operation in the following code are the two lists to be appended, and the third parameter is the resulting list:

```
append([], List, List).
append([Head | List_1], List_2, [Head | List_3]) :-
          append(List_1, List_2, List_3).
```

The first proposition specifies that when the empty list is appended to any other list, that other list is the result. This statement corresponds to the recursion-terminating step of the ML append function. Note that the terminating proposition is placed before the recursion proposition. This is done because we know that Prolog will match the two propositions in order, starting with the first (because of its use of the depth-first order).

The second proposition specifies several characteristics of the new list. It corresponds to the recursion step in the ML function. The left-side predicate states that the first element of the new list is the same as the first element of the first given list, because they are both named Head. Whenever Head is instantiated to a value, all occurrences of Head in the goal are, in effect, simultaneously instantiated to that value. The right side of the second statement specifies that the tail of the first given list (List_1) has the second given list (List_2) appended to it to form the tail (List_3) of the resulting list.

One way to read the second statement of append is as follows: Appending the list [Head | List_1] to any list List_2 produces the list [Head | List_3], but only if the list List_3 is formed by appending List_1 to List_2. In LISP, this would be

```
(CONS (CAR FIRST) (APPEND (CDR FIRST) SECOND))
```

In both the Prolog and LISP versions, the resulting list is not constructed until the recursion produces the terminating condition; in this case, the first list must become empty. Then the resulting list is built using the append function itself; the elements taken from the first list are added, in reverse order, to the second list. The reversing is done by the unraveling of the recursion.

To illustrate how the append process progresses, consider the following traced example:

```
trace.
append([bob, jo], [jake, darcie], Family).

(1)  1 Call: append([bob, jo], [jake, darcie], _10)?
(2)  2 Call: append([jo], [jake, darcie], _18)?
(3)  3 Call: append([], [jake, darcie], _25)?
(3)  3 Exit: append([], [jake, darcie], [jake, darcie])
(2)  2 Exit: append([jo], [jake, darcie], [jo, jake,
                     darcie])
(1)  1 Exit: append([bob, jo], [jake, darcie],
                    [bob, jo, jake, darcie])
Family = [bob, jo, jake, darcie]
yes
```

The first two calls, which represent subgoals, have List_1 nonempty, so they create the recursive calls from the right side of the second statement. The left side of the second statement effectively specifies the arguments for the recursive calls, or goals, thus dismantling the first list one element per step. When the first list becomes empty, in a call, or subgoal, the current instance of the right side of the second statement succeeds by matching the first statement. The effect of this is to return as the third parameter the value of the empty list appended to the second original parameter list. On successive exits, which represent successful matches, the elements that were removed from the first list are appended to the resulting list, Family. When the exit from the first goal is accomplished, the process is complete, and the resulting list is displayed.

The append propositions can also be used to create other list operations, such as the following, whose effect we invite the reader to determine. Note that list_op_2 is meant to be used by providing a list as its first parameter and a variable as its second, and the result of list_op_2 is the value to which the second parameter is instantiated.

```
list_op_2([], []).
list_op_2([Head | Tail], List) :- list_op_2(Tail, Result),
                                  append(Result, [Head], List).
```

As you may have been able to determine, list_op_2 causes the Prolog system to instantiate its second parameter with a list that has the elements of the list of the first parameter, but in reverse order. For example, ([apple, orange, grape], Q) instantiates Q with the list [grape, orange, apple].

Once again, although the LISP and Prolog languages are fundamentally different, similar operations can use similar approaches. In the case of the reverse operation, both the Prolog's list_op_2 and LISP's reverse function include the recursion terminating condition, along with the basic process of appending the reversal of the CDR or tail of the list to the CAR or head of the list to create the result list.

The following is a trace of this process, now named reverse:

```
trace.
reverse([a, b, c], Q).

(1) 1 Call: reverse([a, b, c], _6)?
(2) 2 Call: reverse([b, c], _65636)?
(3) 3 Call: reverse([c], _65646)?
(4) 4 Call: reverse([], _65656)?
(4) 4 Exit: reverse([], [])
(5) 4 Call: append([], [c], _65646)?
(5) 4 Exit: append([], [c], [c])
(3) 3 Exit: reverse([c], [c])
(6) 3 Call: append([c], [b], _65636)?
(7) 4 Call: append([], [b], _25)?
(7) 4 Exit: append([], [b], [b])
(6) 3 Exit: append([c], [b], [c, b])
(2) 2 Exit: reverse([b, c], [c, b])
(8) 2 Call: append([c, b], [a], _6)?
(9) 3 Call: append([b], [a], _32)?
(10) 4 Call: append([], [a], _39)?
(10) 4 Exit: append([], [a], [a])
(9) 3 Exit: append([b], [a], [b, a])
(8) 2 Exit: append([c, b], [a], [c, b, a])
(1) 1 Exit: reverse([a, b, c], [c, b, a])

Q = [c, b, a]
```

Suppose we need to be able to determine whether a given symbol is in a given list. A straightforward Prolog description of this is

```
member(Element, [Element | _]).
member(Element, [_ | List]) :- member(Element, List).
```

The underscore indicates an "anonymous" variable; it is used to mean that we do not care what instantiation it might get from unification. The first statement above succeeds if Element is the head of the list, either initially or after several recursions through the second statement. The second statement succeeds if `Element` is in the tail of the list. Consider the following traced examples:

```
trace.
member(a, [b, c, d]).
(1) 1 Call: member(a, [b, c, d])?
(2) 2 Call: member(a, [c, d])?
(3) 3 Call: member(a, [d])?
(4) 4 Call: member(a, [])?
(4) 4 Fail: member(a, [])
(3) 3 Fail: member(a, [d])
(2) 2 Fail: member(a, [c, d])
(1) 1 Fail: member(a, [b, c, d])
no

member(a, [b, a, c]).
(1) 1 Call: member(a, [b, a, c])?
(2) 2 Call: member(a, [a, c])?
(2) 2 Exit: member(a, [a, c])
(1) 1 Exit: member(a, [b, a, c])
yes
```

16.7   Deficiencies of Prolog

Several problems arise in using Prolog as a logic programming language. Although it is a useful tool, it is neither a pure nor a perfect logic programming language.

16.7.1   Resolution Order Control

Prolog, for reasons of efficiency, allows the user to control the ordering of pattern matching during resolution. In a pure logic programming environment, the order of attempted matches that take place during resolution is nondeterministic, and all matches could be attempted concurrently. However, because Prolog always matches in the same order, starting at the beginning of the database and at the left end of a given goal, the user can profoundly affect efficiency by ordering the database statements to optimize a particular application. For example, if the user knows that certain rules are much more likely to succeed than the others during a particular "execution," then the program can be made more efficient by placing those rules first in the database.

Slow program execution is not the only negative result of user-defined ordering in Prolog programs. It is very easy to write statements in forms that cause infinite loops and thus total program failure. For example, consider the following recursive statement form:

```
f(X, Y) :- f(Z, Y), g(X, Z).
```

Because of Prolog's left-to-right depth-first order of evaluation, regardless of the purpose of the statement, it will cause an infinite loop. As an example of this kind of statement, consider

```
ancestor(X, X).
ancestor(X, Y) :- ancestor(Z, Y), parent(X, Z).
```

In attempting to satisfy the first subgoal of the right side of the second proposition, Prolog instantiates z to make ancestor true. It then tries to satisfy this new subgoal, coming right back to the definition of ancestor and repeating the same process, leading to unending recursion.

This particular problem is identical to the problem a recursive descent parser has with left recursion in a grammar rule, as discussed in Chapter 3. As was the case with grammar rules in parsing, simply reversing the order of the terms in the right side of the proposition above eliminates the problem. The trouble with this is that a simple change of term ordering should not be crucial to the correctness of the program. After all, the lack of the need for programmer concern for control order is supposedly one of the advantages of logic programming.

In addition to allowing the user to control database and subgoal ordering, Prolog, in another concession to efficiency, allows some explicit control of backtracking. This is done with the cut operator, which is specified by an exclamation point (!). The cut operator is actually a goal, not an operator. As a goal, it always succeeds immediately, but it cannot be resatisfied through backtracking. Thus, a side effect of the cut is that subgoals to its left in a compound goal also cannot be resatisfied through backtracking. For example, in the goal

```
a, b, !, c, d.
```

if both a and b succeed but c fails, the whole goal fails. This goal would be used if it were known that whenever c fails, it is a waste of time to resatisfy b or a.

The purpose of the cut then is to allow the user to make programs more efficient by telling the system when it should not attempt to resatisfy subgoals that presumably could not result in a complete proof.

As an example of one use of the cut operator, consider the member rules from Section 16.6.7, which are repeated below:

```
member(Element, [Element | _]).
member(Element, [_ | List]) :- member(Element, List).
```

If the list argument to member represents a set, then it can be satisfied only once (sets contain no duplicate elements). Therefore, if member is used as a subgoal in a multiple subgoal goal statement, there can be a problem. The problem is that if member succeeds but the next subgoal fails, backtracking will attempt to resatisfy member by continuing a prior match. But because the list argument to member has only one copy of the element to begin with, member cannot possibly succeed again, which eventually causes the whole goal to fail, in spite of any additional attempts to resatisfy member. The solution to this inefficiency is to add a right side to the first statement of the member definition, with the cut operator as the sole element, as in

```
member(Element, [Element | _]) :- !.
```

Backtracking will not attempt to resatisfy member but instead will cause the entire subgoal to fail.

Cut is particularly useful in a programming strategy in Prolog called **generate and test.** In these programs, the goal consists of subgoals that generate potential solutions, which are then checked by later "test" subgoals. Rejected solutions require backtracking to "generator" subgoals, which generate new potential solutions. As an example of a generate and test program, consider the following, which appears in Clocksin and Mellish (1984):

```
divide(N1, N2, Result) :- is_integer(Result),
                  Product1 is Result * N2,
                  Product2 is (Result + 1) * N2,
                  Product1 =< N1, Product2 > N1, !.
```

This program performs integer division, using addition and multiplication. Because most Prolog systems provide division as an operator, this program is not actually useful, other than to illustrate a simple generate and test program.

The predicate is_integer succeeds as long as its parameter can be instantiated to some nonnegative integer. If its argument is not instantiated, is_integer instantiates it to the value 0. If the argument is instantiated to an integer, is_integer instantiates it to the next larger integer value.

So, in divide, is_integer is the generator subgoal. It generates elements of the sequence 0, 1, 2, ..., one each time it is satisfied. All of the others are the testing subgoals—they check to determine whether the value produced by is_integer is, in fact, the quotient of the first two parameters, N1 and N2. The purpose of the cut as the last subgoal is simple: It prevents divide from ever trying to find an alternative solution once it has found *the* solution. Although is_integer can generate a huge number of candidates, only one is the solution, so the cut here prevents useless attempts to produce secondary solutions.

Use of the cut operator has been compared to the use of the goto in imperative languages (Van Emden, 1980). Although it is sometimes needed, it is possible to abuse it. Indeed, it is sometimes used to make logic programs have a control flow that is inspired by imperative programming styles.

The ability to tamper with control flow in a Prolog program is a deficiency because it is directly detrimental to one of the important advantages of logic programming—that programs do not specify how solutions are to be found. Rather, they simply specify what the solution should look like. This makes programs easier to write and easier to read. They are not cluttered with the details of how the solutions are to be determined and, in particular, the precise order in which the computations are done to produce the solution. So, while logic programming requires no control flow directions, Prolog programs frequently use them, mostly for the sake of efficiency.

16.7.2 The Closed-World Assumption

The nature of Prolog's resolution sometimes creates misleading results. The only truths, as far as Prolog is concerned, are those that can be proved using its database. It has no knowledge of the world other than its database. Any query about which there is insufficient information in the database to prove absolutely is assumed to be false. Prolog can prove that a given goal is true, but it cannot prove that a given goal is false. It simply assumes that, because it cannot prove a goal true, the goal must be false. In essence, Prolog is a true/fail system, rather than a true/false system.

Actually, the closed-world assumption should not be at all foreign to you—our judicial system operates the same way. Suspects are innocent until proven guilty. They need not be proven innocent. If a trial cannot prove a person guilty, he or she is considered innocent.

The problem of the closed-world assumption is related to the negation problem, which is discussed in the following subsection.

16.7.3 The Negation Problem

Another problem with Prolog is its difficulty with negation. Consider the following database of two facts and a relationship:

```
parent(bill, jake).
parent(bill, shelley).
sibling(X, Y) :- (parent(M, X), parent(M, Y).
```

Now, suppose we typed the query

```
sibling(X, Y).
```

Prolog will respond with

```
X = jake
Y = jake
```

Thus, Prolog "thinks" jake is a sibling of himself. This happens because the system first instantiates M with bill and X with jake to make the first subgoal, parent(M, X), true. It then starts at the beginning of the database again to match the second subgoal, parent(M, Y), and arrives at the instantiations of M with bill and Y with jake. Because the two subgoals are satisfied independently, with both matchings starting at the database's beginning, the response above appears. To avoid this, X must be specified to be a sibling of Y only if they have the same parents *and* they are not the same. Unfortunately, stating that they are not equal is not straightforward in Prolog, as we will discuss. The most exacting method would require adding a fact for every pair of atoms, stating that they were not the same. This can, of course, cause the database to become very large, for there is often far more negative information than positive information. For example, most people have 364 more unbirthdays than they have birthdays.

A simple alternative solution is to state in the goal that X must not be the same as Y, as in

```
sibling(X, Y) :- parent(M, X), parent(M, Y), not(X = Y).
```

In other situations, the solution is not so simple.

The Prolog not operator is satisfied in this case if resolution cannot satisfy the subgoal X = Y. Therefore, if the not succeeds, it does not necessarily mean that X is not equal to Y; rather, it means that resolution cannot prove from the database that X is the same as Y. Thus the Prolog not operator is not equivalent to a logical NOT operator, in which NOT means that its operand is provably true. This nonequivalency can lead to a problem if we happen to have a goal of the form

```
not(not(some_goal)).
```

which would be equivalent to

```
some_goal.
```

if Prolog's not operator were a true logical NOT operator. In some cases, however, they are not the same. For example, consider again the member rules:

```
member(Element, [Element | _]) :- !.
member(Element, [_ | List]) :- member(Element, List).
```

To discover one of the elements of a given list, we could use the goal

```
member(X, [mary, fred, barb]).
```

which would cause X to be instantiated with mary, which would then be printed. But if we used

```
not(not(member(X, [mary, fred, barb]))).
```

the following sequence of events would take place: First, the inner goal would succeed, instantiating X to mary. Then Prolog would attempt to satisfy the next goal:

```
not(member(X, [mary, fred, barb])).
```

This would fail because member succeeded. When this goal failed, x would be uninstantiated because Prolog always uninstantiates all variables in all goals that fail. Next, Prolog would attempt to satisfy the outer not goal, which would succeed, because its argument had failed. Finally, the result, which is x, would be printed. But x would not be currently instantiated, so the system would indicate that. Generally, uninstantiated variables are printed in the form of a string of digits preceded by an underscore. So the fact that Prolog's not is not equivalent to a logical NOT can be, at the very least, misleading.

The fundamental reason why logical NOT cannot be an integral part of Prolog is the form of the Horn clause:

$$A \text{ :- } B_1 \cap B_2 \cap \ldots \cap B_n$$

If all the B propositions are true, it can be concluded that A is true. But regardless of the truth or falseness of any or all of the Bs, it cannot be concluded that A is false. From positive logic, one can only conclude positive logic. Thus the use of Horn clause form prevents any negative conclusions.

16.7.4 Intrinsic Limitations

A fundamental goal of logic programming, as stated in Section 16.4, is to provide nonprocedural programming; that is, a system by which programmers specify what a program is supposed to do but need not specify how that is to be accomplished. The example given there for sorting is rewritten here:

sort(old_list, new_list) $\subset$ permute(old_list, new_list) $\cap$ sorted(new_list)
sorted(list) $\subset \forall j$ such that $1 \leq j < n$, list(j) $\leq$ list(j+1)

This can easily be written in Prolog. For example, the sorted subgoal can be expressed as

```
sorted ([]).
sorted ([x]).
sorted ([x, y | list]) :- x <= y, sorted ([y | list]).
```

The problem with the sort process above is that it has no idea of how to sort, other than simply to enumerate all permutations of the given list until it happens to create the one that has the list in sorted order—a very slow process, indeed.

So far, no one has discovered a process by which the description of a sorted list can be transformed into some efficient algorithm for sorting. Resolution is capable of many interesting things, but certainly not this. Therefore, a Prolog program that sorts a list must specify the details of how that sorting can be done, as is the case in an imperative or functional language.

Do all of these problems mean that logic programming should be abandoned? Absolutely not! As it is, it is capable of dealing with many useful applications. Furthermore, it is based on an intriguing concept and is therefore interesting in and of itself. Finally, there is the possibility that new inferencing techniques will be developed that will allow a logic programming language system to efficiently deal with progressively larger classes of problems.

16.8   Applications of Logic Programming

In this section, we briefly describe a few of the larger classes of present and potential applications of logic programming in general and Prolog in particular.

16.8.1   Relational Database Management Systems

Relational database management systems (RDBMSs) store data in the form of tables. Queries on such databases are often stated in relational calculus, which is a form of symbolic logic. The query languages of these systems are nonprocedural in the same sense that logic programming is nonprocedural. The user does not describe how to retrieve the answer; rather, he or she only describes the characteristics of the answer. The connection between logic programming and RDBMSs should be obvious. Simple tables of information can be described by Prolog structures, and relationships between tables can be conveniently and easily described by Prolog rules. The retrieval process is inherent in the resolution operation. The goal statements of Prolog provide the queries for the RDBMS. Logic programming is thus a natural match to the needs of implementing an RDBMS.

One of the advantages of using logic programming to implement an RDBMS is that only a single language is required. In a typical RDBMS, a database language includes statements for data definitions, data manipulation, and queries, all of which are embedded in a general-purpose programming language, such as COBOL. The general-purpose language is used for processing the data and input and output functions. All of these functions can be done in a logic programming language.

Another advantage of using logic programming to implement an RDBMS is that deductive capability is built in. Conventional RDBMSs cannot deduce anything from a database other than what is explicitly stored in them. They contain only facts, rather than facts *and* inference rules. The primary disadvantage of using logic programming for an RDBMS, compared with a conventional RDBMS, is that the logic programming implementation is slower. Logical inferences simply take longer than ordinary table look-up methods using imperative programming techniques.

16.8.2   Expert Systems

Expert systems are computer systems designed to emulate human expertise in some particular domain. They consist of a database of facts, an inferencing process, some heuristics about the domain, and some friendly human interface that makes the system appear much like an expert human consultant. In addition to their initial knowledge base, which is provided by a human expert, expert systems learn from the process of being used, so their databases must be capable of growing dynamically. Also, an expert system should include the capability of interrogating the user to get additional information when it determines that such information is needed.

One of the central problems for the designer of an expert system is dealing with the inevitable inconsistencies and incompleteness of the database. Logic programming appears to be well suited to deal with these problems. For example, default inference rules can help deal with the problem of incompleteness.

Prolog can and has been used to construct expert systems. It can easily fulfill the basic needs of expert systems, using resolution as the basis for query processing, using its ability to add facts and rules to provide the learning capability, and using its trace facility to inform the user of the "reasoning" behind a given result. Missing from Prolog is the automatic ability of the system to query the user for additional information when it is needed.

One of the most widely known uses of logic programming in expert systems is the expert system construction system known as APES, which is described in Sergot (1983) and Hammond (1983). The APES system includes a very flexible facility for gathering information from the user during expert system construction. It also includes a second interpreter for producing explanations to its answers to queries.

APES has been successfully used to produce several expert systems, including one for the rules of a government social benefits program and one for the British Nationality Act, which is the definitive source for rules of British citizenship.

16.8.3 Natural Language Processing

Certain kinds of natural language processing can be done with logic programming. In particular, natural language interfaces to computer software systems, such as intelligent databases and other intelligent knowledge-based systems, can be conveniently done with logic programming. For describing language syntax, forms of logic programming have been found to be equivalent to context-free grammars. Proof procedures in logic programming systems have been found to be equivalent to certain parsing strategies. In fact, backward chaining resolution can be used directly to parse sentences whose structures are described by context-free grammars. It has also been discovered that some kinds of semantics of natural languages can be made clear by modeling the languages with logic programming. In particular, research in logic-based semantics networks has shown that sets of sentences in natural languages can be expressed in clausal form (Deliyanni and Kowalski, 1979). Kowalski (1979) also discusses logic-based semantic networks.

SUMMARY

Symbolic logic provides the basis for logic programming and logic programming languages. The approach of logic programming is to use as a database a collection of facts and rules that state relationships between facts, and to use an automatic inferencing process to check the validity of new propositions, assuming the facts and rules of the database are true. This approach is the one developed for automatic theorem proving.

Prolog is the most widely used logic programming language. The origins of logic programming lie in Robinson's development of the resolution rule for logical inference. Prolog was developed primarily by Colmeraur and Roussel at Marseille, with some help from Kowalski at Edinburgh.

Logic programs should be nonprocedural, which means that the characteristics of the solution are given but the complete process of getting the solution is not.

Prolog statements are facts, rules, or goals. Most are made up of structures, which are atomic propositions, and logic operators, although arithmetic expressions are also allowed.

Resolution is the primary activity of a Prolog interpreter. This process, which uses backtracking extensively, involves mainly pattern matching among propositions. When variables are involved, they can be instantiated to values to provide matches. This instantiation process is called *unification*.

There are a number of problems with the current state of logic programming. For reasons of efficiency, and even to avoid infinite loops, programmers must sometimes state control flow information in their programs. Also, there are the problems of the closed-world assumption and negation.

Logic programming has been used in a number of different areas, primarily in relational database systems, expert systems, and natural language processing.

BIBLIOGRAPHIC NOTES

The Prolog language is described in several books. Edinburgh's form of the language is covered in Clocksin and Mellish (1997). The microcomputer implementation is described in Clark and McCabe (1984).

Hogger (1984) is an excellent book on the general area of logic programming. It is the source of the material in this chapter's section on logic programming applications.

REVIEW QUESTIONS

1. What are the three primary uses of symbolic logic in formal logic?
2. What are the two parts of a compound term?
3. What is the general form of a proposition in clausal form?
4. Give general (not rigorous) definitions of *resolution* and *unification*.
5. What are the forms of Horn clauses?
6. What is the basic concept of declarative semantics?
7. What are the three forms of a Prolog term?
8. What are the syntactic forms and usage of fact and rule statements in Prolog?
9. Explain the two approaches to matching goals to facts in a database.
10. Explain the difference between a depth-first and a breadth-first search when discussing how multiple goals are satisfied.
11. Explain how backtracking works in Prolog.
12. Explain what is wrong with the Prolog statement K **is** K + 1.
13. What are the two ways a Prolog programmer can control the order of pattern matching during resolution?
14. Explain the generate and test programming strategy in Prolog.
15. Explain the closed-world assumption used by Prolog. Why is this a limitation?
16. Explain the negation problem with Prolog. Why is this a limitation?
17. Explain the connection between automatic theorem proving and Prolog's inferencing process.
18. Explain the difference between procedural and nonprocedural languages.
19. Explain why Prolog systems must do backtracking.
20. What is the relationship between resolution and unification in Prolog?

PROBLEM SET

1. Compare the concept of data typing in Ada with that of Prolog.
2. Describe how a multiple-processor machine could be used to implement resolution. Could Prolog, as currently defined, use this method?
3. Write a Prolog description of your family tree (based only on facts), going back to your grandparents and including all descendants. Be sure to include all relationships.
4. Write a set of rules for family relationships, including all relationships from grandparents through two generations. Now add these to the facts of Problem 3, and eliminate as many of the facts as you can.

5. Write the following statements in Prolog:
    a. If Fido is a yellow Lab, then Fido is a dog.
    b. If it is Tuesday and it is February, then there is school.
    c. If Fred is a male and Fred is your parent, then Fred is your father.
    d. If X is your parent, then X is your father or X is your mother.
6. Explain two ways in which the list-processing capabilities of Scheme and Prolog are similar.
7. In what way are the list-processing capabilities of Scheme and Prolog different?
8. Write a comparison of Prolog with ML, including two similarities and two differences.
9. From a book on Prolog, learn and write a description of an occur-check problem. Why does Prolog allow this problem to exist in its implementation?

PROGRAMMING EXERCISES

1. Write a Prolog program that finds the maximum of a list of numbers.
2. Write a Prolog program that succeeds if the intersection of two given list parameters is empty.
3. Write a Prolog program that returns a list containing the union of the elements of two given lists.
4. Write a Prolog program that returns the last element of a given list.

Bibliography

ARM. (1995) Ada Reference Manual, ISO/IEC/ANSI 8652:19 Intermetrics, Cambridge, MA.

ACM. (1979) "Part A: Preliminary Ada Reference Manual" and "Part B: Rationale for the Design of the Ada Programming Language." *SIGPLAN Notices*, Vol. 14, No. 6.

ACM. (1993a) History of Programming Language Conference Proceedings. *ACM SIGPLAN Notices*, Vol. 28, No. 3, March.

ACM. (1993b) "High Performance FORTRAN Language Specification Part 1." FORTRAN Forum, Vol. 12, No. 4.

Aho, A.V., R. Sethi, and J.D. Ullman. (1986) *Compilers: Principles, Techniques, and Tools*. Addison-Wesley, Reading, MA.

Aho, A.V., B.W. Kernighan, and P.J. Weinberger. (1988) *The AWK Programming Language*. Addison-Wesley, Reading, MA.

Ambler, A.L., D.I. Good, J.C. Browne, W.F. Burger, R.M. Cohen, C.G. Hoch, and R.E. Wells. (1977) "Gypsy: A Language for Specification and Implementation of Verifiable Programs." Proceedings of the ACM Conference on Language Design for Reliable Software. *ACM SIGPLAN Notices*, Vol. 12, No. 3, pp. 1–10.

Andrews, G.R., and F.B. Schneider. (1983) "Concepts and Notations for Concurrent Programming." *ACM Computing Surveys*, Vol. 15, No. 1, pp. 3–43.

ANSI. (1966) *American National Standard Programming Language FORTRAN*. American National Standards Institute, New York.

ANSI. (1976) *American National Standard Programming Language PL/I*. ANSI X3.53–1976. American National Standards Institute, New York.

ANSI. (1978a) *American National Standard Programming Language FORTRAN*. ANSI X3.9–1978. American National Standards Institute, New York.

ANSI. (1978b) *American National Standard Programming Language Minimal BASIC*. ANSI X3.60–1978. American National Standards Institute, New York.

ANSI. (1985) *American National Standard Programming Language COBOL*. ANSI X3.23–1985. American National Standards Institute, New York.

ANSI. (1989) *American National Standard Programming Language C*. ANSI X3.159–1989. American National Standards Institute, New York.

ANSI. (1992) *American National Standard Programming Language FORTRAN 90*. ANSI X3.198–1992. American National Standards Institute, New York.

Arden, B.W., B.A. Galler, and R.M. Graham. (1961) "MAD at Michigan." *Datamation*, Vol. 7, No. 12, pp. 27–28.

Backus, J. (1954) "The IBM 701 Speedcoding System." *J. ACM*, Vol. 1, pp. 4–6.

Backus, J. (1959) "The Syntax and Semantics of the Proposed International Algebraic Language of the Zurich ACM-GAMM Conference." *Proceedings International Conference on Information Processing*. UNESCO, Paris, pp. 125–132.

Backus, J. (1978) "Can Programming Be Liberated from the von Neumann Style? A Functional Style and Its Algebra of Programs." *Commun. ACM*, Vol. 21, No. 8, pp. 613–641.

Backus, J., F.L. Bauer, J. Green, C. Katz, J. McCarthy, P. Naur, A.J. Perlis, H. Rutishauser, K. Samelson, B. Vauquois, J.H. Wegstein, A. van Wijngaarden, and M. Woodger. (1962) "Revised Report on the Algorithmic Language ALGOL 60." *Commun. ACM*, Vol. 6, No. 1, pp. 1–17.

Ben-Ari, M. (1982) *Principles of Concurrent Programming*. Prentice-Hall, Englewood Cliffs, NJ.

Birtwistle, G.M., O.-J. Dahl, B. Myhrhaug, and K. Nygaard. (1973) *Simula BEGIN*. Van Nostrand Reinhold, New York.

Bobrow, D.G., L. DeMichiel, R. Gabriel, S. Keene, G. Kiczales, and D. Moon. (1988) "Common Lisp Object System Specification X3J13 Document 88-002R." *ACM SIGPLAN Notices*, Vol. 17, No. 6, pp. 216–229.

Bodwin, J.M., L. Bradley, K. Kanda, D. Litle, and U.F. Pleban. (1982) "Experience with an Experimental Compiler Generator Based on Denotational Semantics." *ACM SIGPLAN Notices*, Vol. 17, No. 6, pp. 216–229.

Bohm, C., and G. Jacopini. (1966) "Flow Diagrams, Turing Machines, and Languages with Only Two Formation Rules." *Commun. ACM*, Vol. 9, No. 5, pp. 366–371.

Bolsky, M., and D. Korn. (1995) *The New KornShell Command and Programming Language*. Prentice-Hall, Englewood Cliffs, NJ.

Booch. G. (1987) *Software Engineering with Ada*. 2nd ed., Benjamin/Cummings, Redwood City, CA.

Bradley, J.C. (1989) *QuickBASIC and QBASIC Using Modular Structures*. W.C. Brown, Dubuque, IA.

Brinch Hansen, P. (1973) *Operating System Principles*. Prentice-Hall, Englewood Cliffs, NJ.

Brinch Hansen, P. (1975) "The Programming Language Concurrent-Pascal." *IEEE Transactions on Software Engineering*, Vol. 1, No. 2, pp. 199–207.

Brinch Hansen, P. (1977) *The Architecture of Concurrent Programs*. Prentice-Hall, Englewood Cliffs, NJ.

Brinch Hansen, P. (1978) "Distributed Processes: a Concurrent Programming Concept." *Commun. ACM*, Vol. 21, No. 11, pp. 934–941.

Brown, J.A., S. Pakin, & R.P. Polivka. (1988) APL2 at a Glance. Prentice-Hall, Englewood Cliffs, NJ.

Bulena, F. (2002) "Programming Microsoft Visual BASIC .NET." Microsoft Press, Redmond, WA.

Campione, M., K. Walrath, and A. Huml (2001) *The Java Tutorial, 3e,* Addison-Wesley, Reading, MA.

Cardelli, L., J. Donahue, L. Glassman, M. Jordan, B. Kalsow, and G. Nelson. (1989) Modula-3 Report (revised). Digital System Research Center, Palo Alto, CA.

Chambers, C., and D. Ungar. (1991) "Making Pure Object-Oriented Languages Practical." *SIGPLAN Notices*, Vol. 26, No. 1, pp. 1–15.

Chomsky, N. (1956) "Three Models for the Description of Language." *IRE Transactions on Information Theory*, Vol. 2, No. 3, pp. 113–124.

Chomsky, N. (1959) "On Certain Formal Properties of Grammars." *Information and Control*, Vol. 2, No. 2, pp. 137–167.

Church, A. (1941) *Annals of Mathematics Studies. Volume 6: Calculi of Lambda Conversion*. Princeton Univ. Press, Princeton, NJ. Reprinted by Klaus Reprint Corporation, New York, 1965.

Clark, K.L., and F.G. McCabe. (1984) *Micro-PROLOG: Programming in Logic*. Prentice-Hall, Englewood Cliffs, NJ.

Clarke, L.A., J.C. Wileden, and A.L. Wolf. (1980) "Nesting in Ada Is for the Birds." *ACM SIGPLAN Notices,* Vol. 15, No. 11, pp. 139–145.

Cleaveland, J.C. (1986) *An Introduction to Data Types.* Addison-Wesley, Reading, MA.

Cleaveland, J.C., and R.C. Uzgalis. (1976) *Grammars for Programming Languages: What Every Programmer Should Know About Grammar.* American Elsevier, New York.

Clocksin, W.F., and C.S. Mellish. (1997) *Programming in Prolog,* 4e. Springer-Verlag, New York.

Cohen, J. (1981) "Garbage Collection of Linked Data Structures." *ACM Computing Surveys,* Vol. 13, No. 3, pp. 341–368.

Converse, T. and J. Park. (2000) *PHP 4 Bible.* IDG Books, New York.

Conway, M.E. (1963). "Design of a Separable Transition-Diagram Compiler." *Commun. ACM,* Vol. 6, No. 7, pp. 396–408.

Conway, R. and R. Constable. (1976) "PL/CS—A Disciplined Subset of PL/I." Technical Report TR76/293. Department of Computer Science, Cornell University, Ithaca, NY.

Cornell University. (1977) *PL/C User's Guide, Release 7.6.* Department of Computer Science, Cornell University, Ithaca, NY.

Correa, N. (1992) "Empty Categories, Chain Binding, and Parsing." pp. 83–121, *Principle-Based Parsing.* eEds. R.C. Berwick, S.P. Abney, and C. Tenny., Kluwer Academic Publishers, Boston.

Dahl, O.-J., E.W. Dijkstra, and C.A.R. Hoare. (1972) *Structured Programming.* Academic Press, New York.

Dahl, O.-J., and K. Nygaard. (1967) "SIMULA 67 Common Base Proposal." Norwegian Computing Center Document, Oslo.

Deliyanni, A., and R.A. Kowalski. (1979) "Logic and Semantic Networks." *Commun. ACM,* Vol. 22, No. 3, pp 184–192.

Department of Defense. (1960) "COBOL, Initial Specifications for a Common Business Oriented Language."

Department of Defense. (1961) "COBOL—1961, Revised Specifications for a Common Business Oriented Language."

Department of Defense. (1962) "COBOL—1961 EXTENDED, Extended Specifications for a Common Business Oriented Language."

Department of Defense. (1975a) "Requirements for High Order Programming Languages, STRAWMAN." July.

Department of Defense. (1975b) "Requirements for High Order Programming Languages, WOODENMAN." August.

Department of Defense. (1976) "Requirements for High Order Programming Languages, TINMAN." June.

Department of Defense. (1977) "Requirements for High Order Programming Languages, IRONMAN." January.

Department of Defense. (1978) "Requirements for High Order Programming Languages, STEELMAN." June.

Department of Defense. (1980a) "Requirements for High Order Programming Languages, STONEMAN." February.

Department of Defense. (1980b) "Requirements for the Programming Environment for the Common High Order Language, STONEMAN."

Department of Defense. (1990) "Ada 9X Requirements." Office of the Under Secretary of Defense for Acquisition, Washington, DC.

DeRemer, F. (1971) "Simple LR(k) Grammars." CACM 14:7, pp. 453-460.

DeRemer, F. & T. Pennello. (1982) "Efficient Computation of LALR(1) Look-Ahead Sets." ACM TOPLAS 4:4, pp. 615-649.

Deutsch, L.P., and D.G. Bobrow. (1976) "An Efficient Incremental Automatic Garbage Collector." *Commun. ACM*, Vol. 11, No. 3, pp. 522–526.

Dijkstra, E.W. (1968a) "Goto Statement Considered Harmful." *Commun. ACM*, Vol. 11, No. 3, pp. 147–149.

Dijkstra, E.W. (1968b) "Cooperating Sequential Processes." In *Programming Languages*, F. Genuys (ed.). Academic Press, New York, pp. 43–112.

Dijkstra, E.W. (1972) "The Humble Programmer." *Commun. ACM*, Vol. 15, No. 10, pp. 859–866.

Dijkstra, E.W. (1975). "Guarded Commands, Nondeterminacy, and Formal Derivation of Programs." *Commun. ACM*, Vol. 18, No. 8, pp. 453–457.

Dijkstra, E.W. (1976). *A Discipline of Programming*. Prentice Hall, Englewood Cliffs, NJ.

Dybvig, R.K. (1996) *The Scheme Programming Language* 2e. Prentice Hall PTR, Upper Saddle River, NJ.

Ellis, M.A., and B. Stroustrup (1990) *The Annotated C++ Reference Manual*. Addison-Wesley, Reading, MA.

Ennals, J.R. (1980) "Logic as a Computer Language for Children." Logic Programming Research Reports. Theory of Computing Research Group, Department of Computing, Imperial College of Science and Technology, London.

Farber, D.J., R.E. Griswold, and F.P. Polansky. (1964) "SNOBOL, a String Manipulation Language." *J. ACM*, Vol 11, No. 1, pp. 21–30.

Farrow, R. (1982) "LINGUIST 86: Yet Another Translator Writing System Based on Attribute Grammars." *ACM SIGPLAN Notices*, Vol. 17, No. 6, pp. 160–171.

Feuer, A., and N. Gehani. (1982) "A Comparison of the Programming Languages C and Pascal." *ACM Computing Surveys*, Vol. 14, No. 1, pp. 73–92.

Fischer, C.N., G.F. Johnson, J. Mauney, A. Pal, and D.L. Stock. (1984) "The Poe Language-Based Editor Project." *ACM SIGPLAN Notices*, Vol. 19, No. 5, pp. 21–29.

Fischer, C.N., and R.J. LeBlanc. (1977) "UW-Pascal Reference Manual." Madison Academic Computing Center, Madison, WI.

Fischer, C.N., and R.J. LeBlanc. (1980) "Implementation of Runtime Diagnostics in Pascal." *IEEE Transactions on Software Engineering*, SE-6, No. 4, pp. 313–319.

Fischer, C.N., and R.J. LeBlanc. (1991) *Crafting a Compiler in C*. Benjamin/Cummings, Menlo Park, CA.

Flanegan, D. (1998) *JavaScript: The Definitive Guide*. O'Reilly Publishing Co., Sabastopol, CA

Floyd, R.W. (1967) "Assigning Meanings to Programs." *Proceedings Symposium Applied Mathematics, in Mathematical Aspects of Computer Science*, ed. J.T. Schwartz. American Mathematical Society, Providence, RI.

Frege, G. (1892) "Über Sinn und Bedeutung." *Zeitschrift für Philosophie und Philosophisches Kritik*, Vol. 100, pp. 25–50.

Friedl, J.E.F. (1997) *Mastering Regular Expressions*. O'Reilly Publ. Co., Sabastopol, CA.

Friedman, D.P., and D.S. Wise. (1979) "Reference Counting's Ability to Collect Cycles Is Not Insurmountable." *Information Processing Letters*, Vol. 8, No. 1, pp. 41–45.

Fuchi, K. (1981) "Aiming for Knowledge Information Processing Systems." *Proceedings of the International Conference on Fifth Generation Computing Systems*. Japan Information Processing Development Center, Tokyo. Republished (1982) by North-Holland Publishing, Amsterdam.

Gehani, N. (1983) *Ada: An Advanced Introduction*. Prentice-Hall, Englewood Cliffs, NJ.

Ghezzi, C., and M. Jazayeri. (1987) *Programming Language Concepts*. 2d ed. Wiley, New York.

Ghezzi, C., and M. Jazayeri (1987) *Programming Language Concepts*. 3d ed. Wiley, New York.

Gilman, L., and A.J. Rose. (1976) *APL: An Interactive Approach*. 2d ed. J. Wiley, New York.

Goldberg, A., and D. Robson. (1983) *Smalltalk-80: The Language and Its Implementation*. Addison-Wesley, Reading, MA.

Goldberg, A., and D. Robson. (1989) *Smalltalk-80: The Language*. Addison-Wesley, Reading, MA.

Goodenough, J.B. (1975) "Exception Handling: Issues and Proposed Notation." *Commun. ACM*, Vol. 18, No. 12, pp. 683–696.

Goos, G., and J. Hartmanis (eds.). (1983) *The Programming Language Ada Reference Manual*. American National Standards Institute. ANSI/MIL-STD-1815A–1983. Lecture Notes in Computer Science 155. Springer-Verlag, New York.

Gordon, M. (1979) *The Denotational Description of Programming Languages, An Introduction*. Springer-Verlag, Berlin–New York.

Gosling, J., B. Joy, and G. Steele. (1996) *The Java Language Specification*. Addison-Wesley, Reading, MA.

Gries, D. (1981) *The Science of Programming*. Springer-Verlag, New York.

Griswold, R.E., and M.T. Griswold. (1983) *The ICON Programming Language*. Prentice-Hall, Englewood Cliffs, NJ.

Griswold, R.E., F. Poage, and I.P. Polonsky. (1971) *The SNOBOL 4 Programming Language*. 2d ed. Prentice-Hall, Englewood Cliffs, NJ.

Hammond, P. (1983) APES: A User Manual. Department of Computing Report 82/9. Imperial College of Science and Technology, London.

Henderson, P. (1980) *Functional Programming: Application and Implementation*. Prentice-Hall, Englewood Cliffs, NJ.

Hoare, C.A.R. (1969) "An Axiomatic Basis of Computer Programming." *Commun. ACM*, Vol. 12, No. 10, pp. 576–580.

Hoare, C.A.R. (1972) "Proof of Correctness of Data Representations." *Acta Informatica*, Vol. 1, pp. 271–281.

Hoare, C.A.R. (1973) "Hints on Programming Language Design." *Proceedings ACM SIGACT/SIGPLAN Conference on Principles of Programming Languages*. Also published as Technical Report STAN-CS-73-403, Stanford University Computer Science Department.

Hoare, C.A.R. (1974) "Monitors: An Operating System Structuring Concept." *Commun. ACM*, Vol. 17, No. 10, pp. 549–557.

Hoare, C.A.R. (1978) "Communicating Sequential Processes." *Commun. ACM*, Vol. 21, No. 8, pp. 666–677.

Hoare, C.A.R. (1981) "The Emperor's Old Clothes." *Commun. ACM*, Vol. 24, No. 2, pp. 75–83.

Hoare, C.A.R., and N. Wirth. (1973) "An Axiomatic Definition of the Programming Language Pascal." *Acta Informatica*. Vol. 2, pp. 335–355.

Hogger, C.J. (1984) *Introduction to Logic Programming*. Academic Press, London.

Holt, R.C., G.S. Graham, E.D. Lazowska, and M.A. Scott. (1978) *Structured Concurrent Programming with Operating Systems Applications*. Addison-Wesley, Reading, MA.

Horn, A. (1951) "On Sentences Which Are True of Direct Unions of Algebras." *J. Symbolic Logic*, Vol. 16, pp. 14–21.

Hudak, P. and J. Fasel. (1992) "A Gentle Introduction to Haskell, ACM SIGPLAN Notices, 27(5), May 1992, pp. T1–T53.

Huskey, H.K., R. Love, and N. Wirth. (1963) "A Syntactic Description of BC NELIAC." *Commun. ACM*, Vol. 6, No. 7, pp. 367–375.

IBM. (1954) "Preliminary Report, Specifications for the IBM Mathematical FORmula TRANslating System, FORTRAN." IBM Corporation, New York.

IBM. (1956) "Programmer's Reference Manual, The FORTRAN Automatic Coding System for the IBM 704 EDPM." IBM Corporation, New York.

IBM. (1964) "The New Programming Language." IBM UK Laboratories.

Ichbiah, J.D., J.C. Heliard, O. Roubine, J.G.P. Barnes, B. Krieg-Brueckner, and B.A. Wichmann. (1979) "Rationale for the Design of the Ada Programming Language." *ACM SIGPLAN Notices*, Vol. 14, No. 6, Part B.

IEEE. (1985) "Binary Floating-Point Arithmetic." IEEE Standard 754, IEEE, New York.

Ingerman, P.Z. (1967). "Panini-Backus Form Suggested." *Commun. ACM*, Vol. 10, No. 3, p. 137.

Intermetrics. (1993) Programming Language Ada, Draft, Version 4.0. Cambridge, MA.

ISO. (1982) *Specification for Programming Language Pascal*. ISO7185–1982. International Organization for Standardization, Geneva, Switzerland.

ISO. (1998) ISO14882-1, ISO/IEC Standard – Information Technology – Programming Language – C++. International Organization for Standardization, Geneva, Switzerland.

ISO. (1999) ISO/IEC 9899:1999, Programming Language C. American National Standards Institute, New York.

Iverson, K.E. (1962) *A Programming Language*. John Wiley, New York.

Jensen, K., and N. Wirth. (1974) *Pascal Users Manual and Report*. Springer-Verlag, Berlin.

Johnson, S.C. (1975) "Yacc—Yet Another Compiler Compiler." Computing Science Report 32. A.T.& T. Bell Laboratories, Murray Hill, NJ.

Jones, N.D. (ed.) (1980) *Semantic-Directed Compiler Generation*. Lecture Notes in Computer Science, Vol. 94. Springer-Verlag, Heidelberg, FRG.

Kay, A. (1969) The Reactive Engine. Ph.D. Thesis. University of Utah, September.

Kernighan, B.W., and R. Pike. (1984) *The UNIX Programming Environment*. Prentice-Hall, Englewood Cliffs, NJ.

Kernighan, B.W., and D.M. Ritchie. (1978) *The C Programming Language*. Prentice-Hall, Englewood Cliffs, NJ.

Knuth, D.E. (1965) "On the Translation of Languages from Left to Right." Information & Control, 8:6, pp. 607-639.

Knuth, D.E. (1967) "The Remaining Trouble Spots in ALGOL 60." *Commun. ACM*, Vol. 10, No. 10, pp. 611–618.

Knuth, D.E. (1968a) "Semantics of Context-Free Languages." *Mathematical Systems Theory*, Vol. 2, No. 2, pp. 127–146.

Knuth, D.E. (1968b) *The Art of Computer Programming*, Vol. I. 2d ed. Addison-Wesley, Reading, MA.

Knuth, D.E. (1974) "Structured Programming with GOTO Statements." *ACM Computing Surveys*, Vol. 6, No. 4, pp. 261–301.

Knuth, D.E. (1981) *The Art of Computer Programming*, Vol. II. 2d ed. Addison-Wesley, Reading, MA.

Knuth, D.E., and Luis Trabb Pardo. (1977) "Early Development of Programming Languages." In *Encyclopedia of Computer Science and Technology*, Vol. 7. Dekker, New York, pp. 419–493.

Kowalski, R.A. (1979) *Logic for Problem Solving*. Artificial Intelligence Series, Vol. 7. Elsevier-North Holland, New York.

Lampson, B.W. (1983) "A Description of the Cedar Language." Tech. Report CSL-83-15. Xerox Palo Alto Research Center, December.

Lampson, B.W., J.J. Horning, R.L. London, J.G. Mitchell, and G.J. Popek. (1977) "Report on the Programming Language Euclid." *ACM SIGPLAN Notices,* Vol. 12, No. 2. (Revised Report, XEROX PARC Technical Report CSL78-2.)

Laning, J.H., Jr., and N. Zierler. (1954) "A Program for Translation of Mathematical Equations for Whirlwind I." Engineering memorandum E-364. Instrumentation Laboratory, Massachusetts Institute of Technology, Cambridge, MA.

Ledgard, H. (1984) *The American Pascal Standard.* Springer-Verlag, New York.

Ledgard, H.F., and M. Marcotty. (1975) "A Genealogy of Control Structures." *Commun. ACM,* Vol. 18, No. 11, pp. 629–639.

Liskov, B., and A. Snyder. (1979) "Exception Handling in CLU." *IEEE Transactions on Software Engineering,* Vol. SE-5, No. 6, pp. 546–558.

Lomet, D. (1975) "Scheme for Invalidating References to Freed Storage." *IBM J. of Research and Development,* Vol. 19, pp. 26–35.

MacLaren, M.D. (1977) "Exception Handling in PL/I." *ACM SIGPLAN Notices,* Vol. 12, No. 3, pp. 101–104.

Marcotty, M., H.F. Ledgard, and G.V. Bochmann. (1976) "A Sampler of Formal Definitions." *ACM Computing Surveys,* Vol. 8, No. 2, pp. 191–276.

Mather, D.G. and S.V. Waite (eds.). (1971) *BASIC.* 6th ed. University Press of New England, Hanover, NH.

McCarthy, J. (1960) "Recursive Functions of Symbolic Expressions and Their Computation by Machine, Part I." *Commun. ACM,* Vol. 3, No. 4, pp. 184–195.

McCarthy, J., P.W. Abrahams, D.J. Edwards, T.P. Hart, and M. Levin. (1965) *LISP 1.5 Programmer's Manual.* 2d ed. MIT Press, Cambridge, MA.

McCracken, D. (1970) "Whither APL." *Datamation,* Sept. 15, pp. 53–57.

Meyer, B. (1992) *Eiffel the Language.* Prentice-Hall, Englewood Cliffs, NJ.

Microsoft. (1991) *Microsoft Visual Basic Language Reference.* Document DB20664-0491, Redmond, WA.

Milner, R., M. Tofte, and R. Harper. (1990) *The Definition of Standard ML.* MIT Press, Cambridge, MA.

Milos, D., U. Pleban, and G. Loegel. (1984) "Direct Implementation of Compiler Specifications." *ACM Principles of Programming Languages 1984,* pp. 196–202.

Mitchell, J.G., W. Maybury, and R. Sweet. (1979) *Mesa Language Manual,* Version 5.0, CSL-79-3. Xerox Research Center, Palo Alto, CA.

Moss, C. (1994) *Prolog++: The Power of Object-Oriented and Logic Programming.* Addison-Wesley, Reading, MA.

Mössenbock, H. (1993) *Object-Oriented Programming in Oberon-2.* Springer-Verlag, New York.

Moto-oka, T. (1981) "Challenge for Knowledge Information Processing Systems." *Proceedings of the International Conference on Fifth Generation Computing Systems.* Japan Information Processing Development Center, Tokyo. Republished (1982) by North-Holland Publishing, Amsterdam.

Naur, P. (ed.) (1960) "Report on the Algorithmic Language ALGOL 60." *Commun. ACM,* Vol. 3, No. 5, pp. 299–314.

Newell, A., and H.A. Simon. (1956) "The Logic Theory Machine—A Complex Information Processing System." *IRE Transactions on Information Theory,* Vol. IT-2, No. 3, pp. 61–79.

Newell, A., and F.M. Tonge. (1960) "An Introduction to Information Processing Language V." *Commun. ACM,* Vol. 3, No. 4, pp. 205–211.

Nilsson, N.J. (1971) *Problem Solving Methods in Artificial Intelligence.* McGraw-Hill, New York.

Osterhout, J.K. (1994) *Tcl and the Tk Toolkit.* Addison-Wesley, Reading, MA.

Pagan, F.G. (1981) *Formal Specifications of Programming Languages.* Prentice-Hall, Englewood Cliffs, NJ.

Papert, S. (1980) *MindStorms: Children, Computers and Powerful Ideas.* Basic Books, New York.

Perlis, A., and K. Samelson. (1958) "Preliminary Report—International Algebraic Language." *Commun. ACM,* Vol. 1, No. 12, pp. 8–22.

Peyton Jones, S.L. (1987) *The Implementation of Functional Programming Languages.* Prentice-Hall, Englewood Cliffs, NJ.

Pratt, T.W. (1984) *Programming Languages: Design and Implementation.* 2d ed. Prentice-Hall, Englewood Cliffs, NJ.

Pratt, T.W., and M.V. Zelkowitz (2001) *Programming Languages: Design and Implementation, 4e,* Prentice-Hall, Englewood Cliffs, NJ.

Rees, J., and W. Clinger. (1986) "Revised Report on the Algorithmic Language Scheme." *ACM SIGPLAN Notices,* Vol. 21, No. 12, pp. 37–79.

Remington-Rand. (1952) "UNIVAC Short Code." Unpublished collection of dittoed notes. Preface by A.B. Tonik, dated October 25, 1955 (1 p.); Preface by J.R. Logan, undated but apparently from 1952 (1 p.); Preliminary exposition, 1952? (22 pp., where in which pp. 20–22 appear to be a later replacement); Short code supplementary information, topic one (7 pp.); Addenda #1, 2, 3, 4 (9 pp.).

Richards, M. (1969) "BCPL: A Tool for Compiler Writing and Systems Programming." *Proc. AFIPS SJCC,* Vol. 34, pp. 557–566.

Robinson, J.A. (1965) "A Machine-Oriented Logic Based on the Resolution Principle." *Journal of the ACM,* Vol. 12, pp. 23–41.

Roussel. P. (1975) "PROLOG: Manual de Reference et D'utilisation." Research Report. Artificial Intelligence Group, Univ. of Aix-Marseille, Luming, France.

Rovner, P. (1986) "Extending Modula-2 to Build Large, Integrated Systems." *IEEE Software,* Vol. 3, No. 6, November.

Rubin, F. (1987) "'GOTO Statement Considered Harmful' considered harmful" (letter to editor). *Commun. ACM,* Vol. 30, No. 3, pp. 195–196.

Sammet, J.E. (1969) *Programming Languages: History and Fundamentals.* Prentice-Hall, Englewood Cliffs, NJ.

Sammet, J.E. (1976) "Roster of Programming Languages for 1974–75." *Commun. ACM,* Vol. 19, No. 12, pp. 655–669.

Schneider, D.I. (1999) An Introduction to Programming Using Visual BASIC 6.0. Prentice-Hall, Englewood Cliffs, NJ.

Schorr, H., and W. Waite. (1967) "An Efficient Machine Independent Procedure for Garbage Collection in Various List Structures." *Commun. ACM,* Vol. 10, No. 8, pp. 501–506.

Scott, D.S., and C. Strachey. (1971) "Towards a Mathematical Semantics for Computer Language." *Proceedings, Symposium on Computers and Automation,* ed. J. Fox. Polytechnic Institute of Brooklyn Press, New York, pp. 19–46.

Scott, M. (2000) *Programming Language Pragmatics.* Morgan Kaufman, San Francisco, CA.

Sebesta, R.W. (1991) *VAX Structured Assembly Language Programming* 2e. Benjamin/Cummings Publ. Co., Redwood City, CA.

Sergot, M.J. (1983) "A Query-the-User Facility for Logic Programming." In *Integrated Interactive Computer Systems,* eds. P. Degano and E. Sandewall. North-Holland Publishing, Amsterdam.

Sewry, D.A. (1984b) "Modula-2 and the Monitor Concept." *ACM SIGPLAN Notices,* Vol. 19, No. 11, pp. 33–41.

Shaw, C.J. (1963) "A Specification of JOVIAL." *Commun. ACM*, Vol. 6, No. 12, pp. 721–736.

Sommerville, I. (1992) *Software Engineering*. 4th ed., Addison-Wesley, Reading, MA.

Steele, G.L., Jr. (1984) *Common LISP*. Digital Press, Burlington, MA.

Stoy, J.E. (1977) *Denotational Semantics: The Scott-Strachey Approach to Programming Language Semantics*. MIT Press, Cambridge, MA.

Stroustrup, B. (1983) "Adding Classes to C: An Exercise in Language Evolution." Software—Practice and Experience, Vol. 13, pp. 139–161.

Stroustrup, B. (1984) "Data Abstraction in C." *AT & T Bell Laboratories Technical Journal*, Vol. 63, No. 8.

Stroustrup, B. (1986) *The C++ Programming Language*. Addison-Wesley, Reading, MA.

Stroustrup, B. (1988) "What Is Object-Oriented Programming?" *IEEE Software*, May 1988, pp. 10–20.

Stroustrup, B. (1991) *The C++ Programming Language*. 2d ed. Addison-Wesley, Reading, MA.

Stroustrup, B. (1997) *The C++ Programming Language*. 3d ed. Addison-Wesley, Reading, MA.

Sussman, G.J., and G.L. Steele, Jr. (1975) "Scheme: An Interpreter for Extended Lambda Calculus." MIT AI Memo No. 349 (December, 1975).

Suzuki, N. (1982) "Analysis of Pointer 'Rotation'." *Commun. ACM*, Vol. 25, No. 5, pp. 330–335.

Tanenbaum, A.S. (1978) "A Comparison of Pascal and ALGOL 68." *Computer Journal*, Vol. 21, pp. 316–323.

Tanenbaum, A.S. (1998) *Structured Computer Organization*. 4 ed. Prentice-Hall, Englewood Cliffs, NJ.

Tanenbaum, A.S., Y. Langsam, and M.J. Augenstein (1990) *Data Structures Using C*. Prentice-Hall, Englewood Cliffs, NJ.

Teitelbaum, T., and T. Reps. (1981) "The Cornell Program Synthesizer: A Syntax-Directed Programming Environment." *Commun. ACM*, Vol. 24, No. 9, pp. 563–573.

Teitelman, W. (1975) *INTERLISP Reference Manual*. Xerox Palo Alto Research Center, Palo Alto, CA.

Thompson, S. (1996) *Haskell: The Craft of Functional Programming*. Addison-Wesley, Reading, MA, 500 pages.

Turner, D. (1986) "An Overview of Miranda." *ACM SIGPLAN Notices*, Vol. 21, No. 12, pp. 158–166.

Turner, D. (1990) (ed.) *Research Topics in Functional Programming*. Addison-Wesley, Reading, MA.

Ullman, J.D. (1998) *Elements of ML Programming. ML97 Edition*. Prentice-Hall, Englewood Cliffs, NJ.

Van Emden, M.H. (1980) "McDermott on Prolog: A Rejoinder." *SIGART Newsletter*, No. 72, August, pp. 19–20.

van Wijngaarden, A. B.J. Mailloux, J.E.L. Peck, and C.H.A. Koster. (1969) "Report on the Algorithmic Language ALGOL 68." *Numerische Mathematik*, Vol. 14, No. 2, pp. 79–218.

Wall, L., T. Christiansen, and R.L. Schwartz. (1996) *Programming Perl, 2e*. O'Reilly & Associates, Sebastopol, CA.

Wall, L., J. Christiansen, and J. Orwart. (2000) *Programming Perl, 3e*. O'Reilly & Associates, Sebastopol, CA.

Warren, D.H.D., L.M. Pereira, and F.C.N. Pereira. (1979) "User's Guide to DEC System-10 Prolog." Occasional Paper 15. Department of Artificial Intelligence, Univ. of Edinburgh, Scotland.

Watt, D.A. (1979) "An Extended Attribute Grammar for Pascal." *ACM SIGPLAN Notices,* Vol. 14, No. 2, pp. 60–74.

Wegner, P. (1972) "The Vienna Definition Language." *ACM Computing Surveys,* Vol. 4, No. 1, pp. 5–63.

Weissman, C. (1967) *LISP 1.5 Primer.* Dickenson Press, Belmont, CA.

Welsh, J., M.J. Sneeringer, and C.A.R. Hoare. (1977) "Ambiguities and Insecurities in Pascal." *Software—Practice and Experience,* Vol. 7, No. 6, pp. 685–696.

Wexelblat, R.L. (ed.). (1981) *History of Programming Languages.* Academic Press, New York.

Wheeler, D.J. (1950) "Programme Organization and Initial Orders for the EDSAC." *Proc. R. Soc. London,* Ser. A, Vol. 202, pp. 573–589.

Wilkes, M.V. (1952) "Pure and Applied Programming." In *Proceedings of the ACM National Conference,* Vol. 2. Toronto, pp. 121–124.

Wilkes, M.V., D.J. Wheeler, and S. Gill. (1951) *The Preparation of Programs for an Electronic Digital Computer, with Special Reference to the EDSAC and the Use of a Library of Subroutines.* Addison-Wesley, Reading, MA.

Wilkes, M.V., D.J. Wheeler, and S. Gill (1957) *The Preparation of Programs for an Electronic Digital Computer.* 2d ed. Addison-Wesley, Reading, MA.

Wirth, N. (1971) "The Programming Language Pascal." *Acta Informatica,* Vol. 1, No. 1, pp. 35–63.

Wirth, N. (1973) *Systematic Programming: An Introduction.* Prentice-Hall, Englewood Cliffs, NJ.

Wirth, N. (1975) "On the Design of Programming Languages." *Information Processing 74* (Proceedings of IFIP Congress 74), North Holland, Amsterdam, pp. 386–393.

Wirth, N. (1977) "Modula: A Language for Modular Multi-Programming." *Software—Practice and Experience,* Vol. 7, pp. 3–35.

Wirth, N. (1985) *Programming in Modula-2.* 3d ed. Springer-Verlag, New York.

Wirth, N. (1988) "The Programming Language Oberon." *Software—Practice and Experience,* Vol. 18, No. 7, pp. 671–690.

Wirth, N., and C.A.R. Hoare. (1966) "A Contribution to the Development of ALGOL." *Commun. ACM,* Vol. 9, No. 6, pp. 413–431.

Wulf, W.A., D.B. Russell, and A.N. Habermann. (1971) "BLISS: A Language for Systems Programming." *Commun. ACM,* Vol. 14, No. 12, pp. 780–790.

Zuse, K. (1972) "Der Plankalkül." Manuscript prepared in 1945, published in *Berichte der Gesellschaft für Mathematik und Datenverarbeitung,* No. 63 (Bonn, 1972); Part 3, 285 pp. English translation of all but pp. 176–196 in No. 106 (Bonn, 1976), pp. 42–244.

Index